Drinking

Drinking

Behavior and Belief in
Modern History

EDITED WITH AN INTRODUCTION BY

Susanna Barrows and
Robin Room

UNIVERSITY OF CALIFORNIA PRESS
Berkeley   Los Angeles   Oxford

University of California Press
Berkeley and Los Angeles, California

University of California Press, Ltd.
Oxford, England

© 1991 by
The Regents of the University of California

Library of Congress Cataloging-in-Publication Data

Drinking : behavior and belief in modern history / edited by Susanna
    Barrows and Robin Room.
        p.   cm.
    Rev. papers from a conference held in Berkeley in 1984.
    Includes bibliographical references.
    ISBN 0-520-05653-1 (alk. paper).—ISBN 0-520-07085-2 (pbk. :
alk. paper)
    1. Drinking of alcoholic beverages—History.   2. Alcoholism—
History.   3. Temperance—History.   I. Barrows, Susanna, 1944–
II. Room, Robin.
HV5025.D75   1991
394.1′3′09—dc20   89-20616
                                                            CIP

Printed in the United States of America

9 8 7 6 5 4 3 2 1

The paper used in this publication meets the minimum requirements of
American National Standard for Information Sciences—Permanence of
Paper for Printed Library Materials, ANSI Z39.48–1984. ∞

Contents

Introduction
Susanna Barrows and Robin Room / *1*

PART 1 • THE MANY WORLDS OF DRINK IN EUROPE AND AMERICA

1. Puritans in Taverns:
Law and Popular Culture in Colonial Massachusetts, 1630–1720
David W. Conroy / *29*

2. Social Drinking in Old Regime Paris
Thomas Brennan / *61*

3. "Parliaments of the People":
The Political Culture of Cafés in the Early Third Republic
Susanna Barrows / *87*

4. The Tavern and Politics in the German Labor Movement, c. 1870–1914
James S. Roberts / *98*

5. Decay from Within: The Inevitable Doom of the American Saloon
Madelon Powers / *112*

⌣ 6. Student Drinking in the Third Reich:
Academic Tradition and the Nazi Revolution
Geoffrey J. Giles / *132*

PART 2 • POLITICS, IDEOLOGY, AND POWER

7. Against the Flowing Tide:
Whiskey and Temperance in the Making of Modern Ireland
George Bretherton / *147*

8. Drunks, Brewers, and Chiefs:
Alcohol Regulation in Colonial Kenya, 1900–1939
Charles H. Ambler / *165*

9. Capitalism, Religion, and Reform:
The Social History of Temperance in Harvey, Illinois
Ray Hutchison / *184*

10. Women and Temperance in International Perspective:
The World's WCTU, 1880s–1920s
Ian Tyrrell / *217*

PART 3 • THE INEBRIATE, THE EXPERT, AND THE STATE

11. Socialism, Alcoholism, and the Russian Working Classes before 1917
George E. Snow / *243*

12. Public Health, Public Morals, and Public Order:
Social Science and Liquor Control in Massachusetts, 1880–1916
Thomas F. Babor and Barbara G. Rosenkrantz / *265*

13. Inebriate Reformatories in Scotland: An Institutional History
Patrick M. McLaughlin / *287*

14. Alcohol and the State in Nazi Germany, 1933–1945
Hermann Fahrenkrug / *315*

PART 4 • PERSPECTIVES ON DRINKING AND
SOCIAL HISTORY

15. From Fasting to Abstinence:
The Origins of the American Temperance Movement
Joel Bernard / *337*

16. The Paradox of Temperance:
Blacks and the Alcohol Question in Nineteenth-Century America
Denise Herd / *354*

17. From Symbolic Exchange to Commodity Consumption:
Anthropological Notes on Drinking as a Symbolic Practice
Marianna Adler / *376*

18. Benevolent Repression:
Popular Culture, Social Structure, and the Control of Drinking
Joseph Gusfield / *399*

Sources for the Social History of Alcohol
Jeffrey Verhey / *425*

Contributors / *441*

Index / *445*

Introduction

Susanna Barrows and Robin Room

SOCIAL HISTORY AND ALCOHOL STUDIES

This volume bears witness to the extraordinarily diverse roles and meanings attached to alcohol in modern history. Purposefully eclectic and interdisciplinary, the volume juxtaposes a number of articles written by sociologists and historians of Western culture from a diversity of perspectives. Although the methodologies of the individual contributions vary, the collection is bound together by a common concern with alcohol and social history in the broadest sense—with the place and meaning of drinking in everyday life and with the varied responses of families, social movements, institutions, political parties, professions, and states to drink. From the assembled essays much can be learned by those with a general interest in historical studies. Troy Duster's felicitous remark that "alcohol is to social science what dye is to microscopy"[1] applies with full force to historical studies: as a ubiquitous part of everyday life and as a potent medium for symbolism, alcohol can indeed serve as a revealing stain on the slide in the historian's microscope, highlighting the structures and relations of a society and the processes of stasis and change.

The Rise of Social History

Since the late 1960s historical research has turned increasingly to the study of social history as a particularly privileged key to understanding the past. The social movements of the 1960s in America and Europe impelled a sizable number of scholars to inquire into the

1

relatively neglected social movements and political conflicts that have characterized the past as well as the present. Be they Marxist or otherwise, these historians began to reconstruct the lives and collective experiences of ordinary people—workers, housewives, peasants, shop-keepers, day laborers, servants. The publication in 1966 of E. P. Thompson's *Making of the English Working Class*[2] became a model for subsequent research; Thompson's focus on the crucial transition from an agrarian to an industrial society, the impact of technological change on the common man and woman, and the emergence of a new con-sciousness provided nothing short of a blueprint for the study of class and the shared experiences of the vast majority of citizens.

Thompson chose to illuminate the characteristic conflicts of agricul-tural and industrial change—whether in the form of strikes, collective protest, or luddism. Within the next decade other historians followed in Thompson's path, studying factory protest in New England, revolu-tionary uprisings in France in 1830, 1848, and 1871, or the growth of trade unionism on both sides of the Atlantic. The harvest was of unquestioned richness: by 1980 a new labor history, distinctly populist in nature, had come of age, focusing less on leaders and select-com-mittee negotiations and more on the unsung rank and file. Political history had taken a new turn as well; Charles Tilly, Eric Hobsbawm, Michelle Perrot,[3] and many others began to uncover a struggle for political power across Europe and the United States that was scarcely described in the traditional recitations of parliamentary infighting, ministerial crises, or presidential politics. Instead, the new history of power scrutinized a far larger range of actors, whose scenarios un-folded in other locales—the shop floor, the food market, the picket line, or the barricades.

The dual focus of this new generation on labor and revolutionary protest vastly enriched the texture of modern history and altered its fundamental liberal interpretation. But however richly drawn were these new pictures of nineteenth-century society, they left unanswered many questions about the lives of ordinary people. Revolutionary crises or strikes were, after all, exceptional moments punctuating dec-ades of less momentous existence. Studying them tended to privilege the world of males over that of females and organized labor over more isolated or independent workers. In addition, they revealed far more about the world of work than about that of leisure—or what Lenard Berlanstein has called off-the-job life. Not surprisingly, in a second wave of research scholars began to explore the broader contours of working-class life, including the family, patterns of sociability, belief systems, religiosity, rituals, and the importance of local community as they shaped the lives of all citizens.

The New Focus on Alcohol in History

These issues, of course, were not wholly new concerns, nor were they wholly separate from the emphasis on work and industrialization. As early as 1845 Engels had suggested in *The Condition of the Working Class* the centrality of the family, religion, and traditional forms of leisure in working-class life.[4] The consumption of alcohol was one of Engels's benchmarks for the increasing exploitation of laborers, the breakdown of communal life, and the demoralization of the working class. Drink, of course, was not his sole—or even primary—focus, but his use of alcohol as evidence for economic and social change and class analysis set a precedent often followed. In this volume Marianna Adler's article belongs, in part, to the theoretical tradition first sketched in Engels's grim early Victorian portrait. Alcohol, in modern society, is a commodity whose attractions are shaped by the rhythms of production and the persuasive nature of advertising. It can serve as an index of demoralization and dominance, but the context surrounding its use is not invariably a tale of degradation and collective decline. To study drinking is also to examine diverse forms of sociability, to listen to the rallying cries for trade unions, socialists, ethnic groups, nationalists, and religious reformers. Such study offers one optic, a rich one, for the broader definition of power and the problematics of social relations, self-help, and social control.

If the new emphasis on social history inevitably led to a focus on drinking as an important part of social life and sociability in most industrial societies, there were also other influences pointing historians toward the history of alcohol.[5] Alcohol issues had been a neglected area in history, in part because of a generational reaction against Prohibition and temperance concerns,[6] resulting in a scholarly distaste for dealing with what were seen as misplaced and bigoted concerns—as a "crusading debauch...carried about America by the rural-evangelical virus."[7] Yet a copious supply was available of the raw material for original historical research in the enormous bulk of archival materials left behind by two centuries of self-conscious concern about alcohol issues. Brian Harrison's brilliant and painstaking study of drinking issues in Victorian Britain offered a stirring model of what could be done with all those materials.[8] As the zeitgeist has turned again to make alcohol issues a respectable concern of progressive intellectuals, historians have energetically set about subjecting the materials of alcohol history to research and interpretation.

Social History and the Social Sciences

Clearly, social historians have now set an agenda that draws much of its language, conceptual categories, and methodology from adjacent disciplines—especially sociology, anthropology, and philosophy. This branch of history has become particularly interdisciplinary and shamelessly eclectic in inspiration. But in the meantime the other branches of the social sciences have reciprocated in paying serious attention to history. American sociology, for instance, which took shape as an offshoot of social work in the early twentieth century, for a long time was a distinctly practical, problem-oriented discipline. With rare exceptions, it did not focus systematically on history—that vast, inchoate data bank of the past—before the 1960s. The migration of European scholars to the United States in the 1930s and 1940s stimulated an interest in the theoretical work of pioneers such as Max Weber, Ferdinand Tönnies, and Emile Durkheim. The broader social and intellectual movements of the 1960s led a number of scholars to the study of Marxism and other conflict perspectives and, by extension, to history; E. P. Thompson's work was read by sociologists as well as historians. In methods courses for graduate students in sociology, historical methods gained a place alongside survey research methods. Meanwhile the growth of such intellectual traditions as symbolic interactionism and ethnomethodology pointed sociologists toward emphases congenial to social historians—toward an attention to symbolic action, outsiders' perspectives, and rituals of daily life. Social historical studies have become a terrain held increasingly in common by history and other social sciences.

History and Alcohol Sociology

Although some sociological work relevant to alcohol studies can be found as early as the turn of the century, sustained attention to the field of alcohol by American sociologists was initiated only in the 1940s and 1950s, by Selden Bacon and his students at the Yale Center of Alcohol Studies. The Yale center was the nucleus of the alcoholism movement—a movement that popularized the term *alcoholism* to replace the older *inebriety* and that, in defining alcoholism as a disease for which treatment should be provided, distinguished it from so-called normal drinking. Bacon's blueprint for a "sociologic study of drinking behavior," however, had insisted on a broad focus on drinking in the context of everyday life rather than a narrow focus only on alcoholism.[9] Alcohol sociology in America has generally kept to this broader view, although such a perspective has often been in considerable tension with the alcoholism movement and with problem-oriented funding agencies. This breadth of focus has generally been lost on the mainstream of American academic sociology, which has tended to regard the subject matter as alcoholism and to treat it as a narrow subfield of social problems, a relatively low-status applied topical area.

Usually, alcohol issues have been handled in classroom sociology with a passing discussion of alcoholism and of skid-row drinkers in a social problems course.

Though cultural variation in drinking practices played a large part in American alcohol sociology in the 1950s and 1960s, relatively little attention was given to their historical dimensions. The most notable exception was Joseph Gusfield's *Symbolic Crusade,* an interpretation of the American temperance movement somewhat in the tradition of those of such contemporaries in historical studies as Richard Hofstadter, viewing the movement as an expression of symbolic conflicts over the hegemonic status of the life-styles of competing social groups.[10] *Symbolic Crusade* served as an exemplar to American sociology in general of the possibilities of historically oriented analysis, and twenty-five years later it remains, as will be seen in some of the papers that follow, a worthy whetstone for new interpretations.

Sociological attention to alcohol history has grown considerably in the last decade, in the wake of Harry Levine's pioneering paper, "The Discovery of Addiction."[11] Adapting the perspectives of Michel Foucault and David Rothman on the "shift of gaze" occurring at the close of the eighteenth century,[12] Levine argued that the concept of addiction arose, along with the temperance movement, in a societal context of increased demands for self-control. In recent years historically oriented social alcohol researchers have moved, in parallel with historians, to open up a number of new territories: the institutional history of nineteenth-century efforts to treat inebriety (see McLaughlin, chapter 13 in this volume),[13] the growth and functioning of state alcohol controls,[14] and the rise of the alcoholism movement and its role in the postwar era.[15] By and large, however, historical sociological work has been more attuned to the histories of ideas of deviance, social and political movements, and social controls in the alcohol field than to detailed work on the social history of drinking patterns, norms, and problems. Until recently, also, the focus has been particularly on American history. To a considerable extent these emphases reflected a critical role alcohol sociologists have played in regard to the modern alcoholism movement.[16]

History and the Alcohol Field

History has also played a subversive role in alcohol studies in recent decades, as perhaps it must with all timeless orthodoxies. From a clinical perspective, history often seems irrelevant or even counterproductive. A clinician's professional style of optimistic pragmatism can better sustain the illusion of progress if current methods can be assumed to reflect an unbroken chain of progress from the past and if potential alternatives can be viewed as novel departures not weighted down with the negatives of the past.[17] To point out, for instance, the recurrent cycles of clinical interest in hypnotism as a treatment for alcoholism may rather take the bloom off the rose of the report of a successful new treatment. In such a clinical perspective, historical studies may be an interesting avocation to be pursued in retirement but have nothing to contribute to practical day-to-day affairs. It is perhaps no wonder that proposals for federal support of historical research baffle clinical researchers on peer review committees.

A consciousness of history had, in fact, been part of the alcohol studies arena from about 1880 to 1930. Scholars affiliated with the temperance movement set out to apply its perspective to the "liquor problem in all ages," as one book title put it.[18] Much can still be learned from the historical material in the magnum opus of temperance scholarship, the *Standard Encyclopedia of the Alcohol Problem*.[19] A scholarly work from the 1920s, *The Origins of Prohibition*, is still widely cited.[20] With the decisive turn of American middle-class youth against temperance by the time of the repeal of Prohibition (1933), this older historical work was quickly and almost universally forgotten.

The timeless orthodoxy of the postwar decades has been that of the alcoholism movement, presenting what it called a new scientific approach to alcoholism as a disease in place of the old "moral" approach. As this governing image of alcohol issues and problems took center stage in the United States in the mid-1940s, the rich sense of alcohol history carried by older generations was occluded. Whereas in its early years the *Quarterly Journal of Studies on Alcohol* had paid substantial attention to history, by the late 1940s in its pages, time in large part stood still. In *Alcohol, Science and Society,* the record of the 1944 Summer School of Alcohol Studies, we can catch a glimpse of the antagonism between a historical consciousness and the new alcoholism perspective. It is the temperance movement representatives at that meeting who had a sense of history and who occasionally embarrassed the lecturers when they assumed, for instance, that temperance and alcoholism treatment had been antagonistic and antithetical.[21] The presentation by Jellinek, an intellectual leader of the new movement, of the symptomatology of alcoholism as a disease was quite devoid of a sense of history.[22] Only later, after a broader international experience at the World Health Organization,[23] and after he was somewhat alienated from the orthodoxy of the alcoholism movement, did Jellinek return to his substantial antiquarian interest in alcohol history.[24]

An intrinsic part of the process, in the social science literature, of gaining distance from the assumptions of the alcoholism movement has been to place it in a historical perspective as part of the larger

sweep of societal concerns about drinking. It was no accident that the
landmark National Academy of Sciences report on Alcohol and Public
Policy carried the subtitle "Beyond the Shadow of Prohibition" and
that the first supporting paper published with the report was a lengthy
interpretation of themes in American alcohol history.[25] Historical work
has thus served as a counterweight for the ahistoricism of clinical and
other alcoholism movement thought. But history, as the articles in this
volume suggest, can serve as more than mere intellectual ballast. A
better understanding of the past has much to teach us about present-
day predicaments, processes, and proposals.

THEMES AND ISSUES IN THE SOCIAL HISTORY OF ALCOHOL

Most of the papers in this volume are revised from papers presented at
a conference on the social history of alcohol held in Berkeley in 1984.
(The discussions at that meeting, along with informative abstracts of
the papers, have been separately published).[26] It was the first occasion
on which a large number of historians and social scientists with interest
in alcohol history were brought together. The scope of the Berkeley
conference was broad, including a good deal of institutional, ideological, and political history as well as social history more narrowly defined. The studies in the present volume are somewhat more closely
bounded to social history as historians would usually define the term.
They have been chosen to exemplify the widening reach of the social
history of alcohol—across different national histories, across mentalities, social movements, and institutional responses, and across different historiographical perspectives and approaches. Somewhat arbi-
trarily, the papers are grouped into four sections, although common
thematic strands twist through all the sections. Some of these strands
have been pulled out for further discussion here.

Drinking Cultures and Subcultures

Drinking, more than most other leisure activities, derives its meaning from its social context and setting. The essentially social nature of
drinking is indicated by the fact that solitary drinking is commonly
considered to be a problematic symptom. The timing, frequency, and,
above all, company of drinkers can tell us a great deal about sociability
and shared values. Unlike many aspects of historical analysis, the world
of working-class drinking has received far more attention than the
drinking culture of their social betters. The well-to-do had the luxury
of privacy and elaborate etiquettes surrounding drinking and dining,
and their consumption remained discreetly hidden from the public
record. For better and for worse, laboring people lacked such luxuries

and private pleasures. For them, drinking was to a large degree a public event that occurred in taverns, inns, pubs, cafés, saloons, or other similar locales. The precise descriptions of the physical settings stand as more than colorful detail; at best, they provide, in Clifford Geertz's phrase, a "thick description" of the amenities that attracted many a client. Customers in colonial New England could find heat, light, food, lodgings, and news of the uneasy relationship between the settlers and the British administration. A century later the American saloon and its counterparts elsewhere often resembled a pleasure palace for the ordinary man, who could find in the more elaborate examples many of the luxuries, such as gas lighting, mirrors, ornate decors and games, that only the rich could install at home.[27] Until after the First World War, newspapers were widely read in taverns, inns, and cafés. With the constant commentary elicited in these settings, so unlike the hushed silence of the public library or gentleman's club, the drinking locales served as a clearinghouse for both local and national news.

A number of essays in this collection take us into these animated, often boisterous settings. Madelon Powers evokes the rise and fall of the American saloon, and Thomas Brennan reconstructs the salty, ribald world of the eighteenth-century Parisian tavern. These settings bear scrutiny for several reasons. They suggest something of the nature and ambience of drinking, but they can also describe other aspects of collective behavior and values. The contributions of James Roberts, David Conroy, and Susanna Barrows document a distinctly political facet of the subcultures of taverns and cafés. Often the authors can give us very clear views of the perceptions of working-class drinking by those higher in the class structure. Sometimes we also get something of a picture of the actual behavior when an author tries to peer through or around the dense filter of the perceptions of the literate concerning the unlettered.

The documentation surrounding working-class drinking establishments was hardly dispassionate or complete. In a number of countries in the nineteenth and early twentieth centuries middle- and upper-class views of working-class drinking were inextricably mixed with antipathy for working-class interests and fears of revolution. Barrows has shown that in nineteenth-century France conservative social theorists focused on the inebriate as one of their major images of the much-feared urban crowd[28] and that the concerns of the willfully small and select French temperance movement were dominated by disapproval of working-class drinking.[29] Patricia Morgan has shown the same concerns carried forward into the twentieth century by the similarly minuscule temperance forces in Italy.[30] In the different political contexts of Wilhelmine Germany and Victorian Britain we can find the same kind of mixture of fear of the drinking masses and paternalistic concerns George Snow describes among the temperance movement doctors of early twentieth-century Russia.

But the concern over drunkenness or excessive drinking was not always drawn neatly along class lines. In his path-breaking study *Drink and the Victorians* Brian Harrison underlined the emergence of a split in perspectives between different elements of the working class.[31] In nineteenth-century Britain, for a working man to join the temperance movement was to declare himself aligned with progressive thought and serious about himself and his children's chances in the world. George Bretherton's essay shows an equivalent divergence in Ireland, as Jill Dodd has suggested for an earlier period in Boston.[32] Often the portion of the working-class most affected—artisans and skilled workers—was precisely that sector that had the resources for, and the tradition of, the heaviest drinking in earlier times. Adler's interpretation in this volume of the changes in the cultural signification of drink suggests that, in this respect, history was on the side of temperance. Certainly, the temperance movement has left behind a record of its view of the situation more complete than the record of the drinker's view—from Ben Franklin's observations of drinking in a London print shop, through Dunlop's chronicle of drink fines and usages, drawn on heavily by Adler, to the contemporary accounts consulted by Powers or Snow. The glimpses we gather of the unregenerate working-class perspective mostly come filtered through other sensibilities—if not through the eyes of the workers' temperate peers, then through the observations of the police and informers, whose findings permeate the contributions of Brennan and Barrows to this volume, or through the portrayals of nineteenth-century novelists from Dickens to Zola.

Another kind of split in perspective occurred in multiethnic countries such as the United States. Roy Rosenzweig has shown the strong divergence in perspectives of the Irish-American and Scandinavian-American workers in Worcester, Massachusetts.[33] Frequently, advocacy of, or agitation against, temperance became a point of demarcation between different ethnicities, as between Boers and British workers in South Africa.[34]

Colonialism offers another instructive arena for conflicting attitude toward drink. The view that subjugated peoples can't hold their liquor entered British thought early in the period of colonial expansion.[35] Whatever reality lay behind the view, it reflected fears of insurrection, which the colonizers associated with irrationality and which reinforced their conviction that access to alcohol was a prerogative of dominion. Where alcohol was previously unknown—in North America, Australia, the Pacific islands[36]—its introduction served as a potent instrument of power for whites in frontier circumstances. As Charles Ambler shows, even where there was some form of indigenous alcohol, the advent of improved transportation and new agricultural and industrial methods often transformed its availability. Lynn Pan has sketched in the use of alcohol in European interests in the long march of colonization of Africa.[37]

As the contributions to this volume suggest, the literature on drinking cultures is by no means complete. We have a sharper picture of urban and plebeian drinking patterns than of rural or bourgeois drinking patterns in the eighteenth and nineteenth centuries. Images of rural drinking were dominated by the picture of the drunken peasant on feast days, a staple of paintings and literature. What was often not noted was that in traditional economies in Europe (and in Kenya as described by Ambler) alcohol was not readily available except on rare celebratory occasions; the pattern was thus one of sporadic heavy consumption. Even in wine-growing countries poor peasants often lacked the resources to drink beverages with much alcohol in them—instead drinking, for instance, piquette, made from the fourth pressing of the grapes. The papers by Conroy and Brennan give us some inkling of the relatively low cumulative annual consumption in the countryside in many traditional societies.[38]

As for the alcoholic consumption of the privileged classes, the literature is scantier still. It is hardly surprising that aristocrats, millionaires, sturdy burghers, leading citizens, or other dominant groups drank as well, and probably more often than the poor. But precious little work has been done on the drinking habits of dominant groups in any past culture. Our ignorance partly reflects where contemporary observers turned their gaze—downward—but it also reflects the concerns of modern social historians, who have scrutinized the populace far more closely than the well-to-do. As the historian Peter Gay has noted, the bourgeoisie has remained virtually unstudied, in comparison with the working classes, the indigent, or the peasantry.[39] Although the drinking of the affluent was less visible to the public eye, and surely less disturbing, it has left countless traces for the historian to track—be they the holdings of private wine cellars, the records of country estates and urban clubs, the celebratory rituals of German fraternities or of British and American residential colleges, the menus of restaurants and ceremonial feasts, or the voluminous diaries and correspondence of contemporaries—and perhaps the richest storehouse for daily customs in the nineteenth century, the novel. Even the casual reader of the works of Jane Austen, Charles Dickens, Emile Zola, or the Goncourt brothers can discover much about the rhythms of eating and drinking and the social valences attached to the consumption of alcohol.

The emphasis in this volume is on symbols, ideologies and cultural meanings of drinking. But, as implied above, the symbolic culture of drink existed in a matrix of circumstances of material production and distribution. Charles Ambler's essay gives attention most explicitly to the material substrata of drinking—issues in the production and distribution of alcoholic beverages—although these issues are woven into the fabric of some of the other essays as well. As Ambler notes, drinking patterns in Kenya were transformed by the cash economy, the changes in agriculture, and the improvements in transportation that came with colonialism. The much greater availability of alcohol allowed it to serve as both an instrument and a symbol of the breakdown of authority relations such as age grading in the traditional society. Related patterns can be discerned in the meaning and cultural position of alcohol in European modern history. In part the temperance movements of the nineteenth century may be interpreted as delayed cultural reactions to the gin epidemic—or, in the case of North America, the whiskey glut—of the preceding century.[40] But improvements in the technology of alcohol production and in transportation have a longer history, one not yet fully told. Although distillation techniques had been known for several centuries in Europe, the shift in the status of spirits from medicine to consumable seems to have begun in the sixteenth century.[41] Control over the production, sale, and taxation of spirits in particular became an arena for struggles among various class interests and with the state in many countries in the eighteenth and nineteenth centuries. As Snow's paper demonstrates with respect to Russia, the class position and political affiliation of nineteenth-century temperance movements in different European countries were deeply affected by the outcome of these struggles.

The increasing commercialization and industrialization of alcohol production intersected with changing tastes and political decisions in the last two centuries to produce drastic alterations in the choice of beverages—for instance, in the United States, from rum to whiskey in the revolutionary era and from cider to beer later.[42] Since improved production techniques usually diffused quickly, commonalities between different national histories of the development of drinking cultures often in part reflect a shared change in the material availability of various drinks.

Societal Responses to Drinking

Along with the social history of drinking, this volume is concerned with the diverse, frequently conflictual responses to drinking. Responses by others to problematic drinking have existed at many levels and taken various forms and modes. Often the response comes in the first instance from those immediately affected—those in the drinker's family or in his or her vicinity. In many places and times the family or bystanders have acted and reacted in relative isolation, without much direct support from others. Sometimes those for whom the drinking becomes defined as a problem—the drinkers themselves or those around them—have organized themselves to cope with, or intervene in, the problems collectively. The community may also respond to problems, by attempting to help, advise, or deter problematic drinkers and by seeking to prevent future problems. Where there are community agencies to respond to drinking problems, their efforts frequently support and reinforce the informal efforts of family members and intimates of the drinker. In nation-states in the modern era, responses to drinking may also come from national, provincial, and other state entities, interacting in a complex way both with the social worlds and institutions of drinking and with the efforts of intimates and communities to cope with drinking problems. As will be seen in the essays in this book, societal responses may take many forms, involving different definitions of the situation and different agencies of control: alcohol problems may be defined, for instance, as the province primarily of clergy, doctors, social workers, or the police.

Of course, responding to problematic drinking presupposes that the drinking has been defined as excessive or troublesome. The questions of how and under what circumstances behaviors are deemed problematic have come to be of great interest in recent years to sociologists and other social scientists studying social problems.[43] Some sociologists, adopting a constructivist perspective, have insisted that what is regarded as problematic is entirely a matter of social definition in a given time and place.[44] Others see the process by which behaviors become problems as involving an interaction between objective patterns and social definitions.[45] Along with such constructivist perspectives has gone an increased interest in the history of social problems, both because the historical record underlines how very differently a given set of behaviors may be defined by the same society in different times and because the perspectives focus interest on the temporal processes of change in societal definitions.

Temperance Movements and Social History. The foreground of historical work on societal reactions to drinking has been occupied by the fact and experience of the temperance movements of the century after 1830. This preoccupation is partly because modern scholarship oriented particularly around alcohol matters has been a specialty of a small list of countries, especially those of North America and Scandinavia, in which temperance movements played a particularly strong role. In a certain sense the modern scholarship may be seen as the residual legatee of the former strength of temperance perspectives. In some countries, notably including the United States, "temperance was the most popular, influential and long-lived social reform movement" of the late nineteenth and early twentieth centuries.[46]

As Ian Tyrrell suggests in this volume, temperance movements were strong all over the English-speaking world in the nineteenth century. If Harrison's seminal social history of English temperance stressed the centrality of temperance in nineteenth-century England, temperance movements found even wider support on the periphery of the English-speaking world. In Scandinavia too, where temperance played an important role in the national histories of the late nineteenth and early twentieth centuries, it was at its strongest on the periphery—in Iceland, Finland, and Norway.[47] In continental Europe the strength of temperance sentiments and organizations varied roughly according to latitude. By the end of the nineteenth century there were important temperance movements in Germany (particularly in the north),[48] the Netherlands, Switzerland, and some Eastern European countries. In his essay Snow shows that temperance issues played a role in the revolutionary situation of early twentieth-century Russia. By contrast, in France and Italy and in other Southern European countries alcohol problems as a public issue tended to be a concern only of tiny elite groups.

There is as yet no synthetic history that attempts to understand where and why temperance was strong. The problem is not a lack of possible explanations but rather an embarrassment of riches. At its inception as a distinct movement specifically concerned with alcohol, in the United States in the 1830s, temperance was clearly associated with Protestantism, specifically with the ferment within American Protestantism known as the Second Great Awakening. Conroy's and Joel Bernard's essays give a sense of the religious antecedents of early American temperance. Temperance clearly made greater headway in Protestant countries than in Catholic ones and among Protestants than among Catholics. In the crosscutting divisions of Switzerland the temperance movement first arose among French-speaking Protestants but found its greatest strength eventually among German-speaking Protestants.[49] But there are some anomalies. As Bretherton underlines, Irish Catholics organized a strong temperance movement. In Protestant countries or groups temperance often came to be associated with dissenting and anticlerical sentiments.[50]

By and large, temperance was strongest in spirits-drinking societies and weakest in wine-drinking societies—which in Europe means stronger in colder climates and weaker in warmer ones. This pattern implies that a strong temperance movement might be seen as a delayed response in societies where traditional drinking patterns had been swamped by the advent of cheap spirits. In addition, temperance seems generally to be associated with industrialization and urbanization— perhaps more exactly with suburbanization. Graeme Decarie has shown the particular association of temperance with larger workforces in Ontario,[51] and Ray Hutchison's essay herein suggests the association with suburbanization in the United States.[52] By contrast, temperance played an extraordinary role in nineteenth-century Iceland, a country that was experiencing no significant industrialization or urbanization.[53]

In most societies temperance started as the concern of a relatively elite group, sometimes about their own drinking but more often about the drinking of others in less privileged positions. In this volume the pattern can by seen in the essays of Conroy and Bernard for the United States (although these illuminate what we might call the prehistory of temperance), Ambler for colonial Kenya, Bretherton for Ireland, and Snow for Russia. The paradox of temperance is that it became strong in precisely those countries where it was taken up as an issue by those with little status and power. In country after country the temperance movement became in its initial decades a powerful organizational and rhetorical weapon of those seeking to change the status quo. Denise Herd has shown here and elsewhere[54] the coincidence of concerns about freedom and about temperance among American blacks before the Civil War. Bretherton's contribution gives one among several available historical examples where temperance became allied with, and a vehicle for, nation building in colonized or dependent nations.[55] Tyrrell's essay underlines the extent to which temperance organizations became a main vehicle for organizing and consciousness-raising among women in English-speaking countries, with Frances Willard and others developing an analysis of women's interests in home protection in antithesis to men's drinking.[56] With respect to the other overarching cleavage of nineteenth-century politics, the conflict of classes, temperance and drinking played a more ambiguous role. In many countries the tavern served its traditional function as a nurturant medium for revolutionary sentiments and movements. In this volume the essays by Barrows and Roberts exemplify this role for working-class movements. Yet in some places the institutions of the temperance movement played a similar role; Irma Sulkunen once remarked that Barrows's description of the functions of café life for workers in nineteenth-century France sounded to her just like a description of Finnish workers at the turn of the century in their temperance clubs.[57] The strong alliance of temperance with working-class movements in Nordic countries carried over to immigrant groups in the United States;[58]

Rosenzweig shows that this alliance within the Swedish community resulted in sharp cleavages between ethnicities in the working class in an American industrial city.[59] Given this diverse experience, it is no wonder that, as Snow shows for Russia, the socialist movement was split at the turn of the century in its interpretation of temperance.[60]

For all these "progressive" movements of the nineteenth century, temperance offered an interpretation of the status quo that helped to raise consciousnesses.[61] For the women's movement in English-language countries in an era of moralization and embourgeoisement, given that drinking was already rendered morally suspect by the early temperance movement, a focus on the problems caused for women by men's drinking effectively counteracted traditional arguments of women's greater irrationality and untrustworthiness. Particularly where the alcohol supply was a profitable monopoly for the central power (as in Finland and Iceland), nation builders in dependent societies could readily portray alcohol as an instrument of domination. Ether drinking attained some of its popularity in late nineteenth-century Ireland as an alternative to paying English government taxes on "parliamentary whiskey."[62] Where organizing around nation building or class conflict was forbidden, temperance organizations often served a surrogate role, as Snow shows for turn-of-the-century Russia.

It is perhaps the fate of the progressive movements of one generation to become associated with the status quo or reaction in succeeding generations. Herd's interpretation of the history of blacks and temperance in the United States gives a dramatic instance, in a circumstance where blacks were necessarily responding to shifts in the political position of temperance in dominant groups. The image of American temperance that is still dominant in American popular consciousness and dominated historical interpretations until recent decades is an image of the mutation of American temperance, two generations after its inception, into a movement allied with illiberal, racist, and reactionary forces in the society.[63] Fahrenkrug's and Giles's essays about drinking and alcohol policies in Nazi Germany explore an extreme version of this situation, where common nineteenth-century social conceptions opened up avenues ultimately pointing toward the extermination camps.

Mutual Help, Medicalization, and Inebriety. The route from temperance to the Nazi policies in Germany lay through another territory of social reaction to drinking that has received substantial attention from historical research: the response of doctors and medical institutions to drinking as a problem. In part this interest reflects and reacts to the governing image with which alcohol matters have mostly been discussed, at least in English-speaking countries, in recent decades: the disease concept of alcoholism. The rise of the modern alcoholism movement has been chronicled for the United States.[64] Although less work as been done on other countries, it seems clear that in many industrial nations—those with an active temperance history—systems of more-or-less medically oriented treatment for alcoholism grew up in the last forty years in the context of the welfare state.[65] Stimulated by these developments, sociologists interested in the history of the medicalization of deviance, along with medical historians, have begun to open up our understanding in an international perspective of the treatment response to alcohol problems in the nineteenth and early twentieth centuries.[66] Patrick McLaughlin's essay in this volume is an original contribution to this development, distinguished particularly by his attention to the inmate's perspective on the institutions he studied. His work has already stimulated collateral analyses of Irish and English inebriate reformatories.[67]

In the earliest manifestations of the temperance movement in the United States, the attention of the artisans and professionals who joined it was focused on their own drinking. The Washingtonian revivals of the 1840s focused attention also on the reclamation of the chronic drunkard, seeking to reform him through a regimen of public testimony, mutual support, and such practical help as lodging and job arrangements. In succeeding decades the revival fervor of the Washingtonians was mostly succeeded by the more closed-ended efforts at mutual support of the temperance fraternities, which became major vehicles of the international spread of the temperance movement in the second half of the nineteenth century. Throughout the period before 1914 a concern with self-help and mutual help for those struggling to deal with their own drinking continued as a temperance theme, although that theme was increasingly overlaid on the one hand with the growing politicization around prohibition and alcohol politics and on the other hand with a professionalization of efforts to treat inebriety, as alcoholism in a general sense was then known.[68]

With a few exceptions, historical work on the self-help and mutual-help strands in the temperance movement has been relatively recent, and the picture we have is still only partial. In many European and English-speaking countries it seems that the earliest institutional arrangements for inebriates were what would now be called halfway houses or recovery homes—small boardinghouses, often under religious or temperance auspices, with a regime of "moral treatment" that today might be termed milieu therapy or a therapeutic-community approach. At their best, the program of such homes benefited from the daily and active efforts of temperance society members and committees.[69] Doctors were frequently prominent in these efforts, but they were not necessarily acting in a professional capacity, and the early homes were rarely headed by doctors or seen as medical institutions.

By the 1870s the balance had changed, and the treatment of inebriates was beginning to be seen as a professional specialty for doctors. One signal was the invention and gradual diffusion of new medical terminology for inebriety—*alcoholism* in 1848, and later such terms as *dipsomania* and *narcomania*. Doctors began to propound typologies of inebriety as part of the differentiation and professionalization of treatment.[70] Medically dominated societies oriented to the new specialty were set up in the United States and Britain. The ideal of treatment, at least for poor inebriates, shifted toward large, medically directed, state-supported asylums set in the countryside, and doctors pressed for powers of compulsory commitment for treatment. In this new environment doctors' prognoses for the success of treatment became more guarded, and theories of the origin of inebriety turned from outward causes such as social conditions or peer pressures to inward defects such as genetic degeneration. There have been a number of historical studies of this inebriates asylum movement among doctors in Britain and the United States, which never attained lasting success and generally disappeared by the end of the First World War.[71] Fahrenkrug's essay in this volume shows that the era of inebriates institutions extended in Germany into the Nazi era. In the light of the British and American studies we can see that Nazi perspectives on the alcoholic did not emerge in a vacuum. The ideologies and practices of Nazi doctors and institutions were to some extent extrapolated from the misanthropic and deterministic medical theories current elsewhere at the turn of the century.

The Social History of Societal Responses. The task for a social historian of responses to problematic drinking is to look beyond the political struggles over prohibition or alcohol controls and medical ideologies of the treatment of inebriety and to comprehend the undercurrents of problem definition and response as they shaped family, work, and community life. This task requires that our attention expand beyond the confines of legislative debates or medical journals. The essays in this volume offer a sampler of material for that expanded view. Bretherton's essay gives us a view of the self-regarding aspect of the temperance impulse—where temperance is a matter more of people seeking to remake their own life than of moral entrepreneurs busy reforming others. Tyrrell provides an exemplary study of the confluence of temperance with other large issues of the time; as he shows, the World's Women's Christian Temperance Union was not afraid to tackle large issues and in its own fashion responded energetically to the milieus of private anguish and depression in which many nineteenth-century women lived. McLaughlin's essay, as noted, offers us a glimpse of the consumer perspective on doctors' efforts to cure inebriety. By the turn of the century discussions of the handling of inebriety involved other professions besides medicine. Thomas Babor and Barbara Rosen-krantz's contribution offers a view of the work of early American sociologists, social workers, and statisticians as they set about the task of observing and measuring drinking customs and alcohol-related problems—work that Madelon Powers also draws on for a picture of the turn-of-the-century American urban saloon. Hutchison's essay outlines what happened when temperance-minded developers, combining doing good with doing well, took practical action to construct a temperance utopia as an alternative to the problems depicted in the reports studied by Babor and Rosenkrantz.

Much work in this area remains for the future. In a larger comparative perspective it is beginning to become clear that the early twentieth-century response to alcohol problems in countries with strong temperance traditions became not so much medicalized as bureaucratized.[72] In Scandinavia, Germany, Switzerland, and the Netherlands the isolated, medically directed asylum on which attention has usually focused was only a small part of the overall system of response to drinking problems.[73] There were at least two other generalized institutional responses. One was the work camp for public inebriates and other vagrants—an institution that survived into the 1960s in Norway[74] and found its analogue in the English-speaking world in the jail farms, run as part of the prison system, that were until the 1960s the main institutional response to public drunkenness in several countries.[75] The other response, of particular importance from the perspective of social history, was the community advice bureau or temperance board. *Fürsorgestellen,* or outpatient advice bureaus for alcohol problems, were an invention of a police captain in the north German town of Herford and spread rapidly through cities and towns in the German-speaking world after 1905. Functioning under a mixture of municipal, religious, and temperance auspices, they served as the nexus between private, informal efforts to control the drinker and formal responses by community agencies. Slightly later the institution of temperance boards, local committees with a mixed mandate of counseling and control for the errant drinker, took on analogous functions in Scandinavia.[76] Studies of the functioning and case records of the advice bureaus and temperance boards can provide much insight into private worlds of troubles around drink.[77] The "treatment of the inebriate," an official noted in 1939 after describing the Swedish system, "has proved a boon and a blessing to family life, mainly on account of the energetic action taken against wife tormentors and house tyrants."[78]

SOCIAL HISTORY AND ALCOHOL POLICY

Historical analyses have great potential to contribute to our knowledge of the causes of alcohol problems and to our understanding of the relationships between alcohol consumption patterns, consequences of drinking, and societal reactions to alcohol problems. A historical perspective allows us to envision and comprehend alternatives to the often-unexamined assumptions and values of our own society and our own time. Beyond that, it allows us to study the process of change as it occurs in a given society or milieu.[79] The closest we can come to demonstrating causation in nonexperimental conditions is through the study of change. No wonder Marc Bloch defined history as the science of mankind in time.

History reveals repeated instances of big shifts in alcohol consumption and alcohol problems, both upward and downward—some of these shifts occurring in a relatively short time. Except for during wartime or other interruptions of the alcohol supply, these shifts in consumption usually reflect a transformation in the cultural position and definition of drinking. A well-known example in American history is the rise of the temperance movement in the 1830s, which was accompanied by a drastic and long-lasting fall in per capita alcohol consumption. Less well recognized is the revaluation of drinking in American culture in the 1920s and 1930s—from a cultural association with working-class, immigrant, regressive life-styles to an association with upper-class, cosmopolitan, progressive lifestyles—which set the stage for the rise in consumption after the Second World War.[80] Although such upward shifts may be largely self-sustaining—in part because of the dependence-creating properties of alcohol, in part because of the vested interests created—downward shifts, if maintained, seem to involve not only a cultural shift in the definition of drinking but also legal control measures with strong popular consent. Father Mathew's crusade transformed the statistics of the alcohol problem in Ireland for a few years,[81] but the effects faded in the absence of reinforcing measures from a popularly based government. By contrast, the apparently increased effectiveness of anti-drinking-driving campaigns in recent years in the United States may be seen as reflecting the synergistic effects of new legislation and the substantial shift in popular sentiment about drinking-driving behavior precipitated by movements such as Mothers Against Drunk Driving.[82] Lagging behind, shaping and in turn shaped by the "long waves of alcohol consumption" that have intrigued alcohol scholars,[83] we may discern similar waves of such societal responses to drinking. In this spirit Jack Blocker has published an interpretation of American temperance movements in terms of five "cycles of reform," with American society presently on the upswing of the fifth cycle.[84]

Historical studies of drinking are thus not simply pleasant distractions or antiquarian pursuits. The exploration of other cultural patterns reveals much of the strangeness of our own customs; a well-chosen contrast between past and present can make history into something of a critical chisel, a tool to chip away at our own preconceptions. As this collection of essays suggests, the consumption of alcohol acquires meaning only when set into a matrix of time, place, class, gender, belief systems, and patterns of sociability. Because so much of historical documentation is embedded in moral commentary and political controversy, the best historical analyses are those that read the past with both skepticism and sympathy.

NOTES

1. Troy Duster, "Commentary," in *Alcohol and Disinhibition: Nature and Meaning of the Link,* ed. Robin Room and Gary Collins, NIAAA Research Monograph no. 12 (Washington, D.C.: U.S. Government Printing Office, DHHS Publication no. [ADM] 83-1246, 1983), 326–330.

2. E. P. Thompson, *The Making of the English Working Class* (New York: Random House, 1966).

3. For example, Charles Tilly, *The Vendée: A Sociological Analysis of the Counter-Revolution of 1793* (Cambridge, Mass.:Harvard University Press, 1976).

4. For instance, Eric Hobsbawm, *Primitive Rebels* (New York: Norton, 1965); Michelle Perrot, *Les Ouvriers en grève: France, 1871–1890,* 2 vols. (The Hague & Paris: Mouton, 1974); Friedrich Engels, *The Condition of the Working Class in England* (1845), trans. W. O. Henderson and W. H. Chaloner (Stanford, Calif.: Stanford University Press, 1968).

5. Jed Dannenbaum, "The Social History of Alcohol," *Drinking and Drug Practices Surveyor* 19 (1984): 7–11.

6. Robin Room, "Alcohol and Ethnography: A Case of Problem Deflation?" with comments and a reply, *Current Anthropology* 25 (1984): 169–191.

7. Richard Hofstadter, *The Age of Reform: From Bryan to F.D.R.* (1955; rpt. New York: Vintage, 1965), pp. 289–90.

8. Brian Harrison, *Drink and the Victorians* (London: Faber and Faber), 1971.

9. Selden D. Bacon, "Sociology and the Problems of Alcohol: Foundations for a Sociologic Study of Drinking Behavior," *Quarterly Journal of Studies on Alcohol* 4 (1943): 402–445.

10. Joseph R. Gusfield, *Symbolic Crusade: Status Politics and the American Temperance Movement,* 2d ed. (Urbana: University of Illinois Press, 1986).

11. Harry Gene Levine, "The Discovery of Addiction: Changing Concep-

tions of Habitual Drunkenness in America," *Journal of Studies on Alcohol* 39 (1978): 143–174.

12. Michel Foucault, *The Birth of the Clinic: An Archaeology of Medical Perception* (New York: Vintage, 1975); David J. Rothman, *The Discovery of the Asylum: Social Order and Disorder in the New Republic* (Boston: Little, Brown, 1971).

13. See *Contemporary Drug Problems* 13 (1986): 387–583, special issue, "Historical Perspectives on the Treatment Response to Alcohol Problems: Case Studies in Six Societies."

14. Klaus Mäkelä, Robin Room, Eric Single, Pekka Sulkunen, and Brendan Walsh, with thirteen others, *Alcohol, Society and the State, Vol. 1, A Comparative Study of Alcohol Control* (Toronto: Addiction Research Foundation, 1981); *Contemporary Drug Problems* 12 (1985): 1–158, special issue, "The Formulation of State Alcohol Monopolies and Controls: Case Studies in Five Nations"; Per Frånberg "*The Swedish Snaps: A History of Booze, Bratt and Bureaucracy*: A Summary," *Contemporary Drug Problems* 14 (1987): 557–611.

15. Carolyn Wiener, *The Politics of Alcoholism: Building an Arena around a Social Problem* (New Brunswick, N.J.: Transaction Books, 1981); Joseph W. Schneider, "Deviant Drinking as Disease: Alcoholism as a Social Accomplishment", *Social Problems* 25 (1978): 361–372.

16. Robin Room, "Sociological Aspects of the Disease Concept of Alcoholism," in *Research Advances in Alcohol and Drug Problems* (New York: Plenum, 1983), 7:47–91.

17. Robin Room, "Drinking and Disease: Comment on 'The Alcohologist's Addiction,' " *Quarterly Journal of Studies on Alcohol* 33 (1972): 1049–1059.

18. Daniel Dorchester, *The Liquor Problem in All Ages* (New York: Phillips and Hunt, 1887).

19. *Standard Encyclopedia of the Alcohol Problem*, 6 vols., ed. E. H. Cherrington (Westerville, Ohio: American Issue Publishing, 1925–1930).

20. John Allen Krout, *The Origins of Prohibition* (New York: Knopf, 1925).

21. Robin Room, "Alcohol, Science and Social Control," in *Alcohol, Science and Society Revisited*, ed. Edith L. Gomberg, Helene Raskin White and John Carpenter (Ann Arbor: University of Michigan Press, 1982), 371–384.

22. E. M. Jellinek, "Phases of Alcohol Addiction," *Quarterly Journal of Studies on Alcohol* 13 (1952): 673–684.

23. Robin Room, "The World Health Organization and Alcohol Control," *British Journal of Addiction* 79 (1984): 85–92.

24. E. M. Jellinek, *The Disease Concept of Alcoholism* (Highland Park, N.J.: Hillhouse Press, 1960).

25. *Alcohol and Public Policy: Beyond the Shadow of Prohibition*, ed. Mark Moore and Dean Gerstein (Washington, D.C.: National Academy Press, 1981).

26. *The Social History of Alcohol: Drinking and Culture in Modern Society*, ed. Susanna Barrows, Robin Room, and Jeffrey Verhey (Berkeley: Alcohol Research Group, 1987) (available from ARG, 2000 Hearst Ave., Berkeley, CA 94709).

27. See, for example, Mark Girouard, *Victorian Pubs* (1975; rpt. New Haven: Yale University Press, 1984).

28. Susanna Barrows, *Distorting Mirrors* (New Haven: Yale University Press, 1981).

29. Susanna Barrows, "After the Commune: Alcoholism, Temperance and Literature in the Early Third Republic," in *Consciousness and Class Experience in Nineteenth-Century Europe*, ed. John Merriman (New York: Holmes and Meier, 1979), 205–218.

30. Patricia Morgan, "Industrialization, Urbanization and the Attack on the Italian Drinking Culture," *Contemporary Drug Problems* 15 (1988): 607–626.

31. Harrison, *Drink and the Victorians*.

32. Jill Siegel Dodd, "The Working Classes and the Temperance Movement in Ante-Bellum Boston," *Labor History* 19 (1978): 511–531; see also George Bretherton, "Independence, Temperance and Irish Manufacture: A Perspective of the Dublin Working-Class, 1829–45," presented at the annual meeting of the Alcohol Epidemiology Section, International Council on Alcohol and Addictions, Dubrovnik, Yugoslavia, June 8–13, 1986.

33. Roy Rosenzweig, *"Eight Hours for What We Will": Work and Leisure in an Industrial City, 1870–1920* (New York: Cambridge University Press, 1983).

34. Wallace Mills, "Cape Smoke: Alcohol Issues in the Cape Colony in the Nineteenth Century," *Contemporary Drug Problems* 12 (1985): 221–247.

35. Craig MacAndrew and Robert Edgerton, *Drunken Comportment* (Chicago: Aldine, 1969); Harry Gene Levine, "The Good Creature of God and the Demon Rum: Colonial and Nineteenth-Century Ideas about Alcohol, Crime and Accidents," in *Alcohol and Disinhibition: Nature and Meaning of the Link*, ed. Robin Room and Gary Collins, NIAAA Research Monograph no. 12 (Washington, D.C.: U.S. Government Printing Office, DHHS Publication no. [ADM] 83–1246, 1983), 405–420.

36. Mac Marshall and Leslie Marshall, "Holy and Unholy Spirits: The Effects of Missionization on Alcohol Use in Western Micronesia," *Journal of Pacific History* 11 (1976): 135–166.

37. Lynn Pan, *Alcohol in Colonial Africa* (Helsinki: Finnish Foundation for Alcohol Studies, vol. 22, 1975).

38. On enslaved blacks in the United States, see Denise Herd, " 'We Cannot Stagger to Freedom': A History of Blacks and Alcohol in American Politics," in *Yearbook of Substance Use and Abuse*, vol. 3, ed. Leon Brill and Charles Winick (New York: Human Sciences Press, 1985).

39. Gay's recent volumes on the bourgeois experience will do much to fill the gaps. For examples of discussions of drinking habits of the affluent, see Irmgard Vogt, "Upper-Class and Working-Class Drinking Cultures in Nineteenth-Century Prussia," abstracted in *The Social History of Alcohol*, 57–58; Timothy G. Coffey, "Beer Street, Gin Lane: Some Views of Eighteenth-Century Drinking," *Quarterly Journal of Studies on Alcohol* 27 (1966): 669–692.

40. William Rorabaugh, *The Alcoholic Republic: An American Tradition* (New York: Oxford University Press, 1979).

41. R. Gordon Wasson, "Distilled Spirits Dissemination," *Drinking and Drug Practices Surveyor* 19 (1984): 6.

42. Peter Park, "The Supply Side of Drinking: Alcohol Production and Consumption in the United States before Prohibition," *Contemporary Drug Problems* 12 (1985): 473–509.

43. Peter Conrad and Joseph Schneider, *Deviance and Medicalization: From Badness to Sickness* (Saint Louis: Mosby, 1980).

44. Malcolm Spector and John I. Kitsuse, "Preface to the Japanese Edition: *Constructing Social Problems*," *SSSP Newsletter* 18, no.3 (1987): 13–15.

45. Robin Room, "Alcohol Problems and the Sociological Constructivist Approach: Quagmire or Path Forward?" presented at the annual meeting of the Alcohol Epidemiology Section, International Council on Alcohol and Addictions, Edinburgh, Scotland, June 4–8, 1984.

46. Dannenbaum, "Social History," 11.

47. Ann Pinson, "Temperance, Prohibition, and Politics in Nineteenth-Century Iceland," *Contemporary Drug Problems* 12 (1985): 249–266; Irma Sulkunen, "Temperance as a Civic Religion: The Cultural Foundation of the Finnish Working-Class Temperance Ideology," *Contemporary Drug Problems* 12 (1985): 267–285.

48. James Roberts, *Drink, Temperance and the Working Class in Nineteenth-Century Germany* (London: Allen and Unwin, 1984).

49. Monique Cahannes, "Swiss Alcohol Policy: The Emergence of a Compromise," *Contemporary Drug Problems* 10 (1981): 37–53.

50. Harrison, *Drink and the Victorians*; Sakari Sariola, "The Finnish Temperance Movement in the Great Lakes Area of the Midwest," *Contemporary Drug Problems* 12 (1985): 287–307.

51. Graeme Decarie, "Prohibitionism, Denominationalism, and the Work Place in Ontario," abstracted in *The Social History of Alcohol*, 161–162.

52. For the association with suburbanization in Australia, see Robin Room, "'An Intoxicated Society?': Alcohol Issues Then and Now in Australia," in John Cavanaugh, Frederick Clairmonte, and Robin Room, *The World Alcohol Industry with Special Reference to Australia, New Zealand and the Pacific Islands* (Sydney: University of Sydney Transnational Corporations Research Project, 1985), 147–215.

53. Pinson, "Temperance in Nineteenth-Century Iceland."

54. Herd, " 'We Cannot Stagger.' "

55. Robin Room, "The Liquor Question and the Formation of Consciousness: Nation, Ethnicity and Class at the Turn of the Century," *Contemporary Drug Problems* 12 (1985): 165–172; Antoni Bielewicz, "Mässigkeitsarbeit der katholischen Kirche und nationale politische Identität in Polen zu Beginn des 19. Jahrhunderts," *Drogalkohol* (Lausanne) 3 (1986): 237–247.

56. Harry Gene Levine, "Temperance and Women in Nineteenth-Century United States," in *Research Advances in Alcohol and Drug Problems*, ed. Oriana J. Kalant, vol. 5, *Alcohol and Drug Problems in Women* (New York: Plenum, 1980), 25–67.

57. Robin Room, "1982 Alcohol Epidemiology Meeting," *Drinking and Drug Practices Surveyor* 18, no.1 (1982): 44–50. Sulkunen's remark is at 48.

58. Sariola, "Finnish Temperance Movement."

59. Rosenzweig, *"Eight Hours."*

60. James Roberts, "Alcohol, Public Policy, and the Left: The Socialist Debate in Early Twentieth-Century Europe", *Contemporary Drug Problems* 12 (1985): 309–330.

61. Jed Dannenbaum, "Anti-Alcohol Mass Movements: The Cross-Cultural Perspective," presented at the Ninety-sixth Annual Meeting of the American Historical Association, Los Angeles, December 28–30, 1981.

62. K. H. Connell, "Ether Drinking in Ulster," *Quarterly Journal of Studies on Alcohol* 26 (1965): 629–653.

63. Denise Herd, "Prohibition, Racism and Class Politics in the Post-Reconstruction South," *Journal of Drug Issues* 13 (1983): 77–94.

64. Wiener, *Politics of Alcoholism*; Room, "Sociological Aspects"; Bruce Holley Johnson, "The Alcoholism Movement in America: A Study in Cultural Innovation," Ph.D. diss., (University of Illinois, Urbana-Champaign, 1973); Ernest Kurtz, *Not-God: A History of Alcoholics Anonymous* (Center City, Minn.: Hazelden Educational Services, 1979).

65. Mäkelä et al., *Alcohol, Society, and the State.*

66. Jim Baumohl and Robin Room, "Inebriety, Doctors, and the State: Alcoholism Treatment Institutions before 1940," in *Recent Developments in Alcoholism*, ed. Marc Galanter (New York: Plenum, 1987), 5:135–174.

67. George Bretherton, "Irish Inebriate Reformatories, 1899–1920: A Small Experiment in Coercion," *Contemporary Drug Problems* 13 (1986): 473–502; Jenny Mellor, Geoffrey Hunt, Janet Turner, and Lynn Rees, " 'Prayers and Piecework': Inebriate Reformatories in England at the End of the Nineteenth Century," *Drogalkohol* (Lausanne) 3 (1986): 192–206.

68. Levine, "Discovery of Addiction"; Baumohl and Room, "Inebriety, Doctors, and the State."

69. Jim Baumohl, "On Asylums, Homes, and Moral Treatment: The Case of the San Francisco Home for the Care of the Inebriate, 1859–1870," *Contemporary Drug Problems* 13 (1986): 395–445.

70. Thomas F. Babor and Richard J. Lauerman, "Classification and Forms of Inebriety: Historical Antecedents of Alcoholic Typologies," in *Recent Developments in Alcoholism*, ed. Marc Galanter (New York: Plenum, 1986), 4:113–144.

71. Baumohl and Room, "Inebriety, Doctors, and the State."

72. Per Frånberg, summary of *The Swedish Snaps.*

73. Pia Rosenqvist, "The Physicians and the Swedish Alcohol Question in the Early Twentieth Century," *Contemporary Drug Problems* 13 (1986): 503–525; Jukka-Pekka Takala, "Ideas and Organizations: Notes on the Finnish Alcoholics Act of 1936," *Contemporary Drug Problems* 13 (1986): 527–554; Ueli Tecklenburg, "The Present-Day Alcohol Treatment System in Switzerland: A Historical Perspective," *Contemporary Drug Problems* 13 (1986): 555–583.

74. Nils Christie, *Tvangsarbeid og Alkoholbruk* (Bergen: Universitetsforlaget, 1960).

75. Room, "Intoxicated Society?"; Robin Room, "Drunkenness and the Law: Comment on the Uniform Alcoholism and Intoxication Treatment Act," *Journal of Studies on Alcohol* 37 (1976): 113–144.

76. Baumohl and Room, "Inebriety, Doctors, and the State."

77. Jukka-Pekka Takala, "Social Consequences of Drinking: Responses to Misuse of Alcohol in Two Rural Towns, 1950–1980," presented at the International Group for Comparative Alcohol Studies Conference on Drinking Patterns and Drinking Problems, Zaborów, Poland, September 22–26, 1986.

78. O. Kinberg, "The Treatment of Inebriates in Sweden," in *The Twenty-second International Congress against Alcoholism, July 30th–August 4th, 1939: Volume of Proceedings* (Helsinki: Raittiuskansan Kirjapaino, 1940–1941), 307–318.

79. Thomas W. Hill, "Ethnohistory and Alcohol Studies," in *Recent Developments in Alcoholism*, ed. Marc Galanter (New York: Plenum, 1984), 2:313–337.

80. Robin Room, "A 'Reverence for Strong Drink': The Lost Generation and the Elevation of Alcohol in American Culture," *Journal of Studies on Alcohol* 45 (1984): 540–546.

81. Gustav Aschaffenburg, *Crime and Its Repression*, trans. Adalbert Albrecht (Boston: Little, Brown 1913), 129.

82. Ralph Hingson, Timothy Heeren, David Kovenock, Thomas Mangione, Allan Meyers, Suzette Morelock, Ruth Lederman, and Norman A. Scotch, "Effects of Maine's 1981 and Massachusetts' 1982 Driving-under-the-Influence Legislation," *American Journal of Public Health* 77 (1987): 593–597.

83. Mäkelä et al., *Alcohol, Society and the State*, 7; Ole-Jørgen Skog, "The Long Waves of Alcohol Consumption: A Social Network Perspective on Cultural Change," *Social Networks* 8 (1986): 1–32.

84. Jack S. Blocker, Jr., *American Temperance Movements: Cycles of Reform* (Boston: Twayne, 1989).

PART ONE

———

The Many Worlds of Drink in Europe and America

ONE

Puritans in Taverns:
Law and Popular Culture in
Colonial Massachusetts, 1630–1720

David W. Conroy

Every member of the group assembled at John Wallis's tavern in Boston on the night of February 6, 1714, was eager to have Samuel Sewall, a member of the Governor's Council and a justice of the Superior Court, join them in celebrating the queen's birthday. On this occasion they had gathered to drink to the queen's health; when Sewall entered the tavern, they rose to drink to his health, and then to the queen's health. Sewall, however, became angrier with each new gesture. He had been summoned by a constable to assist in quelling a tavern "disorder" and insisted that the company of drinkers disperse immediately. But the drinkers refused to leave, replying that they "must and would stay upon that solemn occasion." After almost an hour of argument, during which time Sewall's associate justice Edward Bromfield threatened to raise the militia to oust them forcibly, they finally departed. But they left only to rendezvous at the home of one of the group and only after demonstrating contempt for one of the highest-ranking officials in the province. As Sewall would later recall in his diary, the company had defied his order to disperse by calling for more drink, and one man actually put on a hat to "affront" him directly. Others mockingly helped Sewall spell their names for future use in court. One cursed the constable for refusing to drink a health. But perhaps the most memorable insult for Sewall was the string of reproaches to the provincial government, including the comment that it had not made "one good law."[1]

Although this particular incident was provoked by a mixed group of visiting English officers and Boston residents, it raises to view a conflict within Puritan culture and Massachusetts society of deeper dimensions than mere friction between Puritan magistrates and Anglican visitors. For almost four generations, from the founding of the colony in the 1630s to 1719, the General Court had sought to regulate closely the number and use of taverns and drink to promote the religiously sanctioned virtues of temperance, work discipline, and frugality. For Puritans, the withdrawal from the unreformed Church of England, the organization of Congregational worship in New England, and the ultimate success of the mission of colonization required a complementary repression of drinking habits and customs common in England. Every man in a position of authority became invested with the duty to restrain consumption among those under his care and government; indiscriminate gatherings of men to drink became symptomatic of disorder in the hierarchy of social control. By defining certain drinking practices as being outside the boundaries of acceptable behavior, clergymen believed they were recapturing a more virtuous past when piety and temperance prevailed. In effect, however, the forty-odd separate series of laws enacted to achieve this goal in the seventeenth century represent an innovative use of law to mold and control popular behavior according to the modern ethic of temperance. Puritan initiatives to control alcohol use thus look forward as much as backward and constitute a crucial era in the emergence of temperance as a social value and the subject of legal attention. Scholars who have considered Puritan legislation have long been aware of the gap that existed between professed ideals and social reality.[2] Yet the degree of control that elected and appointed officials exercised over alcohol use, and the extent to which they succeeded in purging Massachusetts society of customs condemned by Puritans in England, remains obscure. Did other patrons of Boston taverns share the opinion expressed in the Wallis tavern concerning controls on the use of drink? And is this the reason that the momentum behind the passage of more legislation and stricter enforcement ground to a halt by 1720?

To assess the impact of legislation on drinking behavior in colonial Massachusetts, it is necessary to understand the social functions of gatherings to drink in the seventeenth century. This task is difficult owing to the dearth of evidence on tavern use by ordinary inhabitants. The sermons, diaries, devotional tracts, and manuals of instruction written and read by ministers and devout laymen have contributed to an ever-richer understanding of the evolution of religious life in New England. But such sources are of limited use in probing the popular culture of tavern assemblies. Indeed, the conversations and actions inside these most numerous and popular gathering places are largely lost to us. Yet the volume of legislation enacted to reduce the tavern to a marginal place in community life and the strident voices raised against its prevailing use together suggest the continuing vitality of this popular culture. Moreover, by the first decades of the eighteenth century taverns began to assume a more explicit political importance. Studies by G. B. Warden and Gary Nash suggest that by the 1720s taverns began to play a role in town and provincial politics.[3] As conflict between the elected assembly and the newly established royal government intensified, taverns became important instruments in the organization of popular antipathy to royal authority. Thus, an examination of the incidence and use of taverns in the face of repeated efforts by lawmakers to limit severely their use should shed light on not only the relative impact of law on traditional customs carried over from England but also the changing configuration of political relationships in the colony after 1689.

This essay surveys this cultural conflict over the course of the seventeenth century in Massachusetts, focusing mainly on Boston. It was in Boston, the cultural and political capital of New England, that magistrates encountered the most difficulty in controlling the incidence of public houses. Licensing records help reveal how Puritan policies in this regard were progressively undermined after 1680. By 1714 the preoccupation with the enforcement of a temperate social order that motivated Sewall's night errand had begun to be replaced by new priorities among a new generation of elected officials.

Sewall enjoyed wine, beer, and cider frequently at meals and on other occasions. His diary affords glimpses of him imbibing at marriage ceremonies and government meetings and when traveling from town to town in connection with his duties as a Superior Court justice. He and other officials responsible for the enactment and enforcement of controls on consumption must not be confused with their nineteenth-century successors. Total abstinence, even from the new beverage of rum introduced for mass consumption by the end of the seventeenth century, was never a Puritan ideal. Moreover, taverns figured prominently in the operation of government, specifically providing a comfortable setting for the convening of Superior and lower court sessions and other public meetings. At the beginning of Sewall's career in government, in the 1680s, John Turner kept tavern for the Boston courts. So many sessions were held there that Turner designated one room as the court chamber. The chamber contained eleven chairs and four tables, where the justices and distinguished spectators probably sat, and three benches and a stool, probably for witnesses and defendants. Sewall himself presided over sessions in George Monck's court chamber in the 1690s. It is not clear whether justices consumed wine, beer, or even rum while hearing cases. Sewall frowned when Monck served fritters to the justices during one session.[4] But food and alcohol were certainly served and consumed by those waiting to go before the court in the other public rooms of Turner and Monck. The authority and dignity of the court obviously rested much more in the persons who convened it than in the chamber in which it was held. The fact that courts of justices met in public houses is a reflection of the structure of authority in colonial society. Government was conceived in familial terms. Heads of private households were called the governors of their families, the smallest unit in a hierarchy of patriarchal figures of authority. Magistrates exercised a broader, but analogous, type of authority when sitting in judgment of local inhabitants in a public house. The exercise of formal administrative and government functions had not yet become detached from the model of family government. Plaintiffs, defendants, and witnesses visited a house to receive justice from magistrates. The scale of social interaction, the number of people who gathered indoors at any one time, did not ordinarily transcend the scale of a house or the services that a house could provide.[5]

Sewall's diary, however, also reveals the boundaries between approved and unacceptable patronage of public houses. Sewall may have spent hours in a court chamber over several days of sessions, but he rarely, if ever, mingled with patrons in the public rooms of Boston taverns. Before the night of February 6 he had never entered the Wallis tavern, even though it was close to his home in the South End. His diary of daily contacts and conversations between the years 1674 and 1729, including thousands of entries, shows a very low rate of patronage by any standard of measurement—only about thirty visits in fifty-five years. Almost all of these instances of patronage involved attendance at a private dinner with the Governor's Council or other officials. In 1697, for example, a "Company of Young Merchants" treated the governor and council at Monck's Blue Anchor Tavern. The merchants escorted the councillors from the Town House in processional display, and most likely they all dined in Monck's court chamber.[6] The same was generally true when Sewall traveled on the Superior Court circuit. In contrast to the low rate of local patronage, he recorded 313 stops at taverns outside of Boston—mainly at taverns in Lynn, Scituate, and Roxbury, staging points north, south, and west—but he rarely engaged in any significant social contact with a tavern-keeper or his patrons. Usually he was welcomed by, or himself sought out, local officials or clergymen. As was the case when he was in residence in Boston, the pages of his diary were filled with conversations with those of high social rank. Of the twenty-five persons most often mentioned in his diary outside of the members of his family, six were ministers and fourteen held high provincial offices, of whom thirteen were graduates of Harvard College.[7]

Sewell's specialized, infrequent patronage exactly corresponds to the ideals enunciated in pulpit and law, the limitation of use to "the right ends" for which public houses were designed—namely, for "the receiving, refreshment and entertainment of travellers and strangers, and to serve publick occasions." The teachings of the church, the only other public gathering place in most towns, mandated similar restraints for all inhabitants. Sewall himself regularly attended Thursday lectures and private prayer meetings as well as Sabbath services. Moreover, he worked hard to enhance the ability of ministers and secular leaders throughout the province to preach and govern from a greater fund of Biblical knowledge. He made a habit of carrying bundles of sermons lately printed from his home to distribute to persons he met by design or chance. His conduct on January 30, 1725, was typical: "Dined at the 3 Cranes, and finished the Court there...left 3 Election Sermons and 3 of Mr. Mayhew's Lecture Sermons with Capt. Phips, viz. 2 for Col. Philips, 2 for Col. Lynde, and 2 for himself."[8] Puritanism was founded on the importance of the study and diffusion of religious texts, and Sewall believed that instruction in, and adherence to, these texts must be the mainspring of community harmony, not the habitual congregation of men to drink. Only within certain limits could the church and tavern coexist peacefully in a well-ordered community.

The commitment of Puritan leaders to the enforcement of a uniform pattern of patronage similar to Sewall's underlay the development and elaboration of legislation to regulate taverns between 1630 and 1720. But just how radical and pervasive a change in social mores such a commitment entailed is defined by contrast to traditional drinking habits deeply rooted in village life in Tudor-Stuart England. Here anthropological models and concepts can be a useful guide to the emerging conflict between advocates of temperance and tavern companies. Although such models must be applied with caution, they can in a general way help to illuminate the social functions of collective drinking in the Anglo-American world in the seventeenth century. Such studies reveal that in village and tribal societies where the production of alcoholic beverages is indigenous to the culture and economy of the locality, the distribution and consumption of drink not only serve as a fundamental source of recreation but also can play a vital role in communal bonding. In communities where kinship ties are the primary relationships shaping loyalties, where a subsistence economy is the basis of survival, and where society itself is conceived and organized in terms of dozens of families, the giving and receiving of drink is often invested with symbolic and emotional significance. Collective drinking to the point of drunkenness is often integrated into crucial intervals in the seasonal cycle of food gathering and harvest, including the local manufacture of drink. On ceremonial occasions the particular sequence, manner, and frequency with which food and drink is given or received can serve to define and reinforce loyalties, obligations, contractual relationships, and delineations of status.[9] This is not to say that drinking always contributed to harmony and never instigated discord; but it could possess a ritualistic dimension totally in keeping with the perpetuation of the cooperation of each member of a community in its survival from year to year.

Judging from the context, level, and manner of consumption in England during the sixteenth and seventeenth centuries, drinking fulfilled similar social functions in the localized society of parish and village. Three quarters of the population lived in villages and hamlets of five hundred people or fewer, and only a small percentage of the total population—the gentry, nobility, and professions—felt the presence of, or had extensive contact with, the king's government in London. Within the close-knit society of villages and market towns alcohol "played a role in nearly every public ceremony, every commercial bargain, every private occasion of mourning or rejoicing." Estimates of consumption drawn from excise figures indicate a rate of almost forty gallons per capita annually, which does not include beer brewed privately.[10] During the sixteenth century religious observance and collective drinking continued to be integrated by the ecclesiastical calendar of festivals and holidays. Many of these observances corresponded to slack work periods in the agricultural cycle. The churchyard was often the site of feasting and dancing at Candlemas, Shrovetide, Mid-Lent, Easter, Mayday, Whitsuntide, and Midsummer. The officers of craft guilds financed "drynkynges" for their members, as did landlords for their tenants and laborers.[11] Drunkenness was acceptable behavior on certain days and weeks when the rhythm of work eased and an entire community could indulge in Brueghelian excess. At such gatherings health drinking was a common custom. A pamphlet published in London in 1682 reveals the degree to which this "ceremony" celebrated personal bonds and obligations in a society structured by patron-client and master-servant relationships. The author condemned the assumption that men who did not drink a series of healths to the king should be suspected of disloyalty to their sovereign or their fellows, for "loyalty and respect to others is not proper to be shewn in so absurd a method." Repudiating the symbolic link between drink and life, he asked, "How can any man drink another's Health?" and "By what new kind of Transubstantiation can his Health be converted into a glass of Liquor?" All of the "modes and ceremonies in drinking" described, including the postures of "prayer standing up, standing bare, sometimes kneeling upon their knees," suggest the symbolic significance of the distribution and exchange of drink in English communities.[12]

Yet, as this pamphlet also indicates, the habitual use of drink in almost every aspect of private and public life had begun to come under concerted attack during the seventeenth century. State initiatives to implement more formal controls over the sale and use of drink were mainly inspired by the fear aroused by the multiplication of taverns and particularly alehouses amid massive disruptions in the organization and customs of community life. The population of England nearly doubled between 1540 and 1640. The enclosure of estates to accommodate shifts in land use forced many tenants off the land to join an increasing number of underemployed, masterless transients moving from parish to parish in search of work. Migration from one community to another no longer took place solely within established kinship networks or between households. The presence of such unemployed transients served to underscore the fact that relationships between patron and client, landlord and tenant, and master and servant within the network of personal bonds and loyalties that constituted society at the local level had become more tenuous, more easily disregarded, more closely attuned to the pursuit of profit and individual advantage in a market economy.[13] The multiplication of alehouses, numbering thirty thousand in England and Wales by one report in the 1630s, began to be perceived as a potential threat to the king's order.[14] Collective drinking no longer served to integrate the social structure in the traditional manner. Groups of idle, masterless men—often hungry and undernourished—lived outside the governance of patriarchal households. State and local authorities became preoccupied with the problem of restoring them to employment and overseership and keeping them out of the alehouses now associated with idleness and rebellion. As more and more men drank as strangers outside of the accustomed social networks of an agricultural society, it is probable that consumption did begin to have more acute effects on physical and mental health. To drink to someone's health even came under question.[15]

James I considered the expansion of regulatory controls over the growing number of alehouses to be a matter of the first priority. In a speech to the Star Chamber in 1616 he declared the "abundance of alehouses" to be one of the most serious offenses in his realm and commanded "all Justices of Peace" to have them "pulled downe." He complained of alehouses as places of "receipt" for "Stealers of my deer" and of horses, oxen, and sheep from the country at large: "There would be no thieves, if they had not their receipts, and these Alehouses as their dennes." On this issue James and Parliament could agree. The Parliament of 1604 introduced and debated eleven bills concerning the regulation and reduction of alehouses. In 1599, 1604, 1608, and periodically thereafter the Privy Council ordered local justices responsible for granting licenses to purge and reduce their numbers.[16] Peter Clark has concluded that the alehouse never became as potent a source of local disorder as its more virulent critics feared in part because of the expansion of administrative controls during the first half of the seventeenth century.[17] Yet no matter how many local purges took place, poverty and consumer demand ensured that the incidence of drinksellers remained high. They continued to be viewed as flashpoints of disorder, especially during grain shortages. The Black Act of 1723, which made poaching a capital offense, was partially inspired by the use of alehouses and taverns on the edge of royal forests and private parks as points of rendezvous and sale for poachers.[18]

The Reformation gave additional momentum to the definition of intemperance and tavern haunting as an issue requiring state action. Puritans in positions of authority at the local and national levels were at the forefront of the agitation for the establishment of more legal controls over the sale of drink; but their attacks on intemperance were just one aspect of a more comprehensive program of reform in church and state. By the 1630s many of the processions and ceremonies such as those on Saint George's Day, Ascension, and Whitsun had disappeared in some localities; but Puritans demanded the elimination of all such celebrations including church ales and Sunday sports. They repudiated the Anglican ecclesiastical calendar altogether and advocated sustained, methodical application to one's calling, whatever the season, excepting only the Sabbath, the only Biblically sanctioned day of rest. For Puritans, the cultivation of a reasoned understanding of the scriptures under the leadership of an educated ministry became the foundation for criticism of the established church as a vast repository of ritual and magic.[19] Although leaders of the reform movement remained as concerned as their Anglican counterparts with the potential threat that taverns and alehouses might pose to constituted authority under certain conditions, they simultaneously sought to reform the structure of church and state in ways that challenged the standing order. Idle, dissolute aristocrats as well as laborers became targets of criticism. Puritans would ultimately prove to be the much greater threat to the stability of the Stuart monarchy than alehouse crowds.

It is against this socioeconomic background of decay and reorganization of traditional institutions that the behavioral ideals reflected in Sewall's diary crystallized into a more demanding religious code. During the first decades of colonization, however, a number of the conditions that had stimulated the articulation of this code were absent. In New England Puritans no longer faced the immediate problem of challenging church and state creeds. By the very act of migration the powerful influence of tradition as embodied, for example, in the Anglican ecclesiastical calendar, was eliminated. Religious holidays such as saint's days that continued to have vitality in England were not revived. Even Christmas passed unnoticed. Almost annually on December 25 Sewall noted in his diary with satisfaction that "shops [are] open as at other times" and that "provisions, Hay, wood, [are] brought to Town." He once chided two boys for playing tricks on April 1 because New England men "came hither to avoid anniversary days, the keeping of them, such as the 25th of Decr."[20] True, a number of efforts to revive such observations occurred after 1680, when the colony lost its charter and the first royal government was installed. But such efforts did not attract a popular following. Sewall noted on Christmas Day, 1685, that "some somehow observe the day" but are vexed because "the Body of the People profane it." He blessed God that there existed no authority as yet "to compell them to keep it." Sewall remained so confident of the lapse of interest in the traditional calendar that he proposed to the Council in 1696 that Tuesday, Thursday, and Saturday be renamed the third, fifth, and seventh days of the week because "the Week only, of all parcells of time was of Divine Institution."[21] The motion did not pass, but the fact that such a proposal could be seriously considered suggests that colonists as a whole, first and succeeding generations, had made a distinct break with the pagan and Christian amalgamation of observations and with the customary use of drink on those days. Although a vast majority of inhabitants continued to labor according to the irregular dictates of season and weather, religious observance was separated from the agricultural cycle without conflict.

Migration also changed the social landscape of drinking. There were no groups of idle, hungry, and masterless men congregating in alehouses and constituting an alternative society separate from the personal control and overseership of the governing hierarchy. Exaggerated fears concerning the alehouse as a seedbed of revolt and disruption no longer had currency. With the exception of Boston most towns in Massachusetts had only one or two licensed houses through the first fifty years of the colony's existence. The low density of settlement helped to sustain personal contact between those of high and low status. It was the sectarian challenges of Antinomians and other splinter groups to the new Congregational establishment that preoccupied magistrates concerned with stability and order.[22] Colonists had left behind the social and economic conditions that had contributed to the emergence of intemperance as an issue in English society.

Public houses, however, remained necessary institutions in the agricultural towns the colonists founded, and the regulation of the use of these taverns remained a priority. The exacting personal standards of the first generation of clerical and secular leaders, the vision of reformed churches becoming the spearheads of reformation, and the messianic impulse to found communities distinctive from those left behind all contributed to the close attention given by the General Court to regulation once the first difficult years had passed. When the court outlawed health drinking in 1639 it stated that such a "useless ceremony" should be abolished "especially in plantations of churches & commonwealths, wherein the least knowne evills are not to be tolerated, by such as are bound by Soleme Covenant to walke by the rule of God's word in all their conversation."[23] Health drinking might have easily continued to be common because Puritan concepts of community life remained grounded in tradition insofar as colonists aspired to re-create consensual communities in which self was subordinate to the common welfare. Although in fact they made distinct breaks with tradition, the past remained their spiritual guide.

The control of taverns also assumed a new importance in the minds of Massachusetts leaders as the implications of the evolution of the colony's institutions became more apparent. What prerogatives should leaders in church and state possess in a society in which distinctions of status were less marked than in England? In the social and institutional context of England Puritan congregations had been an embattled subculture. Theoretical arguments concerning the degree to which ministers should share power with the laity drew on Calvinist doctrines but were also influenced by the immediate need of dissenting clergy to gather support from the laity in resisting harassment from the state. In Massachusetts, however, ministers sought to moderate the trend toward "democratical confusion" by investing the pulpit with more formal powers. The Cambridge Platform drawn up in 1646 delegated to the clergy certain prerogatives over the definition of doctrine and the admission of new church members, but the vital power of ordination and dismissal remained in the control of individual congregations. Local churches also negotiated the salaries of their ministers.[24] As long as a minister could inspire his congregation to piety, his position was a commanding one. But by stripping the church of the power and majesty of the ecclesiastical hierarchy, of rich ornament and distinctive architecture, Puritans divested the ministry of the accoutrements, emblems, and symbols of authority. Hence levels of tavern patronage assumed an immediate importance as a measure of a minister's influence over his congregation and of the success or failure of his performance. Puritan ministers were charged with the responsibility of purging church and community of ritual folk practices of communal significance; but at the same time they had become more dependent than their Anglican counterparts on their congregations for financial support and continuance in office. Unrestrained, uninhibited conversation in taverns respecting the style and content of a minister's preaching could have serious consequences for his position in the community.[25]

Regulation became vital in a colony in which local and colonywide systems of government allowed for wider participation in the choice of rulers. The opportunity to acquire property opened up the traditional restrictions on the franchise that prevailed in England. As with the organization of church government, secular leaders sought to amend and qualify trends toward the decentralization of power. Voting privileges for some offices were limited to church members, a buttress to dominance by the pious and those who controlled admission to membership. But participation in local elections always outstripped the more restrictive franchise in England, as did the number of officials (relative to population) elected annually. In the society that Massachusetts colonists had abandoned, only a tiny percentage of the patrons of the more than thirty thousand public houses possessed any formal right to participate in the government of their communities. English justices and members of Parliament feared crowd actions and riots instigated in tavern assemblies, not election results. But almost an opposite ratio quickly became applicable to the some two hundred public houses in the colony by the end of the century. Of about one thousand adult males resident in Boston in 1683, approximately one hundred were elected to some type of office. It has been estimated that about 70 percent of free adult males in Boston were eligible to vote in town elections in 1687, although only a minority regularly did so.[26] Deference and the belief in a divinely ordained hierarchy of superiors and inferiors influenced all elections. Few men possessed the time and skills necessary to fill the most important offices. Nevertheless, political power had become decentralized in each community and in the General Court. If popular behavior became corrupted in taverns, if rulers did not conform to the ideal character of a good ruler, the consequences could be more serious for the conduct of public affairs, not to mention the goals motivating colonization, than in England.

Magistrates instituted controls over the sale of drink during the first decades of the colony, but not in any alarmist fashion. The chief method of control was the licensing system. The procedures developed over the course of the seventeenth century drew on English practice in many respects but were engrafted into institutions of government that departed from English models in significant ways. In 1633 any person wishing to sell wine or distilled liquors simply asked permission from the governor or deputy governor. The growth and dispersal of population and the formation of new towns and county courts stimulated the elaboration of more systematic procedures. The General Court ordered every town in 1639 "to present a man to be allowed to sell wine and stronge water." The court delegated the authority to grant licenses to the quarter courts staffed by appointed justices in the 1640s. Participation by town selectmen in the approval of those licensed apparently remained vague until a law of 1681. For the future "the selectmen of all towns shall approve of all persons to be licensed before licenses be granted to any of them by the County Court."[27] By this law licenses had also to be renewed annually. Continuance of a license became conditional on annual review of conduct. With this law the fundamental importance of the town as opposed to the county as the primary administrative agent of colony authority was recognized by the inclusion of selectmen in the licensing process.

Part of the impetus to restrict licenses to those carefully screened by selectmen and justices, to make licenseholders quasi-public officers of regulation in their respective communities, was the effort to restrict access to the increasingly diverse and potent beverages available for consumption. Changes in drink manufacture and consumer taste are difficult to trace. Generally speaking, however, the seventeenth century witnessed an expansion in the trade of alcoholic beverages and the raw materials for their manufacture, culminating in the emergence of rum and molasses as vital components in the Atlantic trading networks established by Boston merchants. What was consumed became less tied to local conditions and products, less entwined with the operation of farming households. At the time of migration beer had gradually begun to supplant ale among the populace at large; wine and distilled liquors were more commonly consumed by people of means. This division is reflected in English distinctions between drinksellers roughly defined by the terms *inn, tavern,* and *alehouse.* The inn was a large establishment that sold wine and distilled liquors and catered mainly to the elite. Taverns also sold wine to a fairly select clientele but did not have the extensive accommodations of the inn. Almost anyone could set up the much more prevalent alehouse, where ale and beer could be bought for consumption in or outside the premises.[28]

In Massachusetts distinctions between establishments were less marked. The terms *tavern* and *inn* described houses where varied beverages, usually including wine, could be consumed and lodgings obtained. Retailers could sell for consumption only "out of doors" or at the purchaser's home. During the seventeenth century each licenseholder was restricted to sales of certain beverages. In 1677 only seven of the twenty-seven people approved by the Boston selectmen could sell wine. The rest sold mainly beer and cider.[29] The General Court sought to ensure the quality of the beer brewed and sold and promote it and cider as the staple alcoholic drinks. Price controls guaranteed that cheap and affordable drink was always available. Such controls also acted as a limit on the amount of malt used in a brew and thus reduced the potency of such beverages. By law of 1637 no person could sell any beer, wine, or other drink for more than one pence a quart. The General Court hesitated in 1679 to outlaw the sale of alcohol at public outdoor gatherings such as militia training days despite reports of drunkenness, but it did order that only "beer of a penny a quart" be sold, presumably to inhibit drinking to the point of drunkenness.[30] Lawmakers considered alcohol to be a staple part of every adult's diet and in no way wished to interfere with the customary use of it at meals and for refreshment. But they did wish to prevent the populace from purchasing high-priced beverages for use beyond basic dietary needs.

The licensing restrictions formed the foundation of the magistrates' efforts to define and enforce a temperate standard of conduct for all inhabitants. It became necessary, however, to supplement this system with a host of other laws because it did not function as intended. The English alehouse, the ubiquitous magnet for laborers in the English countryside, was not so easily abolished in Massachusetts. Retailers' houses continued to function as alehouses in that their proprietors allowed drinking on the premises. Laws enacted in 1639, 1654, 1661, and the 1690s testify to their social importance as gathering places. The office of tithingman, created in the 1670s for purposes of general moral regulation, became specifically responsible for the discovery of unlicensed houses and those violating the terms of their licenses.[31] No matter how carefully screened, sworn, and bonded, licenseholders generally did not conceive of themselves as moral watchdogs of drinking behavior but continued to preside over, and contribute to, the perpetuation of popular traditions in the use of drink.

Much of the information about these traditions comes from the laws enacted to prohibit them. In 1639 the General Court decreed that any person who "directly or indirectly by any color or circumstance drink[s] to another" would be fined. Health drinking was not just an occasion for the consumption of a series of drinks but a custom associated with "profane" postures and pagan ritual. Formal covenants proscribing drunken oaths and conversation must now be the basis for defining social relationships. This law, however, was so universally disregarded that it suffered repeal in 1645. Efforts to purge the exchange of drink in labor contracts and agreements met the same fate. A decree in 1633 ordered all laborers to work the entire day, an indirect reference to the practice of drinking at intervals during the day. When William Whyte was fined for selling beer without a license, he defended himself by saying that his intentions had been "only to brew a little small beere, for ye Collyers and other workmen," they "being Destitute of necessary Things for ye purpo[se]" and without which they could not "so comfortably proceede in their workes." By law of 1645 laborers could not be given drink as part of their wages. Yet consumption continued to punctuate the course of labor, evident by the fact that it was deemed necessary in 1672 to forbid the "allowance of licquors or wine every day, over and above their wages" even though some "refuse to work" without it.[32] Laborers continued to expect and demand the provision of drink as a condition of employment and an obligation of the employer.

When the General Court sought to restrict the volume of drink consumed at taverns and eliminate drunkenness, violation and evasion of the law became routine practice. "Excessive drinking" punishable by fine was defined in 1645 as the allowance of above one half-pint of wine to one person at one time.[33] This action was part of the court's effort to repress the consumption of wine in favor of beer and cider and prevent drinking to the point of drunkenness. Yet evidence indicates that all types of alcohol were commonly drunk in large quantities from vessels above one half-pint in the seventeenth century. A 1682 pamphlet published in London is instructive here. The author cites instances of persons carrying "pails of drink into the open fields," of alewives serving "pots" of drink, of a vintner "standing in his door with a pot in his hand to invite guests," of "certain Gentlemen drinking Healths to their Lords, on whom they had dependence," and of one laying hold on a "pot full of Canary Sack" asking, " 'What will none here drink a Health to my Noble Lord and Master?' "[34] Boston tavern-keepers served beverages by quarts and pints more often than any other quantity judging from inventories of the 1680s and 1690s. John Turner did have three quarter-pint and four half-pint vessels, but he served wine and other liquors more often in his six wine quarts, four beer quarts, and eleven pints in the 1680s. Witnesses waiting to be called into Turner's court chamber violated the drinking laws even as justices sat in the other room. Nicholas Wilmot had only eight pint pots as opposed to twenty-one quart pots, Captain William Hudson five pots less than a pint and eighteen of a pint and more, and George Monck four half-pints as opposed to sixteen pints and quarts.[35] Two of these taverns were settings for court sessions. The majority of other tavernkeepers may have possessed a more narrow range of vessel sizes. True, pots of drink were often passed around or used as punch bowls would be later, but travelers often drank alone. The overall impression is one of large quantities consumed over an extended period of time.

The laws are, of course, an imprecise means of describing drinking behavior by the populace at large. Perhaps evasion was characteristic of only a minority of colonists during the first decades of the colony.

Certainly a number of statutes targeted particular age and occupational groups such as mariners, servants, apprentices, laborers and youths—groups who probably sought tavern fellowship as a release from subordination in other settings. In 1651 the General Court complained of various "corrupt persons...who insinuate themselves into the fellowship of the younge people" and encourage them to drink to "the grief of their parents, masters, teachers, tutors, guardians, overseers."[36] Such laws do suggest that the elected representatives of a temperate majority were simply trying to discipline an intemperate minority. It is difficult to draw a profile of the most frequent offenders because a majority of drinking offenses could be heard by individual justices. Yet a consideration of the laws as a whole, together with the incidence of licensed houses, indicates that "excessive" drinking was characteristic of a broad segment of society, not just particular groups. The repeated recourse to law itself suggests that magistrates and deputies could not rely on heads of households and employers to discipline those under their government to the degree desired. What leaders defined as intemperance may have been considered by a majority of patrons to be traditional and natural levels of consumption. Alcohol use did not interfere with the accomplishment or quality of the manual labor most colonists performed on farms or in shops but only extended it over a longer period of time. In any case, the court by its own admission could not contain consumption within levels considered acceptable. In 1648 the deputies admitted that "excess" drinking continued despite all the "hoalsome laws provided and published." In a preface to a 1651 law they explained the need for more legislation by stating that "notwithstanding the great care" the court had taken to suppress drunkenness, "persons addicted to that vice finde out ways to deceve the laws." Again in 1664 the court became "sensible of the great increase of prophaneness amongst us." Edward Ward, a critical visitor to Boston in 1682, was struck by the widespread evasion of the laws respecting drink and taverns; he wrote that "all their laws look like Scarecrows" compared to their habits, for "the worst of drunkards may find Pot companions enough, for all their pretences to Sobriety."[37]

The stability of local and colony government, the ability of John Winthrop and other leaders to solve the problems of institutional definition as they surfaced, together with high levels of church membership, made the seeming ineffectuality of temperance laws during the first fifty years of the colony little more than an irritant for most leaders—a visible flaw in a society conceived as a model of reform, but not a source of alarm. Given the scholarly zeal of ministers for discovery and dissemination of the Word, they remained more sensitive to the issue of tavern regulation. By the 1680s, however, they hammered on the theme of intemperance from less secure positions. Declining numbers of applicants for church membership eroded their social and political influence and automatically stirred new anxiety over the influence of drinking fellowships. David Hall has shown that the second generation of ministers confronted more contention in their churches, faced increasing difficulties in securing adequate salaries from their congregations, and were consequently less likely to continue as minister to one church for the duration of their careers.[38] The polarization of some towns over the location of meetinghouses contrasted with the easy multiplication of taverns to accommodate the dispersal of population over a wider land base. Nathaniel Saltonstall, deputy to the General Court from Haverhill, complained to the Essex County justices on this issue in 1696.

> I always thought it great prudence and Christianity in our former leaders and rulers, by their laws to state the numbers for publique houses in towns, and for regulation of such houses....But alas, I see not but that now, the care is over....I pray what need of six retailers in Salisbury, and of more than one in Haverhill, and some other towns, where the people when taxes and rates for the country and ministers are collecting with open mouth complain of povertie and being Rudely[?] dealt with, and yet I am fully informed, can spend much time, and spend their estate at such blind holes, as are clandestinely and unjustly petitioned for, and more threaten to get licenses.[39]

Inhabitants seemed ready to support a higher incidence of taverns but quarreled over the expense of support for the church.

The clergy increasingly resorted to the delivery of jeremiads, scathing denunciations of intemperance with the promise of God's awful judgement. Increase Mather warned his congregation in 1673 that they might drink the "conscience into a deep Sleep, but when their souls shall awake in the midst of Eternal Flames, all the wounds received by this sin will be felt with a witness."[40] But such a strategy had its dangers, for if a minister elicited no response from his congregation, no change in habits, the jeremiad might be turned against him in mockery of his claims. Samuel Danforth did succeed in stimulating a revival and a renewal of the church covenant in 1676 and again in 1705 in Taunton. The possibility of a different outcome to his efforts, however, was implicit in the provisions of the covenant renewal, namely the reform of unnecessary patronage and expressions of "contempt" for the "Magistracy and Ministry." Benjamin Wadsworth took a more conciliatory approach in a later sermon, enumerating the "useful" functions of taverns and even of rum on certain occasions "lest I should be mis-interpreted, or be thought to run into extreams." Cotton Mather observed in 1708 that the use of rum "may not be amiss for many laboring men, especially when Extream Heat, or Extream Cold, Endangers them in their Labours." Yet if Mather could have prevented the importation and manufacture of rum, he would have done so, for it threatened "a Confusion to all Societies" and would subvert "Good Order" everywhere. The "Votaries of Strong Drink will grow so numerous, that they will make a Party against anything that is Holy, and Just, and Good."[41] Danforth spelled out the threat to secular officers as well. If the "Drinking party is so potent as to prevail over the Small Number of Sober Men, that are the Remnant of God's People in the Land, then none Shall be improved in offices of trust but Such as Work at, favour and countenance this Vice."[42]

Deputies to the General Court did respond to clerical admonitions for lax enforcement, for after 1680 the colony received several shocks to its stability that made leaders more concerned with the maintenance of order at all levels of society. The Crown had been hostile to the defiant claims of the colony to autonomy since its founding. But only after the restoration of the Stuart monarchy did efforts begin to abridge self-government in all the colonies and particularly in Massachusetts. The 1629 charter was voided in 1686, replaced by the government of the Dominion under the hated Edmund Andros, only to be overthrown in 1689 upon news of the Glorious Revolution. The interim government after 1689, which never possessed any real legitimacy, was in turn replaced by a new charter making Massachusetts a Crown colony. A royal governor arrived in 1692 to rule together with an elected council and assembly. In all, Massachusetts experienced six major changes in the structure and personnel of government at the provincial level between 1686 and 1694. The restriction of the franchise to church members ended, and many leaders became more concerned with the restive and assertive posture assumed by many colonists during the overthrow of Andros and in the years that followed. Ministers interpreted the problems of the colony as divine punishment for immorality. It seemed more imperative than ever to promote reformation through the imposition of additional control over drink and taverns.[43]

By the 1680s applicants for licenses were required to obtain approval from both selectmen and justices. In the 1690s the process underwent further revision. By law of 1698 the date on which licenses could be considered and renewed was limited to the first session of the Court of General Sessions on an annual basis. Licenses could not be renewed to any "that the Selectmen shall except to." By establishing a special licensing session when all applicants could be considered together at one time, the assembly took back part of the power delegated to the county authorities in the 1640s, for at any other time of the year applicants had first to petition the governor, council, and assembly for authorization to go before the justices.[44] These procedures were in some ways more rigorous than those of England, where county justices almost alone controlled the issuance of licenses. In Massachusetts the assembly increased the number of officials involved in the process ostensibly to tighten and enhance the impact of regulation. But this imposition of new regulations involved the delegation of power in the licensing process to town selectmen, officials in some cases elected by the very people who defied the laws respecting drink. After the 1680s this decentralized structure of political authority, on the one hand, and the persistent efforts of the assembly to mobilize all officials to enforce the laws, on the other, came into conflict more directly.

The assembly of town deputies had already recognized the weakness of regulation at the local level by its decision to seize the licensing system in 1681 and make it work as intended. Deputies decided to reduce and fix the number of licenses in the entire colony, from forty-five to twenty-four in Boston and to one in every other town in the colony except for six seaport towns. This action reduced the incidence of public houses in Boston from one for every 133 inhabitants to one for every 250 according to population figures in 1687. But this order only exacerbated the already existing problem of unlicensed houses. George Monck and four other Boston tavernkeepers who had survived the purge and were attempting to conform to the laws complained to the assembly that a "great number" of Bostonians "presume openly in Contempt of Authority to Violate & breake the whole some Laws Established amongst us...And without Lycense or paying to the Publique doe dayly and frequently draw & sell by Retail Wine, Syder and all other Liquors at their pleasure without controle." They also allowed drinkers to "Set & Drinke, play and Revell in their houses at any time as long & as often as they please."[45] The same year the assembly allowed five more to be licensed in Boston. By the end of the decade the legal number had crept back up to forty-three, though the population of Boston remained stable. Eighteen of the licenses were held by widows, although widows had been the major victims of the purge of 1681. By 1696, just before the enactment of the new licensing restrictions, seventy-four people held licenses, or approximately one public house (taverns and retailers) for every hundred inhabitants.[46] Saltonstall complained of the rise in incidence of licenses in Essex County at the same time. Sewall and other members of the government did not contribute much to the custom of Boston drinksellers between 1670 and 1720, but they found profit in the habitual patronage of a small number of customers.

Passage of a spate of new laws in 1693, 1695, 1696, and 1698 accompanied reform of the licensing system. The levying of excise taxes on a regular basis after 1690 was partially motivated by the goal of reducing the consumption of the increasingly popular distilled liquors. The principal targets of taxation were wine and rum. By the excise of 1698 the levy on wine ranged from six to twelve pence a gallon; for beer, ale, and cider it was one shilling and six pence a barrel.[47] At the annual licensing session justices estimated the amount each would sell in the ensuing year. Every licenseholder also had to keep accounts. Given the chronic evasion of the laws before the excise levies, it is no surprise that these laws included detailed reiterations of penalties for unlicensed sales and monetary incentives for informers. The excise taxes, however, did nothing to halt the increasing popularity of rum, for by 1712 the assembly took the radical step of banning the sale of all distilled liquors in taverns.

Again in 1698 the assembly considered intervention in the licensing system to fix the number of public houses even as it passed new laws to tighten the system. Though the deputies to the assembly supported the action, the governor and council voted against it, perhaps in recognition of social realities. In 1704 the governor, council, and assembly reminded the justices of the county sessions, and probably the Boston selectmen as well, that "for many Years Last past the General Assembly, as well as the Ministers in the several parts have...laboured to prevent the Growth of Intemperance and Debauchery by all possible means and amongst others by abridging the Number of public houses in Boston, Charlestown, and Salem the principal seaports for the prescence of seamen and strangers." The letter also instructed the justices to take particular care that only "persons of good reputation be licensed" and that "licenses be given to Men & no Widows Who Cannot Support the Government of their Houses."[48] At the same time the assembly considered fixing the number of licenses once again. Later, in 1710, it ordered a reduction in all country towns to one innholder and one retailer "unless the selectmen of the town shall judge there is need for more for the better accommodation of travellers."[49] Although some degree of discretion was allowed selectmen, they came under pressure to justify each license.

With this series of new laws and initiatives in the 1680s and 1690s the assembly began to test the limits of law as an instrument of social reform and control. On the one hand, the deputies expressed confidence in their ability to maintain and perpetuate a political system informed by habits of deference when they enacted new laws on top of old ones. In addition, the new legislative surge is indirect testimony to the willingness of voters to reelect representatives who enacted widely evaded and unpopular laws, laws that affected the very core of social

life. On the other hand, by repeatedly charging all elected officials to
enforce the laws vigorously, the assembly came close to exposing the
weakness of the force of law relative to the force of popular resistance.
The feeble state of regulation is implicit in the 1695 warning to all
officials that if they were convicted of "taking any bribe, fee, received
directly or indirectly, to connive at, conceal, or not to present or inform
against any person or persons being licensed to retail" for consumption out of doors only; or if they concealed people who allowed
drinkers to gather in their houses or who sold without license, those
officers must "pay three times the value. . . received as a bribe."[50] Such
warnings narrowed the degree of discretion allowed officials responsible for enforcement and moved them into the category of lawbreakers
themselves. The assembly could maintain the authority of law by compelling the machinery of enforcement stretching beneath it—justices,
selectmen, constables, tithingmen, grand jurors—to enforce its statutes, but it also risked multiplying the instances of confrontation between elected officials and the populace at large.

Considered against this overview of the escalation of temperance
agitation, Sewall's confrontation with the Wallis tavern company assumes new meaning. By the end of the seventeenth century Boston had
become a major stimulus to the enactment of more legislation because
of its growth into a commercial seaport. A rising proportion of mariners and transients with little or no identification with Puritan social
ideals made Boston the site of polar extremes in patterns of tavern and
drink use. Boston merchants, some hostile to the Puritan establishment, regarded rum as a vital component in the emerging Atlantic
trading system that enabled Massachusetts to dispose of its produce.[51]
More than those of any town, Boston selectmen faced a difficult task in
enforcement. Under pressure from the assembly they did make an
effort. The seventy-four houses licensed in 1696 dropped to a low of
sixty in 1705 at about the time the assembly considered seizure of the
system. The same year the assembly refused to approve five applicants
for licenses who had won approval from county justices, declaring "it to
be their opinion that there are more than enough of Such lycenced
Houses Already, and that the new granting of more will be of Ill
Consequence to this Town." The number did rise again to seventy-two
by 1708 but then fell back to sixty-one in 1710. In 1709 the selectmen
refused even to consider sixteen petitions because "there [are] more
than enough" public houses. They decided to refuse renewal of another nineteen licenses in 1710 in response to the act for reducing "the
over great number of Lycenced Houses." Whereas the population of
Boston increased from approximately sixty-seven hundred in 1700 to
ten thousand by 1720, the selectmen had held the number of licenses

steady. As of 1718 seventy-four people held licenses. The same had been true in 1696, twenty-two years earlier.[52]

Efforts to curb the consumption of distilled liquors, especially rum, also continued. Saltonstall warned justices in 1696 of prospective licenseholders laying in stocks of rum and molasses and of procuring "licenses for something which they will enlarge to any and everything which [it] is not." Cotton Mather warned of the total destruction of good order. Wadsworth spoke in terms close to modern clinical diagnoses of alcoholism. He thought it "easy to give instances of Persons... that by excessive drinking of rum, have been brought into languishing circumstances, yet they have so Crav'd Rum, that they could not be without it."[53] In 1712 the assembly took the radical step of banning the sale of rum in taverns. Boston selectmen also tried to conform to this policy. They admitted James Pitson, a "Cyderman" from London, as an inhabitant in 1714 and approved his petition to retail. The selectmen explained that the "motive" behind the admission was that "ye Skillfull managemt of Cyder may prove a Common benefit." A year later they warned William Cutlove, a distiller from London, to leave the town "in as much as more of that Imploym't is not needful in this town."[54]

Selectmen and lesser town officials also participated in the patrols and visits of officials authorized and recommended by the assembly in every town. In January 1707 councillors, justices, selectmen, and overseers of the poor met together and agreed to "Vissit the Familyes of this Town on Wednesday the 5th of Febry next, in Order to prevent and redress disorders." Eight teams were organized consisting of two or three councillors and justices, a selectman, a constable, and a tithingman. Such agreements were regularly made at least once a year during the next decade. Most of the visits took place during the day, after which officials gathered at the Town House in order to compare and discuss their findings. By agreements made beginning in 1712, councillors and justices also walked and inspected at night. Some of the most prominent men in the province led these processions of lesser officials: Major John Walley, councillor and justice of the Superior Court; Paul Dudley, attorney general and justice of sessions; Colonel Elisha Hutchinson, councillor and justice; Edward Bromfield, justice of the Superior and sessions courts; Samuel Sewall, councillor and justice of the Superior Court.[55] Watches, constables, and tithingmen had become insufficient. The social and political elite of the province sought to make themselves more visible in every household in the growing town.

Sewall and his associate justices and councillors expected that their presence would invest the offices of constable and tithingman with more dignity and authority, on the one hand, and place pressure on them as well as selectmen to aggressively pursue enforcement, on the other. The personal involvement of men like Sewall in these patrols and visits became a means to close the gap implicit in the 1690s legislation, which repeatedly ordered all officials in a descending hierarchy of authority to uphold the laws vigorously but simultaneously categorized many of them as potential offenders through provisions for their prosecution for taking bribes.[56] From the 1630s on Puritan magistrates and deputies had gradually constructed a hierarchy of regulation from justices and selectmen down to tithingmen and paid informers. Now this abstract structure of regulation was to be put in motion, made visible in the streets, by the eminence of men such as Sewall.

These inspections and tours did have an impact on the order of the town, judging from the small number of minor disorders recorded by Sewall in his diary. Even Guy Fawkes Day passed unnoticed on November 5, 1709, when Sewall patrolled. In 1715 he dispersed some players of ninepins at the northern edge of the town, but "generally, the Town was peaceable and in good order." At no time did Sewall encounter the degree of defiance displayed at the Wallis tavern. These patrols, however, were also well publicized and anticipated. Moreover, Sewall and others deemed it necessary to extend the time they were active. In 1712 the members of the council, justices, and selectmen resident in the town agreed to walk at night "for the space of eight weeks ensuing."[57]

Yet even as selectmen participated in these various efforts to promote and enforce temperate behavior, they encountered direct and indirect resistance that must have forced them to doubt the efficacy of their own actions. When the visitation policy began in 1707, twenty-six of the sixty-three licensed public houses in the town were operated by widows, most of whom needed to move as much alcohol as possible to subsist. The selectmen were under pressure to grant licenses to the poor to keep them off the rolls of public relief. Moreover, the number of licenses that selectmen initially decided not to renew suggests that a majority of houses routinely operated outside the law. Between 1703 and 1718 selectmen objected to the renewal of over seventy licenses. As of 1714 twenty-eight of eighty tavernkeepers and retailers had faced difficulties in renewing their licenses or would face them in the future. Almost all of the objections to renewal were eventually withdrawn.[58] Acquiescence by selectmen indicates that they recognized the limits of their ability to use their power of approval to compel conformity to law. Holding the number of licenses to a minimum also meant rejecting a growing number of applicants. Between 1712 and 1715 more than three hundred petitions met rejection, whereas only 128 were approved. Meanwhile selectmen had become uneasy over the high price of grain. In 1711 a crowd prevented merchant Andrew Belcher from exporting it from the town. But the assembly kept the pressure on by enacting in 1712 the "Act Against Intemperance, Immorality and Prophaneness, and for Reformation of Manners," which included the radical ban on the sale of distilled liquors in taverns.[59]

Such a drastic ban, however, only served to expose further the underlying weakness of these new actions. Approximately two-fifths of the thirty-nine Boston tavernkeepers in 1615 probably were in compliance with the law, according to excise levies made in 1715. David Copp, for example, had 126 gallons of cider in stock at the time of his death in 1718 and paid three pounds excise in 1715. Sarah Wormall, licensed from 1716 to 1721, had only twelve gallons of wine as opposed to 157 of cider. Neither had any rum or brandy. Nathaniel Emons had 189 gallons of cider and only one gallon of brandy in 1721.[60] Beer does not figure in large quantities in any inventories in the early eighteenth century. This fact suggests that although cider remained the basic alcoholic drink, rum may have begun to replace beer as a popular alternative. Using Copp's excise as a measure, fourteen other tavernkeepers also served mainly cider.

Fifteen other tavernkeepers, however, paid more than ten pounds excise, an indication that the 1712 ban was a dead letter as soon as it was enacted. Thomas Gilbert, for example, paid sixteen pounds excise and had in his cellars 218 gallons of rum, 319 of wine, and 982 of cider. In 1717 Edward Durant had no cider in stock at all but did have 204 gallons of rum and other spirits. Samuel Mears, licensed from 1708 to 1726, drew on 326 gallons of rum and brandy and only sixteen of cider. Thomas Selby, proprietor of the Crown Coffee House from 1714 to 1725, paid twenty-five pounds excise, the highest in 1715. He had more than fifteen hundred pounds worth of alcohol in stock in 1725, including almost seven hundred gallons of rum and more than six thousand gallons of wine. He alone had approximately one-half gallon of wine for every man, woman, and child in Boston.[61] High as his excise was in 1715, it accounted for only 5 percent of the total excise payments made by tavernkeepers and retailers. Perhaps the greatest index of shifts in consumption is the subsequent career of James Pitson, the London ciderman admitted as resident in 1714 to promote cider. Pitson, however, proceeded to acquire a license to keep a tavern and sell distilled liquors on King Street near the Town House. At his death in 1737 he still sold mainly cider but also sold rum, canary, and sherry.[62] In 1712, when the assembly sought to ban the sale of rum in taverns, it may not have been the most common drink in Boston, but the direction in rum consumption is clear. Over the course of the eighteenth century rum would become a staple provision of employers to their laborers.[63] It is probable that Wadsworth decided to be conciliatory on the issue of rum in his 1716 sermon in the face of such widespread disobedience of the law. But he still asserted that drink-sellers had become "more dangerous to the Publick, than so many Indians on the Frontiers" and that rulers "should not only Talk of a Reformation, but diligently & heartily Indeavour it."[64]

The momentum for reformation, however, was dissolving in the face of popular resistance. Selectmen must also have become aware during these years of the mounting pressure to eliminate the office of tithing-man, elected annually to help enforce the laws and allowed to claim informer's fees. Selectmen appointed seventy-three to office in 1676, but their numbers were steadily reduced in succeeding decades by sentiment apparently asserted in town meeting. In 1701 Boston deputies received instructions from the town meeting to modify the strict oath required of tithingmen. By this date they numbered less than twenty. Six were fined for refusing to take the oath in 1710. Those who did serve were not active. Of the fifty-nine drink- and tavern-related offenses that came before the Suffolk sessions between 1712 and 1719, only four involved tithingmen. Although they were named as part of the eight teams organized to visit families in 1707, it is doubtful that they walked with other officials after 1710 because they were not mentioned in succeeding agreements. By 1727 Boston and seven other Suffolk towns refused to elect them at all.[65] Informer's fees could not compensate for isolation from drinking fellowships. Reluctance and then refusal by town meetings to elect these drink enforcement officers must have had a significant impact on the ability and willingness of selectmen to adhere to the policies of the assembly.

The series of attempts on various fronts to close the widening gap between Puritan social mores and reality only exposed officials and laws to contempt by the populace at large. The 1712 Act Against Intemperance—in some ways the most alarmist, emphatic, and severe of all the laws enacted between 1630 and 1720—was also the last piece of major legislation on the subject until after the Revolution. Whether members of the assembly realized the implications for law enforcement if they passed more legislation is not a matter of record. Yet it is clear that by progressively defining the popular use of taverns and drink as illegal or excessive, and by placing pressure on all officials to enforce the laws personally, the members of the assembly propelling the crusade against intemperance forward had transformed the law from a tool promoting order into a spark to disorder, from an expression of their authority into a stark exposure of the limits of their authority. By one means or another they had come to the conclusion articulated by

Robert Breck, a Marlborough minister, in an election sermon in 1728. "Though our Legislature enact ever so many good Laws for the regulation of the morals of the people," he stated, "unless you [the people] do your part...to make choice of Such for your Grand Jurors, Tythingmen, etc. [who will] bring the transgressors to open shame and punishment [then] all our laws for the reforming of the manners and morals of a corrupt people are insufficient and our lawmakers labor in vain."[66] This sermon came one year after the Boston town meeting failed to elect tithingmen at all.

A more complete break with the momentum behind the agitation for reformation came in 1719 when the pent-up demand for licenses in Boston began to be answered. The number of public houses licensed jumped from seventy-four to eighty-eight in 1719 and to 134 by 1722 before leveling off—an 81 percent increase in four years. The number would have increased in any case because of population growth, but the sharp rise is an indication of a new policy. So is the rate of approval by selectmen. Whereas between 1714 and 1718 they approved only eighty-eight, or 31 percent, of the 285 petitions for licenses put before them, in the five years after 1719 they approved 245, or 82 percent, of those received.[67] The assembly made no attempt to intervene. Never again would it try to fix the number of licensed houses in Boston or any other town during the colonial period. Massachusetts had turned a corner not only in the enforcement of drinking laws but also in the relationship between Puritan morality and public policy.

This allowance of a higher incidence of public houses was not merely acquiescence by selectmen and justices to licensing policies resembling those of England, to the Anglicization of Massachusetts society in respect to alcohol control. Evidence strongly suggests that the reversal of policy also represents part of a change in the relationship between rulers and ruled. The rather decentralized structure of authority that had taken root in the seventeenth century had originally been a spur to the elaboration of legal controls; and for most of the seventeenth century the relative unity of leaders in outlook and purpose had contributed to their willingness to enact laws in the face of chronic evasion. The promotion of temperance remained an attribute of the good ruler exercising paternal guidance over the people.

With the installation of royal government in the 1690s, however, and especially after the appointment of Joseph Dudley to the governorship in 1702, partisanship began to characterize the operation of provincial government. Dudley became unpopular at all levels of society for his arbitrary methods of leadership and his suspected use of his office for private gain. Elisha Cooke and Elisha Cooke, Jr., led the opposition to the "court" faction that supported Dudley and his successor, Shute, and became the champions of the old charter, which Cooke, Sr., had unsuccessfully tried to save. Though the evidence is sparse and fragmentary, G.B. Warden has made a convincing case that the junior Cooke and his allies transformed the Boston town meeting into a local base of opposition to royal authority. He appears to have organized a secret political club known as the Boston Caucus to mobilize popular support for caucus members standing for election at town meetings. Beginning in 1719 Cooke and his allies were regularly elected to office. Cooke himself served as moderator almost continuously till his death and also represented the town in the assembly. He would later be accused of treating Boston patrons to thousands of pounds' worth of drink to consolidate control in the 1720s.[68]

The steep climb in the number of licenses approved by selectmen corresponds exactly with the year that Warden believes the caucus assumed control of Boston politics. Cooke himself owned a tavern on King Street as well as properties throughout the town.[69] By approving 170 applications for licenses between 1721 and 1723 and dramatically increasing the number actually licensed, the selectmen allied with Cooke probably hoped to cement ties of clientage with the populace as a whole in every street and alley. The caucus appears to have used drink and licenses in a manner similar to those "ambitious men" described later by John Adams in connection with Braintree politics: "An Artful Man, who has neither sense nor sentiment may by gaining a little sway among the Rabble of a Town, multiply Taverns and Dram shops and thereby secure the Votes of Taverner and Retailer and of all, and the Multiplication of Taverns will make many who may be induced by Phlip and Rum to Vote for any Man whatever." Drinkers grew "attached to the Taverner who is attached to his Patron both by Gratitude and Expectation."[70] Selectmen had initially been delegated power over the approval of licenses in order to strengthen regulation in the seventeenth century; those elected in Boston between 1700 and 1718 had done so. Beginning in 1719, however, a new board of selectmen appears to have reversed temperance policy as part of an effort to solicit popular support on other issues. The distribution of drink to seal contracts of mutual obligation, never completely eradicated in Massachusetts, had resurfaced within the relatively decentralized structure of electoral politics in the colony.

Something of the emerging character of tavern discussions in Boston is implicit in an incident that came before the Suffolk sessions in 1721. One of Elisha Cooke's opponents became so incensed with something he said or did in Richard Hall's tavern that he struck him. News of the incident spread quickly through Boston. Christopher Taylor, a mariner who admired Cooke, began to walk through the streets "in an insolent, daring, and menacing manner" and on meeting Thomas Smith, a pewterer, asked, " 'What do you applaud the thing [,] do you Justify the Ac[ti]on of Mr. Yeamans beating...Mr. Cooke....They have begun with us, they have taken us by the beard, they are come to Clubb Law....Why don't he come out to me, I wish I could See the Dog come out, a God, I would have some of his Blood.' " Almost by stage design Governor Shute happened to pass up King Street in his coach, and Taylor turned and said to him, " 'By God I will face ye,' " and "without any motion of respect boldly faced him in his Coach." Taylor then accosted several others in the street and told one that he "was for the old Charter and would loose ten lives if he had it in that Account."[71] The same year Governor Shute wrote to the Board of Trade that the "common people of this Province are so perverse, that when I remove any person from the Council, for not behaving himself with duty towards H.M. or His orders,...he becomes their favorite, and is chose a Representative."[72] It is likely that after 1720 many Boston officials entered taverns not to disperse the gatherings there but to cultivate their support with treats of liquor.

Throughout the seventeenth century Puritan leaders had sought to restrict the use of taverns and drink not only to promote piety and work discipline but also to insure that the leveling influence of tavern gatherings did not affect the hierarchical structure of authority. The persistent revival of efforts by the assembly to reduce the incidence of licensed public houses and levels of consumption testify to the hegemony of leaders who exercised the kind of paternal authority expected of the good ruler. Such rulers did succeed in helping the clergy to purge the church and the calendar year of the drinking festivals and holidays, which had customarily marked the passage of seasons in the agricultural society of England. Moreover, even after 1720 clerical attacks on intemperance continued to help define Massachusetts as a society always in need of reform, perpetually falling short of even minimum standards of virtuous behavior—a society in motion.[73]

Yet to some extent the efforts of the first generations of Puritan leaders had always been doomed to frustration. They attempted to enforce restrictive standards of drink use while still preserving traditional models of community life. Within the consensual and hierarchical towns established by the colonists, the distribution and exchange of drink within the social structure continued to define membership, mutual obligations, and dependence. The ultimate failure of the laws to restrict the use of taverns and drink to the degree desired is a reflection of the broader social functions that they continued to fulfill in the integration of community life. Drink, particularly rum, might indeed be abused by individual colonists to the point of deterioration of health, but collective drinking had not completely lost its traditional communal connotations. By 1720 magistrates such as Sewall had tested the limits of law as a means of enforcing the nascent modern ethic of temperance, on the one hand, and the preservation of a traditional structure of authority, on the other. They retreated to a more moderate stance on the issue of alcohol control.

A new social process had begun to emerge within popular assemblies in taverns. The 1720s witnessed not only an expansion in the incidence of licensed houses and a relaxation of restraints but also an end to censorship of the press and an expansion of the use of print to mold and shape public opinion. Conflict between the assembly and royal government did much to spur this expansion. By 1737 Pitson had thirty-one pamphlets and eighty-eight books on his barroom shelves. Secular issues and ideas began to compete with religious instruction.[74] Massachusetts taverns did become distinctive from their English counterparts, not because of a lower incidence of taverns or lower levels of consumption but rather because they would become instruments for the more complete integration of local patrons into active political participation over the course of the eighteenth century.

NOTES

1. *The Diary of Samuel Sewall, 1674–1729*, ed. M. Halsey Thomas (New York: Farrar, Straus and Giroux, 1973), 2:741–742.

2. David H. Flaherty, "Law and the Enforcement of Morals in Early America," in *Perspectives in American History*, ed. Donald Fleming and Bernard Bailyn (Cambridge, Mass.: Charles Warren Center for Studies in American History, Harvard University, 1971), 5:237.

3. G. B. Warden, "The Caucus and Democracy in Colonial Boston," *New England Quarterly* 43 (1970): 19–45; Gary B. Nash, *The Urban Crucible: Social Change, Political Consciousness, and the Origins of the American Revolution* (Cambridge, Mass.: Harvard University Press, 1979), chap. 4. "Popular culture" is not a neat analytical category. In some ways it is an awkward euphemism, but no more so than "Puritan culture" or indeed "intellectual history." Here I simply use it to name a pattern of behavior, custom, and belief shared by many Massachusetts colonists to varying degrees but nevertheless condemned in sermon and law as being outside the boundaries of virtuous and godly behavior.

4. Suffolk County Probate Records, 9:47, 14:3; Sewall, *Diary*, 1:253.

5. The Town House also had chambers for the courts, and a new court chamber was opened in 1713, but taverns continued to be used in Boston and in country towns in conjunction with court houses built in the eighteenth century. Sewall, *Diary*, 2:609, 711, 713, 1026.

6. The rate of patronage was compiled from the entire diary. The local rate is almost too low to be credible. Possibly Sewall did not mention many

visits, but since he did faithfully record mundane events and conversations and always noted tavern stops when traveling, the diary is used here to represent the pattern of patronage typical of the devout elite of the colony. Sewall, *Diary*, 1:379.

7. Compiled from Sewall, *Diary*, vols. 1–2.

8. *The Acts and Resolves, Public and Private, of the Province of Massachusetts Bay, 1692–1714* (Boston, 1869), 679; Sewall, *Diary*, 2:1026.

9. For example, see A. I. Richards, *Land, Labour, and Diet in Northern Rhodesia: An Economic Study of the Bemba Tribe* (Oxford, 1939), 76–87, 135–143, 366–380; Clarence H. Patrick, *Alcohol, Culture, and Society* (Durham, N.C.: Duke University Press, 1952), chap. 2; Thomas W. Hill, "Ethnohistory and Alcohol Studies," in *Recent Developments in Alcoholism*, ed. Marc Galenter, (New York: Plenum, 1984), 2:313–337; also relevant is Mark A. Tessler, William M. O'Barr, and David H. Spain, *Tradition and Identity in Changing Africa* (New York: Harper and Row, 1973), passim; for connections to late medieval and early modern English society, see Keith Thomas, "Work and Leisure in Pre-Industrial Society: Conference Paper, Discussion," *Past and Present* 29 (December 1964): 50–66.

10. Peter Laslett, *The World We Have Lost: England before the Industrial Age*, 2d ed. (New York: Scribner's, 1973), chaps. 1–3; Keith Thomas, *Religion and the Decline of Magic* (New York: Scribner's, 1971),17.

11. Peter Clark, "The Alehouse and the Alternative Society," in *Puritans and Revolutionaries: Essays in Seventeenth-Century History Presented to Christopher Hill*, ed. Donald Pennington and Keith Thomas (Oxford: Clarendon Press, 1978), 47–72; Charles Phythian-Adams, "Ceremony and Citizen: The Communal Year at Coventry" in *Crisis and Order in English Towns, 1500–1700: Essays in Urban History*, ed. Peter Clark and Paul Slack (Toronto: University of Toronto Press, 1972), 57–85.

12. *A Warning Piece to All Drunkards and Health Drinkers Faithfully Collected from the Works of English and Foreign Learned Authors of Good Esteem, Mr. Samuel Ward and Mr. Samuel Clark, and Others...* (London, 1682).

13. For an overview, see Lawrence Stone, *The Causes of the English Revolution, 1529–1642* (New York: Harper and Row, 1972), 67–76; Edmund S. Morgan, *American Slavery, American Freedom: The Ordeal of Colonial Virginia* (New York: Norton, 1975), chap. 3; Peter Clark, "Migration in England during the Late Seventeenth and Early Eighteenth Centuries," *Past and Present*, 83 (May 1979): 57–90; Harris Gray Hudson, *A Study of Social Regulations in England under James I and Charles I: Drink and Tobacco* (Chicago: University of Chicago Libraries, 1933), 4–20; Clark, "Alehouse."

14. Hudson, *Social Regulations*, 12.

15. *Warning Piece to All Drunkards*.

16. Hudson, *Social Regulations*, 11.

17. Clark "Alehouse," 61–64.

18. The continuing connection between alehouses and poaching is apparent in E. P. Thompson, *Whigs and Hunters: The Origins of the Black Act* (New York: Pantheon Books, 1975), and Douglas Hay, "Poaching and the Game Laws on Cannock Chase," in *Albion's Fatal Tree: Crime and Society in Eighteenth-Century*

England, by Douglas Hay, Peter Linebaugh, John G. Rule, E. P. Thompson, and Cal Winslow (New York: Pantheon Books, 1975), 189–253.

19. For an overview of the various ways in which Puritans attacked and undermined traditional values and beliefs, see Christopher Hill, *Society and Puritanism in Pre-Revolutionary England* (London: Secker and Warburg, 1964), and Thomas, *Religion and The Decline of Magic.*

20. Sewall, *Diary,* 2:736, 1:351, 2:920.

21. Sewall, *Diary,* 1:90, 351; see also 1:481, 502, 588, 2:627, 701.

22. Middlesex County Court Records, 1686–1688, 39–40; Edmund S. Morgan, *The Puritan Dilemma: The Story of John Winthrop* (Boston: Little, Brown, 1958).

23. *Records of the Governor and Company of the Massachusetts Bay in New England,* ed. Nathaniel B. Shurtleff (Boston, 1853), 1:271.

24. David D. Hall, *The Faithful Shepherd: A History of the New England Ministry in the Seventeenth Century* (New York: Norton, 1974), chaps. 1–5, esp. 102–120.

25. Benjamin Wadsworth, *An Essay to Do Good* (Boston, 1716), 10.

26. T. H. Breen, *The Character of the Good Ruler: Puritan Political Ideas in New England, 1630–1730* (New York: Norton, 1974), chaps. 1–2, B. Katherine Brown, "The Controversy over the Franchise in Puritan Massachusetts, 1959 to 1974," *William and Mary Quarterly,* 33 (1976): 212–241; G. B. Warden, *Boston, 1689–1776* (Boston: Little Brown, 1970), 31–32; Nash, *Urban Crucible,* 29; Haverhill town records reveal the way in which the franchise could expand according to the circumstances beyond what the law allowed. In 1681 a complaint was made that a motion to build a new meetinghouse was defeated because of the "additional & wilful votes of many prohibited by law from voting." George W. Chase, *History of Haverhill, Massachusetts, 1640–1860* (Haverhill, Mass., 1861), 136, 168, 204.

27. Sidney Webb and Beatrice Webb, *The History of Liquor Licensing: Principally from 1700 to 1830* (London: Cass, 1963), 1–48; *Records of the Governor,* 1:106, 140, 279–280, 2:100, 188, 276, 277–278, 3:427–428, 5:305; for the development of county government, see George Lee Haskins, *Law and Authority in Early Massachusetts: A Study in Tradition and Design* (New York: Macmillan, 1960), 32; the reorganization of the courts under the new charter is covered by Hendrig Hartog, "The Public Law of a County Court: Judicial Government in Eighteenth-Century Massachusetts," *American Journal of Legal History* 20 (1976): 282–291.

28. Clark, "Alehouses," 48–50.

29. *A Report of the Record Commisioners of the City of Boston, Containing the Boston Records from 1660 to 1701* (Boston, 1881), 109.

30. *Records of the Governor,* 1:213–214, 258, 2:100, 286, 4(1): 59, 4(2): 344, 5:211.

31. *Records of the Governor,* 1:279–280, 4(1): 203, 4(2): 37, 5:448; *Acts and Resolves,* 1:190–191, 328, 5:448; up through 1700 the manner in which licenseholders were categorized varied. In 1682 they were divided into wine taverns, innholders, and retailers; in 1691 the terms used were taverns, alehouses, and retailers. The two basic distinctions were (1) between those taverns that could sell wine and those limited to beer, ale, and cider; and (2) between those

allowed to sell for consumption on the premises and those forbidden to do so. By 1700 the categories had been simplified to innholders and retailers. What appears to distinguish Massachusetts from England is the effort to restrict a large percentage of licenseholders (all retailers) from allowing consumption in their houses. *Boston Records from 1660 to 1701*, 76, 156, 207, 215; Records of the Suffolk County General Sessions, 1702–1712, 8.

32. *Records of the Governor*, 1:271, 2:121, 1:108–109, 2:100, 4(2): 510, 4(1): 59–60, 347; William Whyte to General Court, May 15, 1646, *Massachusetts Archives*, vol. 111, *Taverns, 1643–1774*, Archives of the Commonwealth, Boston, Mass., 13.

33. *Records of the Governor*, 2:100.

34. *Warning Piece to All Drunkards.*

35. Suffolk County Probate Records, 9:47, 374, 74–75, 14:3–4; *Records of the Governor*, 2:100.

36. *Records of the Governor*, 4(1): 59–60.

37. *Records of the Governor*, 2:257, 4(1): 203, 4(2): 100; *Acts and Resolves*, 1:679; Edward Ward, *Letter from New England concerning Their Customs, Manners, and Religion Written upon Occasion of a Report about a Quo Warranto Brought against That Government* (London, 1682), 3, 7.

38. Hall, *Faithful Shepherd*, chap. 8.

39. Nathaniel Saltonstall to Justices of Quarter Sessions in Salem, December 26, 1696, Prince Collection, Massachusetts Historical Society.

40. Increase Mather, *Wo to Drunkards* (Cambridge, Mass., 1673).

41. Samuel Danforth, *Piety Encouraged* (Boston, 1705), 23; Samuel Danforth, *The Woful Effects of Drunkenness* (Boston, 1710), 25–26; Wadsworth, *Essay to Do Good* (Boston, 1716), 2; Cotton Mather, *Sober Considerations, on a Growing Flood of Iniquity* (Boston, 1708), 5, 15.

42. Danforth, *Woful Effects*, 25–26.

43. William Pencak, *War, Politics, and Revolution in Provincial Massachusetts* (Boston: Northeastern University Press, 1981), chap. 2; Breen, *Good Ruler*, 199–202, 210–226.

44. *Acts and Resolves*, 1:679–680.

45. *Records of the Governor*, 5:305, Petition of Tavernkeepers to General Court, July 9, 1684, *Massachusetts Archives*, 111:48; Population figure taken from Nash, *Urban Crucible*, 407.

46. *Boston Records, from 1660 to 1701*, 171, 203–204; List of Licenses Granted in Suffolk County, March 30, 1696, *Massachusetts Archives*, 111:57.

47. *Acts and Resolves*, 1:32, 342–346, 475–477, 680.

48. Proposals for Regulating Innholders and Retailers, June 8, 1698, *Massachusetts Archives*, 111:63; Order of General Court concerning Innholders, June 27, 1704, *Massachusetts Archives*, 111:76.

49. *Acts and Resolves*, 1:664.

50. *Acts and Resolves*, 1:191.

51. Bernard Bailyn, *The New England Merchants in the Seventeenth Century* (New York: Harper, 1964), 129, 130, 187; *The Indictment and Tryal of Richard Rumm* (Boston, 1724), 15–17.

52. Compiled from Records of Suffolk County Sessions, 1702–1712,

1712–1719; *A Report of the Record Commissioners of the City of Boston, Containing the Records of Boston Selectmen, 1701–1715* (Boston, 1884), 47, 91–92.

53. Saltonstall to Essex Quarter Sessions, Massachusetts Historical Society; Mather, *Sober Considerations*, 15–16; Wadsworth, *Essay to Do Good*, 8.

54. *Records, 1701–1715*, 218, 227; *Acts and Resolves*, 1:679–680.

55. *Records, 1701–1715*, 55–56, 62, 67.

56. *Acts and Resolves*, 1:664.

57. Sewall, *Diary*, 2:627, 719, 795; *Records, 1701–1715*, 171.

58. Records of Suffolk County Sessions, 1702–1712, 156–157; *Records, 1701–1715*, 33–35, 46, 63, 91–92, 111–112, 166, 187, 212, 231; *A Report of the Records Commissioners of the City of Boston, Containing the Records of Boston Selectmen, 1716–1736*, 6, 20, 40.

59. Compiled from *Records, 1701–1715*; *Records, 1701–1715*, 106, 161–162; Nash, *Urban Crucible*, 77; *Acts and Resolves*, 1:679–680.

60. Records of Suffolk County Sessions, 1712–1719, 93; Suffolk County Probate Records, 21:351–352, 22:528, 370.

61. Suffolk County Probate Records, 21:561, 20:388–389, 27:269, 25:530.

62. *Records, 1716–1736*, 27; Suffolk County Probate Records, 34:360–364.

63. A writer to the *New London Gazette* in 1769 stated that "it is now an established custom among our day labourers, that their employers afford not less than an half pint of the choice West India Spirits for one day's consumption." January 20, 1769, *New London Gazette*, no. 271.

64. Wadsworth, *Essay to Do Good*, 20, 22.

65. David H. Flaherty, *Privacy in Colonial New England* (Charlottesville: University Press of Virginia, 1972), 195–200; Records of Suffolk County Sessions, 1712–1719, October 31, 1727, 123; *Records, 1701–1715*, 62.

66. Robert Breck, *The Only Method to Promote the Happiness of a People and Their Posterity* (Boston, 1728), 41.

67. Compiled from Records of Suffolk County Sessions, *Records of Boston Selectmen, 1701–1715*, and *Records of Boston Selectmen, 1716–1736*.

68. Breen, *Good Ruler*, chap. 7, Warden, "Caucus and Democracy"; Nash, *Urban Crucible*, 87.

69. Suffolk County Probate Records, 34:241–242.

70. L. H. Butterfield, ed., *Diary and Autobiography of John Adams* (New York: Atheneum, 1964), 1:128–129, 190–192, 205–206.

71. Records of Suffolk County Sessions, 1719–1725, April 4, 1721, 80–81.

72. Quoted in Breen, *Good Ruler*, 223n.

73. The social dynamism inherent in the Puritan ethic is surveyed by Edmund S. Morgan, "The Puritan Ethic and the American Revolution", *William and Mary Quarterly*, 3d series, 25 (1967): 3–43.

74. Clyde Duniway, *The Development of Freedom of the Press in Massachusetts* (Cambridge, Mass.: Harvard University Press, 1906), chap. 6; Nash, *Urban Crucible*, 85–86; Suffolk County Probate Records, 34:360–361.

TWO

Social Drinking in Old Regime Paris

Thomas Brennan

Drink often serves as a barometer of the health of an individual, class, or society. We tend to see widespread drunkenness as a sign of trouble —an indication of a deeper social malaise that is causing alcoholic excess. Thus, historians speak of drink as a drug and of drunkenness as solace or escape from problems that lie deep in the society.[1] This equation of drink with something sinister is an old one. At least as early as the sixteenth century French writers identified drunkenness as a scourge that troubled the state. Historians and writers since then have pointed to drunkenness as a sign of the dissolution of public morals, particularly those of the poor. Yet their emphasis on drunkenness obscures, in my opinion, the importance of wine in people's diet and in their culture. The consumption of alcohol, particularly social drinking in taverns, provided the structure of popular sociability and gave a ritual form to public and communal comportment. If we are accurately to assess the health of Old Regime society, we must recognize the social and cultural role of drinking and taverns.

The traditional portrait of alcohol consumption, especially consumption in cabarets, has been one of excess. The poor supposedly got drunk at every occasion, especially on Sundays, when they would leave Paris to drink in the suburbs. "In Paris, regiments of drunks return to town from the suburbs every night, staggering, beating the walls.... The drunkenness of the Parisian people is abominable and horrifying."[2] This contemporary description is still echoed by historians today; for example, Jacques Saint-Germain wrote in 1965, "Too often workers passed their evenings at the cabaret; drunkenness was consid-

ered a social scourge by the government."[3] The taverns both inside and
outside the city earned the reputation of "Bacchic stews" where the
populace went to get drunk.[4] Historians have long depicted cabarets
and their clientele in this fashion; even as the Old Regime ground to a
halt, Sébastien Mercier was proclaiming his abhorrence of taverns—the
"receptacle of the dregs of the populace."[5] Mercier disdained the
cabaret just as he despised its popular customers. He was content to
portray both as wine-soaked and criminal. Nineteenth-century historians, reflecting their society's horror of alcoholism and a drunken
proletariat, maintained this depiction of the eighteenth-century cabaret.[6] Most modern historians of Paris have not gone much beyond this
caricature of the drunken and disorderly patrons of the Parisian cabaret.[7] If we wish to understand the implications of drink in the Old
Regime, we will have to do more than rely on Mercier, as so many have
done. The impact of alcohol depended on how much was actually
drunk, how often, and how it functioned in popular culture. The
answers to these questions reveal that the tavern was far more than a
place to get drunk; alcohol was more than a drug or an escape; and
drunkenness was still far from an epidemic. Rather, alcohol served as a
symbol of community and an idiom of social exchange. If its consumption resulted at times in drunkenness, the central aim of drinking was
sociability.

The ideal place to begin a discussion of drinking would be with an
extensive set of fiscal records documenting how much alcohol Parisians consumed. The tax on alcohol entering the city was a major
source of income both to the crown and to the tax farms, and a sizable
bureaucracy existed simply to keep track of the Parisian wine trade. Yet
the surviving records of this tax are fragmentary and isolated and offer
little encouragement toward making a comprehensive assessment of
the amount of alcohol sold or consumed in Paris. The fact that emerges
most clearly is that alcohol in Paris meant wine, above all else. Reports
from 1700 to 1708 indicate that the average importation of wine into
the city was more than half a million hectoliters a year, whereas imports
of spirits were less than 3 percent of that amount. Given a population
of roughly half a million, the per capita consumption of wine would
have been about 120 liters, but since France was fighting a brutal war
for most of that decade, the figure is probably abnormally low.[8] Reports
from 1719 to 1721 put per capita consumption closer to 160 liters.
Figures for consumption in 1637 were 155 liters per capita. The
amount of wine consumed around mid-century, calculated from taxes
for the years 1744–1757, was practically identical to wine consumption
earlier in the century, but the population had undoubtedly grown.
Figures cited by Arthur Young for the last decades of the Old Regime

were little above those at the beginning of the century (not including the 17 percent that he added to account for fraud, which had probably been fairly constant over the century), whereas the population had increased by some 30–40 percent. Thus, per capita consumption would seem to have been declining, toward 102 liters per annum by the second half of the century.[9] This decline can be compared to a similar decrease in consumption figures for Lyon: from 201 liters per annum at the beginning of the century to 150 liters at the end.[10]

The decline in Parisian consumption may perhaps be explained by considering that wine sold at *guinguettes,* the taverns in the suburbs beyond the tax barriers, was not included in these tax figures. Ramponeau's *guinguette* alone sold more than a thousand hectoliters a year, and the rest of the *guinguettes* in his parish brought the figures up to twenty-one thousand hectoliters sold in 1766 and thirty thousand hectoliters sold by the end of the Old Regime.[11] Consumption figures indicate that although the amount of wine sold in the city, at cabarets, remained fairly constant, business increased rapidly beyond the tax barriers. Clearly, per capita consumption of wine was not decreasing overall. In all probability it stayed at least as high as the 1630 level of 155 liters, before *guinguettes* became popular. Even then the figure does not include wine sold fraudulently. The wine taxes provoked a massive fraud in wine entering Paris itself. Tax men were suborned, walls were secretly pierced by pipelines, and a hundred different schemes kept the tax farm waging a ceaseless and unsuccessful war to control the traffic in wine.[12] A more realistic figure for per capita consumption could easily be more than 155 liters of wine a year. Moreover, since that average is for the whole Parisian population, it is certain that adults drank more. But how often did they drink, and how much at a time?

The price of wine and the frequency of consumption are essential elements in a proper understanding of the amount of wine consumed. The price of a *pinte* (slightly less than a liter) remained between eight and twelve sous for most of the eighteenth century. With wages at about thirty sous a day or less for most workers, a daily liter would have meant roughly a third of a worker's pay spent on wine—an unlikely apportionment. In fact, Lavoisier estimated that a craftsman spent on average 15 percent of his income on wine, which would have allowed him half a liter each day.[13] Furthermore, a medical treatise from the end of the century offered one-tenth to one-half liter as the range of normal—and healthy—consumption.[14] The skilled artisan or master craftsman, making two or three times the wages of a laborer, was obviously in a better position to add wine to his diet. Indeed, judicial records indicate that by comparison he drank in taverns more often.[15]

Most people, then, could drink only a modest amount of wine on a regular basis. Alternatively, they could have done all of their drinking on Sundays, filling themselves up on cheap wine in the suburbs and making do with hangovers for the rest of the week. A variety of contemporary authors have stressed the latter syndrome—Vadé, Cailleau, and the inevitable Mercier—and historians have tended to accept them.[16] The records of Parisians filing complaints with the police, however, suggest that most drinking was done in the city, where cabarets were patronized steadily throughout the week. The receipts of daily sales for one wine merchant on the rue Neuve-de-Cléry show that his business was fairly constant; his busiest days came in no particular pattern. The account book of a wine merchant in 1749 records that the number of people drinking on credit (a very different figure from total sales but indicative of the level of business) was roughly the same every day.[17] Other wine merchants kept account books of individual customers buying wine on credit which give a general idea of individual attendance. Twice a week seems to have been common; of course that is a minimum figure, for men patronized more than one establishment regularly and did not always drink on credit.[18] People appear to have gone often, if not to the same cabaret, then to some cabaret.

Police records give a similar impression that men went to cabarets in the city frequently and throughout the week. The artisans and shopkeepers could best afford this expense, but the working poor went almost as often. They came to the cabaret several times a week at least, not imbibing much but stopping only to "drink a glass." Some spent their Sundays drinking in the suburbs, and the number making the trip appears to have increased through the eighteenth century. The distance to the suburbs made the outing inconvenient, however, and police records suggest that there was much less business there than in the city. Drinking in the tavern in the city—at the neighborhood cabaret—seems to have been both regular and moderate. The brief respites taken during the working day and tavern visits in the evening, common in depositions with police, were generally not long enough for serious drinking.

Little more can be discovered about the amount of wine consumed or the frequency of trips to taverns. The questions of drunkenness—its prevalence and its implications—must be addressed indirectly, then, through sources and records that do not lend themselves to quantification but offer rich insight into the significance of alcohol consumption. Various sources, as well as common sense, suggest that people did become intoxicated. Yet there are discrepancies in these sources, differences of interpretation and definition, that reveal how complex the problem of analyzing drunkenness really is. Government and church, the elites and the common people, all yield different and sometimes contrasting perspectives on the question. Through the study of these various perceptions of drunkenness, as well as the light each perception sheds on the realities of the problem, it may be possible to reconstruct the meaning of drinking and drunkenness in the eighteenth century.

DRUNKENNESS

Drunkenness, we are told, did not appear as a problem until the seventeenth century in France. "One does not perceive in France, before the end of the sixteenth century, any trace of the profound and general anxiety which the word alcoholism [alcoolisme] causes in us today."[19] This statement from the historian of wine and vines, Roger Dion, is not easily dismissed, nor is his conclusion that drunkenness (ivrognerie) increased rapidly after the sixteenth century. The principle evidence, for Dion, of a rise in drunkenness was the assertion of the fact by Bernard de Laffemas in several works published at the end of the sixteenth century describing the problems besetting the country. Laffemas pointed particularly to "the intoxications [les yvrogneries] which very often ruin households and families" and blamed the recent extension of the problem on the number and indiscipline of taverns.[20]

The very terminology used by Laffemas, however, illustrates the difficulty of understanding early modern drunkenness. The most common word for drunkenness in the Old Regime, ivrognerie, covered a wide range of human conditions. It referred to everything from intoxication to alcoholism, and its more precise definition, "habit, or practice, of getting drunk [habitude de s'enivrer]," does little to clarify its meaning.[21] Few in the Old Regime spoke of ivrognerie as a medical problem, nor is the term alcoolisme introduced until the nineteenth century, though one jurist just before the Revolution defined ivrognerie as an "inveterate passion for drink."[22] Most contemporaries referred to ivrognerie as a vice, emphasizing its moral dimension. Furthermore, the word denoted nothing specifically about the scale of the problem. The vagueness of the vocabulary reflected the ambiguity of contemporary perceptions. Thus, before concluding that alcoholism, or even drunkenness, was increasing, it is essential to examine what the sources were talking about.

Laffemas's work had been preceded only a few years before by an essay on drunkenness describing the problem in very different terms. Michel de Montaigne considered drunkenness a "gross and brutish vice" but one that "costs our conscience less than the others."[23] For Montaigne, drunkenness was considered in terms of men rather than economy, though he noted that drunkenness was "less malicious and harmful than the other [vices], which almost all clash more directly with society in general." Nor did he perceive drunkenness as a wide-spread problem among his compatriots. He described the "French style of drinking" as "at two meals [a day] and moderately, for fear of your health" and even argued that "we should make our daily drinking habits more expansive and vigorous."[24] Between Laffemas, a mercantilist, and the skeptic Montaigne there was little agreement; they do not appear to have used the same terminology in the same way. The *Ivrogneries* of Laffemas were, arguably, habitual drinking on the scale of alcoholism. *Ivrognerie* for the tolerant Montaigne seems closer to a moral failing, a weakness of minor and occasional proportions, with no sense of permanent degeneracy. The books of Laffemas may well reflect a new awareness of mercantilist principles rather than a discovery of changed conditions in society.[25]

The vocabulary of drunkenness gained little precision in the following two centuries, nor did social commentaries refine their understanding of the problem. The mercantilist perception of wine echoed in the writing of Colbert, who condemned wine for being a "great obstacle to work" and taverns for "having no principle other than idleness and debauchery."[26] The work of eighteenth-century magistrates, such as Duchesne's *Code de la police,* identified drinking as a cause of indigence: "In those places where there is a superabundance of wine which is not exported...the low price of wine means that the common people are drawn into the cabarets,...leave their work, their business, and become miserable." The *Dictionnaire économique* also blamed the poverty of "peasants and artisans" on cabarets.[27] The volumes on jurisprudence in the *Encyclopédie méthodique* at the end of the century addressed the subject of *"l'ivrognerie,* above all in cabarets and other public places" as the responsibility of the police. "This vice is one of the most hateful and most common among the populace [*peuple*]....[It is] equally a vice that the police ought to prevent since it renders subjects incapable of fulfilling their duties to society."[28] Duchesne and Colbert reiterated the principles of social utility already formulated by Laffemas.

The definition of *ivrognerie* in the *Encyclopédie,* however, appearing at about the same time in the eighteenth century as Duchesne's *Code,* was virtually copied out of Montaigne. Thus, the parallel traditions of utilitarian disapproval and classical tolerance existed still and were little closer to each other in their judgments. Elsewhere in the *Encyclopédie* the authors described the ill effects of an excess of wine on the balance of solids and liquids in the body and the "impotence in venereal exercise of men lost to drunkenness."[29] Yet the philosophes no more condemned drunkenness than did Montaigne.

The *Encyclopédie* did go beyond Montaigne in one important aspect. What for Montaigne had been a vice was for the philosophes an offense against reason. "One should conclude that drunkenness...is not always a fault, against which it is necessary to be on one's guard; it is a breach that one makes in natural law which orders us to preserve our reason." The abuse of wine produced "irrationality [*la déraison*]"; "let one stiffen his reason as much as he will, the least dose of an intoxicating liquor suffices to destroy it."[30] Although such objections did not seriously alter the generally tolerant tone of the *Encyclopédie* definition, the identification of intoxication with irrationality reveals an important theme in early modern perceptions of drunkenness. "Drunkenness [*ivresse*]...is a brief madness," explained an influential eighteenth-century treatise on the police, "all the worse...for being voluntary."[31] Still, drunkenness as irrationality had little in common with the mercantilist objections of Laffemas or Duchesne. For Duchesne, drunkenness separated a man from society; for the philosophes, it separated man from humanity.

The church used a vocabulary of drunkenness that was similar to that of the philosophes while expressing a censure that equaled that of the mercantilists. The doctors in theology of the Faculty of Paris, in instructions to confessors in 1721, assured them that *ivrognerie* was a mortal sin.[32] They went on to describe various manifestations of the sin, distinguishing those who drank to the point of "losing the light of reason" from those who drank "beyond need and even beyond propriety" and those who "heat their head" and were unable to "fulfill the duties of their profession." Thus the single term *ivrognerie* referred to anything within a wide range of intoxication, from incidental to uncontrollable. Yet their methods for dealing with the problem of drink suggest that the doctors were aiming particularly at those suffering from a physical reliance on alcohol.

Drunkards, especially those with a head "so weak that a small quantity of wine is capable of intoxicating them," the doctors thought should be told not to drink at all. No drunkenness was to be tolerated, and "frivolous excuses," such as the "invitation of a friend to drink" or the "conclusion of a business deal," was not to be accepted. However, those who were "so accustomed to drink that they fall into a swoon when they are deprived of it" were to be allowed to drink moderately if they had shown a desire to avoid drunkenness and a "firm resolution to work effectively to conquer little by little the unfortunate necessity in which they are put by their drunkenness." Thus, the church combined an awareness and condemnation of drunkenness with the philosophes' concern for reason. The theologians spoke of drink and "the light of reason" earlier even than the *Encyclopédie*. Their position undoubtedly influenced many in the society.

The government had long since expressed its official condemnation of drunkenness. An ordinance on the punishment of drunkards (*ivrognes*) in 1536 declared that "whoever shall be found drunk [*ivre*]" was to be put in prison on a diet of bread and water for a first offense and whipped for recurrences.[33] Such severity was intended to curb the excesses of the drunkard, the "idleness, blasphemy, homicides, and other damage and harm which comes from drunkenness [*ébriété*]." Thus, the drunkard, for the government, was a potential trouble-maker, but it is not clear whether the ordinance referred to alcoholics or to anyone found drunk.[34] It further stated that "if by drunkenness or the heat of wine drunkards commit any bad action, they are not to be pardoned, but punished for the crime and in addition for the drunkenness at the judge's discretion." Drunkenness, then, was seen as an aggravating circumstance not unconnected to other crimes.

The ordinance against drunkenness was enforced only fitfully. Commissioners occasionally noted in their reports that a suspect was ine-briated and might even weigh that fact in their judgments. In a fight between two people who blamed each other for the initial aggression, it was the person who "besides appeared drunk [*pris de vin*]" that was sent to prison.[35] Yet such incidents were infrequent, and the police inspect-ing taverns at night made little effort to arrest those who were found drunk.[36] Someone found drunk on the street at night might be incar-cerated—particularly if it was a woman—but for being out at night rather than for drunkenness. Thus, an inspector who had come across a person "sleeping on the street dead drunk [*mort ivre*]" at midnight arrested not only the drunk but also two friends who were trying to get him home.[37]

Unlike ordinances on closing hours for cabarets and cafes or edicts against taverns serving alcohol during mass, the ordinance against drunkenness was not incorporated into the litany of ordinances deal-ing with cabarets—and with morals in general—that was repeated and repromulgated regularly throughout the Old Regime. There was no reissuing of the edict against drunkenness in the eighteenth century and probably none in the seventeenth.[38] If drunkenness was truly a scourge after the sixteenth century, the government did not consider it serious enough to necessitate renewing the law.

Elite perceptions of drunkenness ranged from broad tolerance to alarmed condemnation. There would seem to have been no common ground for understanding the meaning or implications of the term. By and large, however, those who harshly condemned drunkenness were talking about the populace; those who expressed toleration were speaking more generally of humanity. The theme unifying these disparate texts and attitudes may simply be that when drunkenness was a problem, it was a lower-class problem. As one historian has remarked, "This official literature [on drunkenness]...reveals the secret of a rage among the upper classes at seeing a social distinction diminish in a consumption from which they hoped the poor would remain excluded as a sign of inferior condition."[39] Once the traditional preserve of the elites, wine was now an item of common consumption, valuable to commoners perhaps for the very reasons that provoked elite commentators. Invested with such significance, wine was clearly both a potent element of popular consumption and aspirations and an acrimonious symbol in elite discourse about society.

Evidence of popular perceptions of drunkenness—the attitudes of the laboring classes of Paris—is more difficult to assess than are official attitudes. The records that addressed drink and drunkenness explicitly derived most often from the extreme cases of alcoholic excess and abuse, the kinds of affairs that warranted legal attention. They offer rich evidence but must be used with caution, for they represent the exceptions to accepted behavior. Such records in the police archives include complaints brought by Parisians against family members for drunkenness, libertinage, and debauchery. Some depositions sought protection from violence, others demanded imprisonment of the culprit, and still others requested the legal division of a married couple's communal property.[40] Such complaints linked drunkenness to a variety of other concerns—taverns, idleness, filial disobedience—that were often more central to people's indignation. These plaintiffs perceived drinking as an escape, an abdication of responsibility, and complained for reasons that were economic as well as moral.

Drunkenness was clearly contrary to plaintiffs' notions of honorable behavior. The way an "honest woman" ought to act, according to a domestic, was "in staying home attentive to her household." Instead, his wife "abandoned her household and her child" and "gave herself to a continual debauch of wine."[41] A barrister felt his wife should apply herself to "maintaining peace and the union with her husband," but she was "given to drunkenness."[42] Here it is drunkenness rather than the cabaret that is opposed to accepted behavior. Thus, a plaintiff styling himself a *marchand-bourgeois* complained about his son-in-law "throwing himself into all sorts of debauchery, coming home late every day drunk [*saoul et pris de vin*]."[43]

A few who complained of libertinage addressed the problem of drunkenness in terms of madness, much as the church had done. A clock maker denounced his wife for having "deranged herself" with constant drink.[44] He described her drinking as "a wicked inclination" and "this habit." His vocabulary was unusually blunt: he said his wife was continually *ivre* and *saoule*. Both of these terms seem to have been reserved for describing serious drinking problems as well as indicating severe disapproval. The complaint of a journeyman mason depicted an equally grave situation. His wife was "given to an excess of wine and brandy" but, more tellingly, was "in a despair so frightful that she wishes to destroy herself." The husband suggested that she had a "spirit alienated...by debauchery of wine."[45] The mason seems to have been moved by a sincere concern for his wife, who had already tried to kill herself and had incurred a serious head injury from falling down while drunk. Hence he asked that she be confined in order to "keep [her] in a place of security." The mason's vocabulary indicates that he had identified his wife's drinking as a kind of madness.

Most complainants objected less to drunkenness than to drinking because of the time and money spent at taverns and the friends and sociability in taverns that kept men away from their work. In the most frequent descriptions the spouse was accused of "spending days and even entire nights in the taverns" or of "going daily to taverns" without really mentioning that he was drunk.[46] "Instead of working and occupying himself with something, he [a merchant] leaves in the morning and does not return until evening, sometimes very late...and passes his time drinking in taverns....Instead of devoting himself to work, [he] does nothing but go for walks, with cane in hand, and debauch himself."[47] Though drunkenness was perhaps implied, it was less important than the fact that the husband spent a great deal of time and money away from his job. Thus, one "abandons his business to pass the day in the tavern," and another "often quits his shop to go play *boules* and to go to the tavern."[48] The Sieur Harcourt gave himself to "drink, gambling and to all pleasures, which causes, on the one hand, the neglect of his commerce and, on the other, a great deal of useless expenses."[49] The time spent at the tavern was evidence of time not spent working and could indicate as well that the husband was "no longer willing to work."[50] In general, then, the tavern represented everything that was antithetical to work; one was either in one's shop or in the tavern.[51]

The tavern was presented in these complaints as a refuge from responsibility and authority. Such complaints of libertinage were in fact as much complaints against a family member for having escaped the family's authority, usually embodied in the father, as they were complaints of misbehavior.[52] Thus, a fruit seller complained that his fifteen-year-old daughter had run away five times and "retires with many libertines to drink in the *guinguettes*."[53] Similarly, a master heel maker accused his son of "refusing to work at his profession and passing the time roaming and in the different quarters and cabarets of Paris where he makes acquaintances whose example can only be dangerous."[54] A wig maker, whose wife had left him "to have greater liberty to live as she likes [*à sa fantaisie*]," complained that she would not apply herself to "keep house as an honest woman" and instead was "given to debauchery."[55] Plaintiffs clearly considered escape from work and responsibilities to be debauched. These complaints were directed as much against the tavern as an escape as against drinking.

Wives took this tone even when they were not making official complaints. They appeared in popular plays scolding their husbands for drinking instead of working: "Drinking is your only employment." Their complaints have a familiar ring: "At the cabaret you pass each instant.... You eat all my money."[56] Wives, as they were portrayed in literature, objected not so much to drinking per se—indeed they joined their husbands readily enough on Sundays—as to drinking on a workday. "Have the holidays come so soon?" one wife taunts her husband.[57] But her concern is unmistakable: "You are reducing us to the poorhouse." This kind of drinking is not necessarily even drunkenness, but it is idleness and an escape from work.

The opposition of work and the tavern is striking. The tavern was already perceived as a haven for the idle. We might question whether husbands preferred the cabaret to their shops because in fact they could get no work. Was not the cabaret an essential element in an economy that did not work to full capacity or employment? Some wives did not see it that way and held the tavern responsible for their families' low income. However, wives did not isolate alcohol as the agent of their problem. Their complaints brought up drunkenness because it made the husband threatening and because it was an expense, but drunkenness itself was not yet singled out as a killer or the destroyer of households, as it would be in later centuries or had already become in England.[58] Instead, it was the tavern, a more complex phenomenon than mere drinking, that was seen as the cause of idleness and unwillingness to work.

The languages of work and of rationality seem to have provided the basic vocabularies with which people of all ranks comprehended drinking and drunkenness, though work figured more prominently. Certainly many of the authors of this period spoke of drunkenness in terms of social utility and work, and some plaintiffs did as well. Yet while those like Duchesne in his *Code* continued to see drunkenness as an offense against a work ethic, both the church and the philosophes condemned drunkenness for destroying the light of reason and for producing irrationality. Some plaintiffs also identified drunkenness as a form of madness. The conjunction of these two languages may perhaps be explained

by the "new sensibility to poverty,...to the economic problems of unemployment and idleness, a new ethic of work," as it has been outlined
by Michel Foucault. It is also, Foucault argues, a sensibility that "included madmen in the proscription of idleness."[59] He describes the fall
of madness from its privileged position in medieval culture because of
the growing repression of all social deviance during the seventeenth
and eighteenth centuries. Foucault has pointed to the conflation in
early modern culture of what he calls unreason and true insanity. The
realm of unreason was populated by "the debauched, spendthrift fathers, prodigal sons, blasphemers, men who seek to undo themselves,
libertines"—in short, by those who resisted the ethic of labor and social
utility. Within this general paradigm of social utility there was a "special
modulation which concerned madness proper,...those called, without
exact semantic distinction, insane, alienated, deranged."[60] Thus, eighteenth-century perceptions of drunkenness reflected the contemporary
connection between social utility and insanity.

If drunkenness was not identified as a widespread problem before
the seventeenth century, as Dion argues, it may be that like poverty,
and perhaps even like madness, it was seen hitherto with more charity.
Drunkenness in Rabelais, for example, is relatively benign—almost
divine—in its access to truth and was similar in that regard to contemporary perceptions of madness.[61] By the seventeenth and eighteenth
centuries, however, it was condemned. Mercantilists and some Parisian
depositions spoke of drunkenness in terms that were identifiably a part
of the language of social utility. References to the debauchery of wine,
to derangement, and to libertinage all indicate an underlying coherence to the perception of drunkenness: drunkenness, whether perceived as idleness or as madness, had been placed outside of the
community of labor.[62] Therein lies the logic of the cabaret/work antithesis. Drunkenness shared the moral opprobrium that was attached to
poverty and unemployment as early as the middle of the seventeenth
century; and in the nineteenth century, when the disease of drink was
baptized *alcoholism,* drunkenness, like madness, became a medical
problem—though unlike madness, it never shed the indictment of
moral debauchery.[63]

Given the changing, sometimes contradictory perceptions of drinking and drunkenness, it is difficult to ascertain how much drunkenness
there actually was in the Old Regime. An English visitor in 1776
declared that "this vice is almost unknown in France."[64] Other contemporary evidence seems to confirm the Englishman's assertion. Jean
Louis Flandrin, a historian who has surveyed seventeenth-century
authors, has concluded that excessive drinking was uncommon in
France, and he argues in support of this that the French customarily

drank their wine mixed with water. He contrasts the East Europeans' reputation for drunkenness with French moderation and suggests that the French used wine as "daily food" rather than as a "social rite of complex signification."[65] Such a description simply will not do for the eighteenth century, however accurate it may be for earlier periods. By the eighteenth century adding water to wine was part of the cure for venereal disease. When one Parisian about whom we know a fair amount was forced to follow this regime, it was sufficiently unusual, at least for him, that his companions immediately divined his malady.[66] Although Parisians certainly drank at meals, it is equally clear that they drank at taverns without eating and between meals. Nor is it accurate to say that drink was not a social rite in Paris, as I shall attempt to demonstrate later in this paper. Still, the seventeenth-century image of the abstemious French makes a great deal of sense in the eighteenth century as well.

It is also true that Parisians drank far less liquor than East European societies appear to have consumed and that they far preferred wine to stronger alcohols.[67] Modern studies suggest that liquor is socially disruptive as much because of its novelty as because of its potency.[68] If it is sold and consumed in nontraditional settings, without ritual forms to control its use, then liquor has no social meaning beyond its intoxicating effects. This situation seems largely to have been avoided in Paris. The relatively small amount of liquor that was consumed in Paris was sold in establishments quite similar to taverns, and this practice seems to have averted the excess caused by gin in England.

What other kinds of evidence do we have about drunkenness? The depositions for marital separations and complaints of libertinage indicate that habitual drunkenness was not unknown, even among the bourgeoisie. But such documents focus attention on the exceptional cases of extreme behavior. Is there any way of looking at more representative behavior? Other depositions exist—vastly more numerous than demands for separation—that present us with more mundane problems and contentions in people's lives. Such depositions suggest that drunkenness was not the problem of epidemic proportions it had become at that time in England, the home of Gin Lane, nor had it produced any serious social dislocation.

The daily complaints about insults and injuries brought before the police *commissaires*, which make up the bulk of the *commissaires'* archive, present evidence in support of the English visitor's pronouncement.[69] These complaints dealt not with habitual drunkenness but with daily social relations and conflicts in taverns, with insults and slander, and with the defense of honor and reputation. They tell about simple intoxication, to the extent that it marked conflicts in taverns and streets.

Accusations of drunkenness are surprisingly rare. Only 3 percent of forty-five hundred tavern customers found in a sample of the police archives were identified as drunk, though the percentage was increasing between the beginning of the eighteenth century and the second half. Some of this reticence was certainly due to the belief that inebriation, particularly if unexpected and extreme, could diminish the gravity of a crime.[70] Hence plaintiffs would not have been eager to speak of factors mitigating an assailant's fault. Yet practically all the testimony—whether from plaintiffs, witnesses, the accused, or even the police—was silent.[71] The very infrequency of any mention of drunkenness in a source where drunken brawls must have occurred is a striking comment on the general attitude toward, if not the extent of, drunkenness.

In the few cases that depositions did mention someone being drunk, it was more as an afterthought or by way of explaining otherwise bizarre behavior. A plaster beater got into a fight because of a head "heated by wine" and spoke in "terms customary to a man who has drunk and who lacks education."[72] Similarly, a wine merchant in a fight with a customer accused her of having "drunk a glass too many, that it was the wine that made her talk."[73] In both cases the drink was deemed responsible rather than the drinker. Intoxication excused sexual misbehavior, as with several plaintiffs who explained that they had been with prostitutes only because they, the plaintiffs, had been drunk. One had "had the weakness to accept the prostitute's propositions, being a bit *remply de vin*"; another conceded that he was "giddy [*étourdi*] from drink."[74] It was the drink that made them weak or giddy and to some extent absolved them.

Why then was drunkenness generally absent from the ways people described themselves and each other? If drinking to the point of intoxication was as prevalent as some authors have suggested, it is curiously hidden in the depositions before the police. This sample of the sociability of cabarets contains little indication of widespread drunkenness and almost no overt reference to it. Perhaps one explanation lies in the popular attitudes toward intoxication. Little of the opprobrium directed at habitual drinking and idleness that was expressed in depositions of libertinage appears in other complaints. Inebriation could exacerbate or mitigate one's behavior, depending on the circumstances, but there is rarely mention of drunkenness or a sense of censure or reproach in these depositions. The stark contrast with complaints of libertinage and separation is due to the difference in patterns of consumption. Unlike the husband or son who spent all his time drinking and was habitually drunk, most people drank sociably and often in moderation. The author artisan Ménétra captures this same dichotomy in his memoires. He flatly condemns fathers, his own and others, who "by their drunkenness [*yvrogneries*] are responsible for the downfall of their children."[75] Yet he expresses evident pleasure in recounting his own "carousing [*ribotes*]." Drinking is a frequent theme in Ménétra's story, but he insists that however much he "sacrificed to Bacchus," he "never sacrificed except in company"—in social drinking.[76] His intoxication and that of his companions is always accidental to their social drinking.

The popular literature of the period also presented drunkenness as often accidental. The drunk was generally a comic figure, harmless, impertinent, victimized perhaps by his wife. There was a good deal of sympathy for him, even when the other characters disapproved. Those disapproving were generally the women—wives or girlfriends of the drunks. Thus, the dramatic tension of a play (this was not sophisticated drama) might center on the hapless hero becoming drunk, unintentionally or through someone's malice, and then having to face a woman's reproach. In both *Le Correspondant de la guinguette* of Caylus and *L'Impromptu des harangères* of Farin de Hautemar a rival gets the hero drunk to discredit him in the eyes of the girl for whom they are vying. The girl is horrified—"she believed that drunkenness was hateful in a young man"—though Caylus pointed out that "this was a simple bourgeoise who did not know the great world of Paris."[77] The girl's father, however, appears more enthusiastic: "You must pardon him; when wine is common, reason is rare, only women are forbidden to drink, because when they once lose their reason they never find it, but a wise man must get drunk at least once in his life, to know what wine he has."[78] The girl's disgust sounds fastidious, and the father appears overzealous. The comedy lay in both extremes opposed to the hero's inadvertent condition. The moral was simple: despite the father's enthusiasm, drunkenness was a mishap, comic perhaps but not particularly objectionable.

The vocabulary of drunkenness found in depositions and complaints illustrates this point. There were many ways to describe the condition: *yvre, plein de boisson, pris de vin, remply de vin, gris*. Half of those persons indicated as drunk were called *pris* or *plein de boisson* or *de vin*—most often *pris de vin*. A third were described as *ivre, saoul*, or *mort ivre*—most often *ivre*. The rest were *gris, trop bu*, or *étourdi*. *Ivre* and *saoul* appear to have been less euphemistic terms than the others: they were preferred by plaintiffs speaking of others, whereas people were far likelier to speak of themselves as *pris de vin*. Depositions often said only that the person "seemed" or "appeared to be" drunk. *Ivre* may have implied too clear a demarcation between drunk and sober. Instead, most people spoke in terms of the drink, that someone was either full of it or taken by it. The vocabulary, then, reflected the tendency to blame the drink for the drunkenness. The implication was that the drink had gotten the better of the drinker, that the drinker had not intended to get drunk.

Evidently, popular culture was also engaged in a discourse about drink. Unlike elite discourse, however, which pilloried drinking and drunkenness in terms of unreason and social utility, popular discourse preferred not to speak of drunkenness and cloaked it in terms of sociability. As Roland Barthes said ironically of the "myths" of this century, "In France, drunkenness is a consequence, never an intention. A drink is felt as the spinning out of a pleasure, not as the necessary cause of an effect which is sought: wine is...the leisurely act of drinking."[79] There are clear parallels with the popular myths of the eighteenth century. The realities behind those myths—the existence and nature of popular drunkenness—remain elusive. Yet the myths themselves are revealing. The elites managed to evoke a world in which the lower orders apparently rejected the values of thrift and hard work. As an external problem, drunkenness conveniently explained the failure of capitalist virtues without challenging their internal logic. Popular myths about drink may get us no closer to the truth, yet anthropologists point to the ability of cultures to impose meaning on, and mold the sensation of, their drinking.[80] If the laboring classes had already created a myth of drinking as conviviality and of drunkenness as accident rather than intention, as seems to be the case, there is reason to believe that this model could in fact shape the experienced nature of drinking just as surely as any biological absolutes of metabolism and alcohol.

I have argued that the line that separated simple intoxication from alcoholism was not clearly understood in the Old Regime; that the very notion of alcohol abuse was in fact only half-formed; and that those who would look for the rise of such excess in the Old Regime must remember that perceptions of drunkenness were evolving and reflecting changes in social values as much as changes in social behavior. I have also argued that the line separating drinking and drunkenness was not clear, but for different reasons. It is hard to imagine that people could not tell when someone was drunk, yet there is a certain reticence about the fact on the part of witnesses, plaintiffs, suspects, and even the police. Their silence on the subject expresses the primacy of drinking over drunkenness, the centrality of drinking in sociability as opposed to the unpremeditated quality of drunkenness. The people of Paris professed not to drink to get drunk and viewed drunkenness as a side effect. Drinking, even to excess, was an essential instrument of tavern fellowship and social relations, and therefore drunkenness was tolerated, but not sought, by those who valued such sociability.

DRINK

If the motives of most people's drinking remain elusive, and if there is little evidence of widespread drunkenness, then drinking must be approached in a different manner. Only by integrating drinking with other activities in the tavern and with other motivations for going to a tavern can it be understood as the laboring classes experienced it. The quick drink with a chance acquaintance and the slower, more leisurely drinking with friends were part of the sociability of the tavern and contributed to the tavern's function as a public and communal space. It is only in conjunction with the other activities in the tavern, to which drinking might be subordinated, that drinking becomes understandable.

Wine was a source of refreshment and food and thus a legitimate end in itself. The drink was important mainly as symbol—as something shared, a sign of friendship, a token of esteem, or a bond. It was common to seal business deals by drinking over them.[81] The church was aware of this practice and warned confessors to discourage it.[82] There is evidence, in fact, that contracts included the price of a concluding bottle at a cabaret, paid for by the buyer.[83] Even prostitutes, on establishing a liaison, suggested that they begin with a drink at the nearest tavern. Thus, the drink was something of a handshake, a courtesy, and a sign of good faith. Wine was offered as a recognition of a favor done or in thanks for a service. One worker, for instance, bought a drink for a man who had just agreed to employ him.[84] The sharing of wine initiated relationships and established a bond between those who partook.

Drinking together was most often a sign of friendship. As an author in the middle of the century wrote, "The man with whom I get drunk is more dear to me than wife or child."[85] The standard, even ritual, expression of witnesses who had been in a tavern, "...having been drinking with my friends in a cabaret," linked friend to drinking, and both to the cabaret. It implied more than just that one often went drinking with friends. The habitual conjunction of the three elements —friends, drink and cabaret—suggest they were perceived as intrinsically related.

The drink functioned as a symbol in several ways. First, it was an offering, a gift. The offer might be reciprocated or not, depending on the relationship of the drinkers. Second, it was a sharing. As a simultaneous consumption, a drink set up a bond of mutual partaking and

fellowship. Third, it was an association. Thus, the members of a group
of drinkers were in some way united by the drinking into a sort of
community. Witnesses referred to groups of drinkers often as a company and occasionally as a society. The sense of community was
strengthened by the fact that wine was generally served in a single
pitcher or bottle. There was, then, a joint possession of wine as each
filled his glass from the pitcher.

Wine acted as a way of integrating persons into a group and defining those who belonged and those who did not. Witnesses spoke of
being given a glass of wine on joining a group of drinkers, as a formal
act of inclusion. One laborer met a group of soldiers in his local tavern
who "offered him a drink of wine, which he accepted and began to
drink with them."[86] If two groups were already drinking separately in a
tavern, they might be brought together by one group offering the
other a drink or by mixing the contents of their pitchers. Two bourgeois prevailed on some friends to join them at their table by taking the
bottle and glasses from their friends' table and carrying them back to
their own, "to admit them to their [the bourgeois'] table, where they
drank all together."[87] Those who had been sent for by a group of
drinkers to join their company were formally presented with a glass of
wine on their arrival.[88] People seem to have used wine consciously as a
token of their immediate community. A refusal to offer wine made this
point just as clearly. When a master pastry maker sat down, unbidden,
at a table with others of his guild, they protested that he had not been
asked; and "since they did not offer him a drink," he ordered a glass
from a waiter, at which effrontery the whole group attacked him.[89] In
another case witnesses remarked that two bakers who had met in a
tavern to argue a dispute did not drink together, as a sign of their
hostility.[90] Wine, offered or withheld, signified the relationship between individuals.

A shared drink could also reestablish ties that had been disrupted.
A falling-out between two master locksmiths was patched up, at the
urging of other guild members, with a drink at a nearby cabaret "with
the design of reconciling them."[91] Two water carriers, both women, met
with their families, having fought the previous day at the fountain. The
two families stood each other to drinks at several cabarets to pacify the
two women, and the families left the last cabaret treating each other as
friends. Here wine was a catalyst as well as a symbol. Its role was
recognized even in jurisprudence: drinking with someone who had
offered an injury was seen as a "tacit...mark of reconciliation."[92]

The power of the symbol is as evident when the offer was refused.
One witness explained that he had refused the offer of a drink by an
accused "because of the suspicion attached to the man and because of

the debauched company he was keeping at his table."[93] The drink would have associated the witness too obviously with a potential murderer. A master glazier seems to have been motivated by no such apprehension when he refused a drink offered by another master glazier and explained that he was looking for someone else.[94] Yet by declining the proffered glass, the glazier was denying a gesture of interdependence and violating the "ethic of generosity."[95] In response the repulsed glazier insulted the first and beat him up. Two lead workers ended up fighting outside a cabaret after one had refused the offer of a glass of wine.[96] A master shoemaker declined a glass of wine from a journeyman coppersmith, saying only that "he had not wished to accept." He does not seem to have known the journeyman well, and the journeyman was drunk (it was the police, not the shoemaker, who mentioned that fact), but it is possible that his refusal stemmed from the social distance between master and journeyman. Whatever the reason, the journeyman waylaid the shoemaker later that evening and broke his leg.[97] An overture of friendship and reciprocity was rebuffed at one's peril.

The language of generosity and reciprocity pervaded most aspects of social drinking. Phrases like "buy someone a drink," "offer someone a drink," or "pay for a pitcher" were common in invitations to join someone at a tavern. A quick drink, *un [coup] de vin*, offered as a salutation, *par politesse*, to someone who briefly joined a drinking group but did not stay long, was considered a gift.[98] Such an offer might be described in depositions as a matter of civility or politeness, yet it also constituted a social exchange that by "strengthening the bonds of kinship, neighborhood, or friendship" was employed by artisans and laborers to achieve a measure of security in their lives.[99]

The reciprocity of buying drinks was generally more narrowly defined. A person's explicit offer to "pay for a pint of wine," when among friends, was usually translated into each paying for himself. His friends would accept and consume his pitcher, and perhaps some more wine, but the bill was paid by all on leaving the tavern. Each man knew how much he had drunk and paid for his share. An equitable alternative sometimes took the more complicated form of friends paying for alternate rounds or bottles at different taverns; people seem to have kept track of what each owed regardless of the method. This is not to suggest that everyone always agreed about the division of the bill; there are occasional complaints against drinking companions who would not "give their part of the expense."[100] Nonetheless, the protocol of paying for drinks reveals a disjunction between the language and practice of generosity. People bought drinks for each other, but generosity lasted only until the group was finished drinking, whereupon each settled his bill individually. A master shoemaker complained that having paid for a round of wine with a friend he had met at a cabaret, the friend refused his "turn to pay for a chopine," and they got into a fight. The friend declared, however, that the shoemaker "had spoken in langue d'oc and called him a swindler" and continued to do so despite being told, "We have known each other for a year and can find each other and I will buy you a drink—I will not be a swindler."[101] The shoemaker was less interested in a future debt than in an immediate reciprocation. The social exchange at this point is more symbolic, perhaps, than it appears to be in a gift of a drink, but we must not doubt its importance.

Between strangers, by contrast, there was no presumption that the cost of drinks would be shared. Invitations to drink were taken at face value, and several plaintiffs maintained that they had drunk only "at the solicitation and request of the person...who had promised to pay the expense."[102] There is indirect evidence as well that men often paid for other men's alcohol. It was a favorite trick of people drinking together who did not know each other to leave without paying, sticking the last of the party with the bill. Bartenders must have been aware of this practice, yet they were quite ready to hold any single member of a party of drinkers responsible for the whole bill.[103] When we do find a person buying someone a drink, it often emphasizes the inequality between them. Usually the inequality was economic, as between employee and employer: thus, people bought wine for their carriage drivers. When men and women were together, the men usually paid. One woman even asserted that "when men are present, they ought to pay."[104] Not everyone felt this way: the woman's escort had expected her to pay since she had invited him. Buying drinks was expensive, yet the etiquette of meeting someone in a bar required it. The offer of a drink was the necessary overture to joining someone; the gift could be reciprocated, but with strangers reciprocation was not presumed. The drink between strangers was less shared than given, thereby expressing a more tentative relationship.

Social drinking in taverns was central to popular culture. It gave substance to the rituals of friendship and social interaction; it was the common denominator of all customers and all activities. A glass of wine, the drink, was an idiom of social exchange. As a gift or as a communion, it bound people together in ties of reciprocity and debt, of friendship and solidarity. Social drinking used the signs and rituals of gifting to cement personal ties and articulate social relations. Such sociability—dense, constant, even political in its concern with neighborhood or professional status and power—is central to the significance of taverns and drink. Drunkenness, by contrast, was the metaphor of a consistent and recurring critique of popular culture by the elites. It summarized the waste of money and time, the idleness and immorality of those in the popular classes who refused to respond to a new ethic of work and self-discipline. Taverns became a symbol of their unrepentant reliance on sociability and public consumption in daily life. Whether seen as social drinking or as drunkenness, drink constituted a battlefield of two conflicting cultures.

NOTES

1. "Scholars commonly associate drink and social distress in describing a society" (Michael Marrus, "Social Drinking in the *Belle Epoque*," *Journal of Social History* 7 [1974]: 116). Marrus gives several examples of historians of the eighteenth and nineteenth centuries to support this point.

2. Louis Sébastien Mercier, *Tableau de Paris*, 12 vols. (Amsterdam, 1782–1788), 12:275–276.

3. Jacques Saint-Germain, *La vie quotidienne en France à la fin du grand siècle* (Paris, 1965), 17.

4. Fernand Braudel, *Capitalism and Material Life*, trans. Miriam Kochan (New York, 1973), 166. He is quoting a verse from the eighteenth century.

5. Mercier, *Tableau de Paris*, 7:238.

6. Attitudes in the nineteenth century are masterfully analyzed in Susanna Barrows, *Distorting Mirrors: Visions of the Crowd in Late Nineteenth-Century France* (New Haven, 1981), 43–73. Surprisingly, Louis Chevalier, *Classes laborieuses et classes dangereuses à Paris pendant la première moitié du XIXe siècle* (Paris, 1928), has little to say about the question, but some of the "historians" of the cabaret writing in the nineteenth century, such as Michel and Fournier, and Colombey, illustrate the point adequately.

7. Taverns and drunkenness are treated briefly—and in most cases synonymously—by Braudel, *Capitalism and Material Life*, 165–166; Robert Mandrou, *Introduction à la France moderne* (Paris, 1974), 302–303; Jeffry Kaplow, *The Names of Kings: The Parisian Laboring Poor in the Eighteenth Century* (New York, 1972), 78–79; Farge, *Vivre dans la rue à Paris au XVIIIe siècle* (Paris, 1979), 70–78; and Saint Germain, *Vie quotidienne*, 17. A notable exception is provided by Daniel Roche in two books on Parisian culture: *Le peuple de Paris: Essai sur la culture populaire au XVIII siècle* (Paris, 1981), translated as *The People of Paris: An Essay in Popular Culture in the Eighteenth Century* (Berkeley and Los Angeles: University of California Press, 1987); and Jacques-Louis Ménétra, *Journal de ma vie*, ed. Daniel Roche (Paris, 1982).

8. Figures for 1700 to 1708 are in Archives Nationales (hereafter AN), G^7 1179. Figures for 1719 to 1721 are in G^7 1182; cited in *Mémoirs des intendants sur l'état des généralités...*, ed. Arthur-Michel de Boislisle (Paris, 1881), 1:501.

9. Orest Ranum, *Paris in the Age of Absolutism* (New York, 1968), 176–178, gives figures for 1637. Marcel Lachiver, *Vin, vigne et vignerons en région parisienne du XVIIe au XIXe siècles* (Pontoise, 1982), 275, gives 610,740 hectoliters as average yearly sales in 1741–1757. For six hundred thousand Parisians, per capita consumption would have been 102 liters. Arthur Young, *Travels in France*

(Garden City, N.J., 1969), 374, gives 656,600 hectoliters per year. To this figure Young added a sixth part again, for the amount of wine that the tax farm was willing to admit slipped by untaxed annually. His computations resulted in per capita consumption of 107 liters. Modern historians are inclined to judge Young's figures for both population and smuggling to be much too low. Beer consumption in the first two decades of the eighteenth century was roughly 12 liters per capita.

10. Georges Durand, *Vin, vigne et vignerons en Lyonnais et Beaujolais* (Paris, 1979), 48.

11. Lachiver, *Vin...en région parisienne*, 267, uses figures from Ch. Mathis, "Belleville et Menilmontant au XVIIIe siècle" (mémoire de maîtrise, 1974).

12. Marcel Lachiver, "Fraude du vin et fraudeurs en l'Ile de France, XVIIIe siècle," *Revue d'histoire moderne et contemporaine* 21 (1974): 420.

13. Wages, of course, varied considerably. Kaplow concludes that the "great majority of the laboring poor had to make do with about 1 livre and 10 sous a day or less" (*Names of Kings*, 54). George Rudé, "Prices, Wages and Popular Movements in Paris during the French Revolution," *Economic History Review* 6, no. 3 (1954): 249, agrees that "few wage earners could afford to buy even the comparatively modest quantity of one quart per day." He cites Lavoisier.

14. Jean Baptiste Pressavin, *L'art de prolonger la vie et de conserver la santé, ou traité d'hygiène* (Lyon, Paris, 1786), cited in Durand, *Vin...en Lyonnais et Beaujolais*, 44.

15. Thomas Brennan, *Public Drinking and Popular Culture in Eighteenth-Century Paris* (Princeton, 1988), chap. 3.

16. Jean-Joseph Vadé, "La pipe cassée," in *Oeuvres de Vadé* (Paris, n.d.). André Charles Cailleau, "Le waux-hal populaire," in *Three Centuries of French Drama*, microfiche ed. (Louisville, 1969). See also George Rudé, *The Crowd in the French Revolution* (Oxford, 1959), 15. Kaplow, *Names of Kings* (New York, 1972), 78–79; Braudel, *Capitalism and Material Life*, 162–175.

17. Archives Départementales de la Seine et la ville de Paris (hereafter AD) D_5B^6 3881; D_5B^6 525.

18. The average frequency of customers' drinking on credit at a particular tavern is actually about once every four days, based on eighty-three customers in eight different taverns over periods of two to six months. This figure understates the amount, of course, because such customers did not always drink on credit. AD D_5B^6 5775; D_5B^6 2704; D_5B^6 525; D_5B^6 248; D_5B^6 4097; D_5B^6 657; D_5B^6 2854; D_5B^6 2521. Although there are many other account books of wine merchants from this period, serious problems arise in interpreting the material, for wine merchants also sold wine to be taken out. In many cases the wine merchants dealt only with wholesale orders of wine to be delivered to customers' houses. Even when the account books list retail sales (for wine sold by the *pinte*, etc.), it is often impossible to tell whether the wine was being consumed in the tavern or taken home. In most of the above cases there are telltale signs, such as food sold with the wine or a note that the customer drank the wine with someone or drank it "dans le jardin," that clarify the issue. But many account books simply cannot be interpreted.

19. Roger Dion, *Histoire de la vigne et du vin en France des origines au XIXe siècle* (Paris, 1959) 488.

20. Bernard de Laffemas, *Source de plusieurs abus et monopoles qui se sont glissez et coulez sur le peuple de France depuis trente ans ou environs* (n.p., 1596), cited in Dion, *Histoire,* 488.

21. *Petit Robert* (Paris, 1972), s.v. "ivrognerie."

22. The *Petit Robert* gives 1859 as the first known use of the word, s.v. "alcoolisme." Susanna Barrows finds the word used first by a Swedish doctor in 1852 (*Distorting Mirrors,* 61). Pierre-François Muyart de Vouglans, *Les loix criminelles de France dans leur ordre naturelle,* new ed., augmented, 2 vols. (Paris, 1780), 1:14.

23. Michel de Montaigne, *The Complete Essays,* trans. Donald M. Frame (Stanford, Calif., 1958), 247.

24. Montaigne, *Complete Essays,* 247.

25. Charles W. Cole, *Colbert and a Century of French Mercantilism,* 2 vols. (Hamden, Conn., 1964), 1:28–39.

26. Ernest Lavisse, *Louis XIV,* 2 vols. (Paris, 1978), 1:217.

27. Duchesne, *Code de la police ou analyse des reglements de police,* 4th ed., (Paris, 1767), titre 12, 1: *Police des pauvres. Dictionnaire economique,* cited in Durand, *Vin... en Lyonnais et Beaujolais,* 44.

28. *Encyclopédie méthodique: jurisprudence,* 10 vols. (Paris, 1782–1791), 10:538.

29. *Encyclopédie, ou Dictionnaire raisonné des sciences, des arts et des métiers,* ed. Denis Diderot and Jean le Rond d'Alembert (Paris, 1751–1765), s.v. "eau" and "vin."

30. *Encyclopédie,* s.v. "yvrognerie."

31. Nicolas Delamare, *Traité de la police,* 2d ed., augmented, 4 vols. (Paris, 1705–1738), 1:612.

32. "Cas de conscience sur l'yvrognerie et sur les danses, décidés par MM. les Docteurs en Théologie de la Faculté des Paris," *Journal des savantes,* 14 April 1721.

33. Edit sur la punition des ivrognes..., Valence, August 1536, in François Isambert, et.al., *Recueil général des anciennes lois françaises depuis l'an 420 jusqu'à la révolution de 1789,* ed. François Isambert, N. Decrucy, Alphonse-Henri Taillandier, et al. (Paris, 1821–1833), 12:527.

34. The *Petit Robert* defines *ivrogne* as "qui a l'habitude de s'enivrer," whereas *ébriété* refers to simple "ivresse." A police report described an officer arresting four *ivrognes* who had gotten into a fight (AN, Y10993b, May 17, 1751). Apparently, anyone found drunk could be an *ivrogne.*

35. AN, Y10139, 29 January 1751. Two domestics were imprisoned "on account of their behavior [in a cabaret], their insolence, and their drunkenness [*ivresse*]." AN, Y9657, 7 January 1761.

36. In fact, relatively few of the reports of these night patrols make any mention of drunkenness in taverns, with exceptions like the report of 21 November 1751 that found "beaucoup d'ivrognes, des soldats... et autres gens suspects" but did not arrest any of them (Bibliothèque de l'Arsenal, Archives de la Bastille [hereafter AB] Ms 10139).

37. AN, Y13166, 12 May 1751.

38. The various eighteenth-century treatises on law—Duchesne and Delamare, for example—find nothing more recent than the 1536 edict to refer to.

Such treatises not only were careful to cite the oldest examples, as precedent, but generally gave the most recent reeditions. Dion, *Histoire*, 488, also comments on this lacuna.

39. Durand, *Vin...en Lyonnais et Beaujolais*, 45.

40. These records actually consist of two distinct legal documents, the *séparation des biens* and the complaint of *libertinage*, which could lead to the police imprisoning someone for immorality.

41. AN, Y14527, 6 October 1731.

42. AN, Y15219, 29 December 1712.

43. AN, Y13926, 20 March 1741; Y14877, 18 April 1691.

44. AN, Y10993b, 20 November 1751.

45. AN, Y12952, 22 November 1751.

46. AN, Y14174, 3 August 1731; Y11228, 12 October 1741.

47. AN, Y13005, 11 January 1781.

48. AN, Y14537, 30 December 1741; Y14877, 21 November 1691; Y11228, 12 October 1741.

49. AN, Y12177, 23 January 1771.

50. AN, Y14527, 25 October 1731.

51. As one witness, a wine merchant, put it, the husband was "at the cabaret as often as at his work" (AN, Y14877, 5 December 1691).

52. Jean-Claude Perrot, *Genèse d'une ville moderne: Caen au XVIIIe siècle* (Paris, 1975), 2:836–838, notes of the *lettres de cachet* he examined that conflict was most often between generations, particularly between a widow and her children.

53. AN Y11178, 9 September 1761.

54. AN Y11947, 6 February 1761.

55. AN Y15219, 21 November 1712.

56. Gaspard Toussaint Taconnet, "Impromptu de la foire," in *Théâtres français* (Paris, 1732–1791), 31:10.

57. Vadé, "La pipe cassée," 22.

58. See Barrows, *Distorting Mirrors*, 70–71, for the nineteenth-century view, particularly Zola's, of alcohol as a fatal legacy. See Hans Medick, "Plebeian Culture in the Transition to Capitalism," in *Culture, Ideology and Politics: Essays in Honour of Eric Hobsbawm*, ed. R. Samuel and Gareth Stedman Jones (London, 1983), 84–112, for a perceptive discussion of Gin Lane. The collection of *lettres de cachet* assembled by Arlette Farge and Michel Foucault, *Le désordre des familles* (Paris, 1982) also sheds light on the French experience of drunkenness. Drunkenness is prominent in these records for many of the same reasons that I have described.

59. Michel Foucault, *Madness and Civilization: A History of Insanity in the Age of Reason*, trans. Richard Howard (New York, 1965), 46, 57; see also chaps. 2 and 3. Foucault mentions drunkenness only briefly.

60. Foucault, *Madness and Civilization*, 65–66.

61. Mikhail Bakhtin, *Rabelais and His World*, trans. Helene Iswolsky (Cambridge, Mass., 1968), 295–296. Voltaire went so far as to call Rabelais a "drunken philosopher, who only wrote when he was drunk [*dans le temps de son ivresse*]" (*Letters on England*, trans. Leonard Tancock, [Harmondsworth, 1980], letter 22).

62. Foucault, *Madness and Civilization*, 58.

63. Barrows, *Distorting Mirrors*, 61.

64. *Observations in a Journey to Paris* (1777), 1:50, cited in Albert Babeau, *Les artisans et les domestiques d'autrefois* (Paris, 1886), 208. Babeau states, "The French artisan, more polite than the English worker, is also more sober than he,...a sobriety animated in part by sentiments of economy" (207–208). On the Gin Lane problem, see T. G. Coffey, "Beer Street: Gin Lane, Some Views of Eighteenth-Century Drinking," *Quarterly Journal of Studies on Alcohol* 27 (1966): 669–683; M. Dorothy George, *London Life in the Eighteenth Century* (London, 1951), 27–42. The Gin Lane problem has been in some ways a paradigm of modern perceptions of drunkenness and the poor in early modern Europe.

65. Jean Louis Flandrin, "La diversité des goûts et des pratiques alimentaires en Europe du XVIe au XVIIIe siècle," *Revue d'histoire moderne et contemporaine* 30 (1983): 70–73.

66. Ménétra, *Journal de ma vie*, 215.

67. Mercier, *Tableau de Paris*, 12:225–227. In 1714 the importation of eau-de-vie and liqueur into Paris was about one-fortieth that of wine. AN G^7 1182–1215.

68. Medick, "Plebeian Culture," 104–106; William B. Taylor, *Drinking, Homicide and Rebellion in Colonial Mexican Villages* (Stanford, 1979), 36–45.

69. I discuss the sources at some length in my book, Brennan, *Public Drinking*. See especially chapters 1 and 3.

70. "Drunkenness [*ivresse*], being potentially the effect of surprise, can also serve, when it is extreme, to render crimes less punishable" (Muyart de Vouglans, *Loix criminelles*, 1:14).

71. A notable exception is the master chandler who declared that he "was drunk [*ivre*] and without reason when he was arrested and not knowing what he was doing, which rendered him absolutely excusable" (AN, Y9668, 28 December 1761). There is no indication what the judge thought of this plea.

72. AN, Y10233, 2 August 1761.

73. AN, Y11238, 23 July 1751.

74. AN, Y15931, 8 August 1731; Y10837, 5 April 1720.

75. Ménétra, *Journal de ma vie*, 192.

76. Ménétra, *Journal de ma vie*, 259.

77. Claude-Philippe de Tubières, comte de Caylus, *Oeuvres badines*, 12 vols. (Paris, 1786), 10:142; Farin de Hautemar, *Impromptu des harangères, opéra-comique* (Paris, 1754), reprinted in *Three Centuries of French Drama*, microfiche ed. (Louisville, 1969).

78. Caylus, *Oeuvres badines*, 10143.

79. Roland Barthes, *Mythologies*, trans. Annette Lavers (New York, 1972), 58–60. I am indebted to David Price for bringing this quotation to my attention.

80. Craig MacAndrew and Robert Edgerton, *Drunken Comportment: A Social Explanation* (Chicago, 1969), 88–89, 165–172.

81. AN, Y10233, 31 October 1760.

82. "Cas de conscience."

83. Communicated to me by Vivian Doz, who is working on *revendeuses* in the Series Y for a *mémoire de maîtrise*.

84. AN, Y12661, 21 September 1761.

85. Caylus, *Oeuvres badines,* 140.

86. AN, Y10086, 5 October 1741.

87. AN, Y10141, 6 April 1751.

88. AN, Y14499, 26 April 1691.

89. AN, Y12952, 6 October 1751.

90. AN, Y14066, 22 December 1741.

91. AN, Y15643, 14 May 1751.

92. Muyart de Vouglans, *Loix criminelles,* 2:313.

93. AN, Y13942, 12 October 1751. A journeyman refused the offer of a drink from a soldier "because of the persons in his [the soldier's] company." The soldier was so "shocked" by the refusal that he attacked the journeyman (AN, Y12100, 10 April 1691).

94. AN, Y13908, 13 January 1728.

95. Ivan Karp, "Beer Drinking and Social Experience in an African Society," in *Explorations in African Systems of Thought* ed. Ivan Karp and Charles S. Beard (Bloomington, 1980), 97. I wish to thank Hans Medick for pointing this article out to me.

96. AN, Y15496, 7 October 1751. Numerous examples can be added to illustrate the anger provoked by refusal of a drink; for example, Y15366, 23 October 1761.

97. AN, Y11178, 14 August 1761.

98. That such an offer was a gift seemed so obvious to a *bourgeois de Paris* who had just been "presented" with a *coup de vin* that when the wine merchant tried to hold him equally responsible for the bill, he presumed it was an insult (AN Y14611, 6 February 1691).

99. See AN, Y13037, 26 November 1691, for the phrases. Medick, "Plebeian Culture," 92, discusses social exchange as an alternative to capitalist values of thrift and saving.

100. AN, Y11238, 26 January 1751.

101. AN, Y15238, 19 February 1731.

102. AN, Y14661, 25 October 1741; Y14661, 20 January 1741.

103. AN, Y11238, 26 January 1751.

104. AN, Y10993b, 21 August 1751.

THREE

"Parliaments of the People": The Political Culture of Cafés in the Early Third Republic

Susanna Barrows

Some time ago the National Archives in Paris discarded, lost, or destroyed what must have been a monumental set of boxes specifically devoted to nineteenth-century French cafés. Whatever the cause, the disappearance of these records suggests a dramatic shift in the official perception of the café. Until the 1880s French governments viewed cafés in the same light as did Honoré de Balzac: they were the "parliaments of the people." But after 1880 the purely political aspects of café culture elicited almost no documentation on the part of French authorities—at least not under the rubric of cafés. What happened in that interstitial space between close official surveillance and bureaucratic oblivion? What happened, in other words, to popular political culture and the attitudes of the French state during the first decade of the Third Republic?

Every textbook of modern French history recounts the events of the *coup de seize mai* as seen from the top and summarized for the nation as a whole.[1] In 1877 the power struggle between an authoritarian president, Maréchal MacMahon, and a republican Chamber of Deputies culminated in the dissolution of the chamber; but despite MacMahon's harsh and efficient measures of political repression, the republicans triumphantly returned a majority in the October elections. This "remarkable" success, in the words of Gordon Wright, "meant that the republicans had somehow infiltrated hundreds of small towns and village councils and had taken control away from the older notables....Evidently some effective political activity had been going on through the 1870s."[2]

The primary arena for many of these republican activities was none other than the café. It was here that the spirit of the republic was to be affirmed in the face of MacMahon's self-styled "moral order." To examine the popular political culture of cafés allows us to ask crucial questions concerning the ultimate triumph of republicanism in the late 1870s. How was the coup viewed in the countryside? Why did the well-developed machinery of political repression fail in 1877? Even more important, what did the *coup de seize mai* mean to the vintner in the Beaujolais, the innkeeper in the Savoie, the skilled laborer in the Vaucluse, or the café waitress in Lyon? What was the conjuncture of change in the 1870s that ultimately tipped the balance in favor of the Third Republic?

The answers to such questions are not as obvious as they might seem. The machinery of café repression had been carefully constructed in the first half of the nineteenth century. Restoration governments rightly feared the cabaret, the café, and related institutions, including the *goguette* and the *auberge,* as prime places for political organization, for the transmission of news and dangerous ideas, and for the mobilization of popular protest. The authorities took care to forbid the singing of political songs, the sale of newspapers and pamphlets, or the recitation of inflammatory poems. By the 1830s a special arm of the law—the *police des débits de boisson*—watched over the drinking establishments of many cities and large towns. In the countryside local minions of the law—the *garde champêtre* and the mayors—served a similar function. During the massive political mobilizations of the Second Republic the café, the *auberge,* and the cabaret were regarded as the great clearinghouses for popular culture.[3]

As cafés grew in number, so did the anxiety of men of order. Hence, when a more sophisticated machinery of political repression was installed in the early 1850s, the café fell victim to new decrees. Napoleon III's orders of December 29, 1851, placed a sword of Damocles over every drinking establishment in France. He gave prefects the discretionary power to close down any cabaret, *auberge,* or café. Napoleon's motives were frankly political; he held cabarets, especially those in the countryside, responsible for "disorders," the rise of secret societies, and what he called the "progress of despicable passions." Under the pretext of politics or immorality any café could now be closed.

By 1855 the number of such potentially subversive forums had been cut from 350,424 to 291,244, and although the charges against cafés were often vague—"badly run" or "bad reputation"—the intent was clear: to stamp out the republican or socialist Left. Prefects, moreover, could do more than close existing cafés; as of 1851 they could also block the establishment of any new *débits* (public houses) on whatever grounds. Although the severe repression of the cafés was moderated during the "liberal" phase of the Second Empire in the 1860s, the prefectoral prerogatives remained on the books.[4]

The next great wave of repression came in the wake of the Franco-Prussian War and the Commune of Paris. Reactivating the existing machinery of repression, President Adolphe Thiers urged a thorough purge of all cafés whose proprietors or clientele had sympathized with the Commune or who dared voice criticism of the new regime. The close surveillance was quickly extended to all aspects of café culture. In November 1872 the minister of the interior lashed out at those "veritable schools of depravity," the café concerts. Prefects were instructed to "repress energetically" any establishment permitting "obscene songs, smutty sketches, and all other items that might compromise morals or the public order."[5] The following year the National Assembly saw fit to declare public drunkenness a crime and to equate obscenity, immorality, and vice with revolution. A new hegemony over the non-political activities of citizens became the order of the day. Forms of café sociability that had been taken for granted during the Second Empire —the right to besot oneself, employ waitresses, install a piano, or sing slightly off-color ditties—were now declared illegal and indeed associated with political subversion.[6] Such a conflation of politics and morals signaled a new phase of state control over the citizen and social space. The new restrictions on cafés presumed to enforce not simply political but, at least in principle, total control over one's public comportment.

When Maréchal MacMahon assumed the presidency on May 24, 1873, the repression of the cafés grew to draconian proportions. His prefects were told to establish a more severe curfew on all drinking establishments (8 or 9 P.M. in the countryside, 10 or 11 P.M. in most cities), to scrutinize all those employing waitresses, and to shut down many of the cafés as a "moral lesson."[7] Any rumor of left-wing sympathies, any hint of unseemly or familiar behavior, could trigger a departmental sweep of the cafés. When a detailed survey of the *brasseries à femmes* in Lyon found that the "eccentrically" dressed women addressed their customers with the intimate *tu* or permitted an occasional squeeze of the waist, all such establishments were outlawed.[8] Anonymous letters denouncing particular *débitants* as "radicals" or morally suspect were sufficient grounds for prosecution and closing, even when the local gendarmes could find no evidence of illegal activity. In such a climate of near paranoid repression it is little wonder that 3,808 additional cafés had disappeared by the end of 1875.[9]

The worst was yet to come. After the *coup de seize mai* in 1877, the Ministry of the Interior telegraphed all prefects to remind them that cafés could not allow the reading aloud of newspapers, professions of political opinion, or political discussions, nor could they display electoral posters, leaflets, or ballots. The prefects themselves were encouraged to use any pretext, however minimal, to shut down a representative sample of *débits*. Merited or not, such firm action would serve as "salutary examples" to the populace.[10]

As the electoral period approached, the repressive machinery moved into high gear. Between May 16 and November 10, 2,219 *débits* were shut down, 1,285 for reasons of "general security" and 934 others for having violated any of the dozens of regulations. Most often the charges were damning and laconic: "a site of political meetings," "a veritable club," "a meeting place of radicals," "infraction of the rules," "badly run," "bad morals," or "open after hours." But how accurately did the formulaic accusations reflect the real activities of the *débits*? Could we assume that, although the language was spare, the victims were indeed properly categorized?

The answer lies in two documents found in the departmental archives of the Haute Savoie and the Marne. In the Haute Savoie fourteen cafés were ordered closed between May and November, half for political reasons, half ostensibly for various nonpolitical infractions, including "badly run," "irregular management," "a record of late closings," or "allowed his niece to run his establishment." But as parenthetical remarks in the document—inserted later and in a different hand—indicate, political motives actually accounted for all fourteen closings: "(mais en réalité pour motif politique)."

Just as the Haute Savoie officially underreported the scope of purely political repression, so did the prefect of the Marne deliberately downplay the political sympathies of his victims when he transmitted his statistics to Paris. One café proprietor, M. Baillet, was originally arrested because "he engaged in propaganda of the most vigorous sort in favor of the radical party." This indictment was subsequently amended to read "Establishment badly run, scene of continual disorders." A certain M. Menonville was first said to be "very hostile to the government; he held a club at his place and continually sought to increase the number of individuals of his own party." On revision this became "M. Menonville is given to drink, his establishment frequented by people of the worst reputation." M. Prin was first described as a "radical of the worst order," but later that description turned into "Prin is always drunk; his *débit* is badly run and frequented by drunkards." M. Lambert's establishment, originally noted as a "place of revolutionary propaganda," was eventually recorded quite simply as "badly run." Clearly, the government's statistics obscure the extent and nature of political activity in cafés; the charges of immorality or lax

management, moreover, are misleading and almost wholly unreli-
able.[11]

But what can we learn from the exceptions—those hundreds of
detailed accounts scattered about the departmental archives? What do
they tell us about café habitués and their patrons in a period of massive
repression? Without question some French citizens in the 1870s hon-
ored the letter and the spirit of the law. How many others simply moved
their political activities into private space or prudently aired their
views beyond earshot of the authorities? Speculation here courts haz-
ard, since for this chapter, as for so many others in the history of
silence, discretion, and whispers, the archives remain mute. They do
record, however, much of the traditional rough music of defiance and
rebellion. Political songs, the meaningful insult, the funeral proces-
sion, the noisy chorus of political toasts or impromptu allegorical
speeches, and even the significant practical joke did not die after the
revolution of 1848; they resurfaced in creative form during the crisis
of 1877.

Many of these political protests were intertwined with the many
rituals that transpired in cafés. Suddenly interrupting his performance
in a café in Gueux (the Marne), a traveling artist told the assembled
audience, "We are being governed by beasts; like kings and emperors,
they are nothing but cowards. They're just like the soldiers of Ver-
sailles; they killed the children of Paris. The good Frenchmen were
those who were part of the Commune."[12] Elsewhere an aged and illiterate widow in Vaison (Vaucluse) encouraged her clientele to read aloud
certain radical newspapers; one of her literate counterparts in the
Isère did the public reading himself.[13] Both were perpetuating a traditional function of the café as the transmitter of written news to a larger
and often illiterate audience. In Courthezon (Vaucluse) M. Avril, who
leased the room above his café to a literary circle, joined the chorus of
seditious cries like "Long Live '93" or "Down with the hunchback runt"
(a popular local nickname for MacMahon), followed by a lusty singing
of the Marseillaise.

Other songs were less venerable, perhaps even more threatening to
the authorities.[14] Gendarmes in Lyon overheard a group of young men
belting out a song whose refrain was "We'll burn the white flag; we'll
slit the throats of all the Carlists" and whose coda featured three cries
of "Vive la République."[15] In another café in the Hérault, which had
received the official sanction for a concert, the performers and audience waited until the police commissioner had stepped outside, then
began to sing "one of the most violent and essentially political of
songs," eliciting bravos from the audience. This song, the report concluded, "had a refrain that was sung at the top of one's voice, 'Let's

sweep all that away,' and one of the couplets concluded with the following words 'Kings, emperors, and prelates, let's sweep all that away.' "[16]
Elsewhere in the Hérault the Café des Fleurs in Mezignan l'Evêque
became the site of local political sing-alongs. During the local fête five
musicians were hired to play for a large audience; the mayor, the
deputy mayor, and a part of the municipal council attended every
performance. According to the police, the crowd sang such songs as
"Robespierre and Marat," "The Storming of the Bastille," and "Ledel
and the Papal Palace," and after each couplet the municipal leaders
shouted for the song to be repeated.[17]

But rebellion was not always cast in lyrical cadence. In Lodève
(Hérault) the café run by M. Brun was condemned by MacMahon's
authorities because of the subversive language of a three-year-old. On
June 11 Brun's young son was asked publicly what he wanted; he
replied with the curt revolutionary slogan *La Commune ou la mort*.[18] In
these times saber-rattling truths streamed out of the mouths of babes;
their elders often modulated their own disaffection into gesture. When
the *garde champêtre* arrived at the café run by M. Espitalié in Quarante
(Hérault), a well-known meeting place for radicals, they interrogated
him for serving clients after hours. Offering no response, Espitalié
merely shrugged his shoulders and gave a "disdainful look." The gesture was sufficient grounds for closing the café.[19] The prize for the
most insolent behavior must surely be awarded to the earthy Arsène
Lambert, proprietor of the village café in Faux sur Coole (Marne).
When on the eve of the October elections two persons offered to give
him posters and ballots for the government's candidate, Lambert first
refused to take any, then changed his mind. "Give me some anyway; I
can use them to *torcher le cul*." (When later interrogated by the police,
he admitted only to having said, "I can use them for rolling my
tobacco.") The same afternoon the town's best known drunk was seen
leaving Lambert's café with a string attached to his leg, trailing behind
him a ballot for the candidate of moral order.[20]

Any of these activities, we must remember, constituted a serious
breach of the law; with the most trivial infraction of regulations a
cafetier risked loss of livelihood, fines, and even prison. Is it surprising,
then, that the archives contain dozens of protestations of innocence—
genuine or otherwise? "I'm not learned enough to be concerned with
politics," said an illiterate *cafetier* in the Rhône. "I'm not political,"
declared another. "I am so politically indifferent that I do not even
take a newspaper," asserted a café proprietor in the Hérault, bolstering
his statement with fifteen signatures of friends and clients.[21] "I care for
my mother and a sick brother," pleaded a *débitant* accused of holding
socialist meetings in his place. Occasionally local priests were pressed

into interceding on behalf of members of their flock. Other proprietors simply passed the buck: "It wasn't I who hung a tricolor outside my café; a twelve-year-old servant did it."[22]

Familiar, too, were the local targets of political anger. In the Côte d'Or the funeral of a local republican allowed the clientele of the cafés of Messrs. Carnet Roux and Baudry to march through the village, demonstration-style, and insult an old local conservative whom the authorities described as "inoffensive." During a ball held in a café in St. Saturnin d'Avignon the young dancers twice paraded across the street to hurl insults at the priests who taught in the Catholic school.[23] The curé of St. Just (Hérault) suffered even worse indignities on the occasion of the town fête. Breaking with tradition, the local *cafetier* decided to hold his ball in the archway that linked his establishment with the rectory. When several local girls refused to attend the ball, their absence was blamed on the curé. The day of the fête someone sighted the curé and screamed, "Kidnap him!" Written insult soon compounded verbal assault. The next day, over the door to the curé's quarters was scrawled "house of young females" and underneath "Gourin," the local word for a woman chaser. In these cases, as in many others, gross insults to the authorities were common, their targets the local representatives of the moral order—priests, rural police, and the like. Who can know what wellspring of political sentiment caused Joseph Jean, *cafetier* in Aubignan (Vaucluse), to insult "with menacing gestures" the local mailman on his appointed rounds?[24]

Not all the actions of café folk were mere reprints of traditional behavior. Consider the resourcefulness of one innkeeper in the Savoie, whose place was invaded by the *garde champêtre* after hours. As they stomped through the doorway, he rushed to the clock and turned the hands backward to a legal hour. Other *aubergistes* in the same department, mindful of the prohibition against serving liquor except during meals, tossed pieces of stale bread on the tables of their customers as the guard opened the door.[25]

Mixed in among these traditional or creative forms of political behavior were tactics that pointed not to the past but to the future. Infuriated by the web of restrictions placed on the cafés as well as the 8 P.M. curfew, which was costing *cafetiers* business, the mayor of Saint Gingolph (an Haute Savoie commune near the Swiss border) decided to take action along with the four other local *cafetiers*. Requesting that their commune be annexed to that haven of liberation, Switzerland, they offered to pay the French government eight thousand francs a year in reparations.[26] Other documents attest to the revolution in literacy of the late nineteenth century. Spreading from the cities into the countryside, petitions circulated in many cafés. Be they calls for the abolition of the National Assembly, testimonies signed by 151 villagers of Tart le Haut (Côte d'Or) swearing to the moral probity of a café proprietress, or a lengthy bill of particulars hostile to MacMahon signed by café regulars in three Burgundian towns, these pages with their large, awkward, or stylized signatures remind us that the world of the written petition was for many a new and unfamiliar part of rural political activity.[27]

However systematic the attack on the political culture of the café, MacMahon's crusade did not silence the world of popular protest. Still familiar with traditional forms of symbolic protest and beginning to exploit the new written, legalistic expressions of discontent, ordinary French people stood at the crossroads between two political cultures; many of these citizens were culturally ambidextrous. MacMahon's ministers were only Right-handed. As men well versed in the moralizing power of the word, they produced sheaves of written instructions to regulate public decorum. When the objects of their scrutiny responded with earthy songs or rituals of disorder, the government felt justified in equating subversion with immorality. The moralizing tone of the authorities may indeed have accentuated the grossness of the rebellion. In such a time even obscenity may belong to the keyboard of popular protest.

By the end of 1877 MacMahon had clearly lost the war on the café. Within weeks of the November departmental elections a new cadre of prefects was instructed to reopen nearly all of the closed cafés. Still smarting from the blatantly partisan nature of the repression, French ministers shied away from employing the machinery of Louis Napoleon's decree. Between 1878 and 1880 most departments watched the number of political closings dwindle to practically none. Fisticuffs exchanged over the prospect of secular education and a raucous shouting of "Vive Henri V" at the Fleur de Lys café in Avignon did attract the censure of the new administration, but these cases stand as rare exceptions to a new tolerance of politics in the café.[28] And once the republicans had secured the Senate in 1879, they chose to discard the revengeful justice of Hammurabi in the interest of constitutional reform.

By July 1880 the law abrogating Louis Napoleon's decree sailed through the Chamber of Deputies almost without debate and received a rare, nearly unanimous vote even in the Senate. Thereafter any person with two and a half francs to spare and a clean civil record could open a café.[29] The sword of the prefects was broken; they could no longer refuse applications for new cafés or close down those considered subversive. To be sure, the authorities continued to monitor *débits* of all varieties, but their eyes were now focused on the nonpolitical facets of café culture—infractions of closing hours, debauchery, prostitution, gambling, drunkenness, and fraud. The sole surviving element of the crackdown on the café was the insistence upon moral order. To read the late nineteenth- and early twentieth-century archival records concerning cafés is to enter the world of satyricon, populated by provocative waitresses and group orgies of a distinctly Gallic nature, to watch the wild dancing gyrations of the young, to listen to a discourse stripped of politics and obsessed with Eros. Actual sexual behavior in cafés almost certainly changed far less than did the anxious perceptions of authorities, but that is another story.

Should we then conclude that the political culture of cafés faded after 1880 into historical memory? Yes and no. The very relaxation of political censorship, the legalization of trade unions, the softening of restrictions on strikes and demonstrations—all enacted by 1885—eventually altered both the content and the genre of political expression. Consequently the arenas of politics became more diverse. Especially for people living in cities, the *salle publique,* the *bourse du travail,* and the *salle des fêtes* came to offer alternative and more commodious space for the large-scale discussion of political and social issues. People changed, too. As literacy became nearly universal, as newspapers declined in price, and as candid public speech became commonplace, men and women had less need to resort to musical, symbolic, or purely oral modes of political representation.

Just as politics swelled in scale and organization, so did the structure of the state. By the mid-1880s government officials began filing political reports in the more efficient, "modern" manner, classifying dossiers by party, organization, event, or person. This was the age and the nation, after all, that gave birth to the mug shot and the fingerprint. At least with respect to the café, the Opportunists were well named; rather than closing the hundreds of *débits* that catered to criminals, "dangerous anarchists," and the like, they preferred to eavesdrop on the suspected enemies of the state.

By 1900 the café could no longer be viewed as the sole parliament of the people. As they made their rounds of the cafés and *auberges,* the *police des débits de boisson* and the *gardes champêtres* rarely bothered to summarize the casual political conversations they overheard at the counters and tables of French drinking establishments. Yet café politics did not disappear with MacMahon; it flourishes in France even today. But the pride of place it had once held—frequented by ordinary people, feared by authorities—was being supplanted by new and diverse networks of political exchange. The café now represented just one of many arenas for politics. In the words of one *patronne,* whose place had been shut down in 1875, "You know how it goes. If the government were forced to close every café where politics is discussed, it would have to close them all."[30] The *patronne* was undoubtedly correct. But the shape and content of those millions of conversations remain mysterious, "not known," in T. S. Eliot's phrase, "because not looked for, but heard, half-heard," in the stillness of the archives.

NOTES

Much of the archival research for this article was carried out while I was a Mellon Fellow at Mount Holyoke College and, in 1983–1984, a Guggenheim Fellow. I am most grateful to those foundations for their support.

1. This crisis was initiated on May 16, 1877, when the president of the Third Republic, Maréchal MacMahon, asked for the resignation of the cabinet headed by the republican Jules Simon. MacMahon's actions, although not explicitly unconstitutional, were widely considered to be contrary to the intent of the Third Republic. Disturbed by a growing majority of republicans in the Chamber of Deputies, MacMahon decided to contest the presumed right of that body to name cabinets. Three hundred sixty-three deputies protested MacMahon's "coup"; siding with the president, the more conservative Senate called for new elections in October. MacMahon's monarchist sympathies were no secret; in the months following the coup, he executed one of the most dramatic purges of French civil servants and administrators yet seen in the nineteenth century, and he drew up a slate of government candidates that included not a single republican. But MacMahon's campaign was to founder at the ballot box; despite his extraordinary measures of repression, the republicans captured a majority in the October elections.

2. Gordon Wright, *France in Modern Times*, 3d ed. (New York, 1981), 238.

3. Archives de la Préfecture de Police, Paris (hereafter cited as APP), DB 174. See also John M. Merriman, *The Agony of the Republic* (New Haven, Conn., 1978) and Maurice Agulhon, *La République au village* (Paris, 1970).

4. Susanna Barrows, "After the Commune: Alcoholism, Temperance, and Literature in the Early Third Republic," in *Consciousness and Class Experience in Nineteenth-Century Europe*, ed. John M. Merriman (New York, 1979), 205–218.

5. Archives Nationales, Paris (hereafter cited as AN), F7 12705–6.

6. Archives Départementales (hereafter cited as AD) Rhône, 4 M 461 (provisional classification), March 19, 1874.

7. AD Haute Vienne, 4 M 154.

8. AD Rhône, 4 M 461, March 19, 1874.

9. APP DB 174 contains the official government reports on the extent of the repression.

10. APP DB 174 and AD Haute Vienne, 4 M 154, October 4, 1877.

11. AD Marne, 82 M 34, November 15, 1877, with later corrections, and AD Haute Savoie, 4 M Police des débits, January 29, 1878.

12. AD Marne, 82 M 34.

13. AD Vaucluse, 4 M 114, November 26, 1877, and AD Isère, 111 M 1.

14. AD Vaucluse, 4 M 114, November 14, 1877.

15. AD Rhône, 4 M 458.

16. AD Hérault, 60 M 8, June 16, 1877.

17. AD Hérault, 60 M 8, July 27, 1877.

18. AD Hérault, 60 M 8, June 12, 1877.

19. AD Hérault, 60 M 8, *rapport* of July 22, 1877.

20. AD Marne, 82 M 34.

21. AD Hérault, 60 M 8, October 19, 1877.

22. AD Rhône, 4 M 458.

23. AD Côte d'Or, 20 M 291, and AD Vaucluse, 4 M 114, October 11, 1877.

24. AD Vaucluse, 4 M 114, September 27, 1877.

25. AD Savoie, 12 M 2. The proprietors of cafés that had been closed often reopened their establishments as *auberges* or restaurants and tried to evade prosecution by serving bread.

26. AD Haute Savoie, 4 M 245.

27. AD Côte d'Or, 20 M 291, and APP DB 174, December 7, 1872.

28. AD Vaucluse, 4 M 114, June 27, 1878. To cite but one example, fifty-four cafés were closed in the Vaucluse between May 16 and November 10, 1877. In 1878 only twelve were shut down; in 1879, eight; and in the first six months of 1880, a mere four.

29. APP, DB 174.

30. AD Côte d'Or, 20 M 291.

FOUR

The Tavern and Politics in the German Labor Movement, c. 1870–1914

James S. Roberts

It is by now a commonplace in the growing literature on the working class and ethnic communities of nineteenth-century Europe and North America that taverns were important social institutions that provided their clientele with much more than food and drink.[1] As primary social centers for workers, artisans, petty tradesmen, and other members of the lower end of the urban social hierarchy, taverns played a multiplicity of roles in the lives of their customers. Some of these roles had political implications, for taverns often became centers of discussion and organization. The potential political importance of tavern life is now generally recognized, but thus far there has been little consideration of the foundations of the relationship between tavern life and political life and its consequences for popular politics. In this chapter I attempt to raise these questions by looking at the role of the tavern in the German labor movement.

In Imperial Germany, where traditions of tavern-based sociability were strong and the increasingly powerful labor movement faced both government persecution and social discrimination, the ties between tavern life and political life were especially significant. But there were also more general reasons for the connection between the tavern and politics, for politics was itself a form of leisure activity. Only a few men and women became "professional" politicians; the rest, if not indifferent, had to fit their political activities into their working, family, and social lives. So it was for hundreds of thousands of men and women who committed at least some of their resources—money, time, and energy—to the organizations of the socialist labor movement: the Social Democratic party (SPD), the free trade unions, and a host of other associations ranging from choral societies to cycling clubs.[2] Such commitments were nurtured in face-to-face encounters that invariably provided social as well as political gratification. The tavern was perhaps the most prominent and characteristic setting in which such encounters occurred. It was there that traditional forms of popular leisure activity fused with modern forms of political organization. This fusion, as we shall see, both nourished and constrained popular politics and thus helped to shape the German labor movement.

1

The term *tavern* encompasses many different kinds of drinking establishments. The provision of food and drink was often all they had in common. There were taverns for the rich and taverns for the poor, country inns and urban *Schnaps* dives, cramped and crowded stand-up bars and spacious beer palaces. There were places for pimps, prostitutes, and petty thieves as well as for respectable workingmen and urban burghers. Nor is this the end of the variation. The ambience of a particular tavern depended on the social characteristics and mix of its clientele. In a large city of many trades, where men from a variety of occupations had frequent occasion to mingle, the character of tavern life must have been considerably different from that in a town dominated by a single industry or firm. Moreover, the opportunity to drink and socialize, if the density of taverns is any indication, varied from place to place and depended on patterns of urban development.[3] But if it is difficult to generalize about the kinds of drinking places German workingmen frequented, it is still possible to suggest some of the reasons for the tavern's prominence as a social institution in the cities and towns of rapidly industrializing Germany.

The tavern was an ancient institution, but the growth of towns, the increase of travel, the expansion of purchasing power, and the easing of state restrictions on economic activity all served to multiply the number of drinking places in the nineteenth century.[4] The number of drinking places (*Gast- und Schankwirtschaften*) in relation to the total population in Germany rose from the 1850s until 1879, when the liberal licensing policy enacted in 1869 was revised. In the eight old provinces of Prussia the number of outlets with permission to sell spirits per thousand inhabitants rose from 2.5 in 1852 to 3.7 in 1869 and 4.8 in 1872. In the new Prussia there were 4.5 drinking places per thousand inhabitants; ten years later there were 5.2. After the revision of the Imperial commercial code (*Gewerbeordnung*) in 1879, the number of drinking establishments declined slightly, but levels remained above those of the 1850s. In both 1886 and 1893 there were 4.8 drinking places per thousand people and in 1911, 4.3.

The tavern met many essential needs, not all of them strictly related to leisure.[5] Taverns provided food, drink, and sometimes lodging. Just as important, they served as reading rooms and meeting halls. In some areas, as in the harbors of Hamburg, taverns were also the sites of highly regularized labor exchanges, the places where workingmen gathered to look for a day's work.[6] But the heart of the tavern was its social life. The tavern was an extension of the domestic milieu. In view of their overcrowded and otherwise miserable housing conditions, working-class communities required forms of social life centered outside the domestic sphere;[7] this the tavern—virtually alone—provided. Other institutions that could meet these needs simply did not exist. The tavern was all the more important because workingmen and their families changed residences frequently.[8] In neighborhoods whose neighbors were constantly changing, the tavern remained, providing at least some measure of continuity.

As a vital social center, the tavern was a natural place for working-men to discuss their aspirations and grievances, both personal and political. Beyond the reach of social superiors, they could develop their ideas unmolested. One man could harden his convictions against another's, and the convinced socialist could try to win converts to the cause. Paul Göhre, the Protestant pastor and later socialist who lived incognito among the workers of Chemnitz in 1891, believed this kind of face-to-face, word-of-mouth agitation to be the most important channel for the dissemination of socialist ideas.[9]

The role of the tavern in the formation of popular political consciousness was crucial because it provided a setting for social relations that were less parochial and less hierarchical than at the workplace. Work-based social ties were strengthened and supplemented after working hours. Taverns provided a setting in which men from a variety of occupations and firms could mingle, sharing their experiences and perspectives. Mill hand and greengrocer, letter carrier and journeyman butcher, wagon driver and ship's carpenter might thus be found together, forced to confront the interests and aspirations that could divide as well as unite them. One source of the potential political importance of the tavern, then, was that the social interactions it housed could be neighborhood-based as well as job-based. The tavern thus helped create social ties that bound together diverse groups of the urban population.

Social life at the tavern was also more egalitarian than at the workplace. Göhre reported that the division of labor within the factory where he was employed was accompanied by a status hierarchy that was visibly manifested in the on-the-job interactions of his fellow workers. But after hours, he reported, social relations took on a different complexion:

> Outside the factory walls the simple hand worker, the machine operator, the trained mechanic were considered to be perfectly equal to the highly skilled fitter. The barriers that the factory inevitably set up between them fell away. In their mutual interactions they were, and understood themselves to be, workers; and the only factors that influenced their personal relationships were common inclinations, shared principles, and the ties of neighborhood.[10]

The tavern was thus one of the few places where workingmen regularly met each other as equals. It was in this face-to-face setting that the day-to-day reality of working-class politics was played out.

2

For the socialist labor movement, the tavern and the social life that centered there were of the greatest importance. The everyday life of socialist politics, the grass roots of the labor movement, remained closely tied to the tavern until after the First World War. The labor movement harnessed the protopolitical energies spawned in spontaneous social interactions within the tavern and channeled them onto the stage of national politics. The importance of the tavern and the social networks centered there was explicitly recognized by Karl Kautsky, a leading figure in the German labor movement. Writing in 1891 to parry the threat of a revived German temperance movement beginning to make inroads even within the socialist labor movement, Kautsky called the tavern "the sole bulwark of the proletariat's political freedom."[11] Without it, he maintained, the proletariat would be deprived of its political as well as its social life, for the two were intimately related:

> If the temperance movement were to reach its goal in Germany and convince German workers en masse to shun the tavern in their free time and confine themselves to the family life [the temperance reformers] depict so enticingly..., then it will have accomplished what the anti-socialist law never even came close to achieving: the solidarity of the proletariat will have been destroyed, it will have been reduced to a mass of disconnected and therefore defenseless atoms.[12]

As Kautsky's remarks suggest, the social networks that came together in the tavern were also the transmission lines of political ideas and the sinews of political organization.

By the 1880s the tavern had become a crucial institution of the labor movement. To be sure, not all tavernkeepers were willing to establish such a relationship, and not all taverngoers were incipient socialists. But where the labor movement took root, the tavern was its organizational center. In cities like Berlin, where the influence of the SPD was great, boycotts could be used effectively to force reluctant or hostile tavernkeepers to open their halls. Problems were more serious when the socialists tried to take their agitation into less hospitable territories.[13] Where tavernkeepers could not be found who were willing to lend their premises to socialist agitation, the movement could make little headway. This was the case, for example, in large areas of the upper Rhineland, where in 1899 meeting places could be found in only six of twenty-three agitational districts.[14]

A genuine symbiosis developed between the party tavern and the labor movement. Despite the dangers of police harassment, especially great during the period of the antisocialist laws (1878–1890), the tavernkeeper who offered his premises to social democrats could expect tangible returns—most important, a regular clientele. The publican's profession was notoriously unstable, and competition was fierce. Affiliation with the labor movement offered a solution to the tavernkeeper's problems. Theodor Bömelburg, a leading figure in the German trade union movement and, after 1903, a member of the SPD's Reichstag delegation, remarked on this situation as late as 1907. "We can usually only get a meeting room at all," he noted, "when half a dozen publicans have already gone bankrupt in the place. And then the publican, already practically ruined, offers his place to the labor movement only to get back on his feet again."[15]

But not all publicans who served the party were motivated by the narrow *Geschäftssozialismus* suggested in Bömelburg's comments. Many, indeed, had entered the trade only after their political dedication had cost them their regular jobs. Setting up shop, whether as tavernkeeper or victualler, provided them with a livelihood and allowed them to continue to serve the labor movement.[16]

The stamp of approval of the labor movement, then, was good for business. The socialist free trade unions and local electoral associations attempted to steer the workers under their influence to taverns with socialist connections. The Berlin *Vorwärts*, for example, regularly published a list of approved establishments for this purpose.[17] They attracted an informal, day-to-day trade and also hosted the meetings of the various organizations affiliated with the labor movement. Meeting rooms were provided rent-free, but their use was accompanied by a tacit obligation to drink (*Trinkzwang*). The consumption of alcohol was therefore a virtual requirement for participation in the socialist labor movement. Nonalcoholic beverages were not widely available, and they were generally more expensive than beer and *Schnaps*.

For its part, the labor movement found a much-needed home in the tavern. Not only electoral associations and trade union locals but a whole host of other organizations affiliated with the labor movement—singing groups, education societies, sports clubs—depended to one degree or another on the tavern.[18] Even the abstinent socialists met there. But apart from the meeting rooms they offered, the taverns that served the labor movement also served as more informal gathering points. By thus providing a setting for a multiplicity of social interactions, they helped perpetuate the encapsulation of the labor movement in a unique subculture apart from the rest of German society.[19] This arrangement was not entirely voluntary, for just as there were taverns that catered to a socialist clientele, there were also those whose doorways warned, "Entry Forbidden to Notorious Socialists!"[20] Thus, though tavern life could bring diverse elements of the urban population together, the specifically socialist tavern cut across the urban social milieu and helped separate socialists from elements of the urban population hostile or indifferent to their cause. The tavern could broaden socially and narrow politically the personal contacts of the adherents of the labor movement.

Labor movement ties to the tavern were especially important during the period of the antisocialist laws, when Bismarck's repressive legislation made formal socialist organizations illegal. The secret life and ultimate vitality of the SPD depended heavily on the tavern in those years, and many socialist tavernkeepers suffered for their devotion.[21] "Without alcohol, without customary drinking practices," wrote the socialist Georg Käferstein some years later, "the labor movement in those years would have had to find another way to achieve its political and economic goals."[22] Even after the expiration of the antisocialist laws in 1890, the dependence of the movement on the tavern was scarcely lessened. In most places there were simply no alternatives. Union-owned meeting and recreational facilities were established in some cities, but these did not begin to provide an adequate number of meeting places. The labor movement had been able to establish only twenty-seven such centers by 1906. A year later Theodor Bömelburg could argue before the SPD congress at Essen that "even in the big cities, the question of meeting places [*Lokalfrage*] has almost nowhere been solved."[23] As Bömelburg's remarks suggest, some socialists were unhappy with the continuing dependence of the labor movement on the tavern and its implicit encouragement of working-class alcohol consumption.

One of the best descriptions of everyday life in a socialist tavern was provided by Edgard Milhaud, a socialist and professor of political economy at the University of Geneva.[24] During the years 1896 and 1897 Milhaud lived in the socialist communities of Leipzig and Berlin, learning the ins and outs of the German labor movement, sharing the lives of militant workingmen and meeting their leaders. In Leipzig Milhaud frequented a socialist tavern run by a man named Jaeger, a former worker who had lost his job as a result of his political activities. His comrades had set him up in his modest enterprise, and they remained his best customers.

Jaeger's was a socialist tavern through and through. Unlike most other establishments, his was not fully a public place. It catered exclusively to socialists; unwanted guests were turned away. Its decor also distinguished it from other taverns. Three pictures hung in the main room: the first depicted the victory of the working class, the second memorialized the victims of 1848, and the third portrayed the socialist Reichstag deputies. Under the pictures were inscribed the words "Our Goal," "The Martyrs to Our Cause," and "Our Representatives." Announcements of meetings, the statutes of local trade unions, and an assortment of socialist periodicals were also found there. In addition, a book peddler visited Jaeger's from time to time. He took subscriptions to socialist publications and sold the books and pamphlets of the labor movement as well as stocking a wide variety of socialist memorabilia. His wares included "matchbooks, emblems, tiepins, and cuff links adorned with portraits of Lasalle, Marx, Liebknecht, or Bebel as well as New Year's greeting cards with photographs of the great leaders." The socialist milieu was thus complete down to the matchbooks and cuff links.

Jaeger's filled each day at noontime. About twenty-five workingmen regularly took their midday meal there. Soup, meat, vegetables, and beer were offered at a cost of fifty pfennig. Mealtime conversation was sparse. Most of the customers preferred to read. Some brought their own copies of the *Leipziger Volkszeitung;* others read the Berlin *Vorwärts*, the official party daily, to which Jaeger's subscribed. By 1:30 in the afternoon, when work resumed, the tavern had emptied. Later in the day customers would gather again—bachelors for another meal, and others to drink, read, and talk. On Saturday night, when some men brought their wives, Jaeger's was filled to capacity. On those evenings interest was especially great in the illustrated and satirical party publications—*Die Neue Welt, Der Wahre Jakob,* and *Die Süddeutsche Postillon.* For Milhaud, these Saturday nights were the occasions of his most fruitful conversations with socialist workingmen.

The combination of easy conviviality and political dedication at Jaeger's and countless places like it was one of the most important day-to-day expressions of the labor movement. The regular meetings of social democratic organizations took place in similar settings. Paul Göhre attended the weekly sessions of one socialist electoral association in Chemnitz in 1891 and recorded his observations.[25] Meetings typically lasted from eight o'clock until midnight. Everyone present was expected to participate and to express and defend his opinions. For the participants, Göhre noted, "these were evenings not of trivial amusements but of strenuous labor; hours invariably of diligent learning, critical thinking, of refreshment and encouragement in their monotonous, unvarying factory lives."[26] Fatigued after a long day's work, a few men would slumber in their chairs. But for the most part the men who spent their free time at these meetings followed the lectures and debates assiduously, enjoying a glass or two of beer and a pipe or cigar.

Here was much of the best in the socialist labor movement—mutual support, self-improvement, a desire to help shape contemporary society, and a sense of belonging not only to a powerful movement but also to an intimate community.[27] These were ties, as Kautsky recognized, on which the labor movement depended. It is no wonder that the majority of German socialists rejected the appeals from within their midst for a radical antialcohol campaign, for in giving up alcohol, they would have had to give up their whole style of political activism and the mutually reinforcing social and political gratifications that tied them to the labor movement.[28]

3

What were the consequences of the symbiosis between the tavern and working-class politics? The most immediate consequence was the political prominence of many tavernkeepers. Their service was often gratefully acknowledged with positions of trust and responsibility in the labor movement. There were hints of this relationship even in the composition of the SPD's Reichstag delegation. Six of eighty-one (7.4 percent) socialist Reichstag deputies in 1906 were tavernkeepers. In the 1890s the proportion had been even higher. In 1892 four of thirty-five socialists in the Reichstag were publicans.[29] I do not mean to argue with Robert Michels that these petit bourgeois elements set the tone of the party or dominated the labor movement, but there can be no doubt that socialist publicans could exercise local influence and that this was one path of mobility within the labor movement.[30]

Another consequence of the relationship between the labor movement and the tavern was the creation and perpetuation of enduring stereotypes about working-class politics and the socialist workingman. Middle- and upper-class observers correctly saw close links between political radicalism and tavern life, but they misunderstood the nature of the connection. According to one view, the symbiosis between the tavern and the labor movement suggested that only under the influ-

ence of alcohol could otherwise-sensible workingmen be won over to
the labor movement at all. Otto von Leixner, for example, a critical
observer of the social democratic milieu of Berlin in the early 1890s,
suggested that the tavern was one of the "most powerful allies of the
social democratic doctrine." He saw in working-class taverns "the principal place for cultivating new disciples."[31] Another view had it that
labor leaders condoned or even encouraged heavy alcohol consumption, knowing that it would help keep the working class in poverty. Only
in this way, it was suggested, could they cling to their dogmas about the
increasing pauperization of the proletariat.[32] Singly or together, these
stereotypes helped create a caricature of the red-nosed socialist that
was at once reassuring and troubling to the middle-class consciousness
—reassuring because it reduced socialism to a species of moral degeneracy, and troubling because it reminded the defenders of the social
and political status quo of the fragility of their own privileged position. But whether rationalizations of existing power arrangements or
expressions of profound cultural insecurities, such stereotypes helped
both affirm and widen the gulf between German workers and the
leading sectors of German society.

The caricature of the red-nosed socialist in turn helped make the
use of leisure a political concern. Emperor William II, for example,
justified his refusal to limit the hours of workingmen in 1890 with
explicit reference to the link between the tavern and politics. With a
shorter working day, he feared, workers would spend more time in the
taverns and thus be drawn all the more surely into the morass of
radical politics.[33] If there was great reluctance to grant workingmen
more free time, there was an equal concern to see to it that what free
time they already had was put to the right use. To this end a variety of
middle-class reform movements and charitable organizations, including the temperance movement, sought to influence the leisure habits
of workingmen and their families.[34] Almost all of them hoped to divert
the workingman from the tavern by creating alternative recreations
and extolling the virtues of domesticity. No single motive underlay
these efforts, but one goal of many reformers was to break the link
between socialist politics and the tavern, as was clearly the case, for
example, in the early home economics movement.

Beginning in the 1880s a diverse group of reformers sought to
address the problems of the urban working-class family by improving
the domestic skills of the workingman's wife. Often idealized as the
mainstay of the social order, working-class housewives could also be
held responsible for its imperfections, including their husbands'
drinking and radical politics. These sentiments were clearly expressed
by Fritz Kalle and Otto Kamp in a prologue to their 1889 report to the

German Association for Poor Relief and Charity (Deutsche Verein für Armenpflege and Wohltätigkeit):

A good part of the misery under which hundreds of thousands of propertyless families suffer stems from the inability of women to run their own households. This deficiency is often responsible when a working-class family is inadequately nourished and when, as a result, strength and willingness to work vanish among young and old alike and illness takes their place; or when the children's and husband's clothing, and the house itself, go to ruin so that both parents and children lose the sense for cleanliness and order, the husband is driven out of the unpleasant home into the tavern, and the children are forced out into the streets. In this way many not untalented men become habitual drunkards and gamblers and many children vagabonds. The horde of unhappy people multiplies; to the detriment of themselves and their dependents, they are filled with hatred, jealousy, and dissatisfaction with God and the world and become willing tools in the hands of revolutionary agitators.[35]

These reformers hoped that by improving homemaking and family life, workingmen could be induced to spend their free time at home rather than in the tavern, and the blandishments of socialist agitators would be neutralized.

The links between the tavern and political life also highlighted and reinforced traditional sex roles. Despite the growing participation of women in the labor movement in the years before the First World War, the SPD and the free trade unions continued to be dominated by men.[36] As late as 1913 there were nearly six times as many men as women in the SPD.[37] Socialist workingmen did little to foster the political education of their wives and daughters or encourage their active participation in the labor movement. Like German men generally, they believed that a woman's place was in the home.

The predominance of men in politics was reinforced by the dependence of the labor movement on the tavern. Although there were no hard and fast cultural norms that completely precluded women from entering the tavern setting, the tavern, like politics itself, was part of the masculine cultural sphere. Many women were reluctant, as a result of their own education and the cultural norms many of their fathers, brothers, and husbands no doubt perpetuated, to enter this sphere, especially alone. This reluctance had to be overcome if women were to take an active part in the labor movement. Adelheid Popp did overcome this obstacle and became a prominent figure in Austrian social democracy, but she recalled in her memoirs how difficult it had been as a woman, even though a convinced socialist, to enter this men's world to attend her first social democratic meeting.[38] In the 1920s German socialist women were still complaining about the links between the drinking place and the labor movement. Speaking for Berlin feminists,. Elise Schreibenhuber asked the party at its 1925 congress to combat the use of alcohol in socialist meetings. "Many women feel themselves shut out of party life," she objected, "because it takes place for the most part in the taverns."[39] Her argument suggested that had working-class politics had its home on culturally more neutral ground, breaking out of the domestic sphere might have been much easier for many women.

4

The tavern, then, was a primary social center for the workers, artisans, and tradesmen who inhabited the cities and towns of Imperial Germany. Alternative institutions that could have met their needs for recreation and conviviality were slow to develop. The tavern and the associational life based on it filled the gap, providing, especially for the male half of the population, one of the principal sources of individual identity and social integration in the urban social milieu.[40]

As social centers, taverns were inchoate political institutions. They helped broaden the social experience of their clientele and expose them to a diversity of ideas and ideals. They formed the nodal points of intersecting social networks, job-based and neighborhood-based, and provided channels of communication that could form the basis of political solidarity.

But beyond these somewhat amorphous protopolitical roles, the tavern could also be given more explicit political functions, as was the case in the socialist labor movement. The potential political significance of tavern life was recognized and exploited by the SPD and the free trade unions. Partly by necessity and partly by choice, they allied themselves with the tavern and made political use of traditional patterns of leisure. Their adherents in turn found in the labor movement mutually reinforcing social and political gratifications. The social ties thus created and maintained provided the thread of continuity between electoral campaigns and strike movements when the rank and file of the labor movement could participate more actively and directly in political events.[41] Without the resiliency these social ties provided, the labor movement would have been diminished both in its significance for its adherents and in its effectiveness in addressing their multifaceted needs.

NOTES

This article originally appeared in German under the title "Wirtshaus und Politik in der deutschen Arbeiterbewegung," in *Sozialgeschichte der Freizeit*, ed.

Gerhard Huck (Wuppertal: Peter Hammer Verlag, 1980), 123–140, and is published here with minor revisions.

1. See, for example, Kathleen Neils Conzen, *Immigrant Milwaukee,. 1836–1860: Accommodation and Community in a Frontier City* (Cambridge, Mass.: Harvard University Press, 1976), 156–158; Brian Harrison, "Pubs," in *The Victorian City: Image and Reality,* 2 vols., ed. H. J. Dyos and Michael Wolff (London: Routledge & Kegan Paul, 1973), 1:161–190; Michael R. Marrus, "Social Drinking in the Belle Epoque," *Journal of Social History* 7 (1974): 115–141; Perry R. Duis, *The Saloon: Public Drinking in Chicago and Boston* (Urbana: University of Illinois Press, 1983); Robert Roberts, *The Classic Slum: Salford Life in the First Quarter of the Century* (Manchester: Manchester University Press, 1971), 93–96.

2. For a useful English-language survey of the German labor movement, see Gary P. Steenson, *"Not One Man! Not One Penny!" German Social Democracy, 1863–1914* (Pittsburgh: University of Pittsburgh Press, 1981).

3. On this point, see Franz J. Brüggemeier and Lutz Niethammer, "Schlafgänger, Schnapskasinos und schwer industrielle Kolonie. Aspekte der Arbeiterwohnungsfrage im Ruhrgebiet vor dem Ersten Weltkrieg," in *Fabrik, Familie, Feierabend. Beiträge zur Sozialgeschichte des Alltags im Industriezeitalter,* ed. Jürgen Reulecke and Wolfhard Weber (Wuppertal: Hammer, 1978), 135–176, esp. 158–165.

4. Statistics on the number of drinking places are derived from the following sources: Abraham Baer, *Der Alkoholismus. Seine Verbreitung und seine Wirkung auf den individuellen und socialen Organismus* (Berlin: Hirschwald, 1878), 242; "Gast- und Schankwirtschaften in Preussen, 1911," *Mässigkeits-Blätter* 30 (1913): 144–145; "Statistik der Schankstätten Preussens," *Mitteilungen des Deutschen Vereins gegen den Missbrauch geistiger Getränke* 11 (1894): 75–77; Zentrales Staatsarchiv (Potsdam), Reichsamt des Innern, nos. 16350, fols. 163–164.

5. For an important contemporary discussion of the importance of the tavern in working-class communities, see Alfred Grotjahn, *Der Alkoholismus. Nach Wesen, Wirkung und Verbreitung* (Leipzig: Wigand, 1898), 230–239.

6. Peter N. Stearns, "The Unskilled and Industrialization," *Archiv für Sozialgeschichte* 16 (1976): 249–282, at 252–253.

7. On working-class housing conditions, see Lutz Niethammer, in collaboration with Franz Brüggemeier, "Wie wohnten Arbeiter im Kaiserreich?" *Archiv für Sozialgeschichte* 16 (1976): 61–134.

8. For discussions of intercity and intracity mobility, see Niethammer and Brüggemeier, "Arbeiter," and Dieter Langewiesche, "Wanderungsbewegungen in der Hochindustrialisierungsperiode. Regionale, interstädtische und innerstädtische Mobilität in Deutschland 1880–1914," *Vierteljahrsschrift für Sozial- und Wirtsschaftsgeschichte* 64 (1977): 1–40.

9. Paul Göhre, *Drei Monate Fabrikarbeiter und Handwerksbursche* (Leipzig: Grunow, 1891), 104.

10. Göhre, *Drei Monate,* 83.

11. Karl Kautsky, "Der Alkoholismus und seine Bekämpfung," *Die Neue Zeit* 9, no. 2 (1891): 1–8, 46–55, 77–89, 105–116, at 107.

12. Kautsky, "Alkoholismus," 107–108.

13. Edgard Milhaud, *La démocratie socialiste allemande* (Paris: Alcan, 1903), 75–76.

14. *Die Sozialdemokratische Partei im Agitationsbezirk Obere Rheinprovinz, 1897–1918*, ed. Günter Bers (Cologne: Einhorn-Presse, 1973), 22–24.

15. *Protokoll über die Verhandlungen des Parteitages der Sozialdemokratischen Partei Deutschlands* (Berlin: Vorwärts, 1907), 373.

16. Robert Michels, *Zur Soziologie des Parteiwesens in der modernen Demokratie. Untersuchungen über die oligarchischen Tendenzen des Gruppenlebens* (Leipzig: Klinkhardt, 1911), 271–272; Dieter Fricke, *Die deutsche Arbeiterbewegung 1869 bis 1914. Ein Handbuch über ihrer Organisation und Tätigkeit im Klassenkampf* (East Berlin: Verlag das europäische Buch, 1976), 265.

17. Milhaud, *Démocratie socialiste allemande*, 75–76.

18. For an innovative study of social democratic associational life, see Vernon L. Lidtke, *The Alternative Culture: Socialist Labor in Imperial Germany* (New York: Oxford University Press, 1985). See also his "Die kulturelle Bedeutung der Arbeitervereine," in *Kultureller Wandel im 19. Jahrhundert*, ed. Günther Wiegelmann (Göttingen: Vandenhoek and Ruprecht, 1973), 146–159.

19. The original statement of the proposition that the social democrats had developed a separate subculture is found in Guenther Roth, *The Social Democrats in Imperial Germany: A Study in Working-Class Isolation and National Integration* (Totowa, N.J.: Bedminster Press, 1963). For more recent research on this subject, see, in addition to the work of Vernon Lidtke cited above, the three anthologies introduced by the following essays: Richard B. Evans, "Introduction: The Sociological Interpretation of German Labour History," in *The German Working Class 1888–1933: The Politics of Everyday Life*, ed. Richard B. Evans (London: Croom Helm, 1982), 15–53; Jürgen Kocka, "Arbeiterkultur als Forschungsthema," *Geschichte und Gesellschaft* 5 (1979): 5–11; Gerhard A. Ritter, "Workers' Culture in Imperial Germany: Problems and Points of Departure for Research," *Journal of Contemporary History* 13 (1978): 165–190.

20. Milhaud, *Démocratie socialiste allemande*, 75.

21. Under the provisions of the antisocialist law publicans who hosted meetings of prohibited organizations were liable to fines, imprisonment, banishment, and loss of their right to do business. For numerous examples of police action against publicans, see Ignaz Auer, *Nach Zehn Jahren. Material und Glossen zur Geschichte des Sozialistengesetzes* (Nuremberg: Verlag der Frankischen Verlagsanstalt, 1913). For one prominent socialist's appreciation of socialist tavernkeepers' contributions to the labor movement in this period, see Wilhelm Blos, *Denkwürdigkeiten eines Sozialdemokraten*, 2 vols. (Munich: Birk, 1914), 2:12.

22. Quoted in Arthur Dix, "Alkoholismus und Arbeiterschaft," *Zeitschrift für Sozialwissenschaft* 2 (1911): 531–556.

23. Michels, *Zur Soziologie des Parteiwesens*, 284n; *Protokoll* (1907), 373.

24. Milhaud, *Démocratie socialiste allemande*, 148–151.

25. Göhre, *Drei Monate*, 89–92.

26. Göhre, *Drei Monate*, 92.

27. Cf. Dieter Dowe's discussion, "The Workingmen's Choral Movement in Germany before the First World War," *Journal of Contemporary History* 13 (1976): 269–296, esp. 272.

28. On the controversy surrounding the drink question in the German labor movement, see James S. Roberts, "Drink and the Labour Movement: The *Schnaps* Boycott of 1909," in *The German Working Class*, 80–107.

29. Michels, *Zur Soziologie des Parteiwesens*, 286.

30. On this point, see Paul Kampffmeyer's discussion of the socialist labor leader Friedrich Ebert, president of Germany under the Weimar Republic, and his activities as a tavernkeeper in Bremen during the 1890s, "Friedrich Ebert: Ein Lebensbild," in *Friedrich Ebert. Schriften, Aufzeichnungen, Reden*, 2 vols., Hg. Friedrich Ebert, jun., ed. (Dresden: Reissner, 1926), 1:58–59. See also Michels, *Zur Soziologie des Parteiwesens*, 270–277. For a rebuttal of Michels's view, see Hedwig Wachenheim, *Vom Grossbürgertum zur Sozialdemokratie. Memoiren einer Reformisten*, Beihefte zur Internationalen wissenschaftliche Korrespondenz zur Geschichte der deutschen Arbeiterbewegung, 1 (Berlin: Colloquium Verlag, 1973), 109.

31. Otto von Leixner, *Soziale Briefe aus Berlin. Mit besonderer Berücksichtigung der sozialdemokratischen Strömungen* (Berlin: Pfeilstücker, 1891), 325. Cf. Brüggemeier and Niethammer, "Schlafgänger," 158–165 passim.

32. Dix, "Alkoholismus und Arbeiterschaft," 531; Wilhelm Bode, *An die Politiker* (Hildesheim: Selbstverlag, 1898), 4–5. For socialist commentary on these stereotypes, see "Beiträge zur Alkoholfrage," *Sozialdemokratische Partei-Correspondenz* 2 (1907): 537–540.

33. See William II, "Vorschläge zur Verbesserung der Arbeiter," cited in Ingeborg Weber-Kellermann, *Die deutsche Familie. Versuch einer Sozialgeschichte* (Frankfurt am Main: Suhrkamp, 1974), 137–138. Cf. Karl Eric Born, *Staat und Sozialpolitik seit Bismarcks Sturz. Ein Beitrag zur Geschichte der innenpolitischen Entwicklung des Deutschen Reichs, 1890–1914* (Wiesbaden: Steiner, 1957), 12.

34. For a discussion of the German temperance movement, see James S. Roberts, *Drink, Temperance and the Working Class in Nineteenth Century Germany* (Boston: George Allen & Unwin, 1984), chaps. 2–4.

35. *Die hauswirtschaftliche Unterweisung armer Mädchen* (Wiesbaden: J. F. Bergmann, 1889), iii.

36. On the position of women in the labor movement, see Jean H. Quataert, *Reluctant Feminists in German Social Democracy, 1885–1917* (Princeton, N.J.: Princeton University Press, 1979), esp. 153–160, 180–187.

37. In 1913 the SPD claimed 841,735 male and 141,115 female members (*Protokoll* [1913], 18). In the free trade unions there were more than ten times as many men as women in 1912 (Quataert, *Reluctant Feminists*, 184).

38. *Die Jugendgeschichte einer Arbeiterin, von ihr selbst erzählt* (Munich: Reinhardt, 1909), 62, 71–72.

39. *Protokoll* (1925), 168.

40. Cf. Lidtke, "Arbeitervereine," 146.

41. Cf. Dowe, "Workingmen's Choral Movement," 272.

FIVE

Decay from Within: The Inevitable Doom of the American Saloon

Madelon Powers

If the saloon was such an important center of social, cultural, and political life for the working class, why then did its millions of regular customers ever allow it to be closed down? Scholars have suggested several reasons for the apparent quiescence of saloongoers in 1920. Their political unsophistication, lack of resources, and sheer inertia were partially responsible, especially when compared to the organization, funding, and fervor of the temperance coalition.[1] Some were reluctant to defend the saloon publicly when so many damning exposés of its connections to vice and political corruption were issuing daily from press and pulpit.[2] Many also were influenced by the onset of World War I, with its belt-tightening sentiment and its anti-German propaganda, often directed at brewers and barkeepers of German descent.[3] Then too there were those who scoffed at the notion that nationwide prohibition could ever actually be enacted or enforced.[4] Yet even these reasons taken together do not seem enough to explain why saloon customers caved in so easily to outside pressure. In years past, laborers and artisans unhappy with official decisions had shown no such reticence in demonstrating their displeasure through rallies, parades, strikes, and even street riots.[5] But where was the saloongoers' esprit de corps when prohibition threatened? The evidence seems to point to decay from within: the significance of the saloon in workingmen's lives had so eroded by 1920 that its customers were simply not sufficiently motivated to mount the required action—spontaneous or organized—to save it.

To understand how the relationship between the saloon and its "regulars" came to be seriously undermined, it is first necessary to consider what that relationship had been. The centrality of the saloon in working-class life from 1870 to 1920 has already been well documented and need only be summarized here.[6] Like taverns throughout history, the primary function of the saloon was to offer the basic amenities of home in a public place. Drink, food, shelter, and companionship have ever been the stock-in-trade of the tavern. Beyond this, the American saloon proved eminently capable of serving its customers' broader needs during the nation's chaotic industrial phase. Backed by influential liquor interests and allied with well-connected machine politicians, the saloon was able to offer the emerging working class a wide array of facilities, services, and contacts often available nowhere else. In time it also became a principal arena for all manner of working-class movements, including labor organization, political action, and immigrant assistance. This is not to ignore the many detrimental effects that the saloon and its wares had on the laboring population. Despite its faults and excesses, however, the saloon was able to earn considerable customer loyalty by serving as both shelter and staging ground for its vast working-class clientele.

Reinforcing and intensifying this customer loyalty was the quality of relationship that typically developed among the regular customers themselves. It is important to keep in mind that the relationship among the regulars of any particular saloon was a personal one and that the sense of group identity among regulars was what made the saloons such influential centers of working-class culture and consciousness. Thus, the astonishing volume of saloon attendance in the late nineteenth century did not mean that people were going willy-nilly to any saloon that was handy. Rather, a great percentage of them were the regular customers of a particular saloon. There were always a number of onetime or occasional patrons who wandered in, but most saloons were kept in business by a steady clientele of perhaps fifty to sixty regulars.[7] It was this constancy of custom and the spirit of camaraderie and cooperation that developed from it that earned the saloon its popular sobriquet of the poor man's club. In the words of Royal Melendy, "The term 'club' applies; for, though unorganized, each saloon has about the same constituency night after night."[8]

Because the saloon was first and foremost a business, it could not provide that degree of exclusivity characteristic of formal clubs, though a stranger was probably made to feel a stranger until he had proved himself acceptable to the regulars.[9] Neither was there a fixed hierarchy or formal set of rules, though the proprietor was an authoritative figure and was known to give the "bum's rush" to patrons who made a nuisance of themselves.[10] Thus, the working-class saloon strad-

dled the line between public and private, order and anarchy, convention and freedom.[11] Compared to the middle-class businessman's club,
the saloon was definitely more accessible and democratic, but the
regulars nevertheless regarded their favorite establishment as their
own. "The saloon...may have no constitution or by-laws," Raymond
Calkins wrote, "but it is still a distinct, compact, sympathetic company
of men."[12]

Several social factors account for the cohesiveness of this sympathetic company. Most fundamentally, the regulars' sense of group identity was rooted in the common circumstances of their personal lives.
Saloongoers were mostly males seeking the fellowship of other men of
similar age, marital status, and economic standing. Their environs
were the streets and tenements of working-class districts where, despite
overcrowding and poverty, people still developed strong feelings of
neighborhood loyalty. Many were immigrants struggling to achieve a
livable balance between ethnic ways and the American way. All were
workingmen who, skilled or unskilled, took a measure of pride in their
labor while condemning the conditions under which that labor was
performed. Such shared factors as working conditions, ethnic background, neighborhood affiliation, marital status, age group, and gender identity provided the basis for the sympathetic relationship among
regulars.[13]

Since this multifaceted relationship that characterized barroom
groups was such an important ingredient in the success of the saloon, it
seems reasonable to speculate that its demise was in some way related
to a deterioration of that relationship. The first decades of the twentieth century brought enormous changes in the circumstances of
workers' lives, which in turn may have placed a demoralizing strain on
the ties that held working-class saloon groups together. A systematic
review of the principal linking factors of sex, age, marital status,
neighborhood, ethnicity, and occupation in the light of changing conditions in urban America after 1900 may help explain why working
men did not more vigorously defend the saloon when its enemies
closed in for the kill.

The first thing to be noted about urban saloongoers is that they
were overwhelmingly male, in demeanor as well as numbers. The
liberal drinking, rough talk, and occasional brawls in which men engaged produced an aura of freewheeling masculinity in which respectable women would have felt both uncomfortable and unwelcome.
Slouching against the bar with one foot on the rail would have been
unthinkable behavior for most "decent" women, let alone spitting into
the cuspidors or allowing their skirts to trail in the beer-soaked saw-
dust. The working-class barroom had for decades been the recognized

domain of the male, a world off-limits under most circumstances to all women, respectable or otherwise. There were a few exceptions to this rule. Working-class women might come in to consume the celebrated free lunch or purchase a quantity of alcohol for consumption else-where, though they ordinarily utilized the side entrance, stayed a limited time, and kept well away from the masculine merriment in the barroom proper. Sometimes family-oriented saloons would feature female proprietors or hired help, but most of these establishments had abandoned working-class districts for the suburbs by the 1890s. Then too there were "fallen" women such as prostitutes and drunkards who gravitated to bars, though they were more likely to be found in slum dives than in the typical working-class saloon.[14] Furthermore, simply to be present was not to belong, and the aforementioned women seldom attained the status of regular in their own right. Men's thinking on this issue seems to have involved an interesting mixture of solicitude and defiance. On the one hand, decent women should be protected from the rough world of men; on the other, the rough world of men should be protected from decent women.

This men-only imperative remained true of most saloons to the end, despite a growing trend among middle-class adults and younger people in general to socialize more frequently and openly with the opposite sex. Had Prohibition not intervened, it is conceivable that the saloon would eventually have had to yield to the trend toward hetero-sexual socializing; certainly most post-Prohibition bars have been so transformed. Before 1920, however, the typical saloon remained stead-fastly committed to its tradition of masculine exclusivity. This policy no doubt suited its older customers but may have rendered it less attrac-tive and even somewhat archaic to some potential younger converts.[15] In a shifting social climate the saloon was holding fast to a traditional style of same-sex socializing that still had millions of adherents but was now receiving a challenge from an emerging modern style in which the object was more to bridge the sexual gap than institutionalize it.

For many regular customers, the fascination with saloons began at a very early age. Often their first impressions of masculinity and the proper pastimes for men had been formulated while peering under a swinging door.[16] Those boys who were put to work at a tender age were quickly introduced to the pattern of factory work and saloon play that the older workers followed. Meanwhile those idle on the streets were also quick to learn that the saloon afforded them the only convenient and hospitable place to congregate.[17] By the early twentieth century, however, better enforcement of child labor laws and school attendance regulations had begun to interrupt the easy flow of youth into saloons. A significant increase in the number of boys' clubs and organizations also assisted in diverting the flow. As Raymond Calkins observed in 1901,

> The importance of providing good clubs and other means of recreation for boys and girls has been appreciated of late years, and no branch of social reform has received more attention....The immediate necessity, then, is to get hold of the child, and in early years create such interests and ideals that the future man and woman cannot be drawn into the lower life of which the saloon is often the exponent.[18]

By the 1910s the proliferation of other amusements such as movie theaters and baseball parks was beginning to siphon off a share of fun-seeking youth.[19] It is important to note, moreover, that schools, community organizations, and competing forms of amusement all introduced boys to activities not ordinarily carried on in saloons, including opportunities for social encounters with girls. Thus, there were an increasing number of points in a boy's life in which alternatives to the saloon presented themselves. To be sure, boys continued to be attracted to the all-male milieu of the saloon, and many of them would become regulars as soon as they were old enough. No longer, however, was the saloon the only game in town, nor even necessarily the most exciting. It was an ominous portent for the saloon to be losing its grip on an increasing number of city boys, for it was the revitalizing force of each new generation that kept the saloon in touch and in power.

In addition to men who had grown up in urban centers, many thousands more were arriving constantly from foreign countries and the American hinterlands between the Civil War and World War I. Owing in part to the large number of male immigrants entering the country unmarried or unaccompanied by their wives, males in this period consistently outnumbered females in the general population.[20] Similarly, there was a preponderance of males in many major cities, such as San Francisco and Chicago.[21] These newcomers, gravitating to saloons in search of companionship, jobs, and big-city adventure, helped swell the ranks of an already-established subculture of professional bachelors, men committed to a life-style of unfettered bachelorhood where females and families had no place.[22] As the twentieth century began, however, this bachelor brotherhood started to decline as an improving economy and a more balanced sex ratio prompted more men to marry, and marry earlier.[23] Though marrying did not by any means preclude further saloongoing, it did reduce that proportion of the male population for whom saloongoing was virtually the only alternative to social isolation. This marrying trend also meant leaner times for those establishments that catered especially to single men, of whom there would henceforth be an ever-dwindling supply.

The married man was not so heavily dependent on saloons for all his social contacts, but by custom and inclination he was still likely to seek out the company of other men when time and opportunity permitted. In the words of Hull House associate E. C. Moore, "The desire to be with his fellows—the fascination which a comfortable room where men are has for him is more than he can resist."[24] For decades this "comfortable room where men are" could be found only at the saloon. The crowded tenement flats where most married men lived with their families were neither comfortable nor practicable for home entertaining. Most men's organizations, meanwhile, were headquartered either in barroom backrooms or in adjacent brewery-owned buildings, with the understanding that members would patronize the host saloon.[25] Though social reformers had begun to establish settlement houses, reading rooms, and other facilities in working-class neighborhoods, these projects were too few and in most cases too restrictive to attract the majority of ordinary workingmen.[26] Thus, if a married man felt inclined to spend a leisure hour in the company of his peers, there was little doubt—and little choice—where he would go. As long as these conditions prevailed, the saloon was assured of a central role in workingmen's lives.

But conditions were changing, particularly in the crowded tenement neighborhoods, where saloons had long enjoyed a virtual monopoly on comfort and modern conveniences. In 1890 reform advocate Jacob Riis had jolted the conscience of a generation of progressive young minds with his exposé of New York tenements, appropriately entitled *How the Other Half Lives*. A host of subsequent writers took up the tenement lament, most notably Lincoln Steffens, whose *Shame of the Cities* in 1904 urgently reissued the call for urban reform. Progressive activists such as Jane Addams started exerting increasing pressure on municipal officials to upgrade and enforce building codes, sanitary regulations, and zoning restrictions.[27] At the same time, several new "model" tenement projects were begun by civic-minded citizens, such as builder Alfred T. White and philanthropist Ellen Collins, often specifically prohibiting the renting of street-level space to saloons.[28] Efforts at urban reform were further boosted by voluntary associations for municipal improvement and by technological advances in the design of public utilities, water and sewage systems, and other essential city services and facilities.[29] Among tenement dwellers themselves, moreover, there was a growing consciousness of the necessity to abandon certain traditional folkways that were inconsistent with healthful urban living. Transplanted rural practices such as sweeping garbage into the streets to decompose, baking bread in ovens dug in the pavement, and even slaughtering sheep in tenement basements had begun to disappear by the early twentieth century.[30] Though tenement life still left much to be desired, many of the worst conditions were being ameliorated, and the lot of the typical family was neither as dismal nor as desperate as it had been in decades past. What was good news for the people boded ill for saloons, however, for their power to attract a regular clientele had always rested in part on the contrast they could offer to workers' substandard living conditions. Henceforth there would be a formidable new competitor on the block: the livable home.

A certain amount of home entertaining and social drinking had always gone on in working-class households, as evidenced by the widespread custom of "rushing the growler" (filling beer pails at saloons for consumption elsewhere).[31] In addition, such ethnic groups as Italians and Jews were by tradition accustomed to socializing with friends and family at home, where the men might indulge in moderate drinking. Since these two groups made up a significant portion of the new immigration that was flooding the cities at the turn of the century, their preference for home entertaining and light drinking posed an increasing threat to saloons. As settlement house director Robert A. Woods remarked of the situation in Boston in 1902, "The saloon business is noticeably falling off. . . where Jews and Italians are displacing a population of Irish origin, both being more temperate races, taking milder liquors, and using them at home."[32] When improvements in tenement dwellings made home entertainment even more feasible and generally appealing, the ominous implications for the saloon were clear; for though it still supplied the alcohol to home gatherings, the quantity consumed might have been less than it would have been had the drinking gone on in the wetter atmosphere of the barroom.[33] Sales by the growler were not always profitable, either, since barkeepers were by custom expected to charge only ten cents (the price of a pint) to fill the customer's pail, whereas the pail itself might well hold much more.[34] But most important of all, the saloon could not depend on the loyalty of its take-out customers as it could on that of barroom regulars, who valued the place as their personal club. And it was customer loyalty, in the last analysis, that kept the saloon in business.

The neighborhood saloon faced competition for the laboring man's free hour not only from home entertainment but also from a growing array of public amusements. Until the 1890s few alternative forms of diversion had been available in tenement districts, and most of those were in any case closely associated with the operation of saloons. Poolrooms, bowling alleys, shooting galleries, and penny arcades situated themselves near drinking establishments and were often adjuncts to them. Vaudeville houses and dance halls typically contained well-patronized bars, and it was often difficult to determine whether they

were entertainment halls offering beer or beer halls offering entertainment. The character of such amusement centers was of a piece
with that of the saloon: the patrons were predominantly male, the
atmosphere rough, and the liquor plentiful. A barroom habitué could
pass among these various establishments and feel that he had never
really left the world of the saloon.[35]

A very different atmosphere characterized the alternate forms of
entertainment that proliferated at the turn of the century, however,
most notably the movie theater, the baseball stadium, the amusement
park, and the uptown cousin of the saloon, the cabaret. Despite their
dissimilarities, these various amusements all promoted an intermin-
gling of sexes, ages, classes, and cultures. By 1920 the blending process
had progressed far enough to produce an identifiable mass or popular
culture in America to which many had contributed and in which all
could participate. The popular pastimes associated with this evolving
national culture were, in the main, activities to which laborers could
bring their families, as in the case of movies and baseball games.
Alcohol, though perhaps present, was not central to most of these
experiences.[36] In contrast stood the saloon, with its emphasis on drink
and its tradition of catering to a single sex, class, and oftentimes ethnic
group as well. Many laboring men no doubt found room in life for both
the saloon and the other amusements, but every hour and dime spent
away from the barroom diminished its centrality in workers' lives and
weakened the ties that held saloon groups together.

The formerly secure position of the saloon in working-class neighborhoods was threatened not only by upgraded living conditions and
public amusements but also by upwardly mobile tenants moving away
from the old districts in droves after the turn of the century. Many were
longtime Irish and German residents of the old immigration who were
moving because they could at last afford to do so and because they were
upset by the influx of new immigrant groups who were changing the
character of their neighborhoods. Territorial tugs-of-war between old
and new residents often ensued, as illustrated by events in the South
Chicago neighborhood of Irondale. First had come the Irish and other
northern Europeans, who established themselves in Irondale tenements in the late nineteenth century. By 1915, however, this original
settlement was being overwhelmed by a steady influx of Italian and
Serbian immigrants, many of whom later recalled having to "fight the
Irish on the corner of 106th and Torrence."[37] Yet hardly had a generation of these newcomers put down roots when they in turn were
challenged by Mexican immigrants, who clashed bitterly with the Italians and Serbians as well as the few remaining Irish.[38] The territorial
conflicts that characterized Irondale after 1900 were mirrored in tene-

ment neighborhoods nationwide as successive waves of immigration drastically rearranged the ethnic landscape of urban America.[39]

For the saloon, the demoralizing effects of neighborhood turmoil and ethnic conflict were particularly damaging since the ties of community and ethnicity were often fundamental to the clublike nature of barroom association. As familiar faces vanished, the last holdouts in many older neighborhood establishments developed a kind of siege mentality that rebuffed newcomers and effectively sealed the doom of the very institutions they were trying to protect.[40] In the midst of this friction in changing communities, the saloonkeeper's position was extremely ticklish, for he was usually reluctant to alienate his old customers and yet fearful of sacrificing the new. Moreover, if the new groups moving in were temperate homedrinkers, like the Italians and Jews who displaced the Irish in Boston's West End and North End, the saloonkeeper could stand to lose his business altogether.[41] The resentment and regret felt by both residents and saloonkeepers were forcefully expressed by Mr. Dooley, the fictional barkeeper-philosopher created by Chicago columnist Finley Peter Dunne in 1892. The locale of Dooley's fictional saloon was the actual Irish neighborhood of Chicago known as Bridgeport, where the incursion of "Polish Jews an' Swedes an' Germans an' Hollanders" proved so unsettling to Dooley and his regulars that he, like many real-life counterparts, decided to sell his establishment and go with the outward flow of his neighbors at the close of the century.[42] Thus, the linking factors of neighborhood and ethnicity, ordinarily assets to the saloon, were in many cases becoming liabilities for those establishments caught in the crossfire between encroaching and retreating groups.

Even more devastating to the stability of saloon life after 1900 was the tendency of working-class organizations, many of them formed in saloons and built on the saloongoing relationship, to remove themselves from barroom backrooms to separate headquarters of their own. In the late nineteenth century workers' groups ranging from singing societies to labor unions had often found that saloons were able to offer them the best, the cheapest, and frequently the only available meeting rooms in the city. As Royal Melendy observed, "The hotels...do not want the man with the soiled clothes and the calloused hands in their rooms. They...meet in saloons..., the churches and schoolhouses being closed against them."[43] The ability of the saloon to offer meeting space was owing to its connections to powerful breweries that owned the buildings in which barrooms were housed as well as many adjacent commercial properties in working-class districts. At the saloonkeeper's discretion these facilities could be offered at very low rates, or even free of charge, to workers' groups as long as the men attending bought a beer or two for the saloonkeeper's trouble. As Raymond Calkins noted, this arrangement of indirect taxation through beer sales could actually cost the workers' clubs far more than if they had rented higher-priced rooms with no saloon connections. When the leader of a 250-member union chapter was confronted with this fact, however, "he admitted the truth of this, and added that he felt that the saloon was detrimental to the serious work of their organization, but said that their members were so much accustomed to the scheme of indirect taxation by collecting most of the actual room rent from trade in beer that they would be alarmed to be directly taxed for a sum actually much smaller than that which they were then paying."[44] Until significantly cheaper facilities for meetings could be found, and until workers' attitudes toward drinking during those meetings could be changed, the role of the saloon as host of neighborhood club life was secure.

Toward the end of the nineteenth century, however, progressive reformers were beginning to exert increasing pressure on city officials to provide more public facilities to groups in need of a decent place to meet. Challenging the laissez-faire notion that it was not the proper function of government to intervene in the people's social problems, progressives like Raymond Calkins insisted that "the duty of the municipality is to provide for the safety and comfort of its inhabitants." Furthermore, he argued, "there is no good reason why the municipality should not seriously consider the propriety of erecting...large plain buildings, which should serve solely as clubhouses for the different organizations in the district that should desire to meet there.... Clubs would come from alleys, back streets, tenements, and saloons."[45] With municipal and school buildings added to the growing number of settlement houses, YMCA chapters, and other privately financed projects, the monopoly of the saloon on desirable meeting places could at last be broken. It would be an uphill battle since many city officials, especially those in the school system, were suspicious of the membership and motives of clubs recruited from "alleys, back streets, tenements, and saloons." Even more important, workers themselves still had to be convinced that it was to their advantage to meet in more sober surroundings than those to which they were accustomed. Progressives could try to pry workingmen free from the grip of the saloon, but success would ultimately depend on the voluntary cooperation of the rank and file of workers' organizations.

Some cooperation was forthcoming from fraternal, ethnic, and benevolent societies after 1900 that adopted an increasingly unfriendly attitude toward saloons in the name of respectability and uplift. The Masons, for example, urged members to ban liquor sellers from their ranks and adopt a commitment to temperance (though not necessarily prohibition).[46] Yet there were limits to the influence that Masons, Odd Fellows, Knights of Pythias, and other organizations could exert on their members and on society generally. Their numbers were large, but their membership nevertheless constituted only a small fraction of the total male population.[47] Many groups were predominantly middle-class, and those joiners who were drawn from the working class tended to be the upwardly mobile artisan elites rather than the more numerous and hard-drinking unskilled laborers.[48] The temperance stand taken in some organizational charters was not always enforced, and a few ethnic lodges took no stand against drinking whatsoever.[49] Furthermore, because many lodges were still forced for financial reasons to utilize facilities connected with saloons, the temptation was great for members to stop off for drinks after their formal meetings were adjourned. As one observer remarked, some societies "hold lodge meetings above the saloon and after-meetings in the saloon below."[50] These drawbacks, combined with the relative infrequency of meetings and social events, meant that fraternal organizations alone could not hope to curb the saloongoing habits of the majority of working-class men. In general, however, they exerted a restraining influence on their own members and provided an alternative way for workers to cultivate the ties that had drawn them to urban barrooms. Moreover, in their attempts to distance themselves from saloons, the fraternal organizations were not alone.

Unions, even more than lodges, had an interest in extricating themselves from the saloons that had in many cases given them their start. Meeting there when no other institution would have them, the unions at first found barrooms extremely useful for recruiting and organizing purposes.[51] As they became more established, however, they soon found the saloon to be a liability. Drinking men disrupted meetings, jeopardized the safety of others in the industrial workplace, and tarnished the public image of organized labor. Equally damaging were the drinking excesses of labor leaders such as William "Big Bill" Haywood and Eugene V. Debs, both of whom eventually restrained their saloongoing habits after fellow organizers pointed out the harm they were doing to the movement.[52] By the 1910s many union leaders had become privately convinced that the saloon was a menace, but few publicly advocated its outright elimination for fear of alienating workers not yet of similar minds and of jeopardizing relations with unions connected with the liquor industry.[53] The leaders could, however, engage in a consciousness-raising campaign by encouraging workers to discuss alcohol-related problems at meetings and recognize that the liquor business, like all capitalist enterprises, was ultimately engaged in the exploitation of the working class.[54]

Convincing workers that saloongoing was detrimental to the cause of labor was complicated by the fact that saloonkeepers and their political allies were often helpful to customers needing jobs, vending licenses, loans, charity, and other assistance.[55] In New York, for example, the Democratic political machine known as Tammany Hall routinely utilized saloons as district headquarters where ordinary workingmen could easily approach local bosses for favors and participate in machine-sponsored political clubs.[56] Many saloonkeepers were themselves machine politicians, such as Chicago boss Michael "Hinky Dink" Kenna, whose saloon, the Workingmen's Exchange, served as an organizing ground for the First Ward Democratic Club from the 1890s to Prohibition.[57] The alliance between saloonists and politicians extended to Republican as well as Democratic machines; in Pittsburgh, for example, Republican boss Christopher "Chris" McGee packed the city government with "bartenders, saloonkeepers, liquor dealers, and others...dependent in a business way upon the maladministration of the law," according to Lincoln Steffens.[58]

Politicians helped saloonkeepers by thwarting bothersome temperance legislation; saloonkeepers helped politicians by contributing to campaign coffers and facilitating contact with local constituents; and working-class men, by patronizing barrooms and arranging to swap their votes for drinks and favors, kept both saloonists and politicians in operation.[59] On the surface this system of practical politics had the appearance of benefiting everyone involved, making it difficult for union advocates to persuade workers that their interests were better served without beer and bossism.

In practice, however, this ostensibly beneficial arrangement was too often subverted by political machines more interested in pursuing government graft and bribes from businessmen than in ensuring the long-term welfare of their working-class constituents. Nowhere was this unhappy truth brought home more forcefully to laboring people than in San Francisco in the early 1900s. A politically savvy lawyer named Abraham Ruef had guided the fledgling Union Labor party to victory in 1901, owing in part to the secret but substantial support of the liquor industry.[60] Ruef, the power behind Mayor Eugene E. Schmitz, pretended to promote the interests of labor. He was particularly famous for dispensing sundry favors to union men and others from his accustomed table in The Pup, one of the so-called French restaurants of the city that offered food and alcohol downstairs and private supper bedrooms on upper floors.[61] But as graft prosecutions of Ruef and his cohorts revealed in 1907, the Union Labor political machine had repeatedly betrayed the interests of unions and the people in favor of the bribe-paying railroads and other business corporations. As the scandal made the headlines, the outrage of workingmen was succinctly expressed in a statement of the United Brotherhood of Carpenters and Joiners: "We repudiate and condemn the action of the gang of boodlers and grafters who have used the name of the labor unions to promote their own ends."[62] As the bitter experience of San Francisco workers demonstrated, then, the long-standing practice of relying on saloon-allied politicians to better the lot of labor could be highly damaging to both the interests and the reputation of the labor movement.

Thus, workers attending union meetings in the early twentieth century were likely to hear many disturbing arguments designed to make them reexamine their relationship to the saloon, its wares, and its backers. The man behind the bar might have helped them obtain jobs, but he represented, and participated in, the kind of good-old-boy employment network—arbitrary, inefficient, and fraught with favoritism—that unions were fighting to eliminate. Furthermore, the saloonkeeper was often hostile to the goals and ideals of the labor movement itself. Unions promoted sobriety and thrift, hardly qualities that would please a liquor seller. They urged workers to vote for reform-minded labor candidates rather than the entrenched machine politicians who protected saloons from temperance crusaders. Most galling of all, unions built their organizations on the occupational ties that had brought saloongoing groups together and then tried to remove the saloon from the equation by banning saloonists from their ranks, criticizing the capitalistic motives of the liquor industry, and moving their headquarters out of saloons at the earliest opportunity. Understandably, then, the saloonkeeper and his allies in the political and business worlds were often hostile to the objectives of the labor movement.[63] It was the hope of union leaders that saloongoers, awakening to that fact, would realize that although the saloon had enabled them to develop the rudiments of labor solidarity, future progress would depend on a transfer of their loyalty from the beer hall to the union hall.

Unionizing efforts reached only a portion of the working class, of course, and even those who were recruited into the movement did not necessarily relinquish their ties to the urban barroom. Yet unions did make it difficult for workers to regard the saloon with the same degree of warmth after 1900 than before. Barroom regulars might scoff at the antisaloon tirades of pious middle-class reformers, but the hardheaded arguments of labor advocates could not be as easily dismissed. Even then most workers were not prepared to reject the saloon simply on the advice of unions, but neither, perhaps, were they prepared to defend it when the final showdown came in 1920. Furthermore, since unions tended to attract those workers most committed to organization and unified action, they may well have wooed away the very men who might otherwise have mounted a more spirited defense of the saloon in the face of Prohibition.

Lack of commitment on the part of saloongoers was not the only reason for the downfall of the saloon. A tremendous array of forces were working against it, including increasingly cutthroat competition within the liquor industry, an upsurge in antisaloon legislation, the initiation of criminal proceedings against machine politicians, and the drive for war-time preparedness and conservation.[64] In the face of this opposition even the most vigorous, well-organized campaign by saloongoers might not have succeeded. Yet the lack of such a campaign almost surely doomed the saloon, for popular support was its last chance in the firestorm that threatened to engulf it in its final years.[65]

In the eyes of most regular customers the saloon never completely fell from grace; on the contrary, many men continued to regard it fondly as their personal club and to patronize it to the end. But something had gone out of the old relationship, when the saloon had stood at the center of everything happening in cities across the country. The secret of its success had always been to capitalize on the disorganized state of urban society in general and the working class in particular. Allied with the machine politicians and backed by the liquor interests, the saloon was able to indulge and exploit the needs of its constituents without serious fear of constraint or competition.

But the confused and wide-open urban conditions that sustained the saloon could not last. It was a great irony, in fact, that the saloon itself helped along the process of working-class self-organization that would be a major factor in its own undoing. By providing an arena in which laborers could cultivate their common ties and develop solutions to their problems, the saloon had effectively hastened the day of its own demise. In time workingmen would begin performing for themselves a great many social, economic, and political functions previously performed for them by saloons. The process was slow, uneven, subject to setbacks, and by no means complete by 1920. Yet it appears to have progressed far enough so that many saloongoers found themselves lacking the whole-hearted commitment necessary to inspire action to save the saloon. Thus, when the Prohibition bulldozer came through, the saloon collapsed not only from pressure without but also from decay within.

NOTES

1. James H. Timberlake, *Prohibition and the Progressive Movement, 1900–1920* (New York: Atheneum, 1970), 149–184.
2. Peter H. Odegard, *Pressure Politics: The Story of the Anti-Saloon League* (New York: Columbia University Press, 1928), 36–77.

3. Timberlake, *Prohibition and the Progressive Movement*, 165.

4. George Ade, *The Old-Time Saloon: Not Wet—Not Dry, Just History* (New York: Long and Smith, 1931), 20.

5. For an account of the volatility and frequency of popular protests in the nineteenth and early twentieth centuries, see Herbert G. Gutman, *Work, Culture, and Society in Industrializing America* (New York: Knopf, 1976), 3–78; Michael E. McGerr, *The Decline of Popular Politics: The American North, 1865–1928* (New York: Oxford University Press, 1986), 12–41, 145–151. According to McGerr, public disenchantment with political theater and the spectacle style of political activism and campaigning became increasingly marked after 1900, owing to such factors as competition from new patterns of leisure and consumption, the growing sophistication of the public through education and the media, and the steady erosion of local community cohesiveness as a result of class stratification and economic expansion.

6. For example, a succinct account of the characteristics and functions of the saloon as well as its place in the history of taverns worldwide is available in Robert E. Popham, "The Social History of the Tavern," in *Research Advances in Alcohol and Drug Problems*, ed. Yedy Israel, Frederick B. Glaser, Harold Kalant, Robert E. Popham, Wolfgang Schmitt, and Reginald G. Smart (New York: Plenum Press, 1978), 4:225–302. The urban saloon and its role as a semipublic institution in two major cities is analyzed in Perry R. Duis, *The Saloon: Public Drinking in Chicago and Boston, 1880–1920* (Urbana: University of Illinois Press, 1983). For a case study of saloons in a single community over several decades, see Roy Rosenzweig, *Eight Hours for What We Will: Workers and Leisure in an Industrial City, 1870–1920* (New York: Cambridge University Press, 1983). An interesting comparison can be made of urban saloons and their frontier counterparts by consulting Elliott West, *The Saloon on the Rocky Mountain Mining Frontier* (Lincoln: University of Nebraska Press, 1979). The transformation undergone by saloons in Denver as that city grew from a frontier outpost to a major urban center is analyzed in Thomas J. Noel, *The City and the Saloon: Denver, 1858–1916* (Lincoln: University of Nebraska Press, 1982) and David Brundage, "The Producing Classes and the Saloon: Denver in the 1880s," *Labor History* 26 (Winter 1985): 29–52. Eastern European immigrants who frequented saloons adjacent to the Chicago stockyards are discussed in Robert A. Slayton, *Back of the Yards: The Making of a Local Democracy* (Chicago: University of Chicago Press, 1986). How employers endeavored to stigmatize and stamp out the saloongoing habits of workers is analyzed in John J. Rumbarger, *Profits, Power, and Prohibition: Alcohol Reform and the Industrializing of America, 1800–1930* (Albany: State University of New York Press, 1989).

7. Ade, *Old-Time Saloon*, 104–105.

8. Royal L. Melendy, "The Saloon in Chicago," part 1, *American Journal of Sociology* 6 (November 1900): 293.

9. This assertion is based on studies of post-1920 bar behavior among regulars, though the retrospective use of evidence is admittedly risky. See, for example, E. E. LeMasters, *Blue-Collar Aristocrats: Life-Styles at a Working-Class Tavern* (Madison: University of Wisconsin Press, 1975), 7; Sherri Cavan, *Liquor License: An Ethnography of Bar Behavior* (Chicago: Aldine, 1966), 211–213; David

Gottlieb, "The Neighborhood Tavern and the Cocktail Lounge: A Study of Class Differences," *American Journal of Sociology* 67 (May 1957): 561.

10. Frederic C. Howe, *Confessions of a Reformer* (New York: Quadrangle, 1925), 54; Ade, *Old-Time Saloon*, 41.

11. For a thorough treatment of the theme of the saloon as a semipublic institution, see Duis, *Saloon*.

12. *Substitutes for the Saloon*, ed. Raymond Calkins (Boston: Houghton Mifflin, 1901), 9.

13. I have identified these six linking factors as the core elements of the saloongoing relationship after reviewing contemporary accounts by saloongoers, barkeepers, journalists, and social commentators as well as the considerable secondary literature on the urban saloon and working-class culture. It is not meant to be an exhaustive list but rather a summary of the most universal and significant constants in barroom interaction, as I argue in my dissertation, "Faces along the Bar: Lore and Order in the Workingman's Saloon, 1870–1920" (forthcoming, University of California, Berkeley).

14. Some representative primary sources dealing with the relationship of women to the saloon include Dorothy Richardson, "The Long Day: The Story of a New York Working Girl," in *Women at Work*, ed. William L. O'Neill (Chicago: Quadrangle, 1972), 258–259; M. E. Ravage, *An American in the Making: The Life Story of an Immigrant* (New York: Harper, 1917), 124–134; Howe, *Confessions of a Reformer*, 51–52; Melendy, "Saloon in Chicago," part 1, 298–299; *Substitutes for the Saloon*, 15. Eugene O'Neill's 1933 play, *Ah, Wilderness!* set in a small Connecticut town on the Fourth of July, 1906, provides a sensitive portrait of a young prostitute in the backroom of a sleazy hotel bar who is both exploited and humiliated by men embracing a double standard of female morality. See Eugene O'Neill, *Ah, Wilderness!* act 3, sc. 1, and act 4, sc. 3. For a different interpretation of the evidence on women in the saloon, arguing for their relative importance, see Duis, *Saloon*, 2–3.

15. By the 1910s social interaction between the sexes was the norm in the cabaret, which, though hardly a working-class institution, was still an important trendsetter that attracted the younger and more adventurous among the laboring classes. See Lewis A. Erenberg, *Steppin' Out: New York Nightlife and the Transformation of American Culture, 1890–1930* (Westport, Conn.: Greenwood Press, 1981), 81–87. Some saloons did try to imitate the cabaret atmosphere with tables, live entertainment, and dance floors, but these efforts did little but incur the wrath of both older saloongoers and antisaloon groups. See Duis, *Saloon*, 293–295.

16. Jack London, *John Barleycorn: Alcoholic Memoirs* (Santa Cruz, Calif.: Western Tanager Press, 1981), 42–43.

17. Melendy, "Saloon in Chicago," part 1, 295.

18. *Substitutes for the Saloon*, 75; for additional information on boys' organizations, see 74–79, 314–320.

19. Robert Sklar, *Movie-Made America: A Social History of American Movies* (New York: Random House, 1975), 4; Gunther Barth, *City People: The Rise of Modern City Culture in Nineteenth-Century America* (Oxford: Oxford University Press, 1980), 177.

20. Between the Civil War and World War I the proportion of males in the population increased from 50.6 percent in 1870 to 51.2 percent in 1890, reaching a peak of 51.5 percent in 1910. Though males continued to outnumber females in 1920, the proportion decreased by 0.5 percent to 51.0 percent, owing to such factors as World War I casualties, the stationing of soldiers overseas, and an increase in emigration (U.S. Bureau of the Census, *Population, 1920* [Washington, D.C., 1922], 2:103–104, 107, 383). Laws restricting immigration were not passed until 1921 and 1924.

21. In San Francisco the ratio of males to every hundred females was 117.1 in 1900, 131.6 in 1910, and 116.6 in 1920. In Chicago the ratio of males to every hundred females was 103.4 in 1900, 106.3 in 1910, and 102.9 in 1920 (U.S. Bureau of the Census, *Population, 1920*, 2:117, 119).

22. Jon M. Kingsdale, "The 'Poor Man's Club': Social Functions of the Urban Working-Class Saloon," *American Quarterly* 25 (October 1973): 485–486, 489.

23. The beginnings of a more balanced sex ratio in the general population was demonstrated by the decrease in the proportion of males from 51.5 percent in 1910 to 51.0 percent in 1920. Similarly, the ratio of males to every hundred females in San Francisco decreased from 131.6 in 1910 to 116.6 in 1920; in Chicago, from 106.3 in 1910 to 102.9 in 1920 (U.S. Bureau of the Census, *Population, 1920*, 2:107, 117, 119). Regarding marital status, the percentage of single males fifteen years of age and older decreased from 40.2 percent in 1900 to 38.7 percent in 1910 and then to 35.1 percent in 1920 (U.S. Bureau of the Census, *Population, 1920*, 2:387). There was also a decline in the median age of males at first marriage, from 25.9 years in 1900 to 25.1 years in 1910 and then to 24.6 years in 1920 (U.S. Bureau of the Census, *Historical Statistics of the United States, Colonial Times to 1970*, bicentennial ed., (Washington, D.C., 1975), 1:19.

24. E. C. Moore, "The Social Value of the Saloon," *American Journal of Sociology* 3 (July 1897): 8.

25. *Substitutes for the Saloon*, 61–62, 72.

26. *Substitutes for the Saloon*, 152–155.

27. Jane Addams, *Twenty Years at Hull House* (New York: New American Library, 1960), 200–238.

28. Jacob August Riis, *How the Other Half Lives* (New York: Hill and Wang, 1957), 218–225.

29. John A. Garraty, *The New Commonwealth, 1877–1890* (New York: Harper and Row, 1968), 192–200, 211.

30. Addams, *Twenty Years at Hull House*, 202, 207–209; Garraty, *New Commonwealth*, 188.

31. "The Experiences and Observations of a New York Saloon-Keeper as Told by Himself," *McClure's Magazine* 32 (January 1909): 305, 311.

32. *Americans in Process: A Settlement Study*, ed. Robert A. Woods (Boston: Houghton Mifflin, 1902), 107.

33. It is difficult to know whether the quantity of alcohol laborers consumed during a typical evening's drinking was greater in the saloon or in the home. Antisaloon groups argued that it was the wide-open, clublike atmosphere of the saloon that encouraged excessive drinking and that if the saloon

were eliminated, the home would have a temperate influence. Saloon advocates, however, asserted that home drinking was the heavier, owing to the greater privacy and freedom from public scrutiny in the home. For a discussion of these opposing views, see, respectively, Marcus T. Reynolds, "The Housing of the Poor in American Cities," *Publications of the American Economic Association* 8 (March and May 1893): 33–34; and Duis, *Saloon*, 274; Henry Barrett Chamberlin, "The Public Bar vs. Private Sideboard," *Chamberlin's* 13 (November 1915): 39.

34. "Experiences...of a New York Saloon-Keeper," 305.

35. *Substitutes for the Saloon*, 22–23, 158–159.

36. Of the large and growing literature on popular pastimes and their homogenizing effects on American society, two comprehensive studies include Barth, *City People*, and Russel Nye, *The Unembarrassed Muse: The Popular Arts in America* (New York: Dial Press, 1970). For a discussion of the challenge to saloons posed by movies, see Sklar, *Movie-Made America*, 3–17; by city playgrounds and stadiums, see Barth, *City People*, 148–191; by amusement parks, see John F. Kasson, *Amusing the Million: Coney Island at the Turn of the Century* (New York; Hill and Wang, 1978), 33–36; by cabarets, see Erenberg, *Steppin' Out*, 5–25. Though few workers could afford to own cars in the period before 1920, saloon proprietors and suppliers nevertheless recognized the potential threat that automobiles posed to their trade; see Duis, *Saloon*, 292–293.

37. From reminiscences of Italian and Serbian immigrants, quoted in William Kornblum, *Blue Collar Community* (Chicago: University of Chicago Press, 1974), 72.

38. Kornblum, *Blue Collar Community*, 72.

39. An overview of the characteristics and consequences of the old immigration versus the new immigration is available in Milton M. Gordon, "Assimilation in America: Theory and Reality," in *The Shaping of Twentieth-Century America*, ed. Richard M. Abrams and Lawrence W. Levine, 2d ed. (Boston: Little, Brown, 1971), 70–89.

40. For an interesting account of a modern bar confronted with the problems of an ethnically changing neighborhood, see Gottlieb, "Neighborhood Tavern," 562.

41. *Americans in Process*, 107.

42. Charles Fanning, *Finley Peter Dunne and Mr. Dooley: The Chicago Years* (Lexington: University Press of Kentucky, 1978), 223–226.

43. Royal L. Melendy, "The Saloon in Chicago," part 2, *American Journal of Sociology* 6 (January 1901): 438.

44. *Substitutes for the Saloon*, 62.

45. *Substitutes for the Saloon*, 72–73.

46. Lynn Dumenil, *Freemasonry and American Culture, 1880–1930* (Princeton: Princeton University Press, 1984), 75–80.

47. By 1901 there were nearly six hundred fraternal organizations nationwide, many with chapters in every major city and claiming an aggregate membership approaching five million. Of these, approximately two and one-quarter million were Masons, Odd Fellows, and Knights of Pythias; two and one-half million were members of forty-seven other national organizations;

the remainder belonged to various smaller societies. See Dumenil, *Freemasonry*, xi; B. H. Meyer, "Fraternal Beneficiary Societies of the United States," *American Journal of Sociology* 6 (January 1901): 650. Yet though fraternal organizations were large, their membership in 1901 still constituted only about one-fifteenth of the male population of the United States and Canada, according to Calkins (*Substitutes for the Saloon*, 64).

48. According to Dumenil's research on Masons belonging to the Live Oak Lodge in Oakland, California, for example, "Between 1880 and 1900, men in white-collar occupations of all levels constituted between 75 and 80 percent of the total. Skilled workers ranged from 15 to 20 percent, while semiskilled workers never comprised more than 5 percent. The bulk of the membership was drawn from the low-level, white-collar group (clerks, salesmen, accountants, etc.) and proprietors (mostly small businessmen such as restaurateurs, contractors, and retail merchants). Live Oak, then did include a number of workingmen, but it was primarily a white-collar, middle-class lodge" (Dumenil, *Freemasonry*, 12–13). Similar statistics on Masons in Boston are reported in Roy Rosenzweig, "Boston Masons, 1900–1935: The Lower Middle Class in a Divided Society," *Journal of Voluntary Action Research* 6 (July–Oct. 1977): 121–122.

49. Melendy, "Saloon in Chicago," part 2, 437; Dumenil, *Freemasonry*, 75–80.

50. An unidentified German minister, quoted in Melendy, "Saloon in Chicago," part 2, 437.

51. Ray Ginger, *Eugene V. Debs: A Biography* (New York: Collier Books, 1962), 305; Melendy, "Saloon in Chicago," part 2, 438. For the history of the Union Labor party of San Francisco and its reliance on the liquor trade for organizing space and funding, see Walton Bean, *Boss Ruef's San Francisco: The Story of the Union Labor Party, Big Business, and the Graft Prosecution* (Berkeley: University of California Press, 1952), 25–26, passim.

52. *The Autobiography of William D. Haywood* (New York: International Publishers, 1929), 228–229; Ginger, *Eugene V. Debs*, 68.

53. Ronald Morris Benson, "American Workers and Temperance Reform, 1866–1933" (Ph.D. diss., University of Notre Dame, 1974), 254–255.

54. Brundage, "Producing Classes," 44–45; Timberlake, *Prohibition and the Progressive Movement*, 89–92.

55. A succinct account of the "kindness and petty privileges" that machine politicians offered their working-class constituents is presented in Lincoln Steffens, *The Shame of the Cities* (New York: Hill and Wang), 205. For a competent overview of machine politicians' methods, see Howard Zink, *City Bosses in the United States: A Study of Twenty Municipal Bosses* (Durham: Duke University Press, 1930), 194–201.

56. *Substitutes for the Saloon*, 10–11, 371–372. A fascinating account of the many services and favors rendered by Tammany boss George Washington Plunkitt in the early 1900s (based on Plunkitt's own diary) is available in William L. Riordon, *Plunkitt of Tammany Hall: A Series of Very Plain Talks on Very Practical Politics* (New York: Dutton, 1963), 90–98. Also informative is Riordon's introductory essay, "When Tammany Was Supreme," vii–xxii.

57. Lloyd Wendt and Herman Kogan, *Bosses of Lusty Chicago: The Story of*

Bathhouse John and Hinky Dink (Bloomington: Indiana University Press, 1967), 164–166, 170, 341, passim. Michael Kenna acquired the nickname Hinky Dink because of his diminutive size. For a street-view photograph of the Workingmen's Exchange, see George Kibbe Turner, "The City of Chicago," *McClure's Magazine* 28 (April 1907): 577. For some statistics on the deep involvement of saloonkeepers and saloons in urban politics, see Odegard, *Pressure Politics*, 248.

58. Steffens, *Shame of the Cities*, 107. In San Francisco a maverick third-party machine, the Union Labor party, came to power under the astute, if corrupt, direction of Abraham Ruef. See Bean, *Boss Ruef's San Francisco*, 12–39.

59. There were of course many instances of abuse and exploitation associated with this arrangement. For example, uncooperative saloonkeepers who resisted paying what one proprietor called the politician's tithe were swiftly punished by machine-ordered police raids and other strong-arm tactics. See "Experiences...of a New York Saloon-Keeper," 306–307. For an instance of saloonkeepers taking unfair advantage of laborers in search of work, see Timberlake, *Prohibition and the Progressive Movement*, 83.

60. Bean, *Boss Ruef's San Francisco*, 19–26.

61. According to historian Walton Bean, the *San Francisco Bulletin* once aptly described the French restaurant as San Francisco's "peculiar institution." Popular for decades with tourists and residents alike, the establishments (about a dozen in the early 1900s) combined elements of the respectable public dining room, the less-respectable saloon, and the decidedly not respectable house of assignation. See Bean, *Boss Ruef's San Francisco*, 26, 29, 50–51. It is noteworthy that Ruef's fondness for The Pup as his informal headquarters did not stop him from threatening to revoke the liquor licenses of its proprietor and the other French restaurateurs unless they permitted the unionization of their employees and paid Ruef large "attorney's fees" to maintain his good will. This extortion scheme would later figure prominently in the graft prosecutions against Ruef, as discussed in Bean, *Boss Ruef's San Francisco*, 51–54, 169–170, 179, 188, 212–213, 221–226, 268–270.

62. Quoted in Bean, *Boss Ruef's San Francisco*, 257.

63. Brundage, "Producing Classes," 44–47; Timberlake, *Prohibition and the Progressive Movement*, 83–84; *Substitutes for the Saloon*, 56–63.

64. A good summary of the many causes contributing to the demise of the saloon is provided in Duis, *Saloon*, 274–303.

65. Even when liquor trade organizations like the United States Brewers' Association tried to rally support through a saloon-based network of Liberty Leagues, they had only sporadic success, for the movement was almost always directed from the top and involved more string pulling in high places than committed grassroots activism. For an account of Liberty Leagues in the early twentieth century, see Odegard, *Pressure Politics*, 245–266. The divided attitudes of organized labor toward the leagues is discussed in Benson, "American Labor and Temperance Reform," 279–284. The public's waning enthusiasm in general for the spectacle style of political activism is discussed in McGerr, *Decline of Popular Politics*, 12–41, 145–151.

SIX

Student Drinking in the Third Reich: Academic Tradition and the Nazi Revolution

Geoffrey J. Giles

Students have been associated with alcoholic excesses since the earliest days of universities. Several of the medieval town-gown riots at Oxford and Cambridge were sparked by drunken disputes. It has been suggested that the medieval German student developed elaborate drinking games in imitation of nobility, whose equal he felt the notion of academic freedom made him. German students in their fraternities set up whole hierarchies of beer empires or beer states with painstaking distinctions of rank among the nobles and courtiers. Many of their beer games show this obsession with status.

The most notorious of these was the so-called pope's game, in which students sat in a circle and were required to drain a whole glass of beer every time a spinning stick came to a stop pointing at their place. Each draught allowed the drinker to advance in rank from soldier or private up through all the ranks of the military and then on through the ranks of the nobility—baron, count, prince, and finally king and emperor. The rank above emperor on the social scale was deemed, with a touch of student humor, to be that of student. If a player succeeded in advancing further to the rank of cardinal, he might eventually be crowned pope. Although it is astonishing that anyone had the capacity to get that far, the coronation itself included an even more severe test: the "pope" was required to sit on a chair, placed on the table, and drink a further twelve mugs of beer during the singing of the twelve verses of the traditional song for the occasion. As if that treatment were not bad enough, he had to attempt to perform the feat with a large sheet thrown over him, under which the assembled company would furiously puff smoke from their pipes in an effort to choke him.[1]

All these games and ceremonies of the German student fraternities were built around the compulsion to drink. It was not a question of a relaxed social evening in which the members took a mug of beer if and when they pleased. On the contrary, they were formal occasions at which the students sat at table in their fraternity caps and uniforms and drank at the command of the president. Moreover, a student was almost certain to commit one of the dozens of misdemeanors that had been dreamt up, such as not emptying the mug quickly enough or spending longer than three minutes away from the table in the bathroom (permission to leave the table had to be sought, in any case, and might well be refused). Each transgression resulted in the imposition of a fine, invariably to be fulfilled, for the general amusement of the assembled company, by the rapid downing of yet another glass of beer by the miscreant. A particularly heavy drinker might be given a mock honorary doctorate by his fraternity brothers with appropriate academic ceremony and become a *doctor cerevisiae et vini* (doctor of beer and wine), which entitled him to include the letters D.C. after his name, usually followed by N.e.B.—*nunc est bibendum* (now is the time to drink). These traditions of compulsory excessive drinking continued to be the predominant characteristic of fraternity life right up to the First World War.

It was only around the turn of the century that a movement to curb such unhealthy practices began in earnest and was quickly embraced by the Wandervogel youth movement, with its back-to-nature philosophy of simplicity and purity. Pamphlets published by the aptly named Moderation Press or by that of the League of the Opponents of Alcohol began to appear on campus by the late 1890s.[2] They had a minimal effect on the established fraternities, but by the 1920s more students were attracted to groups promoting abstinence in the austere atmosphere of postwar Germany. Still, the only student group that actually obligated its members to total abstinence from alcohol and tobacco was the Catholic Hochland organization, founded in 1925 deliberately to attack the use of alcohol by students. Although there were fifteen local associations by 1927, they only comprised a total of 180 student members.[3] The influence of the Hochland may have been muted, but there was a definite general shift of attitude during the 1920s away from heavy drinking. One strong reason for this shift was the economic hardship suffered by a large proportion of the student body during the Weimar Republic.[4] Even the writer of an enthusiastic essay about student drinking customs in 1931 noted the change. In the past neither exhortations, sermons, threats or actual punishments on the part of the authorities had exercised any lasting effect on the alcoholic excesses; but the abstinence movement had arisen within the student body, and this provenance appeared to give it special poignancy. Would the trend continue? The historical evidence of the past several centuries seemed to the wistful alumnus author of the essay to suggest the contrary.[5]

The National Socialist Students' Association (NSDStB) was founded in 1926 to provide a vehicle to spread the ideas of the Nazi party among the student body. Initially it stood firmly opposed to the fraternities as representatives of the establishment, which the Nazis wanted to destroy. The fraternity associations certainly dominated student politics through their superior organization of student election campaigns, and this domination set the NSDStB against them in a struggle at the university for the center of the political stage. The outdated customs of the fraternities became an issue inasmuch as the Nazi student group, by contrast, held out the promise of aggressive political action to students who felt increasingly threatened as a social group in the ostensibly less stratified democratic republic. The Nazis attempted to portray the fraternity students as ossified relics inappropriate to the new politicized era. Drinking was rarely mentioned, though Hitler himself, in a rare pronouncement about students, did propagate a subsequently oft-repeated bon mot, that the student of the future would be judged not by his capacity for beer but by the degree of his sobriety.[6]

Hitler's personal distaste for alcohol is well known, although he was not a total abstainer. A phobia against alcohol was not one of his more rabid fanaticisms. After all, the party was founded in a bar, and beer halls played a vital part as meeting places in the growth of the Nazi movement. Hitler's position on the matter was more an attempt to exude an aura of asceticism (just as he also let it be known that he was a vegetarian and a nonsmoker) and demonstrate the strength of his will to the man in the street. Several other leaders considered it proper or expedient to emulate him. Such a public face came easily to Heinrich Himmler, who in his own craving for status had joined a prestigious drinking fraternity as a student but had successfully petitioned for exemption from the drinking bouts because of his sensitive stomach.

Within the Nazi party heavy drinking does not seem to have been a particular issue before Hitler's accession to the chancellorship of Germany in January 1933. The Great Depression and the financial sacrifices demanded of the party members and storm troopers left them with little beer money. After the seizure of power, however, the Nazi rank and file insisted on the spoils of victory and went on what amounted to an eighteen-month binge, which ended only with the murder of SA leader Ernst Röhm in June 1934. The national head of the Nazi Students' Association, Oskar Stäbel, was obliged to issue a sharply-worded decree in June 1933, which hinted at uniformed NSDStB members reeling drunkenly through the streets all over Germany. Stäbel wrote:

It must be particularly stressed that every party member ought to be able to avoid having *Heil Hitler* bellowed at him by drunken students. If certain students fall into this state, then they would do well not to advertise their membership in the NSDStB in such an importunate fashion. One would think that such a circular would be superfluous in our ranks. But since these incidents have been multiplying, especially lately, I shall in future take the necessary measures against such provocateurs.[7]

There is, however, no evidence that he actually did anything. Indeed, the main thrust of the decree was not to forbid participation in alcoholic student celebrations but to ensure that NSDStB members attended in civilian clothes. Stäbel, a fraternity alumnus himself, is a good example of a Nazi student who wanted not so much to destroy the old elite (in this case the fraternities) as to take it over and control it. The liberty to drink oneself under the table was regarded as part of the trappings of success and power, a manifestation of elite status. Stäbel, who was subsequently dismissed for embezzling student funds to maintain an ostentatious life-style, did not practice the wider decorum that he preached.

The junior student leaders did not always follow the example of their führer either. A report from July 1933 took to task the leader of a student labor camp for going back to bed with a hangover the morning after a weekend party, having sent his squads marching off to the worksite with picks and shovels.[8] Such bad examples detracted from the idealistic self-image of the Nazi movement. The 1933 party rally at Nuremberg, at the end of Hitler's first summer as chancellor, deteriorated into a veritable orgy of celebration for many Nazis. The orders for participants at the Nuremberg rally the following year emphasized that "one thing holds true above all else for this occasion: a National Socialist does not get drunk." This slogan was printed boldface in oversize letters and underlined heavily as well. The party did not want to face another huge bill for damages, as it had in 1933, with thousands of drinks left unpaid for, countless beer mugs stolen as souvenirs, and public transport defaced with graffiti. The memorandum had even to draw attention to the disgusting condition in which toilets were left at the 1933 rally.[9]

Hermann Fahrenkrug identifies in chapter 14 of this volume three common categories of state intervention in alcohol-related incidents: traffic violations, criminal offenses, and offenses against public order. But as the following examples show, in Nazi Germany there was no consistency in treatment or punishment. Nevertheless, drunkenness was not viewed as a particularly serious offense, more as an embarrassment. Alcoholic excesses were only rarely used by the party as an excuse to rid itself of a burdensome member. The national leader of the German Students' Union, Andreas Feickert, was suspended from his office in February 1936 ostensibly because of a prosecution for drunk driving (by all accounts a particular concern of the party), though this incident had in fact been known by the Ministry of Education for months. It had taken no action before, but now there were political reasons for doing so, which made the ministry search out a convenient pretext.[10] It is not clear whether Feickert in fact had a serious drinking problem; but what is certain is that he was working under extraordinary pressure, which may have resulted in heavy drinking. The pace of student politics between 1933 and 1936 was hectic; the task of nazifying the student body in short order was an enormous one. Already in the spring of 1933, in the first flush of victory, the regional Nazi student leader for northern Germany, Reinhold Schulze, had suffered a nervous breakdown. The intergroup rivalries between Nazi organizations for control of the student body drove many student leaders to the brink of despair and, as much as the desire for ostentation, may have led many of the leaders to excessive consumption of alcohol.

Drunkenness could be a serious enough misdemeanor to warrant expulsion from the Nazi party. This ultimate disgrace was suffered by Heinz Haselmayer in 1936, after he had given a public speech in Holland at Haarlem in an evidently intoxicated state. The central issue here was that the party had been brought into disrepute; even worse, the scandal had erupted outside of the borders of Germany. However, after a lengthy appeals process Haselmayer managed to have himself reinstated by asserting that his bizarre behavior and perhaps slurred speech had in fact been caused by the strain of his schedule of speaking engagements and the effects of strong coffee on an empty stomach. It took him more than two years to convince the Supreme Party Court, during which he somehow succeeded in making the chief witness, a nurse, reverse her original damaging assessment of his behavior.[11]

The incidence of drunkenness was common enough among rank-and-file storm troopers in 1933 for a clause to be included in the SA rule book reminding them that they would be punished if inebriation prevented them from carrying out orders while on duty. Furthermore, article 12 stated that drunkenness would not be treated as an extenuating circumstance for other transgressions but would actually increase the severity of the punishment.[12] If this was true in the SA, it was not always the case in the regular courts of law, as two examples from the academic world demonstrate. They concern professors at the University of Hamburg, both of them historians and both of them among the leading exponents of National Socialist ideology in the university. They had performed sterling service for the party cause, and the party had every reason to support them. But in 1936 both became victims in entirely separate cases of the SS campaign to stamp out homosexuality. In the case of Professor Alfred Schüz the court, searching for a way of acquitting a loyal party member and wounded war veteran from charges that he had in part admitted, declared that such an offense by such a man could only be explained by the effects on him of alcohol.

The court found a number of reasons to acquit Professor Otto Westphal of similar charges, primarily using an argument of *nulla poena sine lege* because the offenses had been committed when the older, more tolerant republican version of the law concerning homosexual offenses was still in effect. It also sought to disqualify the evidence of the chief prosecution witness, a male prostitute, on the grounds of his inferior character. However, it is interesting that one of the central points in Westphal's defense was, again, that he at times drank to excess. He blamed the political infighting at the university and the opposition to his attempts at radical politicization for this intemperance, asserting that by the summer of 1934, when the first homosexual encounter had occurred, his nerves were almost completely shattered. To escape the poisonous atmosphere, he did much of his scholarly writing (so ran his extraordinary claim) in the bars of the Hamburg nightclub district, the Reeperbahn, working till late into the night and then drinking fairly heavily as a sleeping aid. All these circumstances were indulgently catalogued in the justification for acquittal by the court, whereas normally the simple denunciation of a male prostitute would have been sufficient to send even an innocent person to a concentration camp.[13] Drunkenness, then, could be interpreted and used by the authorities in different ways in accordance with the situation.

The battle of Nazi Students' Association with the old student fraternities offers some examples of this. In May 1935 fraternity students in Göttingen pulled down from a maypole the swastika ribbons decorating it, which were of course a new embellishment of an old tradition. The NSDStB refused to accept the excuse that this action was harmless, drunken horseplay and chose to interpret it as a "politically interesting and revealing deed."[14] By contrast, the Nazi student leadership did not downplay the tipsy condition of some Heidelberg fraternity students in 1935, who began blowing across the mouths of half-empty champagne bottles in a local bar to whistle down a radio speech by Hitler. This admittedly rowdy behavior gave rise to a vituperative press campaign that specifically focused on the irresponsible and besotted nature of the fraternity world as a whole. The press was soon filled with monocled caricatures of the students unsteadily clutching champagne bottles to their breasts. Much capital was made out of the alleged decadence of the old student elite on this occasion.[15]

In November 1936 the student leadership was reorganized under the influence of the SS, and the new leaders tried to infuse the student body with the kind of discipline and propriety meant to characterize the SS itself. The struggle with the fraternities took on a more subtle aspect, and the old student customs, even those involving drinking, were no longer summarily rejected. Fraternities had always sought to keep up close relationships with their alumni, on whom they depended for financial support, and a number of social occasions for former members punctuated the academic calendar. Especially popular was the *Frühschoppen,* a kind of brunch at which the central element was wine. Financial constraints made it necessary for the NSDStB as well to court the alumni, and the Nazis' quasi-fraternities began holding their own *Frühschoppen.*[16] In addition, at the rushes of these Nazi fraternities a plentiful supply of beer was on hand to make the potential recruit feel at home; members were assigned to individual newcomers to "keep them supplied with drinks and cigarettes."[17]

Dueling had long been a common practice of certain types of fraternity, and members could enhance their prestige by fighting in them. Therefore, students would use the slightest pretext to provoke a duel, such as a rude taunt hurled by the member of a rival fraternity in a bar. To the new student leadership in 1936, however, the insult of a student in his cups did not count. They did not wish to excuse the insult; rather they wanted to protect the sanctity of dueling from such flippancy. One of their earliest steps in November 1936 was to issue the following decree: "Drunkenness is unworthy of a German citizen. Therefore no drunken person who has been insulted in this condition has the right to demand satisfaction. If a German citizen while drunk affronts the honor of another, this insult may never be avenged with blood."[18] On the whole this kind of step pleased the fraternity alumni because it appeared that the Nazis were taking the old traditions seriously, indeed treating them more conscientiously than the fraternities themselves had lately done.

A lead article appeared in the national student newspaper in February 1939 on the need for self-control regarding alcohol and tobacco; it was a sign at least that the student leaders perceived a problem among German youth. One concern of the writer was that student fraternity traditions had spread to associations of apprentices, and the heavy drinking was damaging productivity.[19] Later in the year an article in the same newspaper under the headline "The Oxford of Today Is

Rotten" deplored the drinking habits of Oxford students and their reportedly rowdy behavior in pubs and restaurants, which often ended in food fights and the destruction of furniture. It was also pointed out to the reader that the Oxonian often dissipated his energies in so-called petting parties: "These petting parties are gatherings with loose women, at which the chief 'amusement' consists of endless drinks and turning out the lights."[20]

To the embarrassment of the Nazi student leaders, a similar "veritable wave of flirting and boozing" was sweeping several German universities around this time, according to the reports of the secret police. With the outbreak of the Second World War the student leaders were more worried than ever about the adverse comment with which the public would surely greet such behavior. Students must not be seen to be idly celebrating while the rest of the population was enduring hardships.[21] Thus, there were also special police campaigns against the so-called swing groups (which included students). Participants were censured not simply because they drank, though that aspect was included in the horrified descriptions of furtive night life the police imputed to these young people, who liked to dance a forbidden, foreign dance, but rather because they were enjoying themselves in private, unofficial ways. This behavior was interpreted by the perpetually nervous political leadership as clear proof of opposition to the regime.

Of course, enjoyment was permissible if there was some purpose behind it. An example was a reception given for foreign students in the plush Hotel Atlantik in Hamburg in May 1944. In the chaotic conditions of the latter stages of the war the student leaders had difficulty in keeping track of students, and the foreigners among them were perennial objects of suspicion. It served as good propaganda to have young people from conquered territories welcomed as students at German universities. There were always rumors, however, that the Bulgarian contingent, for example, included many communists. Therefore, it was especially necessary to keep a close watch on them. Regrettably, their whereabouts were not always known. What better way of bringing them out of the woodwork than by laying on a lavish reception? The evening was indeed a huge success and "the atmosphere exceptionally lively owing to a substantial allowance of vermouth and spirits as well as an ample supply of cigars and cigarettes." Here the Nazis actually used drinks as a lure, despite the official coolness about indulgence in alcohol. Unknown foreign students who had missed the party stopped by the Nazi student leader's office for days afterward, begging to be invited to the next occasion.[22]

At some student parties during the war, however, overindulgence in alcohol allowed feelings about the Nazi regime to surface that were best left hidden. There was a terrible fuss in the summer of 1943 at the University of Jena, resulting from a party held by a group of medical students during the course of which a bust of Hitler was destroyed. This incident naturally drew the attention of the Gestapo. No effort was spared by the dean of the Faculty of Medicine (who had been in charge of the event) or the rector of the university to prove that it had not been a political demonstration but was merely the result of excessive drunkenness. To buttress the argument, the precise alcoholic intake of the culprit was listed. He had drunk "one glass of champagne, one glass of red wine, three of schnapps, four beers, at least three more of schnapps, another four beers and then apparently further small amounts of alcoholic drinks." The university asserted that in the light of this imbibing, it was not surprising that the student had sprayed his companions with a fire extinguisher, ripped a soap dispenser off the washroom wall, and finally flung the bust of the führer (on which another student had written "You arse!") down the lavatory steps, where it smashed to smithereens.

Punishment for this escapade had necessarily to be exemplary and severe to convince the Gestapo of the political loyalty of all concerned. The student in question was sent to prison for two years, and even the dean was put under house arrest for six weeks. How had it been possible for the students, others of whom had also destroyed (fortunately less sacrosanct) objects, to lay their hands on such quantities of alcohol? They had managed it by saving their rations from the army over an extended period, even exchanging cigarettes for beer coupons to increase the stockpile. The rector noted solemnly that a recurrence of such a disgrace could only be prevented if alcohol were removed altogether from the student scene.[23]

In addressing this remark to the minister of education, however, the rector was not speaking to a friend of prohibition, for Bernhard Rust was himself an alcoholic. If anyone had doubted it, nowhere was his alcoholism more apparent than at the annual rectors' conference that very year in Salzburg. Minister Rust tried to deliver his speech of welcome to the assembled university heads at dinner on the first night in an obvious state of inebriation. He doubtless annoyed diners and kitchen staff alike by rambling on for over an hour between the soup and the main course, which could not be served till he had sat down after a maudlin and pathetic apology for his total failure as a minister. The rectors were treated on another evening to the spectacle of the minister clambering onto the table in an attempt to elude his aides and give a foreign-policy speech on Italy, a subject about which he, cut off from Hitler's inner circle, knew little. His civil servants, with great presence of mind, burst in chorus into a lusty rendering of a traditional student drinking song about the Romans to drown him out. It was one of those interminable songs, with literally dozens of verses, so that every time Rust tried to launch into his speech, they were able to strike up a fresh stanza. At last the minister had to admit defeat, descending from the tabletop and staggering out of the room, red in the face.[24]

With the minister of education setting such an example, there was little likelihood of any initiative from the top in curbing student drinking. The Reich Student Leadership was much more conscientious in encouraging moderation, but in such a way that the leaders looked like killjoys. For in attempting to suppress the undoubtedly colorful (though hardly salubrious) student drinking customs, they offered nothing in their place beyond dreary evenings of political instruction and German folklore, which kept the students away in droves. It was a characteristic of these leaders that they lacked lively ideas with which to fasten the attention of the students. As the old fraternities were gradually banned during the 1930s, the students did not come over to the NSDStB. Student drinking may have declined in these Nazi fraternities, but students were not attracted to them. Freshmen had certain role expectations about university life, and drinking parties were an indispensable part of it for many.

It was typical of the Nazi movement in general to be essentially conservative in outlook rather than truly revolutionary, as its members liked to imagine. It embraced old values sufficiently to regard indulgence in alcohol still as a symbol of elite status. The Nazi party was the elite after 1933 and resented when the old elites like the fraternities continued, for example, to drink champagne at the initiation of new members, a practice abandoned by the party. Symbolically such a rite of passage suggested that the fraternity was still somehow more attractive than the Nazi organizations at the university.

The attitude of National Socialists toward alcohol was, then, an ambivalent one. They resented the fact that the old elites and their customs did not die out overnight, condemning the former while lacking an appealing substitute for the latter. The old fighters of the movement had looked forward to enjoying eventually such perquisites as these. The drunken excesses of Nazis in 1933 had caused such adverse publicity that it was necessary to remind the rank and file of the philosophy of self-denial or, at the very least, self-control. Yet as long as public embarrassment did not result, the leaders of party and state were usually ready to turn a blind eye. Enough of them, certainly among the civil servants, had been fraternity students themselves to view the student drinking bouts nostalgically and enjoy the alcoholic reunions of fraternity alumni. Their own background did not lead them to believe that there existed a problem sufficiently serious to warrant vigorous reform.

The Nazi leader in charge of German physicians, Gerhard Wagner, did lead a campaign against alcoholic excess (while admitting that he himself liked his glass of wine or beer). He viewed the question, however, exclusively in racial terms. People's bodies did not primarily belong to them but to the state, and alcohol abuse both reduced national productivity and damaged the racial stock (he was especially concerned about the effects on pregnant women, though he believed smoking to be even more serious).[25] In light of the increase in the consumption of spirits in Nazi Germany from 397,000 hectoliters in 1933 to 761,000 hectoliters in 1939 (a 92 percent increase) the success of his efforts is questionable.[26]

What chance would reform have had anyway in the hands of unrepentant alcoholics like Rust or Robert Ley, head of the political organization of the Nazi party and of the German Labor Front, who had been given behind his back the further title of Reich Boozer? Ley was himself a former fraternity student and probably began his heavy drinking while at university. There must have been hundreds of similar alcohol abusers turned out by the German fraternities decade after decade.

The lack of concern about alcoholism is astonishing, though in the case of the Nazis it is at least consistent with their social Darwinism: if a person lacked the self-discipline to keep his drinking habits from harming him, then there was obviously some inherent flaw in his character, and society should be pleased that he had revealed himself as unfit to fill a responsible position in the Nazi state. Yet as has been seen, the Nazis did not act on this belief with regard to the upper echelons of party and state, and the treatment of alcohol-related offenses elsewhere varied unpredictably. Detailed investigation of individual cases still needs to be carried out before these diverse and contradictory responses can be fitted into a reliable conceptual model of the alcohol question in Nazi Germany.

NOTES

1. Alfred Bienengräber, "Studentische Trink- und Kneipsitten," in *Das akademische Deutschland*, ed. Michael Doeberl et al. (Berlin: C. A. Weller Verlag, 1931), 2:108.

2. E.g., Theobald Ziegler, *Der Kampf gegen die Unmässigkeit auf Schule und Universität* (Hildesheim: Mässigkeitsverlag des Deutschen Vereins gegen den Missbrauch geistiger Getränke, 1898); A. Fick, *Studententum und Abstinenz* (Basel: Verlag der Schriftstelle des Alkoholgegnerbundes, 1903).

3. Rudolf Degen, "A New Form of Student Life in Germany: 'Hochland' and Its Activities," *The International Student* 24, no. 4 (January 1927).

4. Michael H. Kater, *Studentenschaft und Rechtsradikalismus in Deutschland 1918–1933. Eine sozialgeschichtliche Studie zur Bildungskrise in der Weimarer Republik* (Hamburg: Hoffman und Campe, 1975), esp. chap. 4.

5. Bienengräber, "Studentische Trink- und Kneipsitten," 112.

6. Adolf Hitler, "Um die Zukunft der deutschen Studentenschaft. Studenten und Politik," *Völkischer Beobachter*, 13–14 February 1927. On the NSDStB and students in general during the Third Reich, see Geoffrey J. Giles, *Students and National Socialism in Germany* (Princeton: Princeton University Press, 1985).

7. Rundschreiben Stäbel no. 9, 8 June 1933, Archiv der ehemaligen Reichsstudentenführung und des NSDStB, Würzburg (RSF) V * 2 alpha 524.

8. Rundschreiben Götz und Heinrichsdorff, 6 July 1933, RSF V * 2 gamma 646.

9. Merkblatt für alle Teilnehmer am Reichsparteitag 1934, n.d., RSF II * phi 23.

10. Vermerk Heinrich, 9 August 1935, Zentrales Staatsarchiv Potsdam REM 868; Rust to Feickert, 21 February 1936, Berlin Document Center (BDC) Parteikorrespondenz Feickert.

11. BDC Oberstes Parteigericht Haselmayer.

12. *Allgemeine Dienstordnung für die SA der NSDAP* (Berlin: J. C. Huber, 1933), Pflichten des SA-Mannes, article 12.

13. Personnel files on Schüz and Westphal in Staatsarchiv Hamburg, University of Hamburg (UniHH) and Hochschulbehörde files.

14. Bericht über das Verhältnis des NSDStB zu den studentischen Vereinigungen, 27 May 1935, RSF II * phi 90.

15. Details of this and another incident in Bundesarchiv Koblenz (BA) R128/73.

16. Cf. an invitation to alumni from the NSDStB Kameradschaft Hermann von Wissmann, 18 June 1939, UniHH o.10.2.17.

17. *Dienstanweisung für die Kameradschaft vom 20.4.1943* (Munich: Amt Politische Erziehung der Reichsstudentenführung, 1943), 15.

18. "Betrunkener kann keine Genugtuung verlangen. Die neue studentische Ehrenordnung," *Hamburger Fremdenblatt*, 25 November 1936.

19. "In corpore sano," *Die Bewegung*, 7 February 1939.

20. "Das Oxford von heute ist morsch," *Die Bewegung*, 24 October 1939. There had been great respect for the officer qualities of Oxbridge students in World War I. This article in part conveyed the message that the British officers in this new war surely could not be as impressive.

21. Meldungen aus dem Reich, 24 November 1939, BA R58/145.

22. Bericht Akademische Auslandsstelle Hamburg, 24 May 1944, RSF V * 2 alpha 532.

23. Rector University of Jena to Reich Education Minister, 12 August 1943, BA R21/439.

24. Kaltenbrunner to Bormann, 16 November 1943, BDC Parteikorrespondenz Rust.

25. Gerhard Wagner, "Nationalsozialistische Gesundheitsführung. Richtlinien des Reichsärzteführers," *Der Schulungsbrief*, V, 12, 1938, 420–427.

26. *Der Schulungsbrief*, VI, 2, 1939, 46.

PART TWO

Politics, Ideology, and Power

SEVEN

Against the Flowing Tide:
Whiskey and Temperance in the Making
of Modern Ireland

George Bretherton

1

For some fifty years beginning in the 1780s a growing number of
anxious people in Ireland worried publicly and loudly about the ever-
increasing rise in Irish whiskey production and consumption. Examples of their complaints are to be found in virtually every newspaper and collection of pamphlets, in private correspondence, and in
government reports.[1] Irishmen from every station in life, as well as
foreign observers from the most casual tourists to those long familiar
with the country, had something to say about the prevalence of alcohol.[2]

Little enough was done about this situation until 1829, when a
Presbyterian minister, the Reverend Dr. Joseph Penny, returned to his
native Ulster with news of that great new American invention, temperance. He brought with him a number of tracts describing this wonder—
perhaps the most important cache of temperance propaganda in history, for it was soon disseminated among the Presbyterian clergy of the
province.[3] Within a few months many of these same clergymen had
established the Ulster Temperance Society, with offices in Belfast, and
by the end of the year a national body, the Hibernian Temperance Society, had been established in Dublin.

When the student of Irish history thinks of the year 1829, it is
usually in relation not to the temperance movement but to Catholic
Emancipation. After much resistance the British government yielded
to a crescendo of popular protest, brilliantly orchestrated by Daniel

O'Connell and his followers, and permitted Emancipation to pass through Parliament. Catholics who were otherwise qualified by the possession of considerable amounts of property—and there were few enough of them—could now sit in Parliament. Over the next ten years some thirty-five Catholics became members of the House of Commons. The immediate political results of Emancipation were modest; the very term in this context seems grandiose to me. Catholics would not have agreed. Emancipation ended the political monopoly of Protestants. So long as only Protestants could hold public office and exercise power, they were the citizens, and Catholics were the despised helots. Catholics regarded Emancipation as a great moral combat won against the determined opposition of the Protestant establishment. It was an enormous psychological victory that liberated all manner of pent-up energies and raised expectations often beyond the limits of reality. For the Protestant ascendancy, the wealthy Protestants of property, it was equally a significant defeat—not so much for its immediate consequences as for what it foretold. In the fight against Emancipation Protestant landlords lost the support of their tenantry in a number of spectacular electoral contests. Would tenants continue to defy the political wishes of their landlords, and might their defiance threaten the landlords' economic and social position as well?

These questions were much on the minds of ascendancy people at the time, and they are relevant to the history of temperance, because most of the leaders of the movement at first came from this caste. Nearly all of them were Protestants of position and property. We can divide these Protestant leaders into three different groups, though all shared the same fear of a colonial elite brought to the realization that its power over the natives is no longer untrammeled.

First, and crucial for what success the early movement enjoyed, were a number of landlords. Irish landlords were not liked by their tenants, who were known for their violent reactions to landlord exactions. For their part landlords had a reputation for crassness and insensitivity to their tenants' needs. If more landlords were not stabbed or shot at by tenants it was because they were away in England or Italy, basking in the luxury of uncaring absenteeism. Their rents, collected by agents or middlemen, who had leased the property for many years, were such as to keep most tenants in dire poverty. When a tenant could no longer pay, he was evicted; there was no trouble finding someone else.

Such was the impression that many people in Britain and Europe had of Irish landlordism and its victims. Like all such impressions, it is something of a caricature and overlooks those landlords who never left Ireland and who tried to treat their tenants with decency and humanity. Still, it is by no means a wildly distorted picture of Irish realities. What is striking about the landlords who took up temperance is the degree to which they departed from this stereotype. Most of them were not absentees. In many ways these men demonstrated considerable concern for their tenants, and they prided themselves on their interest in the land and its people. The landlords from this group, who spent much time away from home, insisted that they did so of necessity, and they chose with care the agents and stewards they left behind.[4]

Most of these temperance landlords hated the middleman system, often said to be a prime example of inefficiency and exploitation, and they brought it to an end as soon as they could on their properties.[5] They were improvers, most of them encouraging the tenants to adopt up-to-date farming methods and often providing the means for them to do so. They were nothing if not paternalists, and many of their acts and attitudes would strike as extremely condescending. Yet when set against the behavior of the rapacious landlord or middleman that many tenants had known and continued to know, the new model landlord was a benevolent and preferred alternative.

The *Irish Temperance and Literary Gazette*, a weekly journal of the Hibernian Society, lauded such men as the duke of Leinster, the premier nobleman of Ireland and the owner of extensive acreage in the rich lands near Dublin. His tenants were fortunate enough to have Leinster and the duchess "residing among them and spending their princely fortune in poor neglected Ireland; what a happy land would this be if all our nobility and gentry acted as they do."[6] Leinster established a temperance society in the village of Maynooth, a short distance from his great estate, Carton. By the fall of 1836 the Maynooth Temperance Society had affiliated with other societies in several nearby villages to form a regional union of about a thousand members, most of them tenants of Leinster and his friends in the neighborhood.[7]

Elsewhere in the pages of the *Gazette* are reports of other active members of the nobility and gentry. Their overall number was never great when measured against those listed in *Burke's Irish Peerage and Baronetage*, but these men were the dominant members of their class. Peers and gentry like Annesley, Clements, Daly, de Vesci, Downshire, Monsell, and Porter were the cream of country society.[8] Obviously, the formidable example they set to others must have carried far beyond their own estates.

It is to their estates that we must look, however, for some insight into the temperance system as managed by the great landlords. Though compulsion was rarely employed—what tenant could long resist his landlord's wishes?—it is clear that most tenants joined a temperance society if their landlord had established one and took an abiding personal interest in it.[9] This interest could be manifested in several ways—by providing a temperance meeting room with clublike facilities, by donating books and other educational materials, and by paying constant attention to the condition of the temperance society and its members.[10] Landlord-tenant get-togethers, none too frequent under the old dispensation, were an important part of the system. Tea parties, soirees, and other celebrations occurred frequently, with the landlord normally in attendance. Tea, a new beverage to many country folk, must have seemed as strange at first as the occasions on which it was served to them by the landlord's wife and daughters.

Soirees were considerably more elaborate affairs than the tea parties and were meant to rival the county balls that the unreconstructed aristocracy still attended. Here the temperate peasantry could ogle the local great in all their finery, proud and confident in the common cause they shared. These soirees had decided ceremonial and symbolic overtones. Often several local societies would come together and meet under the presidency of some local magnate, who would be installed in solemn state like a king on his throne. In the fall of 1837 the *Gazette* reported on the anniversary celebration of the Carbury and Edenderry Temperance Society, which enjoyed the patronage of the marquis of Downshire and John Brownrigg, two great landlords in the vicinity. Brownrigg, senior magistrate of the King's County, presided. The assembly room "was lighted by three large chandeliers filled with wax lights, tastefully ornamented with wreaths of evergreens and artificial flowers, and no pains were spared to render the whole scene worthy of the occasion. At the head of the room the royal arms of England and Ireland were splendidly emblazoned, surmounted by the harp of Erin and the imperial crown." Beneath the escutcheon was the chair occupied by Brownrigg. "Covered with crimson and gold," it rested "upon a platform elevated several feet from the level of the room, over which we observed, amidst festoons of flowers and evergreens, the appropriate motto of 'Good will towards all Men.' "[11]

The loyalties and affinities celebrated here are obvious. Not so apparent is the novelty of such rites. Rack-renting landlords, who dealt with a people bereft of all political rights and any belief in their future, had no need for this sort of thing. An aristocracy that had to prove its fitness for leadership and its place in society would need to coax its tenantry into patterns of behavior that, though still submissive, were indicative of a basic alteration in landlord-tenant relations. Tea parties, soirees, temperance balls, and these little deference rituals were a sign of changing times.

Among the second group of temperance supporters we find a dif-

ferent outlook. This group consisted of large employers—factory owners, mine owners, millers, carters, and canal and railway proprietors.
Whereas landlords were central to Irish society, entrepreneurs were
marginal. Temperance entrepreneurs wanted to demonstrate that the
Ireland of popular imagination, inhabited by lazy, garrulous, drink-
sodden peasants, was a thing of the past. The country was ripe for
industrial and commercial development, especially once the dead
hand of landlordism had been lifted; these entrepreneurs had decided
stereotypes of their own. Perhaps their greatest contribution to the
cause came in creating propaganda for a new Ireland, one that looked
rather like England propelled forward by its great industrial revolution.[12] Their vision attracted interest across the water and helped to
focus attention on the temperance movement in Ireland.

Curiously, what success large employers had in encouraging temperance among their own employees was the result of attitudes and circumstances similar to those found on the estates of temperance landlords. Consider the cotton mill belonging to David Malcolmson near
Portlaw, County Waterford. It employed nearly five hundred workmen
and was one of the most successful industrial enterprises in the entire
country. When one remembers that the Irish textile industry, except
for linen, was then in the doldrums, Malcolmson's accomplishment
becomes all the more remarkable, and there is no plausible explanation
for it apart from the area of employer-employee relations.[13] Malcolmson was a true paternalist: the head of a vast family of workers, he
concerned himself with every aspect of their work and lives. He paid
good wages and permitted his people a much shorter working day than
was usual at the time.[14] From all accounts his employees respected him
and worked hard. Presumedly, they were all sober folks, for they were
required to join the factory temperance society. Outright compulsion
seems to be missing, but considerable pressure was used to get miners
to enroll themselves in temperance societies at the several collieries
belonging to the Mining Company of Ireland. Though the proprietors
were in far-off London, local supervisors in Tipperary and Waterford
seem to have taken some interest in the welfare of the men in the pits.
If there were some complaints about a truck system of payment being
introduced as part of the temperance system in the colliery community
at Bonmahon, the men on the whole appear to have been better paid
and more contented than other miners in the country.[15] Admittedly,
coal-mining operations in Ireland were few and far between, and those
of the Mining Company of Ireland were the only ones consistently to
show a profit.

The third group of temperance Protestants was related to the first,
urban cousins to the great landlords. Scions of old ascendancy fami-

lies, these wealthy Dublin lawyers, doctors, bankers, and clergymen came from what has been called the old middle class.[16] Physicians and clergymen from this group had daily contact with the urban poor, who had increased tremendously in number since the turn of the century as more and more people fled the countryside. These migrants brought little with them besides their poverty, and they soon put a strain on what charitable resources existed in their new communities. The problem was particularly acute in Dublin, where in 1829 the Society for the Relief of Sick and Indigent Room-Keepers—the title fairly describes the clientele—gave assistance to 13,674 persons, a number that would have appalled the eighteenth-century founders of the organization. Yet two years later the society had to provide for more than twenty-five thousand persons.[17] The principal Dublin charity, the Mendicity Institution, was "down to its last penny" in both 1828 and 1839, and in an effort to encourage contributions and save itself, "its directors were driven to the heart-rending necessity of parading the wretched inmates of the institution through the streets of the city with the hope that the exhibition of such a massive misery, while it filled the minds of the humane and benevolent with sorrow, would arouse the charity and the sympathy of the most callous and thoughtless."[18]

The crisis was compounded by the lack of a poor law and the likelihood of the imminent enactment of such a law, which would have established a mandated system of poor relief paid for from the taxes of the urban middle class. What do the misfortunes of the Dublin charities and the coming of a poor law have to do with temperance? A great deal, for the temperance movement seemed to point the way out of the confusion surrounding the debate over poverty.[19] In other words, temperance offered straightforward and simple answers to the problem for men who believed that if drinking did not lead to poverty, it certainly worsened the condition of the poor and tended to make that condition intractable. Furthermore, temperance was cheap since it threw the poor man back on his own resources and taught him that his intemperance was the cause of his poverty. Some concerned persons, like the editor of the leading Irish temperance journal, believed that the temperance system obviated the need for both voluntary charities and public relief entirely, asserting that "temperance societies are nothing more nor less than institutions for the prevention of pauperism, disease and crime."[20]

Not surprisingly, such people were disappointed when the pauper population of Dublin failed to enroll en masse in the new temperance societies. They woke one morning to find that the poor were still with them, along with the debt-ridden charities of the city and a new poor law. For the middle-class inhabitants of Dublin, poverty would continue to be expensive.

2

For the first seven or eight years of its existence the temperance movement was dominated by landlords, and the rest followed. Ulster was an important exception. There vigorous organizations existed in town and country alike. Though temperance was by no means the exclusive concern of Protestants at this early date, the leadership of the movement was in Protestant hands. Within a few years the situation would change remarkably as the late 1830s gave way to the 1840s.

First, the movement took off in the towns and cities of the south, where it had lacked much force, and in its newly invigorated state it had considerable impact on the countryside. Second, many Catholic clergymen, who had been rather aloof toward the movement, became active missionaries of temperance. Soon they dominated most temperance organizations in the south. A mass movement took the place of a lobby. What wealthy Protestants had fashioned from their own worries and anxieties was snatched away and used against them by their enemies. To many it appeared as if the great drama of the 1820s was having a rerun, with priests leading their flocks away from the landlords along the path of nationalist politics toward a new Ireland. Can this final phase of the great Irish temperance movement be interpreted in this light? Not exactly.

Let us look at what happened in the cities, especially Dublin and Cork. From 1837 to 1840 temperance activity escalated sharply in the two largest towns of Ireland: more people joined temperance societies, more temperance societies and other organizations such as reading rooms and coffee houses were established, and more tracts were circulated with a much greater effect than before.[21] In addition, the mood of this phase of the movement was one of confidence and enthusiasm. The second wave of temperance recruits went about converting others with great élan. They were not interested in preserving the traditional social and economic hierarchies of town or country or warding off a poor law but in bringing their fellow citizens into a movement that called for an all-consuming commitment. They had discovered the only true principle of temperance and had fashioned from it a new discipline sufficient for all the requirements of life itself. These new temperance people were teetotalers.

Of course, the movement had passed through the same evolution in America and England, and this pattern would be repeated elsewhere. The moderation system did not work well, and that failure suggested more drastic measures. Yet there are other factors worth considering regarding this important transition in the history of the Irish movement.

Most of the teetotal newcomers came from humbler backgrounds than their moderationist predecessors. The typical Cork or Dublin teetotaler was either a young professional man, a tradesman (in Irish usage a shopkeeper or someone who worked at a trade), an artisan, or a journeyman or apprentice.[22] Since the newcomers reacted strongly against the hierarchical nature of Irish society and the way society in their respective cities was dominated by a tiny elite, it is not surprising that they rejected a temperance system associated with that elite. As teetotalism itself is a radical response to a difficult problem, so the teetotalers of Dublin and Cork were political and social radicals. Temperance societies were not instruments of social control, to be manipulated by landlords or their urban kinsmen troubled by difficult tenants or servants, but brotherhoods for those who wanted a fundamental transformation in Irish society.

The assault on the old moderationist system aimed at several points where that system was most vulnerable. The old pledge that forbade the use of whiskey or other spirits, though allowing wine or beer, caused no difficulty for the port-loving upper classes. Fine wines continued to grace the dinner tables of the rich while the lower orders were denied their whiskey.[23] Moderationist gentlemen even kept brandy and whiskey on hand for their unconverted guests. High society remained unruffled by the temperance movement. Total abstainers were quick to charge moderationists with hypocrisy, saying that they were not truly committed to the movement they had launched. This criticism could be extended, with some disservice to logic, to all members of the upper classes: if the temperate rich had done little with their moderation system, look at all the rich and wellborn who had not joined it and had done precisely nothing. Arguments like these served as surprisingly effective attacks on a corrupt and oligarchical society.

Teetotal attitudes toward confirmed drunkards or alcoholics and toward the antislavery cause, then at its peak in the British Isles, are also revealing. Confirmed drunkards were pariahs, and moderationists wanted little to do with them, declaring that their societies were meant for people of an essentially sober nature who needed a little order and direction in their lives. Total abstainers, however, sought out alcoholics and, when they could get them to stop drinking, paraded them at teetotal meetings as triumphant examples of the new system. Some reformed drunkards, as they called recovered alcoholics, went on to become star attractions on temperance platforms, living examples of what teetotalism could do and what the moderation system had neglected. Brian Harrison has written eloquently about these aspects of the teetotal movement in England, and what he has to say holds true for Ireland as well.[24]

Yet there are some special points that need to be made clear in the Irish case. For many Irish teetotalers, the history of their country and its people was the history of every reformed drunkard writ large. Crushed, degraded, turned into an outcast by a social and economic system that drove him to drink, he hit bottom and was at last saved. Recovery brought strength and hope to the drunkard turned teetotaler, but he would never forget that he had been a slave to drink and would forever do what he could to help others recover their liberty. Analogies to slavery, images and metaphors drawn from the antislavery cause, fill the rhetoric of Irish teetotal advocates at this time. John Hockings, a well-known reformed drunkard from England, told a Dublin audience in the spring of 1838 that he was proud that he had joined the movement "for the liberation of slaves." Though he was referring to the antislavery movement, he went on to tell his audience what they instinctively knew, that there were "white slaves as well as black."[25] At another meeting in Dublin a man named Flynn remarked that gentlemen concerned with the black slaves of Jamaica would do well "to look to the slaves at home."[26] In Cork a teetotaler asserted that drunkenness itself "was the greatest slavery"—not a self-inflicted servitude, as was sometimes said, but an evil imposed on the lower orders by the upper classes.[27] A little parable told by a temperance man at a Dublin meeting in 1837 was repeated many times over the next few years. The ancient Spartans, it seems, at certain appropriate times exhibited drunken helots to their children so that they might be taught to recognize and despise true servility.[28] The Spartans had created a class of drunken, fawning slaves to serve them; the Irish upper classes had done no less to their fellow countrymen.

The onus of responsibility had shifted; it was the rich, not the poor, who were guilty. Antiaristocratic and antidifferential propaganda poured forth from the teetotal press in the late 1830s, by which time the movement had spread from town to country, where the moderationists had flourished and teetotalism would reign supreme. In 1841 a country teetotaler could write in doggerel what was felt to be increasingly true of a peasantry grown temperate and more socially and politically aware:

The gentry in the lurch are left;
The people march before them,
As patterns of sobriety,
Good order and decorum,
The temperate poor are nobler far
Than roaring, roystering grandees are.[29]

3

In the spring of 1838 one of the leading teetotalers of Cork, William Martin, got his friend Theobald Mathew to join the Cork Total Abstinence Society. Martin was a Quaker and Mathew a priest. Few of the

Catholic clergy had involved themselves in a movement where land-lords and urban radicals struggled for control. Father Mathew, then, was something of a catch. He thought he could do the cause some good, and he was right. John Francis Maguire, a local temperance advocate and Father Mathew's biographer, declared that he managed to enroll 156,000 new members in the Cork Total Abstinence Society and its many new branches during the first year of his leadership. By 1842 the organization claimed six million members, 75 percent of the population of the country.[30] Though these figures were exaggerated—it is impossible to say by how much—they point to an incredible effort and a phenomenal success. Even if these numbers are halved, they are still impressive. Where else could temperance ever claim such a victory?

More to the point, how was this triumph possible? Few people doubted that the great growth in the movement was the result of Father Mathew's own labors. He stood head and shoulders above his contemporaries, the author of a "mighty moral miracle."[31] As a priest he was certainly a logical choice for a leadership position in a movement whose membership was heavily Catholic, yet some of his attributes made the choice a particularly fortunate one. For years he had ministered to the poorest of the working people of Cork, a population swollen by the migration of many displaced cotters and farm laborers from the countryside. These people and their friends and relations throughout southwest Munster regarded him as a saint. If he urged them to give up drinking, many would listen. Without quite realizing it, Father Mathew was in a position to turn a fairly lively local organization into an important regional, and finally a national, movement as word of his temperance activities spread to the countryside.

He was helped enormously by his extensive contacts among clergy and lay people. These contacts reached throughout the country to a number of bishops, some of whom were close friends of his or of his family, and to many members of the lower clergy he had met during a priesthood of more than thirty years. The fact that as vicar-general of the Capuchin order in Ireland he was free of immediate episcopal control was also important. It gave him the freedom to go where he wanted and make what arrangements he needed in order to preach temperance. Soon his clerical friends began to write to him, asking that he pay their parishes a visit with the idea of starting a temperance society. Introductions to other priests followed, and by 1839 Father Mathew was writing to more and more clergymen offering his services as a temperance advocate.[32]

If some pastors were at first less than enthusiastic, there was a way to interest them. Father Mathew had a great deal of money at his disposal.

It was unusual for a priest, let alone a Capuchin friar who had taken a vow of poverty, to be well supplied with funds, but he was not a typical priest or monk. His family was a distinguished and noble one. His aunt was heiress to a great fortune that she promised to leave to him. For a time generous donations poured in from wealthy benefactors of the movement, making Theobald Mathew something of a temperance broker, able to call whole new societies into being with a timely gift to a priest eager to repair a church or even build a new one. There were all sorts of projects he supported, from temperance reading rooms to temperance bands. The former needed quarters and books and newspapers, the latter instruments, which proved to be far more popular and far more costly.

The system, if we can call it that, worked something like the Catholic Association, which had fought for Emancipation. Father Mathew played the role in which Daniel O'Connell had been cast, touring the country and preaching temperance wherever he went while enrolling batches of new recruits. The priests who joined the movement served as local organizers, as they had done for the Catholic Association, only instead of collecting the penny-a-month subscriptions from the faithful that went to O'Connell in Dublin, they took part in the distribution of Father Mathew's considerable largesse.[33]

Father Mathew's supporters among the laity were of a different sort. Most of them were Protestants; whenever the opportunity arose, he never failed to give credit to "the very first who had ever come forward to support him in this great work, members of the Society of Friends, Protestants and Presbyterians."[34] Whom did he have in mind? As the movement began to prosper, he thought less about the assistance given by William Martin, a fair example of an urban teetotal radical, and more about the help he got from Charles Bianconi, who ran one of the most important coaching companies in the country, or Lord Landsdowne, who was one of the greatest landowners of Ireland. His background, his manner, and his social connections helped secure their support. "Father Mathew was the pink of a gentleman," declared his biographer.[35] Daniel Owen Madden, the famous essayist, noted "his great suavity of manners" and added, "To the higher classes he was exceedingly respectful, and was always considered by them as one of their order."[36] Large employers and landlords, whose interest had flagged as the movement passed under the control of radical teetotalers, felt a lot better with Father Mathew at the helm. He was one of them, and he viewed the movement much as they did. Temperance was a means of bringing the upper and lower orders together, of healing the wounds of class and religious cleavage.

It was hoped that the new movement would create a sober work force and tenantry as well. For a time temperance landlords and employers were in the habit of dispatching their worst backsliders to Cork, telling them not to come back without one of Father Mathew's temperance medals.[37] By the later months of 1839 it occurred to these people that they might do well to reverse the process. The mountain was too big, and Muhammad would have to come to it. As a result, Father Mathew's temperance tours took in many of the great estates, towns, and cities where tenantry and workers could be gathered as well as the parishes in which he was welcome. Yet it is no good pretending that what happened can be explained simply in terms of his ability to deal with priests and landlords alike. The number of people who pledged exceeded all possible expectation as thousands of converts became millions.

One of the reasons for Father Mathew's involvement in the first place was the belief that temperance was the key to national regeneration. The thought was hardly novel; many teetotalers talked of how temperance would revive and strengthen Ireland, but Father Mathew laid special stress on the spiritual aspects of regeneration. The teetotal pledge became a sacred commitment and the temperance movement itself a great crusade. What matters more than Mathew's perception of the cause is the reaction of the men and women who took the pledge, for they welcomed a great crusade and accepted temperance in that spirit. They expected something like a miracle as well. When one considers that they attributed to Father Mathew thaumaturgical powers, despite his denials, the great acceleration in pledge taking is more understandable. Father Mathew, it was believed, could heal the sick, restore shaken faith, and stop the drunkard's drinking. This last miracle ability was a specialty, but his followers had no doubt he could work the others too. Of all the stories told about his adherents, one reveals—in terms comic though exaggerated and surely apocryphal—the degree to which Mathew was invested with magical powers by a people with great expectations. One day he thought he saw among the batches waiting to pledge someone who had been to see him just the day before. When he asked the man, he was told that yes, it was so. The man went on to explain that he had come back because the pledge had not worked. Immediately after taking it he drank a glass of whiskey, and it went down just as easily as it always had.

Drinking and pledging went hand in hand in other ways. Many of the people who came to him were drunk. Naturally his enemies had a field day. According to the high Tory paper, the *Dublin Evening Mail*, "the disciples of Father Mathew reel from the tap-room to the platform or the altar, as the case may be, brutalised with the vice they are about to renounce and take vows of sobriety with lips still moist with the liquor of intemperance."[38] Even Father Mathew's friends had to admit "that it was of very common occurrence to see a tipsy or even a drunken man take the pledge."[39] John Francis Maguire explained that such drunkenness resulted from a sort of leave-taking ritual: "With tears in his eyes, and even heart-rending sobs, more than one poor fellow tossed off his last pint of porter, or swallowed at a mouthful his 'last glass of whiskey.' "[40] Even so, elation mingled with sorrow in these rites, as the pledge taker expected a great transformation in his life— the sick would be healed, Ireland would prosper, its people would be made spiritually and physically whole. All would be changed utterly. The pledge was for such a people a great millenarian moment, which many would repeat again and again and again.

4

If the temperance movement captured the imagination of the country and filled many people with new hope, it left those hopes largely unfulfilled. Attempts to give explicit political meaning to the movement under the auspices of O'Connell's repeal campaign brought a reinvigorating second wind and a crisis in its wake. When Father Mathew said, "Ireland free is Ireland sober, and Ireland sober is Ireland free," he meant precisely that, nothing more nor less. He disliked O'Connell and his brand of nationalism, and it broke his heart to see his temperance bands marching off to repeal meetings.[41] Political controversy had compromised the cause. When the repeal campaign collapsed in 1843, much of the élan of the movement died with it. The onset of Mathew's own debilitating illness a few years later left his rearguard leaderless.

What remained was several significant results and an important legacy. The temperance movement did realize to an appreciable extent its basic purpose—not, of course, in turning Ireland into a nation of teetotalers, as Father Mathew would have liked, but in helping to create an atmosphere in which moderate, as opposed to excessive drinking, became the norm. Though Ireland still bears the stigma of a stereotype that harks back to the eighteenth and early nineteenth centuries, many people from that time would find the relative sobriety of post-Mathewite Ireland remarkable.

Father Mathew had two other goals in mind, which were to a considerable extent contradictory. The point has already been made that his notion of national regeneration was spiritual in nature—in fact, implicitly Catholic. He hoped to use the temperance movement to bring the people in closer touch with religion. The Catholic church in Ireland was not yet the great power it would become later. It had not enough

priests, churches, or money to serve its community. The funds at
Father Mathew's disposal helped many priests out of their most pressing difficulties. One can argue that what has been called the devotional
revolution, the process by which the fabric and organization of the
church were reordered so as to relate it more closely with its parishioners, can be traced back to the Mathewite movement.[42] Whatever the
number of churches built or repaired as a result of his efforts, Father
Mathew's movement did a great deal to strengthen the church and
instill a sense of pride and confidence among its members.

Father Mathew also wanted to heal the rift that had been widening
since Emancipation by finding a way of bringing Catholics and Protestants together. He thought temperance might be that way. Religious
hatred often masked class tensions, such as those that set landlords and
tenant against each other. Mathew, a Catholic from a landlord family,
was especially aware of the distrust and animosity that marred relations between the haves and have-nots of the countryside. The pre-
Mathewite phase of the movement had been dominated by a few
landlords who had exhibited what was for Ireland a rare interest in
their tenants' futures. Father Mathew encouraged those tendencies,
and under his leadership temperance became a well-oiled engine of
paternalism.

Did the movement serve landlord interest? Did it contribute to social
peace and harmony in the countryside? Over the short term the answers must be yes. All sorts of testimony attest to the fall in violent
drink-related crime and disorder.[43] Ireland became a much more
peaceful place as a result of the temperance campaign. While Father
Mathew still lived, the great potato famine struck the country. He
spent his last years appealing to the government for aid and organizing
famine relief; still, nearly one million people starved to death or died
of famine fever.

Though temperance helped create an era of good feeling between
landlord and tenant, it failed to improve relations between Catholics
and Protestants generally. Despite the appearance of good fellowship
and cooperation, including strenuous attempts to keep the movement
free of sectarian bias that extended to the most scrupulous sorts of
arrangements concerning meetings, reading rooms, and the like, the
teetotal alliance was severely strained as a result of growing sectarian
discord.

Considering that teetotalism began to spread like wildfire among a
Catholic population, the mode of its organization with priests playing a
decided role, it is little wonder that the whole movement began to look
parochial. Some teetotal priests welcomed the change, either because
they saw it as an expression of growing Catholic strength or because

they had been disturbed by the strongly Protestant flavor of the pre-Mathewite movement. Indeed, several clergymen put themselves at the head of parish temperance societies, the better to fight Protestant proselytism among their flocks.[44]

Publicists who climbed on the bandwagon often aggravated the issue by pointing to the way the temperance cause had prospered under Catholic auspices. The *Dublin Evening Post*, edited by F. L. Conway, took this line, congratulating "the Catholic clergy of Ireland, who must after all be the chief instruments in this blessed work." While Protestants had been in control, the whole affair "had smealt to[o] strongly of the conventicle." The sensible thing for Protestants to do was to go among their own unconverted; they should preach temperance in the Orange Lodges, "and the miserable dupes that attend them would be restored—in one word—to their sense."[45]

Protestant sentiments mirrored Catholic ones. Mathew's brand of temperance was a mishmash of ritual and fakery, a mumbo jumbo for drunkards and crazed fanatics; there was no real sense or meaning left in it. Furthermore, many people who had worked hard to propagate temperance resented upstarts like Conway telling them what to do. Several old stalwarts founded the Protestant Total Abstinence Society in Dublin in May 1840. The Reverend J. P. Sargent, its first vice president, pointed out that a number of Dublin dissenters had begun the good work in their city many years before. He was certain that all at the inaugural meeting shared his delight that the cause was at least attracting the interest of Catholics—so much so that they (the Protestants) might be left to themselves and their own societies where they could pray as Protestants, an activity they had once forsworn to entice Catholics to their meetings. He was sorry if those Catholics who were in the habit of attending were upset "at our new form of meeting but now our first duty lies to our fellow Protestants."[46]

Little scenes like this one were repeated all over the south of Ireland; the reaction in the Protestant north was even more emphatic. There it was said that "the temperance Reformation is the John the Baptist, or the forerunner of a great revival of religion," and "the only true temperance is the temperance of the Bible."[47] Such attitudes, though exclusive, were mild in comparison with the ugly feelings that sometimes found expression in threatening words and violence. Father Mathew never visited the Protestant heartland of Ulster. Though he was not going to find many recruits there, it was the Catholic bishops who warned him off. They told him that any temperance tour he might make in their part of Ireland could end in riot and bloodshed and that no one could guarantee his safety.

The temperance movement, then, left a legacy of bitterness and a growing polarization between the two religious communities. As the Mathewite movement reached its peak in the south, it became more decidedly a political movement, much to Father Mathew's chagrin. Temperance and nationalist politics were now tied together, a connection that became yet more obvious in the great temperance revival of the 1880s. Furthermore, the temperance of this later period was exclusively linked with the Catholic church. The pledger's medal had become a badge of militant Catholic nationalism. In Ulster this process happened in reverse. As the cause became more purely sectarian, it served to foster separatism among the Protestants of the province. This great movement in strengthening and institutionalizing religious and regional differences played a considerable part in bringing about the tragic division that exists within Ireland today.

NOTES

I would like to thank Montclair State College for an award from their Summer Stipend Fund that greatly assisted in the preparation of this essay.

1. *Fifth Report of the Commissioners of Inquiry into the Collection and Management of the Revenue Arising in Ireland; Distilleries, Parliamentary Papers* (1823), vii; *Report from the Select Committee on the Employment of the Poor in Ireland; Parliamentary Papers* (1823), vi; *Third Report on the State of Ireland; Parliamentary Papers* (1825), viii; *First Report of Evidence from the Select Committee on the State of the Poor in Ireland; Parliamentary Papers* (1830), vii.

2. For example, Charles Haliday, *An Inquiry into the Influence of the Excessive Use of Spiritous Liquors in Producing Crime, Disease and Poverty in Ireland* (Dublin, 1830), Royal Irish Academy Pamphlet Collection; Johann Georg Kohl, *Travels in Ireland* (London, 1844), 180–192.

3. P. T. Winskill, *The Temperance Movement and Its Workers: A Record of Social, Moral, Religious and Political Progress* (London, 1891), 1:50.

4. W. A. Maguire, *The Downshire Estates in Ireland, 1801-1845* (Oxford, 1972), 42, 71–74, 172–173, 225–227.

5. Maguire, *Downshire Estates*, 225–227. Edward Maclysaught, *The Kenmare Manuscripts* (Dublin, 1942), xi.

6. *Irish Temperance and Literary Gazette*, January 7, 1837.

7. *Irish Temperance and Literary Gazette*, November 12, 19, 1836, January 7, 1837.

8. *Irish Temperance and Literary Gazette*, September 16, November 12, February 18, 1837.

9. Robert Browne Clayton, *A Few Facts and Observations, Illustrative of the Baneful Effects of Intoxication in Ireland; Showing the Necessity and Benefit of Temperance Societies* (Bristol, 1830), 1–10, Royal Irish Academy Pamphlet Collection.

10. *Irish Temperance and Literary Gazette*, November 19, 1836.

11. *Irish Temperance and Literary Gazette*, September 16, 1837.

12. *Hibernian Temperance Society, Paper F. Calculations, Shewing the Extensive*

Encouragement Which Could Be Given to Manufactures in Ireland with the Money Spent on Whiskey (Dublin, 1830); W. Neilson Hancock, *Is There Really a Want of Capital in Ireland?* (Dublin, 1848), Royal Irish Academy Pamphlet Collection.

13. Dr. Andre Fitzpatrick believes that Malcolmson's ties with a number of fellow Quakers in England permitted him to break into the trade there. If so, one wonders why other Irish Quakers in the textile business did not make use of those connections.

14. *Irish Temperance and Literary Gazette*, January 13, 1838.

15. *The Miner, a Poem Founded on the Facts Connected with the Present State of the Temperance Cause in Bonmahon, in the County of Waterford* (Waterford, 1841).

16. R. S. Neale, "Class and Class Consciousness in Early Nineteenth-Century England: Three Classes or Five?" *Victorian Studies* 12 (September 1968): # 7ff.

17. "Statistical Report upon the Principal Charitable Institutions in the City of Dublin," in *First Report of His Majesty's Commission of Inquiry into the Condition of the Poorer Classes in Ireland, Parliamentary Papers* (hereafter *Whately Commission*), vol. 30 (1836), 3a.

18. *Twenty-Second Annual Report of the Managing Committee of the Institution for the Suppression of Mendicity in Dublin (for the Year 1839)* (Dublin, 1840), Royal Irish Academy Pamphlet Collection.

19. *Whately Commission*, vol. 30 (1836), appendix (C), part 2, p. 9, vol. 24, appendix (G), "Report on the State of the Irish Poor in Great Britain"; [Charles Haliday], *Observations on the Habits of the Labouring Classes Suggested by Mr. G. C. Lewis' Report on the State of the Irish Poor in Great Britain* (Dublin, 1836), 40.

20. *Irish Temperance and Literary Gazette*, June 17, 1837.

21. *Dublin Weekly Herald*, November 2, December 28, 1839.

22. *Dublin Weekly Herald*, June 1, 22, July 6, 20, August 3, September 7, October 26, 1839.

23. *Dublin Weekly Herald*, January 16, 1840.

24. Brian Harrison, *Drink and the Victorians: the Temperance Question in England, 1815–1872* (London, 1971), 107–126.

25. *Irish Temperance and Literary Gazette*, May 5, 1838.

26. *Dublin Weekly Herald*, January 23, 1841.

27. *Dublin Weekly Herald*, June 26, 1841.

28. *Irish Temperance and Literary Gazette*, October 7, 1837.

29. *Dublin Weekly Herald*, January 2, 1841.

30. John Francis Maguire, *Father Mathew: A Biography* (New York, 1887), 111.

31. Samuel Carter Hall, *Ireland: Its Scenery and Character*, (London, n.d.), 1:27. James Birmingham, *A Memoir of the Very Rev. Theobald Mathew, with an Account of the Rise and Progress of Temperance in Ireland* (Dublin, 1840), 12–20.

32. There are hundreds of these sorts of letters among the Mathew Papers, Capuchin Archive, Raheeny, County Dublin; see also John Nolan, Vice President of Saint Mary's Temperance Society, to the editor, *Limerick Chronicle*, November 23, 1839.

33. *Cork Total Abstainer*, May 22, 1841; Eugene O'Reilly, P.P., to the Very Rev. Theobald Mathew, Navan, August 9, 1840, Mathew Papers.

34. *An Accurate Report of the Proceedings of the Very Rev. Theobald Mathew in the*

Cause of Temperance When Eight Thousand Persons Took the Pledge (Dublin, 1840), Haliday Pamphlet Collection, vol. 1783, Royal Irish Academy.

35. Maguire, *Mathew*, 64.

36. Daniel Owen Madden, *Ireland and Its Rulers since 1829*, (London, 1845) 1:279–280.

37. *Dublin Weekly Herald*, November 2, 1839. The temperance medals were to cost Father Mathew a great deal of money and many problems. The custom of giving medals to new converts was enthusiastically adopted, if not actually begun, by a few members of the aristocracy, such as Lord Annesley, who liked to distribute temperance medals to the children of his tenants. *Irish Temperance and Literary Gazette*, March 17, 1838.

38. *Dublin Evening Mail*, January 24, 1840.

39. Maguire, *Mathew*, 130.

40. Maguire, *Mathew*, 130–131.

41. Theobald Mathew to Thomas Cooke, Esq., April 28, 1846; idem to Miss N. A. Greg, n.d.; idem to E. Carolan, Esq., n.d., all Mathew Papers.

42. Emmet Larkin, "The Devotional Revolution in Ireland," *American Historical Review* 77 (June 1972): 627ff.

43. Outrage Papers, 1839–1842, State Paper Office, Dublin Castle.

44. *Dublin Evening Post*, January 9, 1840; *Dublin Weekly Herald*, July 3, 1841.

45. *Dublin Evening Post*, November 9, 1838.

46. *Dublin Weekly Herald*, August 15, 1840.

47. *Ulster Missionary*, July 1, 1841; *Christian Patriot*, September 21, 1839.

EIGHT

Drunks, Brewers, and Chiefs:
Alcohol Regulation in Colonial Kenya,
1900–1939

Charles H. Ambler

From the earliest years of the colonial intrusion in the central region of Kenya British officers complained repeatedly and vehemently of the dangers posed by endemic drunkenness in the rural districts under their authority. They traced a striking increase in alcohol use, seeing this rise as the product of the disintegration of traditional social and economic relationships and as a source of disorder. In report after report officials characterized intemperance as the cause of disrespect, indolence, and criminality. Initially the British responded to this perceived threat simply by attempting to suppress the production, sale, and consumption of local beer in certain areas and to particular segments of the population. In the years after the First World War, however, officials developed new perceptions of the roles and importance of beer brewers, sellers, and drinkers. Gradually the administration abandoned its earlier, and largely fruitless, efforts to impose prohibition and moved increasingly toward the regulation of brewing and drinking. My basic concern in this essay is to relate the evolution and application of these policies to the shadowy reality of alcohol production and use in rural central Kenya in the period prior to the Second World War. Examination of the complex interplay between the evolving norms of alcohol use and official policy not only reveals changing drinking patterns but also provides insight into the varied and complex processes through which a new—colonial—order was superimposed on the small-scale peasant societies of Kenya.[1]

1

Central Kenya occupies the country sloping away from the foothills of the Nyandarua range and Mount Kenya some one hundred miles to the east and south.[2] During the nineteenth century, as today, most of the inhabitants of the region adhered to cultural traditions associated with one of several closely related Bantu languages—Kikuyu, Embu, Meru, and Kamba. But these larger ethnic bonds had little practical importance. Societies throughout the region were small in scale, tightly knit, and highly autonomous. Local economies were based in arable farming; but all families had at least some livestock, and some wealthy men owned substantial herds. Though such notables sometimes possessed considerable influence, authority essentially remained in the hands of the elders, who maintained their positions through control over labor and surplus.[3]

Alcoholic beverages were regularly consumed in all nineteenth-century central Kenyan communities. No child was initiated, no marriage arranged, no planting or harvesting begun, no important case decided without the preparation, consumption, or offering of beer. Alcoholic drinks had both ritual and social significance. When a homestead was opened, for instance, neighbors assembled to drink and socialize, but first a gourdful of beer was hung in the house and drops sprinkled across the yard to honor ancestors. Similarly, the presentation and consumption of beer in the course of marriage negotiations sanctified the new bond between families and lineages.[4]

Across central Kenya customary law closely regulated the preparation and consumption of beer. Although conventions varied somewhat from society to society, women usually were expected either to abstain or only to drink sparingly. In some areas they were excluded not only from drinking but also from any involvement whatsoever in the preparation of beer.[5] As a rule, young men prepared beer, whereas drinking itself remained the exclusive preserve of elders.[6] Excepting occasional ritual drinks, men were meant to avoid beer until they had married and had children of circumcision age. It was held to be both unhealthy and dangerous to permit youths to drink. Machakos people complained that beer "settles in the legs."[7] More pointedly, a Kikuyu proverb warned youths that "one goes to fight holding a spear, not a container of beer."[8]

The right to drink was a mark of the privileges and responsibilities of the rulers. Beer parties provided opportunities for elders to let down their guard and forget their duties.[9] But the consumption of beer in the course of consideration of community matters also gave symbolic weight to such deliberations. When a man sent word to his peers that he had brewed beer, it signaled his wish to discuss an important issue. As Ivan Karp has pointed out, the ensuing beer party provided a context in which conflicts could be aired and various points of view expressed.[10] The presentation to guests of large amounts of beer demonstrated a man's access to labor and raw materials and hence his wealth, influence, and position.[11]

Few men could afford to brew large quantities of beer on a regular basis. Although some beer was made from millet or honey, most was prepared from sugarcane. The cane was first cut into long pieces, which were crushed with large wooden mortars. The juice was then squeezed from the pulp, filtered, and allowed to ferment in large calabashes for a day or so until it was ready to drink.[12] Given the technology available, substantial amounts of labor were required to produce beer in quantity; thus it is likely that manpower would only occasionally have been diverted to this task. In any case beer could only be brewed during those seasons when the raw materials could be had in adequate quantities, particularly in the drier sections of the region where extensive cane cultivation was not practicable and where the elders depended more on honey than on cane for beer production.[13] The seasonal pattern of supply encouraged sporadic but heavy drinking. Since the beer itself was highly perishable, drinkers were encouraged to consume large quantities at one time. Thus, despite the fact that cane beer did not have a high alcoholic content, drinking parties often ended in general intoxication.[14]

Scholars have generally taken the view that drinking in preindustrial societies was a highly integrated activity and that drunkenness, where it occurred, fell well within the bounds of accepted and responsible behavior.[15] Certainly, it was the case that the tightly knit communities of central Kenya had little tolerance for antisocial conduct of any sort. But even if obnoxious drunkenness was largely kept in check (or out of sight), the possibility remains that individuals sometimes struggled with alcohol addiction.[16] Those proverbial warnings against drinking among youths at least suggest that societies conceived of alcohol consumption as potentially dangerous.

2

Beginning about 1890 the advance of British power gradually drew the small communities of central Kenya within the economic and political structures of the emerging colonial state. Early in the new century vast tracts of land adjacent to central Kenya were set aside for white commercial farming, while at the same time the British established their capital on the southern margin of the region, at the new settlement of

Nairobi. As a result the sometimes violent pace of imperial expansion accelerated. By 1910 at least the pretense of colonial control had been asserted everywhere in central Kenya. Soon thereafter the acute competition for labor and supplies occasioned by the outbreak of the First World War forced the administration to consolidate its position. Throughout the region the British ruled through designated local leaders, generally called chiefs or headmen. Although the colonial authorities made an effort to select influential individuals as their local representatives, in fact the new chiefs possessed little traditional legitimacy. They were in effect low-level colonial bureaucrats and thus fundamentally creatures of the new order.

The progressive incorporation of central Kenyan communities in a colonial economy rapidly undermined the stability of established drinking practices. The creation of bulk transport facilities and the related extension of externally based retail trade networks into the region gave central Kenyans regular and relatively easy access to imported processed sugar. These developments also permitted the importation of mechanical cane crushers. A trader in Kitui had set up one of these ox-driven mills as early as 1910.[17] By 1914 more than fifty-five were in operation in neighboring Machakos District processing locally grown cane.[18] Some of the sugar produced was exported, but considerable amounts were sold to consumers in the immediate areas. In fact, all across central Kenya it was the sale of sugar and the introduction of cane mills that propelled the expansion of trade during the early colonial years.[19] The rising demand for agricultural produce and labor also provided the opportunity for residents of rural communities to earn the money necessary to buy sugar and even the mills themselves.

It was a relatively simple task to produce beer from refined sugar. The elimination of hand crushing removed many of the complications of brewing, sharply reduced the amount of labor involved in beer preparation, and thus ultimately lowered the price. In addition, seasonal constraints on beer making were largely removed; imported refined sugar was available throughout the year, as for the most part was sugar processed from locally grown cane.[20] The ease and speed with which beer could be produced from purchased sugar much increased the opportunities for surreptitious brewing and drinking. Moreover, the growth of the sugar trade put access to the raw materials of beer production outside the realm of the household economy and hence beyond the control of elders. At the same time wage labor gave growing numbers of male youths—traditionally forbidden to drink beer—the cash to buy sugar.

It was the common assumption among European observers that

these changes sustained a substantial increase in alcohol consumption —an increase that was marked by a striking and ominous rise in the incidence of disruptive drunken behavior.[21] This "problem" of drunkenness is well known, of course, to those who have studied labor migration and urbanization in colonial Africa, but it was the rapid expansion of drinking in the rural areas that preoccupied the Kenyan administration. A more measured assessment, including the study of oral records, suggests that drunkenness was actually far less pervasive than colonial reports suggest. Nevertheless, even if the official hysteria was largely misplaced, the actions taken by the state to control alcohol were in some cases far-reaching in their effects.

3

Almost from the inception of colonial rule in the mid-1890s British officials saw drunkenness among the African population as a serious problem. As early as 1897 the administrator of Machakos District, John Ainsworth, described drinking in that area as "excessive,...too awful."[22] In fact, colonial reports for the period before 1920 preserve a regular litany of claims of alcohol abuse.[23] Not surprisingly, when the responsibilities of chiefs and headmen were laid down in the Native Authority Ordinance of 1912, prominent among them were the regulation of beer preparation and beer drinking.[24]

With the foundations of their authority still tenuous, officials assumed there was a close causal relationship between drinking and disorder. Administrators repeatedly linked drunkenness to instances of violence. In 1910 in the Migwani section of Kitui District the son of the local chief supposedly killed a man in the midst of a "drunken brawl."[25] The officer in charge in Dagoretti in southern Kikuyuland reported five cases of alcohol-related murders or attempted murders during 1912.[26] Much greater attention, however, was focused on the supposedly disruptive social impact of drinking among youths.

According to official reports, changes in customary drinking practices came rapidly. As early as 1910 an officer stationed in Kiambu District, just north of Nairobi, went so far as to assert that "the old tribal restrictions as to the age limit for beer drinking have largely disappeared, the younger men drink now."[27] In the same area two years later intoxication was seen as the source of "constant fighting and disorders created by the young natives in the District."[28] Similar comments appeared regularly in reports from most sections of the region during the years from about 1910 until the end of the First World War. Accounts of the seriousness of the drinking varied considerably, but the "drunkenness problem" was defined with remarkable consistency.

Colonial officials argued that alcohol emboldened youths to assert their independence and defy the elders—the result being a general breakdown in "tribal discipline." In an effort to combat what was viewed as a volatile situation, the administration attempted, beginning in 1912, to impose increasingly restrictive regulations governing beer preparation and consumption.

British efforts to control the alcohol consumption of Kenyan Africans in effect date from the 1890 Act of Brussels, which among other provisions forbade the export of spirits to East Africa.[29] Whereas substantial amounts of liquor were imported to fill the demands of the growing population of white settlers, the colonial administration apparently acted consistently and forcefully to keep such liquor out of the hands of Africans. By 1907 the first feeble attempts had been made to devise legislation regulating the manufacture and sale of locally produced "native intoxicating liquors."[30] During the same period chiefs and headmen were empowered to impose temporary bans on drinking and on ceremonies, such as circumcisions, during which heavy drinking commonly occurred. But it was not until 1912 that the first efforts were made to apply permanent restrictions aimed specifically at combatting what were regarded as dangerous alterations of customary consumption patterns.[31]

Late in that year officials in Kiambu District set down a series of rules governing the use of alcohol. The most important of these new regulations was the complete prohibition of drinking imposed on men under the approximate age of thirty. In addition, the administration banned "purposeless drinking bouts" for people of any age and made nuisance drunkenness an offense. Substantial fines were set for violators: first offenders were to pay fifteen rupees, second thirty, and third seventy-five, at a time when the salary of a typical laborer generally amounted to no more than five or six rupees for an entire month's work. Similar restrictions were adopted in Nyeri in 1913 and in Embu and Machakos in 1916.[32]

These regulations apparently did little to change behavior or produce revenue since enforcement (usually the responsibility of chiefs and headmen) was sporadic or nonexistent. At best, illicit drinking was done less openly.[33] Recognizing this failure, officials began in 1916 to shift the direction of their assault on alcohol toward restrictions on access to the essential raw material of brewing—sugar. In that year the Machakos administration not only placed age limitations on drinking and abolished the use of beer in local court hearings but severely limited imports of refined sugar and banned the operation of crushing mills outright. The same regulations were applied in part in Kitui and Kiambu districts as well, leading—according to an official report—to an immediate 80 percent reduction in beer sales.[34]

Despite these early claims of success, by 1918 beer drinking in Kiambu was once again described as pervasive. At a large public meeting at Dagoretti the provincial commissioner felt moved to place his greatest emphasis on "the evils of excessive drinking."[35] In the official view a bad situation was made worse by the return home of thousands of young men recruited as carriers for service in the military campaigns against German forces in East Africa. These youths, the official argument went, were wasting their time and money on drink at a time when the region was feeling the combined painful effects of severe drought and the global outbreak of influenza. The local Kiambu administration restated existing age restrictions and extended regulations establishing the occasions for which beer could be produced and the amounts permissible. Drunkenness in any circumstance was made an offense for men and women of all ages. During 1919 and 1920 the other Kikuyuland districts, Fort Hall and Nyeri, adopted similar rules.[36]

By 1920 a complex of regulations severely limited the legal production and consumption of alcoholic beverages. Although these regulations were often ignored, the colonial regime nevertheless possessed powerful and effective weapons of control. In the countryside British officials might find it impossible to enforce absolute compliance with the new rules of consumption, but the administration, with its commanding power over the structures of the colonial economy, clearly did have the capacity to restrict beer production by cutting off supplies of raw materials.

4

The "epidemic of drunkenness" in Central Kenya apparently had as much to do with official insecurities and frustrations as with actual alcohol abuse. The administration regarded control of drinking as a major task of its local agents, but actual descriptions of increasing alcohol consumption, though frequently alarmist, appear only irregularly in colonial records.[37] Examined as a body, these reports are both inconsistent and vague. Indeed, the striking absence of specific evidence of disruptive drunken behavior suggests that the preoccupations of particular administrators lay behind many of the sensational claims of excessive drinking. Oral records contain a similar lack of information on alcohol use, but what there is places drinking squarely within the context of socially condoned activities. The fact that testimonies have little to say about drinking, or about the seemingly harsh regulations imposed to control it, suggests that these were not issues that pressed heavily on people's lives.[38]

In interviews former chiefs and other minor functionaries of the

colonial regimes (as well as members of their families) only rarely
mentioned enforcement of alcohol ordinances in descriptions of their
duties. Certainly, new patterns of drinking were emerging, but it does
not appear that these changes translated at that point into anything
resembling a threat to the social order. Given the clear correlation
between reports of rising drunkenness and periods of social unrest, it
seems fair to assume that colonial administrators often sought to explain away more complex phenomena with charges of alcohol abuse.

In fact, colonial administrators often did not understand a great
deal of what went on in the communities surrounding their posts.
Although many were keen students of ethnology, most carried with
them stereotypical and highly simplistic preconceptions of African
mentality and behavior. Common among these ideas was the notion
that Africans could not hold their liquor.[39] But Europeans and Africans had markedly different attitudes as to what constituted appropriate drinking behavior. What Europeans regarded as obnoxious drunkenness Africans generally placed within the limits of acceptable
conduct. As William Taylor has pointed out, Europeans have traditionally placed great emphasis on their ability to function "normally"
whatever the amount they may have drunk.[40] But in the societies of
central Kenya drinkers did not mind losing control; in fact, they
relished it. Anthropologist Gerhard Lindblom noted that in Machakos
around 1910 it was common to observe beer party participants "considerably the worse for liquor." He recalled as well that on such occasions "the *atumia* [elders], generally so careful about their dignity,
forget it, and sing, babble and gesticulate in a way that is very amusing."[41]

Early British administrators generally took a less benign view of
drunken behavior. To them, drinking made Africans both unpredictable and dangerous, in the process eroding the veneer of obeisance
that made control possible. To the rulers (although probably not to the
ruled), drunkenness suggested the fragility of the intricate networks of
collaboration that permitted one or two British officials to rule vast
districts with apparent ease. Hence, the regulations on drinking imposed after 1912 generally included some antinuisance provisions
prohibiting flamboyant, if harmless, behavior, such as incoherent
speech, inability to stand, and walking about "naked and shouting and
in public."[42] Even more obvious was the intent of a regulation that
made elders subject to fines if they drank before meetings with administrative officers or when officers were visiting their locations.[43] There
was considerable irony in this concern for African drunkenness since
beginning at this time a segment of the white population of Kenya was
earning a well-deserved reputation for flamboyant drug and alcohol
abuse.[44]

Of course, drinking among whites did not appear to interfere with the preservation of order. The assumption among Europeans was that alcohol dissolved whatever rationality Africans possessed; hence, Africans who had been drinking could be expected to be rude, insolent, and even rebellious. For example, officials in Nyanza in western Kenya maintained that stalwart supporters of the Dini ya Msambwa protest movement were excessive drinkers.[45] The evidence concerning central Kenya reveals no similar assertion of a link between drinking and political activism, but it is surely significant that the periods of most rigorous alcohol regulation, from 1916 to 1920 and again in the late 1920s, corresponded to periods of unusual social and political unrest.

Not surprisingly, the particular target of alcohol prohibitions was young males of the warrior age. Across central Kenya the warrior class enjoyed a kind of privileged existence. Its carefully cultivated dress and demeanor suggested narcissism, self-confidence, and even arrogance—qualities that were little valued at district headquarters. Youths devoted themselves especially to dancing; in the words of one elder, "the task of the *mwanake* [youth or warrior] was first to be a fighter and next to dance."[46] They spent long hours preparing their clothing, hair, and ornaments and practicing for communal dances that could go on for days.

Administrators saw the fever pitch of these dances as inherently dangerous. According to one report, "the dance is characterized by extreme licentiousness and lawlessness. The dancers become very excited and reckless. For this reason more serious crimes are expected at this time."[47] British officials did not suggest that dances were the occasion for excessive drinking, but they did view the two activities similarly—as sources of disorder. Moreover, they responded to each in much the same way. Beginning as early as 1910 the administration restricted participation in dances and in some cases banned them outright. Officials argued that such steps were warranted by the necessity of maintaining order within the context of a putative tribal system.[48] Notwithstanding the claims made about the preservation of traditional authority relationships, the basic objective of the administration in its attempts to restrict dancing—and drinking—was the domestication of the warrior class. In the Kiambu District records the 1912 notice of the complete prohibition of warrior dances was placed in a file labeled "Prohibiting Acts or Conduct Likely to Cause a Riot."[49] By 1919 the authorities in Fort Hall District were even considering forbidding youths to wear traditional warrior headdresses.[50]

Measures taken to control brewing and drinking were meant not only to preserve order but also to encourage the free flow of labor out of peasant communities. In the official mind drinking simply encouraged a strong natural inclination to sloth. Evaluations of colonial func-

tionaries frequently linked laziness to alcohol. In 1910 the governor
told a meeting of chiefs in Kiambu that if "they idled away their time
and went to beer drinks, they would be taxed very heavily."[51] Greater
attention was focused, however, on the role of drinking in discourag-
ing young men from engaging in wage labor. Repeatedly during the
period from 1910 to 1920 the issues of work and drink were connected
in official reports and in records of public meetings.

By 1912 the rapid expansion of both public works and white settler
agriculture had created considerable competition for labor in Kenya.
Private employers as well as many colonial officials charged that young
males formed a kind of leisure class, spending their time drinking and
attending dances instead of seeking work. Youths from Machakos and
Kitui districts—areas that provided significantly fewer migrant laborers
than other parts of central Kenya—were singled out as particularly
"indolent."[52] Faced with the delicate task of encouraging labor recruitment, local officers looked with special disfavor on any able-bodied
young men engaged in brewing or drinking beer. However, the relationship between alcohol consumption and participation in the wage
economy was complicated. To young men, part of the attraction of
seeking a job was the opportunity that such work provided to get out
from under the control of elders, to do the things that were frowned on
at home—such as drinking. In fact, employers often used the availability of alcohol as a lure to attract workers.[53]

The desire to drink was probably more likely to draw youths into
wage labor than it was to keep them at home, but administrators
nevertheless continued to cite drinking as an explanation for the failure of local populations to conform to the objectives of the colonial
system. Thus, it is hardly surprising to find that as pressures on the
labor force built toward the mass wartime impressment of carrier
recruits, regulations governing alcohol production and use became not
only increasingly harsh but increasingly removed from reality as well.
A 1917 description of the highlands districts noted that such a large
proportion of the population had left to go to work that it was possible
to walk "for miles in the heart of the reserve without seeing a young
able-bodied native anywhere."[54] Yet at the same time officials in these
areas continued to point to drinking by youths as a serious problem in
labor supply.

Even if they exaggerated the incidence and disruptiveness of increased drinking by youths, the British were certainly right to relate
changing drinking habits to deep generational tensions. Still, alcohol
was not really the cause of these conflicts. Whatever its scale, increased
beer drinking was essentially just an emblem of far more fundamental
change. Certainly, it was wishful thinking on the part of officials to

imagine that by stamping out illicit alcohol consumption among young men, they would restore the hegemony of the elders.

Basic British policies, aimed at achieving the integration of rural communities in a larger colonial political economy, inexorably undermined established institutions, fragmenting the traditional patterns of authority in the countryside. A Kiambu elder summed up the situation at a public meeting in 1912: "After returning from work in the towns and wearing clothes our young men are spoilt. They are different men. Those who return from monthly work are as yet unspoilt, but they don't bring their money to their fathers as before, they disobey the orders of the elders and think only of themselves."[55] Wages in the hands of youths implied a threat to the control of elders over the circulation of women and bridewealth, the fundamental basis of their authority. Ultimately, young men who did not depend on their fathers for wives were free to act—and hence drink—as they pleased.[56]

The harder the administration struggled to preserve (or invent) traditional local political institutions, the clearer it became to all that authority flowed from the central government. In these circumstances designated headmen and chiefs rapidly monopolized power in their particular localities, and the elders found themselves increasingly marginalized. It is hardly surprising to find that some elders themselves began to press the administration for restrictions on alcohol consumption, notably by youths and women. Indeed, to confirm this support, the administration cleverly dispersed to the elders a portion of the fines collected for violations of alcohol-related offenses.[57]

Ironically, the decline of the elders was reflected in changes in their own drinking behavior. Previously the presence of beer at council meetings had signified the importance of the deliberations that would take place. Under the colonial order elders continued to command respect, but in practice they became increasingly irrelevant. Beer drinking among elders was likewise robbed of its political and judicial significance. Beer parties became largely social, their frequent incidence a sign of boredom and the need of companionship. Describing Kikuyuland in the 1920s, a Roman Catholic missionary wrote, "Whenever there happens to be a beer drink on, a new sense of vigor seems to pervade [the elder's] limbs.... To him that day is a red letter day in a grey life that completely holds him in bondage. At other times he sits quietly on his stool waiting his time to pass over.[58]

5

In the period between the wars the state approach to alcohol restriction gradually shifted away from the previous uneven and somewhat hysterical attempt at suppression toward a more comprehensive policy of management and regulation. In the early 1920s drinking was rarely an issue. Officials were content to congratulate themselves on the success of existing rules, going so far as to attribute the supposed prosperity of peasant communities to controls on sugar production and sales.[59] Beer drinking came to be thought of less as a threat to colonial authority than as a symbol of the survival of archaic custom. In one official's words, "The young natives returned from contact with civilisation [after the First World War] to find that their elders were still steeped in Ancient Law, Bribery, Superstition and Tembo [local beer]."[60] Administrative records frequently describe as drunkards those chiefs who were regarded as unprogressive. This view was generally shared by the considerable number of central Kenyans—mostly young men—who became Christians during this period. As one man recalled, "I left all traditional ways of life and decided to join the Christians. Before, I had been drinking beer and dancing and other bad things."[61] Protestants took an increasingly strong stand against any involvement in brewing or drinking. To both traditionalists and Christians, the term *drinker* became a shorthand label for those who resisted conversion to Christianity.[62]

Beginning in 1925 pressures for restrictions on alcohol began to build again. Local representative councils in both Kitui and Embu urged a tightening of the prohibitions against drinking by youths. Over the next several years complaints appear of excessive drinking in Kitui, Fort Hall, and Embu districts, but the official response was relatively restrained. Rules governing sugar trading were enforced with renewed vigor, and in 1927 crushing mills were closed down throughout Kikuyu Province. As during the years between 1912 and 1920, drinking and dancing were linked, and repeated attempts were made to ban youth dances, especially in Kitui. Once again, the assault on drinking reflected an intensified demand for labor. However, officials increasingly acknowledged that restrictions on youth activities actually had little impact on the flow of workers out of their communities.[63] Nevertheless, the labor issue was not irrelevant since the scale and methods of recruitment at the time were such that dislocation and attendant discontent were inevitable.[64]

This period was in fact one of considerable political unrest. During 1926 and 1927 the opposition program of the Kikuyu Central Association (KCA) attracted growing support, especially in Fort Hall—precisely the area that was the focus of alcohol regulation. It turned out, however, that the administration did not fall back on antidrinking and antidancing measures in its response to this challenge. As political conflict built toward a climax in the crisis over female initiation in

1929–1930, the drinking question simply faded from official notice. Alcohol reappeared as an issue only sporadically during the 1930s. Age limitations and restrictions on sugar trading, although frequently ignored, remained in force; but officials no longer appear to have regarded the control of drinking as a serious problem. Notwithstanding the discontent created by unemployment and depressed commodity prices, officials made only scattered attempts to regulate the activities of youths. Of the attempts that were made, the large proportion occurred in those districts—notably Kitui and Embu—that were most insulated from such difficulties.[65] Presumably, it was in these more remote areas, where the continuity in warrior organization was strongest, that youths seemed to represent the greatest threat to stability.

During the late 1920s and 1930s state alcohol policy increasingly emphasized regulation over prohibition. Largely abandoning earlier attempts to suppress production and consumption, the administration moved instead to make beer a weapon of colonial hegemony. The beer trade had played a critical role in the expansion of the central Kenya exchange economy during the first decades of the colonial period. By and large the first generation of shopkeepers—both aliens and local men—had built their businesses on the purchase, refining, and resale of sugar.[66] Brewing itself did not become highly commercialized in most areas, but in those rural communities adjacent to Nairobi and the estates of the white highlands, local entrepreneurs did begin to prepare beer for Sunday sales.[67]

When the colonial authorities imposed alcohol control regulations, they attacked those men whose interests were most clearly aligned with their own. The 1927 closing of sugar mills in Fort Hall met with "bitterest opposition from the mill owners," men who gave strong support to most colonial policies.[68] That the ordinarily subservient local representative council approved the measure only by a vote of eleven to nine indicates the importance that sugar refining had in the emerging local economy.[69] Not surprisingly, the reformist Kikuyu Central Association took up the cause of the mill-owners, many of whom apparently were KCA members. Moreover, the KCA was also well aware of the possible long-term implications of alcohol control. The leaders were familiar with the systems of municipally owned and run beer halls that had been established elsewhere in Africa and argued forcefully that in rural Kenya bars should be in private, African hands.[70]

After about 1930 the Kenyan administration increasingly eschewed its previous piecemeal approach to alcohol control in favor of a more comprehensive regulatory strategy. In future, alcohol policies would systematically favor the interests of those men—like mill owners and members of the KCA—whose positions were closely tied to the development of the colonial economy. In his study of Rhodesian mineworkers Charles Van Onselen has shown how an alliance of state and capital smashed the local beer trade and introduced a system of monopolies within the confines of the labor compounds.[71] In rather different circumstances Kenya followed a parallel course. Beginning about 1930 a series of ordinances steadily restricted legal brewing to relatively few officially designated marketplaces.[72] In that setting, under the close supervision of the local chief, beer production could be licensed, regulated, and taxed, and drinking could be controlled. Confining consumption to specified sites also reduced the possibility that social drinking could provide the context for resistance or opposition.[73]

Ultimately, the policy of licensing alcohol outlets discouraged the informal beer trade in the countryside, subordinating previously autonomous economic activities to the spatial model of the colonial political economy. In the long run this process drew central Kenyans ever more securely within a highly centralized colonial system but at the same time made the cultural definitions of drink and drinking more compatible with the structures and ideology of that system. Beer was increasingly viewed as a commodity. The growing use of imported machinery and raw materials in beer production was an early stage in a gradual separation or alienation of producer and product, marked especially by the steady loss of the ritual significance of beer.[74] The migration of the locus of alcohol production and consumption from the homestead to the marketplace was accompanied not only by the commoditization of local beer but also by an association (in terms of both time and place) between drinking and a specifically defined period of leisure—in opposition to work.[75] Thus, as colonial society matured, the control of drinking became less a means of social control and more the instrument of economic "development."

NOTES

Abbreviations

CO   Great Britain, Colonial Office
KNA   Kenya National Archives
DC   District Commissioner
ADC   Assistant District Commissioner
PC   Provincial Commissioner

1. William Taylor examines many of these issues in *Drinking, Homicide and Rebellion in Colonial Mexican Villages* (Stanford, Calif., 1979), 28–72. I provide an overview to the study of the history of alcohol in Africa in Charles Ambler,

"Africa: Mapping the Historical Terrain of Drink" (Paper presented at the University of Florida history seminar, March 1987). José Curto has published a bibliography of works related to alcohol in Africa in *African Affairs* 88 (1989).

2. The region comprises present-day Kiambu, Murang'a, Nyandarua, Nyeri, Kirinyaga, Embu, Meru, Kitui, and Machakos districts. It encompasses considerable ecological diversity: at one extreme, farmers on Mount Kenya lived at elevations of seven thousand feet in areas of high rainfall and rich volcanic soils; at the other, residents of eastern Kitui District worked poor soils in dry country below three thousand feet.

3. This description is drawn from Charles Ambler, "Central Kenya in the Late Nineteenth Century: Small Communities in a Regional System" (Ph.D. diss., Yale University, 1983), chap. 2.

4. C. Cagnolo, *The Akikuyu: Customs, Traditions and Folklore* (Nyeri, Kenya, 1933), 57. Trouble later developed when abstemious Christian men refused to provide required token offerings of beer to their prospective fathers-in-law. See E. N. Wanyoike, *An African Pastor: The Life and Work of the Rev. Wanyoike Kamawe, 1888–1970* (Nairobi, 1974), 67–69.

5. L. S. B. Leakey, *The Southern Kikuyu before 1903* (London, 1977), 1:288–289; Gerhard Lindblom, *The Akamba in British East Africa* (Uppsala, 1920), 519.

6. Simeon Njage, Runyenges, Embu District, interview with author. Oral evidence is cited by informant's name and area of residence. All testimonies were collected by the author during 1977 and 1978. Transcripts are deposited in the Kenya Archives and at the University of Nairobi.

7. Lindblom, *Akamba*, 520.

8. Cagnolo, *Akikuyu*, 104.

9. This freewheeling attitude toward drinking corresponds to the notion of drunkenness as time out advanced by Robert Edgerton and Craig MacAndrew, *Drunken Comportment: A Social Explanation* (Chicago, 1969), 137.

10. Ivan Karp, "Beer Drinking and Social Experience in an African Society: An Essay in Formal Sociology," in *Explorations in African Systems of Thought*, ed. Ivan Karp and Charles S. Bird (Bloomington, Ind.: 1980), 83–119; see also Leakey, *Southern Kikuyu*, 1:287–291.

11. Wealthy men had beer prepared to reward work parties. See Carolyn Clark, "Women and Power in Nineteenth Century Kikuyu," *Africa* 50 (1980): 366; and Njuthwe son of Rumbia, Mwandu, Mbeere, Embu District, interview with author.

12. Lindblom, *Akamba*, 518–519; and Cagnolo, *Akikuyu*, 114–115.

13. Kitui District, Annual Report, 1913, DC/KTI/1/1/1, KNA; Lindblom, *Akamba*, 498. Walter Sangree has identified a seasonal pattern in frequency of beer parties in Tiriki in western Kenya ("The Social Functions of Beer Drinking in Bantu Tiriki," in *Society, Culture and Drinking Patterns*, ed. David J. Pittman and Charles R. Snyder [New York, 1962], 15).

14. Lindblom, *Akamba*, 521. According to William Taylor, in traditional Mexican societies moderation was defined by the frequency of drinking (and restrictions on who was permitted to drink) rather than how much was consumed when drinking occurred (*Drinking, Homicide and Rebellion*, 30).

15. See especially Robert Netting, "Beer as a Locus of Value among the

West African Kofyar," *American Anthropologist* 66 (1964): 375–384; see also Dwight B. Heath, "A Critical Review of Ethnographic Studies of Alcohol Use," in *Research Advances in Alcohol and Drug Problems* 2 (1975):1–92.

16. It is important, of course, to separate alcoholism from drunkenness (David G. Mandelbaum, "Alcohol and Culture," *Current Anthropology* 6 (1965): 281–293). In the case of the Kofyar, Netting states, "Not only is alcohol addiction absent but the social and personal costs of drunkenness have been significantly limited; there is no drinking problem" ("Beer as a Locus of Value," 375).

17. Kitui District, Quarterly Report, September 1910, DC/MKS.1/3/3, KNA.

18. J. Forbes Munro, *Colonial Rule and the Kamba: Social Change in the Kenya Highlands, 1889–1939* (Oxford, 1975), 89.

19. See the trade figures found in colonial reports. Note, in particular, Kitui District, Annual Report, 1916, DC/KTI/1/1/1, KNA; Simeon Njage, Runyenges Market, Embu District, and Saleh Shaban, Embu Town, interviews with author.

20. Sugar produced from the mills could be stored for later use, whereas the juice produced by the former method had to be used immediately (Simeon Njage, Runyenges Market, Embu District, interview with author).

21. Some more-recent scholarship perpetuates this view; see Lynn Pan, *Alcohol in Colonial Africa* (Helsinki: Finnish Foundation for Alcohol Studies, 1975).

22. John Ainsworth, diary, Rhodes House Library, Oxford, Mss. Afr. S 377–378, entry for 4 October 1897 (microfilm, Yale University Library).

23. For an early example, see United Kingdom, Public Record Office, Colonial Office, Report of Capt. Aylmeron, Kitui District, November 1907, CO 533/32.

24. K. L. Buell, *The Native Problem in Africa* (New York, 1928) 1:362n. The present essay deals specifically with central Kenya, but officials in other regions of the colony expressed similar concerns, particularly those stationed at the coast. Indeed, it was asserted that up-country men who sought work at the coast were being infected there with the plague of drunkenness (Colonial Office, East Africa Protectorate, Annual Report, 1909), 29. See also Thomas J. Herlehy, "Drink and the State: Palm Wine, Alcohol, and Development at the Kenya Coast, 1897–1980" (Walter Rodney Seminar Paper, Boston University African Studies Center, 2 April 1984).

25. Kitui District, Quarterly Report, September 1910, DC/MKS.1/3/1, KNA.

26. Dagoretti Political Record Book, vol. 1, 1908–1912, 26 November 1912, KBU/76, KNA. Defendants may have been aware that Europeans were likely to punish less severely crimes committed under the influence of alcohol (Edgerton and MacAndrew, *Drunken Comportment*, 149).

27. H. R. Tate, July 1910, Kiambu Political Record Book, part 2, KBU/98, KNA.

28. ADC, Kiambu, 17 June 1912, Kiambu Political Record Book, part 2, KBU/107, KNA.

29. Buell, *Native Problem*, 2:942.

30. East Africa Protectorate, Annual Report, 1908, 19.

31. Kitui District, Quarterly Report, December 1909, DC/MKS.1/3/1, KNA.

32. Report, 26 November 1912, Dagoretti Political Record Book, vol. 1, 1908–1912, KBU/76; Kiambu Political Record Book, part 2, KBU/107; Embu Political Record Book, PC.CP 1/5/1; DC, Nyeri, 4 September 1913, Minute Paper no. 19, 1913, PC Kenya Province, PC/CP/6/1/1, all KNA. See also Munro, *Colonial Rule*, 89. For wage rates, see A. Clayton and D.C. Savage, *Government and Labour in Kenya, 1895–1963* (London, 1974), 49. East African currency was converted to Sterling at a fixed rate of fifteen rupees to one pound.

33. Memo, Re: Beer Drinking, 14 November 1916, Dagoretti Political Record Book, vol. 2, 1913–1919, KBU/77, KNA. See also ex-Senior Chief Kasina son of Ndoo, Mwingi Market, Kitui District, interview with author.

34. East Africa Protectorate, Annual Report, 1917, 20. Munro, *Colonial Rule*, 89.

35. ADC, Dagoretti, 10 February 1918, Dagoretti Political Record Book, vol. 2, 1913–1919, KBU/77, KNA.

36. ADC, Dagoretti, 1 February 1918, Dagoretti Political Record Book, vol. 2, 1913–1919, KBU/77; DC, Kiambu, 17 June 1918, Dagoretti Political Record Book, vol. 2, 1913–1919, KBU/77; DC, Fort Hall to Chief Native Commissioner, 28 April 1920, Fort Hall Political Record Book, PC/CP.1/7/1, all KNA.

37. Marshall Clough, "Chiefs and Politicians: Local Politics and Social Change in Kiambu, Kenya, 1918–1936" (Ph.D. diss., thesis, Stanford University, 1978), 213.

38. Isaka Muragari son of Njathumba, Kagaari, Embu District, interview with author. The impact of regulation was much greater at the coast, where the production and trade of palm wine played a critical economic role (Herlehy, "Drink and the State").

39. Buell, *Native Problem*, 1:154. The European apprehension was reflected in the fact that before 1934 Kenyan Africans were not even permitted to work as barmen in white establishments (Kenya Colony and Protectorate, Report of the Liquor Licensing Committee, 1934, East Africa Pamphlet Collection [microfilm, Yale University Library]).

40. Taylor, *Drinking, Homicide and Rebellion*, 41.

41. Lindblom, *Akamba*, 521.

42. Report, 26 November 1912, Dagoretti Political Record Book, vol. 1, 1908–1912, KBU/76, KNA.

43. Rules applied under the Native Authority Ordinance, 11 November 1912, Kiambu Political Record Book, part 2, KBU/107, KNA.

44. See James Fox, *White Mischief: The Murder of Lord Erroll* (New York, 1983).

45. Audrey Wipper, *Rural Rebels: A Study of Two Protest Movements in Kenya* (Nairobi, 1977), 196–197.

46. Kamwochere son of Nthiga, Ngandori, Embu District; also, Kinyenye son of Mbuvi, Migwani, Kitui District, interviews with author.

47. DC, Kiambu, 17 September 1915, Kiambu Political Record Book, part 1, sec. 2, KBU/87, KNA.

48. Kenya Colony, Native Affairs Department, Annual Report, 1923; 17 June 1912, Kiambu Political Record Book, part 2, KBU/107, KNA. In fact, elders kept fairly strict control over these dances. Mutinda son of Ruanyaki, Ivurori (Mbeere), Embu District, interview with author.

49. November 1912, Kiambu Political Record Book, part 2, KBU/107, KNA.

50. DC Fort Hall to PC, 21 November 1919, Fort Hall Political Record Book, PC/CP.1/7/1, KNA.

51. Newspaper report, 26 March 1910, excerpted in Kiambu Political Record Book, part 1, sec. 1, KBU/81, KNA.

52. See East Africa Protectorate, Native Labour Commission, 1912–1913, *Evidence and Report*, 19–21; East Africa Protectorate, Annual Report, 1911, 47. See also Munro, *Colonial Rule*, 89.

53. PC, Central Province to PC, Nyanza, November 1942 in PC, Nyanza, Circular to DCs, 25 November 1942, Nyanza Province Daily Correspondence, L & O 10/4/225, KNA. On the implications of the use of alcohol to attract workers, see Charles Van Onselen, *Studies in the Social and Economic History of the Witwatersrand, 1886–1914*, vol. 1, *New Babylon* (New York, 1982), esp. 60.

54. Kenya Province, Annual Report, 1917, 20, PC/CP.4/1/1, KNA.

55. "The Kikuyu Point of View," ADC, Dagoretti, 12 December 1912, Dagoretti Political Record Book, vol. 1, 1908–1912, KBU/76, KNA.

56. P. P. Rey has noted, however, that the elders sometimes fought this process by inflating bridewealth. "The Lineage Mode of Production," *Critique of Anthropology* 3 (1975): 78. For evidence of this process at work in central Kenya, see Wanyoike, *African Pastor*, 70–71.

57. DC, Fort Hall to Chief Native commissioner, 28 April 1920, Fort Hall Political Record Book, PC/CP.1/7/1; Report, 26 November 1912, Dagoretti Political Book, vol. 1, 1908–1912, KBU/76, KNA.

58. Cagnolo, *Akikuyu*, 119.

59. "History of Fort Hall," entry for 1924, DC/FH.6/1, KNA; United Kingdom, Parliament, Sessional Papers, "Kenya: Tours in the Native Reserves and Native Development in Kenya," Acting Governor to Colonial Office, 5 August 1925, Cmd. 2573 (1926), vol. 9.

60. "History of Fort Hall," entry for 1919, PC/CP.1/7/1, KNA. Capitalizations as in original.

61. Johana Mbarire, Kigaa, Embu District, interview with author.

62. Kabare [Kirinyaga District] Station Logbook, 1910–1937, entry for 10 May 1923, CMS 1/639, KNA (Church Missionary Society Deposit); Sangree considers the relationship between drinking and conversion at some length ("Social Functions of Beer Drinking," 19).

63. Kitui District, Native Council Minutes, 6 and 26 October 1925, DC/KTI.9/1; Kitui District, Annual Report, 1926, DC/KTI/1/1/2, KNA. Kenya Colony, Native Affairs Department, Annual Report, 1927, 58–59. Embu District, Native Council Minutes, 3 August 1925, Embu County Council.

64. See Sharon Strichter, *Migrant Labour in Kenya: Capitalism and African Response, 1895–1975* (London, 1982), 48.

65. Embu District, Native Council Minutes, 8 August 1934 and 13 No-

vember 1942, Embu County Council. Muhammad Ali Sunkar, Mwingi, Kitui District, interview with author. "History of Fort Hall," entry for 1936, DC/FH.6/1; Kitui District, Annual Reports, 1934 and 1936, DC/KTI/1/1/4; and Embu District, Annual Report, 1936, DC/EBU/1/2, KNA. Kenya Colony, Native Affairs Department, Annual Report, 1926, 20.

66. Simeon Njage, Runyenges, Embu District, and Saleh Shaban, Embu Town, interviews with author. Journal de la Mission de Notre Dame de la Redemption à Kombé, 1912–1920, held at R.C. Mission, Kabaa, Machakos District, entry for 11 May 1913. Kitui District, Annual Report, 1916, DC/KTI/1/1/1, KNA.

67. Memo, A.D.C., Dagoretti, 14 November 1916, Dagoretti Political Record Book, vol. 2, 1913–1919, KBU/77, KNA.

68. Kenya Colony, Native Affairs Department, Annual Report, 1927, 6–7.

69. "History of Fort Hall," entry for 1927, DC/FH.6/1, KNA.

70. DC, Fort Hall, to PC, 6 March 1928; Colonial Office response to KCA petition dated 2 January 1930, "Kikuyu Central Association (1928–1930)," PC/CP.8/5/3, KNA.

71. Charles Van Onselen; *Chibaro: African Mine Labour in Southern Rhodesia, 1900–1933* (London, 1976), 167.

72. Kenya Colony, Annual Report, 1930, 55. Kitui District, Annual Report, 1934, 12, DC/KTI/1/1/4, KNA.

73. I have examined the use of alcohol regulation by colonial authorities to exercise control over African communities in several papers. See Charles Ambler, "Legislating Leisure in Colonial Kenya" (Paper presented at the annual meeting of the Canadian African Studies Association, Kingston, Ontario, May 1988; "Alcohol, Racial Segregation, and Popular Politics: Northern Rhodesia (Zambia) in the Colonial Era" (Paper presented at the annual meeting of the American Historical Association, San Francisco, December 1989; and "Alcohol, the Control of Labor, and Urban Culture on the Northern Rhodesia Copperbelt, 1920s–1964" (Unpublished paper, 1989). This last paper will be included in a forthcoming collection of essays on alcohol, the state, and labor control in southern Africa, edited by Jonathan Crush and Charles Ambler, to be published by the Ohio University Press. The issue of alcohol and labor control in South Africa has been explored in Van Onselen, "Randlords and Rotgut," in *Social and Economic History of the Witwatersrand*, 44–102; and in Paul la Hausse, *Brewers, Beerhalls, and Boycotts: A History of Liquor in South Africa* (Johannesburg, 1988).

74. See Michael T. Taussig, *The Devil and Commodity Fetishism in South America* (Chapel Hill, N.C., 1980), esp. 13–38; Marianna Adler, chapter 17 in this volume.

75. For discussion of leisure and work time, see Van Onselen, *Chibaro*, 170; Keith Thomas, "Work and Leisure in Pre-Industrial Society," *Past and Present* 29 (1964): 50–66.

NINE

Capitalism, Religion, and Reform: The Social History of Temperance in Harvey, Illinois

Ray Hutchison

The rise and fall of the temperance movement in the United States during the nineteenth century has gained increased attention since Joseph Gusfield's (1963) interpretation of temperance as a response "to the conflicts between divergent subcultures in American society." As a mass social movement temperance had its greatest impact before the Civil War. Afterward emphasis shifted from voluntary abstinence to the forced prohibition of alcohol products, and temperance became fused with the evangelical movement, woman suffrage, and labor issues. Thus, by the end of the 1800s temperance had evolved from individual commitment to a broader social vision of the ideal community and society.

Numerous temperance towns—communities planned, financed, and settled by followers of the temperance life-style—were established in the last quarter of the nineteenth century. In these communities the social ideals of temperance were translated into physical structures that would stand as moral outposts against an increasingly threatening world. The temperance town remains a physical image of the social and political goals of the movement, a permanent representation of the ideal community created by temperance values.

This essay concerns Harvey, Illinois, a temperance town some twenty miles south of the Chicago Loop founded by Turlington Harvey, a wealthy Chicago businessman. In its ideological focus Harvey was similar to other temperance towns of the era, sharing a commitment to the moral values of temperance and a reaction against social problems brought on by the change to an urban industrial society. The following pages present a brief social history of a planned industrial community devoted to the values of temperance and industry, focusing on the following questions: What persons or groups of persons were responsible for the founding of the temperance community? How did the economic base of the community affect the social composition of the town and the relative success of temperance life-styles? Who settled the community and what were the social backgrounds of early residents? What factors account for the eventual abandonment of temperance ideals?

THE TEMPERANCE TOWN

The decades marking the end of the nineteenth century brought important changes to the American landscape. Immigrants from Eastern Europe flooded the industrial cities, creating problems of social and moral control. Urban areas grew rapidly and experienced serious problems of pollution and overcrowding. New social movements appeared as populist parties spread from the American Midwest, the Socialist party emerged in the industrial cities, and urban political reform began to take hold.

Those years are also important in the history of the temperance movement. The Women's Christian Temperance Union (WCTU) grew in numbers and political influence. In 1884 a separate branch of the WCTU was established to include members of the black evangelical movement, and Amanda Smith (an early black temperance leader) traveled through Europe and Africa to spread the temperance message; Frances Willard rose to prominence and visited Europe to meet with temperance leaders; and in 1891 the first world congress of the movement was held in Boston. By the early 1900s many states had already passed prohibition legislation in response to the changing emphasis from actual temperance education, stressing voluntary abstinence, to political lobbying for prohibition, or forced compliance.

At the intersection of these different social forces—industrial expansion, immigration, political and social reform, and a shift from temperance to prohibition—are the temperance towns established in different parts of the country in the late 1800s. Although many early suburbs passed ordinances outlawing saloons in the 1890s (see Duis 1983), the temperance towns were entirely new settlements planned, financed, and populated by followers of the temperance movement. Prohibition Park, New York, began as a summer colony for temperance followers in Manhattan and was financed by New York businessmen; Vineland, New Jersey, was founded by Charles Landis, a land developer from Philadelphia; Harriman, Tennessee, was a land development founded by General Clinton B. Fisk, the Prohibition party presidential candidate in 1888 (Furnas 1965, 324–326). Palo Alto, California, was a temperance town begun by Mrs. Leland Stanford; Demorest, Georgia, was advertised in the *Union Signal* as a "city of refuge" from the problems of urban life. Harvey, Illinois, by contrast, was a planned industrial community. Surprisingly little is known of these settlements; they are not mentioned in the standard literature on temperance. The few primary sources of information concerning these communities are found in a book written by the founder of the Vineland Colony (Landis 1903) and in advertising supplements, short editorials, and news stories appearing in the *Union Signal*.[1]

This lack of attention is striking given the large volume of scholarly work devoted to other experimental communities in the United States. As Dolores Hayden (1979, 9) notes, "Communitarian thinking was most popular between 1820 and 1850, decades of agitation for abolition, labor rights, equitable land distribution policies, women's rights, educational reform, and penal reform." Literally hundreds of settlements appeared across the country, a movement that has been studied in numerous books beginning as early as 1870 and continuing to the present.[2] These experiments aimed at the restructuring of both interpersonal and socioeconomic relationships. Early participants viewed themselves as social architects redesigning society in response to problems posed by the industrial revolution (Hayden 1979, 9). In describing the emergence of similar experiments in England, Dennis Hardy (1979, 1–2) notes, "The communities derive their mandate, not so much from a spontaneous response to local grievances, as from a total vision of an alternative reality. They represent the efforts of groups of people who are agreed on the nature of an alternative society, and on the efficacy of the community as a method of achieving it. Communities can, therefore, be seen both as a method of social change and as an end in themselves."

Restrictions concerning alcohol were frequently ambivalent and contradictory. Religious settlements incorporated varying degrees of abstinence, and alcohol was one of many products whose consumption was limited. Yet some communities manufactured alcohol: the New Harmony Colony in Indiana, for example, brewed beer, owned a distillery, and produced wine (Arndt 1975). Although other forms of behavior, particularly sexual arrangements, have received extensive attention (Foster 1981), the position of alcohol in the overall social organization of these communitarian experiments has not been studied.

It is necessary to draw a distinction between the temperance town of the 1890s and earlier communitarian settlements. Although similar to communitarianism in its response to the problems of industrialization and the need of social reform, the temperance vision was narrower in practice. Its goal was to promote temperance values within the contours of the existing society and economic arrangements. In this sense the temperance town is more directly related to model company towns in England and the United States. As John Garner (1984, 5–6) notes:

> Company towns were developed, administered, and owned in their entirety by a single enterprise. Those which were comprehensive in design with a physical layout that included landscaping, community facilities, safe and sanitary factories, good houses, and programs for maintenance have been labeled as models....The goal of these companies was to protect their industrial investment through comprehensive planning and site control and to secure employees by offering attractive working and living conditions.

Hardy (1979, 11) further describes the English model towns developed by wealthy industrialists as "paragons of capitalist industrial society—conscious attempts to re-establish the assumed harmony of village life in an industrial setting."

Garner makes an important distinction between company towns and corporate towns such as Lowell, Massachusetts, and Manchester, New Hampshire. The corporate town was initially planned by a single company, although later growth occurred through the private market. The difference has important consequences:

> Orderly development ensues only when a single enterprise exercises control over an entire town site; and this is not the case in the corporate town, where many companies, each acting independently, were permitted to build with little or no coordination. The founding interest eventually became a land and utility company, abandoning site supervision through lease or sale to other businesses or developers. A destruction of order—not order—resulted, as the quality of their environments rapidly deteriorated. (Garner, 1984, 6–7)

The development of such corporate towns have been studied in Holyoke, Massachusetts (Green 1939), and Lowell, Massachusetts (Coolidge 1942).

The temperance town appears as a compromise between the company town and the corporate town. Harvey was wholly owned and developed by the Harvey Land Association, which controlled the location and type of industry in the community. Temperance was enforced by restrictive clauses in the original property deeds; control over the local housing market was meant to influence which groups would live in the community. But the land association rapidly shifted focus to land and utility interests and soon lost administrative control over community affairs. The temperance town sought to overlay moral controls with outside economic development. The fortunes of the community would depend on the strength of commitment and moral values of its inhabitants.

THE HARVEY LAND ASSOCIATION

Turlington Harvey was born in Durhamville, New York, in 1834. Although apprenticed as a carpenter, he later attended the Oneida Seminary. Harvey came to Chicago in the 1850s and opened a lumber mill on South Canal Street. The company moved to a larger plant at Twenty-second and Morgan, where Harvey pioneered the concept of railroad lumbering—purchasing large tracts of forest land in the south and northwest and shipping the fresh-cut lumber directly to his mill in Chicago. Harvey gained additional recognition for refusing to allow the mill to open on the Sabbath (Hotchkiss 1900, 387–388).

Harvey was elected president of the Relief and Aid Society in 1866 and helped organize the delivery of building and food supplies immediately after the Chicago fire in 1871. He served as president of the Young Men's Christian Association from 1871 to 1873 and again from 1876 to 1878. Later he would become vice president of the Chicago Evangelical Society and was friends with Dwight L. Moody and others in that organization, including persons from the Evanston temperance group.

By the end of the 1880s Harvey had formed plans to build a temperance town in the Chicago suburbs. Whereas the city was already expanding rapidly to the west, the southern edge was undeveloped. Ten years earlier A. G. Spalding, the sporting-goods magnate, had formed the South Lawn syndicate to develop land at the junction of the Grand Trunk Western and Illinois Central railroads some twenty miles south of the city, although this initial effort met with little success. Harvey began purchasing land in the South Lawn tract in 1889 and then sold it to the newly formed Harvey Land Association in June 1890. An additional five hundred acres was purchased from Spalding in 1891, and the new town was officially registered under the name of Harvey in May 1891 (Kerr 1962, 16–17; also Zimmerman, 1938, 11).

At first glance the Harvey Land Association represents a peculiar mixture of business and social interests—an unlikely aggregation of business and professional leaders, financiers and capitalists, and religious and social reformers. Turlington Harvey was president; F. H. Revel, the Boston publisher of religious books and periodicals, was a vice president. Dwight L. Moody was one of the original investors and sat on the board of directors. Other members included bankers and businessmen, and at least one person also sat on the board of directors of the Pullman Corporation. Common interests were formed by religious, social, and political values that produced a belief in temperance and industry (a return to the work ethic) as a solution to the social problems of capitalism in the Gilded Age. The group resembles those Brian Harrison (1971) identifies as the temperance industrialists.

It is necessary to place the principles guiding the founders of Harvey within the broader social currents of the time. It was a period when many still believed that industrial capitalism and Christian values could be fused to work for the good of the community as a whole (Foster 1975; Kasson 1976). In this and other considerations the efforts of Turlington Harvey parallel those of George Pullman, who had built his corporate showcase town five miles further north in 1882. The vision of American industrialists and capitalists was to provide a community free from working-class vices such as saloons and labor unions (see Ashton 1978). Writing in 1915, Graham Taylor offered an insight into the capitalists' logic in the first study of industrial suburbs:

> Some company officials act on the belief that by removing workingmen from a city it is possible to get them away from the influences which foment discontent and labor disturbances. The satellite city is looked to as a sort of isolation hospital for the cure of chronic "trouble."...if the plants were moved out to the suburbs, the workingmen should not be so frequently innoculated with infection. (1915, 23–24)

The labor disturbances of the late 1870s had been put down only with the use of federal troops in Chicago, Saint Louis, Baltimore, Philadelphia, Pittsburgh, and other industrial cities. The movement of industry to the suburbs appeared to be the most efficient method of escaping labor difficulties in the cities. Thus, temperance and industry were fused and emerged as a popular ideology for dealing with the social problems of the day.[3]

The original plans of the Harvey Land Association, as reported in the souvenir booklet prepared for the Columbian Exposition (the 1893 World's Fair in Chicago), called for the development of an extensive industrial base of some one hundred manufacturing firms of varying size to provide employment for a town of twenty-five thousand persons (Harvey Land Association [1893], 37–38). Industries were attracted to Harvey by the ready access to major rail lines. Located beyond the Chicago city limits, manufacturers could escape city taxes. Because the land association owned not only the residential land but industrial land around the railroads as well, strict control was maintained over the types of industry allowed to settle in the community. For many years, and particularly in the period before 1895, industries were actually invited to settle in Harvey.

Two separate industrial areas were planned, each separated from adjacent residential areas by the railroad tracks. A municipal power plant was built, water and sewer lines laid out, and a streetcar line established. Public services were owned and operated by holding companies that received franchises from the city. These holding companies represented corporate subsidiaries of the land association and its original group of investors (similar to the corporate structure in Pullman). This arrangement had built-in conflicts and was not always successful. When the new waterworks plant did not pass the first tests, the city council hired an independent consulting engineer to conduct further tests; the land association, however, telegraphed that his services were not required.

Fundamental to the plans of the Harvey Land Association was the creation of a working environment that would attract disciplined and skilled workers to the community. But the land association also sought to assure residents of the community job security in local industry. Thus, official contracts with industries that located in Harvey included a clause wherein the manufacturer "covents and agrees that it will at all times in hiring employees give preference to persons living upon land owned or controlled by the Harvey Land Association or its grantees, and that it will, so far as is practicable, limit its employment of help to persons living upon land owned or controlled by said Harvey Land Association or its grantees" (Harvey Land Association [1893], 16–17). This covenant signals an important break with the efforts of other industrialists. The land association sought a social contract wherein the Christian residents of Harvey might be protected from unscrupulous employers and economic hardships. Employment security was stressed in a promotional booklet: "And to crown all: The influence of a legal and strongly worded covenant in favor of employment in the great industrial concerns on which the prosperity of the town is based." The booklet further emphasized that these industries "are diversified in interest. Harvey's eggs are not all in one basket, and dullness in one branch of trade will not affect the town disastrously as is often the case where a community is dependent, or nearly so, upon one industry" (Harvey Land Association [1893]).

TEMPERANCE: THEME AND VARIATIONS

The themes of sound moral virtues, a pastoral setting, and reliable employment are repeated in the official literature on the town—the advertisements, souvenir booklets, and fliers published by the Harvey Land Association. The promotional souvenir book, published in forty thousand copies in 1893, plainly stated that the "founders believe that the highest good for both the employer and the employe' requires the absolute prohibition of the saloon. This will keep some people out of the town, but it will be a strong inducement for others to become residents. It is the 'others' who are preferred." The distinction between temperance values and those of the outside world could hardly be stated more succinctly. The community was described as "a veritable city of refuge":

Here is a chance for the man who is toiling in hot, dusty city factories, living in crowded rooms, without a breath of fresh air, to work in large, roomy buildings, and OWN a home in a purer atmosphere....For the homeseekers—men with families to support who are looking for a place in which they can make a healthful home, where the moral surroundings are the best, where there is no fear of saloon influences on the rising generations, and where there are excellent educational privileges, Harvey presents such inducements as offered by no other town or city in America....[It is] a place where, safe from temptation, [residents] can sit under their own vine and catalpa tree, with no one to molest them or make them afraid.

The original deeds to residential property sold by the Land Association contained a clause that would enforce temperance and its associated moral values (Harvey Land Association [1893]):

If the purchaser uses any part of the property for the purpose of permitting any intoxicating drink to be manufactured, sold or given away upon said premises, or permits gambling to be carried on therein, or creates any house or other place of lewd and immoral practice thereupon, he, his heirs, executors, administrators and his assigns shall be divested of the entire estate and it shall revert to the party of the first part.

Viewed from the distance of nearly a century, the promotional literature of the Land Association is striking in the obvious attempt to merge the values of Protestant asceticism with those of industrial capitalism in a romantic, pastoral setting. For many in the temperance movement, communities such as Harvey filled a growing need and were indeed to become cities of refuge, if only for a brief moment.

The Calling
The "two basic principles" of temperance and industry (as they were identified in land association publications) figured predominantly in the promotion of the community. In the spring of 1891 advertisements and announcements concerning the community appeared regularly in the *Union Signal,* the weekly journal of the Women's Christian Temperance Union. In the March 5 issue, for example, a full-page advertisement carrying the headline "Harvey, Illinois, The Magic City," with a

description of the town and its location, announced that two new manufacturing firms (the Conner Core Drilling Company and the Grinnell Wagon Works) had just contracted to move to Harvey.

Reaction to the community was overwhelming, and Harvey quickly attracted hundreds of families from across the United States. The missionary zeal of the land association was fully matched by the religious fervor of its followers. An early resident gave the following description of the decision to move to Harvey:

> In the spring of 1892 I was living with my parents and sisters on a farm near Amity, Missouri. It was on a Sunday afternoon after we had returned from church and Sunday School and were reading the papers we received there that my sister exclaimed, "Father, here is a town, a temperance town near Chicago. Let us go there—we will have better opportunities..." That was the beginning. We talked of little else until my father and sister came to Harvey the following September. (Kerr 1962, 17)

Descriptions of the community suggest that in these years Harvey was every bit the respite from life in the industrial city of the nineteenth century that the land association declared it to be. One resident recalled that "there were families from many states, fine friendly folk attracted here from far and near because it was to be a Temperance town, with factories where men could earn good wages and where their children could grow up surrounded by the best influences" (Kerr 1962, 32).

The Mission

The Harvey Land Association clearly saw a larger mission, for which the physical town of Harvey would provide a base. Advertisements in the *Union Signal* spread the image of the community across the country, and people did in fact come from many different states. During the Columbian Exposition the land association acquired offices in the Rookery Building in downtown Chicago. Salesmen were assigned to each train carrying visitors to the World's Fair. Special excursion trains ran south along the Illinois Central lines past Jackson Park (site of the fair) to take visitors to the industrial city of Pullman. It is said that more than three million persons visited Pullman in 1893; many of them continued on to Harvey to view the temperance community set up by the land association (see Kerr 1962).

The religious mission of the land association is perhaps best shown in its planning for the Columbian Exposition. In 1892 the land association published a flier asking for subscriptions to finance construction of a World's Fair hotel. The architect's drawings showed the hotel to be a city block in size, four stories high, with an inner courtyard, fountain, and gardens. It would serve as headquarters for "clergymen, teachers, Christian workers, Sunday school folks, and Temperance people" attending the fair and would accommodate five thousand guests. The exposition was scheduled to run for twenty-six consecutive Sundays, and the land association planned to sponsor revival meetings in a ten-thousand-seat outdoor theater constructed in a nearby forest. It should be noted that the temperance hotel and revival auditorium have precedents in other temperance experiments: Prohibition Park in Staten Island had an auditorium that seated four thousand persons (Furnas 1965, 325–326), and Temperance hotels had been common in England (Harrison 1974) and the eastern United States (Furnas 1965, 104–105) in the mid-1800s.

Whereas the activities of the land association are described in secondary sources, there is no further mention of the World's Fair hotel. The hotel flier is in fact the last official publication of the land association in historical archives. Although the hotel was never built, the plan demonstrates both the expanding temperance mission and the merging of commercial and religious interests in the temperance town.

Land Speculation

The industrial community of Harvey was different both in scale and purpose from temperance towns in other areas of the country. It was intimately connected to the growth and expansion of manufacturing in the Chicago region and was also part of the land speculation taking place in suburban areas opened up by commuter railroads. The Harvey Land Association regularly advertised residential lots in newspapers and fliers. Housing lots were located in the fourteen hundred acres of land purchased from the earlier Spalding syndicate. But other investors quickly bought up the adjacent land and advertised in the *Union Signal* alongside the land association. The W. W. Brown Company advertised that while its property was not within the legal boundaries of Harvey, the community had not yet been fully incorporated, and when final boundaries were drawn up the new suburban tracts it was selling were sure to be included. On the same page the Charles French company offered land both within the community and in adjacent tracts and built a large apartment-house and rooming-house complex for workers (*Union Signal*, March 5, 1891, 16).

Other land speculators attempted to out-do one another and the land association itself. One development south of Harvey was advertised as the "Beautiful Park Addition" to the Temperance town. Prominent reference was made to the director of the company, J. P. Bishop, who was also the chairman of the Cook County Prohibition Committee (*Union Signal*, March 19, 1891, 16). The Walter Thomas Mills Company offered land

Fig. 9.1. Advertising poster of the Harvey Land
Association, c. 1892

east of the community and noted in larger print that there were "no
Sunday excursions" to Harvey. Moreover, the streets in this development
were named Willard, Fisk, Lathrop, and West after national leaders of
the temperance movement (*Union Signal,* March 5, 1891, 4).

The Harvey Land Association countered by reminding readers of
the *Union Signal* that only those housing lots actually owned by the land
association had access to public services and were protected by the
employment covenant. Other real estate developers, it warned, could
offer no such guarantees. This approach is nicely summarized in one
of the early fliers (Fig. 9.1):

> Take special notice of Harvey's Corporation Lines, and BUY INSIDE THESE
> LINES, where main sewers, water-works, trees, parks, and boulevards are
> furnished without any assessments to purchasers of lots....
>
> ...All the manufacturers in Harvey are bound by contract to give the
> preference to workmen who live INSIDE THE LINES. (Harvey Land Associ-
> ation, 1892a)

The conflict is an interesting one—serious because it involved the use of capital improvements by outside corporations that had not contributed to their costs, but moderated by the common interests of at least some of the outside developers in expanding the temperance community. This same approach was taken by the *Union Signal* itself in an editorial. The editors noted that it was good that more land was being made available for all those interested in contributing to the new experiment and emphasized that the new developments were living up to the high standards of the land association, as shown by the commitment to name streets after prominent leaders of the movement. Readers of the newspaper were urged to invest while there was still an opportunity to purchase land in and around Harvey (March 5, 1891, 13).

Residential lots in Harvey were priced from $150 to $700, and the land association offered financing with a 25 percent down payment with semiannual installments. To aid working families who might want to join the community, special loans of $1,000 were available to build $1,000 wood-frame Victorian homes on $400 lots. A more modest plan was offered for $500, including a five-room cottage constructed on a $175 lot.

The land association was quick to point out that residential land was a good investment, and many lots were sold on a speculative basis. Land was sold not only through personal visits to Harvey (travel costs from other cities and states were reimbursed) but through the mail with a $50 deposit (mail purchases were guaranteed a refund if the lots did not meet later approval). The fourteen city blocks located south of the downtown area sold out within ninety days after they were offered in 1891.

The land association actively promoted home ownership for the working class and in this sense operated differently from the Pullman Corporation. But home ownership in the community was obviously approached from a broader perspective emphasizing both pastoral ideals (relaxing under the catalpa tree in your own front yard) and moral virtue. Thus, home ownership became part of the ideal community where the interests of the working man and capital would be joined for the common goal of a temperance community. The Marxist critique of home ownership is certainly on target here—the working-man with his own home is more likely to remain on the job, more susceptible to the demands of the workplace and the social order, and more inclined to participate in the maintenance of the community (see Stone 1979).[4]

Control over the original land resource was an important feature of the community. Industrial areas were separated from residential space,

TABLE 9.1 Place of Origin for Early Households in Harvey,
Illinois, 1890–1900

	Households	Persons	Persons per Household	Percent
Scandinavia	11	64	5.8	18.5
Great Britain	8	30	3.8	8.7
Other Western European	10	53	5.3	15.3
Eastern European	3	15	5.0	4.3
Chicago area	3	16	5.3	4.6
Midwest	21	83	3.9	24.0
Eastern United States	14	69	4.9	19.9
Western United States	1	3	3.0	0.9
Total	73	359	4.8	100.00

SOURCE: Place of birth recorded in public records (birth and death certificates), City Clerk's
Office, Harvey, Illinois.

and the location of different types of businesses was closely regulated.
The creation of residential lots and housing packages of different size
and value also influenced the location of different groups of persons
within the community. The planned development of the town, controlled in most every aspect by the land association, was intended to
create the ideal community where two years earlier there had been only
open prairie. It is significant that this planning resulted in a stratified
social order not very different from that of the society the reformers
were attempting to replace.

SOCIAL COMPOSITION OF THE TEMPERANCE TOWN

Information from records in the city clerk's office allows us to reconstruct the social background of early residents (shown in table 9.1).
This population was drawn from three distinct groups: native-born
families from the Midwest (24 percent of the total), those from other
states (almost 21 percent), and foreign-born residents from Western
European countries (43 percent). These figures suggest a population
base of persons of Anglo and Western European heritage similar to
that of the American population of the period (Hutchison, 1984).

By 1894 ten churches had been established in the community. As
shown in table 9.2, these congregations emphasize the Western European and Protestant heritage of the community. Eight of the churches
present in the community by 1900 were Protestant; only one was
Catholic. Two of the congregations were German speaking (one until
1917, the second until 1940), and two were Swedish. The Catholic

TABLE 9.2   Religious Congregations in Harvey, Illinois, 1900

	Year of Organization	Year Building Constructed
Union Chapel[a]	–	–
First Congregational	1890	–
First Baptist	1890	1892
Swedish Methodist[b]	–	1891
German Evangelical[c]	1891	1891
Swedish Lutheran[b]	1891	1892
Academy Methodist	1891	1893
Honore Methodist	1891	1897
First Christian	1892	1895
Free Methodist	1892	1899
Ascension Catholic	1894	1894
African Methodist[d]	1896	(1902)
Trinity Lutheran[c]	1897	(1902)

SOURCE: *Harvey, Illinois, History: 1890–1962*, ed. Alex Kerr, 119–147.
[a]Constructed by the Harvey Land Association but never used as a religious center.
[b]Swedish-language congregation.
[c]German-language congregation.
[d]A second congregation of Black Evangelical Baptists was organized around 1900 as well.

parish was Irish. The religious composition of the population in Harvey is significant when we compare the ethnic composition of Chicago and the Calumet region during the same period.

The decade from 1890 to 1900 was marked by the immigration of large numbers of Eastern European families to the United States. By 1900 more than sixty thousand Poles had immigrated to Chicago, and fourteen parishes had been established (City of Chicago 1974, 47–49). Other Eastern European groups included Italians (27,000) and Czechs and Slovaks (36,000); in total more than 20 percent of the Chicago population in 1900 was of Eastern European stock (City of Chicago, 1974, 24–26).

Harvey, by contrast, contained few Eastern Europeans in 1900, despite the rapid growth that had occurred in the previous decade. The containment of the Eastern European population outside the community may be explained by the social milieu of the temperance town itself. As Gusfield (1963, 55–56) noted, by the end of the nineteenth century the temperance movement had "widened the cultural gap between native and immigrant by placing each as opponent to the other's way of life. The American Protestant and immigrant Catholic were not simply two people of somewhat different cultures.... The political confrontation between native and immigrant was a real one, based on cultural differences." Although Eastern Europeans would move to Harvey in the early 1900s, they were not a part of community life in the early years.

The social values of the temperance community may also help explain the early appearance of blacks in Harvey. Before the Civil War the temperance movement had been associated with the abolition movement, and in later years many black evangelical leaders were active in the temperance movement on a national and even international level. The first black congregation in Harvey, organized in 1896 (just four years after the founding of the town), was associated with the African Methodist Evangelical church. Amanda Smith, a noted evangelical leader who traveled throughout the United States, Europe, and Africa to spread the teachings of the temperance movement, established an industrial school for orphaned black children in Harvey. Temperance values as a way of life thus produced a somewhat unique aggregation of ethnic and racial groups in the early industrial community.

Industry and Employment

The occupational distribution of the working population reveals a good deal about the characteristics of industrial communities at the turn of the century. Nearly two-thirds (61.6 percent) of the local population was employed in industrial jobs including a wide range of positions from managers and office personnel (white-collar workers) to skilled craftsmen and common laborers. The physical construction of the community required many persons in the building trades—contractors, carpenters, plasterers, painters, and the like (17.1 percent of the employed population). A significant number of persons was employed in other jobs required for a dynamic and growing community—farmers, storekeepers, and professionals (18.3 percent) (Hutchison 1984).

Industrial enterprises at the turn of the century employed what today appears as an interesting assortment of personnel. Office workers (bookkeepers, purchasing agents and salesmen, correspondence secretaries) and managerial personnel accounted for the relatively few white-collar workers. At the bottom end were large numbers of common laborers necessary for unloading raw materials and transporting finished products. Machinery in the manufacturing plants ran on steam power, which required unskilled and semiskilled workers to transport coal and maintain the furnaces; the rolling mills needed additional laborers to carry pigs of iron and other materials.

But the most striking feature of employment in Harvey was the large number and wide variety of skilled craftsmen required by factories manufacturing even rather primitive products. Two manufacturers produced cast-iron stoves. Molds for the castings were produced by pattern makers according to design specifications, and the firing of the raw iron in the blast furnaces required specially trained personnel. Each mold was hand-set by skilled craftsmen, usually in boxes of sand, and the iron molders oversaw the pouring of the molten iron into the molds. The finished castings were then removed and brushed by hand. Semiskilled assemblers (stove mounters) assembled the castings, laborers handled the iron pigs, and colliers stoked coal and other materials for the furnaces (Walker 1966).

As Marxist scholars have pointed out, the advance of industrial capitalism came about largely at the expense of the skilled worker; the origins of the factory system are found not in technological advances in the industrial process but in the increased control over the labor force given to the capitalist owner (Marglin 1974). The early factories in Harvey are fairly typical of industrial development of the time, where skilled craftsmen were grouped together under a single roof to produce products for the industrial capitalist. In this respect social patterns in the temperance town closely resemble those in other industrial communities.

Social Class and Residential Space

In New York, Chicago, Philadelphia, and other cities identifiable patterns of residential segregation had emerged by the end of the nineteenth century (Gutman 1966; Pessen 1978; Thernstrom 1964). The basis of segregation could be either income or race and ethnicity, although the two were closely associated. Centralized planning by the land association might be expected to result in new patterns of residential settlement. At the local level temperance should be viewed as an egalitarian movement stressing the integration of all elements of the community for a common goal. To what extent might the new community develop patterns of residential settlement different from those of other industrial cities?

Harvey supported a number of diverse residential environments, from apartments in the downtown area to single family homes and small farms on the outskirts of town. The Buda Company built a large apartment building for its employees (known as the Buda Flats), and other entrepreneurs constructed apartments and hotels. The various land and housing packages arranged by the Land Association produced a de facto separation of working groups on the basis of size and cost of housing.

The residential location of social class groups in Harvey reveals distinct residential neighborhoods. Business and professional families lived in the center of the community, in the large housing structures built by the land association. Middle-class white-collar families (office and management personnel) followed a similar residential pattern. Many of the industrial workers continued to live in two worlds, working in the factories while raising cows, poultry, and crops on their land—a pattern common to workers in many other industrial settings of the early 1900s (see Braverman 1974; Ewen 1976).

The residential segregation by social class described here corresponds to the pattern of housing development set in motion by the land association. Two-story family homes were built in the blocks adjacent to the business district at the center of the community. Smaller four-room worker cottages were constructed further from the downtown area. These alternative housing packages, given prominent mention in all the promotional literature published by the land association because they would allow virtually every working family to purchase its own home, resulted in a pattern of segregation by social class. The larger homes in the center of the community were purchased by upper status groups, dominated by families of native and Western European origin. Smaller homes around this central core were purchased by white-collar and skilled workers (predominantly Western European). The unskilled working class, with relatively fewer resources at its command, was less likely to settle in housing developed by the land association and instead moved into older housing at the fringe of the town. These neighborhoods also corresponded to the areas of settlement by the newer Eastern European immigrants.

In both ethnic and class composition the temperance community in Harvey was similar to that of the national movement. Isetts (1979) has shown that the Hillsboro Women's Temperance Crusade, which led to the formation of the WCTU, was largely formed by Ohio women and other native-born women whose husbands were members of the social elite (cf. Epstein 1981). Tyrrell (1979) indicates that the leaders of temperance reform in Worcester were similarly industrial entrepreneurs and skilled craftsmen. And Bordin's (1981, 163–175) analysis of the social background of the leadership of the WCTU demonstrates that more than 80 percent were native-born whites of English, Irish, and Scotch ancestry; nearly all were from Protestant backgrounds; and more than 60 percent came from households where the husband was an attorney, clergyman, businessman, or educator. This analysis is not meant to overemphasize ethnic and religious differences within the community; as Tyrrell notes, temperance reform was much more than simply a matter of ethnic conflict: "Rather, it was part of a widespread movement to discipline society and to create a society of predictable individuals devoted to self-improvement. By no means opposed to industrialization, temperance reform was rather the product of that crucial transition to an urban-industrial, commercial society" (Tyrrell 1979, 46).

Although the land association might pursue certain limited social reforms to guarantee employment opportunities and private owner-ship of housing for the resident workforce, it could not guarantee the social and physical integration of different groups in the community. The social programs underlying the formation of the community were designed to operate within the private market economy of the Gilded Age, and within such a framework could offer only limited modifica-tions to the emerging social structure of the community. The conse-quence was a work force stratified by ethnic background and residen-tial segregation based on social status.

LOCAL GOVERNMENT AND POLITICS

As one might expect from the history of the community, the dominant force in Harvey in its early years was the land association, yet Harvey did not function like a company town.[5] Although the centralized plan-ning and moral proscriptions of the land association were the founda-tion of the town and would provide the hub for local leadership, the land association was itself absentee-owned and exercised little direct control over day-to-day activities.

It is assumed in much of the literature that political life in the manufacturing towns of the Gilded Age was dominated by the local economic elite—by the petty capitalists who had built factories, accu-mulated wealth, and established political hegemony. This process of economic concentration created a crisis for local government in the early 1900s when small family-owned businesses were swallowed up by large corporations and local economic interests withdrew from local politics. The trajectory from local capitalism to absentee ownership is generally equated with corporate indifference to local affairs. But the situation in Harvey was very different.

In the 1890s there were thirteen dominant economic units in Har-vey—the land association, the local bank, and eleven industries. Of the eleven industries, eight had been founded elsewhere before moving to Harvey, and four maintained central offices in Chicago. Of the twenty-two members of the economic elite identified by Carol Rahn (1980) during this period (those persons exercising direct control over the dominant economic interests in the community), only ten actually lived in Harvey. Thus, most of the economic elites were not eligible to hold public office, but of the ten who were, six served in political positions. In the early years more than half of the city council members were

workingmen from the community. Although economic interests were
actively involved in some community issues—such as the establishment
of public schools, important for providing a skilled, loyal, and sober
work force—they were not overtly visible.

The major concern of local government in the early years of Harvey
was apparent—the physical development of the community and particularly the provision of public services. By 1895 an underlying conflict
in the community had come to the surface, and the ten-year struggle
over the temperance clause that would earn Harvey the nickname of
the little ewe lamb of prohibition had begun.

The Fight for Prohibition

In 1893 a businessman with the unfortunately Irish name of
McLatchy opened an amusement hall and saloon at 155th and Halsted,
just east of the land association property. Lucy Page Gaston led an
effort to annex this property to Harvey, a dry town, thus effectively
closing the saloon (Zimmerman 1938). The movement was defeated,
but the mayoral election of 1895 developed into a battle over prohibition. Although temperance forces won, electing Jonathan Mathews to
two one-year terms as mayor, Mathews refused to run again in 1897. In
May 1897 a new mayor favorable to the saloon interests, Clark W.
Ranger, took office, and in July a new ordinance legalizing liquor sales
came before the city council. The vote was split among the eight
councilmen, and Ranger cast the tie-breaking vote allowing liquor
licenses. In September a public referendum was held, and temperance
was reinstated by a small majority. A series of court cases would keep
the issue in the forefront of public attention throughout the early
1900s.

Kenneth Beers, publisher of the *Harvey Citizen* in the 1890s, carried
on an editorial campaign in support of prohibition. Perhaps most vocal
in the attempt to rid the community of the saloon menace was Lucy
Page Gaston, member of the Women's Christian Temperance Union
and later founder of the Anti-Cigarette League (she is said to have
coined the term *coffin nail*). Her brother, Edward Page, was founder of
the World Prohibition Federation in London (Kerr 1962). Efforts to
protect the temperance clause in the original Harvey property deeds
was finally declared unconstitutional in the Cook County courts.

The protracted struggle over prohibition during the early history of
the town had important consequences. Harvey was founded as a temperance community, and many persons had been attracted to it by the
promise of a life-style fashioned around the religious and social values
of the movement. The land association had been straightforward when
it stated that although some might not be attracted to a community

without saloons, "it is the others who are preferred." Thus, the defeat of temperance threatened the symbolic image of the community, and the attempt to reinstate prohibition became a crusade to save the town.

The Disrupted Economy

From this brief portrait Harvey appears as an industrious community of religious persons sharing common values and a belief in a better way of life through temperance. But by 1900 the economic foundation of the town had been severely tested and found wanting. The provision of skilled jobs in local industry was integral to the plans of the land association; early promotional brochures made frequent mention of guaranteed employment in the community and noted that the economy of Harvey was diversified and not dependent on a single industry. Hence, the effects of the depression of 1893–1898 cut through the social and economic fabric of the community.

The depression began with a panic in the financial markets in the fall of 1893 and spread rapidly throughout the economy. By 1894 fully 18 percent of the working population in the United States was jobless, and the number would remain above 12 percent through 1898. The iron and steel industries were particularly hard hit. In 1894 the *Commercial and Financial Chronicle* reported that "never before has there been such a sudden cessation of industrial activity. Nor was any section of the country exempt from the paralysis. Mills, factories, furnaces, mines nearly everywhere shut down in large numbers, and commerce and enterprise were arrested in an extraordinary degree...and hundreds of thousands of men thrown out of employment" (Sobel 1968, 260). Virtually every industry in Harvey would be affected by either the fall in iron and steel prices or the declining purchases of rail equipment and farm machinery. The following description of the effect of the depression years of the 1890s by one early resident parallels that of the financial newspapers and offers a sociological analysis of the impact on the moral fiber of the community itself: "In some respects I believe that Harvey suffered more from the depression which ran its course from 1893 to 1900 than it did in the last depression, 1929. During these trying years the price of real estate declined in many instances 50 percent and many Harvey people lost their homes. Many more lost faith in Harvey and moved elsewhere" (Kerr 1962, 33).

DECLINE OF THE TEMPERANCE TOWN

From 1891 to 1893 Harvey grew at a phenomenal rate, attracting persons from across the country seeking a new way of life safe from the

menace of the saloon. By 1894, however, plans for further development had been halted by the onset of the depression. In the late 1890s
temperance itself became a political issue. Although conflict over temperance may have solidified the reputation of the community, it also
inflicted damage. By 1900 the two guiding principles of the community—industry and temperance—had both been challenged and found
insufficient.

References to Harvey as a temperance community disappear by
1900. The community does not appear in any of the temperance
literature; it is not mentioned in Frances Willard's autobiography, the
temperance encyclopedia, or other primary or secondary works. Although Lucy Page Gaston and Edward Page are sometimes mentioned
in the literature, they are minor figures, and their early history is not
discussed. There is little in the town today to indicate the unique
circumstances surrounding its founding.

The failure of Harvey as a temperance town is not in itself surprising. Utopian settlements of various kinds were common in nineteenth-
century America, but the majority of these experiments failed. Other
temperance towns shared a similar fate: by 1910 none of the original
temperance communities founded in the 1800s remained intact. Given
the ultimate failure of the attempt by the land association at social
reform and urban planning, it is necessary to ask why the temperance
experiment was unsuccessful, and what significance (if any) the history
of Harvey may have for understanding the temperance and prohibition movements at the turn of the century.

Economic Crisis

The most obvious explanation for the decline of temperance is the
economic crisis brought on by the depression of the 1890s. The largest
industries in Harvey manufactured railroad equipment and farm machinery—two of the areas most heavily affected by the downturn in
economic activity. The initial effect was the loss of employment for
industrial workers, followed by a decline in commercial and retail
activity in local businesses. Unemployed workers, unable to maintain
mortgage payments to the land association, lost their homes. Many
persons moved elsewhere to look for work. Contemporary accounts
indicate the devastating impact of the depression on the local economy.

Although the depression resulted in unemployment and business
losses for the community as a whole, there was an important symbolic
dimension to this crisis as well. The Harvey Land Association virtually
guaranteed stable employment to local residents as part of a new social
contract. Promotional literature had stressed that the economy was
diversified and not dependent on any single industry. Many persons

sold their homes and possessions in other states before moving to Harvey. When the land association was unable to fulfill its obligation to temperance followers, the social contract was irreparably destroyed. To suggest that people simply lost faith in the community may be an understatement: for many, their belief in a better and more secure way of life guaranteed by temperance values had been shattered.

But the economic crisis provides in some ways too easy an explanation. The depression did produce serious problems for the industrial community, but the end of temperance in Harvey was not the only possible outcome. Indeed, crisis and conflict might instead have caused local officials to pool resources and reaffirm the moral values that guided the community. Hence, we must focus on the broader social processes that influenced events in Harvey. The most significant of these forces were the structural problems of administrative control by the land association and the decline of temperance as a social movement. These problems may be cited as contributing causes to the decline of the community, and both would have threatened the long-term viability of the town even had the economic collapse of 1893 not taken place.

Community Planning

The structural problem confronting Harvey was how to preserve temperance values while actively promoting continued economic development. The temperance town represents a compromise between the corporate town and utopian community. As in the utopian community, local residents were united by a common belief system and lifestyle that differentiated them from the outside society. Economic development, by contrast, depended on integration into the national market economy and the continued success of many different industries (rather than a single economic concern, as in the traditional company town). In Harvey the founding business interests evolved into a landholding and utility company, thereby relinquishing control over site supervision and the day-to-day administration of community affairs (Garner 1984, 6–7). This process of economic concentration emphasized short-term financial gains over longer-term interests in social reform and social control. But this decision was to have serious consequences.

By 1895 the land association had clearly lost influence over local events: in that year prohibition was defeated in a city council vote and later passed in a public referendum by only a small margin. That temperance became a public issue brought before the city council is significant in itself. It is difficult, for example, to imagine such a vote taking place in Pullman (where liquor sales were confined to the

company-run Florence Hotel). Had the land association exercised direct control over local politics in Harvey, the preservation of temperance probably would not have become a political issue. But the large
number of votes in favor of liquor trafficking in the public referendum
indicates that many people in the community did not favor temperance. Since temperance followers were not likely to have switched their
allegiance on this issue, which persons would support legislation allowing saloons into the community?

Harvey's success as a manufacturing and employment center and
the continued diversification of economic activity planned by the land
association were themselves important factors in the decline of temperance. It is likely that not enough temperance followers could be
brought to the community to meet the needs of employers, and economic expansion by itself must have attracted workers to the community who did not favor temperance. Local business may of necessity
have become less discriminating in their hiring practices, employing
persons from both within and outside the community. Some of the
newer firms did not share the same commitment to temperance as the
founding organization. But these changes could not have gone unnoticed. Local businesses would have had to violate the employment
clause in their own contracts requiring them to give preference to
Harvey residents—that is, temperance followers. Thus, the Harvey
Land Association, as the founding agent and major corporate entity
within the community, must bear responsibility for the failure to regulate properly the activities of local businesses.

It is important not to overlook other long-term social changes confronting the community. The depression may simply have hastened the
decline of the small family-owned industries with ideological commitments to the community in favor of large corporate interests that saw
little immediate value in promoting a temperance life-style. Other
temperance towns (such as Greely, Colorado) experienced similar conflicts between communitarian idealism and interests and economic
development (Hayden 1979), suggesting that even had the community
survived the crises of the 1890s, other problems would have reappeared in later decades.

One might question the long-term viability of the social contract
between the land association and local employers when confronted
with the need for a new supply of labor. The commitment of local
businessmen to temperance ideals appears paramount in this analysis.
Perhaps, as Garner (1984) suggests, orderly development is possible
only when a single interest exercises control over an entire town site.
Without the strong centralized control of the land association, the drift
away from temperance may have been an irreversible process.

By the end of the nineteenth century the WCTU and other social movements concerned with the alcohol problem in the United States had come to focus on prohibition rather than personal abstinence as a solution to the alcohol problem. Attention had shifted from local to national and even international concerns, from community action to a national political movement and international missionary efforts (see Tyrrell 1991). For citizens of Harvey this shift may have resulted in a decision to carry on the temperance battle through direct (state and national) legislation rather than the appellate (local) courts—perhaps a realistic strategy given the success of prohibition efforts in many states during the 1880s.

What impact did such a change in political strategy have within the community? Two local figures in the prohibition fight, Lucy Page Gaston and Edward Page, refocused their efforts at social reform on a broader societal and even international level. Local leaders may have felt the temperance struggle in Harvey had been lost, perhaps as a consequence of economic disruption and the changing composition of the population. An attempt was made to salvage the moral issues of temperance by appealing to the more powerful forces of statewide and national legislation.

Although Harvey and other temperance towns relied on prohibition rather than abstinence to ensure social conformity, Harvey was born of the temperance movement and promoted through the temperance media. There are other direct linkages: Turlington Harvey was actively involved in the Chicago Evangelical Society and the YMCA; Frances Willard and others from the WCTU attended lectures at both organizations. Thus, the fortunes of the temperance towns may also be linked with the rise and decline of the WCTU in the 1890s.

There is evidence of an internal crisis in the WCTU during this period. The national membership drive slowed noticeably after 1892, and the national Anti-Saloon League was formed the following year. In 1893 the *Union Signal* asked whether the limit of growth had been reached (Bordin 1891, 140). Personality conflicts and power struggles also took their toll. Although an attempt to unseat Frances Willard at the 1896 national convention failed, she received only 387 of 436 votes instead of the unanimous affirmation of previous conventions (Epstein 1981). Conflicts in the national organization must have drained considerable energy from local efforts to preserve the temperance cause in towns such as Harvey. Roberts's comments concerning the decline of Temperance in nineteenth-century Germany appear relevant to the United States as well: "The social, economic, and political crisis of the immediate pre-revolutionary years undermined the appeal of a movement which promised so much but could do so little to offset the hardships faced by small farmers and urban craftsmen. The promise that the individual could control his own destiny and that virtue would be rewarded was belied by the course of events" (Roberts 1984, 39).

The WCTU encountered political opposition from several sources in the 1890s. When faced with serious challenges to basic premises, an ideological movement must either reform its goals or affirm its basic principals. By the 1890s the WCTU had made significant progress by joining with American labor movements, influencing public school curricula and forming an international organization. Given this success, the need for a reaffirmation of basic principles at the grass roots may not have been apparent, and questions of reforming the goals of the movement become more difficult to answer—although in Harvey the need for such an effort might well have made the difference between the success and failure of the temperance town.

Commitment to Temperance

The temperance era in Harvey was short-lived. If the ultimate goal of the land association was to establish a permanent temperance settlement, the social experiment was a failure. The above analysis focused on the contributions of economic depression, lack of planning control by the land association, and ideological shortcomings of the temperance movement itself; but we should also examine the commitment mechanisms within the temperance town, which may have made the social experiment more or less likely to succeed.

Utopian movements attempt to build an ideal community within a select group of persons sharing common values and beliefs. The resulting settlements have the specific purpose of serving as a model for the larger society. Thus, the temperance town would be the ideal community governed by the moral values of a temperance life-style. The success of such movements depends on the ability of the community to foster commitment to its social ideals. There are, however, many different methods of fostering commitment, from vows of chastity and poverty in certain religious communities to communal ownership of the means of production in socialist settlements.

Rosabeth Kantor (1972) analyzed the variety of commitment mechanisms used by communitarian settlements in the United States from 1800 to the present. Successful communes isolated themselves from the dominant society and required substantial sacrifices from new members. Isolation was achieved by physical location (in rural areas outside the social mainstream) or by restrictions on contact with the outside world (vows of silence among religious groups). Personal sacrifices included abstinence (vows of chastity, for example, although abstinence from alcohol was more common) as well as financial sacrifices (turning one's resources over to the community at large). Communes that altered traditional social structures (replacing the family unit with alternative sexual arrangements) thereby helped prevent divisiveness between members. Successful communes found a means of replacing the pursuit of individual self-interest through the collective commitment to common goals; unsuccessful communes were those that attempted minimal social changes while maintaining extensive social contacts with the dominant society.

To what degree did the commitment mechanisms found in the temperance town encourage the future success of the community? For the initial residents of Harvey, commitment was registered by the very decision to move to the town. Many families did so at great personal sacrifice, selling their property and severing ties to relocate from other states. These voluntary actions correspond to some of the commitment mechanisms described by Kantor—renouncing personal possessions and terminating earlier social ties. There is no reason to question the sincerity of these actions.

But even though individual commitment to temperance ideals in Harvey may be evident, it has little to do with commitment to a specific community or group of persons. Although a person may have felt that he or she shared certain important values and beliefs with others in the community, such attachments were easily transferred to another group or location (such as another temperance town in another area of the country). The lack of commitment to Harvey as a physical entity (rather than to temperance per se) is demonstrated by the number of persons who left during the depression years rather than remaining to confront the economic and ideological crisis challenging the community.

The land association did not possess the social and political controls necessary to develop commitment among new residents. The temperance clause included in property deeds had no effect on personal beliefs. Persons could not be required to give up their possessions. The land association could not regulate sexual behavior. Successful communes isolated their inhabitants from the influences of outside society; Garner (1984, 60–61) notes that "spatial separation between towns can induce social introspection, and company towns acquired special advantages in shaping public opinion because of their isolation.... Isolation in regard to paternalism made it easier for management to regulate other activities as well, such as temperance and politics." But Harvey was not isolated from the outside world—indeed, integration of the local economy with that of the Chicago region meant that extensive contacts were maintained.

Could the Harvey Land Association have generated greater commitment? Short of such measures as requiring residents to turn over their property to the community or renounce formally behaviors and values at variance with temperance, it would appear that the land association was powerless to develop the type of commitment mechanisms found in communitarian settlements. The lost opportunity was the failure to exercise greater control over what groups were allowed to live and work in the community, as was done in other company towns. Once a heterogeneous community developed, it was difficult to enforce particular ideologies or value systems. By maintaining a democratic and open community, the land association ensured that Harvey would develop a diverse population with competing value systems. The problem was in not anticipating the threat to temperance values in this policy.

SIGNIFICANCE OF THE TEMPERANCE TOWN

Students of utopian and communitarian settlements often adopt a romanticized and noncritical stance when evaluating the success of the social experiment. The usual conclusion of such studies is that even if a settlement survived for only a short time, it must still be significant because it had some lasting impact on those persons involved. In the concluding section to this analysis of Harvey (and, by extension, other temperance towns of the late nineteenth century), a more critical approach must be taken. Were temperance towns successful in creating a new life-style based on temperance values?

In *Crusade against Drink in Victorian England,* Lillian Shiman (1988, 161–169) describes Birstal, a small town in Yorkshire, as a "total temperance community" where teetotalers were committed to creating a community that would take care of all the needs of its members. The symbolic center of the community was the Temperance Hall, where public lectures and weekend celebrations reinforced the temperance life-style. In addition to Sunday sermons, the Temperance Hall hosted the Bright Hour for women on Monday afternoons, the Band of Hope for children Wednesday mornings at 7:30 and 8:30, the Band of Hope Saturday recreation meeting, choir practices three times a week, and annual meetings with other temperance societies. Of the annual meetings Shiman (1988, 163–164) writes, "These joint meetings of the district temperance societies were more than pleasant gatherings; they were an integral part of the fabric that united members. They were the means for bringing teetotal families of the district together and were instrumental in promoting alliances and marriages among them." The temperance community in Harvey lacked this symbolic center and was unable to develop the "total temperance community" that the founders envisioned.

In Harvey temperance did not create a new way of life but instead reproduced patterns of social class and ethnic stratification within the larger society. Temperance towns such as Harvey had little, if any, effect on state or national temperance efforts—indeed, they are generally ignored in both primary and secondary sources concerning temperance history. Temperance produced little unique in the way of town planning. In discussing Pullman, Stanley Buder (1967a) notes that the town plan was close-ended and self-contained, with no provision for later growth or flexibility; it was a static design of little practical interest for planners. The same is true of planning efforts in Harvey. Dolores Hayden's (1976, 274) characterization of the Union Colony in Greely, Colorado, a temperance town founded in the spirit of Christian socialism, seems appropriate for Harvey as well: "The Union Colony translates this spirit into town planning, and the end result is an average American town with a single idealistic episode in its early history."

What, then, is the significance of the temperance town? To a limited extent the legacy of temperance as a progressive, liberal reform movement may be seen in the later development of the town. In 1912 Harvey was the first municipality to approve a commission form of government by popular referendum. In the 1920s it was viewed as a model suburb, with the lowest rate of delinquency and the best school system in the region. But from a long-term perspective there is little lasting influence from the temperance period, and perhaps the parallel with Pullman should again be noted.

The lasting importance of Harvey is that the town stands as a historical record of the attempt to establish a planned industrial community based on temperance reform. Although there are many such examples of industrial temperance settlements in Great Britain, most temperance towns in the United States were rural settlements isolated from the growing industrial centers. In Harvey temperance followers sought to establish an ideal community largely nativist in character—indeed, the early motto of the WCTU had been "For God and Home and Native Land"—which maintained class differences and provided only limited social mobility for the working class. Social class differences were symbolically restructured in geographic space, with the middle class (in Western Europe) living in larger homes near the center of the community and the working class (in Eastern Europe) confined to smaller bungalows around the periphery. Temperance in Harvey represented liberal social reform carried out within the structures of the existent society—but with relatively little questioning of the larger values and purposes of that society. As a consequence the temperance town only reproduced patterns of class and ethnic segregation of nineteenth-century America.

The possible explanations for the decline of temperance in Harvey at the turn of the century raise several interesting hypotheses for temperance scholars. If the prolonged economic depression of the 1890s is responsible for the decline of temperance, then temperance communities in regions of the country less dependent than the Midwest on industrial employment should have survived into the 1900s. If Harvey's dependence on regional economic and labor markets increased external pressures against temperance, communities in more rural areas of the country should have been more successful. And if the lack of commitment mechanisms is ultimately responsible for the decline of temperance in Harvey, then those communities that more strictly limited residence to the followers of temperance should have been more successful in preserving temperance values.

The historical record in Harvey demands more extensive comparative work on the development of temperance towns in other areas of the country. Temperance towns of the 1890s allow us to study the impact of temperance on the lives of the common man and woman. What new opportunities were presented by the temperance movement? How did the community respond to changes in the national temperance organization? Current information is too limited to determine if Harvey is representative of other temperance towns or is a unique case. The relevant questions are the same as those outlined in the introduction: Who were the founders and what were the motives for settlement? Were the towns centrally planned, and if so, by whom? What groups settled in the community, and where did they come from? What were the means of economic support for the community, and what factors were responsible for their decline? What role did the temperance town play within the temperance movement generally? And what lasting contribution, if any, did the temperance town make to American society at the turn of the century?

NOTES

An initial version of this material appears in my doctoral dissertation (Hutchison 1985). It was revised for a presentation to a faculty colloquium at the University of California, San Diego, in June 1983. I must thank Joseph Gusfield for the incentive to complete this work while I was a visiting faculty member at UCSD and for the suggestion that it be presented at the Social History of Alcohol conference in Berkeley. Two anonymous reviewers provided valuable suggestions for this final version.

1. J. C. Furnas (1965, 323–326) gives a brief sketch of Prohibition Park (New York), Greely (Colorado), Harriman (Tennessee), and the Vineland Colony (New Jersey), but these towns are not mentioned in other standard works on the temperance movement: Bordin 1981; Duis 1983; Engelmann 1979;

Epstein 1981; Gusfield 1963; Harrison 1971; Longmate 1963; Odegard 1928; Timberlake 1963. Donovan (1955) is a secondary work dealing with land speculation in Harriman, Tennessee, in the early 1890s.

2. Early studies of communitarian settlements include Noyes 1870, Nordhoff 1875, and Lockwood 1905. More recent work includes Bestor 1950, Foster 1981, Halloway 1951, Hardy 1979, Hayden 1979, Kantor 1972, and LeWarne 1975.

3. Although the relationship between the rise of labor unions and working class militancy in the late 1880s and the decentralization of industry to the suburbs has been noted in Marxist work (e.g. Stone 1978), the full impact of the social disturbances of the late 1870s on this process has not been adequately documented. Armed conflicts on the streets of Chicago in 1877 produced a good deal of hysteria when the media reported that a Red War had begun and Chicago was in the hands of the communists. These events must have influenced George Pullman's decision to locate the new factory buildings for the Pullman Palace Car Company outside of the city, and the origin of the industrial suburbs of Chicago may be dated from the construction of the new industrial community by the shores of Lake Calumet in 1881–1883. The 1877 conflicts are described in a contemporary account by Allan Pinkerton ([1878] 1969) and have been studied in detail by Robert Bruce (1970) and Phillip Foner (1974).

4. Carol Rahn (1980) has suggested that the home ownership plan in Harvey was an intentional effort on the part of the Land Association to distance itself from mounting public criticism of the Pullman Company, which maintained strict control over housing. But the timing of this conclusion may not be accurate: early reports from the economist Richard T. Ely and Jane Addams of Hull House in the 1880s were generally favorable toward Pullman housing policies, and widespread criticism of Pullman would await the strike of 1893–1894. Thus, the housing efforts of the Harvey Land Association from 1890–1893 may best be viewed as the result of planning efforts that saw home ownership as a positive benefit rather than a simple response to criticisms of Pullman policies.

5. Rahn (1980) covers the history of local politics in Harvey. My analysis builds on her work in identifying local elites during the Land Association period (1890–1899).

REFERENCES

Arndt, Karl J. R. 1975. *A Documentary History of the Indiana Decade of the Harmony Society, 1814–1819.* Indianapolis: Indiana Historical Society.

Bestor, Arthur E. 1950. *Backwoods Utopias: The Sectarian Origins and the Owenite Phase of Communitarian Socialism in America, 1663–1829.* Philadelphia: University of Pennsylvania Press.

Bordin, Ruth. 1981. *Women and Temperance: The Quest for Power and Liberty, 1873–1900.* Philadelphia: Temple University Press.

Braverman, Harry. 1974. *Labor and Monopoly Capital: The Degradation of Work in the Twentieth Century.* New York: Monthly Review Press.

Bruce, Robert. 1970. *1877: Year of Violence.* Chicago: Quadrangle Press.

Buder, Stanley. 1967a. *Pullman: An Experiment in Social and Industrial Order.* New York: Macmillan.

———. 1967b. "The Model Town of Pullman: Town Planning and Social Control." *Journal of the American Institute of Planners* 33 (January): 2–10.

City of Chicago. 1974. *Historic City: The Settlement of Chicago.* Chicago: Department of Planning.

Coolidge, John P. 1941. *Mill and Mansion: A Study in Architecture and Society in Lowell, Massachusetts, 1820–1865.* New York: Columbia University Press.

Donovan, William F. 1955. "Real Estate Speculation in Cardiff and Harriman, 1890–1893." *Tennessee Historical Quarterly* (September).

Duis, Perry R. 1983. *The Saloon: Public Drinking in Chicago and Boston, 1880–1920.* Urbana: University of Illinois Press.

Engelmann, Larry. 1979. *Intemperance: The Lost War against Liquor.* New York: Free Press.

Epstein, Barbara Leslie. 1981. *The Politics of Domesticity: Women, Evangelism, and Temperance in Nineteenth-Century America.* Middletown, Conn.: Wesleyan University Press.

Ewen, Stuart. 1976. *Captains of Consciousness.* New York: McGraw-Hill.

Foner, Philip. 1974. *The Great Railroad Strike of 1877.* New York: Monad Press.

Foster, Edward Halsey. 1975. *The Civilized Wilderness: Backgrounds to American Romantic Literature, 1817–1860.* New York: Free Press.

Foster, Lawrence. 1981. *Religion and Sexuality: Three American Communal Experiments of the Nineteenth Century.* New York: Oxford University Press.

Furnas, J. C. 1965. *The Life and Times of the Late Demon Rum.* London: W. H. Allen.

Garner, John S. 1984. *The Model Company Town: Urban Design through Private Enterprise in Nineteenth Century New England.* Amherst: University of Massachusetts Press.

Green, Constance M. 1939. *Holyoke, Massachusetts: A Case History of the Industrial Revolution in America.* New Haven, Conn.: Yale University Press.

Gusfield, Joseph. 1963. *Symbolic Crusade: Status Politics and the American Temperance Movement.* Urbana: University of Illinois Press.

Gutman, Herbert. 1966. *Work, Culture, and Society in Industrializing America.* New York: Random House.

Halloway, Mark. 1951. *Heavens on Earth: Utopian Communities in America, 1680–1880.* New York: Library Publishers.

Hardy, Dennis. 1979. *Alternative Communities in Nineteenth Century New England.* New York: Longman.

Harrison, Brian Howard. 1971. *Drink and the Victorians: The Temperance Question in England, 1815–1872.* London: Faber and Faber.

Harvey Land Association. [1892a]. "Harvey! Two Miles South of Chicago City Limits." Advertising flier. Chicago Historical Society.

———. [1892b]. "World's Fair Subscriptions." Advertising flier. Chicago Historical Society.

———. [1893]. *The Town of Harvey, Illinois: Manufacturing Suburb of Chicago, Aged Two Years.* Published by Harvey Land Association.

Hayden, Dolores. 1979. *Seven American Utopias: The Architecture of Communitarian Socialism, 1790–1975.* Cambridge, Mass.: MIT Press.

Hoffman, Charles. 1956. "The Depression of the Nineties." *Journal of Economic History* 16 (June): 137–164.

Hotchkiss, George W. 1900. *Industrial Chicago: The Lumber Interests*. Chicago: Goodspeed.

Hutchison, Ray. 1984. "Black Suburbanization: Social Change in an Industrial Suburb." Ph.D. diss., Department of Sociology, University of Chicago.

Isetts, Charles A. 1979. "A Social Profile of the Women's Temperance Crusade: Hillsboro, Ohio." In *Alcohol, Reform, and Society: The Liquor Issue in Social Context*, ed. Jack S. Bl₋ :ker, Jr., 101–10. Westport, Conn.: Greenwood Press.

972. *Commitment and Community: Communes and Utopias*
. Cambridge: Harvard University Press.

ilizing the Machine: Technology and Republican Values in
ew York: Grossman.

Harvey, Illinois History: 1893–1962. Harvey, Ill.: First

The Founders Own Story of the Founding of Vineland, New
ineland Historical and Antiquarian Society.

1975. *Utopias on Puget Sound, 1885–1915*. Seattle:
on Press.

5. *The New Harmony Movement*. New York: Appleton.
. *The Water Drinkers: A History of Temperance*. London:

hat Do Bosses Do? The Origins and Functions of
Production." *Review of Radical Political Economics* 6

(1965). *The Communistic Societies of the United States*.
ocken Books.

. *History of American Socialisms*. Philadelphia: Lippincott.
essure Politics: The Story of the Anti-Saloon League. New
ty Press.

Three Centuries of Social Mobility in America. Lexing-

69. *Communists, Tramps, and Detectives*. Reprint. New

Elites and Social Change: A Case Study of Harvey,
artment of Sociology, University of Chicago.
ink, Temperance, and the Working Class in Nineteenth
Century Germany. Boston: Allen & Unwin.

Shiman, Lillian Lewis. 1988. *Crusade against Drink in Victorian England*. London: Macmillan.

Sobel, Robert. 1968. *Panic on Wall Street: A History of America's Financial Disasters*. New York: Macmillan.

Stone, Michael. 1978. "Housing, Mortgage Lending, and the Contradictions of Capitalism." In *Marxism and the Metropolis: New Perspectives in Urban Political Economy*, ed. William Tabb and Larry Sawers. New York: Oxford University Press.

Taylor, Graham R. 1915. *Satellite Cities: A Study of Industrial Suburbs*. New York: Appleton.

Thernstrom, Stephen. 1964. *Poverty and Progress: Social Mobility in a Nineteenth Century City.* Cambridge: Harvard University Press.

Timberlake, Joseph. 1963. *Prohibition and the Progressive Movement.* Cambridge: Harvard University Press.

Tyrrell, Ian R. 1979. "Temperance and Economic Change in the Antebellum North." In *Alcohol, Reform, and Society: The Liquor Issue in Social Context,* ed. Jack S. Blocker, Jr., 45–65. Westport, Conn.: Greenwood Press.

———. 1991. "Women and Temperance in International Perspective: The World's WCTU, 1880s–1920s." Chapter 10 in this volume.

Union Signal. 1891. Vol. 17, nos. 10–12. March 5, 12, 19.

Walker, Joseph E. 1966. *Hopewill Village: The Dynamics of a Nineteenth Century Iron Making Community.* Philadelphia: University of Pennsylvania Press.

Zimmerman, J. T. [1921]. "Early History of Settlement in Thornton Township." Typescript. Harvey Public Library, Harvey, Ill.

TEN

Women and Temperance in International Perspective: The World's WCTU, 1880s–1920s

Ian Tyrrell

The 1885 national convention of the American Woman's Christian Temperance Union was depicted by contemporary reformers as a most auspicious occasion. That year abstainers celebrated the completion of one hundred years of temperance agitation, dated from the appearance of Benjamin Rush's *Inquiry into the Effects of Spirituous Liquors* in 1784. What would the new century hold? Frances Willard, the dynamic and charismatic national president, told her adoring followers that the "second temperance century" would witness the export of temperance reform around the globe, spearheaded by her recently created World's Woman's Christian Temperance Union.[1]

Though the hundred years that followed hardly fulfilled Willard's expectations, the meaning of her 1885 address has been lost on historians, both American and non-American. Internationalism has been a persistent and obscure theme in temperance reform. Willard's grandiose vision was not exceptional among temperance advocates. Ernest Cherrington's World League against Alcoholism in the 1920s is one example; the fraternal orders, such as the Sons of Temperance, which spread from the United States to the British empire in the mid-nineteenth century, provide other cases.[2] This essay explores the international dimension and its limits and poses new questions for the comparative history of temperance and drink questions through a case study of the World's WCTU as an international organization.

Frances Willard first suggested a World's WCTU in 1883, though not until late in 1884 did the first world missionary, Mary Clement Leavitt, depart from San Francisco on a journey that would lead her to all continents and take eight years to complete. When Willard first proclaimed an international campaign, there was no tangible organization. Only in 1891 did a world convention assemble to approve a constitution. Conferences were then held biennially until 1897 and triennially thereafter, except during World War I. In all, fourteen conventions were held between 1891 and 1931. The membership was declared to be half a million by 1895 and more than one million in the 1920s, though records of dues paid yield lower figures. In 1910 there were 435,000 dues-paying members, of whom almost 46 percent were non-American. By 1927 the organization had 766,225 members, but proportionately the American contribution had risen more rapidly in the 1920s as part of the drive to preserve national prohibition. (Just under 43 percent of members were non-Americans in 1928.) The World's WCTU also sent out fifty-four missionaries in the footsteps of Leavitt, some outdoing her in distance traveled, years spent in the work, and eccentricity.[3]

The membership figures point to a genuinely international dimension to the activity of temperance women in forty-two countries by the 1920s. The second and third presidents of the World's WCTU were Englishwomen, Lady Isobel Somerset and Lady Rosalind Carlisle, both titled aristocrats. The missionaries were recruited not just from the United States but also from England, Scotland, Australia, New Zealand, South Africa, Scandinavia, India, and China. Superintendents of its "departments" of work were also chosen from a variety of affiliates. Unlike the International Council of Women, organized in 1888, the World's WCTU was not an umbrella group of separate reform organizations but a relatively integrated society pursuing common policies and sharing a common organizational framework, ideology, and international leadership. Support for this organization was, like for other international women's groups of the time, strongest in the Anglo-Saxon world. But in contrast to its competitors the World's WCTU also operated in the mission stations of American and British evangelical churches in China, Japan, India, and the Pacific islands.

The World's WCTU was an important conduit of international communication on all questions of interest to woman reformers. Material published in the *Union Signal,* the British *White Ribbon,* or the World's WCTU *White Ribbon Bulletin* was reprinted in other national and local temperance papers sponsored by the WCTU. The *Union Signal* was itself popular in those areas that did not have their own national or regional papers and among WCTU leaders everywhere. Other WCTU publications, such as the pamphlets, speeches, and books of Frances Willard, were also widely circulated. One method of spreading the teachings of the organization was through medal contests named for the prohibitionist William Jennings Demorest. Under this system children were entered in contests to win Demorest medals by reciting temperance material. In such countries as Australia and New Zealand the material came from American temperance publications, especially the WCTU *National Educator.*[4]

Personal communication was also used for the dissemination of WCTU principles. Friendships made during Leavitt's global missionary tour, for example, persisted for twenty years until the death of the correspondents; women who met at conventions visited one another and corresponded in the same fashion. These links were not simply between the American WCTU and various World's WCTU auxiliaries. Similar exchanges took place between, for example, Australian and New Zealand temperance women and between the organizations in Australasia and South Africa.[5]

Through these personal contacts and publications the World's WCTU served as a medium for the exchange of ideas and institutional arrangements. The introduction of police matrons, for instance, began with the efforts of the American WCTU prison reformer Susan Barney in the late 1870s and was popularized in Britain through Barney's trip there in 1895. Barney herself went on a world tour in the interests of temperance and prison reform in 1897–1898, but her ideas were also transmitted by women she had met during her time in England. Florence Balgarnie, a British temperance reformer impressed with Barney's schemes, succeeded in having matrons introduced into police stations in Sydney, Australia, in 1902.[6]

Especially valuable was the role of the World's WCTU as a transmitter of information on the woman suffrage question. In some areas where the organization took root, there were either no suffrage organizations at all or their influence was severely restricted. In such cases franchise propaganda had to be spread through WCTU sources. Much suffrage propaganda published in Australasia in the 1890s came from American WCTU publications, though they were often adapted for local conditions. Australian WCTU franchise departments used the examples of Colorado, Wyoming, and Idaho to justify the granting of woman suffrage in the colonies and received firsthand information on the benefits of woman suffrage to the temperance cause from such visiting American missionaries as Mary Leavitt and Jessie Ackerman.[7]

The flow of propaganda operated in reverse as well. With the granting of woman suffrage in New Zealand in 1893 and South Australia in 1894, Australasia became an experiment in votes for women that American WCTU propagandists could exploit. Writing on "the new international movement for woman's suffrage" in the *Union Signal* in 1902, Jane Stewart proclaimed that in the new federal government of Australia "the question of woman's political equality" was "on a higher plane than in any other part of the world." American suffrage workers were willing, like those elsewhere, to use the example of victories in other countries to raise spirits in their own ranks and force their own governments into action out of shame. If suffrage was suitable for South Australian women, why withhold it from their American sisters?[8]

The World's WCTU also distributed literature on the alcohol issue itself. Especially in the early 1920s the organization set out to explain to non-Americans the benefits of national prohibition in the United States and strove to counter "wet" views that might be gleaned from sections of the American media. It was in the interests of the American WCTU to promote such campaigns because the importation of foreign liquor was an issue of concern to all who sought to enforce the Volstead Act. But the American WCTU emphasized its desire to spread the benefits of prohibition to other countries. "It would be criminally selfish in us as Christian temperance women," wrote Anna Gordon, national WCTU president in 1920, "to content ourselves with ridding our own land of the greatest enemy of the home and of childhood." To attain the result of world prohibition, American and British lecturers toured Europe, Latin America, and Australasia, proclaiming that those regions would be dry within a decade.[9]

World prohibition was only the final phase of a long campaign to spread the principles of abstinence and restrictive legislation to countries other than the United States. In the 1880s Mary Leavitt had campaigned wherever she went against the use of barmaids, and those efforts were ultimately successful through the agitation of local WCTUs in Cape Town, South Australia, and Victoria before World War I.[10] This issue tied in with a general offensive against the perceived threat of woman drinkers. Reports in Australia, Britain, and the United States indicated that WCTU members believed an increase was occurring in the number of women drinking between 1890 and 1914. Yet the evidence that WCTU reports used was drawn almost exclusively from Britain; neither Americans nor Australians thought it essential to produce their own evidence. The threat of parallel trends in other English-speaking countries was enough to raise hysteria and indicated the considerable extent to which WCTU propaganda treated the organization as an indivisible international unit.[11]

This example does not mean that the non-American affiliates were merely imitative. The original decision to form a world organization was stimulated by the fact that church groups, American travelers, and others had begun to form unions outside the United States before 1883 and that these groups had urged Willard to coordinate the international movement. Similarly, ideas and institutional changes sometimes flowed from non-American affiliates to the American and world organizations. The home-protection slogan was first applied to the temperance movement by Letitia Youmans of the Ontario WCTU and later adopted by Willard in her offensive to gain voting rights for women.[12]

When historians have noted these international dimensions to WCTU work at all, they have favored trivial or superficial explanations. For Ruth Bordin, Willard's growing international commitment in the 1890s flowed from her personal attachment to Isobel Somerset of the British Women's Temperance Association. Mary Earhart argued similarly but also repeated the Willard line of the 1880s that she had been "converted" to internationalism "overnight" by exposure to the horrors of the opium dens of San Francisco.[13] These and other views fail to explain the long history of American temperance reformers' concern, going back to the 1820s, with a global evangelism. Within the WCTU an international impulse was manifest as early as 1876, when the first Woman's International Temperance Convention was held in Philadelphia. These international convictions stemmed from the close connection between temperance and evangelical religion. Whereas WCTU links with evangelical churches are well documented, the implications of foreign missionary work for an international women's temperance campaign have not been followed up by historians.[14] Almost all of the women the WCTU sent out as international lecturers or world missionaries had participated in the foreign missionary societies. They had either gone to do gospel work in the so-called uncivilized world and were then recruited for the WCTU or had expressed a desire at an early age to become involved in such work. Their proselytizing for the World's WCTU sometimes constituted a secularization of the missionary motivation, sometimes an embodiment of its religious fervor.[15]

The missionary impulse was linked to the issue of Western imperialist expansion in Asia, Africa, and Latin America. The political dissection of large portions of the globe in the interests of European colonial powers coincided with the expansion of Western cultural influence, of which the World's WCTU was both a beneficiary and a source. Protestant missionaries in the 1880s sent back first-hand accounts of the impact of the West on the "native races" of Africa and cited the spread of Christianity and the introduction of "alcoholic poisons" as tandem and contradictory developments. WCTU women joined in the condemnation. In 1885 Willard pointed out that "habits of social drinking are a greater harm to the natives than our missionaries can by any means offset."[16]

As much as the impact of European penetration on "these helpless people," the World's WCTU leaders feared the reciprocal influence of a corrupted colonial world on the metropolitan countries. Isobel Somerset believed that if vice prevailed in India, the officers and enlisted men of the British army would bring home to Britain the bad habits acquired in the service of empire.[17] Even before the acquisition of former Spanish territories in 1898, American WCTU officials wondered whether their own country could escape contamination. Lower moral standards might spread from Europe and Asia through improved communications, foreign travel, and immigration; thereby the status of women in the United States might eventually be affected by the moral diseases of imperialism. This connection was made by Willard as early as 1883, when she noted the development of the Pacific Coast of the United States, the spread of commerce, and the migration of Chinese, with their opium smoking, to California.[18]

The strategy adopted to deal with these problems had Britain as its centerpiece. Since Britain was the leading colonial power, the reform of drinking habits there would, it was hoped, entail an automatic international influence. Willard stressed "the momentous value of strengthening the white-ribbon movement in the central country of the English-speaking race, with its mightly outreach of power to its great colonies."[19] Underlying this assessment was the worldview of social Darwinism: the Anglo-Saxon race was destined to lead the world to a higher stage of evolution and eventually to world federation. Women had a crucial role in strengthening the Anglo-Saxon race for this moral struggle through the universal application of their maternal morality.[20]

Support for this grandiose program cannot be explained as a simple reflection of the level of alcohol abuse in various societies. The connections between women, drink, and abstinence were mediated through the intervening variables of evangelical Christian motivations and through a host of issues important to women. Unlike the Woman's Crusade in Ohio in 1873–1874, which was closely and directly linked to the incidence of drinking among relatives of temperance women,[21] the World's WCTU canvassed the whole spectrum of reform issues, thus complicating the construction of a simple connection between drinking and temperance activity in the 1880s and 1890s.

It is widely known that the WCTU after the 1880s was indeed interested in many reform causes loosely linked to temperance under the do-everything policy of Frances Willard. Much more obscure is the extent to which this policy was closely associated with the internationalization of the WCTU program. The inclusion of opium as a drug to be suppressed was a critical decision in the broadening of the WCTU beyond a narrow temperance base, and adoption of the antiopium position was closely tied to Willard's international aspirations. David

Courtwright's *Dark Paradise* makes clear that opium smoking was spreading in the United States in the 1870s and that whites as well as Chinese were beginning to be affected.[22] When Willard turned her attention to opium smoking, her concern thus reflected the actual shifts in the patterns of opium consumption. Nonetheless, if she was concerned primarily with the actual incidence of opium addiction among white middle-class women Courtwright identifies as the most common opium takers among the native-born, her justifications did not reveal it. Nor did she single out for emphasis the problem of opium taking within the United States. Her international outlook and evangelical messianism focused on the larger world problem of opium use that the opium dens in San Francisco only dimly evidenced.

If the WCTU was to become a worldwide organization, Willard argued, it would have to attack those drugs of concern in each area of the globe. This strategy entailed a modification of the WCTU program. In "working up" the new organization, Willard announced, "we must carefully study the adaptation of methods to varying climates and nationalities, no less than to prevailing habits of brain poison. One of the best results to be obtained...will, perhaps, be this: That all stimulants and narcotics will finally be included in our pledge, as alike the enemies of that sacred instrument of thought, the human brain."[23] By 1886, the American and World's WCTU executives had endorsed Willard's suggestion. Whereas the home protection campaign had sundered restrictions on WCTU political activity within the United States, the opium campaign helped internationally to breach restrictions on the types of social issues the WCTU could legitimately embrace.

Just as opium was considered crucial to non-Western temperance mobilization, so too was the purity question raised to an almost equal importance for the recruitment of temperance women in Europe. The 1886 "plan of proposed work" for the World's WCTU coupled temperance and purity, probably because the document had been drafted in the context of a British presence at the American WCTU convention in that year. The purity question was at the time of much greater importance in Britain than temperance as a women's issue.[24] This sentiment the World's WCTU hoped to tap. Willard put the point directly in relation to continental Europe in 1893: "In no portion of the world has the W.C.T.U. found it so difficult to gain a foothold." Since European women could not be easily won over to a crusade against drink, the WCTU must first, Willard argued, work in alliance with Josephine Butler, leading opponent of prostitution legislation in Britain, and build on Butler's connections with European purity workers. The World's WCTU could thereby "involve their sympathies as women."[25]

Apart from these tactical concerns, the purity issue was of relevance to the American WCTU for entirely American reasons; but these reasons cannot be divorced completely from European influences. Spasmodically in the 1880s, and in hysterical form by 1900, fears developed of an influx of foreign white slaves and of native-born girls falling victim to foreign pimps. There was also the issue of how to deal with the prostitution question in the United States and the relevance of European experience to those debates. Mark Connelly has shown that the issue of regulation versus abolition of prostitution continued to haunt purity debates in the United States even though regulation ceased after the 1870 Saint Louis experiment. These debates were conducted with close reference to the existence of regulatory systems in several European nations. The regulationist controversy was not settled in an intellectual sense until 1914, with the publication of Abraham Flexner's *Prostitution in Europe*. Thus, right up to World War I it was important for supporters of Willard's "white life for two" to have knowledge of international aspects of prostitution reform and to campaign in Europe, India, and East Asia if purity forces in the United States were to remain dominant.[26]

Modern historians depict the social purity campaigns of the nineteenth century as repressive attempts to force a middle-class morality on working people. Purity crusaders denied the sexuality of women, accepted male dominance, and treated woman prostitutes in a misleading and damaging way as victims.[27] These charges contain a large degree of truth; but the international campaign of the WCTU also linked antiprostitution reform with related work emphasizing the cross-cultural subordination of women and proposed through purity a form of women's emancipation. The WCTU noted that prostitution placed restrictions on women that were not equally applied to men who engaged in sexual "indulgence" and linked this analysis to practices in non-Western societies that illustrated the inferior legal and cultural status of women. These included child marriage and the treatment of widows in India, the geisha system in Japan, polygamy in a variety of countries, the veil in the Arab world, and foot binding in China. Attacking these practices involved an identification of interests with culturally and racially diverse peoples. Emma Brainerd Ryder's book on "marital slavery" in India was widely distributed in the WCTU, "for what one class of women can endure during thousands of years other women can afford to know." WCTU women in Australia grieved for, and sent money to help, "the sorrowladen little wives of India" after a visit from Ryder in 1895. Women there and in other countries joined in the Ramabai Associations (sponsored by, among others, Frances Willard) to help high-caste Hindu widows receive an education. The founder of that movement, Pundita Ramabai, was an Indian WCTU

lecturer, a friend of Willard's, and a senior figure in the World's
WCTU. The Reverend Anna Shaw stated the assumption on which
such campaigns rested: "It was not possible for any one woman to sink
beneath the dignity of womanhood and the plane upon which God
intended she should live without all other women being more or less
affected thereby."[28]

Another venture, the work of the peace and arbitration department,
had more obvious international implications. This branch of work was
established on the national American level in 1887 and within the
World's WCTU in 1891. Its energetic coordinator was Hannah Clark
Bailey, a wealthy Quaker woman who had contacts in the British and
American peace movements. As Frank L. Byrne has observed, the work
of Bailey's department constituted "the greatest women's peace movement of the nineteenth and early twentieth centuries."[29] By 1894
twenty-four states had adopted departments, and this total rose to
thirty-three by 1910. As early as the 1890s peace work under WCTU
auspices was going on in twenty different countries. The organization
sent representatives to most international peace congresses held before 1914. Although World War I naturally put international campaigns for peace to their severest test, it is significant that peace
resolutions continued to be a major topic at WCTU conventions in the
1920s, with the World's WCTU campaigning for a league of nations
and a world court.[30]

Liquor was the other major issue requiring an international component. The World's WCTU tried to shape the policies of Western governments on the export of liquor to colonial areas by providing some
of the "facts" on which temperance assessments of imperial policies
were based. Thus, Mary Leavitt supplied some of the information for
the hostile account of the penetration of European liquor in East
Africa in *The Cyclopedia of Temperance*. WCTU workers attended international conferences that discussed this question, including the Universal
Races Congress of 1911, and the many International Congresses on
Alcoholism. Moreover, the World's WCTU lobbied the American and
British governments for action from 1890 onward in a joint campaign
with missionary societies and the evangelical churches.[31] How far
church groups in general and the WCTU in particular influenced
governmental policies is difficult to measure. What the church campaigns did achieve was the publicizing of the issue in the metropolitan
centers of empire, and a succession of international conferences culminated in the total prohibition of certain types of cheaper spirits under
the covenants of the League of Nations after World War I.[32]

These issues could be agitated in a more-or-less self-contained way;
but what held the membership together and defined the limits of the

World's WCTU appeal was insistence on total abstinence and Christian profession. These common denominators of reform meant not only total abstinence in countries where a partial pledge would have elicited more support but also a virtual injunction against regulation of the liquor traffic. The efficacy of prohibition thus became a controversial point, defining the membership and limiting the capacity of the world organization to respond to changing conditions and circumstances in the way that Willard had originally suggested. Although prohibition was not enjoined on members, there was an implicit understanding that members everywhere must refrain from measures hostile to American conceptions of prohibition.

A major controversy did break out over this issue when the Gothenberg system of state ownership of the liquor business won support in several European affiliates of the WCTU. The most controversial challenge to the prohibitionist faith came from Isobel Somerset. She was forced to resign from the presidencies of both the British Women's Temperance Association and the World's WCTU because of her decision to support public management in Britain through the Temperance Legislation League in 1906. Her replacement, Lady Rosalind Carlisle, was a staunch supporter of prohibition.[33] Insistence on prohibition was not, however, an American imposition on the world organization since indigenous support for legal action in many affiliates was considerable, particularly after the American drive for national prohibition gained momentum around 1907. Non-American locals imported American WCTU workers to tell of the advantages of national prohibition and pushed for their own closest approximations to the dry millennium.[34] This was particularly true in Australasia and Scotland, but in much of Europe advocacy of prohibition profoundly limited the WCTU's appeal. The organization never confronted the strategic implications of its prohibitionist sentiments and turned instead to cultures that seemed more receptive to ideas of abstinence. India, Japan, Burma, and China were, after the turn of the century, regarded as more promising, and the efforts of the WCTU in the non-Anglo-Saxon world increasingly concentrated in these regions.[35]

How important were the international aspects of temperance work for the WCTU membership? Certainly, it is necessary to distinguish between the enthusiastic statements of support in the *Union Signal* and the actual commitment of money, time, and personnel to the World's WCTU and to temperance work on an international scale. It is also important to distinguish between those who made a career in reform and those who simply joined a local temperance society. For the leadership of the women's temperance movement at the national and international levels, the work of the World's WCTU was of considerable importance. International work did impinge on national policies.

A case in point was the lynching controversy of the mid-1890s. The American WCTU had passed a straightforward antilynching resolution at its 1893 convention, but in 1894 it coupled an attack on lynching with a denunciation of the "unspeakable outrages" that "have so often provoked such lawlessness." To antilynching groups, the WCTU appeared to be excusing the behavior of southern white mobs. Ida Wells, a young negro woman temperance and antilynching activist, took her opposition to this resolution to the British Women's Temperance Association, alleging that Willard had changed her stand to placate her southern constituency.[36] The franchise superintendent of the BWTA, Florence Balgarnie, took up Wells's criticisms and secured demands for a change to the American policy from one-tenth of the six hundred BWTA auxiliaries. Though the Somerset-Willard forces still controlled the BWTA, the annual conference in 1895 and the World's WCTU convention held in London at the same time did pass stronger antilynching resolutions. This pressure in turn influenced the American WCTU, where the offending resolution was rescinded. Thereafter Willard and her supporters in both Britain and America made clear their unequivocal opposition to lynching. Willard denied that she had bowed to pressure from Wells and Balgarnie, but the evidence suggests otherwise. Wells was unable to influence the American WCTU when she appeared before its national convention in 1894. Only after the issue erupted into a major controversy on the international level did Willard and her American colleagues shift ground. Though the evidence is only circumstantial, it appears that Willard was prepared to offend her supporters in the American South when forced to choose between them and international influence in the women's temperance movement.[37]

A second issue that demonstrated the power of international issues was social purity. In 1897 Somerset, then vice president of the World's WCTU as well as president of the BWTA and a close confidant of Willard's, wrote to the *Times* of London sanctioning a British government plan for the reintroduction of the registration of prostitution in India on behalf of the British army garrisons there. WCTU opinion everywhere was stunned by the association of a WCTU leader with the idea of regulation. Nonetheless, Willard stuck by her friend, and the American WCTU in turn supported Willard despite misgivings. Willard did not approve Somerset's scheme but refused to ask for her resignation, believing that Somerset was simply too important to the movement to be lost over any other issue than total abstinence.[38]

Ultimately Somerset retracted her support of regulation, but what has been obscured in this controversial story is the role of non-American WCTU affiliates in the eventual demise of Somerset and in the elimination of the regulationist taint from the WCTU. The impression has been given that the American WCTU was responsible for the eventual resolution of the crisis. It is true that the American Mary Leavitt organized some of the opposition to Somerset,[39] but most of Leavitt's factional fighting against the Willard-Somerset axis took place on the international level, and the crucial opposition to Somerset came from WCTU groups in Sweden, Canada, Australia, New Zealand, South Africa, India, and Britain.[40] Opposition was so widespread because many of these countries had recent experience of the Contagious Diseases Acts regulating prostitution or feared that they would be introduced everywhere in the British empire if successful in India. The threat of WCTU leaders in Canada, Australia, and other affiliates to resign from the World's WCTU was what forced Somerset to recant.[41]

Thus far the complexities of support for the World's WCTU among a coterie of national and international leaders have been illustrated. At the local level the World's WCTU was, not surprisingly, unable to touch the WCTU constituency as profoundly as local issues did. The closure of a liquor outlet or a municipal campaign for prohibition or against prostitution might be inspired by reading of a similar episode elsewhere, but it was a different matter to expect local unions to involve themselves continuously in international work. They never did.

Yet before concluding that the World's WCTU was of peripheral importance to the rank and file of the American WCTU, several examples of the level of commitment can be probed. More than a million women signed the so-called polyglot petition against alcohol and other drugs by 1895.[42] (The size of the petition was swelled by six million "attestations" from interested groups signing on behalf of members.) Though World's WCTU national affiliates paid dues to that organization only haphazardly before 1891, by 1900 contributions were comprehensive. Local unions around the globe contributed generously but unevenly to such projects as the Temperance Temple in Chicago because the foreign unions wanted to be identified with that architectural symbol of WCTU achievement. Others contributed to Somerset's Duxhurst Retreat for alcoholic women in Britain, even though such contributions bore no specific benefits for the contributors.[43]

Examination of minutes of WCTU locals in Australia, the United States, and Canada reveals that local members experienced the World's WCTU largely through the visits of international workers, the polyglot petition, occasional selection of delegates to world conventions, and the reading of material in the *Union Signal* and the *White Ribbon Bulletin*. The international work was also built into the local WCTU ritual through the singing of the movement's anthem, "All Round the World the White Ribbon Twined," the inclusion of World's WCTU organizational activities among the topics of the month regularly treated, and the World's WCTU collection day on which funds were raised.[44]

One measure of non-American support apart from the payment of affiliation dues was the reception given to visiting missionaries. In such places as Australia, New Zealand, Britain, Canada, and South Africa local supporters paid the way of the visitors. Some missionaries boasted that they had never spent a cent of American or World's WCTU money on their travels. Within the United States, too, there was support for these missionary campaigns. Three thousand dollars was raised by voluntary contributions for Leavitt's trip in about a year, compared to seven thousand dollars in dues paid to the national WCTU.[45]

The most explicit test of support for the World's WCTU outside the United States occurred in Britain between 1891 and 1893, when considerable resentment of American domination arose. The BWTA split badly over the issue. Somerset stood on one side with Willard's support, and the conservatives opposed to Americanization and the do-everything policy aligned themselves on the other. The subsequent fate of the two groups after the split suggests that alignment with the World's WCTU, or at least support of its policies, was more acceptable to British temperance women than a policy of isolation. The British Woman's Total Abstinence Union, formed by opponents of Somerset, never captured the rank and file of the BWTA, and support peaked at about twenty-one thousand members in 1903. At the same time the BWTA, affiliated with the World's WCTU, had 114,000 members and grew continuously from 1893 to 1914, reaching a peak membership of 160,000 at the outbreak of war.[46]

Where there was support for a World's WCTU, it did not necessarily rest on reform grounds alone since a major theme in international work was travel. In an age of accelerated communications it was possible as never before for intrepid women to travel virtually unaccompanied to almost any country. The World's WCTU enabled travel to be linked to concepts of service and to the enlargement of women's prestige and physical accomplishments. The exploits of Leavitt and others ranked with those of the great nineteenth-century male explorers and missionaries. Leavitt was, Willard said, "our white ribbon Stanley." Though women at home in their middle-class drawing rooms could not, with few exceptions, hope to compete with such herculean feats, they could read about them and learn about foreign countries at the same time. The pages of the *Union Signal* were filled with material detailing the lives, customs, physical appearance, and geographical peculiarities of the peoples and nations that Leavitt and her several dozen emulators contacted during the long period of WCTU cultural imperialism from 1884 to the end of the 1920s. BWTA members, for example, could follow Agnes Slack's 1914 tour of Italy through such never-to-be-forgotten tourist experiences as visits to Capri and the

ruins of Pompeii and could gasp at the illustrations of the great art
works of the Renaissance and the gardens of Italian villas.[47]

Such examples illustrate the diverse appeal of international work
but hardly change the fact that the average WCTU member's interests
were localist and that national and international issues touched her
only intermittently or peripherally. That observation is not, however,
to undermine the significance of the World's WCTU but to suggest that
it was of importance primarily to the elite of international leaders and
that the organization was used as a vehicle of statecraft by women who
regarded themselves as the women's equivalent of statesmen and international celebrities.

If the significance of this point is to be fully understood, the organization must be linked to the conceptual framework of the historiography of Frances Willard and the American WCTU. Typically the WCTU
has been depicted as going through a number of temporal stages. The
earliest was under Annie Wittenmyer from 1874 to 1879, devoted
almost completely to temperance. The second was Willard's do-everything policy from 1880 to 1898. There followed a third period in which
the WCTU became a narrower organization focused heavily on prohibition after Willard's death. In the light of Joseph Gusfield's work, we
could add a fourth stage covering the declining years of the postprohi-
bition period.[48]

Yet the WCTU can also be conceived in spatial terms as a set of
overlapping local, national, and international societies. This idea of a
hierarchy of WCTUs may contribute to a reassessment of the more
typical temporal conception. Despite divergences of interpretation on
many other issues, Mary Earhart, Janet Giele, Ruth Bordin, and Barbara Epstein all share the view that the late 1890s marked a watershed
in WCTU history away from progressive policies toward a narrower
focus on prohibition.[49] This view has not yet been convincingly established, largely because it rests on a lopsided attention to the Willard
period. Ultimately this question will have to be settled by detailed work
on the post-1900 WCTU, but it is worth noting that these authors give
little or no attention to international issues. Internationalism was an
important commitment in both the Willard and post-Willard periods;
for example, peace work in the World's WCTU was more widely undertaken after 1900 than before. If we focus on the international sphere,
the organization does not look quite as narrow after 1900 as it has been
portrayed, nor does the WCTU seem to be as clearly declining in
prestige as is often argued.

This model of a World's WCTU depicts an organization led by a
relatively small group of leaders of the national WCTUs, temperance
missionaries, and superintendents of departments of work. These

leaders were in close contact with one another and developed strong emotional ties of friendship that sustained the international effort. This elite of World's WCTU workers in effect used the numbers and the financial support of affiliated unions to create a structure for exercising power and influence for themselves and on behalf of "womanhood." As she announced to the BWTA in 1894, Willard and her supporters in the World's WCTU "were organizers of force among women."[50] Willard herself admitted that the organization operated on different levels and that it was legitimate to conceive of it on the international plane as an elite, not a grass-roots, movement. A good deal of the work was heavily subsidized in the first ten years by the national WCTU executive in the United States with the tacit approval of the rank and file. The World's WCTU constitution and forms of organization were both drafted by a small group of interested officials and only later approved by national conventions. "In all new movements," Willard explained in justifying her high-handed approach, "it is necessary that a few who grasp the situation should exercise whatever power is needed in order to set the wheels...in motion."[51] Not until after her death in 1898 did the organization become fully responsible to its members in a constitutional sense.[52]

The World's WCTU proclaimed that it was the largest grouping of women in the world, and the size of its membership certainly was impressive by the standards of contemporary voluntary organizations.[53] Yet numbers were not worshiped for their own sake so much as for their propaganda value when lobbying governments. The polyglot petition was used in this way, but demonstrations of mass support were supplemented by attempts to wield influence indirectly through access to powerful persons. The aristocratic leaders of the British temperance women were especially valued because of their connections to the actual seats of power in that country and because of their wealth. Both Carlisle and Somerset contributed heavily to the World's WCTU coffers and gave secretarial support to Willard. Moreover, through Somerset's good offices the Salvation Army in Britain contributed a quarter of a million signatures to the polyglot petition.[54]

Willard hoped to duplicate the British pattern elsewhere and boasted of the ubiquitous influence of World's WCTU emissaries. The organization had representatives at the royal court of Sweden; the German leader Ottilie Hoffmann was favorably received by the kaiser; Jessie Ackerman claimed to know most of the "potentates of the East"; Mary Leavitt used her status as a curiosity to gain access to King Leopold of Belgium to discuss the ill-treatment of "natives" in the Congo.[55]

International connections helped boost the prestige of the elite of temperance leaders, particularly that of Frances Willard. Children in some Chinese mission schools sat in classrooms in which her picture was posted on the walls; in Wales miniature photographs of Willard were said to be carried by lonely crofters; letters testifying to her fame and influence came from many countries; newspapers reporting WCTU conventions called her "the world famous temperance lecturer."[56] Willard was adored by her followers in the United States, but outside the American WCTU her supporters competed to perpetuate the Willard cult after her death, naming buildings and children after her. She was "the queen of temperance," according to one report, and another ranked her work as "more successful than that of any living statesman."[57]

These examples did not involve the exercise of much real power, however. What attracted women to the World's WCTU was the prospect of greater influence abroad than at home. Non-American members were especially impressed with how strong the American organization was and how articulate and forceful its leaders seemed. But what beckoned American WCTU officials was the potential of other countries for realizing the power of women at a time when the United States still failed to grant full equality. They praised Australasian suffrage and looked to Britain for influence because of the undoubted talent and resources of BWTA leaders. At a time in the 1890s when temperance reform seemed increasingly frustrated in the United States, Willard and her supporters envied the British system of government. British women had just one parliament and Westminster to confront. Willard could not envisage that this system would prove as profound an obstacle to the aspirations of the WCTU as the federal system in the United States.[58] When the drive for national prohibition gained momentum and women received the vote in several states after 1911, the American desire for external influence began to subside; but this sentiment was replaced by increasing foreign interest in United States laws and institutions among temperance women.

The World's WCTU was thus an organization in which the grass nearly always seemed greener somewhere else. Discontent with purely American action or any other national solution to temperance problems, and identification of women's interests in "advanced" countries with those where the subordinate position of women was more explicit and pronounced, help provide a commentary on the status of women in nineteenth-century liberal democracies. Though historians such as Evans and Grimshaw have depicted that status as high and placed the WCTU in the broad coalition of liberal reform movements, the persistent search for influence on the international stage was a reflection of discontent with women's material condition and power in Anglo-

American society. Connection of their own subordination with the more severe disabilities of women in non-Western societies points to a strain in WCTU thinking that could not be accommodated within the framework of liberal-individualist reform.[59]

The contemporary reassessment of the WCTU, begun by Ruth Bordin in her *Women and Temperance* (1981), has, like that of other women's movements, been constructed against a background profoundly influenced by contemporary feminism. Some historians have measured the WCTU in terms of its contribution to the emancipation of women and the embodiment of feminist goals. International agitation helped develop the sense of woman's solidarity that Willard called "the wide sisterhood of the World's W.C.T.U."[60]

Yet the WCTU on either the national or the international level cannot be linked in any simple way with a progressive tradition by depicting temperance women as the ancestors of modern feminist thinking. Women's consciousness was harnessed to a hierarchical, evangelical impulse that valued service and self-sacrifice over the achievement of individual aspirations. The missionary campaigns were expressions of this mentality of service to others, the Anglo-Saxon race, and "humanity" rather than strategies for the advancement of women's interests alone. Moreover, by its insistence on Christian abstinence and prohibition the World's WCTU erected barriers that divided the potential sisterhood and, along with its emphasis on a bureaucratic and matriarchal hierarchy, undermined the egalitarian aspects of the movement. On the international level, therefore, the WCTU was caught in the contradiction between its own critique of gender subordination and the logic of its cultural imperialism.

A need exists for further comparative analysis of the cultural exports of the American temperance movement. (We need to know more, too, about the diffusion of the British Rechabites and Bands of Hope, which were of considerable significance in the British empire especially.) Yet the arguments advanced here concerning women's temperance do not necessarily apply with the same force to mixed or male societies. The Sons of Temperance and the Good Templars were both plagued by schisms that destroyed their international coherence. The World League against Alcoholism may be a better case for comparison, but according to its latest historian, it was American-dominated throughout and hardly merits being termed an international organization.[61]

Women's organizations are another matter. It might be profitable to examine in comparative context an organization like the International Woman Suffrage Alliance. Carrie Chapman Catt, its moving force, regarded international work as important for women and, like woman temperance reformers, presided over international conferences and toured the world between 1911 and 1913 on behalf of woman suffrage. Catt's organization and others, like the Women's International League for Peace and Freedom, may owe something to the example of the World's WCTU.[62]

Women who were deprived of the vote had special reasons for working internationally from the 1880s to the 1920s. American women "desire" to feel "love and respect" for "their land and government," the American WCTU remonstrated in 1898. But how could women who did not vote—while "ignorant" foreign males were readily admitted to the franchise—have a full measure of respect for their country? Exclusion from the suffrage was, they said, calculated to lessen feelings of pride and patriotism. Ellen Sargent, a California suffragist, was prompted by one defeat at home to ask, "Who that realises the situation can be patriotic?"[63] Willard touched such discontents in her World's WCTU and her polyglot petition. She manipulated the sentiment that women were "outside [the nation state's] barriers" to create a surrogate international community that gave women the prestige and power they lacked at home. The enfranchisement of women, which quickened in pace in a number of countries after 1910, cut across such feelings and helped integrate women more firmly into their respective national political communities by the 1920s. But a strain of international action persisted in such organizations as the Women's International League for Peace and Freedom and in Anna Gordon's drive for world prohibition.[64]

This essay has focused on international organization and has sketched some elements of an international history of women's temperance. International analysis is certainly not a category that must logically exclude comparisons of the national histories of women's temperance. That too remains to be done and must be integrated into an international and comparative history. But when we come to compare these different national histories, it would be well to remember that they are not self-contained and that at times women have regarded international issues as important. It is also worth keeping in mind the flow of ideas that have been exchanged and that constituted the cultural context of actions not entirely national in motivation or derivation. In addition, the movement of personnel and the loyalties they carried with them must be considered. Globe-trotting temperance missionaries provide the best examples, but there was also the identification of the WCTU in certain areas with expatriate English and American communities involved in business, church work, and government. Nor can the contribution of emigration be neglected. The leaders of the WCTU in Australia and South Africa were frequently British in origin, whereas in Canada both British and American migrants served the WCTU.[65] In leadership, in ideology, in sentiment, in organization, we are not comparing completely self-contained national experiences. We are entering the territory of international history.

NOTES

1. *Annual Minutes of the National Woman's Christian Temperance Union, 1885* (Chicago: WCTU, 1885), 63, 91 (hereafter cited as *Annual Minutes, NWCTU,* with appropriate year); *Union Signal,* 8 January 1885, 10.

2. On the World League, see Susan Mary Brook, "World League against Alcoholism: The Attempt to Export an American Experience" (M.A. thesis, University of Western Ontario, 1972), 39–40, 60, 65ff. On the international activities of the Sons of Temperance, see Donald W. Beattie, "Sons of Temperance: Pioneers of Total Abstinence and Constitutional Prohibition" (Ph.D. diss., Boston University, 1966).

3. Cf. Janet Giele, "Mary Greenleaf Clement Leavitt," in *Notable American Women: A Biographical Dictionary,* 3 vols., ed. Edward T. James, (Cambridge, Mass.: Harvard University Press, 1971), 2:384. Membership figures come from *White Ribbon Bulletin for Asia* (August 1895), in Scrapbook 58, Woman's Christian Temperance Union Historical Files, Evanston, Ill.; *Proceedings of the Fifteenth International Congress against Alcoholism...1920,* ed. Ernest Cherrington (Washington, D.C., and Westerville, Ohio, 1921), 130; *Report of the Eighth Convention of the World's Woman's Christian Temperance Union...1910* (n.p., 1910), 212; *Report of the Thirteenth Convention of the World's Woman's Christian Temperance Union...1928* (n.p., 1928), 22; *Union Signal,* 11 August 1928, 4.

4. Ian Tyrrell, "International Aspects of the Woman's Temperance Movement in Australia: The Influence of the American WCTU, 1882–1914," *Journal of Religious History* 12 (1983): 292–294, for a case study of WCTU literature in Australia; Phillida Bunkle, "The Origins of the Woman's Movement in New Zealand: The Women's Christian Temperance Union 1885–1895," in *Women in New Zealand Society* ed. Beryl Hughes and Phillida Bunkle (Sydney and Auckland: Allen and Unwin, 1980), 58; *Addresses, Reports, and Minutes of the Twenty-seventh Annual Meeting of the British Women's Temperance Association...1903* (London: British Women's Temperance Association, 1903), 128.

5. Mary C. Leavitt to Ruth Stevens, 20 July 1907, and Leavitt to Flora Brentnall, [1907], in "Second Book of Records of the Woman's Christian Temperance Union of Queensland Begun in 1910," WCTU Headquarters, Brisbane, Australia; J. J. G. Carson, *Emilie Solomon, 1858–1939* (Cape Town: Juto, [1941]); Alice Palmer to Frances Willard, 3 February 1895, roll 18, Woman's Christian Temperance Union Historical Series, microfilm ed.

6. *White Ribbon* (London), July 1902, 108; *Standard Encyclopedia of the Alcohol Problem,* 6 vols., ed. Ernest Cherrington (Westerville, Ohio: American Issue, 1924–1930), 1:261; Frances Willard, *Woman and Temperance* (Hartford, Conn.: Park, 1883), 586.

7. Anthea Hyslop, "Temperance, Christianity and Feminism: The Woman's Christian Temperance Union of Victoria, 1887–1897," *Historical Stud-*

ies, no. 66 (1976): 42; Clara Colby to Caroline Severance, 17 September 1906, box 14, Severance Papers, Huntington Library, San Marino, Calif.; Paul E. Fuller, *Laura Clay and the Woman's Rights Movement* (Lexington, Ky.: University Press of Kentucky, 1975), 33, 86, 177, 178.

8. *Union Signal,* 19 January 1893, 9; 16 October 1902, 3; 22 December 1910, 8; 20 December 1893, 4; *Woman's Herald* (London), 21 September 1893, 481.

9. *Union Signal,* 25 November 1920, 2.

10. "Farewell Letter Sent to the Women's Christian Temperance Unions of Australasia, April 1885," in *Report of the Hon. Sec. of the World's Woman's Christian Temperance Union* (Boston, 1891), 64–65; *Ninth Report of the World's Woman's Christian Temperance Union...1913* (n.p., 1913), 32; *Union Signal,* 12 August 1920, 7; Keith Dunstan, *Wowsers* (Melbourne: Cassell, 1968), 80–86.

11. *Union Signal,* 17 December 1903, 9; 25 October 1906, 8; *Seventh Annual Records...Woman's Christian Temperance Union of Victoria...1894* (Melbourne: Spectator, 1895), 20.

12. Ruth Bordin, *Woman and Temperance: The Quest for Power and Liberty, 1873–1900* (Philadelphia: Temple University Press, 1981), 88, 141, 145, 159; Richard Evans, *The Feminists: Women's Emancipation Movements in Europe, America and Australasia, 1840–1920* (London: Croom, Helm, 1977), 60; Frances Willard, *Glimpses of Fifty Years* (Chicago: Woman's Temperance Publishing Association, 1889), 401; *Our Union* (Chicago), August 1876, 12; September 1878, 4; *Union Signal,* 2 November 1893, 8–9.

13. Bordin, *Woman and Temperance,* 141; Mary Earhart (Dillon), *Frances Willard: From Prayers to Politics* (Chicago: University of Chicago Press, 1944), 340.

14. See Barbara Welter, "She Hath Done What She Could: Protestant Women's Missionary Careers in Nineteenth-Century America," *American Quarterly* 30 (1978): 624–638.

15. This information on the motives of the missionaries is based on biographical data for fifty-four WCTU missionaries and lecturers. These sources are far too scattered and various to cite. Much information can be drawn from the *Union Signal,* the files of the World's WCTU in Evanston, Illinois. A collective biography of these women appears in my "Woman's World / Woman's Empire," manuscript in possession of the author.

16. *Union Signal,* 1 January 1885, 6; *Report of the American Secretary of the World's Woman's Christian Temperance Union, 1890* (n.p., 1890), 40; *Annual Minutes, NWCTU, 1886,* 52.

17. Lady Henry Somerset, *Our Position and Our Policy* (Hutchings, 1893), 56.

18. *Annual Minutes, NWCTU, 1883,* 66.

19. *Annual Minutes, NWCTU, 1892,* 157; see also *Woman's Herald,* 23 February 1893, 9.

20. *Annual Minutes, NWCTU, 1885,* 63; *Report of the First Biennial Convention of the World's Woman's Christian Temperance Union...1891* (n.p., 1891), 14.

21. Jack S. Blocker, Jr., "Separate Paths: Suffragists and the Women's Temperance Crusade," *Signs* 10 (Spring 1985): 460–476.

22. David Courtwright, *Dark Paradise: Opiate Addiction in America before 1940* (Cambridge, Mass.: Harvard University Press, 1982), 70.

9

23. *Annual Minutes, NWCTU, 1894*, 63.

24. See Judith Walkowitz, *Prostitution and Victorian Society* (New York: Cambridge University Press, 1980); *Annual Minutes, NWCTU, 1886*, 52, 90.

25. *Minutes of the Second Biennial Convention and Executive Committee Meetings of the World's Woman's Christian Temperance Union...1893* (Chicago: Woman's Temperance Publishing Association, 1893), 51; *WWCTU Eighth Convention*, 25.

26. Mark Connelly, *The Response to Prostitution in the Progressive Era* (Chapel Hill: University of North Carolina Press, 1980), 81–86.

27. For a summary, see Linda Gordon and Ellen DuBois, "Seeking Ecstasy on the Battlefield: Danger and Pleasure in Nineteenth Century Feminist Sexual Thought," *Feminist Review*, no. 13 (1983): 42–54.

28. *The Shield* (London), August 1899, no pagination; *Woman's Herald*, 23 February 1893, 522; *Union Signal*, 22 March 1906, 5; Charlotte B. DeForest, *The Woman and the Leaven* (West Medfield, Mass.: Central Committee on the United Study of Foreign Missions, 1923), 187, 190; *Standard Encyclopedia of the Alcohol Problem*, 6:2927; Tyrrell, "International Aspects," 289; Pratima Asthana, *Women's Movement in India* (Delhi: Vikas, 1974), 46–47.

29. Frank L. Byrne, "Hannah Clark Johnson Bailey," in *Notable American Women*, 1:84.

30. *Report of the Eleventh Convention of the World's Woman's Christian Temperance Union...1922* (n.p., 1922), 33; Hannah Clark Bailey to Caroline Severance, 15 April 1899, box 14, Severance Papers; Bailey, "Third Biennial Report of the Peace and Arbitration Department," in Hannah Clark Bailey Papers, roll 2, microfilm, Swarthmore College; *Annual Minutes, NWCTU, 1887*, 84.

31. *Cyclopedia of Temperance and Prohibition* (New York: Funk and Wagnalls, 1891), 13; Anna Gordon to William Jennings Bryan, 13 December 1913, in World's Woman's Christian Temperance Union Archives, Evanston, Ill.

32. *Report of the Tenth Convention of the World's Woman's Christian Temperance Union...1920* (n.p., 1920), 139; Mattie E. Phillips to Frances Willard, 19 December 1891, and Emiline Hicks to Willard, 29 November 1891, roll 17, WCTU Historical Series; *Union Signal*, 11 October 1906, 8; *WWCTU Eighth Convention*, 41, 209; Lamar Middleton, *The Rape of Africa* (London: Robert Hale, 1936), 88, 134–138, 257; Raymond L. Buell, *The Native Problem in Africa*, 2 vols. (New York: Macmillan, 1928), 2:942–953; Alan Burns, *History of Nigeria*, 8th ed. (London: Allen and Unwin, 1972), 236–240.

33. Lady Henry Somerset to Mrs. William Harvey, 29 October 1906, Lady Cecelia Roberts to Harvey, [1904], and Hannah Whitehall Smith to Sister Annie [Mrs. William Harvey], 30 January 1904, in Women's Temperance Papers, Fawcett Library, London; [Rosalind Carlisle], *Sir Wilfred Lawson on "Disinterested Management" of the Liquor Traffic*, pamphlet collection, United Kingdom Alliance, London.

34. *Union Signal*, 19 February 1920, 6; 16 December 1920, 7; 14 October 1920, 11; *White Ribbon Signal* (London), 1 November 1913; *Alliance News* (London), 3 July 1909; *Report of the Twentieth Convention of the Dominion Woman's Christian Temperance Union* (Ottawa, 1918), 29, 44.

35. *WWCTU Eighth Convention*, 21.

36. Cf. Barbara Epstein, *The Politics of Domesticity: Women, Evangelism, and Temperance in Nineteenth-Century America* (Middletown, Conn.: Wesleyan Univer-

sity Press, 1981), 124; Wells's side of the story is told in Alfreda M. Duster, *Crusade for Justice: The Autobiography of Ida B. Wells* (Chicago: University of Chicago Press, 1970), 201–212.

37. On Balgarnie, see *Standard Encyclopedia of the Alcohol Problem*, 1:261; on the controversy in the WWCTU, see *Fraternity*, February 1895, 54–57; *Anti-Caste*, March 1895, 4–6; *London Daily News*, 19 June 1895; and *Lady Henry Somerset's Statement Concerning Accusations of Miss Florence Balgarnie*..., in scrapbook 13, WCTU Historical Files, Evanston. *Providence Rhode Island News*, 10 September 1897; *Report of the Fourth Biennial Convention, and Minutes of the World's Woman's Christian Temperance Union...1897* (London: White Ribbon, 1897), 92.

38. *WWCTU Fourth Convention*, 27–34; Kathleen Fitzpatrick, *Lady Henry Somerset* (Boston: Little, Brown, 1923), 177–187.

39. Earhart, *Willard*, 362–363.

40. This point is illustrated in the extensive correspondence between WCTU officials and Josephine Butler, the British opponent of licensed prostitution, in the Josephine Butler Papers, Fawcett Library.

41. Newspaper clipping, 4 February 1898, "Tail of W.C.T.U. Can't Wag Dog," [*Chicago Tribune*], scrapbook 76, WCTU Historical Files, Evanston; *The Shield*, March 1898, 91.

42. *Union Signal*, 28 February 1895, 8; 14 March 1895, 6; 27 June 1895, 7.

43. *A Brief History of the Woman's Christian Temperance Union in South Africa* (Cape Town: Townshend, Taylor and Snashall, 1925), 31.

44. Minutes, Vassar (Tuscola Co.) WCTU, 1889–1895, in roll 47, WCTU Historical Series; Newmarket, Ont., Woman's Christian Temperance Union Minutes, 1897–1899, WCTU Headquarters, Toronto, Canada; WCTU, Duarte, Ca., Papers, 1909–1934, University of California, Los Angeles, Library; Minutes of the Brisbane Central Woman's Christian Temperance Union, 1894–1903, WCTU Headquarters, Brisbane, Australia; Petersham WCTU Minute Book, 1907–1966, in Woman's Christian Temperance Union of New South Wales Records, Mitchell Library, Sydney, Australia.

45. *Annual Minutes, NWCTU, 1886*, 88; *Annual Minutes, NWCTU, 1891*, 205; *Report of the Hon. Sec. of the World's WCTU*, 63.

46. *Addresses, Reports, and Minutes of the Thirty-eighth Annual Meeting of the British Women's Temperance Association...1914* (London: BWTA, 1914), 84; *Eleventh Annual Report of the Woman's Total Abstinence Union for the Year 1903–1904* (London: BWTAU, 1904), 66; *Addresses, Reports and Minutes of the Seventeenth Annual Meeting of the British Women's Temperance Association...1893* (London: BWTA, 1893), 27–68.

47. Willard, *Glimpses*, 431; *White Ribbon*, June 1914, 86.

48. Susan Dye Lee, "Evangelical Domesticity: The Origins of the Woman's National Christian Temperance Union under Frances E. Willard" (Ph.D. diss., Northwestern University, 1980), 437, 363–367; Joseph Gusfield, "Social Structure and Moral Reform: A Study of the Woman's Christian Temperance Union," *American Journal of Sociology* 69 (1955): 227–230; Epstein, *Politics of Domesticity*, 144–146; Janet Giele, "Social Change in the Feminine Role: A Comparison of Woman's Suffrage and Woman's Temperance 1870–1920" (Ph.D. diss., Radcliffe College, 1961), 279, 290.

49. In addition to the references to Lee, Giele, and Epstein in n. 48, see Bordin, *Woman and Temperance,* 151–155; Earhart, *Willard,* 367.

50. *Woman's Signal* (London), supplement, 17 May 1894, 351.

51. Quoted in Somerset, *Our Position and Our Policy,* 43.

52. Executive minutes, 8 June 1903, World's WCTU Archives.

53. Frances Willard, *The World's Woman's Christian Temperance Union: Aims and Objects* (London, 1893), 4.

54. *White Ribbon Bulletin,* September 1921, 2; Charles Roberts, *The Radical Countess* (Carlisle, Eng.: Steel Bros., 1962); *WWCTU Ninth Convention,* 22; *Union Signal,* 13 November 1891, 4; Fitzpatrick, *Somerset,* 145–146.

55. *WWCTU Fourth Convention,* 48; Roberts, *Radical Countess,* 66; *Report of the Hon. Sec. of the World's WCTU,* 53; *Los Angeles Times,* 10 July 1937, 5; *White Ribbon,* December 1904, 22.

56. D. J. Thomas to Willard, 24 March 1893, roll 19, WCTU Historical Series; *Report of the Sixth Convention of the World's Woman's Christian Temperance Union...1903,* (n.p., 1903), 45; *Saint Louis Post-Dispatch,* 21 March 1896, in scrapbook 72, p. 80, WCTU Historical Files, Evanston; Anna Gordon, *The Beautiful Life of Frances E. Willard* (Chicago: Woman's Temperance Publishing Association, 1898).

57. *Chicago Post,* 16 November 1896; [Isobel McCorkindale], *Golden Records: Pathfinders of Woman's Christian Temperance Union of N.S.W.* (Sydney: John Sands, 1926), xiii; Katherine Lent Stevenson to Willard, 27 January 1898, roll 24, WCTU Historical Series; Mary S. Logan, *The Part Taken by Women in American History* (Wilmington, Del.: Perry-Nalle, 1912), 657.

58. *Woman's Signal,* 17 May 1894, 350–351; Tyrrell, "International Aspects," 297; Bunkle, "Women's Movement in New Zealand," 56–58; *Canadian White Ribbon Tidings,* 1 December 1906, 729; *Minutes of the Nineteenth Convention of the Woman's Christian Temperance Union...Cape Town...1910* (Cape Town: Townshend, Taylor and Snashall, 1910), 6; *Annual Minutes, NWCTU, 1886,* 30, 90. There was opposition in the American WCTU to elements in Willard's pro-British strategy in the 1890s—not to international work but rather to Willard's long personal absence from the United States and to her close links with the controversial reformer Lady Henry Somerset. See *Daily News,* 21 October 1893, in scrapbook 66, p. 56, WCTU Historical Files, Evanston, Ill.; Bordin, *Woman and Temperance,* 142, 145, 208 n. 14; Earhart, *Willard,* 352–366.

59. Cf. Evans, *Feminists;* Patricia Grimshaw, *Women's Suffrage in New Zealand* (Auckland: Auckland University Press, 1972); Grimshaw, "Women and the Family in Australian History," in *Women, Class and History,* ed. Elizabeth Windschuttle (Melbourne: Fontana, 1980), 37–53.

60. Willard, *Glimpses,* 434; cf. Bordin, *Woman and Temperance;* Epstein, *Politics of Domesticity;* Wendy Mitchinson, "The WCTU: 'For God, Home, and Native Land': A Study in Nineteenth Century Feminism," in *A Not Unreasonable Claim: Women and Reform in Canada, 1880s–1920s,* ed. Linda Kealey (Toronto: Women's Press, 1979), 152–167.

61. Brook, "World League," 39, 40, 60, 65; Beattie, "Sons of Temperance," 112, 114, 116. The only historical study approaching the temperance movement from a systematically comparative perspective is Ross Evans Paulson,

Women's Suffrage and Prohibition: A Study in Equality and Social Control (Glenview, Ill.: Scott, Foresman, 1973).

62. Studies of the "international sisterhood" wrongly ignore the WCTU. See Edith Hurwitz, "The International Sisterhood," in *Becoming Visible: Women in European History,* ed. Renate Bridenthal and Claudia Koonz (Boston: Houghton, Mifflin, 1977), 327–345; Rebecca Sherrick, "Toward Universal Sisterhood," *Women's Studies International Forum* 5 (1982): 655–661. On Catt, see Mary Grey Peck, *Carrie Chapman Catt: A Biography* (New York: Wilson, 1944).

63. *Annual Minutes, NWCTU, 1898,* 66; Ellen Sargent to Caroline Severance, January 1910, box 23, Severance Papers.

64. Frances Willard, *The Polyglot Petition* (Chicago: WTPA, [1893]), 3; *Union Signal,* 23 November 1922, 3, 25 November 1920, 2.

65. For the expatriate culture, see *WWCTU Eighth Convention,* 202; *Report of the Hon. Sec. of the World's WCTU,* 21–22; *Union Signal,* 14 March 1895, 6; and the files of the World's WCTU Archives, Evanston. British and American leadership of the Australian WCTU is discussed in Tyrrell, "International Aspects," 298–299. For Canada, see Willard, *Woman and Temperance,* 598; Mary Sanderson to Anna Gordon, 15 December 1913, in World's WCTU Archives; clipping on Addie Chisholm, in scrapbook 33, WCTU Historical Files, Evanston, Ill.; *Union Signal,* 6 August 1891, 4; and *Prohibition Leaders of America,* ed. Benjamin F. Austin (Saint Thomas, Ont., 1895). On South Africa, see *Minutes of the Eleventh Convention of the Woman's Christian Temperance Union...Cape Town ...1902* (Cape Town, 1902), 9; *Brief History of the Woman's Christian Temperance Union in South Africa,* 6, 9, 14.

PART THREE

The Inebriate,
the Expert, and the State

ELEVEN

Socialism, Alcoholism, and the Russian Working Classes before 1917

George E. Snow

The struggle against alcoholism is no more than an expedient, the breaking of a single link in the chain of the political oppression and capitalist exploitation of the working class.

V. G. Chirkin, remarks to the
First All-Russian Temperance Congress,
December 31, 1909

One of the most compelling and interesting European reform movements in the period before 1917 was the antialcohol or temperance cause. Yet although the movement in Russia was similar in many respects to the wider European one, at the same time there were elements in it that were wholly lacking in the European—anti-Semitism, state sponsorship, and, since the drink trade and the revenues from it were controlled by the state, an unmatched degree of politicization. It is precisely this last aspect that made the question of socialism and temperance in Russia most pointed.

Russian consumption of alcohol is almost proverbial, a habit attested to by the historical literature before 1917. It has been attributed variously to climate, lack of a safe water supply, democratic folkways, and other causes.[1] However, in the modern period great importance attaches to the revolutionary changes that began to transform Russian society in the latter half of the nineteenth century—urbanization, industrialization, and increased population pressures. Research drawing on cross-cultural models points to alcoholism as an expression of anxiety about the dislocation caused by an increasingly complex social environment or, alternatively, as a means of feeling powerful for those who knew themselves to be powerless in the face of incomprehensible economic forces.[2] Whatever the causes, though, whenever alternate bouts of intense labor and idleness accompanied by drinking were carried over into the small artisanal industries and thence to larger urban industries, they led to severe problems and much attendant criticism by middle-class observers, who sought various means of curbing such behavior.

Nonetheless, the limits of discourse on the relationship between socialism and temperance were established by the appearance in 1846 of Friedrich Engels's *Condition of the Working Class in England in 1844*. Drawing on the so-called environmentalist critique put forward as early as the 1830s by the British socialists, Engels established a direct causal relationship between alcoholism and industrial capital. Given the pollution, crowding, poor ventilation, and bad food with which the working class had to contend, he concluded that one of the few pleasures remaining to its members was alcohol abuse. Moreover, he believed that all irregular behavior of the lower classes—fornication, prostitution, and vice—resulted largely from this universal solvent of social bonds, that they were all, in sum, so many attempts by the "degraded victims" of the bourgeois regime to find escape.[3] In short, alcoholism was an epiphenomenon that would end when the social order based on capitalist exploitation ended, and neither Marx's contradictory views nor the antitemperance positions of the German Social Democrats managed to erode this view.[4]

At the same time an indigenous Russian antialcohol tradition had begun to develop. Among its founders was the tortured figure of I. G. Pryzhov, a failed revolutionary and an admitted alcoholic.[5] In a series of brilliant but erratic articles and a major book on the history of the *kabaks* (taverns) in Russia, Pryzhov attacked drinking as a misery visited on the Russian people. However, his focus was both disturbed and disturbing, for, in addition to being a richly detailed history of the origins and development of the relationship between drinking houses and drunkenness, his work was imbued with an unabashed anti-Semitism: he blamed the drunkenness of the Russian people on Jewish tavernkeepers and their exploitative designs.[6]

Yet Pryzhov made no real attempt to discuss the alcoholism of the workers and the poor as part of a wider socioeconomic problem. The first expression of such concern came from a group of medical doctors who comprised the editorial board and contributing staff of the journal *Arkhiv sudebnoi meditsiny i obshchestvennoi gigieny* (Archive of Forensic Medicine and Public Hygiene). In his research on Saint Petersburg factory workers, Reginald Zelnik has shown that these doctors not only were interested in measures for protecting public health but were concerned with the high incidence of drinking and addiction to drinking among the working population as well.[7]

This link was made more direct in an article entitled "Concerning the Matter of Food and Shelter of Workers at the Factory of the

Merchant Egorov," which appeared in *Arkhiv* of 1871 under the signature R. In the author's view inadequate wages, substandard living quarters, and poor food all led the physically exhausted worker to alcohol as a way of reviving his strength, as a stimulus to help him continue through prolonged periods of work, or as a psychical (psiknicheskii) means of putting him in a condition where he could "resolve the sharp contrasts of his otherwise ordinary life." In place of this vicious cycle R. called for the establishment of a factory inspectorate by the government to be independent of the factory owners and vested with supervisory powers over all sanitary conditions. Among the two dozen sanitation tasks he proposed as part of its mission was to see that workers did not work while intoxicated and in general to oversee the sobriety of the workers. In closing, the anonymous author candidly pointed out that the economic conditions of the workers had to be improved before any of the sanitary improvements would have any meaning. Thus, in addition to healthy, edible food and clean, dry, and warm quarters, a norm for workers' wages should be established.[8]

R.'s references to western European models as examples of industrial labor legislation and his overt and specific championing of the urban working class, filtered through a prism of Marxian analysis, clearly established the tradition of the Engels-environmentalist critique in the Russian antialcohol movement. Further, this identification of the alcoholism of the laboring classes as an effect of industrial capitalism continued in the pages of *Arkhiv* until 1872 and then in its successor until 1885, *Sbornik sochinenii po sudebnoi meditsine, sudebnoi psikhiatrii, meditsinskoi politsii, obshchestvennoi gigiene, epidemiologii, meditsinskoi geografii i meditsinskoi statistike* (Collection of Works on Forensic Medicine, Forensic Psychiatry, Medical Policy, Public Hygiene, Epidemiology, Medical Geography and Medical Statistics). Nor did it cease when the latter, in turn, was superseded from 1885 to 1889 by *Vestnik sudebnoi meditsiny i obshchestvennoi gigieny* (Herald of Forensic Medicine and Public Hygiene) and from 1889 to 1917 by *Vestnik obshchestvennoi gigieny, sudebnoi i prakticheskoi meditsiny* (Herald of Public Hygiene, Forensic and Practical Medicine).[9]

This continuity was further underscored by the work of the physician F. F. Erisman, who for many years was identified with the cause of public health in Russia. Indeed, his article "Basement Dwellings in Saint Petersburg" not only developed the same thematic elements as were raised by R. but did so in language that was strikingly similar.[10] Throughout his long career in Russian public health this Swiss-born activist took the lead in attempting to bring the evils of alcoholism before the public, ultimately succeeding to the extent that he convinced the Twelfth International Congress of Physicians in 1896 to establish a special division on alcoholism as a medical problem.[11]

The growing interest in public health and concern about public alcoholism led to the founding in 1877 of the Russian Society for the Protection of Public Health (Russkoe obshchestvo okhraneniia narodnogo zdraviia). However, owing to the Russo-Turkish War, it did not have its first general sessions until 1882 and from the outset reflected diverse and even contradictory tendencies. The society was divided into five broad working sections; the first, the biological section, was assigned "the study of those questions of natural science that are connected with the interests of public health." That section was therefore not only the scientific center of the entire society, encompassing chemistry, physics, physiology, pathology, bacteriology, and other sciences, but also the arena in which the question of socialism and alcoholism would be fought out.[12]

Although such an outcome was not necessarily inevitable, there were strong currents within the society that made such confrontations likely. It embraced in its ranks government officials and other luminaries—for example, provincial governors and members of the nobility—as well as many figures active in the fight for public health at all levels, including a growing number of local antialcohol activists. The issues of alcoholism and the means to combat it were repeatedly raised at the meetings of the society. They were raised too in the sessions of the organizations of physicians allied in the public-health cause—for example, in the zemstvo-oriented Society of Russian Physicians in Memory of N. I. Pirogov (established in 1883) and the periodic Congresses of National Psychiatrists beginning in 1887.[13] Alcoholism was equally a frequent topic in the pages of the growing number of professional medical journals in this era—publications including the society's own *Zdravie* (Health) as well as such specialized ones as *Vrachebnaia gazeta* (Medical Daily), *Obozrenie Psikhiatr* (Psychiatrist's Review), *Russkii vrach'* (Russian Physician), *Zemskii vrach* (Zemstvo Physician), and *Zhurnal nevropatologii i psikhiatrii imeni S. S. Korsakova* (Journal of Neuropathology and Psychiatry in Honor of S. S. Korsakov) and the more general *Vestnik trezvosti* (Temperance Herald) and *Trezvost' i berezhlivost'* (Temperance and Thrift).

This rising tide of concern also led the society to create the Special Commission on the Question of Alcoholism and the Means for Combatting It, under the aegis of its biological section in 1898. The commission was the longtime project of the Saint Petersburg psychiatrist M. N. Nizhegorodtsev, who served as its first—and virtually indefatigable—chairman, and enjoyed the patronage and support of Prince Aleksandr Ol'denburg.[14] It viewed its mandate as multifaceted, not only to investigate the physiological effects and treatment of alcoholism, but to approach it as a problem with various social, legal, and political ramifications as well.[15] Nizhegorodtsev envisioned and assembled a socially and politically diverse organization that included city and zemstvo public-health physicians, temperance-minded psychiatrists of the Juridical Society of Saint Petersburg University and the Society of Neuropathologists and Psychiatrists at Kazan University, lawyers, teachers, clergymen, and university professors of several disciplines.[16]

The very diversity of such an organization meant that the commission had to strike a balance between the "moderate" and "possibilist" political approaches of (after 1905) Duma politicians such as A. Ia. Gololobov and Baron A. F. Meyendorf and those of advocates of public health and temperance such as N. B. Vvedenskii, D. A. Dril', Dr. I. M. Dogel', D. N. Borodin, barrister and editor of the temperance journal *Trezvost' i berezhlivost'*, and Dr. N. I. Grigor'ev, founder and editor of *Vestnik Trezvosti*. It also had to accommodate the socialist temperance advocates, men equally involved in the antialcohol struggle at that time but with a significantly different perspective from those just mentioned. Interestingly, these men would also remain actively involved in public-health and antialcohol measures under the Bolsheviks: V. M. Bekhterev, G. I. Dembo, L. S. Minor, E. M. Dement'ev, A. M. Korovin, and N. F. Gamalia.[17]

This list is by no means exhaustive, but the distinction between the two groups is clear-cut and important to note. At first their similarities appear to be such that to insist on basic differences would seem pedantic and artificial. For example, both groups focused squarely on industrial capitalism as one of the chief causes, if not the main cause, of what they termed the curse of Russia. Both were concerned about the alcoholism and the dislocation of the urban working class, its low economic status, its generally poor diet, its miserable working conditions, its low morality, public exhibitions of intoxication, and alcohol-related crime. Similarly, neither group concerned itself overmuch with alcoholism among the middle classes or even within their own group, the intelligentsia. However, in distinguishing their respective approaches, the model developed by Joseph R. Gusfield is instructive and useful. The former group favored what Gusfield calls assimilative reform, wherein the reformer is sympathetic to the plight of the urban poor and critical of the conditions produced by industry and the factory system; such a reformer feels his own social position to be affirmed by a temperance cause that invites the drinker to follow the reformer's habits and to lift himself to middle-class respect and income.[18] Thus, although advocates of assimilative reform stressed the need for better housing, better food, and higher wages for the working class, they also called attention in their proposals and their work to the need for moderation (*umerennost'*), thrift (*berezhlivost'*), and morality (*nravstvennost'*) as instruments of self-help by which the poor and downtrodden alcoholic masses could raise themselves up. Consequently, of the thirteen permanent subcommissions that the commission established, the educational and judicial were among the most active.

A sampling of the various subjects of the commission's early sessions bears out this orientation and attests as well to the emphasis some commission members placed on the role of religion and the Russian Orthodox church in helping the workers overcome their addiction to alcohol.[19] Yet from their perspective education remained an issue of great importance—particularly early antialcohol training for school-age children along with the establishment of legal norms—as did the definition of legal limitations on the civil rights of alcoholics.[20] In addition, there were efforts by such figures as N. I. Grigor'ev to link the onset of communicable diseases such as tuberculosis with overconsumption of alcohol and D. A. Dril' and P. Ia. Rosenbach to develop a connection between alcoholism and criminality. Rosenbach argued that certain categories of crime were the direct result of altered psychological states brought about by alcohol "poisoning" rather than the result of socioeconomic conditions. Although only substituting one level of causation for another, this argument, along with the accompanying statistical data presented by E. N. Tarnovskii, clearly purported that alcoholism produced specifically nonpolitical crimes—unpremeditated murder, rape, and assault—rather than political ones; hence if alcoholism were eliminated, crime would also disappear.[21]

Another concern of this group was the conditions and housing of the workers; but expressions of concern, in the main, stopped far short of a call for the total restructuring of society. For example, both Dril' and Grigor'ev were especially troubled by the plight of the handicrafts worker (*remeslennyi rabochii*) in Saint Petersburg. Dril' pointed out that these workers had been put in an unfavorable position by economic forces they neither understood nor were able to control. That position, he explained, led to comparatively high rents and high food prices, which in turn produced crowding, poor food, and a generally low standard of living. Such living conditions, in combination with their unattractive conditions of work, he maintained, led to "narcotism" on their part, primarily in the form of alcoholism. But Dril' was no proponent of a narrow environmentalist approach. He argued that it would do no good to deprive these workers of alcohol under the contemporary working conditions, for they would only find other means of poisoning themselves. Instead, the conditions themselves must be changed gradually through the efforts of government and society. Foremost, therefore, among his solutions were the further development of labor legislation, its application as far as possible to all branches of labor, and the establishment of a strict and multifaceted supervision to see that such legislation was enforced. Other measures of primary importance included, in his view, the creation of trade schools and the elimination of crafts apprenticeships along with the construction, on a strictly commercial basis, of inexpensive and comfortable housing for the workers.[22]

Similarly, Dr. N. I. Grigor'ev, after detailing the working and living conditions of workers in small crafts shops and linking those conditions directly to alcoholism, went only as far as to recommend the establishment of government regulations to control more effectively the relations between owners and workers and improve conditions in the shops. In this context he saw the absolute necessity for creating a special inspectorate to prevent from succumbing to the lure of the *kabak* not just the underage apprentices but their older fellow workers in the shops as well.[23]

These approaches both individually and collectively were certainly progressive but not revolutionary. In fact, Dril' finally achieved the launching of a project for the construction of low-cost worker housing in Saint Petersburg with the aid of public and private financing in 1906.[24] Such accomplishments undoubtedly stood as models of cooperation but hardly represented a revolutionary thrust. Instead, the assimilationist orientation and essentially middle-class philosophy are manifest throughout the words and deeds of such men. By contrast, the antialcohol socialists were determined to turn the issue into a means of attacking the existing order itself.

A number of antialcohol advocates, finding in Engels's environmentalist analysis of the link between the capitalist order and alcoholism a convenient and ready-made tool that not only fit their sociopolitical views but appealed to their sense of causal tidiness as well, allied themselves quite early with revolutionary socialism. Yet they did not receive much ideological ammunition from Russia's "professional" revolutionaries—at least not at first and not from the Social Democrats. Indeed, what is most notable in the position taken by Lenin on the question of alcoholism is that, in the tradition of Marxian socialism, he addressed himself to the subject in an ambiguous fashion. For example, in attacking the theories of the *narodnik* V. I. Postnikov in the latter's *Peasant Farming in South Russia* (1891), Lenin specifically dismissed alcoholism and drunkenness as valid explanations for the poverty and lack of material well-being among the masses.[25] Further, in

Lenin's most noted work, *The Development of Capitalism in Russia,* he lashed out at the agrarian socialists who criticized alcoholic behavior of urban workers, again implicitly rejecting alcoholism as a negative factor in their lives. He strongly implied that it, along with other factors of urban life, might even be progressive in relation to the life and values of the villages the workers had left.[26]

Lenin made his most explicit statement on alcoholism when he tied it with the liquor monopoly introduced by the government in 1894. Contrasting the promises made for this reform by its defenders—"increased revenues, improved quality [of liquor] and less drunkenness" —Lenin pointed out that "instead of less drunkenness, we have more illicit trading in spirits, augmented police incomes from this trading, the opening of liquor shops over the protests of the population...and increased drunkenness in the streets."[27] In his view the monopoly was a target less for its encouragement of alcoholism than for its dual effect both as an indirect tax burden on the people and as a bureaucratic contrivance that deprived the peasant communes of revenues they would have otherwise obtained from the licensing of private liquor sales.[28]

Other movements on the left of Russian society also kept the question of temperance from becoming the exclusive preserve of the assimilationists. First were those *narodnik* critics of the capitalist order who were making their views felt on the question of alcoholism in the Russian zemstvo movement, with Dr. G. M. Gertsenshtein, among others, calling the attention of the intelligentsia to the ruinous effects of alcoholism on the rural population.[29] Then, too, workers groups themselves were assuming an ever-greater awareness of alcoholism as a problem that affected them acutely and were therefore cooperating among themselves to fight this peril.[30]

The socialist antialcohol advocates felt justified, given these trends, in criticizing the views of men like Dril' and Grigor'ev as utopian and pious. In contradistinction to the assimilationist view on the role of education in the antialcohol struggle, the socialist physician I. I. Ianzhul, for example, advocated the "education of the workers to their economic hardships" instead. This undertaking was important, he stressed, since the more the masses were aware of their exploitation, the easier it would be for them to improve their lives through the revolutionary struggle.[31] Further, as G. I. Dembo insisted, the root cause of alcoholism among the working classes was economic—the capitalist system itself—and only secondary were the Russian people's customs and traditions of alcohol consumption, customs that were themselves fed by ignorance, lack of intellectual development, and the absence of healthy entertainment.[32]

Others turned to questions of the awareness of the working class. A. M. Korovin, in numerous articles and public lectures, attacked the dangers of alcoholism on the human physiology and attempted to make these dangers comprehensible to the intelligentsia and uneducated laymen alike.[33] At the same time, however, he put great emphasis on the growth of worker temperance groups in Saint Petersburg (1890), Odessa (1891), Rybinsk (1893), Moscow (1895), and Tula and Astrakhan (1898) as signs of growing worker activism, strength, and political and social consciousness.[34]

The question of political rights was also of central importance to them. Starting from the general premise—again articulated by Dembo —that the "lack of political rights [by the Russian people] must be recognized as one of the leading principles of the struggle with alcoholism," the socialist antialcohol advocates had little difficulty in finding specific instances of this lack.[35] One such area was the forced detention of alcoholics in special hospitals. Since the subject of the violation of individual civil rights naturally arose in connection with this issue, the socialists acidly pointed out that, in view of the Russian peoples' general lack of civil and personal liberties, discussion of it was pointless.[36] In addition, they described as unacceptable official government "half-measures" to combat alcoholism. Among these were the official temperance committees (Popechitel'stvo o narodnoi trezvosti) and the entire system of the government alcohol monopoly, of which they were an integral part.[37]

One area where both assimilationists and socialists agreed, however, was on the importance of a much wider, national forum that would draw together all antialcohol groups in Russia—in short, an all-Russian antialcohol congress.[38] This theme was beat steadily in various publications throughout the first decade of the twentieth century, which stressed the need for such a congress to help develop definitive plans for combatting alcoholism and formulate concrete legislative proposals to deal with it. Similar demands were made in other forums as well, particularly in the chambers of the imperial Duma and the Council of State after 1905.[39]

In the face of both public and private pressures the minister of the interior, P. A. Stolypin, decided on a course of concessions that would lead to the convocation of a series of public forums on issues of concern to Russians—among them the First All-Russian Congress on Combatting Alcoholism.[40] In addition, the government permitted the simultaneous convocation of the Third Congress of National Psychiatrists, which, like the Anti-Alcohol Congress, was to be held in Saint Petersburg. Several joint sessions of these two decidedly antialcohol bodies took place.[41]

By early 1909 the Commission on the Question of Alcoholism had moved to form an organizational committee chaired by Nizhegorodtsev, with Dril' as deputy chairman. This committee was composed largely of men who were assimilationist in their approach to the alcohol problem. Nevertheless, it did count among its fifty-one members several socialists, including V. M. Bekhterev, G. I. Dembo, A. M. Korovin, and L. S. Minor.[42] However, only one of the socialist antialcohol advocates was made a member of the Bureau of the Organizing Committee (Biuro organizatsionnago Komiteta), which was designed to shape the agenda of the organizational committee—the ubiquitous Dembo. Indeed, Professor Dril' and D. N. Borodin appeared most often in various specialized work groups of the bureau, a clear indication of the commission's desire to have the congress hew a moderate line. This desire was further underscored by the stated intention of the congress to "seek the most effective possible means for combatting popular alcoholism" and at the same time "eschew the views of all political groups."[43]

In preparation for the congress the commission contacted more than sixteen thousand different institutions, societies, and persons with a request to attend and present reports.[44] These organizations ranged from the Society for the Protection of Public Health and its various national branches to the Academy of Science, the various Russian universities, the Female Medical Institute, zemstvo and city institutions, Guardianships of Popular Sobriety (the official temperance committees noted above), public and private temperance groups, educational societies, medical societies, legal societies, and statistical and industrial societies. Additional invitations were sent to persons known for their work in the study of alcoholism or with groups involved in cognate activities.[45]

Among the groups contacted were numerous workers' educational and self-improvement organizations throughout Russia, some of which either were directly associated with the various factions of Russian socialism or were ones in which various socialist factions were strongly represented. Thus, the congress undeniably represented an opportunity too good to be missed by any potential opposition group in Russia for many reasons, chief among them the fact that open forums for political discourse had been totally lacking before 1905. Even after the creation of the imperial Duma, that discourse had remained confined to extremely narrow limits—limits that precluded matters touching on the tsarist taxation and budgetary systems. Given the intimate connection between the tsarist government and the vodka monopoly, as well as the increasing tendency among assimilationist and socialist antialcohol critics to associate both with the rising levels of alcohol consumption and alcoholism, the potential of the congress as a forum for airing simultaneous condemnations of the government, the monopoly, and alcoholism was great.[46]

The Social Democratic party certainly recognized this potential. In an article entitled "Toward the Congress for the Struggle with Alcoholism" the party newspaper *Sotsial' demokrat* demanded the "active participation" of all Social Democratic organizations in "preparing the workers for using the Congress to tie the *private* question of alcoholism with the general aims and tasks of the workers movement" (italics mine).[47] Thus, in the months before the convocation of the congress, members of the Social Democratic fraction of the Third Duma, workers clubs, workers educational and cultural societies, and Social Democrat–dominated trades unions throughout Russia engaged in furious organizational activity to produce an agenda that would enable them to air their views.[48]

A major part of this activity was the selection of delegates to represent the various socialist-affiliated workers groups at the congress. In all, some forty-three persons were eventually chosen for this task—the so-called Workers Group or Workers Delegation—with some twenty-four of them representing Saint Petersburg alone, two from Moscow, three from Riga, and two from Baku. The remaining thirteen came from scattered urban and industrial centers.[49]

At the same time the socialist press editorially encouraged its future delegates to use the congress as a forum "to struggle with those opportunistic members who would conceal the class tasks of the protetariat." Further, they were exhorted to "underscore the fact" that alcoholism was a "social ailment (*nedug*) of capitalist society, built on exploitation, and one that can be destroyed only with the destruction of capitalism itself." In addition, the Baku party intoned, "only the overthrow of the capitalist order and its replacement by a socialist one will destroy alcoholism."[50]

This already-militant mood was further exacerbated by two events just prior to the opening of the congress. The first was a report on measures for combatting alcoholism circulated under the aegis of the Saint Petersburg Bolshevik party organization at a public meeting held two days before the congress and attended by both workers of the city and some of the socialist delegates to the Congress. Not surprisingly, the report, which was received with great enthusiasm, condemned both the tsarist system for its fearful exploitation of the working class— of which its administration of the liquor monopoly was a major part— and the upcoming congress. Of the two, in fact, the report reserved the strongest condemnation for the latter, along with the measures it espoused, branding them as bourgeois, hypocritical, and for show (*litsemerno-pokaznoi*). Instead, it called on the Workers Delegation to the congress to disclose for all the world the true causes of alcoholism.[51] The second event was the arrest of twelve members of the Workers Delegation by the tsarist police. It was to have reverberations during the congress, constituting a major subtheme of the socialists and forming the basis of the indictment leveled against the regime by the Workers Delegation—its fear of the truth, which socialists told, about the true nature of Russian alcoholism.[52]

At the congress itself the basic strategy of the Workers Delegation was to emphasize the points that had already been developed in the socialist press. This strategy focused largely on two major areas: first, the close connection between alcoholism and socioeconomic conditions, and second, the definition of alcoholism as both a hygienic and a social problem. An associated question involved the future of the government-operated Guardianship of Popular Sobriety and whether they should be given over to "popular" control. Delegation efforts in all of these areas were made much easier because never more than a third of the 453 delegates to the congress was present at any one time, even when all three of its major working sections met jointly. Further, since the vast majority of the work of the congress was done by its respective sections in relatively small groups, it was easy for a cohesive and fairly united body such as the Workers Delegation to dominate its deliberations.

In thus exercising an influence on congress proceedings out of all proportion to its membership, the Workers Delegation also had the full support of those socialist physicians who were in attendance as representatives of other groups and whose positions on the alcohol question had anticipated their own by many years. In fact, toward the close of the congress, when the Workers Delegation walked out in protest over changes made in one of its resolutions, a number of these physicians exited the meeting with them in a gesture of support. Even N. F. Gamalia, himself a witness to these events and later a noted figure in Soviet medicine, categorized the entire congress as a confrontation between temperance advocates, financiers (the representatives of various Government ministries, especially the Ministry of Finance) and the politicians (the Workers Delegation and its associates).[53]

The bulk of criticism and remarks by these delegates focused on subjects in the congress's second section, Alcoholism and Society, as well as on one area of the third section, Measures for Combatting Alcoholism.[54] The general direction of their thinking in the latter area was indicated at one of the very first joint sessions when O. A. Kaspar'iants, a Saint Petersburg teacher and member of the Workers Delegation, joined the debate on alcoholism in the schools and alcoholism among school-age children. With the ringing declaration that there was no "single panacea" for such a disease as alcoholism, Kaspar'iants maintained that rather it was the result of factors inherent in the social and political order, "from the capitalist order itself": low wages, long working days, unsanitary conditions both on the job and in the homes of the workers, the absence of nutritious food, and the general lack of political rights by the workers. Change these, he asserted, and the elimination of alcoholism at all levels of Russian society would follow.[55] Similarly, at the same session V. P. Miliutin, a fellow member of the Workers Delegation, attacked the assimilationist D. N. Borodin for his report on the Gothenburg system (a Swedish system of limited-dividend corporations having local monopolies for the retail sale of liquor) by explicitly linking the government liquor monopoly—or *any* governmental monopoly—with the "systematic poisoning of the people." He therefore called for the transfer of the Guardianship of Popular Sobriety into the hands of "representative institutions" as the only means of making these bodies into an effective check on the alcoholization of the people.[56]

The same strategies were followed, too, in the smaller gatherings of the congress. At a joint session of the first and second sections on December 31, V. A. Posse, a moderate temperance advocate, contended that the chief importance of the struggle with alcoholism lay in the improvement of the human personality that was gained by abstinence. To this clearly reformist argument V. G. Chirkin cynically retorted that, on the contrary, the struggle was no more than "an expedient, the breaking of a single link in the chain of the political oppression and capitalist exploitation of the working class."[57] Chirkin was in fact so vitriolic and outspokenly revolutionary in his approach that he was one of the few speakers to be prohibited from delivering his own report to the congress several days later.

In addition to their efforts in the open debates, however, the members of the Workers Delegation gave seven reports of their own, reports in which they focused their efforts on showing the economic and social causes of alcoholism while criticizing government measures combatting it. Kaspar'iants's report, "Alcoholism and the Baku Workers," drew extensively from the data obtained from a questionnaire distributed in Baku before the congress. Again, not unsurprisingly, he concluded that such factors as the length of the working day, wages, and the roughness (*grubost'*) and difficulty (*tiazhest'*) of labor greatly influenced alcohol consumption by the Baku workers. But equally deleterious in his view was the political repression that since 1905 had "taken away everything from the masses except the *kabak*."[58] Such was also the thrust of S. I. Kanatchikov's "Workers and the Temperance Society" and A. E. Lositskii's "Alcoholism among the Saint Petersburg Workers in Dependence on Wages," based on data received from yet another questionnaire distributed in Saint Petersburg before the Congress.[59] Both were grounded firmly in the assumptions found in the work of the German author Alfred Grotjahn.[60] The Workers Delegation was vocal as well as instrumental in the adoption by the Congress of resolutions that not only specifically condemned the government liquor monopoly but also advocated the transfer of control of the controversial Guardianship of Popular Sobriety from the Ministry of Finance to the zemstvos.[61]

In the main these resolutions were somewhat more radical than many of the delegates desired and indeed led to the angry withdrawal of the Government representatives from the Congress. Further, their radical stance led to the arrest of seven more members of the Workers Delegation several days after the end of the Congress.[62] But more important, the activity of the Workers Delegation, its high level of revolutionary rhetoric, and the inevitable further politicization of the alcohol question put Nizhegorodtsev and others of the moderate and assimilationist approach in an awkward position. Often some of them were forced into rhetorical postures not dissimilar from those of the socialists lest the antialcohol movement be stolen from them under their noses.[63]

Yet it was the further politicization of the alcohol question that had been the aim of the socialists from the very beginning. Certainly this was the view of the *Sotsial demokrat*.[64] Their success in this task served as the basis for a steady commentary in the socialist press from this point onward. Rather infrequent before the congress of 1909–1910, it now began to focus more on the liquor monopoly, the All-Russian Congress on Alcoholism itself, and, later, the 1912 congress dominated by representatives of the Orthodox church.[65]

The end of the controversial congress did not, however, eliminate the controversy over worker alcoholism. The proponents of the assimilationist and the socialist approaches continued their polemics on the subject right up to the outbreak of World War I. The former are perhaps best represented by the work of the antialcohol activist S. A. Pervushin entitled *An Attempt at a Theory of Mass Alcoholism in Connection with the Theory of Demand: Toward the Question of the Construction of a Theory of Alcoholism as a Mass Phenomenon*, which appeared in 1913.[66] Thoroughly assimilationist in tone and content, Pervushin's work, drawing on German, French, and English economic and sociological treatises as well as Russian materials, emphasized, in addition to the elements of the socialist-environmentalist critique, the importance of custom, traditional usage, mood, lack of education, and excess funds among workers as causes for high alcohol consumption.[67]

By contrast, the socialists continued their attempt to link alcoholism and the capitalist system: witness the publication in 1913 of the combined research efforts of A. Lositskii and I. Chernyshev based on the questionnaires distributed to the workers of Saint Petersburg before the congress, complete with detailed tables and charts intended to give a statistical foundation to their views.[68] Moreover, socialist physicians kept the issue before various professional congresses in the years before World War I in terms that differed little from those articulated from the podiums of the First All-Russian Congress on Combatting Alcoholism or, for that matter, from those expressed in the pages of the socialist press. Dr. A. M. Korovin, addressing the Moscow Society of Factory Physicians in late 1910, emphasized the necessity for all physicians to "awaken the masses to the knowledge of the relationship between alcoholism and their own situation." Both he and L. S. Minor continued these efforts in the immediate prewar years.[69]

With the outbreak of World War I the government unilaterally legislated prohibition of the manufacture and sale of alcoholic beverages, but it did not by any means bring an end to alcoholism in Russia. In Tushino, near Moscow, there was so much vodka available by 1916 that it was no longer profitable for peasants to make home brew; and before the February 1917 revolution not an evening or a Sunday passed without vodka or beer.[70] In southern Russia, too, an observer noted that drunkenness, fighting, and even killings were frequently connected, and even during the first heady days of November 1917 drunkenness, disorder, and near chaos was commonly observed in Saint Petersburg.[71]

Clearly, then, one can deduce from these few examples that the analysis of the alcohol problem by the antialcohol socialists, the Social Democratic party and its press, and the Workers Delegation had not been valid. After everything, the end of the tsarist regime, the government liquor monopoly, and even the system of industrial capitalism in Russia did not result in a decline in the alcoholism of the people. Of course, whether the antialcohol message of the Russian socialists would have been more effective in the long run if it had not been so politicized is impossible to say. It is equally impossible to maintain that they were not wholly sincere in their belief that a combination of scientific method in the treatment of alcoholism and a solution to the "political" question would produce salutary results in, or a solution to, Russia's age-old alcohol problem. However, their conscious, and sometimes cynical, use of the alcohol problem as a club with which to beat the tsarist regime and the regime of industrial capital was in the long run self-defeating. By insisting on putting the question in largely political terms, by tying what was increasingly coming to be known as a disease independent of class, rank, or material well-being to purely economic and social causation, they made a solution independent of these categories impossible.

Many social anthropologists and historians have in fact emphasized that the prevalence of alcoholism depends as much on cultural tradition as on social organization. As Brian Harrison has pointed out, industrialization by no means created the problem of urban intemperance; recreational drinking sometimes does result directly from squalor, overwork, and underpay but sometimes also from the possession of funds without an accompanying tradition that ensures their constructive application and from the possession of leisure time whose incidence is insufficiently predictable to ensure its rational use.[72] Furthermore, contemporary research has shown that alcoholism and drunkenness persist even in the most equitable of social orders where many of the social conditions fostering it have disappeared. Thus, the stress by Russian antialcohol socialists on following Engels's environmentalist approach and blaming alcoholism on a faulty social structure formulated an equation with which contemporary Soviet historians and social scientists have found it difficult to deal.[73]

NOTES

1. See, for example, James H. Billington, *The Icon and the Axe: An Interpretive History of Russian Culture* (New York: Knopf, 1965); Anatole Leroy-Beaulieu, *The Empire of the Tsars and the Russians*, pt. 1, *The Country and Its Inhabitants* (New York: Arno Press, 1969); I. G. Pryzhov, *Istoriia kabakov v Rossii* [A history of taverns in Russia], 2d ed. (Kazan, 1914); Louis Skarzynski, *L'alcool et son histoire en Russie. Etude économique et sociale* (Paris: Librairie Nouvelle de Droit et de Jurisprudence, 1902); and George Vernadsky, *A History of Russia*, vol. 1, *Ancient Russia* (New Haven: Yale University Press, 1943).

2. Donald Horton, "The Functions of Alcohol in Primitive Societies," *Quarterly Journal of Studies on Alcohol* 4 (1943): 199–320. The anxiety hypothesis was subsequently recast to suggest that what Horton called anxiety was really the structural instability of society. See, for example, Peter B. Field, "A New Cross-Cultural Study of Drunkenness," 48, 74, in *Society, Culture and Drinking Patterns*, ed. David J. Pittman and Charles R. Snyder (New York: J. Wiley, 1962); Olav Irgens-Jensen, "The Use of Alcohol in an Isolated Area of Northern Norway," *British Journal of Addiction* 65 (1970): 181–185.

3. Friedrich Engels, *The Condition of the Working Class in England in 1844*, ed. and trans. W. O. Henderson and W. H. Chaloner, (Stanford, Calif.: Stanford University Press, 1968), 115–116, 142–143, 284.

4. For Marx's views on temperance advocacy and the function of drink establishments, see Karl Marx, "Economic and Philosophic Manuscripts of 1844," 121–122, and "The Communist Manifesto," 35, in *Basic Writings on Politics and Philosophy* (New York: Anchor Books, 1959); for the attitudes of the German socialists, see Karl Kautsky, "Der Alkoholismus und seine Bekamp-

fung," *Die Neue Zeit. Wochenschrift der Deutschen Sozialdemokratie* 9, pt. 2, no. 30 (1890–1891): 108; for the polemical exchange which revealed the conflict of opinion over this question, see Ferdinand Simon, "Zur Alkoholfrage," *Die Neue Zeit* 9, pt. 1, no. 15 (1890–1891): 583–590, and "Herr Kautsky Entgegen," *Die Neue Zeit* 9, pt. 2, no. 36 (1890–1891): 309–315.

5. See Abbott Gleason, *Young Russia: The Genesis of Russian Radicalism in the 1860s* (Chicago: University of Chicago Press, 1980), 365.

6. Ivan Gavrilovich Pryzhov, "Ocherki po istorii kabachestva" [Essays on the history of tavernkeeping], in *Ocherki, Stat'i, Pis'ma* [Essays, articles, letters] (Moscow, Leningrad, 1934), 193, and Pryzhov, *Istoriia kabakov.*

7. Reginald Zelnik, *Labor and Society in Tsarist Russia: The Factory Workers of St. Petersburg, 1855–1870*, (Stanford, Calif.: Stanford University Press, 1971); Dr. Gorman, "O p'ianstve v Rossii" [On alcoholism in Russia], *Arkhiv sudebnoi meditsiny i obshchestvennoi gigieny*, no. 1, sec. 3 (1868): 52ff; Dr. Val'kh, "K voprosu o p'ianstve v Petersburg" (Concerning the question of alcoholism in Saint Petersburg), *Arkhiv sudebnoi meditsiny i obshchesvennoi gigieny*, no. 4, sec. 5 (1870): 11–15.

8. R., "Po povodu dele o pishche i pomeshchenii rabochikh na fabrike kuptsa Egorova" [Concerning the matter of food and housing of workers at the factory of the merchant Egorov], *Arkhiv sudebnoi meditsiny i obshchestvennoi gigieny*, no. 1, sec. 3 (1871): 133, 134–135; 139–142.

9. See P. E. Zabliudovskii, *Istoriia otechestvennoi meditsiny. Meditsina v period kapitalizma. Razvitie gigieny, voprosy obshchestvennoi meditsiny* [History of national medicine. Medicine in the period of capitalism. The development of hygiene, questions of public medicine] (Moscow, 1956), 20.

10. See F. F. Erisman, "Podval'nyia zhilishcha v Peterburge" [Basement dwellings in Saint Petersburg], *Arkhiv sudebnoi meditsiny i obshchestvennoi gigieny*, no. 3 (September, December 1871): 37–85, 1–56.

11. "Ot redaktsii" [From the editors], *Vrach'* no. 11 (1896): 326 and "Ot redaktsii," *Nevrologicheskii vestnik* 3, no. 4 (1896): 177. See also I. V. Bokii, I. N. Piatnitskaia, and A. M. Shereshevskii, "Problemy patogeneza, kliniki i lecheniia alkogolizma na meditsinskikh s'ezdakh v Rossii" [Problems of the pathogenesis, hospitalization, and treatment of alcoholism at medical congresses in Russia], *Zhurnal nevropatologii i psikhiatrii imeni S. S. Korsakova* 77, no. 2 (1977): 279–283.

12. E. I. Lotova, *Russkaia intelligentsiia i voprosy obshchestvennoi gigieny. Pervoe gigienicheskoe obshchestvo v Rossii* [The Russian intelligentsia and questions of public hygiene. The first hygienic society in Russia] (Moscow, 1962), 15. See also *Trudy Russkago obshchestva okhraneniia narodnago zdraviia. Ustav obshchestva.* [Works of the Russian Society for the Protection of Public Health. Regulations of the society], vol. 1, (Saint Petersburg, 1884).

13. Piatnitskaia, and Shereshevskii, "Problem patogeneza," 279–283.

14. E. I. Lotova, *Russkaia intelligentsiia*, 167. See also G. I. Dembo, *Ocherk deiatel'nosti kommissii po voprosu ob akogolizma za 15 let, 1898–1913. Osoboe pribavlenie k Trudam postoiannoi kommissii po voprosu ob alkogolizme pod redaktsiei M. N. Nizhegorodtseva* [Sketch of the activity of the commission on the question of alcoholism for 15 years, 1898–1913. A special supplement to the Works of the

permanent commission on the question of alcoholism under the editorship of
M. N. Nizhegorodtsev] (Saint Petersburg, 1913), 18.

15. Dembo, *Ocherk*, 5.

16. *Trudy komissii po voprosu ob alkogolism. Zhurnaly zasedanii i doklady* [Works
of the commission on alcoholism. Journals of the sessions and Reports] (Saint
Petersburg, 1900), 1:i.

17. See, for example, two articles by N. N. Bazanov, "G. I. Dembo—vidnyi
sotsial-gigienist i organizator sovetskogo zdravookhraneniia (k 100-letiiu so
dnia rozhdeniia)" [G. I. Dembo—eminent social-hygienist and organizer of
Soviet health care (on the centenary of his birth)], *Sovetskoe zdravookhranenie* 32,
no. 1 (1973): 75–78; and "Grigorii Isaakovich Dembo" *Bol'shaia meditsinskaia
entsiklopediia* (Moscow, 1928), 8:607–608; E. N. Fokina, "Iz istorii bor'by s
alkogolizmom v Rossii (raboty A. M. Korovina, 1865–1943)" [From the history
of the struggle with alcoholism in Russia (the works of A. M. Korovin,
1865–1943)], *Sovetskoe Zdravookhranenie* 21, no. 8 (1962): 60–64; Kh. I.
Idel'chik, "Problema bor'by s alkogolizmom v nauchnoi i obshchestvennoi
deiatel'nosti professora L. S. Minora (k 125-letiiu so dnia rozhdeniia)" [Prob-
lem of the struggle with alcoholism in the scientific and public activity of
Professor L. S. Minor (toward the 125th anniversary of his birth)], *Sovetskoe
zdravookhranenie* 40, no. 3 (1981): 63–66; and *Bol'shaia Meditsinskaia Entsiklopediia* (Moscow, 1931), s.v. "Minor, Lazar Solomonovich," 18:396–397.

18. Joseph R. Gusfield, *Symbolic Crusade: Status Politics and the American
Temperance Movement* (Urbana: University of Illinois Press, 1969), 6.

19. See D. G. Bulgakovskii, "Rol' pravoslavnago dukhoventstva v bor'be s
narodnym p'ianstvgm" [Role of the Orthodox clergy in the struggle with
popular alcoholism], *Trudy komissii*, 22d session, 6 October 1899, 5:309–316,
547–566; P. I. Poliakov, "Pravoslavnoe dukhovenstvo v bor'be s narodnym
p'ianstvom" [The Orthodox clergy in the struggle with popular alcoholism],
Trudy komissii, 22d session, 6 October 1899, 5:309–316, 567–586.

20. On the former question, see L. B. Skarzynski, "Antial-kogolizm v shko-
lakh," [Antialcoholism in the schools], *Trudy komissii*, 26th session, 22 December 1899, 5:335–345, 479–516; on the latter, see "Zhurnal zasedanii iuridi-
chesko-psikhiatricheskoi subkomissii" [Journal of the sessions of the
judicial-psychiatric subcommission], *Trudy komissii*, 1st session, 9 December
1898, 5:354–363; 2d session, 20 January 1899, 5:364–372; 3d session, 17
February 1899, 5:372–379; 4th session, 17 March 1899, 5:379–387; 5th session, 2 April 1899, 5:387–392.

21. Dembo, *Ocherk*, 39–43.

22. See D. A. Dril', "Nikotoryia prichin massovago alkogolizma i vopros o
sredsvakh bor'by s nim" [Some causes of mass alcoholism and the question of
the struggle with it], *Trudy komissii*, 10th session, 24 October 1898 (Saint Petersburg, 1899), 2 (1): 100–108; 2 (2): 92–110.

23. See N. I. Grigor'ev, "O p'ianstve sredi masterovykh v S-peterburg,"
[Concerning alcoholism among the craftsmen of Saint Petersburg], *Trudy komissii*, 2: 100–108, 111, 118–119.

24. See Dembo, *Ocherk*, 59–60.

25. V. I. Lenin, "New Economic Developments in Peasant Life," *Collected
Works*, 4th ed. (Moscow, 1963), 1:71.

26. V. I. Lenin, *The Development of Capitalism in Russia*, 2d ed. (Moscow, 1964), 579.

27. V. I. Lenin, "Casual Notes," *Collected Works*, 4th ed. (Moscow, 1964), 4:407.

28. V. I. Lenin, "Concerning the State Budget," *Collected Works*, 4th ed. (Moscow, 1961), 5:332 and "Casual Notes," 4:408.

29. G. M. Gertsenshtein, "K voprosu ob otkhozhikh promyslakh" [Concerning the question of seasonal industries], *Russkaia mysl'*, 1887, no. 9.

30. N. I. Grigor'ev, for example, in his early work *Russkiia obshchestva trezvosti. Ikh organizatsiia i deiatel'nost v 1892–1893* [Russian temperance societies. Their organization and activity in 1892–1893] (Saint Petersburg, 1894) cites the existence of numerous private and factory-based temperance groups complete with fine schedules for recidivism, oaths of abstinence, and sets of rules for members. See also Semen Kanatchikov, *Iz istorii moego bytiia* [From the history of my life] (Moscow, Leningrad, 1929), 21, 65–66, whose memoirs reveal both the development of a "revolutionary consciousness" and a growing awareness of the dangers of alcoholism.

31. See "Prenie po oboim dokladom" [Debate on both reports], *Trudy komissii*, 10th session, 24 October 1898, 2(2): 103.

32. G. I. Dembo, "Prichiny alkogolizma" [The causes of alcoholism]. *Trudy komissii*, vol. 10, *Prilozhenie* [Supplement]. See also Dembo, *Ocherk*, 55–56, and idem, *Alkogolizm i bor'ba s nim* [Alcoholism and the struggle with it] (Saint Petersburg, 1909), 34.

33. E. N. Fokina, "Iz istorii bor'by," 60–64.

34. A. M. Korovin, "Dvizhenie trezvosti v Rossii" [The temperance movement in Russia] *Trudy komissii*, 25th session, 8 December 1899, 5:335–341, 439–470.

35. Dembo, *Alkogolizm i bor'ba s nim*, 9.

36. See "Zhurnal zasedanii," 5:372–379.

37. See, for example, N. Zhedenov, *Kazennaia, obshchestvennaia i chastnaia prodazha vina. Ikh ekonomicheskoe i nravstvennoe znachenie* [State, public, and private sale of wine. Their economic and moral Importance], (Saint Petersburg, 1896), and G. I. Dembo, *Kratkii ocherk deiatel'nosti s-Peterburgskogo Popechitel'stva o narodnoi trezvosti, 1898–1908* [A short sketch of the activity of the Saint Petersburg Guardianship of Popular Sobriety, 1898–1908] (Saint Petersburg, 1908), among numerous other works.

38. A. M. Korovin, [Untitled], *Zhurnal nevropatologiia i psikhiatr'*, 1902, no. 1–2: 289–290.

39. See V. M. Bekhterev's speeches to the Congress of National Psychiatrists, *Trudy 2-go s"ezda otechestvennykh psikhiatrov* [Works of the Second Congress of National Psychiatrists], (Kiev, 1907), 28–52; I. D. Strashun, *Russkaia obshchestvennaia meditsina v period mezhdu dvumia revoliutsiiami, 1907–1917* [Russian public medicine in the period between the two revolutions, 1907–1917] (Moscow, 1964), 136–152; 3d State Duma, *Stenograficheskie otchety* [Stenographic Reports], 11th session, 11 November 1907, 602–636, 641–644ff; *Ibid.*, 14th session, 7 December 1907, 849, 861–862, 876; Gosudarstvennyi Sovet [Council of State], *Stenograficheskie Otchet* [Stenographic Report], 3d session, 5 December 1907, 118, 129–140; 8 December 1907, 196, 208; M. I. Friedman, *Vinnaia*

monopoliia [The liquor monopoly], vol. 2, *Vinnaia monopoliia v Rossii* [The liquor monopoly in Russia] (Petrograd, 1916), 596–608.

40. Kh. I. Idel'chik, M. I. Aruin, and A. I. Nesterenko, "Vserossisskoi s"ezd po bor'be s p'ianstvgm," [The All-Russian Congress on Combatting Alcoholism], *Sovetskoe zdravookhranenie* 31, no. 2 (1972): 61.

41. I. D. Strashun, *Russkaia obshchestvennaia meditsina*, 139ff.

42. "Spisok chlenov organizatsionnago komiteta 1-go vserossiisskogo s"ezda po bor'be s p'ianstvom," [List of the members of the organizational committee of the First All-Russian Congress for Combatting Alcoholism], *Trudy pervago vserossisskogo s"ezda po bor'be s p'ianstvom, S-Peterburg, 28 dekabria, 1909g–6 ianvaria, 1910g* (Saint Petersburg, 1910), 1:3–5.

43. "Obshchii plan' organizatsii pervago vserossisskago s"ezda po bor'be s p'ianstvom" [General plan of organization of the First All-Russian Congress for Combatting Alcoholism], article 2, *Trudy pervago. . .s"ezda*, 1:7.

44. "Obshchii plan," article 2, 1:7; see also N. F. Gamalia, "O I vserossisskom s"ezde po bor'be s p'ianstvom" [Concerning the First All-Russian Congress for Combatting Alcoholism], *Sobranie sochineniia* [Collected works] (Moscow, 1958), 3:32.

45. "Obshchii plan," article 3, 1:7–8.

46. Idel'chik, "Problema bor'by," 64; see also L. K. Dymsha, "Kazennaia vinnaia monopoliia i eia zhachenie dlia bor'by s p'ianstvom" [The state liquor monopoly and its importance for combatting alcoholism], *Trudy komissii*, 19th session, 10 March 1899, 4:337–360; D. N. Borodin, "Vinnaia monopoliia (ekonomicheskoe i nravstvennoe zhachenie reformy)" [The liquor monopoly (the economic and moral significance of the reform)], *Trudy komissii*, 11th session, 4 November 1898, 3:133–179.

47. "K s"ezdu po bor'be s p'ianstvom" [Towards the Congress for Combatting Alcoholism] *Sotsial demokrat*, no. 9, 13 November/31 October 1909.

48. P. V. Barchugov, *Revoliutsionaia rabota bol'shevikov v legal'nykh rabochikh organizatsiiakh (1907–1911)* [The revolutionary work of the Bolsheviks in legal and illegal workers organizations (1907–1911)], (Rostov, 1963), 277ff.

49. Barchugov, *Revoliutsionnaia rabota;* see also I. Letunovskii, *Leninskaia taktika ispol'zovanie legal'nykh vserossiiskikh s"ezdov v bor'be za massy v 1908–1911 godakh.* [The Leninist tactic of utilization of legal all-Russian congresses in the struggle for the masses, 1908–1911] (Moscow, 1971), 38; B. Ia. Stel'nik, *Bakinskii proletariat v gody reaktsii* (1907–1910 gg.) [The Baku proletariat in the years of reaction (1907–1910)] (Baku, 1969), 176.

50. Letunovskii, *Leninskaia taktika*, 37–38; Stel'nik, *Bakinskii proletariat*, 176.

51. G. V. Kniazeva, *Bor'ba bol'shevikov za sochetanie nelegal'noi i legal'noi partiinoi raboty v gody reaktsii, 1907–1910* [Struggle of the Bolsheviks for the combination of illegal and legal party work in the years of reaction, 1907–1910] (Moscow, 1967), 120.

52. Lotova, *Russkaia intelligentsiia*, 172.

53. N. F. Gamalia, "O I vserossiiskom s"ezde," 3:32–33.

54. "Programma 1-go vserossiiskogo s"ezda po bor'be s p'ianstvom" [Program of the First All-Russian Congress for Combatting Alcoholism], *Trudy pervago. . .s"ezda*, 1:11, 12.

55. "Protokol vecherniago soedinennago zasedaniia vsekh trekh sekstii 30 dekabriia, 1909g." [Protocol of the evening joint session of all three sections, 30 December 1909], *Trudy pervago...s"ezda*, 1:114–115.

56. "Protokol," 1:116.

57. "Protokol soedinennago zasedaniia I i II sektsii, 31 dekabriia 1909g." [Protocol of the joint session of the first and second sections, 31 December 1909], *Trudy pervago...s"ezda*, 1:120–121. See also the remarks of A. I. Predkaln'e, *Trudy pervago...s"ezda*, 1:118, Chirkin in "Protokol zasedaniia vsekh trekh sektsii 31 dekabriia, 1909g.," *Trudy pervago...s"ezda*, 1:128, and Romanov in "Protokol zasedaniia 3-i sektsii 31 dekabriia 1909g.," *Trudy pervago...s"ezda*, 1:131–132.

58. D. A. Kaspar'iants, "Alkogolizm i bakinskie rabochie" [Alcoholism and the Baku workers], *Trudy pervago...s"ezda*, 2:834.

59. See S. I. Kanatchikov, "Rabochie i obshchestva trezvosti" [The workers and the temperance societies], *Trudy pervago...s"ezda*, 1:214; A. E. Lositskii, "Alkogolizm sredi peterburgskikh rabochikh v zavisimosti ot zarabotka" [Alcoholism among the workers of Saint Petersburg in Dependence on Wages], *Trudy pervago...s"ezda*, 1:230ff.

60. Alfred Grotjahn, *Alkohol und Arbeitsstätte* (Berlin, 1903).

61. Strashun, *Russkaia obshchestvennaia meditsina*, 144; see also *Trudy pervago ...s"ezda*, 1:1–10.

62. Barchugov, *Revoliutsionnaia rabota*, 285.

63. Strashun, *Russkaia obshchestvennaia meditsina*, 144; Lotova, *Russkaia intelligentsiia*, 174.

64. "Pokhmel'e posle p'ianogo s"ezda," [Hangover after the alcoholic congress], *Sotsial demokrat*, 1910, no. 11:5.

65. For a sampling of this commentary, see N. Baturin, "Velikaia piteinaia reforma" [The great drink reform], *Pravda*, no. 21, 24 May 1912; "P'ianye s"ezdy," [The alcoholic congresses], *Pravda*, no. 92, 1912; "Sluchainye zapiski" [Occasional notes], *Pravda* (95), 1912; B. Ivanov, " 'Zvezda' i 'Pravda' i rabochee dvizhenie, 1908–1913gg" [Zvezda and Pravda and the worker movement, 1908–1913], in *Iz epokhi 'Zvezdyi' i 'Pravdyi' (1911–1914)* [From the Epoch of Zvezda and Pravda (1911–1914)], vol. 2 (Moscow, 1922).

66. S. A. Pervushin, *Opyt teorii massovago alkogolizma v sviazi s teorii potrebnostei (k voprosu o postroenii teorii alkogolizma, kak massovago iavlenie)* [An attempt at a theory of mass alcoholism in connection with a theory of mass (toward the question of the formation of a theory of alcoholism as a mass phenomenon)] (Saint Petersburg, 1913). References here are to the edition published as part of the *Trudy* of the Permanent Commission on the Question of Alcoholism, 1913, 13(2): 68–154.

67. Pervushin, *Opyt*, 13(2): 125–134, 149–154.

68. A. Lositskii and I. Chernyshev, *Alkogolizm peterburgskikh rabochikh* [Alcoholism of the Saint Petersburg Workers] (Saint Petersburg, 1913).

69. See A. M. Korovin, "Bor'ba s alkogolizmom kak neobkhodimoe uslovie pri uluchenii rabochego byta," [The struggle with alcoholism as a necessary condition for the improvement of the worker's life], *Vrachebnaia gazeta*, 1910, no. 19:23; E. N. Fokina, "Iz istorii bor'by," 63; Idel'chik, "Problemy bor'by," 65–66.

70. Diane Koenker, *Moscow Workers and the 1917 Revolution* (Princeton, N.J.: Princeton University Press, 1981), 63.

71. Iu. I. Kir'ianov, *Rabochie iuga Rossii, 1914–fevral' 1919* [The workers of South Russia, 1914–February 1919] (Moscow, 1971), 104; and Jan H. Yarovsky, *It Happened in Moscow* (New York: Vantage Press, 1961), 103.

72. See, for example, Peter Laslett, *The World We Have Lost* (New York: Scribner's, 1965), 75; Brian Harrison, *Drink and the Victorians: The Temperance Question in England, 1815–1872* (Pittsburgh: University of Pittsburgh Press, 1971), 393.

73. M. G. Field, "Alcoholism, Crime and Delinquency in Soviet Society," in *Sociology: The Progress of a Decade,* ed. Seymour Martin Lipset and N. J. Smelser (Englewood Cliffs, N.J.: Prentice-Hall, 1961), 577.

TWELVE

Public Health, Public Morals, and Public Order: Social Science and Liquor Control in Massachusetts, 1880–1916

Thomas F. Babor and Barbara G. Rosenkrantz

Heavy drinking and disapproval of intemperance were both character-istic of mid-nineteenth-century Americans. Changes in demography, economics, and politics had by the 1880s altered the environment that shaped attitudes toward alcohol and drunkenness, and charity and religious organizations withdrew from their once-dominant reformist positions. More accurately, social controls once primarily identified with pietistic philanthropy now were adopted by professionals in medi-cine, law, and business. Temperance reformers preferred to speak through such organizations as the Social Science Association. As these men and women worked to secure a less volatile ideological foundation for assessment and management of the alcohol problem in Massachu-setts, their arguments were frequently distinguished by self-conscious reference to research and even greater deference to statistics.

In this essay we focus on the contributions made by social re-searchers to the public debate surrounding alcoholic beverage control (ABC) legislation in Massachusetts before the enactment of national prohibition. In the late decades of the nineteenth century major re-views of the Massachusetts local option system could ignore moral postures previously considered essential to the debate (Thomas 1965; Tyrrell 1979; Wines and Koren 1898; Koren 1910). We review the large amount of empirical evidence that was generated by social research to characterize the nature, dimensions, and causes of alcohol problems in the commonwealth between 1880 and 1916 and point to some of the effects of various measures intended to restrict the use of alcohol.

In many respects Massachusetts served as the first laboratory of social research on the American alcohol problem. With its long tradition of philanthropy and social activism, Massachusetts was preeminent in medical research, public-health policy, welfare legislation, and institutional treatment for mental disorder (Rosenkrantz 1972). The commonwealth was also a focal point for temperance reformers, second only to Maine in enacting statewide prohibitory legislation (1852), and the first state to experiment with the local option as an alternative approach to alcoholic-beverage control (1881). It is therefore not surprising that social scientists would be attentive to the alcohol problem in Massachusetts and that the evidence they generated would play an important role in the debate over public policy.

Our review of social research in the thirty-five years before national prohibition responds in part to the questions contemporaries asked: How extensive was the alcohol problem in Massachusetts? Did ABC legislation influence the incidence and prevalence of alcohol-related problems? Although social scientists of the early twentieth century used less familiar words, they too wanted to learn what the data they collected revealed about the social epidemiology of alcohol use in those crucial decades.

We are also interested in why these studies were undertaken, what interests and constituencies were served by publication of the findings, and what aspects of alcohol abuse appeared most accessible to intervention. In particular we wish to know how scientific authority influenced temperance reform and prohibition sentiment in Massachusetts.

ALCOHOL RESEARCH IN MASSACHUSETTS

Thirteen studies, summarized in Table 12.1 were selected after an extensive survey of temperance publications, legislative investigations and reports, medical and scientific journals, and materials issued by the alcoholic beverage industry. Selection depended on the explicit intent of the investigators to generate and interpret different kinds of "empirical" data as the foundation for their argument and published report.

The sponsors of these studies may be classified into three groups. The first reflects the interests of the alcoholic beverage industry, represented here by investigations sponsored by the United States Brewers' Association (Koren 1910; Thomann 1884). Founded in 1860, the Brewers' Association developed into the most powerful interest group in the nation concerned with the protection of the alcoholic beverage industry from the incursions of the prohibitionists and politicians. Its main organ of communication was an annual yearbook containing summaries of convention proceedings, a digest of state and national

ABC legislation, and reviews of alcohol-related scientific literature both popular and technical. In exceptional cases the Brewers' Association commissioned original studies.

Persons and groups affiliated with academic institutions constitute the second category of social scientists investigating the alcohol problem (Wines and Koren 1898; Calkins 1901; Bowditch and Hodge 1901; Cole and Durland 1901; American Statistical Association 1907). Five studies in this category were sponsored by the Committee of Fifty, which evolved out of a group of fifteen persons who began meeting in 1889 to discuss social research. In 1893 they enlarged to fifty and concentrated on the alcohol problem. New members were recruited primarily from eastern cities. Meetings were held twice yearly in New York City. Eight participants came from Massachusetts, including Charles W. Eliot, president of Harvard, and the statisticians Francis Amassa Walker and Carroll D. Wright. Walker was president of the Massachusetts Institute of Technology, and Wright was chief of the Massachusetts Bureau of Labor Statistics until he went to Washington in 1888 as the first commissioner of the Federal Bureau of Labor. Their first order of business was to appoint subcommittees to study the physiological, economic, legislative, and ethical aspects of the alcohol problem. Four reports were published under the authority of the committee between 1898 and 1904.

A third category of sponsorship was organizations or institutions interested in the alcohol problem for reasons related to public policy. Here we include the Massachusetts state legislature, which commissioned a series of studies from state agencies (Woods et al. 1910; Murray et al. 1914) and bureaus (Wadlin 1896).

As Table 12.1 indicates, the investigations covered three general areas: social epidemiology, that is, the distribution and determinants of alcohol-related poverty, crime, and mental disorder; the effectiveness of alcohol control policies and prevention measures; and legal management and medical treatment of the public inebriate. Though all the studies included here focused on Massachusetts, a number were also concerned with other states (Wines and Koren 1898; Thomann 1884; Calkins 1901; Koren 1899).

Epidemiological Studies

Three studies (Thomann 1884; Koren 1899; Wadlin 1896) were conducted for the purpose of estimating the prevalence of alcohol use and problem drinking among paupers, criminal offenders, and mental patients. The first study, Gallus Thomann's *Real and Imaginary Effects of Intemperance,* was published in 1884 under the aegis of the Brewers' Association. Its aim was to evaluate the "statistical basis" of the

TABLE 12.1 Compendium of Social Science Research Studies Relating to the Epidemiology, Prevention, or Treatment of Alcohol Abuse in Massachusetts, 1880–1916

Designer/Researcher (Year of Publication)	Sponsor/Publisher	Period Studied	Rationale	Method
Thomann (1884)	U.S. Brewers' Association	1854–1883	To provide a statistical basis for understanding relations between alcohol, mental illness, poverty and crime	Testimonial letters from institutional officials; descriptive statistics on prevalence
Calkins (1896)	Committee of Fifty	c. 1895	To report on "substitutes for the saloon" in Boston	Qualitative analysis; descriptive statistics on drinking establishments, pool rooms, clubs, etc.
Wadlin (1896) Mass. Bureau of Statistics of Labor	Mass. State Legislature	1894–1895	To ascertain the number of commitments to all penal and charitable institutions resulting from use of alcoholic beverages	Personal interviews relating to 31,738 cases of pauperism, crime, and insanity
Wines and Koren (1898)	Committee of Fifty	1875–1894	To evaluate the local option system in Massachusetts in relation to other state approaches to alcohol beverage control	Qualitative analysis; descriptive statistics on arrests for public intoxication and prostitution
Koren (1899)	Committee of Fifty	1896–1898	To determine the proportion of pauperism, destitution, and crime attributable to alcohol, and its distribution by class and race	National survey of institutional officials; personal interviews with prisoners and welfare clients
Cole and Durland (1901)	Committee of Fifty	c. 1900	To describe Boston agencies currently serving as functional substitutes for the saloon	Descriptive inventory of drinking fountains, lunch rooms, reading rooms, parks, gymnasiums, men's clubs, temperance societies, public baths and rescue missions

Source	Organization	Dates	Purpose	Methods
Bowditch and Hodge (1901)	Committee of Fifty	1885–1899	To evaluate and critique "scientific temperance instruction" in Massachusetts public schools	Testimonial letters from U.S. and foreign medical authorities; opinion surveys of teachers
No author (1907)	American Statistical Association	1891–1906	To evaluate the application of Massachusetts 1891 probation law in cases of public intoxication	Descriptive statistics on arrests and disposition through probation, release or sentencing
Parmelee (1909)	Russell Sage Foundation	1898–1907	To describe and critique penal methods for dealing with public inebriates in eight Boston municipal courts	Structured interviews with 650 drunkenness offenders regarding age, ethnicity, occupation, etc.
Woods et al. (1910)	Mass. State Legislature	c. 1908	To evaluate state penal system in relation to disposition of public inebriates and treatment of alcoholism	Qualitative analysis; descriptive statistics on public inebriates and habitual alcoholics
Koren (1910)	U.S. Brewers' Association	1881–1909	To evaluate the Massachusetts local option system of alcoholic beverage control	Qualitative analysis; descriptive statistics on voting trends, enforcement, arrests, etc.
Murray et al. (1914)	Mass. State Legislature	c. 1913	To evaluate causes and costs of public intoxication in state; critique penal system and review treatment options	Qualitative analysis, descriptive statistics
Anderson (1916)	Boston Medical and Surgical Journal	c. 1915	To provide a social and clinical description of "the alcoholic as seen in court"	Interviews with a random sample of 50 "habitual" and 50 "periodic" drinkers

prohibitionists' assertion that insanity, pauperism, and crime were principally attributable to intemperance. A major part of the study was devoted to information obtained from a mail survey of fifty-four asylums, of which four were Massachusetts institutions. The survey, sent to every insane asylum in the country, asked for a yearly count of the male and female patients whose "insanity was caused by intemperance." These data, listed in an appendix along with the accompanying written responses of many hospital superintendents, provide important insights into the contemporary meaning of this diagnostic category during the latter part of the nineteenth century. Thomann's analysis consisted of computing the proportions of intemperance diagnoses in each hospital based on total admissions for the reporting year falling closest to 1883. The reports from Massachusetts institutions are representative of those obtained from other United States asylums: Boston Lunatic Hospital, 9.6 percent; Taunton Lunatic Asylum, 3.8 percent; Danvers Lunatic Asylum, 12.2 percent; the McLean Asylum, 3.8 percent. Without going "behind the returns," the compiler concluded that "on the average, intemperance is the cause of insanity in seven cases out of one hundred" (Thomann 1884, 25).

The remainder of Thomann's book is devoted to a discussion of evidence implicating alcohol as a cause of pauperism and crime. Data obtained from the 1875 Massachusetts state census are reviewed with those of other sources to ascertain the amount of pauperism caused by intemperance. Arguing that "intemperance is either the effect—not the cause—or merely one of the contributive causes" in most cases of alcohol-related pauperism, Thomann nevertheless accepted the figure of 24 percent suggested by other studies. In the case of crime statistics he argued that inebriety and alcoholic insanity were frequently put forward by otherwise-sober criminals as an excuse for their misconduct. Thomann gave special attention to the relative sobriety observed among the beer-drinking Germans, whom the brewers were fond of contrasting to other, less temperate ethnic groups.

The 1895 *Report of the Massachusetts Bureau of Statistics of Labor* (Wadlin 1896), the second of the three epidemiological studies, far from being an isolated excursion into survey research, is the culmination of a series of earlier reports dealing with pauperism, crime, drunkenness and liquor selling (Bureau of Statistics of Labor 1877, 1880, 1881). In this monumental study, commissioned as part of the commonwealth's continuing efforts to cut back ballooning budgets, the relation of drinking to crime, pauperism, and insanity was ascertained by questions put directly to the respondent. It epitomizes the inductive statistical method that was applied with increasing frequency by social scientists in the investigation of social problems. The report consists almost entirely of frequency tables describing the numbers of paupers, persons arrested, and mental patients whose conditions were caused by "intoxicating liquors." Over a twelve-month period beginning in August 1894, personal interviews were conducted with all persons admitted to state-supported prisons, asylums, and welfare institutions—a total of 21,738 cases.

The description in the report of 3,230 paupers receiving public support shows poverty to be concentrated among males (81.5 percent) and the foreign-born (68.5 percent). Of the 1,019 American citizens born paupers, only 29.9 percent had both parents born in the United States. Thus, 90.6 percent of all paupers were first- or second-generation immigrants. Of the foreign-born paupers, 58.3 percent of the men and 42.3 percent of the women were Irish. The majority of them (56.1 percent) were concentrated in Suffolk County, whose population was primarily from Boston. The survey of paupers' drinking habits revealed that 19.7 percent of adult men and 6.6 percent of adult women were classified as excessive drinkers, a category of drinker defined as "all who are completely under the influence of the drinking habit—who are, in fact, common drunkards" (Wadlin 1896, 41). Among the foreign-born classified according to country of origin, the Irish had the highest proportion of excessive drinkers.

In the bureau report the analysis of public intoxication is treated in the context of criminal arrests. Public intoxication accounted for 68 percent of the 18,232 convictions made during the twelve-month period under study. Men were more likely to be drinking when arrested than women, but women were more likely to be classified as excessive drinkers. Of the groups compared, the Irish had the highest proportion of their own group arrested while under the influence and designated as excessive drinkers. Moreover, the Irish more frequently admitted excessive drinking and attributed their pauperism to alcohol. German, Russian, and Italian arrestees had the smallest proportions of excessive drinkers and drinking.

Approximately sixteen hundred mental patients were interviewed during the study period. Native-born asylum patients were found to have a lower proportion of insanity "due to the use of intoxicating liquors" (33.6 percent of men, 9.1 percent of women) than naturalized and alien patients (44.3 percent of men, 15.2 percent of women). The proportion of excessive drinkers in these groups was almost identical to these figures, suggesting that the criteria for attributing insanity to intemperance were closely related to evidence used to determine excessive drinking.

The conclusion of the report emphasized the tenor of objectivity that was pronounced from the beginning, deliberately setting the study off from previous consciously moral arguments and even from traditional medical assessments of excessive drinking that had tangled with questions of willpower and habit. In words reminiscent of Lemuel Shattuck's report to the legislature on sanitary conditions in the commonwealth a half century earlier, the Bureau of Labor Statistics argued that it was not in its "province...to draw deductions from the results of this investigation...or to apply the evidence presented to the support of any theory of the regulation or prohibition of the liquor traffic....Our end is reached if the figures tell their story so plainly that its meaning is unobscured" (Wadlin 1896, 415).

A Study of the Economic Aspects of the Liquor Problem (Koren 1899) is the third epidemiological study outlined in Table 12.1. The Committee of Fifty appointed John Koren, a statistician in the Department of Labor, special agent of its economic subcommittee. Among other things, his charge was to investigate the contribution of alcohol to pauperism and crime. Although initially trained as a Lutheran minister, Koren had studied the Gothenburg system of liquor control in Germany and was experienced in the analysis and interpretation of social data associated with alcohol. Later he was to work directly for the Brewers' Association, an affiliation that tainted the objectivity of his findings in the eyes of the prohibitionists (Gordon 1916).

In 1896 Koren made a nationwide survey of charity organizations to gather statistics for the study of intemperance among paupers. He believed that there was a "natural tendency to underestimate this cause [of poverty] on account of the very difficulty of getting the facts" and the desire to give doubtful cases the benefit of the doubt "lest the statement that the applicant has become poor through liquor should prejudice his case when he applied for relief" (Koren 1899, 14). While admitting that the "personal equation" may have thus biased the returns, Koren felt that conservative and liberal views would cancel each other. Moreover, since response to a questionnaire was the basis for inclusion in the study, official cooperation rather than inmates' social characteristics determined the population of the study.

Data were obtained from a survey mailed to forty-six charity organizations, of which six were located in Massachusetts. A total of 29,923 cases were recorded by the thirty-three institutions reporting over a twelve-month period. The questionnaire stipulated that poverty could not be attributed to drink unless the connection was direct and immediate, that is, "unless drink led to loss of employment, prevented the person from getting a situation, or unless he was known to drink to excess" (Koren 1899, 15). Of the more than sixteen hundred Massachusetts cases reviewed, 37.5 percent of the male paupers and 10.0 percent of the female paupers were judged to have their poverty caused directly by intemperance, and 7.7 percent of the men and 33.2 percent of the women were found to have their condition caused indirectly by the intemperance of their parents or spouses. To the extent that these aggregate trends are consistent from one independent sample to another, they imply a certain degree of reliability in the procedure. The estimates are remarkably close to the findings of the 1896 bureau report, which attributed 39 percent of pauperism directly to the paupers' drinking and 10 percent to the drinking of others. Also consistent with the bureau report, Koren found the smallest proportion of paupers among the Italians, Russians, Austrians, and Poles and the highest proportion among the Irish.

Studies of the Public Inebriate Problem: Prevention, Treatment, and Rehabilitation

Between 1907 and 1916 at least five studies were published dealing with the disposition of public-drunkenness offenders within the Massachusetts penal system. A review of the probation system was made by the American Statistical Association (1907) during Carroll Wright's presidency of the Washington-based organization. After 1891 Massachusetts used probation as an alternative to fines or imprisonment. As its use increased, probation officers were given the authority, in 1905, to arrange for conditions permitting the release of first-time and occasional offenders without arraignment.

The purpose of the ASA study was to document the extent to which the probation law was applied uniformly throughout the state. A survey of sixty-nine municipal, police, and district courts was conducted to determine the number of cases released, given probation, or sentenced to prison. The results indicated wide variation in the proportion of cases given probation, with the larger courts favoring more lenient practices; drunkenness offenders were dealt with more harshly in rural areas than in cities, and there was little attempt to treat the infrequent inebriate more leniently than the recidivist.

The next two studies of the penal system (Anderson 1916; Parmelee 1909) develop the theme of differential treatment for occasional and chronic drunkenness offenders, arguing forcefully for institutional alternatives to imprisonment. M. F. Parmelee's study *Inebriety in Boston* was published as a Ph.D. dissertation by Columbia University in 1909. A total of 650 cases, randomly selected from eight courts, were investigated through a seventy-seven-item interview schedule. The primary aim was to describe the social and demographic characteristics of drunkenness offenders in relation to those of the general population. Drunkenness offenders were more likely than the male population of Boston to be single, foreign-born, and Irish. They were also younger.

Whereas the Boston male population between thirty-five and forty-four years of age constituted 22 percent of the population, more than 34 percent of the drunkenness offenders were classified in that age range. Almost all of those arrested worked in manual trades, the greatest proportion (36.5 percent) being unskilled laborers and teamsters. Twenty-three percent were found to be illiterate, in contrast to an estimated 4 percent of the Boston population. Nearly three-fourths admitted to being arrested previously for drunkenness.

The remainder of Parmelee's dissertation was devoted to a discussion of the causes and prevention of inebriety, along with a critique of the Massachusetts penal system. Parmelee invoked hereditary theory both to explain drunkenness and to serve as a guide in its elimination. He suggested, for example, that the Irish were less sober than the Jews because the former race had not used alcohol as long as the latter; as a consequence the Irish had not undergone the kind of natural selection that would have eliminated from their race "those who have a strong craving for drink." Other explanations advanced to explain inebriety include industrial conditions, especially unemployment, lack of recreational alternatives to the saloon, and physiological craving.

According to Parmelee, the failure of statewide prohibition to control inebriety argued for a solution based on "alcoholic selection": "By eliminating these inebriates from society they are prevented from propagating themselves and thus in course of time this type of inebriate would be eliminated from society" (Parmelee 1909, 64). To accomplish this selection, Parmelee recommends sentencing habitual drunkards to hospitals or asylums for an indefinite period of therapeutic work and medical treatment.

In a study similar in nature but less drastic in its recommendations, *The Alcoholic as Seen in Court*, Anderson (1916) provides a medical-psychiatric description of the alcoholic arrestee. His analysis is based on a random sample of fifty "habitual" and fifty "periodic" drinkers having long records of drunkenness arrest. Ninety percent were found to be unemployed or minimally employed, 100 percent indicated impairment in physical or mental performance, 37 percent were diagnosed as feebleminded, 7 percent gave evidence of insanity, and 32 percent revealed a "psychopathic constitution." Anderson concluded that, given these grave physical and mental handicaps, the best interests of the individual would be served by medical rather than penal treatment. He recommended prolonged hospital care and farm colony treatment for the habitual or chronic alcoholic and suggested that the periodic alcoholic should be "incorporated back into society by means of well-directed medical and social service methods" (Anderson 1916, 11).

The last two studies devoted to the problem of the public inebriate were commissioned by the state legislature (Woods et al. 1910; Murray et al. 1914). In 1909 the trustees of the Foxborough State Hospital were asked to "report upon the treatment of inebriates in Massachusetts." James Ford, an instructor in the Department of Social Ethics at Harvard, was appointed by the trustees to review court and institutional procedures for the treatment of drunkenness offenders and to recommend improvements in current practices. The report (Woods et al. 1910) began with a review of police statistics, which in 1908 attributed 60 percent of all arrests and 65 percent of all convictions to drunkenness. The discussion of arrest procedures suggested that these figures may only have represented the tip of an iceberg, given the likelihood that nonoffensive drunks were ignored and only blatant violators arrested. Ninety-two percent of those arrested were men, and almost 50 percent were foreign-born. Most of these cases, perhaps as many as 65 percent, were recidivists, or "rounders." The cost to the state was estimated to be in excess of one million dollars, or 71 percent of the prison budget. This estimate did not take into account economic losses, effects on property and public morality, or "the heritage of abandoned or degenerate offspring" left to future generations.

The report concluded its introduction by noting that the existing penal system for inebriates was inadequate and often self-defeating: too many multiple offenders were released, and too few were followed by probation officers; the poor were imprisoned for failure to pay fines, but imprisonment failed as a correctional measure. Despite the passage of a statute providing for the commitment of habitual drunkards to Foxborough for treatment, only 305 cases were referred in 1908, many of these "defectives" and inappropriate cases. Further, the report noted that although six thousand women were arrested for drunkenness in 1909, there were no facilities at Foxborough or in the penal system for female inebriates, who were therefore sent to insane asylums.

To correct this situation, the Foxborough trustees recommended a differential, graded approach to drunkenness offenders. Occasional and accidental inebriates would first receive a combination of release, probation, and fines. Pathological cases in their early stages were to be sent to Foxborough or to a similar treatment facility. Incurable, chronic inebriates were to be given indeterminate sentences and sent to a proposed detention farm colony located in a rural setting "free of the temptations of alcohol."

In 1913 the state legislature appointed yet another commission "to investigate the subject of drunkenness in this commonwealth and the best means of correcting or controlling that evil" (Murray et al. 1914). With the assistance of Harvard's James Ford, this commission held public hearings and visited correctional facilities in various parts of the state. The year 1913 witnessed the greatest number of drunkenness arrests in the history of the commonwealth, far exceeding the highest rates recorded prior to the repeal of Prohibition. The report began with what had by then become a familiar list of the social costs of alcohol: organic diseases, premature deaths, accidents, loss of labor, poverty, and insanity. Expressing a view closely resembling the conclusion of the 1910 report of the Foxborough Trustees, the commission criticized the present penal system for not releasing occasional inebriates, implying that the arraignment practices of clerks and probation officers may have been motivated less by duty than by the fees collected when the arrestee was held over for trial. Because persons unable to pay their fines were typically imprisoned, the report stated that "imprisonment for drunkenness is not only too severe as a penalty upon the drunkard and his family, but is also generally ineffectual as a deterrent or as an agent of reformation" (Murray et al. 1914, 16). Despite the existence of Foxborough and other hospital facilities, delirium tremens and other acute emergencies were usually treated in the jails by city physicians.

The commission concluded in 1914 that prevention of drunkenness should take precedence over cure. To this end the report considered seven alternatives. First, it advanced state prohibition and then rejected it as inexpedient because of entrenched drinking habits and the infringements on personal liberty. A second solution considered and rejected was the elimination of private profit from liquor sales since it would undoubtedly be opposed by both the liquor interests and the prohibitionists. Other solutions proposed include rigorous enforcement of existing laws governing illegal liquor selling; amendments to existing laws (such as regulation of liquor sales by druggists without prescription); temperance instruction in the public schools; substitutes for the saloon, such as neighborhood centers; and the removal of more general causes of drunkenness, such as "evil heredity," bad housing conditions, poor working conditions, and poverty.

Studies of Alcohol Control Policies and
Other Prevention Measures

The third type of social research conducted in Massachusetts during this period consists of three evaluations of the local option system (Wines and Koren 1898; Koren 1910; Wadlin 1896), two studies of functional "substitutes for the saloon" (Calkins 1901; Cole and Durland 1901), and one study of temperance instruction in the public-school system (Bowditch and Hodge 1901).

The Restrictive System in Massachusetts, 1875–1894 was published as part of the first report of the Committee of Fifty, *The Liquor Problem in Its Legislative Aspects* (Wines and Koren 1898). The Massachusetts study was conducted by John Koren of Boston, who worked for the sub-committee on the legislative aspects of the drink problem between 1894–1895.

This investigation began with a review of the development of Massachusetts liquor legislation following the return of the license system in 1874. This system, better known as local option, gave towns and cities the right to decide whether the trade in alcoholic beverages should be permitted. Using Boston and North Adams as examples of large and small cities in the commonwealth, Koren contrasted current regulatory methods with earlier attempts, giving special attention to their apparent association with drunkenness arrest statistics. As the capital city and a growing metropolis, Boston became a major focus of both alcohol-related problems and ABC legislation. Between 1875 and 1894 four different licensing procedures were implemented in an attempt to control illegal sales and reduce the number of drinking establishments. After the repeal of statewide prohibition in 1873 licensing commissioners were appointed by the mayor. In 1880 this power was entrusted to the police commissioners and later to a metropolitan board to remove licensing power from political influence. According to Koren, these changes and the subsequent imposition of the strict "high license" law of 1888 had little tangible effect on the sobriety of Bostonians. Similarly, a review of arrest statistics for the entire state did not support the common assumption that Massachusetts had become more sober since the adoption of the local-option law.

In 1910 John Koren published an extension of his analysis of the Massachusetts local-option system, this time in the *Year Book of the U.S. Brewers' Association* (Koren 1910). The accumulation of ten additional years of experience with local option did not change Koren's major conclusions about its lack of effectiveness. If the spread of prohibition from rural dry areas to urban wet areas is taken as the criterion of success, then local option was thought to have made little progress since its inception. The dry vote remained remarkably constant during this period (Howie 1933). Koren also points out that even the rural dry votes, which accounted for approximately half the number cast in each yearly local-option election, reflected more of a preference for "home expediency" than for total abstinence. That is, many localities, particularly those in the immediate vicinity of Boston, voted dry to exclude the saloon, knowing full well that spirits and beer could be purchased from druggists, kitchen bars, or private clubs, or could be imported from Boston. Although advocates of prohibition never failed "to find satisfactory evidence of diminution of drunkenness under a no-license

TABLE 12.2   Average Monthly Arrest Rate for Towns and Cities
Changing from License (Wet) to No-license (Dry) or Vice Versa
in a Twelve-Month Period Beginning August 20, 1894

		Drunkenness		Other Offenses	
	N	Wet Months	Dry Months	Wet Months	Dry Months
Wet to Dry Changes					
Towns	13	2.0	2.3	3.0	3.6
Cities	2	50.9	19.9	37.8	26.8
Dry to Wet Changes					
Towns	19	9.4	2.6	5.3	2.9
Cities	3	182.9	60.3	69.7	45.4

SOURCE: Data compiled from Wadlin 1896, 234–253.

regime,...an examination of the evidence in regard to the advantages gained...has proved negative" (Koren 1910, 117).

Of direct relevance to an evaluation of Koren's conclusions regarding the effect of local prohibition of drunkenness arrests is a review of police statistics included in the bureau report of 1896 (Wadlin 1896). During the twelve-month period under study fifty-three cities and towns (with a combined population of 1,275,163) voted to permit alcohol under the local-option system; 260 localities (having a combined population of 924,066) did not permit the sale of alcohol (that is, voted to maintain a no-license policy). Forty additional cities and towns (representing 300,974 persons) changed from one system to the other during the course of the year. Summarizing arrest data, the report showed that license cities and towns had a greater number of drunkenness arrests (36.2 per thousand) than no-license localities (9.94 per thousand), with the towns and cities that switched taking an intermediate position (13.6 per thousand). This comparison may be misleading because of the disproportionate influence of larger cities, which were predominantly wet, so the report presents arrest data in monthly averages for all 353 Massachusetts jurisdictions. A summary of an important part of those data is presented in table 12.2.

Data abstracted from localities that switched from one system to the other provide a means of controlling for possible differences in wet and dry enforcement practices as well as in the baseline numbers of public inebriates. Wet localities, for example, may have had stringent enforcement practices rather than a large number of public inebriates. The analysis of local-option changes within the same localities presumably held enforcement practices constant while at the same time permitting study of factors associated with the direction of change.

The generally close relationship between drunkenness arrests and other offenses may be explained by the fact that the latter category included many offenses where drunkenness was also involved. In general, drunkenness arrests were two to three times more frequent in wet months than in dry months; regardless of the direction of change, fewer arrests were made in cities during dry months for both drunkenness and other offenses. Wet towns voting dry give no evidence of having changed their arrest rates, conceivably because their base rates were so low initially. Towns voting to go wet, however, experienced an almost fourfold increase in drunkenness arrests. Paradoxically, the base rate for drunkenness arrests does not appear to have been a factor in determining the direction of change in the local-option vote. Wet localities voting dry had lower crime rates than dry localities voting wet. Dry towns with an already-high tolerance for drunken comportment tended to vote wet, and wet towns with low tolerance seem to have voted dry. Contrary to the conclusion drawn by Wines and Koren (1898), these data indicate that local-option legislation did exert a significant and immediate effect on drunkenness arrests.

Two additional studies (Calkins 1896, 1901; Cole and Durland 1901) pertaining to Massachusetts were conducted under the auspices of the Committee of Fifty's Subcommittee on the Ethical Aspects of the Liquor Problem. The first was conducted by the Reverend Raymond Calkins, a Harvard student, the second by William Cole and Kellogg Durland of South End House in Boston. Both studies proposed to identify competitive alternatives to the saloon that might be promoted as more wholesome activities than drinking. The studies began with the assumption that the insidious influence of the saloon was related less to the addicting nature of alcohol than to its role as the "poor man's club." Calkins's method consisted of surveying the city to count the numbers of drinking and nondrinking social establishments and estimate the number of persons frequenting these establishments. The daily patronage of licensed saloons was estimated by the foot patrolmen most familiar with the saloons in their districts, whereas the clientele of substitute establishments (pool rooms, coffee rooms, lunch rooms, reading rooms, and private clubs) was determined by Calkins's own participant observations. To these data Calkins added statistics on drunkenness arrests and population density, compiled separately for each of the sixteen Boston police districts. The findings indicated first that in a city counting 156,530 adult male residents, 606 licensed saloons served an estimated 226,752 patrons a day. The enormous disparity between the adult male population and the number of saloon patrons is perhaps explained by the heavy representation of visiting and working suburbanites and the likelihood that many persons were counted more than once. Nevertheless, a conservative bias may compensate for these inflationary tendencies since the many unlicensed establishments of the city were not included in the survey. By contrast, lunch rooms accommodated 47,565 patrons, pool rooms 22,650, and the rest less than sixteen thousand a day. Because the saloon exerted an overwhelming influence on the social lives of its patrons, Calkins concluded that religious and secular organizations should make a concerted effort to provide substitutes and that this activity should be complemented by stricter enforcement of the liquor laws and a reduction in the density of drinking establishments. Cole and Durland (1901) are more specific in their recommendations, suggesting that gymnasiums and public baths would be useful substitutes for the saloon in Boston.

SOCIAL SCIENCE, TEMPERANCE REFORM, AND PUBLIC HEALTH

The social origins of intemperance and the social consequences of drunkenness received new and more powerful articulation as early as 1880 as the language of social science was used to identify and analyze alcohol-related crime, poverty, and mental illness. At the turn of the century industrial expansion, urban growth, and foreign immigration created the context in which the concerns of medicine, public health, and social science converged. George Rosen (1976) has argued that the social sciences in considerable degree have their origins in the health field. Although medical and public-health professionals emphasized prudent prevention of many contagious diseases through bacteriological diagnosis and immunization, the reservoir of more recalcitrant illness appeared to be rooted in behavioral and environmental determinants. In the early twentieth century social scientists saw the potential for public support in exposing the evils of poverty, child labor, and tenement life through the development of social surveys and the application of statistical methods to the identification and analysis of social data, the equivalents of microorganisms. Social researchers were in a position to bring the skills of their trade to such vexing problems as prostitution and drunkenness, societal and personal problems that had obvious health consequences.

Temperance advocates found allies among the social scientists being wooed by university presidents to establish research and graduate programs, and social scientists saw new and complementary professional opportunities in guiding public policy and institutions. The temperance movement gave social researchers a field for study that had heretofore been dominated by physicians. The overriding conviction that emerged from public debate over prohibition was the necessity of preventing or at least reducing the social disease and disorder associated with excessive drinking. Social researchers used this situation to chart an independent course, borrowing ideology with a certain eclectic innocence from public-health officials (Rosenkrantz 1972), social-gospel reformers (May 1949), and university professors like Francis G. Peabody.

Peabody taught social ethics at Harvard. As a member of the Committee of Fifty he inspired James Ford, Raymond Calkins, and other young investigators of the liquor problem as they searched for "the principles of ethics through the observation and analysis of moral facts" (Potts 1965). The social survey generated the facts that were needed to make informed decisions and enlightened social policy. Methodological self-consciousness distinguished these studies, in part reflecting the self-esteem that grew with newly acquired professional status. Recognition by university faculties and eager legislators meant a lot to social investigators who had no well-established discipline to back them up.

Within this context the social survey provided a useful means of generating facts that were needed for enlightened social policy, though the naiveté of underlying assumptions about the cause and character of pathology is painfully obvious. It seems that old facts can easily be the host to new data, which assimilate dissonant information rather than replacing or correcting established wisdom. Thomann's study (1884) is instructive because it accepts the nineteenth-century nosology in which "insanity caused by intemperance" accounted for asylum admissions when drunkenness was itself considered a disease as well as when use of alcohol was designated as the cause of disease. Legal, psychiatric, and social distinctions among these categories had altered the demographic and diagnostic characteristics of asylum inmates in the several decades before Thomann's study. Despite Thomann's manifest concern for precision and objectivity, he was not particularly concerned about this ambiguity, though he included a warning from the superintendent of the Taunton Asylum that the statistics included "cases of alcoholism properly so-called, and also those whose mental disturbance of whatever type was supposed to have resulted from the excessive use of alcoholic liquors" (Brown 1883, 114). Thomann's data represent a social reality that we find patently misconstructed, for he could reconcile what now appear to us as naive observations about the causal relations of social disorder and personal behavior. Rarely criticized or qualified, the statistics were accepted at face value by policy-makers.

Despite methodological limitations and inferential biases, these studies of the social epidemiology of alcohol problems indicate that there was a basis for the general perception that drinking problems in Massachusetts required a social response. This does not mean that the data supported the prohibitionists' exaggerated claims, but there was relative agreement among the estimates provided by three conservative (wet) investigators, Thomann, Wadlin, and Koren, that drunkenness was prevalent. These studies also showed a rather robust association between alcohol problems and the social characteristics of the drinker.

The profile of the prototypical problem drinker that emerges from almost all of these studies is one of a middle-aged, single, unskilled, beer-drinking, foreign-born male who comes into frequent contact with the agents of social control and social welfare. The extent to which this profile depicts a persecuted social drinker or a diseased and dependent alcoholic is a question that goes to the core of temperance history. Was the alcohol problem in Massachusetts a social construction of the temperance reformers and social scientists, or would it have existed without them?

To answer this question, it would be valuable to determine whether there was evidence for systematic discrimination against the foreign-born in the legal processing and treatment of inebriates. It is evident from the studies reviewed that arrest and sentencing procedures varied tremendously over time across jurisdictional boundaries. For this reason most authors considered the drunkenness statistics to be an inaccurate indicator of the effectiveness of ABC laws. Some authors contended that only the most blatant cases of public intoxication and disorderly conduct were subject to arrest (Woods et al. 1910), whereas others suggested that personal gain may have been involved in bringing cases to trial (Parmelee 1909). None of the authors who evaluated the penal system between 1907 and 1916 identified systematic discrimination against particular ethnic groups.

If such discrimination was institutionalized within the criminal justice system, one might expect to find the biases reflected in fines and sentencing procedures. Data relevant to this issue were fortunately collected in 1895 by the Bureau of Labor Statistics. Drunkenness was punished more often by fines than by imprisonment, whereas the reverse was true of other types of crime. A combination of fines and imprisonment was used more frequently when the crime was committed under the influence of alcohol. Foreign-born inebriates were no more likely to be imprisoned than natives (45.1 percent vs. 47.8 percent), nor were they forced to pay greater fines ($6.03 vs. $6.07). When imprisoned for drunkenness, the foreign-born served no longer than the native-born. When convicted of being drunk while committing another crime (usually assault), the foreign-born were less likely to be imprisoned, and their fines and sentences were lower as well. The pattern is mixed regarding other crimes: the foreign-born were less likely to be imprisoned; if imprisoned they received shorter sentences, but if fined they were required to pay more dearly. These aggregate statistics, therefore, do not give evidence of an institutionalized pattern of discrimination against the foreign-born, at least at the level of sentencing.

Nonetheless, to better test the relationships between ethnicity and drinking behavior and explain the apparently disproportionate contribution of Irish Bostonians to the alcohol problem in Massachusetts, it would be desirable to have evidence of the distribution of alcohol problems according to indicators other than those used in the studies reviewed here. One such measure is the death rate from alcohol-related diseases (alcoholism and liver disease) made available in the 1890 federal census. Data concerning cause of death are notoriously inaccurate, and diagnosis is certainly subject to implicit social assumptions, but the data reported show that the Irish led all other ethnic groups in Boston in alcohol-related deaths, followed by the English and the Germans. Italians and Russians were found to have extremely low rates (Room 1968).

That the lower socioeconomic strata in general, and the Irish in particular, were disproportionately represented in alcohol problem statistics is not surprising in view of what is known about nineteenth-century demographic trends and the social ecology of the urban metropolis from 1880 to 1916. During this period Boston experienced explosive population growth primarily owing to the in-migration of young males from Ireland, Southern Europe, and Eastern Europe (Thernstrom 1973). In the late nineteenth century these highly transient blue-collar workers made up one-third of the population and one-half of the male labor force. The Irish of Boston had twice the proportion of unskilled manual laborers as other nationalities. The population of urban immigrants was heavily concentrated in industrial and commercial areas served by cheap tenement housing and numerous saloons. Calkins's (1896) survey of Boston saloons showed that saloon density was associated with the number of daily drinkers and drunkenness arrest rates. His observations may seem intuitively obvious, but they confirm that the public inebriate problem was indeed closely related to the density of urban saloons, whose clientele were disproportionately Irish.

The policy implications drawn from these studies seem to rely as much on the ideological position of the researcher as on the persuasiveness of the data. Koren's (Wines and Koren 1898; Koren 1910) failure to recognize the value of Wadlin's (1896) data concerning the effects of local-option laws on drunkenness arrests suggests a selective bias consistent with his affiliation with the Brewers' Association. In several studies racial and hereditary theory was invoked to interpret problem statistics and data obtained from public inebriates (Parmelee 1909; Woods et al. 1910; Murray et al. 1914). Although there is some suggestion that the state farm colony may have been employed to sequester "moral degenerates" to prevent their propagation (Woods et al. 1910; Murray et al. 1914), the treatment of alcoholic mental patients in Massachusetts took different forms from the openly eugenic policies enacted in California (Fox 1978).

By the last quarter of the nineteenth century, Massachusetts voters and politicians had rejected statewide prohibition as a workable solution to the alcohol problem. Nevertheless, the management of alcohol and drunkenness continued to dominate the political agenda in the commonwealth into the twentieth century, and concern grew in other states as well. In southern and midwestern states prohibition was a more popular solution than in the urban northeast. The experience of Massachusetts was special because there was significant agreement that the Irish were the major source of trouble. Even though protagonists were less unanimous about the remedy, the policy studies considered in this review suggest that one solution was to modify ABC statutes. Another was to shift responsibility to the medical and social welfare agencies, which were at first only too eager to succeed where the penal system had failed. Local option appears to have satisfied neither the drys nor the wets, but it may have been a useful political compromise that removed from the state the onus of taking sides for or against prohibition. Throughout this period social science research was increasingly cited in the public debate to support both wet and dry positions (Howie 1933).

In conclusion, it has been observed that policymakers use scientific data as a drunk uses a lamppost—more for support than for illumination. This metaphor is perhaps appropriate for summarizing the policy implications of social research conducted on alcohol during this period.

Partial support for this research was provided by a grant from the National Institute on Alcohol Abuse and Alcoholism (no. 1K01AA00025). The authors would like to thank Margaret Hausman and Amy Wolfson for their assistance. Barbara G. Rosenkrantz was a fellow at the Stanford University Center for Advanced Study in the Behavioral Sciences when this paper was completed and gratefully acknowledges support of the Center by the National Endowment for the Humanities and the Andrew Mellon Foundation.

REFERENCES

American Statistical Association. "Massachusetts Probation System: Its Administration and Operation." *Quarterly Publications of the American Statistical Association* 10 (March 1907): 236–252.

Anderson, Victor V. "The Alcoholic as Seen in Court." *Boston Medical and Surgical Journal* 74 (1916): 492–495.

Bowditch, Henry P., and George F. Hodge. "Report on the Present Instruction on the Physiological Action of Alcohol." In *Physiological Aspects of the Liquor Problem*, edited by W. C. Atwater, John S. Billings, Henry P. Bowditch, R. H. Chittenden, and William H. Welch, 1:1–136. Boston: Houghton Mifflin, 1901.

Brown, W. Letter to G. Thomann, November 20, 1883. In *Real and Imaginary Effects of Intemperance*, by Gallus Thomann, appendix A, "Correspondence Relative to Insanity Caused by Intemperance," 116. New York: U.S Brewers' Association, 1884.

Bureau of Statistics of Labor, *Report for 1877.* Part 5; *Pauperism and Crime.* Boston: Bureau of Statistics of Labor, 1877.

———. *Report for 1880.* Part 3, *Statistics of Crime, 1860–1879.* Boston: Bureau of Statistics of Labor, 1880.

———. *Report for 1881.* Part 2, *Statistics of Drunkenness and Liquor Selling, 1870–1879.* Boston: Bureau of Statistics of Labor, 1881.

Calkins, Raymond. *Substitutes for the Saloon.* Boston: Houghton Mifflin, 1901.

———. "Summary of a Report on Substitutes for the Saloons in the City of Boston." *The Forum,* July 1896.

Cherrington, Ernest H., ed. "Massachusetts." In *Standard Encyclopedia of the Alcohol Problem.* Vol. 4. Waterville, Ohio: American Issue Press, 1928.

Cole, William I., and Kellogg Durland. "Substitutes for the Saloon in Boston." In Raymond Calkins, *Substitutes for the Saloon,* 321–337. Boston: Houghton Mifflin, 1901.

Fox, Richard. *So Far Disordered in Mind: Insanity in California, 1870–1930.* Berkeley and Los Angeles: University of California Press, 1978.

Gordon, Ernest G. "Two Footnotes to the History of the Anti-Alcohol Movement." *Studies and Documents of the Anti-Alcohol Movement,* no. 2. Boston, 1916.

Howie, Wendell D. "Three Hundred Years of the Liquor Problem in Massachusetts." *Massachusetts Law Quarterly* 18, no 4 (1933): 75–285.

Koren, John. *Economic Aspects of the Liquor Problem.* Boston: Houghton Mifflin, 1899.

———. "Local Option in Massachusetts." In *The Year Book of the United States Brewers' Association,* 96–123. New York: U.S. Brewers' Association, 1910.

May, H. *Protestant Churches and Industrial America.* New York: Harper, 1949.

Murray, M. J., Irwin H. Neff, W. Rodman Peabody, E. E. Southard, and E. O. Childs. *Report of the Commission to Investigate Drunkenness in Massachusetts.* House no. 2053. Boston: Wright & Potter, 1914.

Parmelee, Maurice. "Inebriety in Boston." Ph.D. diss. Columbia University, 1909.

Potts, David B. Social Ethics at Harvard, 1881–1931: A Study in Academic Activism, In *Social Sciences at Harvard, 1860–1920*, edited by P. Buck, 91–128. Cambridge, Mass.: Harvard University Press, 1965.

Room, Robin. "Cultural Contingencies of Alcoholism: Variations between and within Nineteenth-Century Urban Ethnic Groups in Alcohol-Related Death Rates." *Journal of Health and Social Behavior* 9, no. 2 (1968): 99–113.

Rosen, George. "Social Science and Health in the United States in the Twentieth Century." *Clio Medica* 11, no 4 (1976): 289–305.

Rosenkrantz, Barbara G. *Public Health and the State: Changing Views in Massachusetts, 1842–1936.* Cambridge, Mass.: Harvard University Press, 1972.

Thernstrom, Stephan. *The Other Bostonians.* Cambridge, Mass.: Harvard University Press, 1973.

Thomann, Gallus. *Real and Imaginary Effects of Intemperance: A Statistical Sketch.* New York: U.S. Brewers' Association, 1884.

Thomas, J. L. "Romantic Reform in America, 1815–1865." *American Quarterly* 17 (1965): 656–681.

Tyrrell, Ian R. *Sobering up: From Temperance to Prohibition in Antebellum America, 1800–1860.* Westport, Conn.: Greenwood Press, 1979.

Wadlin, Horace G. *Relation of the Liquor Traffic to Pauperism, Crime, and Insanity.* From the 26th annual report of the Massachusetts Bureau of Statistics of Labor. Boston: Wright & Potter, 1896.

Wines, Fredrick H., and John Koren. *The Liquor Problem in Its Legislative Aspects.* Boston: Houghton Mifflin, 1898.

Woods, Robert A., Edwin Mulready, Philip R. Allen, Frank L. Locke, Timothy J. Foley, and W. Rodman Peabody. *Drunkenness in Massachusetts: Conditions and Remedies.* Special report of the Board of Trustees of the Foxborough State Hospital. Boston: Wright & Potter, 1910.

THIRTEEN

Inebriate Reformatories in Scotland: An Institutional History

Patrick M. McLaughlin

On 26 August 1901 Peter Black, a fisherman from Kirkwall in the Orkney Islands, was admitted to the State Inebriate Reformatory at Perth, Scotland. He was to be among the first people—and one of only a few men—to be subjected to an experimental regime for the management of habitual drunkenness. This chapter provides an account of the experiment, a case study of the operation of inebriate reformatories in Scotland.[1] The characteristics of these institutions, the regime of "reform" pursued within their walls, the effectiveness of this regime, and public policies relating to the reformatories are all discussed, as are the characteristics of those who, like Peter Black, were the focus of this regime. The aim of the study is not merely to reconstruct something of the reality of life in these institutions but also to locate and explain the institutions in terms of the wider social and political context.

Drunkenness was a fact of life in nineteenth-century Britain: for many Victorians, mass intemperance was the common denominator that linked many of the social problems that blighted their brave new industrial world. The specific development of so-called Inebriates Acts as an attempt to curb the worst excesses of the urban poor was influenced by the interplay of three more-or-less parallel developments— temperance, the rise of the medical profession, and the emergence of an institutional ideology.

The temperance movement is the best-known, and certainly the most enduring, expression of concern about the problems of mass intemperance. Begun in Scotland as a response to a perceived decline in moral standards, particularly in the urban industrial heartland of the Central Lowlands,[2] the temperance movement spread quickly south of the Border, and throughout the nineteenth century it campaigned vigorously to keep the drink question before the public and, more important perhaps, before the legislators in Parliament. In the latter half of the nineteenth century the movement enjoyed some considerable success as a parliamentary lobby. The fact that parliamentary committees reported on "the prevailing vice of intoxication" on at least three separate occasions and that various pieces of legislation were introduced to control, or more often merely to regulate, the use and abuse of alcohol[3] was due in part to the activities of temperance groups such as the United Kingdom Alliance.

Medical interest in alcohol problems in Britain is usually traced from the publication in 1804 of Thomas Trotter's *Essay, Medical, Philosophical, and Chemical, on Drunkenness.*[4] However, this seminal work had only a limited impact on a medical profession that had yet to consolidate its position in society, and in fact medical opinion did not contribute significantly to the drink question until the last half of the nineteenth century. Even then, it is unlikely that the medical profession would have involved itself with the alcohol problems were it not for the example of a small group of doctors who vociferously promoted their views through, for example, the *British Journal of Inebriety.*[5]

However, the medical profession did become active in the struggle to win recognition for alcohol problems and to involve the state in the provision of facilities for the "care and treatment of habitual drunkards."[6] The most tangible outcome of this developing relationship between medicine and the state was the introduction, between 1879 and 1900, of a series of acts—the so-called Inebriates Acts—that allowed for the establishment of "retreats" and "reformatories" for the treatment of alcoholism. As the inspector for Scotland explained:

> The intention of the [1898] Act is not explicitly stated, but presumably it is (1) to protect the community against inebriate offenders; (2) to provide facilities for their reformation. The implication from the terms of the Act, is that both these objects are better attained by relatively prolonged detention than by repeated committal, which has been proved useless by long experience.[7]

The demand for new and more effective response to the habitual drunkard came from doctors, temperance activists, and reformers generally; the translation of that demand into legislative action was influenced, if not determined, by the ascendancy of an institutional ideology that had emerged during the late eighteenth century. The history of this institutional ideology in Britain and Europe has been discussed in relation to prisons and asylums,[8] but many of its features can be identified in the more mundane institutional structures of the nineteenth century such as the inebriate reformatories. The rationale that lay behind the development of confinement for the criminal and the insane could be readily applied to the habitual drunkard.

With the consolidation of an industrial capitalism founded on factory production, industrial discipline, and the virtues of sobriety, modesty and industriousness were held to be at a premium. New disciplines emerged from and spread across factories, armies, schools, and prisons. These disciplines, according to Foucault, created the minute, hierarchical distribution of persons in time and space; the exact control of segmented activities; the combination and articulation of individual energies; and the seriation of time. Such discipline made the periodic instruction and regulation of the mind and body more possible.[9]

For those who would not or could not adapt to industrial discipline, who sought to escape whether into drunkenness or into crime, the institutional option provided new specialized factories of reform and discipline—prisons, asylums, workhouses, and reformatories of various descriptions. By the last quarter of the nineteenth century the machinery of a modern criminal justice system was already finely tuned to the surveillance and regulation of all manner of deviant behavior. The groundwork had been done; all that was now required was the legislation that would allow some "rational system for responding to the problem of habitual drunkenness" to operate within this institutional framework.

The Departmental Committee of 1872 had taken the first steps when it recommended some element of coercion to reinforce the "reformative power" of voluntary admission to retreats, a recommendation that was not acted on until the introduction of the Inebriates Act of 1898. However, if the intention of the 1898 act was to institute a coercive system of confinement, it was confinement with a difference—confinement that, initially at any rate, seemed to draw more from the North American farm school than from the conventions of the prison system.

THE INSTITUTIONAL ENVIRONMENT

[The Secretary for Scotland]...earnestly hopes...that a fair and reasonable experiment of the Act may prove, not only that a large percentage of these unfortunate inebriates are capable under careful and humane supervision of reformation and restoration to useful lives, but that ultimately both the Imperial and the local Exchequer and local funds will in this way be relieved by a sensible decrease in the population now located in our prisons and poorhouses.[10]

The first (and perhaps the only) "fair and reasonable experiment" was undertaken by the city of Glasgow. Glasgow was in many ways the obvious candidate for participation in the experiment: forged in the furnace of the industrial revolution, the city possessed in full measure all of the social problems that were attendant on the rapid growth of an urban industrial environment. Drunkenness was commonplace. An observer of the city in 1889 was of the opinion that "Glasgow was probably the most drink-sodden city in Great Britain. The Trongate, Argyle Street, and, worst of all, the High Street, were scenes of debauchery.... There were drunken brawls at every street corner and a high proportion of the passers-by were reeling drunk."[11] The city fathers, it seems, did not dissent from this view. The town clerk, reporting on the main provisions of the 1898 act, noted that in the twelve months since January 1899 eighty-seven persons (twelve men and seventy-five women) had been convicted on at least three occasions of being drunk and incapable, a fact that would have made them eligible for admission to an inebriate reformatory had such an institution been in existence at the time. The corporation therefore decided to form a subcommittee "to enquire and report as to any available buildings which might be suitable for an Inebriate Reformatory of moderate size."[12] As a result Girgenti Home was licensed as a certified inebriate reformatory for the reception of fifty-eight women (an earlier license had been for both men and women), and the reformatory opened in January 1901.

Girgenti Home was in reality a farm, situated in the Ayrshire countryside some twenty miles southwest of Glasgow and four miles from the nearest town. The inmates were housed in two buildings. The majority were accommodated in the home proper, but six places were provided in a separate building some distance from the principal part of the reformatory with the intention of providing selected inmates with an environment "more resembling home life"—a kind of limited parole.

The next reformatory to be licensed was established some twenty-five miles down river from Glasgow, at Greenock on the Firth of Clyde. In common with its larger neighbor, Greenock had long had a reputation for drunkenness, particularly among its shipbuilders, fishermen, and distillery workers. By contrast, the town could also claim a considerable reputation in the area of temperance innovation. The earliest recorded temperance society was founded in Greenock in 1818, and John Dunlop, the father of the British temperance movement, was a well-known and respected citizen of the town.

The Greenock Reformatory was also situated in the countryside, at a sufficient distance to discourage inmates from casual encounters with their former associates or life-styles. Licensed in 1903 to receive thirty women, the buildings at Greenock were already well equipped for their purpose, having operated as a refuge for "fallen women" since 1853. Although it received financial support from both the Greenock and, on occasion, Dundee town councils, the Greenock Reformatory was run as a charitable society.

These two certified inebriate reformatories formed the major provision in Scotland under the Inebriates Act. Girgenti was the largest and most innovative of the reformatories, and Greenock, though never as large as the Glasgow home, was the longest-lived of the reformatories, being in continuous operation from 1903 to 1921. There were other reformatories, certainly, all located in much the same environment and run along similar lines: the Lanarkshire Home at East Kilbride, eight miles south of Glasgow, operated from 1904 to 1910; the Scottish Labour Colony Association provided facilities in the border countryside at Dumfries; the latest, and smallest, reformatory in Scotland began work at Seafield, Aberdeen, in 1906 with accommodations for just eight women. Among them these three institutions could accommodate twenty-eight persons, including all the places for men, but they were never fully utilized, and their overall contribution was minimal.

The decision to locate the inebriate reformatories in more-or-less rural surroundings was not in response to any articulated policy directive, but neither was it a coincidence. The preference for country locations was a reflection of a strongly held belief in an association between deviance and the contaminating influences of urban living, particularly for those who were thought to be socially or morally inadequate. Men (and presumably women), it was felt, could be driven to drunkenness by the very proximity of temptation in the town or city. Thus, Ramsay MacDonald referred to "the fearful and devilish temptation of the public house, with its flaring lights, its genial welcome, its boon companionship, and its abominable drug that makes the present unreal and throws an evil glamour over the minds of men."[13] In a similar vein the reports of the inebriate reformatories made frequent reference to the contaminating influence of the urban environment:

> They chafe under restraint...and long to return to the old life they misname "freedom." They are the means of leading away others who are morally weak, who know right from wrong, but have not the will power to do right. Started in life as 'inefficients,' or having drifted to an environment where drink and immorality are inseparable, they turn to drink as an aid to their vicious life, and as a solace for all their ills.[14]

The physical separation of inmates from these "occasions of sin" and the beneficial effects of outdoor labor and recreation were widely considered to be prerequisites for the reformation of habitual drunkards. But, of course, theories about the contaminating effects of urban life were not new, and in fact they had been used widely in North America to justify the rural location of both inebriate homes and more general institutions of correction. In Britain the reformatory movement was certainly aware of, and no doubt influenced by, these developments in North America. There was an abiding interest in what was happening across the Atlantic. The Select Committee of 1872 not only heard evidence from two representatives of inebriates institutions in Philadelphia and New York State but also sent one of its members on a fact-finding tour of the United States and Canada.[15]

In addition to the five certified inebriate reformatories already mentioned, there was the State Inebriate Reformatory at Perth. This institution differed in many respects from the certified reformatories. It was established to deal with two types of inmate: those convicted, under section 23 of the 1898 act, of an indictable offense, and those transferred, under section 6 of the act, to state custody on account of their disruptive behavior in a certified reformatory. Perth was also unlike the other inebriate reformatories in terms of its environment. The State Inebriate Reformatory was located not on a farm but within the walls of Perth prison.

The state reformatory consisted of two divisions—one for male inmates and one for female inmates. The women's reformatory was housed in the disused "female lunatics block," which provided, in the opinion of the superintendent, "an ideal residence for female inebriates." Another part of the prison was converted for use by male inmates.[16] Both divisions had their own entrances and were intended to be separate from the prison proper. In reality, however, the separation of reformatory life from prison life was less clear-cut since prison staff seem to have played an important part in the day-to-day routine of the institution, escorting the inmates on "outings," supervising them at work, and so on. In the final years of the reformatory this separation became even more blurred, as a prison officer (a store warden at Perth) appears to have had effective control of the running of the reformatory. Throughout the period the state reformatory was operated subject to the rules and regulations of the Prisons (Scotland) Act of 1877 as if it were a prison.

REFORMATORY LIFE AND REGIMES OF REFORM

The operation of the inebriate reformatories raises many questions. What was daily life like for the reformatory inmates? What were the strategies adopted by these institutions in an effort to care for and control—and reform—habitual drunkards? How did the various institutions adapt admission policies and management procedures in attempting to meet their objectives? What sorts of people were admitted to the reformatories? How did they adapt to, and come to terms with, the regime? And, perhaps most important, how successful was the regime in reforming those persons committed to its care?

It is a fairly easy task to explain the routine of the institution: the secretary for Scotland issued regulations for the management and discipline of reformatories in Scotland,[17] and the annual reports of the reformatories give a clear picture of how these guidelines were interpreted. The annual reports in particular are replete with details about the inmates' daily routine, diet, work, and recreation. From these reports it seems that all the reformatories, including the state reformatory, employed similar uniform, almost regimented, standards of institutional life. A typical day in the life of, say, Peter Black would begin at about 6 A.M. with prayers and continue thus:

7 A.M.   Breakfast
7:45 A.M.   Work
12 P.M.   Dinner
1 P.M.   Work
5:30 P.M.   Tea
6:30 P.M.   Recreation and "private work"
8:45 P.M.   Prayer
9 P.M.   Bed
9:30 P.M.   Lights out

The strategy of reform favored by the reformatories can be summed up in one phrase: it was a regime of prayers and piecework. Even the fairly short period of recreation allowed to the inmates was given over to the demands of the factory or the pulpit. Recreation periods were generally times of self-improvement: learning the skills of literacy and numeracy, in which many of the inmates were sadly deficient and which were increasingly important in the industrial world outside the reformatory. Such free time as remained was taken up by visits from the ladies committee, lectures (usually on biblical themes), concerts, and "amusements, such as draughts, dominoes, ping pong, etc."

The Reformatories had little to recommend them to the modern advocate of the therapeutic community. There was no counseling beyond the constant religious exhortations that served mainly to impress on the wrongdoer her guilt in the eyes of both society and deity:

Treatment is essentially the same as that for mental disorders, because inebriety is closely allied to insanity in causation, etc. "A healthy mind in a healthy body" is the whole aim of the treatment. To gain this we must have (a) total abstinence (b) the removal of predisposing and exciting causes (c) the restoration of the general tone of body and mind (d) full employment of body and mind. I believe in keeping the inmates in constant employment, and...as much as possible in the open air.[18]

It is an interesting aside to the treatment regime in the reformatories that despite the involvement of the medical profession, there was very little reliance on drugs as a cure for habitual drunkenness. Curiously, whereas they were willing to borrow from the experience of others with regard to management techniques, the Scottish reformatories stayed well clear of contemporary fads of so-called cures for alcoholism. Although medical opinion within the reformatories held that inebriety should not be considered a crime, or even a social evil per se, "but rather a distinct disease with well-known symptoms requiring treatment, like other diseases of the nervous system,"[19] there was a general reluctance to endorse any of the available drug treatments. The inmates, had they known anything of the plethora of cures, might well have been thankful for their doctors' want of initiative in this area. Such cures ranged from simple nerve tonics and the American gold cure of Dr. L. E. Keeley to bizarre concoctions of webs of black spiders (in one-gram pills, of course).[20] Dr. Cunningham, the medical officer at the Girgenti Home, did run one drug trial. On the recommendation of a medical friend he dosed twenty-two patients with a mixture of quinine, ammonium, and aloin plus one tablet of atrophine sulphide daily. The "willing patients" suffered sickness, vomiting, general stomach upsets, and attacks of diarrhea (aloin is a bitter and fairly strong purgative) during the month-long experiment, but their general health and mental well-being was said to have greatly improved. Two years after this experiment, however, all but three of the "patients" had relapsed.

It was back to the Bible and reliance on the therapeutic and reformative value of hard work. The work regime itself was, predictably, focused on those domestic tasks that were necessary for the upkeep of the institution and that supposedly prepared the inmate to return as a useful member to society. Gardening, sewing, knitting, cooking, cleaning, making doormats, and doing laundry—especially doing laundry— were jobs the women were set to do, jobs that would equip them for a role, as wife and mother, many had already rejected in the most dramatic fashion. The annual reports had a penchant for obscuring the true marital status of many of the inmates, recording that the majority of the women (and therefore the majority of inmates) were married. Even the most cursory glance at the available inmate files gives the lie to this official view, making it plain that many of these women had abandoned their families—or had been rejected by them—even before they entered the reformatory.

The male inmates were employed in many of the traditional tasks associated with prison labor—mending nets, sewing mailbags, and doing joinery work and the heavier labor associated with the general maintenance of the institution. There is also some indication that at least a few men had been involved in public works, reclaiming bog land and roadways. It is not clear, in the case of the state reformatory, whether work on the roads was carried out in association with convict labor. However, it is unlikely to have been a long-term venture, given that in Scotland the use of congregate labor on public works was not generally approved of because it was felt to be detrimental to public morale and industriousness. Russell Dobash has noted that "the Scots rejected the 'signifying spectacle' of convicts labouring for the public good, at least within their own country. They did, however, send thousands of convicted Scottish males to England to serve sentences of penal servitude in the hulks and 'convict prisons' such as Dartmoor."[21] Much as they may have favored the idea, however, the managers of the inebriate reformatories in Scotland were not in any position to dispose of their charges to the warehouses of the English system. Nevertheless, they were as determined as the prison authorities that their institutions should pay their way, and to this end they involved the reformatories in socially necessary and useful labor.[22]

Now, to get back to those laundries. Excepting Girgenti, which dabbled in just about everything, and the state reformatory at Perth, which operated under somewhat tighter security, two of the three remaining reformatories were in business as full-blown commercial laundries. The Greenock Reformatory had been operating as a laundry before it was licensed, as had the Seafield Home in Aberdeen on a smaller scale, and one of the first actions of the managers after the institutions were licensed was to increase the scale of production by introducing new machinery. The importance of this commercial venture is obvious from an examination of the financial returns of the various reformatories. Whereas the others, including the state reformatory, were operated at a considerable loss (and were therefore heavily dependent on government funds), Greenock and Aberdeen showed a tidy profit thanks to their commercial interests. Where the Girgenti Home could only earn a few pounds from the proceeds of inmate labor, Greenock could show a yearly profit from their laundry of nearly £200. The importance of the business is also reflected in the costs of maintaining reformatory inmates. It cost about £40 a year to keep an inmate in the state reformatory (approximately £10 more than the average cost of imprisonment), £80 at East Kilbride, and £53.40 at Girgenti but only £44.20 at Seafield and Aberdeen and £33.33 at Greenock. The government inspector commented frequently, and favorably, about the Aberdeen and Greenock laundries. In 1914, a year after it had extended its laundry operations, the inspector had this to say of the Greenock Reformatory: "A great improvement in the premises of the institution has taken place since my last report. It consists of the building of a large, airy, and modern laundry. As the majority of the inmates are employed at laundry work, this addition will be beneficial, not only from an industrial point of view, but also from a sanitary point of view."[23]

The inspector might have gone further with his benediction, adding that the laundry, and indeed work in general, was also beneficial from the management point of view. Institutional labor was used not only to impress inmates with the habits of industrial discipline, prepare them for a useful life upon release,[24] reform them, and make a profit; it was also an important means of social control: "So long as the inmates are kept fully employed they give little trouble, but when idle their management becomes difficult."[25] Yet even when there were "difficulties," labor, or rather the deprivation of work for a period of time, continued to be a powerful weapon in the reformatories' armory of control. The regulations forbade corporal punishment and limited the more severe forms of prison punishment, but the managers made full use of the punishments left to them: deprivation of work, reduction of diet, and isolation were the favored techniques. On occasions those in charge of the reformatories sailed a good deal closer to the punitive wind: "She became very foul mouthed, abusive and disruptive of her clothing and had to be put in a canvass jacket, and put on bread and water for a time (two days)"; "On admission she charged that the superintendent at Greenock struck her on the face till she was black and blue and knocked out a tooth. The medical officer reported no signs of bruising but a tooth had been broken, though he could not say how."[26]

At another level the work, specifically the work in the laundry, accorded closely with the general concern with health and social cleanliness. The reformatories practiced few of the admission rituals associated with entry into prison. Nevertheless, on admission inmates were subjected to a medical examination, bathed, and dressed, as often as not in clothes supplied by the reformatory. This purification was carried out for the explicit purpose of protecting the inmates, but to a lesser or greater extent it also served to humiliate them, to undermine their identity as individuals.[27] In the same way the daily routine of cleaning both the institution and oneself was more than hygienic: it was a tangible expression of the power of the state, acting through its agents, to supervise even the minutiae of institutional life. Within this generalized concern with sanitation and hygiene the concept of laundry work might have seemed particularly reformative. Cleanliness was associated with inner order; dirtiness was indicative of indolence and indiscipline. If through their work in the laundry the inmates should come to learn the value of cleanliness, it was believed they would also be impressed by the need for method and order in their lives.

THE INMATES' TALE

The reformatories may be fairly categorized as places where a reformative regime of hard work and religious exhortation was applied to a group of people who were certainly not renowned for their ability to articulate grievances. From an investigation of the characteristics of those admitted to the reformatories it is clear that they constituted a fair cross-section of the most socially, politically, and economically vulnerable groups in the society. It might seem reasonable to expect that "devoid of will, resistance, requirements, and needs," such inmates would conform to the demands of the institution. After all, they were reasonably well cared for, well fed, and decently housed. The conditions under which they existed may have been somewhat Spartan, but they were better than most were used to and far better than life under any prison regime of the day. That was the official view at least. But it was a view that ignored the reality of the inmates as people, as individuals whose lives were necessarily located within the context of their own culture and community. Arrested by the police, processed by the courts, and in most cases imprisoned at some point before finally being interned in an inebriate reformatory, many of the inmates had experienced intense personal crises. We should not be surprised, therefore, that disturbances were commonplace. The official accounts do not provide a great deal of information about levels of inmate resistance beyond citing the broad categories of misdemeanors for which punishments were awarded. However, from this admittedly limited information it is clear that most of the offenses were against the fabric of the institution (breaking up furnishings, tearing clothing, and so on) or against the requirements of order and discipline. Assaults, whether on other inmates or on reformatory staff, were recorded only infrequently. Those who were not being disruptive inside the reformatory appear to have devoted a good deal of their time to breaking out of it. Girgenti Home, for example, recorded more than 120 escape attempts in its nine years of operation, nearly one-quarter of which were successful.[28]

Although for the most part they appear to be rather mundane, even trivial expressions of personal angst, it is clear that these disturbances posed significant problems for the management of the reformatory system. The state reformatory, being the ultimate sanction *within* the system, bore the brunt of these problems. Originally intended for the reception of those who had been convicted of an indictable offense but who, because of their habitual drunkenness, had been sentenced to a term in an inebriate reformatory, the state reformatory received on average only seven inmates a year under section 23.[29] The majority of inmates detained at Perth, therefore, were drawn from among the ranks of the "unmanageables" of the certified reformatories, a situation that pleased the administrators at the state reformatory not at all. The superintendent at Perth recorded his thoughts on the transfer of yet another unruly inmate from the certified reformatories thus: "This is another of the Girgenti 'unmanageables.' I regret that we have been sent this class of inebriate as it prevents, in great measure, the adoption of proper reformatory principles in the Establishment. We cannot classify, and all must be held under almost penal restrictions for the sake of the 'incouragables.' "[30]

This concern about the "class of inebriate" being sent to the reformatory was not peculiar to Perth. All the reformatories to some degree complained about the "clients" that were referred to them by the courts. They all had an ideal group in mind, one that offered the institution (and the internee) the best hope of effecting a reformation. This client group consisted of "persons who, while habitual drunkards, are of such character and disposition that it may be reasonably expected, if cured of their intemperance, they would be able to take their places in society as self-supporting citizens."[31] In the Second Annual Report on Girgenti the medical officer wrote: "In my opinion...unless patients come under the scope of the Act at an early age, the results of treatment cannot be satisfactory when they are admitted physical wrecks, with shattered constitutions and distinct evidence of mental weakness."[32]

The preference for young, reasonably uncorrupted, well-motivated inmates is easily understood, but it is in marked contrast to the actual pattern of admissions that favored older, more chronic offenders. However, since the reformatories were either public institutions or were dependent on public funding, they were in effect required to accept anyone: reformatories admitted chronic offenders not through choice but because they were obliged to do so. The class of offender scheduled in the act limited "its operation to the street pest, drunken prostitute, and thief, and the drunken flotsam and jetsam of our towns."[33]

But if the Inebriates Act set out, or delimited, the class of persons who could be subject to its provisions, it did not specify that these groups had to be dealt with under that act. The act was simply a piece of enabling legislation, and in practice it was used against only a select

group of persons. The most striking feature of this differential enforcement was the way in which the act was used against women, one
might say almost to the exclusion of men. The ratio of male to female
inmates in the certified inebriate reformatories was about 1:32.[34] The
ratio at Perth was nearer 1:3, but after the closure of the male division
in 1915 no more men were accepted into the reformatory network.

This focus on women is interesting not simply for the insight it
provides on the operation of the act, and indirectly on the role of these
women in the society, but also because it goes some way toward explaining the problems encountered by the reformatories in their
attempts to contain these inmates. Carswell (1901) offers a simple
explanation for the disproportionately high level of female inmates—
poverty. The usual method of dealing with drunkenness-related offenses, then as now, was to impose a fine. Those who could pay the fine,
or who were prepared to forfeit their bail,[35] escaped the system comparatively unscathed. Those who could not, well, they would normally
be faced with no more than a short prison sentence. Again Carswell
suggests that sheriffs (judges) favored this option for men because they
were reluctant to separate a breadwinner from his family for a prolonged period of time. "It is a serious matter to take a bread-winner
away from his family. The worker who gets drunk on a Saturday night
and pays his fine of seven shillings and sixpence on Monday morning is
not a suitable man to take away and shut up for three years."[36] Habitually drunken women, by contrast, had frequently severed family ties
and with them, in the eyes of respectable society, their right to be
considered as "real women."

Although these considerations may have influenced the decision of
sheriffs referring people to reformatories, they clearly do not provide a
full explanation of why the reformatories took so many women. Indeed, the dearth of places for the reception of men would suggest that
the women-only policy was not so much an unforeseen consequence of
the operation of the act as a conscious decision on the part of those
responsible for administering the reformatories and perhaps on the
part of the government. Such a response could not be justified by
reference to the excessive drunkenness of women as compared with
men. On the contrary, of the drunkenness-related offenses known to
the police at this time only about one-third were committed by women:
23,712 drunkenness-related offenses were reported in Glasgow in
1906, for example, and of these just 7,049 were committed by women.
What was perhaps more influential than the drunkenness of women
was that Victorian society's preoccupation with (and fear of) women's
sexuality continued to hold sway. The family continued to be seen as
the mechanism par excellence through which sexuality—and hence

women—could be controlled. Women who challenged this view of the
world by their so-called wanton behavior threatened the very fabric of
the society and had therefore to be responded to. The control and
reformation of drunken women was just one aspect of this response.

The procedure necessary to commit someone to an inebriate reformatory against his or her will was both cumbersome and expensive, and
it seems unlikely that the courts would have been willing to evoke such
procedures in dealing with cases of simple drunkenness. Most admissions, therefore, would have to have been voluntary in the sense that
persons involved would have been persuaded to agree to their committal. Even allowing for a relatively lax system of confinement within the
reformatory, is it likely that any but the naive and the desperate would
have agreed to being detained in such places for a period of two to three
years? Some clearly were desperate: an inmate at Greenock made several applications for admission to the state reformatory, declaring that
she "would like to be all her time in prison."[37] The majority, however,
had no such perverse desire. They were in the reformatory because they
had been persuaded (or pressured) into agreeing to their detention,
perhaps because they were led to believe that they would be helped
there rather than simply treated as prisoners.

Women in general, and women of the lower working class in particular, were more vulnerable to the kinds of pressure exerted by the
courts, if for no other reason than that, as Carswell implies, they often
had only limited financial resources. However, beyond these judicial
considerations there was another, more pragmatic reason for the differential emphasis on women. Two of the reformatories had in earlier
lives been houses of refuge for fallen women: coincidentally, these
institutions, at Greenock and Aberdeen, were also the ones that had
most need of female labor (laundry work not being considered suitable
for men). Just in that moment when Victorian attitudes toward prostitution were becoming ambivalent, especially about the need to lock up
prostitutes,[38] these houses of refuge saw in the Inebriates Act an opportunity for bureaucratic survival (and perhaps for the continuation of
the fight against prostitution as part of some hidden agenda). At
Greenock and Aberdeen they seized the chance, and fallen women
made way for their drunken sisters.

The operation of the act clearly caused a great deal of resentment
among inmates and the idea that they were being treated as prisoners
(contrary to some promise or commitment?) was a common expression
of this rancor. Peter Black, for example, complained bitterly of being
treated as a "criminal prisoner" and being "locked-up during the day
when not employed outside."[39] Another reformatory inmate, in a letter
to her mother, conveyed strongly this feeling of having been somehow
cheated by the system:

I am keeping in very good health I am thankful to say but I am very downhearted when I think of all I have to stand from day to day and from year to year and I have to say nothing whether I am right or wrong and for nothing I ought to be outside working and treated with kindness and respect and getting paid for my work, but to work hard from day to day and not even get a kind word I shall never forget this as long as ever I live, if I had done a crime I would have first taken it as a punishment and said nothing but to be ordered about and never anything to look forward to why it is even worse than the very beasts. My one prayer is to have my health and I will put up with the rest for it is an awful place to have anything wrong with you.[40]

As if to demonstrate the completeness of state supervision of her life, even this expression of despair was silenced—the woman's mother never received the letter, which was suppressed by the authorities.

This ability of the state to direct people's lives is perhaps best illustrated by the movement of inmates within the reformatory system and among the reformatories and other institutions. Although this information does not offer any access to inmate consciousness per se, it does give some indication of the conflict that existed between the formal and informal control of even the most routine aspects of a person's life. Nowhere is this conflict more obvious than in the almost arbitrary nature of movements within and among institutions. The revolving door that has proved such an evocative image in the context of contemporary discussions of alcohol-related issues was already spinning freely in the early years of this century, confining the poor and the stigmatized within a complex and expanding network of institutions. The progress of persons within this institutional network can be traced through the sparse entries in the inmate files. The following history of events in the life of one woman inmate presents an extreme, but by no means atypical, illustration. Before being sent to an inebriate reformatory, this woman had been imprisoned on twenty-nine occasions for periods ranging from three to thirty days. She was sentenced to three years in Girgenti Home on 16 July 1901:

10 October 1901	transferred to State Inebriate Reformatory, Perth.
14 April 1902	"The P.C. [Prison Commissioners] have the honour to report that Irene Tait, at present an inmate of the State Inebriate Reformatory at Perth, has become insane."
21 October 1902	Removed to Woodilee Asylum, Glasgow. "Beyond a slight blunting of the finer intellectual and moral faculties," the psychiatrist at Woodilee could find "no sign of insanity."

10 June 1903	Returned to State Inebriate Reformatory.
14 September 1903	Readmitted to Woodilee Asylum, Glasgow.
16 July 1904	Liberated.
18 July 1904	Arrested (drunk and incapable), fined 2/6d (15p) or three days imprisonment.
8 November 1904	Transferred from Duke Street Prison, Glasgow (sentenced to seven days imprisonment for using obscene language) to Woodilee Asylum.
5 December 1904	Discharged from Woodilee Asylum.
28 June 1905	Sentenced to seven days imprisonment (drunk and incapable).
29 June 1905	Transferred from Duke Street Prison to Woodilee Asylum, Glasgow, as "insane and dangerous."
5 July 1905	Discharged from Woodilee Asylum on expiry of prison warrant. "Readmission same day chargeable to Parish."

From the court to the prison, the asylum, the inebriate reformatory, and back to the court—the circus seems to be explicable not so much in terms of any sociomedical diagnosis, or even some crude classification, as in relation to the inmate's failure to come to terms with institutional reality, an explicit or tacit refusal to allow herself to be institutionally managed:

> [She] commenced at 5 this morning [before the prison was open] to smash all furniture...without doubt an insane person. No jury would convict her, in face of her history, if one of her outbursts resulted in a serious or fatal injury....She has proved over and over again that she is unfit to take care of herself but she is regularly dismissed [cured?] from Asylums....Is it not time this farce ended?[41]

THE FAILURE OF THE INEBRIATE REFORMATORY

For the Girgenti Home, the farce ended on 7 March 1907, when Glasgow Corporation approved a recommendation to "discontinue, at the earliest possible date, the use of Girgenti Home as an Inebriate Reformatory." The immediate reason for this recommendation was Parliament's repeated refusal to amend the Inebriates Act so as to make it easier to admit people to a reformatory and, once admitted, easier to transfer "unmanageables" to the state reformatory or to prison. The proposed amendments also sought to shift the burden of caring for those habitual drunkards who were "beyond hope...of benefiting by the care of a Certified Inebriate Reformatory" from the reformatory to the parish council.[42]

Glasgow's resolve to close the Girgenti Home was further strengthened by the decision of the government to reduce the level of grant support from 10*s*. 6*d*. (52p) to 7*s*. (35p) per inmate per week. Faced with a 43 percent cut in its Treasurer grant, the Girgenti Home was forced to concede that the costs incurred in operating the reformatory were out of all proportion to the benefits accruing. Girgenti finally closed in 1909 and was followed within the year by the closure of the Lanarkshire Reformatory at East Kilbride. Greenock and Aberdeen, being to some extent protected from the financial hardship that so affected the others, carried on throughout the years of the First World War, only to go into decline in the confusion of the postwar period. By 1921 all the reformatories, including the rump of the state reformatory, had closed, and the experiment came to an end.

It is tempting to see the demise of the reformatories as the consequence of insuperable practical difficulties: the procedural complexities of committal, the difficulty of attracting a "better class" of inebriate, properly motivated and with a good chance of reformation, the lack of any proper system of aftercare, and of course the shortage of resources all were cited in an attempt to explain the less-than-successful operation of the Inebriates Act. Certainly, the reformatories were under an obligation to justify their considerable expenditure. Girgenti and East Kilbride were particularly vulnerable in this respect since they were totally financed by the public purse and were therefore under pressure to economize by keeping costs to a minimum. Yet if the reformatories were to justify themselves, they could do so only in relation to their stated aims: they had to demonstrate their success in rehabilitating habitual drunkards. In the light of what has already been said about the "chosen client group" and the practical limitations of the system, it should come as no surprise to learn that the reformatories were incapable of demonstrating any degree of success in this area. The failure of the reformatories to live up to their promise was obvious even to their most vociferous supporters. Only a small proportion of those admitted to the certified reformatories were considered to be successes by the reformatories' own criteria. The position in the state reformatory was, predictably, worse:

> It is worthy of note that out of 50 inmates received from Certified Inebriate Reformatories there have been only two cases of reformation, which emphasizes the fact that real reformatory work, which consists largely in an appeal to the higher moral faculties, can have little or no

success with such cases, the majority of whom consider their detention a gross injustice instead of appreciating the great efforts made for their reformation.[43]

But to assess the history of the reformatories merely by reference to their success, or lack of it, in the rehabilitative field is to accept perforce the official view of what these institutions were about, to see the episode as an essentially benign series of events confounded by unfortunate, or unintended, consequences. If we are to understand why the reformatories failed, we must look beyond the walls of the institution and consider the social and political constraints within which the system was supposed to operate. The reformatories, after all, were not altruistic institutions detached from the social structure; they were very much a part of the society and reflected the dominant ideology of that society. To survive at all, the reformatories had to win support, and it was clear, even before the experiment began, that this support would have to be predicated on something more than a (dubious) functional capacity to control drunkenness. To have garnered a wider appeal, the reformatories would have had to insinuate themselves into the larger strategy that was addressing not merely deviance and crime but the wider social crisis of the period as well. In short, the reformatories were of necessity an adjunct to, rather than a radical departure from, the extant policies of the criminal justice system. Whatever the fine phrases about fair and reasonable experiments, this was clearly meant to be the case. Outlining the history of the Inebriates Act, the inspector for England and Wales presented the rationale of the act in the following terms:

> How necessary it was that some curative or restraining power should exist capable of direct application to the drunkards themselves,... something applicable to inebriates more powerful than mere temperance teaching; something stronger and more physical, something that could make them reform, or, failing reform, could ensure their detention and care for the benefit of the community.[44]

The juxtaposition of the concepts of reform, punishment, and containment is a recurring theme in much of the social commentary at this time. The chief constable of Greenock, while praising the reformatory for giving so many women a chance of reformation, "a chance which many have taken advantage of," is clearly (and more realistically) more impressed by the success of the reformatory in clearing "the streets of the Town of many women who are drunken pests."[45]

The inebriate reformatories made a bid (albeit rather late) for recognition as a legitimate element within a modern network of social control. The acceptability of the institutional option had already been confirmed by the establishment of separate institutions for juvenile offenders and asylums for the mentally ill and, most forcefully, by the ascendancy of the prison, whose towering presence had become the ultimate symbol of the power of the state. But whereas these institutions were gradually absorbed into the fabric of society, to become part and parcel of the institutional inheritance, the inebriate reformatories disappeared. Like so many other contenders, they succumbed to the vagaries of philanthropic style and public policy.

In part the problem lay with the reformers themselves—with their inability to clearly define the problem, its fundamental causes, or the precise nature of the punitive solution. The disparate groups that were involved with the system included doctors, legislators, administrators, and temperance reformers (who were themselves a mixed bag) as well as those involved in operating and administrating the reformatories at a local level. All of these groups had ideas about what the problem was and about the blend of punitive and therapeutic treatment that was necessary for reformation, if indeed reformation was their goal. But there was often little consensus on such issues, and the reformers were never able to resolve the conflict between organizational (bureaucratic) and individual goals. Whereas the medical officer at Girgenti, for example, might express the view that "inebriety is a distinct form of mental disorder...requiring medical care and treatment," the convenor of the city council, the man with ultimate responsibility for the reformatory, could express equally firmly the belief that "inebriety has not been proved a disease."[46]

The response of the medical profession to the reformatory experiment is particularly instructive because although the British Medical Association played its part in the agitation that resulted in the passage of the Inebriates Act, it was never particularly interested in the problem of habitual drunkenness. In part this neglect can be explained by the availability of resources and the perceived need, or understandable desire, to focus these resources on areas that offered the best prognosis. The inmates of the reformatories came close to bottom on any list of priorities. Even those who had an interest in the general area of alcohol abuse, including the medical officers attached to the reformatories, preferred to concentrate on helping the alcoholic—the well-motivated and articulate private patient of the licensed retreat—rather than be involved with the dirty work of the reformatory. Dr. Dunlop, the inspector for Scotland and a medical adviser to the Prison Department, gives an indication of medical preferences in this area in his annual report for 1909: "Retreats have been found to be of value as curative institutions for the treatment of habitual inebriety, and reformatories...as places for the segregation and control of drunken pests and to some extent as curative institutions. The 'recovery' rate in well conducted retreats is found to approach fifty per cent, and that of the reformatories to be about seven per cent."[47]

It has been asserted that the Inebriates Act testified to the seriousness of medical interest in the problem, clearing the way for the eventual acceptance of the medical model of alcoholism.[48] But it must also be said that medical and psychiatric interest in the area is not (and historically was not) widespread. Alcohol-related problems continue to be viewed with ambivalence, calling forth feelings of anger and disgust such as were associated with mental illness a generation ago or syphilis at the turn of the century.[49]

But the indifference of the medical profession alone did not kill off the reformatory system. The inebriate reformatories could have survived without the enthusiastic support of the medical fraternity: they could even have survived in the face of medical hostility. The central plank of the medical critique of the reformatories was that they were a therapeutic flop. Certainly, for those who still saw caring and curing as the primary issue, the fact that the reformatory was little more than a glorified combination of poorhouse and prison was proof enough of the failure of the entire system. However, as has already been shown, there were many people already convinced of the value of segregating habitual drunkards, and for them the therapeutic argument was of secondary importance, if not totally irrelevant. Whatever their faults, the reformatories could still offer a convenient way of getting rid of inconvenient "pests." The reformatories could have taken a great deal of criticism and survived, just as the prison survived criticism of its functional shortcomings, but only if, like the prison, they could attract the continued support of the propertied and powerful. In short, the inebriate reformatories could operate only with the purposeful backing of the state.

The parliamentary debates that preceded the introduction of both the Habitual Drunkards Act of 1879 and the Inebriates Act of 1898, the regulations for the management of reformatories, the official reports, and contemporary commentaries on the implementation of the 1898 act all lead to one seemingly irrefutable conclusion: the government of the day had no intention of providing either the leadership or the resources necessary for the effective implementation of the Inebriates Act. Carswell observed that "[the act]...was admittedly a bit of experimental legislation, and Parliament never puts heart into experimental legislation, except, perhaps, when it is legislating for Ireland."[50] The lack of commitment is not entirely explicable in terms of the novelty of the legislation; after all, there were plenty of similar institutions already in existence providing places for the mentally ill, for prostitutes, and for juvenile offenders. No, the government was chary of lending its support to this latest venture for a number of social and political reasons. First, there was still a fairly general suspicion of any measure that tended to extend governmental authority. For this reason provision for the compulsory detention of habitual drunkards was excluded from the Habitual Drunkards Act of 1879. Second, the government bowed to pressure in passing the Inebriates Act of 1898, but this yielding did not mean that they were entirely happy about the situation or that they were truly committed to implementing the act. These two aspects, the lack of commitment and the avoidance of anything that might be construed as excessive state interference, were brought together in the provisions of the act. The Inebriates Act of 1898 was a piece of permissive legislation. It contained no requirement, no national or local government obligation, to provide reformatories, and in fact there does not seem to have been any real expectation that they would be operated by the state (except in the specific case of the state reformatories). The state would license and supervise the general operation of the reformatory system, and it would contribute to the costs of reformatories, but otherwise the expectation was that the institutions would be taken over by the private sector.

Beyond finances and control other factors contributed to the half-hearted response of the government. The early years of the twentieth century witnessed a softening of attitudes toward poverty and some forms of social deviance. The nineteenth-century reformers were inclined to see the abolition of drunkenness or prostitution as their ultimate goal. By the first quarter of this century this goal had been supplanted by the view that, however undesirable, such deviance was an enduring feature of society and had therefore to be subjected to legislative control and regulation. Even if evils such as intemperance could not be eliminated, their worst effects could be ameliorated with proper treatment. However, there were now few people who continued in the belief that the inebriate reformatories could offer a regime of treatment that was both convenient and effective. No one would have argued that institutions for the insane or the criminal were unnecessary, but increasingly this argument was raised in relation to drunkenness: was it really necessary to lock up drunks for the protection of society? By contrast, there were (and had always been) those who advocated alternative strategies for combatting intemperance. Stronger licensing restrictions such as were introduced during the First World War,[51] greater control of availability and cost of alcoholic drink, and more private facilities for those who wanted to tackle their drink problem—these were the "novel innovations."

At the same time the drink question itself had become somehow less urgent; indeed, it had virtually ceased to be a live issue by about 1918.

Why this waning of interest? Perhaps it was simply because drunkenness itself declined, so the problem was in a sense less visible. Certainly by 1926 the number of prosecutions for drunkenness-related offenses was less than 30 percent of the 1906 figure.[52] Or was it that in the changing social, economic, and political climate of postwar Britain there were more urgent issues to be discussed, more urgent social problems to be attended to? Whereas the drink question had been the consuming passion of Victorian society, the new century was to have a new preoccupation—mass unemployment. During the 1908 licensing debate, for example, a Labour M.P., Victor Grayson, demanded an adjournment to consider the more pressing question of unemployment. "There are thousands of people dying in the streets," Grayson declared, "while you are trifling with this Bill."[53] Whatever the reason, drunkenness was no longer *the* social problem. Against this background, with other putative social problems competing for official recognition, the inebriate reformatories appeared less and less relevant.

POSTSCRIPT

Between 1901 and 1921 the inebriate reformatories attempted to change, or at least to extend the repertoire of, the societal response to habitual drunkenness. The underlying rationale of this "attempt to institute more rational methods for dealing with habitual inebriates" can be traced to the ideological and policy changes that were being formulated during the first half of the nineteenth century. The rise of an institutional ideology, which was itself based on new knowledge provided by the social sciences, and the shift of gaze away from overt punishment of the body to reformation of the deviant's soul heralded a new optimism about the nature of individual deviance and about the ability of society to control it. As Foucault noted, "The day was to come, in the nineteenth century, when this 'man' discovered in the criminal would become the target of penal intervention, the object that it claimed to correct and transform, the domain of a whole series of 'criminological' sciences and strange 'penitentiary' practices."[54]

The most potent symbol of this ideology was of course the prison and the new penology of reformers like John Howard and Elizabeth Fry. By way of contrast it could easily be argued that the inebriate reformatories were relatively unimportant—worthy of no more than a footnote in the history of moral reform.[55] Nevertheless, the history of the reformatories and of their failure contains some important lessons for the contemporary management of habitual drunkenness. Whereas it is easier to explain the development of the inebriate reformatories than to say how that history might be relevant to the present or might influence the future, a number of interesting parallels can be drawn between the reformatory system and changes in the management of public drunkenness that have been proposed in the Criminal Justice (Scotland) Act of 1980.

Section 5 of the 1980 act purports to offer an alternative to the criminal justice processing of public drunkenness by improving the availability of nonlegal options and providing an initial step toward eventual decriminalization of drunkenness. There is not space here to discuss the implications of the act in any detail, but in some aspects of its implementation decision makers might benefit from an understanding of the previous experimental legislation in this field. Practical difficulties will arise relating to the implementation of the provisions of the act, the chosen client group, the nature of the treatment regime, the utility (desirability) of coercive control, and so on. In this respect the aims and objectives of section 5 of the 1980 act are no more clearly articulated than those of the Inebriates Act of 1898. The conflict between organizational and individual goals has not been resolved, and the opposing claims of the sociomedical and criminal justice models have barely been recognized and far less satisfactorily dealt with. Beyond the practical difficulties, however, the major obstacle to the successful implementation of an alternative strategy for the management of drunkenness is (and historically has always been) the lack of purposeful governmental support.

Lord Mansfield, introducing the bill in the House of Lords, described clause 5 (section 5 of the act) as "an enabling power, for use as resources become available, permitting the police to take drunk offenders to a detoxification facility, instead of arresting them."[56] Like its ancestors, this piece of permissive legislation is designed to allow greater involvement of the private sector in the management of social deviance. Again, there is a comparison with the reformatory system in that the government has allowed for only a minimal investment of public funds to help provide for the establishment and operation of so-called detoxification facilities. In the light of this restricted funding and the fact that only one facility "designated for the reception of drunken persons" has been established since the act was implemented in 1981, it is difficult to believe that the government has any more intention of allowing a "full and fair experiment" of the provisions of section 5 than earlier governments had with regard to the Inebriates Act. Tim Cook provides a nice summary of the situation: "When one sees the failure of government to act in any significant way on the recommendations of various reports of this or the last century...then one is forced to ask once more—just what is the problem?"[57]

NOTES

1. Scotland and England were separate nations until joined by the Act of Union in 1707. This treaty guaranteed the continuation of distinct Scottish institutions in the areas of religion, education, and law, with separate, though frequently analogous, administrative arrangements. Therefore, although the provisions of the Inebriates Act of 1898 were virtually identical in both countries, the operation of the reformatories differed considerably. For one thing, the English reformatories tended to be much bigger than those in Scotland. The largest of the English reformatories could boast three hundred beds and the average reformatory more than one hundred. Scotland's largest certified reformatory, Girgenti Home, was small by comparison, having places only for fifty-eight women.

2. John Dunlop, the cofounder of the antispirits movement, cites this concern as the raison d'être for the early temperance crusade. On a visit to Europe in 1828 Dunlop had been shocked to find that France, a country with few of the benefits of the Protestant Reformation, was in no way morally inferior to Scotland. He was forced to conclude that "the superiority of our [Scotland's] religious and civil institutions was evaded and neutralised by the intemperance of our inhabitants." (*Minutes of Evidence Taken before the Select Committee on Drunkenness*, Parliamentary Papers, 1834, 8:394).

3. Cf. *Report of the Select Committee on Drunkenness*, Parliamentary Papers, 1834, viii; *Report of the Select Committee on Habitual Drunkenness*, Parliamentary Papers, 1872 (242):ix; *Department Committee on the Treatment of Inebriates*, 1893–1894, Cd. 7008, xvii. The first legislative "success" was achieved in Scotland with the passing of the so-called Forbes MacKenzie Act of 1854. However, it is the enactment of the Licensing Act of 1872 that is generally cited as the high-water mark of nineteenth-century temperance agitation (see Brian Harrison, *Drink and the Victorians* [London: Faber, 1971]).

4. Trotter's work in its original form was submitted as a doctoral dissertation at Edinburgh University in 1788 ("De ebrietate, ejusque effectibus in corpus humanum"). It was almost two decades before it was published in a more generally accessible form.

5. *The British Journal of Inebriety* was established in 1892 to promote the awareness of "alcoholism" in Great Britain. The journal, now the *British Journal of Addiction*, has been continuously active in this area for more than ninety years.

6. MacLeod, Roy M. "The Edge of Hope: Social Policy and Chronic Alcoholism," *Journal of the History of Medicine and Allied Sciences* 22, no. 3 (1967): 215–245.

7. *Fifth Report of the Inspector for Scotland, under the Inebriates Acts*, 1907, Cd. 4408, xii, 1237:834.

8. See, for example, Michel Foucault, *Madness and Civilisation: A History of Madness in the Age of Reason* (London: Tavistock, 1967); idem, *Discipline and Punish: The Birth of the Prison* (London: Allen Lane, 1977); Michael Ignatieff, *A Just Measure of Pain: The Penitentiary in the Industrial Revolution, 1750–1850* (London: Macmillan, 1978); Andrew Scull, *Museums of Madness: The Social*

Organisation of Insanity in Nineteenth Century England (London: Allen Lane, 1979).

9. Foucault, *Discipline and Punish.*

10. Scottish Office Circular, 22 February 1899.

11. Quoted in C. A. Oakley, *The Second City* (Glasgow: Blackie, 1947), 233.

12. Glasgow Corporation Minutes, 15 May 1899.

13. James Ramsay MacDonald, *Character and Democracy* (London: Wesleyan Methodist Union, 1907), 45.

14. *Second Annual Report of the Inebriate Reformatory Known as Girgenti Home* (Glasgow: Glasgow Corporation, 1902), 17.

15. In the autumn of 1871 Donald Dalrymple, M.P., the chairman of the committee, spent two months visiting inebriate institutions in the United States and Canada. He visited nine institutions in all (eight in the United States and one in Canada) and reported his findings before the committee. In his account of these North American institutions, he stressed both the voluntary nature of most admissions (94 percent of patients were self-referrals) and the limitations it placed on successful treatment: "Patients being voluntary, may leave before they are fit to go, deeming and calling themselves cured though they are not so, because he [the medical officer] has no power to turn the key on them; if he had possessed this power many cases would have been saved that were lost" (*Report of the Select Committee on Habitual Drunkenness*, 81). Despite the force of Dalrymple's evidence and the recommendation of the committee, no compulsory measures were introduced in the Habitual Drunkards Act of 1879, which was passed as a result of this inquiry.

16. The male division of the state reformatory was "lent to the Military Authorities" in October 1915 for use as a detention barracks. From that date the reformatory system was employed exclusively for the "benefit" of women. (Perth State Inebriate Reformatory; Superintendent's Journal, 1915, Scottish Records Office, Edinburgh).

17. The secretary for Scotland issued various regulations and guidelines from time to time concerning the operation of the inebriate reformatories. The most important ones, the rules by which the institutions were (or were supposed to be) run were "General Regulations for the Management and Discipline of Certified Inebriate Reformatories in Scotland," 1905, Cd. 2437, lxv, 189; *Regulations for the Rule and Management of the State Inebriate Reformatory*, 1900 Cd. 92, lxix, 193.

18. *Sixth Annual Report, Girgenti Home* (Glasgow: Glasgow Corporation, 1906), 19.

19. *Fifth Annual Report, Girgenti Home,* (Glasgow: Glasgow Corporation, 1905), 21.

20 David C. Barrows, "Inebriety in the Gay Nineties," *Drinking and Drug Practices Surveyor* 15 (November 1979): 15–56 passim.

21. Russell Dobash, "Labour and Discipline in Scottish and English Prisons: Moral Correction, Punishment and Useful Toil," *Sociology* 17, no. 1 (1983): 30.

22. There does not appear to have been any shortage of such labor, particularly after 1914, when the inmates were set to work doing their bit for the war

effort. The precise nature of the war work that could be undertaken in the reformatories is not mentioned in any of the annual reports, but, given the nature of the institutions, it seems likely that it would have involved the manufacture of items of uniform.

23. *Eleventh Report of the Inspector for Scotland under the Inebriates Acts, 1914–1915*, Parliamentary Papers, 1916, Cd. 8380, xi, 99.

24. It is of course questionable whether the majority of reformatory inmates would have been judged employable under any circumstances, but there is little evidence that reformatory "training" improved their job opportunities on release. Of the few hopefuls that were placed in employment after their liberation, most entered service, doing menial tasks around the homes of their middle-class benefactors. Only one woman inmate of the Greenock Reformatory is recorded as having found work in a laundry, despite all the supposed training in this type of work.

25. *Annual Report of the Inebriate Reformatory, Greenock*, 1909.

26. *Superintendent's Journal, State Inebriate Reformatory, Perth*, 1901; ibid., 1915.

27. The medical examination might have proved particularly embarrassing or humiliating for many women because, in spite of a clear ruling that wherever possible the doctor in a female reformatory should be a woman, virtually all of the medical staff were men.

28. In fairness to the institution it should be pointed out that, unlike in prisons, there was never more than the minimum of staff necessary for the general training and supervision of the inmates. The reformatories did not have the human or technical resources necessary to prevent or discourage escape attempts. Girgenti, for example, was a forty-five-acre farm and lacked even a boundary fence.

29. Most of the admissions to the state reformatory under section 23 were for child neglect (and habitual drunkenness). This situation contrasts sharply with that in England, where there were not only a great many more admissions under section 1 (the English equivalent of section 23) but also greater variety in the crimes for which persons were admitted. An average of about thirty-two persons a year were sent to reformatories in England and Wales under section 1, and although child neglect was again the single most frequent reason for admission, persons had been convicted of crimes ranging from manslaughter and theft to attempted suicide.

30. *Superintendent's Journal, State Inebriate Reformatory, Perth*, 1902.

31. John Carswell, "The Working of the Inebriates Act," *Journal of Mental Science*, October 1901, 9.

32. *Second Annual Report, Girgenti Home* (Glasgow: Glasgow Corporation, 1902), 9.

33. Carswell, "Working of the Inebriates Act," 3.

34. Bretherton makes similar observations about the predominance of women within the Irish reformatory system. George Bretherton, "Irish Inebriate Reformatories, 1899–1920: A Small Experiment in Coercion," *Contemporary Drug Problems*, 1986, forthcoming.

35. The practice of forfeiting bail was so common as to be regarded as normal—the equivalent of an on-the-spot fine for drunkenness. Between 1900

and 1914, on average, approximately 30 percent of those charged with drunkenness-related offenses chose to forfeit their bail in lieu of a fine.

36. Carswell, "Working of the Inebriates Act," 7.

37. Inebriate Reformatory Inmate Files, 1909, Scottish Records Office, Edinburgh.

38. Cf. Judith Walkowitz, *Prostitution and Victorian Society: Women, Class and the State* (New York: Cambridge University Press, 1980).

39. *Superintendent's Journal, State Inebriate Reformatory, Perth,* 1901.

40. Inebriate Reformatory Inmate Files, 1915, Scottish Records Office, Edinburgh.

41. Governor, Duke Street Prison, Glasgow, 1904, in Inebriate Reformatory Inmate Files, Scottish Records Office, Edinburgh.

42. *Second Annual Report, Girgenti Home* (Glasgow: Glasgow Corporation, 1904).

43. *Annual Report of the Prison Commissioners for Scotland for 1914,* 1915, Cd. 7927.

44. *Report of the Inspector under the Inebriates Acts, 1879 to 1900, for the year 1908,* 1910, Cd. 5044, xxxvi, 789.

45. *Annual Report of the Inebriate Reformatory, Greenock,* 1914.

46. Carswell, "Working of the Inebriates Act," 1.

47. *Seventh Report of the Inspector for Scotland under the Inebriates Acts, 1909,* 1910, Cd. 5364, xxxvi, 848.

48. Cf. Jim Orford and Griffith Edwards, *Alcoholism* (Oxford: Oxford University Press, 1977).

49. Cf. H. S. Abram and W. F. McCourt, "Interaction of Physicians with Emergency Ward Alcoholic Patients," *Quarterly Journal of Studies on Alcohol,* 25 (1964): 679–688. Phil M. Strong, "Doctors and Dirty Work: The Case of Alcoholism," *Sociology of Health and Illness* 2, no. 1 (1980): 24–47.

50. Carswell, "Working of the Inebriates Act," 2.

51. There was a widely held belief during the early years of the war that drunkenness among the armed forces and among munitions and other workers in vital industries was having an adverse effect on the nation's morale and on the war effort. "Drink is doing more damage than all the German submarines put together," declared Lloyd George in a speech in North Wales in February 1915 (quoted in Ian Dounachie, "World War I and the Drink Question: State Control of the Drink Trade," *Scottish Labour History Society Journal* 17 (1982): 1. To combat this "menace," the government set up a Central Control Board (Liquor Traffic) with powers to supervise all aspects of the drink trade. The typical licensing restrictions imposed by the board limited opening hours of public houses to two hours at midday and three hours (6 P.M. to 9 P.M.) in the evening. In Scotland, unlike in the rest of the United Kingdom, the restrictions were extended over virtually the entire country (see T. N. Carver, *Government Control of the Liquor Business in Great Britain and the United States* [New York: Oxford University Press, 1919]).

52. Although arrest statistics must always be treated with a great deal of circumspection, the downward trend is so dramatic that it is difficult to explain simply in terms of changes in policing practices. In 1906 there were more than

116,000 prosecutions for drunkenness-related offenses; twenty years later this figure had fallen to around 32,000.

53. Quoted in Harrison, *Drink and the Victorians,* 405.

54. Foucault, *Discipline and Punish,* 74.

55. In a country that prosecuted, fined, or imprisoned thousands of people for drunkenness-related offenses, the inebriate reformatory usually confined no more than a few dozen. In the twenty years under review fewer than six hundred inmates were admitted to reformatories. Even with these small numbers the reformatories had so little impact that it is difficult to give any functional explanation of their existence. Certainly, to view these institutions as major or necessary agencies of social control would be a gross distortion of reality.

56. *Parliamentary Debates,* House of Lords, 5th ser., vol. 404, 15 January 1980.

57. Tim Cook, *Vagrant Alcoholics* (London: Routledge & Kegan Paul, 1975).

FOURTEEN

Alcohol and the State in Nazi Germany, 1933–1945

Hermann Fahrenkrug

Germany needs the strength of every single man for the development of its national and economic freedom. Therefore, no German has the right to impair his strength through alcohol abuse. Such action is detrimental not only to himself, but to his family, and above all, to his people.

Heinrich Himmler, SS leader and
chief of the German Police, 1938

In this matter we must proceed in accordance with our National Socialist principle: radical, or not at all!

Dr. E. Ley, chief of the main office of
National Health, National Socialist German
Worker's Party (NSDAP, 1939)

The following study treats the formation and effects of the social control of alcohol in Germany during the Third Reich. The student of this problem enters an extensive terra incognita. Neither social nor medical historians have, to my knowledge, concerned themselves with it; hence there is no preliminary work in the collection of historical materials or their sociological interpretation for the scholar to fall back on. For my sources I have selected National Socialist writings on the problem of alcohol from the archives of the Prussian State Library in Berlin and the Catholic Charity Library in Freiburg. In my investigation of this massive quantity of material I concentrated on the varying contemporary conceptualizations of the alcohol question and the solutions that were to be derived from them. In my analysis of sources I have attempted to transcend purely historical description and have undertaken an interpretation informed by the sociological theory of modernization.

Explaining German fascism through the categories of social modernization is by no means something new. Ralf Dahrendorf and a series of

young social historians in Germany,[1] as well as Barrington Moore, David
Schoenbaum, and others in the United States,[2] have advanced the thesis
that the thrust to modernization of German industrial capitalism was
effected by the National Socialist state. The National Socialist "brown
revolution" broke up precapitalist estate relics, ties to religion, regional
and legislative bonds, and ties to left-socialist organizations. According
to these authors, modernization came about at that time through a
far-reaching rationalization of all spheres of life (a definition of modernization developed early in the twentieth century by Max Weber).[3]

Crisis-prone German industrial capitalism at the end of the 1920s
required a reorganization—a purposive harmonization of the economy
and the state in the context of a fascist system. Forced social integration was attained through a strict principle of management and production, an increasingly rational organization of labor, the employment of science and technology as productive resources, and a severe
disciplining of the labor force. Furthermore, the state intervened
through positive law in the purposive administrative apparatus that
encompassed institutions of social control. All of these activities produced a vast economic and military potential with which Germany
could regain its lost position of world power.

On the level of individual action, part of the modernization process
and one of the input requirements of modern social systems, according
to Weber, was to induce members of a society to adjust to the systemic
imperative of conducting as self-controllable and rational a life-style as
possible. This adjustment would be realized through disciplined professional work and through the process of social reproduction (in other
words, through the family and child rearing). It seems evident that
under crisis conditions modern system requirements can only be guaranteed through authoritarian or fascist means.

The nucleus of the so-called alcohol question at that time consisted in the collision of traditional drinking habits with the above-
mentioned system imperatives of modern society. This collision began
already with the onset of modernization in German society in the last
quarter of the nineteenth century. The twelve-year interlude of the
Third Reich offers the chance to study the conflict (and the radical
attempts at its solution) between alcohol abuse and the requirements of
modern times under socially extreme conditions (economic crises,
accelerated modernization, totalitarian state, and war).

Jürgen Habermas has described in detail an additional aspect of the
sociological theory of modernization—the pathology of the modern.[4]
Weber had already indicated the self-destructive tendencies of social
rationalization (overcomplexity, bureaucratization, alienation of men
in a disenchanted, materialized world). Habermas, in the Critical

Theory tradition of the Frankfurt school, adopted these categories and further developed them to fit modern social pathologies. Simply stated, the process of modernization—the progressive "colonization of traditional life worlds" by the system imperatives of the economy and the state—has pathological side effects. The visions sketched by litera- ture, philosophy, and Critical Theory of a perfectly managed world that goes to ruin through its own destructive dynamic and ungovern- ability are, according to Habermas, not purely fictional. In other words, Habermas sees as possible a world where a totalitarian system unifies its subjects through purposive rationality and domination and where their life relations fall into the iron bondage chamber previously evoked by Weber, from which there is no escape. It may appear as an exaggeration to want to subsume certain excesses of Nazi alcohol control under these manifestations of the pathology of the modern. But how else is one to understand the fact that as a "publicly danger- ous inebriate" in the National Socialist state, one could end up in Auschwitz—that the state could deny someone (and that person's po- tential descendants) the right to exist?

GOVERNING IMAGES OF ALCOHOL PROBLEMS IN THE THIRD REICH

Alcoholic beverages possess not only a chemical structure but also a social definition that is of importance for understanding the public perception of, and reaction to, the use of alcohol. Whether the basic substance is conceived of primarily as a food, a poison, or an everyday domestic drug directly affects its production, distribution, and con- sumption. The classic polarization of definitions is found in the Nazi alcohol literature. These range from positive—food, stimulant, and remedy—to negative—narcotic, germ poison, addictive drug, and na- tional poison (*Volksgift*). Opposed to these extreme characterizations is the frequent description of alcoholic beverages as poisons of pleasure (*Genussgifte*) or, more moderately, as pleasure drugs. The fact that the leading Nazi journal on alcohol problems was itself titled *The Poisons of Pleasure* clearly indicates the importance of this characterization of the substance. Yet at the same time the characterization is ambivalent, as the following quotations from Friedrich Meggendorfer make clear. On the one hand, Meggendorfer recognized that the principal reason for the use of alcoholic beverages was "the property of alcohol to lift the mood and turn troubles and worries into cheerfulness and good humor."[5] Alcoholic beverages are thus primarily pleasure drugs that in small quantities promote conviviality and consequently have socially integrative effects. Yet on the other hand, "one defines a poison as a substance that is able to produce harmful effects upon living creatures, especially upon men. If temporary impairment of functioning and the enjoyment of life can validly demonstrate the poisonous nature of a substance, then one must state that alcohol is a poison for man."[6] As a poison, the substance possessed a simultaneous potential for misuse that could become dysfunctional for persons as well as for the system.

A typology of drinking styles and inebriate types in Nazi Germany, including their deviance and problem designations, remains inevitably fragmentary in view of the multitude of alcohol modes treated. It was difficult for the Nazis to bring order to the universe of drinking. The following reconstructed overview produced on the basis of Meggendorfer's handbook article seems to me to convey the state of the conceptualization of the problem at the time. It lists the phenotypes of alcohol use and abuse recognized by the Nazis:

nonuse/abstinence
moderate alcohol use (customary and for enjoyment; unproblematic)
nonalcoholic alcohol abuse (all forms of deviance under the influence of alcohol)
acute alcoholism (normal or pathological intoxication, alcohol poisoning)
periodic alcoholism (dipsomania from psychopathological predisposition)
chronic alcoholism—alcohol addiction (instinctual predisposition towards alcohol, constitutionally endowed)
progressive nonaddictive alcohol abuse with organically, psychically, and socially harmful consequences; existing on an environmental as well as a genetic basis

The etiology of alcoholism variants with respect to alcoholic beverages was conceived of as a cross between intrinsic and extrinsic factors. According to Meggendorfer, "In the case of alcoholism, which is not itself a disease proper, and cannot in an overall sense be characterized as a disease, the circumstances are more complicated than in the case of normal disease symptoms."[7]

Without alcohol there is no alcoholism. This truism was also valid for the Nazis. Yet the presence of a great flood of alcohol and permissive drinking habits cannot in itself explain the appearance of alcoholism, for only a relatively small percentage of the population lapses into alcoholism.

It [alcoholism] must therefore consist in a dependent relation between disposition and environment, insofar as circumstances in which the environment is unfavorable, slight errors of dispositions, deficient understanding, slight changes of mood, or dysbulia, and the inability to pursue the higher ends of life, for example, would lead to alcoholism; whereas in a favorable environment more severe mental and physical deficiencies and defects of hereditary predisposition must be present in order nevertheless to break off the craving for drink.[8]

Consequently, the hereditary disposition to alcoholism did not exist within a simple alcoholism gene but rather coincided with the disposition toward various mental disorders, psychopathies, and mental and bodily inferiorities. Alcoholics were now not only "drinking mental cases" but also constitutional psychopaths. Accordingly, alcoholism was believed to lead to "prostitution, crime, and waywardness."[9] The two hundred thousand to three hundred thousand alcoholics estimated by Meggendorfer to exist in the Third Reich were therefore classified either as pure environmental alcoholics (30 percent) or as genetically inferior constitutional alcoholics (with the subcategories *mental cases, psychopaths,* and *criminal antisocials* totaling 70 percent). These characterizations already suggest the contemporary solutions.

It must be stressed, however, that the Nazi conceptualizations of alcohol problems were not exhausted by individual-level deviance. Constant increase in per capita consumption formed a clearly recognizable background to the alcohol question. Statistics, however rudimentary, revealed an increase in beer, wine, and spirit consumption after 1933.[10] Nazi authors recognized this trend. Werner Bracht, for example, in his standard work *Alkohol, Volk und Staat,*[11] described a clear connection between the availability of alcoholic drinks, the increase of alcohol consumption, and the mortality rate of the population.

Nazi authors incessantly repeated the theme of social damages resulting from alcohol abuse. In particular, "disruption of domestic happiness through the influence of alcohol and crime, traffic accidents and alcohol, and a weakening of work and productive ability" were, together with the disruption of public order, moral decline, and economic loss, problems conceptualized on an explicitly social level.[12] For example, one contemporary author suggested that the costs of the economic disturbance of the national wealth through mortality, morbidity, damage to property, subsequent costs for public care and social control, and a series of indirect additional costs could be estimated at 7.5 billion reichsmarks—socially unjustifiable in comparison to the 624 million reichsmarks of state income from liquor taxes.[13] From the standpoint of modern social bookkeeping the alcohol question appeared to be a heavy burden for the National Socialist state.

THE FORMATION OF ALCOHOL CONTROL IN NAZI GERMANY

The control measures of the Nazi state against alcohol abuse may be divided into two groups, in keeping with the above-mentioned conceptualizations of alcohol deviance, as having either an environmental or constitutional basis. On the environmental side the cause of, and guilt for, alcohol abuse lay not only with the consumer but also with the "offerer and encourager"—the alcohol industry and the trade—which did its share to raise the level of consumption. In the beginning phase only the anticapitalist workers' wing of the National Socialist party emphasized the profit seeking of alcohol capital as the real problem in the alcohol question. This emphasis proceeded in connection especially with so-called Jewish alcohol capital, which, according to a paranoid conspiracy theory, was progressing with its strategy of injuring the German race through the alcohol poison.[14] That a general ban of alcohol was, however, no theme for the Nazis is demonstrated by the agreement with the alcohol suppliers. The strained labor market and the difficult financial situation of the state prohibited a reduction of alcohol production and distribution. The state could not do without the jobs provided by the alcohol industry and the finances provided by the tax on alcohol. Hence a compromise was reached between economic considerations and the health burden of mass alcohol consumption: "At the same time, we need not surrender ourselves to any kind of utopian demands, but rather we, along with those responsible for the economy, quite plainly have to develop measures which, upon further consideration, contribute not only to the control of the health of the German Reich but also to its economic leadership."[15]

This course was followed with determination. On the one hand, the classic control instruments of the production and distribution of alcoholic drinks (fiscal policy, licensing) were employed; some ailing branches of the alcohol industry (wine and champagne producers, innkeepers) even obtained state assistance. On the other hand, the state developed new techniques to control the excesses of "liberal" alcohol capitalism. The Nazis introduced the restriction and censorship of advertising, protections against press coercion and economic straightjacketing (tied-house system), as well as strict licensing and police control of pubs (legal measures against irresponsible proprietors). Moreover, the National Socialist state demanded that the alcohol industry and the drink trade reorganize nonalcohol drink production and distribution through measures such as unfermented fruit utilization and the alcohol-free restaurant.

On the consumer side the palette of control measures against alcohol deviance was many-colored. In the region of nonalcoholic deviant drinking, the National Socialist state intervened in three areas: public order, traffic safety, and criminality. Whoever repeatedly disturbed the public order in an alcohol-related offense found himself quickly seized and supervised. He (or she) would be exposed first to police measures and then to public assistance measures. So-called irresponsible drinkers were detected by the local National Socialist administration,[16] admonished by the police, forbidden to drink in pubs, entered in the drinker lists that appeared in the daily newspapers, and identified and registered in the public care centers. They could, if required, be declared legally incapacitated, whereupon they might be transferred to a sanitarium or to a work home. Dangerous cases might even be brought to a concentration camp.[17] Alcohol-deviant recipients of public relief were reported to their agencies and found themselves without any further financial support. Alcohol-related traffic offenses were a special interest of the Nazis from the very beginning, and the criminalization of such acts against society brought about the introduction of Widmark's blood analysis test to the entire nation in 1938.[18]

I have already referred to the intrinsic connection between alcohol, crime, and racial inferiority established by the Nazis. Whoever gave his criminal or antisocial disposition free reign under the influence of alcohol ran the danger of being stigmatized a "criminal and publicly dangerous habitual inebriate" and being treated as such. In his defense he could not again refer to the condition of intoxication that had hindered his insight into the wrongness of the committed act. The newly created "Law against Dangerous Recidivists and Measurements for Protection and Reform" of January 1934, created the new category of full drunkenness. Whoever drank deliberately or negligently could be punished with fines or a prison sentence of up to two years for offenses committed under the influence of alcohol. Instead of prison he could alternatively be sent to a sanitarium or to a workhouse. Whoever did not wish compulsory treatment could, according to this law, "for the greatest possible utilization of his still-existing work strength" be brought to a suitable place of "secure custody."[19] This clause frequently meant a stay in a concentration camp.[20]

The showpiece of Nazi legislation for the long-term radical solution to the genetic foundation of the alcohol problem was the "Law for the Prevention of Descendants affected by Hereditary Disorders" of 1933. With this law "grave alcoholism" became a hereditary condition alongside such classic diseases as hereditary mental deficiency, schizophrenia, insanity, hereditary epilepsy, congenital chorea, hereditary blindness and deafness, and serious bodily deformity. For these diseases, sterilization of the affected person was urged. This law applied only to the "hereditary" class of the alcoholic population and was not thought of as a direct measure in the fight against alcoholism but rather as a preventive act for the protection of the future national strength of the state. Alcoholics were to be preventively sterilized, in spite of a conscious skepticism concerning whether alcoholism was really a hereditary dis-

ease, because there was present in them, as Rüdin and Gütt expressed
in their commentary on the law, "a mental and ethical inferiority so that
the descendants of these individuals are undesirable for a multitude of
reasons."[21] Simply put, the Nazis held the view that "alcoholism is not a
real disease, but only a symptom, an effect of various abnormal and
pathological hereditary conditions." Thus, according to them, "grave
alcoholics in the majority of cases in their circle of blood relations have a
selection of pathological hereditary types of various kinds: psychopaths, the mentally deficient, the retarded, criminals, antisocials, public
wards, prostitutes, drunkards, the mentally ill, epileptics, hysterics, and
so on."[22] Sterilization consequently signified pulling out the roots of
hereditary alcoholism: "Through the sterilization of inebriates, the
number of mentally inferior individuals for coming generations is reduced and with that the number of inebriates from the hereditary
pool."[23]

Legal proceedings legitimized state intervention into the individual's
reproductive abilities. The law required that a petition for sterilization
be presented to the court of race hygiene. The person concerned, in the
case of someone legally incapacitated by his ward, may have petitioned
voluntarily, but principally petitioning was done by medical officers or
administrators of control institutions concerned with alcohol problems.
A tribunal composed of a judge and two doctors decided after presentation of the case whether there existed the presence of grave alcoholism.
In contrast to real hereditary diseases, no biological or medical evidence of the hereditary nature of the alcoholism was necessary; rather,
vague indications of alcohol abuse sufficed. These manifested themselves, in the view of most courts, in alcohol-related diseases (both
bodily and mental), punishable behavior, the need to rely on public
assistance, mental incapacitation, the neglect of obligations to family
and state, reduced productive ability, social decline, and general social
incapability. The court decided each case by a simple majority (90
percent positive) and could, if the concerned person resisted, order
police enforcement of the ruling.

A rough estimate suggests that 5–10 percent of the approximately
three hundred thousand diagnosed alcoholics were sterilized on the
basis of this law.[24] Thus, between twenty thousand and thirty thousand
inebriates were affected, only a small percentage of the 150,000–
200,000 cases marked for sterilization by the racial hygiene specialists
and the Nazi health management. Studies show among reasons for
sterilization alcoholism ranked fourth, after mental deficiency, schizophrenia, and epilepsy and that, in contrast to the other conditions,
sterilized inebriates in the overwhelming majority of cases (nine out of
ten) were men between the ages of thirty and forty and came particularly from the lower class.[25]

In the second commentary on the law of 1937 the definition of grave alcoholism hinted at a dangerous tendency toward extending the diagnosis to all socially undesirable alcohol-deviant population segments. Now the individual's complete personality, his social behavior, and that of his family were viewed as decisive. Whoever possessed a weak will or an unstable personality, was antisocial, or drank in a deviant fashion did not need to manifest the symptoms of chronic alcoholism to be deprived of his reproductive ability under this law.

The commentary already suggested the later projects of the "Social Incapability Law," under whose scope all inebriates would fall. Little is known about the implementation, execution, and response to this law. Although the organized alcohol opponents at this time expressed approval of the law (except Catholics, who were against sterilization on religious grounds), the "professional ban" on would-be parents was rather discomforting for many Germans. Like the search for pure Aryan genealogy, it now became necessary to search one's ancestry for hereditary diseases, inferiorities, and grave alcoholism. And who could be certain that in the chain of generations all relatives twice removed would prove negative?

Not only were "constitutional alcoholics" deemed a menace to the people and race and forbidden to increase the population by establishing families, but "environmental alcoholics" now also began to feel aggression from the Nazi state. Marriage and the procreation of children was made complicated for them by the "Marriage Health Law" of 1935. It forbade marriage

> if one member of the engaged pair suffers from a mental disturbance, for this makes the marriage undesirable for the nation. Those with alcoholism of every form and cause, or ongoing mental disturbances, make a beneficial coexistence in the community impossible for both the married couple as well as for the children; they endanger the orderly raising of children and the economic situation of the family; they prevent and complicate adjustment to the community.[26]

Alcoholics consequently had difficulties obtaining the newly instituted certificate of marriage ability from the public health office. There hopeful young couples were advised, depending on the difficulty of the case, to keep the number of children low, to dispense with children, or not to marry at all. Although marriage could not legally be prevented, undesirable inebriates were disqualified from initial financial help in the form of government loans. The new marriage law of 1938 went even further and incorporated the possibility of terminating by divorce marriages broken through alcohol abuse.

Hereditarily diseased or inferior alcoholics could not be cured; hence the Nazis refused treatment or public assistance for members of this group. But what was to be the course of action with the "environmental alcoholics" (30 percent of all alcoholics), particularly considering that the nation urgently needed them during the war after 1939? A consultation, treatment, and public-assistance system was created for them on the national level by the state, the party, and independent organizations. Where counseling and an attempt to influence certain environmental factors (such as workplace and housing) were insufficient, the following steps were taken:[27]

1. open psychiatric treatment
2. sanitarium stay in a free or confined institution with emphasis on therapeutic activities
3. commitment to a special institution of a workhouse character

The sole goal of all forms of treatment was alcohol abstinence. Before commitment to an institution, alcoholics were always entitled to treatment. The course of treatment depended on the individual case.

> The more environmentally produced and the less hereditarily conditioned the alcoholism—the less time it has existed and the longer the treatment can last—the better the outlook for a successful sanitarium treatment. Inversely, the outlook worsens for intrinsically psychopathologically rooted disorders, longer-range alcoholism, and short-duration treatment. Time and time again, recidivist, undisciplined, unsocial inebriates prove unsuitable for sanitarium treatment.[28]

According to the yearbook of the alcohol question of 1941, there existed twenty-five such sanitariums for inebriates, partly set up and administered by independent antialcohol organizations, the churches, or the state:

> They are spread throughout the entire Reich so that in every region, in every Prussian province, they are available. They are effective on the whole according to their principles of work therapy, submitting their patients to household, agricultural, and forestry work in the area around the sanitarium, letting them exercise, go through a deep cure, serving mostly vegetable and bland food, and instructing and educating them on all aspects of the alcohol question, some through religion and confessional practices, but all under the control and care of a medical specialist.[29]

In spite of such promising measures, all treatment of inebriates and public assistance remained under the suspicion of being only "symptomatic therapy." The best and longest sanitarium treatment could perhaps free the alcoholic from his addiction, but it could not alter his inferior hereditary disposition. Sterilization remained therefore the only "radical therapy," the specific contribution of National Socialism to the solution of the alcohol question.

MODERNIZATION AND MANAGEMENT OF
ALCOHOL-RELATED PROBLEMS IN NAZI GERMANY

In the following discussion I will attempt to describe more precisely the relations between the National Socialist state and its alcohol control policy. For the purposes of simplification, I will investigate the problem in three phases:

1. inventory taking and forced coordination of the German alcohol opposition, 1933–1935
2. intensification of alcohol control during the years of the economic and military upsurge and blitzkrieg, 1936–1941
3 total war, 1942–1945

The Acquisition of Power in the
Alcohol Question, 1933–1935

If one divides the German antialcohol movement of the first third of the century into three parts, a socialist-Marxist workers' fraction, a liberal-democratic fraction, and a conservative-authoritarian bourgeois fraction, without doubt one can trace a continuity of ideas from the latter to the new conceptualization of the alcohol question in the National Socialist "revolution." From 1933 on, because of the zeitgeist —especially the fascist racial theories—radical solutions could be realized. To be sure, the racial hygiene laws introduced by the Nazis after only a few months in power had an intellectual pedigree. Social Darwinist thought of a social biology, which adapted the categories of the eternal struggle for existence, survival of the fittest, natural selection, racial decadence, and the elimination of the unfit to social processes, belonged since the nineteenth century to the worldview of the German bourgeoisie.[30] The sterilization law of 1933 had been discussed in the Prussian assembly without, of course, finding a political majority. The ideological background of the racial biological legislation can be traced back even further. In Ernst Rüdin's lecture to the ninth antialcoholism conference of 1903, "Alcohol in the Vital Function of Race," alcoholism was already indicated as a "direct or indirect consequence of inferior or pathological heredity."[31] Internment of the drinker, sterilization, the prohibition of marriage, and even induced abortion appeared suitable to Rüdin for creating "every possible barrier" through which the "fetus of an inebriate could hardly pass."[32] Is it an accident that thirty years later Rüdin would be the author of the commentary on the Nazi law for the prevention of descendants of those affected by hereditary disorders?

The National Socialists were also in agreement with the conservative bourgeoisie in rejecting the socialist-Marxist view of the alcohol question. In spite of occasional concessions to the importance of "environmental factors" in the etiology of alcoholism, the focal point of the National Socialist weltanschauung was

> in the victory over the environmental teaching—that dogma that we men would be bodily, psychologically, and mentally characterizable in each case as the result of environmental influences. If one were convinced of that now, the social predicament of the individual would in most cases have its causes in the ruling social order, as Marxism in particular maintains. So all along we have been of the opinion that all this has its causes in hereditary disposition.[33]

The proletarian alcohol opponents and their institutions were therefore as exposed to persecution as the workers' movement. The liberal-democratic faction of the alcohol opponents also found itself criticized, although less threatened. The Nazis reproached them for esteeming too highly the freedom of the individual. The classic bourgeois-liberal legal tradition, which protected the alcohol business against state intervention, lacked "the ethics of the total state of National Socialist character; it bypasses the extraordinary danger of alcohol for the race and nation in a liberal overvaluation of the individual."[34] For the Nazis believed that the principle of the common good before self-interest should also apply in the alcohol question.

A further error of the "liberal-Marxist time," namely, "replacing the concept of the inebriate with that of the diseased alcoholic...and substituting for the guilt of the individual the collective guilt of society,"[35] would also have to disappear in the National Socialist state. For the Nazis, "the inebriate consequently no longer appears from the start as a pitiful, sick individual, but rather as a weak-willed, dissolute, or vice-addicted subject, who with all available means must be guided back to the discipline of a responsible life."[36] Alcohol deviants were branded with the stigma of "antisocial psychopathology," which, despite all equations with the sufferers of hereditary diseases, never disappeared. Logically, inebriates should have fallen under the planned "Social Incapability Law" (Antisocial Law) of the 1940s.

Another dangerous consequence of this liberal concept of alcoholism as a disease was that

> one could imagine that through welfare and public assistance, the uncontrollable swarms of alcoholic families and similar antisocial elements could be raised to a level of respectability. So today, the high number of antisocials who in many cases are alcoholics is partly the result of their increased reproduction and the spoon-feeding of their children by misguidedly sympathetic public aid and charity.[37]

Inspired by such thinking, the Nazis closed many public alcohol treatment centers or transformed them into institutions of repressive social control against so-called antisocial inebriates.

The "Law for the Standardization of Matters concerning Public Health" of 1934 constituted for the tradition-rich German temperance and abstinence movement a partially forced, partially voluntary synchronization with the "brown revolution." First, the left-socialist and Marxist organizations were dissolved. At that time the Nazis planted—according to the new "führer principle"—NSDAP functionaries on the board of directors of the bourgeois antialcohol organizations to force them to conduct themselves in accordance with National Socialist principles.[38] The old Main Reich Office against Alcoholism of 1925 was formally dissolved and replaced already in 1933 by the Reich Society for the Struggle against Alcoholism, which forcibly merged under its roof all nonofficial alcohol opponents. The National Socialist state titled these measures "Organized Struggle against Addictive Substances."[39] Simultaneously, on the regional and district level "work societies for the struggle against alcoholism" were established. The party itself took action toward solving the alcohol question through its public welfare and health offices, which, on the instruction of the party leaders, had to take over the responsibility of directing health propaganda. The German Association against Alcoholism, the temperance society founded in 1883, enjoyed the particular goodwill of the Nazis. Renamed the German Society against Alcohol Abuse, it was clearly set on an official party course. From 1937 it was instructed by the NSDAP leadership to take over the struggle against alcohol abuse "as long as it concerns the education, enlightenment, and schooling of nonalcoholics."[40] State health offices, party organizations, and those traditional alcohol opponents "brought in line" in the Reich Society formed the trio of alcohol control.

In 1939, with the shadow of war already looming, the organizational structure was changed yet again. A new Central Reich Office against Alcohol and Tobacco Dangers was created in Berlin, for which the reich minister of health was directly responsible. This office coordinated all measures of the struggle against alcohol abuse:

> The Reich Office is cooperating with all possible agencies of party and state, expertly advising them and supporting them in their efforts to struggle against the dangers of pleasure drugs and narcotics. The Reich Office is working on all aspects of the pleasure drug problem as far as all connected questions of prevention, public assistance, and damages are concerned. In addition, the Reich Office is conducting scientific research in all aspects of the field.[41]

A modern administration for the solution of the alcohol question was therewith created.

Modern Performance-Oriented Society, the
National Socialist State, and the Alcohol Question, 1936–1941

With the onset of the four-year plans in 1936 (designed to bring the German people the greatest economic success) the alcohol question began to extend beyond the boundaries of the problem of racial hygiene. The Nazis' "biological overall view" of people and state asserted the importance of the general health of the individual for the health and power of the nation. As the president of the reich health office expressed it:

> Our future will be a hard struggle for the existence of the German people. Our nation can only be developed if we protect the German people, our most valuable asset, through responsible health leadership and legislation, from bodily and mental damage. The healthy man alone is the source of every national achievement, and with that also of national power. This health leadership would therefore be a duty to our people.[42]

> What was already seen decades ago by some individuals gradually begins to fulfill itself: thoughts about a quantitative and qualitative human economy leads of necessity to a healthy and productively capable national economy.[43]

It seemed evident to the Nazis that, economically, no newly founded nation could have a future with alcoholics, cripples, and sufferers from hereditary diseases and that only thoroughly healthy comrades would be suitable for such a state. Health was now for the National Socialist doctors

> that constitution of man that enabled him to bring to completion the tasks that life, profession, family, and people demanded from him—therefore the functionally highest form of his bodily and mental productive capability. The human ability was from then on the foundation of the total state, and the will to achieve and the productive capability alone decided the social value of a man. Antisocial people did not follow the course of work and were therefore social enemies.[44]

It is understandable, given these prerequisites, that the question of the influence of alcohol consumption on "productive ability" now came to be of central importance to the National Socialist health leadership. According to a thoroughly scientific study, Graf maintained that over time alcohol neither furnished energy nor increased productive ability; rather, it had a horsewhip effect on the subject, numbing the signs of fatigue and mobilizing reserves—in effect, harming the organism. Psychic performance readiness sank under the influence of alcohol. Under conditions of mechanized or automatic work (such as on assembly lines) small quantities of alcohol could probably reduce full nervous tension, but this effect disturbed the thoroughly necessary action readiness. It was also clearly demonstrated for Graf that the danger of accidents—especially in street traffic—increased as a result of alcohol consumption. His conclusion: "Alcohol enjoyment must be rejected in relation to work on the basis of deep scientific insight into the effects of alcohol, as well as on the basis of the recognition of the redesigning of the work process through the development of technology."[45]

Along with these insights, National Socialist medicine discovered "sudden drops of efficiency" for workers around the age of forty, for which, they said, definite drinking patterns were responsible. Education for a healthy life-style was now directed against alcohol abuse. As previously mentioned, this education was the task of the National Socialist health leadership—to be attained through giant propaganda campaigns. Plans were developed to introduce a health pass for every German, in which data concerning a person's health and work suitability would be entered. The idea of storing this data (to which drinking patterns would naturally belong) on computer punch cards and making them accessible to all state agencies and private users demonstrates the tendency and modernity of the National Socialist totalitarian claim to complete control of personal life-conduct (*Lebensführung*). The zealous German worker did not, however, wait for the intervention of the control institutions; rather, he voluntarily took part in the rationalization of the German economy through the self-rationalization of his life-style.

Where the usability of a man for work was the final criterion for health, conditions of labor scarcity required that "even a defective, injured organism reduced in its power, but still accomplishing work, must not in any case feel valueless and superfluous."[46] The selection of inebriates according to their ability to work became, therefore, the new principle of the National Socialist solution to the alcohol question and led straightaway to the "cure through work" or, for the incurable, to "annihilation through work" in concentration camps.

The Alcohol Question under Wartime Conditions, 1939–1945

Under wartime conditions the alcohol field in Nazi Germany was transformed into a section of the inner front. As Erich Ley stated in 1939, "The fighting fitness of our people, how it suffers under the poisons of pleasure! Not only do we not have the workingmen, but it aggravates the situation that many of our people are aging tremendously early."[47] The Nazi approach was racial and hygienic. Already in

1935 Rüttig had stressed the defensive political dimensions of the alcohol question: "A people of idiots and degenerate weaklings can still be great in numbers, but it will go to ruin in the long run if other hereditarily strong nations do not first finish it off."[48]

To mobilize the last productive reserves for the economy and the military, the selection of those fit for work and military service stiffened. Unproductive "deadweight individuals" fell victim at that time to euthanasia measures. The statement of a Nazi doctor, "I do not know of any more sick individuals, only the living [workers and soldiers] and the dead," applied to alcoholics as well as to other groups. The new reich minister of health and simultaneous leader of the Reich Office against Alcohol and Tobacco Dangers, Conti, announced in his 1939 war proclamation:

> Next to the service duty of the soldiers of our Wehrmacht stands the civil service duty of every German. A part of this civil service is health duty. Every German man and woman has to live healthfully and avoid anything that can endanger or damage health. The struggle against alcohol and tobacco dangers is thereby not only an urgent task of health leadership and administration; it also serves the acquisition and the strengthening of German defense power.... You also help through your work to protect and strengthen the German family where it is threatened by drug use, and thereby you raise the inner resistance ability of our people.[49]

In 1939 Nazi Germany appeared better prepared than other belligerent nations for the wartime increase in alcohol problems.[50] The centralization of the antialcohol work, the so-called health duty campaign, and the racial hygiene measures had well prepared the population for alcohol shortages and price increases. The supreme command of the armed forces ordered the sobriety of its troops and obtained their understanding. The alcohol industry submitted to stricter production and distribution regulations and accepted the increased war taxes on alcohol. The majority of Nazi comrades readily bore their war sacrifice of alcohol.

For deviants, a worse time was certainly dawning. Already marginalized during peacetime as hereditary inferiors, psychopaths, and antisocials, they were now declared by the leadership to be dangerous enemies of the German people. Whoever disturbed the delicate social order under war conditions—for example, by engaging in a drunken brawl in an air raid shelter, causing alcohol-related traffic accidents in a blackened-out zone, or neglecting his work duty under the influence of alcohol—could be arrested and brought to a concentration camp for security detention. The public inebriate assistance agencies concerned themselves less with cure or treatment than with security measures for the protection of the public.[51] This happened through a cooperative response of the public assistance and the antialcohol associations with the police and through a network of dedicated and trained social workers.

Under extreme war conditions modern alcohol control showed its true face: "For the registration of alcoholics and dangerous alcoholics, especially early registration," declared Police Major Messer of the reich office, "no dangerous alcoholic, no person who has fallen under the influence of alcohol may...remain unknown to the state and party."[52] A giant machinery was set up, including forms such as the following: "Briefly, and to the point, the undersigned reports that [name] is viewed as alcohol diseased or a dangerous alcoholic and it is desired that this is to be confidentially made known." Called on to deliver this opinion were

> the doctor, the leader of a hospital-sanitarium, the health insurance organization, the national insurance office, the professional association of private insurance organization, the responsible agency of the main office for public welfare, the German work front, in the first place the party with its members and associations, the local government, the criminal court, the surrogate's court, or special court, the state prosecutor, in particular the police authorities, the welfare office, the youth office, the emergency care center, the plant manager, the shop steward, the factory nurse, the community nurse, and many others, above all each member as well of the entire nation.[53]

In the context of this project the handling of the alcohol question was reclassified from the area of hereditary diseases to the criminal political program of the extermination of "socially extraneous unfit individuals [antisocials]." In Hans Werner Kranz and Siegfried Koller's 1941 suggestion for "a law for the deprivation of civil rights for the defense of the nation [antisocial law]" the inebriate was included alongside recidivist criminals, work-dodging welfare recipients, prostitutes, and vagabonds.[54] Alcoholics too were not capable of "complying with the minimum requirements of the community in their personal, social, and national behavior" and were therefore socially incapable. Among those minimum requirements was the duty to protect and support the honor, strength, and achievement of one's own people. Here it becomes clear how strongly the "community ability," and therefore the right of existence, of an individual in the National Socialist system was connected with his or her labor and reproductive ability. The passage of alcohol control from the medically arranged hereditary disease law to the newly assembled "Social Inability Law" combined the existing measures of sterilization, prohibition of marriage, and security detention so as to reach a "final solution" of the alcohol question. Socially incapable inebriates received the degrading punishment of complete exclusion from national life and were surrendered to "annihilation through work."[55]

CONCLUSION

The history of the German alcohol question during the Third Reich is the history of the intervention of a total fascist state in the classic alcohol-related problems of modern societies. Within the National Socialist worldview the propagandized conceptualization and solution of the alcohol question was reactionary in its ends but revolutionary in its means. It brought about the application of the modern inherent tendency of end-rational social molding of society and its members, according to the imperatives of economy and the state, to forms of alcohol control. In their program of alcohol control the Nazis wanted, on the one hand, to utilize the advantages of alcohol as a means of social integration and, on the other, to eliminate the disadvantages of mass alcohol consumption for system integration through measures of repressive social control and biological prevention. The racist theoretician Max von Gruber once labeled the core of the alcohol question, "Alcohol harms too many, but kills too few." The National Socialist state attempted to modify this law of nature by practical rational intervention, out of which emerged a further chapter of the pathology of the modern.

NOTES

1. R. Dahrendorf, *Society and Democracy in Germany* (Garden City, N.J.: Doubleday, 1967); H. Matzerath and H. Volkmann, "Modernisierungstheorie und Nationalsozialismus," in *Theorie in der Praxis des Historikers,* ed. Jürgen Kocka, *Geschichte und Gesellschaft,* Sonderheft 3 (Göttingen: Vandenhoeck & Ruprecht, 1977), 88–116; D. Peukert, *Volksgenossen und Gemeinschaftsfremde* (Cologne: Bund Verlag, 1982).

2. Barrington Moore, *Social Origins of Dictatorship and Democracy* (Boston: Beacon Press, 1969); David Schoenbaum, *Hitler's Social Revolution: Class and Status in Nazi Germany, 1933–1939* (Garden City, N.J.: Doubleday, 1966).

3. Max Weber, *The Protestant Ethic and the Spirit of Capitalism,* trans. Talcott Parsons, with a foreword by R. H. Tawney (New York: Scribner's, 1930); Max Weber, *Economy and Society,* ed. Guenther Roth and Claus Wittich, trans. Ephraim Fischer (Berkeley and Los Angeles: University of California Press, 1978).

4. Jürgen Habermas, *Theorie des kommunikativen Handelns,* 2 vols. (Frankfurt: Suhrkamp Verlag, 1981).

5. Friedrich Meggendorfer, "Der schwere Alkoholismus," in *Handbuch der Erbkrankheiten,* ed. Arthur Gütt, vol. 3 (Berlin, 1940), p. 279.

6. Ibid., 278.

7. Ibid., 301.

8. Ibid.

9. Ibid., 299.

10. Ibid., 271; Theo Gläss, *Das Konto des Alkohols in der deutschen Volkswirtschaft* (Berlin, 1935), 13–17; F. Goesch, "Verbrauch alkoholischer Getränke in Deutschland, 1913–1938," *Forschungen zur Alkoholfrage* 48 (1940): 32.

11. W. Bracht, *Alkohol, Volk und Staat* (Berlin, 1941), 7ff.

12. E. Bruns, *Partei, Gesundheitsführung und Alkoholmissbrauch* (Berlin, 1938), 7ff.

13. Gläss, *Das Konto des Alkohols.*

14. Hans Reiter and Günther Hecht, *Genussgift, Leistung, Rasse* (Berlin, 1935); see especially Günther Hecht, "Alkoholmissbrauch und Rassenpolitik," 14–34.

15. Hans Reiter, "Alkohol, Nikotinmissbrauch und gesundes Volk," in ibid., 17.

16. Gerhardt Feuerstein, "Rauschgiftbekämpfung, ein wichtiges Interessengebiet der Gemeindeverwaltungen," *Die Alkoholfrage* (1936): 16ff.

17. *Die Alkoholfrage* (1934), 118ff., and 242ff.; *Die Alkoholfrage* (1935): 38ff. and 233ff.

18. *Die Alkoholfrage* (1935): 231; *Die Alkoholfrage* (1938), 94

19. K. Thode, "Trunksuchtsbekämpfung," *Die Alkoholfrage* (1935): 111.

20. See *Die Alkoholfrage* (1934): 58; and *Die Alkoholfrage* (1935): 43ff.

21. Ernst Rüdin and Arthur Gütt, "Der Begriff des schweren Alkoholismus im Gesetz zur Verhütung erbkranken Nachwuchses," *Die Alkoholfrage* (1935): 82; see also D. Kathe, "Alkohol und Rassenhygiene." *Die Alkoholfrage* (1937): 141ff.

22. K. Weymann, "Die Alkoholfrage und die Reform des Strafrechtes," *Die Alkoholfrage* (1933): 162.

23. F. Lenz, "Die Alkoholfrage in ihrer Bedeutung für die Rassenhygiene," in *Die Alkoholfrage* (1933): 175.

24. H. Nachtsheim, "Das Gesetz zur Verhütung erbkranken Nachwuchses aus 1933 in heutiger Sicht," *Deutsches Ärzteblatt* (1962): 1640–1644.

25. W. Fichtmuller, "Das Gesetz zur Verhütung erbkranker Nachwuchses 1933–1945" (Diss. med., Erlangen, 1972).

26. Meggendorfer, "Der schwere Alkoholismus," 436.

27. Thode, "Trunksuchtsbekämpfung," 118–120.

28. Meggendorfer, "Der schwere Alkoholismus," 359.

29. Werner Bracht, *Alkohol, Volk und Staat*, 94ff.

30. G. Baader, "Zur Ideologie des Sozialdarwinismus," in *Medizin und Nationalsozialismus*, ed. G. Baader and U. Schulz (Berlin, 1980), 39ff.

31. E. Rüdin, "Der Alkohol im Lebensprozess der Rasse," in *Politisch-anthropologische Revue* 2 (1903–1904): 553–566.

32. Ibid., 563.

33. Hecht, "Alkoholmissbrauch und Rassenpolitik," 30.

34. R. Kobelt, *Alkoholismus im neuen Recht* (Berlin, 1934), 23.

35. Thode, "Trunksuchtsbekämpfung," 110.

36. Ibid.

37. Hecht, "Alkoholmissbrauch und Rassenpolitik," 30.

38. Theo Gläss, "Zum Stand der alkoholgegnerischen Arbeit in Deutschland," *Forschungen zur Alkoholfrage* 42 (1934): 97–108; Theo Gläss, "Der Kampf gegen die Alkoholgefahren in Deutschland 1936/1937," *Forschungen zur Alkoholfrage* 45 (1937): 169–181.

39. G. Feuerstein, *Organisierte Suchtmittelbekämpfung—warum und in welcher Form* (Berlin, 1936).

40. Gläss, "Der Kampf gegen die Alkoholgefahren," 172.

41. Quoted by Theo Gläss, "Deutsche Arbeit gegen die Alkoholgefahren," *Forschungen zur Alkoholfrage* 49 (1941): 1.

42. Reiter, "Alkohol, Nikotinmissbrauch und gesundes Volk," 11.

43. H. Reiter, *Das Reichsgesundheitamt, 1933–39* (Berlin, 1939), 205.

44. O. Graf, "Akloholgefahren und seelische Gesundheit," *Die Genussgifte* (1940), 106.

45. O. Graf, "Neue Anschauungen über die Einwirkung des Alkoholgenusses auf die Arbeitsleistungen," *Alkoholfrage* (1937): 226.

46. Thode, "Trunksuchtsbekämpfung," 140.

47. E. Ley, "Der Kampf gegen die Genussgifte beginnt," *Alkoholfrage* (1939): 102.

48. W. Rüttig, "Rassenpflege und Alkoholmissbrauch," *Alkoholfrage* (1935): 7.

49. Conti-Aufruf, quoted in Gläss, "Deutsche Arbeit gegen die Alkoholgefahren," 2.

50. R. Hercod, "Krieg und Alkohol," *Alkoholfrage* (1939): 77ff.

51. O. Graf, *Trinkerfürsorge und Rauschgiftbekämpfung im Krieg* (Berlin, 1940).

52. W. Messer, "Zur Erfassung Alkoholkranker und Alkoholgefährdeter, besonders die sogenannte Früherfassung," *Die Volksgifte* (1942): 85ff.

53. Ibid., 89.

54. H. W. Kranz and S. Koller, *Die Gemeinschaftsunfähigen*, 2 vols. (Giessen, 1941).

55. Ibid., 75.

PART FOUR

———

Perspectives on Drinking
and Social History

FIFTEEN

From Fasting to Abstinence: The Origins of the American Temperance Movement

Joel Bernard

Writing in the late nineteenth century, the biographer of the English liberal reformer Richard Cobden explained his subject's enthusiasm for the pseudoscience of phrenology by remarking that "to accept phrenology to-day would stamp a man as unscientific, but to accept it in 1835 was a good sign of mental activity."[1] Something similar might be said of the movement to abolish the use of alcohol. Throughout most of the twentieth century the temperance movement has had the reputation of a cranky fad. But it was without question the most popular American mass movement of the nineteenth century, enlisting a variety of eminent and sensible men and women in a long-enduring national crusade. It therefore merits reexamination as to why so many mentally active people engaged so much energy in such an apparently —at least to modern eyes—unscientific venture.

Within the past decade social historians in particular have begun to detail both the extent of early American drinking and the broad appeal of the temperance movement. One provocative work has argued that widespread drinking in the "alcoholic republic" was intimately linked with the anxieties and aspirations of the new American nation.[2] Historians interested in the transition from a preindustrial to an industrial work ethic have discovered in the attempts of employers to instill temperance in their employees a key element in the transformation of work discipline.[3] Quantitative political historians have pointed to the importance of temperance beliefs in influencing voting behavior and even in reorienting the American party system.[4]

Scholars of the temperance movement itself have generally focused on the organizations that first arose in the 1820s to promote voluntary abstinence from spirits and on their successors that pressed for legal prohibition of all alcoholic beverages.[5] They have described the evolving tactics of the movement, investigated the social background of its supporters, and drawn inferences about its goals and motives. But they have been less concerned with exploring continuities between secular temperance attitudes and earlier legal and religious responses to drinking. In this regard they have accepted the premise of supporters of the movement that it represented a fundamentally new approach to an unprecedented problem. We are frequently told, for example, that earlier eras were untroubled by the moderate use of alcohol, even though virtually every American colony attempted to limit, if not prohibit, drinking among certain classes such as servants, apprentices, slaves, and Indians.[6] It has been suggested that the amount of drinking in early nineteenth-century America created a unique problem that the temperance movement arose to solve, even though religions as diverse as Islam, Buddhism, and Hinduism, widely separated temporally and geographically, have long imposed stringent controls on alcohol consumption among all or some of the faithful;[7] even though, as G. R. Owst notes, the prevailing vice of drunkenness was a staple of the "language of complaint" of medieval English preachers, who gave the impression that craftsmen got drunk "at least once a week";[8] and even though, in sixteenth-century Germany, there already existed a medical literature on alcoholism.[9]

This evidence, to cite only a few instances, suggests that we must not confuse the extent of deep concern about drinking—which in Christianity goes back at least to the Bible—with the specific tactics and ideology adopted by the American temperance movement. Rather than viewing the temperance movement as a self-evident response to an unprecedented social problem, we first need to clarify the religious —especially Protestant—rituals and beliefs that associate a variety of sins, including intemperate drinking, with abstinence from a range of things. Then we might see how the long-term evolution of these beliefs interacted with more historically specific problems and interests—in effect, how they were colored by, if not imposed by, the social landscape of nineteenth-century America.

This approach involves tracing historical attitudes toward the sin of intemperate drinking before showing how the particular virtue of abstinence from alcohol (temperance) was constructed to solve an old problem. In the first part of this essay I draw attention to the striking psychic (or emotional) continuities between earlier religious and later, more secular, attitudes toward drinking and abstinence. In the next part I suggest how these underlying emotional continuities found new intellectual justification by the early nineteenth century through a process akin to the evolutionary natural selection of species: they were more "fit" for the American social environment. I also suggest briefly how changing circumstances in the early republic led to novel tactics for the promotion of the new virtue of temperance.

1

It is frequently difficult to explain the original, vivid psychology of historically remote rituals that endure as routine observances for centuries. Dietary restrictions and other taboos have figured prominently among the beliefs of many religions, and they figured in the religious practices of early modern Europeans. The liturgical calendar of the Catholic church and its reformed Protestant offshoots consisted of annual cycles of fasting and feasting. These cycles explicitly commemorated the life of Jesus and the lives of the saints, and they implicitly conformed to the seasonal rhythms of nature. But above all else, the alternation of holy mourning and celebration ritualized the humble psychological comportment of the faithful toward God, providing expressions of the belief in his direct interventions in human affairs. Seasons of thanksgiving expressed the belief that good fortune was the divine reward for human righteousness; seasons of fasting and prayer acknowledged that affliction was divine punishment for human sin.[10]

The most direct access to the psychological sources of fasting (or thanksgiving) is provided not by annual holy days but by the "occasional" days proclaimed by ecclesiastical authorities or civil magistrates for special reasons. These proclamations often set out explicitly reasons for which fasting was felt to be appropriate. Frequently a fast-day proclamation recited the nature of the recent afflictions, which it acknowledged as divinely ordained punishments for enumerated sins. The sins, or "provoking evils," varied somewhat within the range of biblical precepts as modified by centuries of canon law and ecclesiastical practice. Examples might be drawn from virtually every European country and its New World colonies. One proclamation from the Dutch New Netherland colony in 1648, for example, recited "sad and doleful tidings from Europe and the Northern and Southern parts of America, severe inundations and floods, fevers whereby thousands are swept away and scarce any to bury the dead, hurricanes, shipwrecks, and famine." It went on to condemn "all iniquity, all false measures and wicked practices, all blasphemy and licentiousness, drunkenness, rioting, swearing, lying, cheating, profanation of God's most holy name and Sabbath," and to declare that "nothing else can be concluded and inferred than that the Holy One of Israel, the Almighty God, being justly provoked to anger and wrath, threatens us for our unrighteous deeds with a just reward,—a reward from the treasure of wrath and righteous vengeance."[11] In 1622, to take an example from another country, the governors of the Virginia Company in England laid blame for the Indian massacre at Jamestown on the "heavy hand of All-mightie God." They believed that the massacre was punishment visited by God on the colonists for "those two enormous excesses of apparell and drinkeing."[12] Accordingly, the Virginia assembly decreed that March 22 "be yeerly solemnized as holliday" to commemorate the deliverance of the colony from an even-greater tragedy. Twenty-two years later a second Indian massacre and the resulting war led the assembly to declare a series of fasts, "the last Wednesday of every month." The idea of monthly fasts on Wednesday had doubtless been suggested by the practice of Parliament, which had initiated a series of monthly fasts two years earlier, at the beginning of the English civil war.[13] In 1703, to take one final example from a region well known for its piety, the royal governor of Massachusetts issued a "Declaration against Prophaneness and Immoralities." He acknowledged the "evi-dent hand and anger of the Great God" as revealed in a series of defeats inflicted by the Indians. He attributed these afflictions to the prevalence of profanity, neglect of public worship, violations of the Sabbath, and especially the "Excessive Tipling and Drinking, which like a Flood even Drowns much of Christianity in several Places." The governor called for a "General REFORMATION," and he set a solemn day of public fasting as a sign of repentance.[14]

The renunciation enjoined by civil and religious authorities on days of fasting and prayer varied, and in view of this variation fasting ought to be considered to have been a predominating mood rather than an invariable custom. The authorities enjoined attendance at church on fast days, as on the Sabbath, and required all citizens to abstain from their normal occupations. It was expected that appropriately somber dress would be worn outside the home and that penitent private reflec-tions and family prayer within the household would accompany these public duties. The public obligations of both annual and occasional fasts were enforced by ecclesiastical or civil courts. So were certain dietary restrictions, although these injunctions were by no means as extreme as those of the ascetic virtuosi of the early and medieval church.[15] Strict fasting—often total abstinence from food and drink during the entire day—was most likely to be practiced as a personal observance for some private cause. More usually fasting entailed the avoidance of certain kinds of food. The main legally enforced prohibi-tion in both Catholic and Anglican countries was that against meat. During Lent, the most prominent annual season of fasting in the Catholic and Anglican churches, authorities enjoined abstinence from meat and sometimes "white meats" (cheese, milk, and eggs); in six-teenth- and seventeenth-century England butchers and victuallers were bound by heavy recognizances not to slaughter or sell meat on the weekly "fish days," Friday and Saturday. Commonly, however, the ex-pectation was that one would take smaller quantities of plain food and drink, simply prepared and possibly cold or reheated. Puritans in New England, for example, enforced no legal dietary restrictions but more strictly enforced the public duties of fast days and the Sabbath, which they insisted—contrary to Anglican writers—was not a feast but a fast.[16]

The ritual of fasting and prayer, either occasionally proclaimed or annually observed, provides one insight into a premodern mentality that viewed natural events, such as earthquakes or droughts, and social occurrences, such as wars or economic depressions, as divinely or-dained. Underlying the rituals and the rationales offered for them was a common psychological reaction to stress. When Christians were anx-ious about their environment, they looked to the communal ritual of atonement through fasting. The connection between sin, suffering, and repentance expressed through self-denial was a form of theodicy, an emotionally satisfying ritual that reaffirmed divine justice. Be-lievers mortified themselves through dietary self-denial to placate God. By explaining suffering or evil in terms of human transgression of divine law, a theodicy left the order of divine justice intact. Contri-tion expiated sin and restored the preafflictive state of the world.[17]

2

To understand the evolution of this mental attitude by the nineteenth-century, we need to pass from an appreciation of underlying emotional similarities to a grasp of historically overlying differences. Two analy-tically separate problems are involved. First, how did awareness of the particular sin of intemperate drinking gain privileged status in Amer-ica during the nineteenth century, dominating all other sins? Second, how did the intellectual rationale and appropriate ritual for condemn-ing the sin of intemperate drinking in fasting and prayer evolve into the new rationales and rituals of the temperance movement? If days of fasting and prayer were appropriate responses to social disorder in an era when various sins (intemperance among others) were considered causes for the wrath of God, how did intemperance itself become the object of a concern so compelling that it enlisted hundreds of thou-sands in specific temperance organizations separate from churches?

Most historians of nineteenth-century temperance assert that the problem of drinking got worse.[18] Although there is no doubt that the amount of alcohol consumed in early nineteenth-century America was high, there is also much evidence that American drinking had always been high, was perceived as a chronic problem well before the temperance movement, and, within certain limits, is perceived as such today. The texts of fast-day proclamations and ministers' jeremiads, the preambles of colonial laws concerning the sale of alcohol, and the proceedings of colonial courts all cite drinking as a source of concern. The intensity with which these concerns were expressed suggests that well before the nineteenth century many men already believed that the amount of drinking done by their contemporaries was excessive and unparalleled. In preambles to the Massachusetts Bay Colony laws alone there were at least a dozen complaints of the prevalence of the "crying sin of drunkenness" between 1635 and 1680.[19] In contemporary America six special reports on alcohol and health presented to Congress between 1971 and 1987 have demonstrated the continuing high proportion of accidents, violent acts, and health problems attributable to alcoholism.[20]

Historians of temperance have too often confused the short-term perceptions of their subjects with the historical long-term. The gravity of any social problem is a matter of relative judgment that depends on men and women's brief experience of the past. A change in the amount of drinking done in America during the nineteenth century was indeed a compelling motive in the founding of the movement. But the fundamental cause of the movement was a change in perception. The mentality that sought divine causes for afflictive events and sought communal responses in churches and religious rituals evolved into a mentality that sought naturalistic explanations for the same events—and ultimately into one that today seeks economic or psychological determinants of the same phenomena. Just as the logic of one era dictated fast days, so that of another era indicated temperance movements, and that of our own creates helping professions to staff social outreach programs.

The general contours of this change are familiar from histories of the rise of the natural sciences, but their implications for social beliefs have been somewhat less explored. Changes in the observance of fasting offer important evidence of similar effects in the world of social explanation. Fast days became annual holidays declared by secular law, mere gestures toward divine control of human events.[21] Whereas formerly it had been sin that provoked God to send social afflictions, increasingly the empirical associations between affliction and sin (now viewed as vicious behavior) were seen as causally determinate. Vice *caused* social and personal misery. This mental reorientation impelled the creation of more economical versions of the traditional Christian vocabulary of sin, versions that had survived more stringent empirical scrutiny.[22]

One feature of the social landscape that impelled this economized vocabulary was the final legal severance of church and state. The abolition of most colonial religious establishments legally sanctioned the existing social fact of denominational competition and altered the influence of organized religion on the state—although New England maintained for almost a half a century after the Revolution the fiction of denominational equality in its "Protestant" establishments. By the last quarter of the eighteenth century it had become common in America to conflate the political and economic vocabularies of republicanism and liberalism with those of Christian sin and redemption.[23] During the 1780s and 1790s new republican legislatures showed little reluctance to use the powers of the state to suppress immoral behavior. In this Protestant republican tradition Christian morality was recast into republican form and justified as the necessary bulwark of popular government. During the decades following the Revolution virtually every state renewed (and sometimes strengthened) its laws against Sabbath breaking, drunkenness, and profanity.[24]

Denominational equality impelled some organizational innovation, for if the church was no longer, even in theory, coextensive with the state, how were the injunctions of religious morality to remain part of daily life? A *religious* problem pondered for millennia by every ecclesiastical establishment in history had in the United States become a *political* problem following the legal separation of church and state. Sporadically, new quasi-religious, quasi-secular organizations emerged, implicitly attempting to surmount theological or ecclesiastical differences, uniting the virtuous to bring pressure to bear on the state. In 1790, for example, the Reverend Nathanael Emmons helped form the Society for the Reformation of Morals in Franklin, Massachusetts. He warned its members that "intemperance, prodigality, luxury, and debauchery not only violate the laws of religion and virtue" but also "effectually [sap] the foundation of freedom, and completely [prepare] a people for the shackles of slavery." If sin flourished, a republic died; if sin were reformed, a republic flourished. A little more than a decade later, Lyman Beecher, a recent Yale graduate, formed a similar society among his parishioners in East Hampton, New York. He declared that "an association of the sober, virtuous part of the community, if that union become extensive, will have irresistible influence to stigmatize crimes, and to form correctly that opinion which is known to possess such influence over the minds of men." The new, more specific aims of these associations amounted to the mutual avowal of a lower Protestant common denominator than theology: a common moral agenda precipitated from differing beliefs.[25]

These local societies for the "reformation of manners" or the "suppression of vice and immorality" were transitional organizations be-

tween churches and single-aim temperance associations.[26] The creation
of a national network of Congregational and Presbyterian churches
fulfilled one necessary condition for turning isolated precedents such
as Emmons's and Beecher's into a national movement. The rise of party
conflict and the outbreak of the War of 1812 provided other necessary
conditions. During and after the war more than a hundred local moral
societies were formed with the aim of compelling the observance of
moral laws.

Moral societies were an odd mixture of voluntarism and coercion.
Voluntary in membership and sensitive to the importance of public
opinion, they nonetheless raised a storm of controversy when they
attempted to supplement law enforcement by informing on other citizens. In their addresses and annual reports they often juxtaposed the
anachronistic rhetoric of the fast day with an emerging naturalistic
condemnation of vice. In 1813, for example, some citizens of Bath,
Maine, asserted that "iniquity abounds, and our country groans beneath the rebukes of the righteous providence of God." They formed a
society "for Discountenancing and Suppressing Public Vices" to discourage immorality legally and by personal example.[27] Although its
membership was voluntary, the society aimed to compel observance of
morality by pressuring local magistrates to enforce existing laws, by
closing down illegal or disorderly taverns, by punishing those who
traveled on the Sabbath, and by fining public swearers. Moreover,
many of these moral societies urged their members to drink moderately, or even to abstain from distilled spirits. One of them, the Massachusetts Society for the Suppression of Intemperance, was the first
organization to focus uniquely on the problem of drinking.[28]

Increasingly justifications for the suppression of intemperance involved recasting as "reasonable," or even "scientific," attitudes toward
sin that had formerly been justified with reference to the authority of
the Bible, the canons of the church, and the secular laws derived from
them. The most important aspect of this new attribution of naturalistic
social meaning to morality was the willingness to theorize about intemperate drinking as the primary (or secondary) cause of social problems
such as poverty, crime, and disease. For millennia moralists had decried
drunkenness and asserted that many drunkards impoverished themselves, committed crimes, and died of drink. But in a God-centered
world they had not sought to show that drinking "caused" poverty,
crime, and disease, which were contingent facts of the divine order. By
the first quarter of the nineteenth century, however, an attenuated but
empirically powerful version of religious morality converged on a
quasi-scientific attitude toward social problems. For example, after pursuing various inquiries into the sources of social misery, a secular

society formed in New York City "for the prevention of pauperism" declared in 1818 that intemperate drinking "in relation to poverty and vice, may be emphatically styled, the *Cause of Causes.*[29]

There were several converging elements in the growing belief that intemperate drinking was the primary cause of social misery. The main requirement for the successful (that is, popularly appealing) transformation of a religious theodicy into a secular ideology was that it meet the needs of a variety of social groups—needs that were only partially determined by economic interests. Instead, different groups viewed particular professional, gender, and class dilemmas through a common lens that focused on intemperate drinking. It was the superiority of the paradigm of intemperance in explaining an array of social problems—from the most specific personal ones to the broadest national ones—that ensured its health and long, if controversial, life in America during the nineteenth century.

One cornerstone of the new ideology was medicine. At the beginning of the nineteenth century medical science was poised between the grand systemic disease theories of the Enlightenment and the germ theory of the late nineteenth century. Eclecticism and casual environmentalism were the symptoms of professional disarray. It was Dr. Benjamin Rush whose well-known *Inquiry into the Effects of Spirituous Liquors,* first published in 1784, helped to particularize the relationship between drinking and disease. One of Rush's most famous bequests to the temperance movement was his "Moral and Physical Thermometer," which expressed in ideographic form the medical meaning of the sin of intemperance (Figure 15.1). On Rush's moral thermometer religious virtues and vices were graduated and correlated with physical conditions as well as secular rewards and punishments. Thus, if a man habitually drank milk and water, Rush implied, he would enjoy health, wealth, and a long life; if he habitually drank spirits, he would finish in the poorhouse or hospital—or on the gallows. Accordingly, the difference between temperance and intemperance was characterized in a way that, broadly speaking, conformed physiology with morality. Increasingly doctors could declare that intemperate drinking was a major predisposing cause of disease.[30]

Another cornerstone of temperance ideology was provided by the pioneering American studies in social statistics. The nineteenth century was the great era of institutional reform, and reformers found in almshouses, penitentiaries, and hospitals large populations with which to test moral intuitions about the causes of social disorder. Doctors, following in the footsteps of Rush, discovered the ravages of drinking in their hospital patients. Public officials gathered statistics to show the high proportion of those imprisoned or receiving relief who were problem

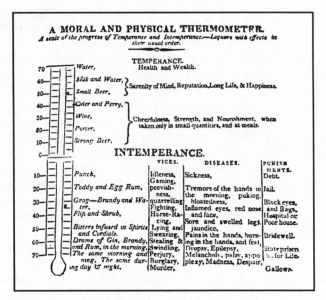

Fig. 15.1. From Dr. Benjamin Rush, *An Inquiry into the
Effects of Spirituous Liquors on the Human Body,
to which is added a moral and physical thermometer*
(Boston, 1790).

drinkers. Well-researched and widely publicized reports on the pauper
systems of Massachusetts and New York, in 1821 and 1824, emphasized
the role of excessive drinking in creating indigence. One report from
Portland, Maine, in 1816 surveyed the town's poor and determined that
of 85 paupers in the local almshouse, 71 had been reduced to indigence
"in consequence" of the intemperance of the head of their household;
of the 118 paupers supplied in their homes, more than one half were
alleged to be poor for the same reason. By 1821 the anonymous author
of a laudatory article on the penitentiary system in the *North American
Review* invoked conventional wisdom to remark that "the unrestricted
manufacture and sale of ardent spirits is almost the sole cause of all the
suffering, the poverty, and the crime to be found in this country."[31]

3

Viewing intemperance as the major American social problem was not
the same as proclaiming the means of solving it, but it was the essential
precondition. The transformation of sectarian and reactionary moral
societies into more broadly based temperance societies was initiated by

a popular evangelical revolution beginning in the 1820s. Having temporarily renounced coercion, the leaders of the movement found new organizational and tactical outlets for their energies. Reacting against partial solutions to intemperance, they turned the goals of the movement away from the suppression of intemperance (a vice) and toward the promotion of temperance—defined shortly as total abstinence from alcohol. The details of this shift, involving parochial issues and organizations especially in New England, need not concern us here. However, once the new ideology was given explicit definition and organizational form, it aroused an enormous national response.

This response was fueled by widespread perceptions of social disorder. Renewed European immigration, westward migration, growing cities, and changes in the structure and scale of work relations all created a fertile soil for social anxiety. Measurable social disorder and drunkenness may or may not have worsened with the expansion of settlement and the growth of industrial capacity, but unquestionably there were brutal and difficult conditions of life in many places. There were also extremely marked national fluctuations of poverty and crime —especially during economic depressions, when men and women were unemployed, and during wars and their aftermaths, when men were first brought into army camps and later demobilized. Reformers pointed quite cogently to the vast expansion of whiskey, and later beer, production, which made alcohol readily available to the poorest and most desperate classes.

Yet it was not in those areas where the problem was most acute that temperance organizations were strongest, either on the frontier or in the cities. Instead, it was in the long-settled towns and villages of New England, New York, and eventually the Midwest—the types of communities where religion had always flourished. As a quasi-religious ideology, temperance appealed to tens of thousands of men and women who also found in it the context for secular self-mastery. Ministers, faced with religious diversity and always preoccupied with the need to shore up virtue, initially sounded the call of moral suasion but were led back to politics by their zealous followers. Doctors still ignorant of germ theory but sensing the role of environmental factors in the etiology of disease stressed the value of abstinence to health. Employers looking to create a docile work force saw in temperance the means to instill labor discipline—and reassure themselves that abstinence guaranteed and justified their own success. Women, accorded a new status of moral superiority and familial authority by writers on domesticity, yet whose continuing inferior legal status was all the more anomalous in an egalitarian age, fixed on alcohol as the major source of marital and familial discord and found in temperance societies an outlet for their political energies. Nativists who disliked the Irish and German immigrants who were changing the complexion of American cities fixed on immigrants' cultural propensity to drink whiskey or beer. Each group, and any person who had witnessed or experienced the tragedy that alcohol wreaked on family and friends, found in alcohol a special lens through which to view misery.

Intemperance "explained" what went wrong in a society of vast potential that still suffered from age-old social problems. Voluntary temperance, and later legal prohibition, proclaimed solutions that would reform society. Had fasting formerly been proclaimed during periods of personal or social anxiety? Then abstinence from alcohol would cure the disorder and misery so prominently displayed in an industrializing society. Had fasting formerly guaranteed the successful conclusion of uncertain personal or social ventures? Then abstinence from alcohol provided psychic assurance of the fruition of personal and social goals in a heterogeneous, mobile society. The taboo against alcohol was a specific, empirically grounded form of fasting made habitual and justified rationally.

An evolutionary dynamic, at once organizational and tactical, informed the subsequent responses of reformers once the fundamental paradigm of total abstinence had been fixed. At every subsequent period after the formation of the first moral societies, temperance advocates had before them the example of the last organizational effort to solve the problem—an effort that had invariably failed. Broad-gauged moral coercion, voluntary moral suasion of drinkers, state laws banning sale and manufacture of alcohol, local option, state prohibition amendments, revivalistic psychodramas of conversion, women's nonviolent direct action, fraternal organizations, political parties, and extrapolitical pressure groups all were touted as new initiatives that mobilized new groups around new tactics after old tactics had failed. Each new initiative was spurred by real crises (such as World War I) or by the recurrent pseudo-crises of electoral politics. Prohibition climbed the ladder of American federal government—town, county, state, and national—retreating one step before advancing two more, until it came to the top: a national constitutional amendment, passed during a world war, to ban the manufacture and sale of all alcoholic beverages for consumption. Then, after a little more than a decade, Prohibition collapsed, the victim of another unprecedented national catastrophe whose very magnitude eroded the perpetually shifting base of its popular support and revealed the insufficiencies of the remedy it proposed. The paradigm could no longer be extended. Like a balloon inflated beyond its capacity, it burst. Prohibition did not bring about a social millennium.

The modern origins of mass organizations to prohibit the use of alcohol lay in this perpetually reinvigorated version of an ancient Judeo-Christian theodicy of suffering. If to modern eyes the explanation was fatally tainted with moralism, we might reflect that our own views of the causes of social misery—to say nothing of our knowledge of the causes and cures of alcoholism—are debatable enough and derive in part from the exhaustion, by historical trial and error, of earlier explanations. The moralistic explanation of social problems was one step along an endless road of social demystification, looking, however partially or incompletely, to the real world for its explanations and no longer to supernatural forces. As John Morley, the biographer of Richard Cobden, suggested for phrenology, if so many mentally active men and women of the nineteenth century committed themselves wholeheartedly to doing away with alcohol, it was in part because temperance and prohibition were, in their own time, "scientific."

NOTES

1. John Morley, *The Life of Richard Cobden* (Boston, 1881), 27.

2. W. J. Rorabaugh, *The Alcoholic Republic: An American Tradition* (New York, 1979).

3. Paul E. Johnson, *A Shopkeeper's Millennium: Society and Revivals in Rochester, New York, 1815–1837* (New York, 1978); Anthony F. C. Wallace, *Rockdale: The Growth of an American Village in the Early Industrial Revolution* (New York, 1978); Allen Dawley, *Class and Community: The Industrial Revolution in Lynn* (Cambridge, 1976); Dawley and Paul Faler, "Working-Class Culture and Politics in the Industrial Revolution: Sources of Loyalism and Rebellion," *Journal of Social History* 9 (1976): 466–480; Faler, "Cultural Aspects of the Industrial Revolution: Lynn Massachusetts Shoemakers and Industrial Morality, 1826–1860," *Labor History* 15 (1974): 367–394; Bruce Laurie, " 'Nothing on Compulsion': Life Styles of Philadelphia Artisans, 1820–1850," *Labor History* 15 (1974): 337–366.

4. Ronald P. Formisano, *The Birth of Mass Political Parties: Michigan, 1827–1861* (Princeton, 1971); Richard J. Jensen, *The Winning of the Midwest: Social and Political Conflict, 1888–1896* (Chicago, 1971); Paul Kleppner, *The Cross of Culture: A Social Analysis of Midwestern Politics, 1850–1900*, 2d ed. (New York, 1970).

5. John A. Krout, *The Origins of Prohibition* (New York, 1925); Joseph R. Gusfield, *Symbolic Crusade: Status Politics and the American Temperance Movement*, 2d ed. (Urbana, Ill., 1986); Norman H. Clark, *Deliver Us from Evil: An Interpretation of American Prohibition* (New York, 1976); Ian R. Tyrrell, *Sobering Up: From Temperance to Prohibition in Antebellum America, 1800–1860* (Westport, Conn., 1979); Robert L. Hampel, *Temperance and Prohibition in Massachusetts, 1813–1852* (Ann Arbor, Mich., 1982).

6. For the restrictions on these groups in colonial New York alone, see the

collection of statutes relating to liquor in New York State Commissioner of
Excise, *First Report* (Albany and New York, 1897), 275–628 passim.

7. For an excellent anthropological overview of drinking practices, see
Beliefs, Behaviors, and Alcoholic Beverages: A Cross-Cultural Survey, ed. Mac Marshall (Ann Arbor, Mich., 1979).

8. G. R. Owst, *Literature and the Pulpit in Medieval England* (Cambridge,
1933), 364, 425–441 passim; see also Keith Thomas, "Work and Leisure in
Pre-Industrial Society" and discussion, *Past and Present* 29 (1964): 50–66.

9. Diethelm, "Chronic Alcoholism of Northern Europe (a Historical
Study)," *Bibliotheca Psychiatrica et Neurologica* 127 (1965): 29–39.

10. On fasting and prayer, see especially William DeLoss Love, Jr., *The Fast
and Thanksgiving Days of New England* (Boston and New York, 1895), which
contains an exhaustive calendar of fast days in the American colonies
(464–515). See also Richard P. Gildrie, "The Ceremonial Puritan Days of
Humiliation and Thanksgiving," *New England Historical and Genealogical Register*
136 (1982): 3–16, and the briefer discussion in Charles Hambrick-Stowe, *The
Practice of Piety: Puritan Devotional Disciplines in Seventeenth-Century New England*
(Chapel Hill, N.C., 1982), 100–101. Among the manuals describing the rituals
for fasting (and thanksgiving) are those of the Anglicans Robert Nelson, *A
Companion for the Festivals and Fasts of the Church of England: With Collects and
Prayers for Each Solemnity,* 10th ed. (London, 1717), and Lewis Bayly, *The Practice
of Piety,* 53d ed. (Boston, 1718). Puritans differed from Anglicans in their
rejection of all but occasional fasting for particular cause; but in fact the
observance of an annual fast day in the spring became customary in New
England. See Love, *Fast and Thanksgiving Days,* Gildrie, "Ceremonial Puritan
Days," Hambrick-Stowe, *Practice of Piety,* and Cotton Mather, *Ratio Disciplinae
Fratrum Nov-Anglorum...* (Boston, 1726). Fuller information about English
fasts may be found in the calendar of royal proclamations by Robert Steele
(supervised by James Ludovic Lindsay Crawford), "A Bibliography of Royal
Proclamations of the Tudor and Stuart Sovereigns...1485–1714," in *Bibliotheca Lindesiana,* vols. 5 and 6 (Oxford, 1910), and Crawford, "Handlist
of Proclamations Issued by Royal and Other Constitutional Authorities,
1714–1910...," in *Bibliotheca Lindesiana,* vol. 8 (Wigan, Eng., 1913). Information about colonial fasts outside New England must be gathered from the
various collections of colonial statutes and from ecclesiastical and church
records as well as from contemporary diaries and journals. For Virginia,
however, see the collection in *Virginia Magazine of History and Biography* 32
(1924): 8–15n. Excellent overviews of the practice of fasting in Christian and
non-Christian contexts may be found in articles by J. A. MacCulloch and A. J.
Maclean in *Encyclopedia of Religion and Ethics,* 13 vols., ed. James Hastings (New
York, 1913–1927) 5:759–765, 765–771.

Christian fasting was primarily, although not always, a form of retrospective
atonement, but it might also be prospective—an oblation, like a sacrifice, to
ensure the success of some hazardous or uncertain venture, such as the launching of a military expedition or the ordination of a minister. My emphasis on the
penitential character of fasting does not exhaust its varied meaning in different
cultures and even in different periods of Christianity. On the development of

Christian fasting through the Middle Ages, see Caroline Walker Bynum, *Holy Feast and Holy Fast: The Religious Significance of Food to Medieval Women* (Berkeley and Los Angeles, 1987) 31–69. In other cultures a wide variety of objects, substances, and types of behavior are tabooed, either periodically or categorically. An encyclopedic discussion of various cultural taboos and restrictions is contained in Edward Westermarck, *The Origin and Development of the Moral Ideas*, 2 vols. (London, 1908), especially 2: 290–345 on dietary restrictions. A recent attempt to explain the concept of taboo is Mary Douglas, *Purity and Danger: An Analysis of the Concepts of Pollution and Taboo* (London, 1978).

11. Love, *Fast and Thanksgiving Days*, 169–170.

12. *The Records of the Virginia Company of London...*, 4 vols., ed. Susan Myra Kingsbury (Washington, D.C., 1906–1935), 3: 666.

13. William Waller Hening, *The Statutes at Large; Being a Collection of all the Laws of Virginia...*, 13 vols. (1819–1823; rpt., Charlottesville, Va., 1969) 1: 123, 177, 206, 263, 289–290, 459–460. On the English fasts, see *Stuart Royal Proclamations*, ed. James F. Larkin, volume 2, *Royal Proclamations of King Charles I, 1625–1646* (Oxford, 1983), 734–736, 734n, 758–760.

14. "A Declaration against Prophaneness and Immoralities" is bound at the end of Samuel Willard, *Israel's True Safety* (Boston, 1704).

15. Bynum, *Holy Feast and Holy Fast*, passim.

16. On the performance of fasting, see Nelson, *Companion for the Festivals and Fasts*, 433, 444–452; Bayly, *Practice of Piety*, 255–268; Mather, *Ratio Disciplinae*, 186–189. Love, *Fast and Thanksgiving Days*, 410–429.

17. The term *theodicy* is usually used to describe an argument vindicating divine government in spite of the existence of evil. In expanding the term to include particular rituals of repentance, I am arguing that the same psychology that underlies the characteristic rationale of a theodicy is expressed in the ritual of the fast day and in derivative movements. My argument depends most centrally on Max Weber, "The Social Psychology of the World Religions," in *From Max Weber: Essays in Sociology*, ed. and trans. H. H. Gerth and C. Wright Mills (New York, 1946), 267–301, esp. 274, 278. On the concept of theodicy, see William Fulton, "Theodicy," in Hastings, *Encyclopedia of Religion and Ethics*, 12: 289–291. I also draw on the work of Anthony Wallace on revitalization movements—attempts to construct more satisfying cultures in the wake of general perceptions of social stress. See Wallace, "Revitalization Movements," *American Anthropologist* 58 (1956): 264–281, and idem, "Paradigmatic Processes in Culture Change," in *Rockdale*, 477–485.

18. Rorabaugh, *Alcoholic Republic*; Clark, *Deliver Us from Evil*. For a different view, see Tyrrell, *Sobering Up*, 28.

19. See *Records of the Governor and Colony of the Massachusetts Bay in New England*, 5 vols., ed. Nathaniel B. Shurtleff (Boston, 1854), 1:213, 271; 2:100, 171, 257; 3:184, 359, 425; 4 (1): 418; 4 (2): 37, 297, 462; 5:211. Comparable concerns in New York are collected in the first report of the New York State Commissioner of Excise, cited in note 6 above.

20. U. S. Department of Health, Education, and Welfare [Health and Human Services], *First [through Sixth] Special Report to the U. S. Congress on Alcohol and Health* (Rockville, Md., 1971–1987).

21. Love, *Fast and Thanksgiving Days*, 251–255, 295–298. On the general problem of rationalization of thought and secularization of religion, see: Weber, "Social Psychology of the World Religions," esp. 293–294; Anthony Wallace, *Religion: An Anthropological View* (New York, 1960), 255–270; and more generally Thomas Kuhn, *The Structure of Scientific Revolutions*, 2d ed. (Chicago, 1970). Although directed toward other ends, Kuhn, "Concepts of Cause in the Development of Physics," in idem, *The Essential Tension: Selected Studies in Scientific Tradition and Change* (Chicago, 1977), 21–30, is very suggestive.

22. Although his dating varies significantly from mine, Perry Miller argued for an analogous change in the New England jeremiad from externally caused sin to internal guilt. See Miller, *The New England Mind: From Colony to Province* (Cambridge, Mass., 1953), esp. 27–39. The sermon form of the jeremiad was one expression of the mentality I am describing, although it was hardly unique to New England. See, for example, Michael McGiffert, "God's Controversy with Jacobean England," *American Historical Review* 88 (1983): 1151–1174.

23. A large body of literature details the eighteenth-century conflation of religious and secular political vocabularies: Perry Miller, "From the Covenant to the Revival," in idem, *Nature's Nation* (Cambridge, Mass., 1967), 90–129; Nathan D. Hatch, *The Sacred Cause of Liberty: Republican Thought and the Millennium in Revolutionary New England* (New Haven, Conn., 1977); Edmund S. Morgan, "The Puritan Ethic and the American Revolution," *William and Mary Quarterly*, 3d ser., 24 (1967): 3–43. The well-known parallel evolution in economic attitudes was first enunciated in Max Weber, *The Protestant Ethic and the Spirit of Capitalism*, trans. Talcott Parsons (New York, 1958). For England, see Joyce Appleby, *Economic Thought and Ideology in Seventeenth-Century England* (Princeton, N.J., 1978); for colonial America, see J. E. Crowley, *"This Sheba, Self": The Conceptualization of Economic Life in Eighteenth-Century America* (Baltimore, 1974); for the new republic, see Drew McCoy, *The Elusive Republic: Political Economy in Jeffersonian America* (Chapel Hill, N.C., 1980).

24. The locus classicus of the secularization of the Anglo-American law of religion and morality by the eighteenth century is "Of Offences Against God and Religion," in idem, William Blackstone, *Commentaries on the Laws of England*, 4:41–65, and a good instance of its influence in postrevolutionary American jurisprudence is the compilation of charges to juries by Pennsylvania judge Jacob Rush (brother of Benjamin Rush), *Charges and Extracts of Charges on Moral and Religious Subjects* (Philadelphia, 1803). A general treatment of the laws regarding morality, focusing especially on Massachusetts, that borrows its structure from Blackstone is Nathan Dane, *A General Abridgement and Digest of American Law...*, 8 vols. (Boston, 1823–1824) 6:664–683. Among the many examples of state laws are *New York Laws* (1788), chap. 42; *Pennsylvania Act of 22 April 1794*. A summary of colonial and postcolonial Virginia is presented in Arthur P. Scott, *Criminal Law in Colonial Virginia* (Chicago, 1930), 357, 361–367.

25. Nathanael Emmons, "The Evil Effects of Sin," in *The Works of Nathanael Emmons, D.D....*, 6 vols., ed. Jacob Ide (Boston, 1842), 2:51–52; Lyman Beecher, *The Practicability of Suppressing Vice, by Means of Societies Instituted for that Purpose...* (New London, Conn., 1804), 9. Such organizations were by no means new. They traced their lineage to English societies for the reformation

of manners of the late seventeenth and early eighteenth centuries. On these, see Dudley W. R. Bahlman, *The Moral Revolution of 1688* (New Haven, Conn., 1957).

26. No secondary work treats moral societies in their full national scope. For contemporary examples, see *Proceedings of a Convention of Moral Societies in the County of Litchfield* (New Haven, Conn., 1815); *Transactions of a Convention of Delegates from Several Moral Societies in the State of New York at Albany* (Albany, N.Y., 1819); New Jersey Society for the Suppression of Vice and Immorality, *Constitution* (New Brunswick, N.J., 1818).

27. Jesse Appleton, *A Discourse Delivered at Bath, May 11, 1813, before the Society for Discountenancing and Suppressing Public Vice...* (Boston, 1813), 22.

28. *Constitution of the Massachusetts Society for the Suppression of Intemperance and Report of the Board of Counsel...* (Boston, 1813).

29. New York Society for the Prevention of Pauperism, *Report of a Committee on the Subject of Pauperism* (New York, 1818), 3–4.

30. See, among many others, Reuben Dimond Massey, *An Address on Ardent Spirits Read before the New Hampshire Medical Society...* (Boston, 1829).

31. Massachusetts, General Court, Committee on Pauper Laws, *Report [of the committee to whom was referred consideration of the Pauper Laws of this commonwealth]* (Boston? 1821), esp. 9, 15, 17, 24, 31–32; "Report of the Secretary of State in 1824 on the Relief and Settlement of the Poor," in Board of Charities of the State of New York, *34th Annual Report*, 3 vols. (Albany, N.Y. 1901) 1:939–943, 950, 965, 970, 983, 986, 987, 994, 1004, 1008–1009, 1017, 1021, 1049; *Report of the Committee of the Society in Portland for Suppressing Vice and Immorality, made at the Fourth Annual Meeting of the Society...* (Portland, Me., 1816); *North American Review*, n.s., 4 (1821): 437.

SIXTEEN

The Paradox of Temperance: Blacks and the Alcohol Question in Nineteenth-Century America

Denise Herd

Alcoholic beverages occupied a key symbolic role in nineteenth-century America. They were the seat of a variety of cultural meanings rooted in the social perception of their psychoactive and behavioral effects. As Harry Levine's well-known paper illustrates, the nature of the sociocultural context was critical in determining whether alcohol was to be regarded as a "good creature" or as a "demon."[1] Each characterization of liquor was tied to the social context and to a particular image of the self.

During the same period African slaves were of immense political and symbolic significance in American culture. Not only was slavery the most inflammatory and long-standing political controversy of the century, but the strikingly different physical appearance and cultural background of Africans gave rise to the expression of a variety of cultural fears and hidden fantasies in Anglo-American culture. Depending on the ideological and social context, blacks were regarded as the epitome of Christian piety and humility or as raving, untamable savages.[2]

The following essay is an attempt to look at the ways in which symbolic characterizations of beverage alcohol and race came together in the nineteenth-century antialcohol movements. The major strains of social thought expressed during the period suggest that the metaphorical synthesis of the two issues gave rise to the two dominant, and yet paradoxical, images of alcoholic beverages characteristic of nineteenth-century alcohol control movements—"alcohol the enslaver" versus "alcohol the disinhibitor." The first summarized the addiction concept of man as a victim of a powerful tempter and master; the second focused on the power of alcohol to release the violent, uncivilized savage within.

CONFLICTING IMAGES OF BLACKS AND ALCOHOL IN THE ANTEBELLUM PERIOD

In the early nineteenth century the ideology concerning blacks and alcohol use was extremely ambiguous. On the one hand, there was a long-standing belief that drunkenness led to disorder and rebellion in the black population. Restrictions on blacks' ability to use or trade in alcoholic beverages and to frequent taverns were incorporated into legal codes as part of the machinery of control to prevent slave uprisings and militancy. The sentiments that inspired antiliquor legislation for blacks are suggested by the colonial statutes of New Jersey, which forbade whites to sell or trade in rum with blacks. It was surmised that the "selling of rum to Negroes" was "productive of disorder." Hence, according to a law of 1685 in West Jersey, "any person 'convicted of selling or giving of rum, or any manner of strong liquor, either to negro or Indian,' except the stimulant be given in relief of real physical distress" became "liable to a penalty of five pounds."[3] Similar provisions restricting the use of spirituous liquors were standard in nearly all colonial governments, including those of Maryland, North Carolina, Georgia, Delaware, Pennsylvania, and New England.[4] At the close of this period, following the American War of Independence, slavery was prohibited or nearly abolished in most northern states.

In the South, however, slavery was firmly embedded in the newly organized states, and the slave codes became more restrictive, particularly with regard to prohibitions on alcohol. Given the large area of nonslaveholding states to the north, the South was more conscious than ever of preventing slave escapes and rebellions that were linked in the planters' minds with drinking and with the fraternizing that occurred in selling and trading alcohol. Eugene Genovese traces the widespread concern over blacks drinking to fears of insurrection rather than to actual drunkenness in the slave quarters. Although liquor use by blacks on the plantation was regarded as a nuisance, the real focus of concern about blacks and alcohol centered in the towns and cities, in which attention fell on the "encouragement to theft, the breaking down of racial barriers, and the camaraderie between blacks and poor whites." In the countryside it was feared that access to liquor provided by slave thieves helped secure protection for runaway slaves and might even encourage insubordination and rebellion among poor whites and blacks: "Grogshops and contact between blacks and poor whites at drinking and gambling parties had long been suspected of playing a role in the Prosser, Vesey, and similar plots."[5]

Corroborating this view, William Freehling points out that planters in the antebellum South remained convinced that "the use of intoxicating liquors" was an important cause "of every insurrectionary movement which has occurred in the United States." The Georgetown conspiracy of 1829 had demonstrated that "ardent spirits and Yankee peddlers were an inflammatory combination."[6] Similarly, Richard Wade argues that whites in southern cities hated and feared grogshops because of the conviction that such Negro gatherings would inevitably lead to insurrections. A New Orleans journalist vividly expressed this sentiment: the shops were "places of temptation to the lower classes, where intoxication can be cheaply purchased, where mobs and caucuses of our Slaves nightly assemble at their orgies, to inflame the brains with copious libations, and preach rebellions against their white masters."[7] In the southern mind both grogshops and abolitionism were like a "devil's pact" aiming to foster negro insurrections that would "maim and murder white families, burn their dwellings and destroy the prosperity of the South."[8]

In contrast to the image of drunken blacks as a rebellious, intractable population, blacks themselves argued that drunkenness was forced on slaves by the slaveholder to weaken their desire for freedom and prevent them from carrying out insurrections. Black abolitionists believed that liquor was used to "narcoticize" the slave population into helpless docility and dissipation. In the words of Frederick Douglass, slavery could only be perpetuated when its victims "have their minds occupied with thoughts and aspirations short of the liberty of which they are deprived.... When a slave was drunk, the slaveholder had no fear that he would plan an insurrection; no fear that he would escape to the north. It was the sober, thinking slave who was dangerous, and needed the vigilance of his master to keep him a slave."[9]

The view that liquor was the foe of liberty reflected a more general strain of antialcohol sentiments expressed by black abolitionists. It was generally believed that "to keep sober was to strike a blow at slavery" and that "drunkenness and pro-slavery always went together whereas antislavery, without exception, was totally abstinent."[10] By the early 1840s a network of black temperance societies was organized; black churches, self-help groups, and political conventions consistently denounced spirituous liquor as a barrier to freedom and a major cause of moral and social degradation.

TEMPERANCE, PROGRESS, AND SOCIAL CONTROL

The conflicting images of alcohol as both liberator and enslaver mirrored the larger ambiguity in the philosophical context of temperance ideas. The rise of temperance reform was associated with a broad diffusion and acceptance of the Enlightenment in American society. The central principle underlying this philosophy was that human society is constantly evolving toward a state of ultimate perfection.[11] The emancipatory ideals of Enlightenment thought were, however, greatly tempered by a focus on order, restraint, and gradualism. Progressive social change was not anarchical; rather, it proceeded under conditions of enlightened self-examination and reason. Education and moral suasion were the proper tools of genuine progress. This philosophy argued that a "free" social order depended on a rigid form of self-government. Persons were charged to rid themselves of violent and irrational impulses. As Levine points out, the external restraints of a rigid feudal society shifted to a preoccupation with control of the self in nineteenth-century America. Temperance became a key metaphor of the new ideology of self-control since it "freed" man to be rational and productive by checking his impulsive, "irresistible" desires.[12]

The temperance movement, reflecting its own humanitarian strains, was associated with a major movement for social reform involving the emancipation of slaves, woman suffrage, and literacy for all. The movement also had implicit overtones of social control of the masses. Protemperance sentiments emerged as early as the mid-eighteenth century when the elite began to lose control of drinking establishments and alcoholic beverages became more available to the common man.[13] The criminalization of public drunkenness occurred in some areas, and many social ills were blamed on the intemperate drinking practices of the poor despite widespread heavy drinking among the upper classes.[14] Temperance values were synonymous with self-restraint and respect for authority.

The temperance movement ushered in new concepts of the physiological effects of alcohol that mirrored the concern with balancing personal freedom with a high degree of self-restraint and social conformity. The temperance model argued that liquor had two equally deleterious qualities. Both inevitably distorted the "will" of the drinker. One, however, inspired images of force and rebellion, whereas the other suggested images of passivity and victimization. From the former perspective liquor was believed to be a powerful agent of disinhibition capable of unleashing violent and irrational behavior in otherwise civilized people. Hence, alcohol was regarded as a cause of crime and violence, a substance that made people commit barbaric and cruel acts.[15] In the latter view alcohol was believed to be a powerfully addicting substance that forced men to drink and left them in a weak, slothful, and thoroughly degraded condition.[16]

The contrasting images associated with alcoholic beverages were adopted by groups with different positions on racial equality. The

image of alcohol and enslavement was stressed by northern abolitionists. The abolitionists regarded blacks as victims of slavery, both to a
physical master and to conditions of social degradation including intemperance. By contrast, the southern slaveholding class magnified
the role of alcohol in rebellion and social disruption. This image
helped justify arguments to maintain slavery and measures for social
control of the black population.

MIRRORS OF REFORM: ABOLITION AND TEMPERANCE

In the early nineteenth century Enlightenment philosophy was used to
buttress the case of abolitionists, who argued that slavery was despotic
and barbarous and a violation of man's natural rights. Slavery violated
the Lockean principle that moral freedom is found in a lack of dependence on the will of others and in unfettered pursuit of enlightened
self-interest. Slavery fostered loathsome dependency in one class and
corrupted another with excessive luxury and power. In Montesquieu's
view there was no utility in slavery; "the institution prevented the slave
from acting virtuously and imparted to the master a cruel and choleric
spirit."[17]

This philosophy occupied a key symbolic and social role in the
temperance movement. Slavery became a primary metaphor for illustrating the specter of intemperance. Drunkenness robbed the drinker
of his ability to exercise freedom of the will. In the eyes of the reformers "the drinker was not free for he was chained to alcohol, bound
to the Demon Rum."[18] Writers asserted that intemperance was a form
of slavery that crippled white Americans to a greater extent than blacks
were hindered by physical bondage.[19]

Abolition and temperance represented two facets of a general movement for social reform in nineteenth-century America. Both were set
in a period of religious fervor, and both were perceived as vehicles for
personal and collective transformation toward a more orderly, humane
society. Through religious conversion it was believed that persons
could rid themselves and society of drunkenness, racial prejudice, and
other social ills.[20]

Although organizations for moral reform had their beginnings
among those who were socially prominent and well educated, by the
1830s they were attracting and recruiting a much broader social constituency. Some aspects of these movements appeared to make them
particularly appealing as vehicles for self-improvement among people
from humbler social backgrounds. First, the reform movements were
infused with a strong egalitarian ethos that welcomed groups like
women and youth, who were traditionally excluded from participating

in public life.[21] Second, they espoused an optimistic doctrine of infinite worthiness and perfectability regarding human beings and society. Reformers believed that social ills such as poverty, crime, slavery, prejudice, and even idiocy could be eliminated through salvation and education. Perfectability was possible to those living under the most depraved circumstances who were imbued with the religious principles of Christ and with the moral precepts of ascetic Protestantism.[22] Third, reformist groups were critical of the existing social order and agitated for a variety of humanistic reforms such as abolition, temperance, woman suffrage, pacifism, and education. Finally, campaigns for moral reform offered programs of social action and organization. Reformers organized self-help and political action groups; they ran newspapers, issued educational tracts, and staged public meetings to inform and sway public opinion.

The message of social change in this reform era, however, was characterized by a strongly individualistic focus. Social ills would be eliminated not by agitating for institutional or political changes but by focusing on moral or religious transformation in individuals.[23] This ethic was highly compatible with the rise of industrial capitalism and the emphasis on developing a class of enterprising, self-reliant, and well-disciplined artisans and laborers.[24]

Taking George Frederickson's view, it seems that the image of blacks in the reform movements reflected the environmentalist, yet strongly individualistic, ethos of the reformers. Reformers argued that wretched social conditions and the "numbing" influence of slavery was sufficient to explain the degraded position of blacks. Henry Clay surmised that "the free people of colour are...the most corrupt, depraved and abandoned element" in the population; but this "is not so much their fault as a consequence of their anomalous condition."[25] Making a similar point, the abolitionist writer Lydia Maria Child concluded, "From the moment the slave is kidnapped, the white man's influence directly cherishes ignorance, fraud, licentiousness, revenge, hatred and murder. It cannot be denied that human nature thus operated upon, must necessarily yield more or less to all these evils."[26]

Counterbalanced against the claim that blacks were degraded by a cruel and prejudicial environment was the belief that they should be in a position to assume self-responsibility for their own development. "What made slavery such a detestable condition was not simply that it created a bad environment; it was a severely limiting condition that was incompatible with the fundamental abolitionist belief that every man was morally responsible for his actions."[27] It was in this vein that abolitionists felt no qualms about exhorting northern free Negroes to improve their lots, believing apparently that a discriminating environment did not fully excuse them from failure to elevate themselves. The national Abolition Society adopted nine "Articles of Advice" to "Free Africans," which urged blacks to "attend church regularly, work diligently at 'useful trades,' respect education, dress modestly, avoid 'frolicking,' 'idleness,' and liquor."[28]

BLACKS AND TEMPERANCE REFORM IN ANTEBELLUM AMERICA

The message of temperance reform appeared to stimulate an overwhelming response in the free black population.[29] According to the limited published accounts of this phenomenon, blacks organized a temperance movement that rivaled the larger movement in scope and intensity.[30]

The popularity of the temperance movement among blacks was indicated by the success of the Colored American Temperance society. Formed in Philadelphia in the early 1830s on the expressed principle of "entire abstinence from the use of ardent spirits," the society had a mushrooming growth, reporting twenty-three branches in eighteen cities within a year.[31] Ohio communities were particularly zealous in support of the temperance movement. In 1840 more than one-quarter of the black population of Cincinnati belonged to either the adult society (450 members) or the youth branch (180 members). Black opposition to drink made it impossible for dissenting blacks to sell intoxicating liquor openly.[32] In Connecticut the State Temperance Society of Colored People was founded. The members of the society pledged to "abstain from the use of all fermented liquors that produce intoxication, as well as all distilled spirits, and not to use them as common drink, nor traffic in them, neither furnish them for other persons thus to use."[33] Adopting an even stronger antiliquor stand at subsequent conventions, the organization became known as the Connecticut Total Abstinence Society in 1836. A similar network of "colored" temperance societies was formed in New England and all along the eastern seaboard. Black newspapers such as the *National Reformer, Freedom's Journal,* and the *Colored American* circulated temperance literature to the black populations in the North and the South.

The enthusiastic level of black support for the temperance movement did not appear to be solely a response to high levels of alcohol-related problems in the black population. Although the evidence on the extent of drunkenness and excessive drinking among antebellum blacks is scanty and conflictual, there is a general consensus that drunkenness and excessive drinking were not a major cause of concern among plantation slaves. In comparison to other groups, writes Genovese, "whites and blacks, southerners and travelers reported no great problems among the slaves. Colonel Higgins reported little drunkenness among the black recruits despite easy access to liquor. Lyell and Mrs. Schoolcraft had long before insisted on the same point.... Rarely, apart from holiday frolics,... did widespread drunkenness occur among slaves, although it did among masters, overseers, and neighboring poor whites."[34] Samuel Cartwright, the New Orleans physician, also asserted that Negroes generally drank very little, and this only for medical purposes or during holiday celebrations.[35]

The temperance speeches given by blacks themselves candidly stated that alcohol use was not more prevalent among blacks than whites when differences in population were taken into account, suggesting that in the minds of reformers alcohol abuse was not the exclusive or key motivation for temperance reform.[36] A speech by Thomas Cole appearing in *The Liberator* illustrates this point:

> I do not believe that the evils of intemperance prevail among us as a people, to any greater extent than among the white class of the community; in fact, I believe that we are less addicted to the use of strong drink. Still we need a reformation in this, particularly; and we ought to abandon those vices which are ruinous to virtue to the improvement of the mind, and progressive elevation of character.[37]

Almost identical sentiments were expressed by J. W. Lewis in a temperance address to the "People of Color of New England." Pointing out that even if "our enemies be our judges, we are not more guilty in this matter than themselves," Lewis stated that drunkenness appeared to be far less common among blacks than whites. "Nay, we believe it will be allowed that it is a much more rare occurrence to see a drunken colored man, than a drunken white man, making due allowance for the numerical distribution existing between the white and colored population."[38]

The above statements suggest that the development of a full-blown black temperance movement was not primarily, or only a response to alcohol-related health and social problems but that it was part of a broader wave of political and social consciousness that swept through the free black population. Two interrelated aspects of the larger temperance movement appeared to make it particularly appealing to blacks. The first factor was the direct connection with the antislavery movement; the second was the value system and organizational program of social betterment offered by the movement.

BLACK TEMPERANCE AND ABOLITION

The connection between abolition and temperance was strong in the minds of many black and white abolitionists. There was a general and well-founded assumption that a supporter of abolition was likely to be a supporter of temperance. In Maine John Krout observed that the one group on which the prohibitionists could always rely was backers of the antislavery movement: "The determined enemies of human bondage wanted to be considered foes of the traffic which enslaved men to the vice, intemperance. They never tired of pointing to the similarity between the two movements."[39] Black leaders invariably linked abstinence with abolition, holding that "to keep sober was to strike a blow at slavery." Jermain Loguen, an ex-slave reformer, did not see much difference in making a man a slave to rum and in making him a slave to a fellow man. William Whipper condemned liquor for its murderous effect on Africa, inducing its peoples to sell their brothers. Jacob C. White, in an address to the Banneker Institute of Philadelphia in 1854, denounced rum as the ruin of the young, "the very class of our peoples to whom we are to look as the warriors who are to fight for our liberty."[40]

Reflecting these themes, convention delegates of the New England Temperance Society of Colored People in 1836 resolved that "the cause of temperance demands our warmest affection and best efforts, on account of its near connexion with the abolition of slavery."[41] The second major convention of the New England society offered the rationale that "the use of intoxicating liquors in our community tends greatly to retard the progress of emancipation, by throwing weapons into the hands of our enemies, which enables them to maintain a strong contest with the friends of our cause."[42] Prominent abolitionists expanded on the rhetoric of the larger movement that alcohol was a powerfully addicting substance that would enslave its victims. The free black was admonished no sooner to "put the intoxicating cup to his lips than he would give his back to the lash of the slave driver."[43] The pledge for black freedmen in most temperance societies resembled that of the American Temperance Union: "Being mercifully redeemed from human slavery, we do pledge ourselves never to be brought into the slavery of the bottle, therefore we will not drink the drunkard's drink: whiskey, gin, beer, nor rum, nor anything that makes drunk come."[44]

TEMPERANCE AS AN IDEOLOGY
OF SOCIAL TRANSFORMATION

As part of the larger goal to achieve emancipation and political equality, blacks fully endorsed the mandate for self-help implied in the larger reform movement. They regarded themselves, and were perceived by others, as a group bound together by certain cultural and historical factors and a common experience of social oppression. The ideology of the larger movement—stressing self-control—was apparently expanded to include self-government for blacks as a collectivity. The pledge to refrain from any socially deprecating behavior—including drunkenness—and cultivate moral and economically stable families was an expression of the overriding sentiment among blacks that they were capable of self-government. Their rationales for temperance were infused with this faith in sharing a common destiny and a collective responsibility for racial betterment.

Temperance activity was thus deemed important for gaining social respectability and improving the overall economic and social position of blacks. An editorial appearing in the *Northern Star and Freeman's Advocate* illustrates a common theme:

> We should show the public now that we are trying to promote one another's interest for the elevation of ourselves and the rising generation... Let the colored people of these United States become a temperate people and they would gain more credit for themselves than all our abolition friends could do for us. Then let us engage in it heart and hand and when it can be said we are a sober, industrious and intelligent people, we shall receive the favor of all classes of the community.[45]

Implicit in the black movement for self-improvement was acceptance of values associated with the Protestant ethic. Black reformers argued that drunkenness negated the emphasis on rationality, education, self-discipline, and hard work, which they believed were the keys to overthrowing slavery and bettering race relations. Drinking was associated with the idle amusements, superstitious religious beliefs, and complacent attitudes that they regarded as part and parcel of the slave system. Liquor inspired brutality in the master class and passivity among the slaves.[46] Frederick Douglass's statement that it was the "sober, thinking" slave who posed a threat to the oppressive slave system is a clear illustration of these attitudes. Douglass argued that under the guise of benevolence, holidays represented one of the cruelest institutions of the plantation system, encouraging frivolity, whiskey drinking, and passivity among the slaves and providing the escape valve for tensions that prevented outright insurrection and rebellion.[47]

The values that Douglass and other black leaders promoted, which today seem accommodating and bourgeois, had at the time a concrete meaning that gave them a sense of genuine militancy. The idea that blacks should be educated, own property, run their own churches and institutions, stage protests against the government, and openly defy state laws was a bold affront to the slave system and indeed to the conventional social hierarchy in America. Obtaining property, for example, had an extremely practical application—blacks would literally buy freedom for themselves and their enslaved compatriots and in turn meet the property requirements for voting.

Education was another value that blacks extolled as a pathway to freedom. The literate slave was a feared one, and specific prohibitions on teaching slaves to read were common throughout the South. In the words of the *Southern Literary Messenger,* quoted in Wade, "To prevent the general instruction of negroes in the arts of reading and writing [thus became] a measure of police essential to the tranquility, nay to the existence of southern society."[48]

Not only was temperance strongly identified with a militant, relentless stream of antislavery protest from white and black abolitionists, but it carried an implicit message of self-determination as well. It provided a means for expressing solidarity and exercising informal mechanisms of social control among blacks within their own communities. The emotional ritual of "signing the pledge" may have solidified commitment to the antislavery cause and to the self-help program necessary to ensure its success. On the basis of the stand taken by the abolitionist preacher Amos Beman in Connecticut it appears that blacks who refused to sign or who broke the pledge were excluded from membership in some churches.[49] Parents were urged to "instruct their children by precept and example, in the principles of total abstinence, and discountenance those shops kept by colored men where intoxicating liquors are sold."[50] Shopkeepers such as David Ruggles encouraged these admonitions by refusing to sell spirituous liquors.[51] Other black businessmen went beyond the usual prohibitions requiring abstinence on the job and demanded nothing less than teetotalism from their employees.[52]

ALCOHOL, SOCIAL CONTROL, AND BLACK DISINHIBITION

If the Enlightenment set the stage for an optimistic period of social idealism and reform, it also laid the groundwork for ideas that culminated in extreme forms of domination of the black population. The emerging natural science model of human behavior paved the way for theories of racial inferiority and social Darwinism that proslavery writers applied to blacks.[53] The preoccupation with order and respect for authority justified more stringent control on slaves. In this context concerns about alcohol began to be associated with an ideology of repression and domination. This was particularly true of the images of the black as a drunken brute that gained wide currency at the turn of the nineteenth century.

Even at mid-century in the slaveholding South whites were voicing concern about the effect of alcohol on blacks. Liquor, it was believed, led to violence and other forms of disinhibition in slaves. The focus of whites on black drunkenness was a means of both controlling the black population and locating the source of disruption outside of the institution of slavery (since they also argued that blacks benefited from slavery and were contented) in the inflammatory nature of liquor and the repressed primitive urges of blacks. This association arose in part from preexisting stereotypes about the primitive and savage nature of Africans.[54] According to Fredrickson, apologists for slavery argued that blacks were naturally wild and bestial, although under slavery they had become "domesticated" and "docile."[55] The conception of man as a double-natured savage was not confined to the enslaved black; as previously suggested, it was a prominent theme in the emerging concepts of the effect of liquor on whites. As Levine points out, the story of Dr. Jekyll and Mr. Hyde "magnificently captured the broader nineteenth century fear of, and fascination with, a liquid which could transform repressed civilized men and women into uninhibited beasts."[56]

The effect of Robert Louis Stevenson's tale drew on the latent fears of losing control in nineteenth-century America. Jordan argues that early impressions of Africans were colored by the same preoccupation appearing earlier in English society. Africans and other "savages" served as "social mirrors" for Europeans, illustrating dreaded flaws they first discovered in themselves but could not speak about. Hence, remarks about the lustful wicked characteristics of African natives were not about blacks; rather, they harped on a theme of external discipline exercised on men who failed to discipline themselves.[57]

Fears about the "savagery" associated with both blacks and alcohol were two manifestations of the growing concern about self-discipline in Anglo-American culture. In the early nineteenth century the vivid synthesis of the two images had not yet fully merged, as they would later, into characterizations of the black as a drunken beast and rapist. After all, in the antebellum North the "degradation" and "primitiveness" of Africans had been attributed to environmental conditions and not to their innate character. Moreover, the institution of slavery along with a stringent series of slave codes constituted a formidable system for the social control of blacks. As a symbol of their relative powerlessness, blacks under slavery were legally prohibited from trading or using alcoholic beverages. However, under Reconstruction, when the social position of blacks was rapidly changing, concerns about black drunkenness came to the forefront.

The arguments of black degeneracy under emancipation were central to popularized depictions of the black as a brute or animalistic fiend at the turn of the century. George Winston's description (1906) of the black "beast" spawned by emancipation and the wild excesses of Reconstruction was a lurid caricature of this theme: "The black brute is lurking in the dark, a monstrous beast crazed with lust. His ferocity is almost demoniacal. A mad bull or tiger could scarcely be more brutal. A whole community is frenzied with horror, with the blind and furious rage for vengeance."[58]

The rise of racist ideology as applied to blacks was a reflection of an overall mood of Darwinist thinking being applied to the lower classes in Europe and to blacks and immigrants in the United States. The philosophy led to the conviction that heredity was the basic determinant of social problems—a belief that culminated in the eugenics movement. In this view education and philanthropy made the masses even more dependent; their only hope was to struggle unaided against the most adverse conditions.[59]

The broad diffusion of these theories was tied to an increasingly conservative view of the social order—one that regarded society as a stratified hierarchy, with the lower, unruly elements being governed by the moral influence of the higher classes. Without the top civilizing layer society would revert to anarchy and primitivism. This stratified view of the social order was traced onto accepted scientific concepts of the body. The nervous system was believed to be arranged in a hierarchical and layered fashion, with earlier and more primitive layers being controlled by a more recently evolved and more highly developed moral center. Under the influence of external pressure or stress the higher governing center would become incapacitated, and the organism would regress to a primitive state. As Levine aptly points out, this idea provided the scientific basis for the concept of alcohol disinhibition. Alcohol provoked violent and uncouth behavior in otherwise civilized people by depressing functions associated with the higher center of the brain and allowing for the expression of repressed primitive urges in the basal nervous system.[60]

PROHIBITION, WHITE SUPREMACY, AND THE DRUNKEN BLACK BEAST

The effect of the saloon upon the negro is disastrous to his industry and good citizenship. And more, the negro fairly docile and industrious becomes, when filled with liquor, turbulent and dangerous and a menace to life, property and the repose of the community.[61]

By the turn of the twentieth century the divergent concerns about black savagery, alcohol disinhibition and social disorder converged in the image of the drunken black beast. Prohibition was urged in order to protect the white populace, particularly females, from the drunken debauches of half-crazed black men. The "negro problem" became a central issue in liquor reform. Sensational newspaper editorials were circulated condemning the liquor traffic as a stimulus for an alleged epidemic of sex crimes as well as the massive wave of lynchings, riots, and other forms of racial violence that swept across the South. For example, *Collier's* ran an article entitled "Mr. Levy's 'Nigger Gin,'" about the cheap gin sold primarily in "negro dives," which by its lewd packaging was believed to incite lurid sexual behavior in black men:

> Obscene titles, obscene labels, advertise by suggestion, by double meanings, that these compounds contain a drug to stimulate the low passions which have made the race problem such a dreadful thing in the South....The viciousness lies in the double meanings, clear to every man who knows the Southern negro, in the pictures of naked white women on the labels, in even greater obscenities.[62]

Violent revenge, it was argued, was the outcome of the "nameless crime" committed by many Negro consumers of gin. Ministers in Atlanta harped on the temptations of prostitution, self-abuse, and Negro women, along with the dooming consequences of whiskey.[63] The renowned Reverend Wilbur Fisk Crafts preached about the devil's girdle of liquor, "which has changed so many Negroes into sensual hyenas" and threatened the safety of white women.[64]

The image of the drunken black brute in the prohibition movement was part of a broader wave of Negrophobia and lower-class repression then sweeping the South. This repression followed a period of severe economic decline, intense labor conflict, and a stream of interracial leftist protest. Arguments about the disinhibitory effects of alcohol on blacks and the lower class in general provided justification for a series of reactionary political measures, including political disfranchisement, racial segregation, and social control of drinking establishments.

Stereotypes about drunken blacks were especially important in the disfranchisement campaigns—campaigns that were supposedly aimed exclusively at blacks but in fact virtually eliminated the poor white vote. Politicians pushed for restrictive voting requirements in the interest of eliminating whiskey-sodden, irresponsible black voters. Charles Crowe reports that one Atlanta prohibitionist, the Reverend Sam Jones, "often called for the expulsion from the polls of the element that 'invariably sells out to the highest bidder.' The vote was worthless to the Negro for 'it is not counted when cast' and the 'Yankees' who organized the whole idea of Negro suffrage had long since admitted to their mistakes. The ballot, Jones concluded, served only to debauch the Negro, prevent the democratic process, and preserve the saloon."[65] Similar sentiments echoed throughout the South, culminating in the denial of voting privileges to thousands of blacks and poor whites.[66]

The lack of a factual basis for the stereotypes of blacks as heavy drinkers and as supporters of the liquor interests is evident in studies of black drinking behavior and in the political positions taken by blacks on temperance issues in the post-Reconstruction period. For example, John Koren's exhaustive analysis of comparative data, "Relations of the Negroes to the Liquor Problem" (1899), stated that "much evidence may be found to support the theory that the type of common drunkard, with an inherited appetite for intoxicants, has not yet developed among the country Negroes." The report concluded that "comparatively few Negroes are habitual drunkards," that "intemperance is only accountable for a small part of the Negro's backward condition, his poverty and anti-social conduct, and that but in exceptional cases is inebriety a barrier to his steady employment."[67] Data from the 1880 census supported these conclusions by illustrating that substantially fewer blacks than whites died from alcoholism—only 0.7 per thousand deaths for blacks, compared to 6.7 for the Irish, 2.7 for the Germans, and 2.5 for whites.[68]

Continuing the legacy of temperance as a means of social improvement, blacks in the post-Reconstruction South also supported temperance organizations and legislation. Hence, in planning a resettlement territory for displaced slaves, a convention of "colored men" meeting in Kansas in 1882 petitioned Congress to "prohibit the sale of all intoxicating liquors as a beverage" in the new territory.[69] Blacks joined white delegates in the Alabama State Temperance Convention of 1881 to appeal for legislative controls on the liquor traffic.[70] They also formed colored departments of the Women's Christian Temperance Union and participated in fraternal organizations such as the Sons of Temperance, the Friends of Temperance, and the Independent Order of Good Templars. However, in the latter organizations they were eventually barred from membership by southern whites who chose to dissolve the orders rather than admit blacks.[71]

In sum, the image of the drunken black beast that emerged in the southern prohibition movement symbolized in graphic form the triangulation of forces that aimed to justify a fixed, hierarchical social system. Darwinist ideology provided both a theory of the innate inferiority of the masses and an evolutionary model emphasizing the naturalness of government by elites. The heightened concern with alcohol served as discourse on fears of social disorder; but primarily it was a means of instituting a series of repressive measures to justify the domination and social control of blacks and poor whites. Whereas the earlier temperance movement had interpreted the issue of order as one of self-control in a society of competitive equals, the later prohibition movement was concerned with imposing order on a population that was frozen in a subordinate status.

FRAGMENTATION OF TEMPERANCE AND
A NEW IDEOLOGY OF BLACK DRINKING

The repressive tactics and conservatism of the southern prohibition movement signaled a fundamental shift in blacks' regard for temperance and "moral" reform generally as an avenue of social advancement. The changes occurred at several levels. First, at the most concrete level, black temperance activity rapidly declined and fragmented after the turn of the century. The issue shifted from a subject of major public discourse to one of individual conscience. There was a growing sentiment among blacks that drinking behavior was a matter for moral suasion but not for regulation by the state. This conviction led a prominent black spokesman to regard prohibition laws as "odious" and harmful to the true aims of temperance.[72]

Second, in the face of conservative repression liberal black reformers who had formerly defended bourgeois values began to show signs of radicalism. As early as the Reconstruction period Frederick Douglass was reversing his position that liquor actually caused poverty among the working classes. In the 1840s and 1850s, he was convinced that the cause of impoverishment of the Irish working classes was intemperance. By the 1880s he argued that the exploitive lien-labor system and extreme poverty would lead to intemperance in the black population. The success of temperance reform, he declared, would depend on the effectiveness of economic reform.[73]

W. E. B. DuBois was a key political figure who came to prominence later than Douglass, but his career illustrates a similar transition. A noted scholar and humanist, he had supported the temperance movement in the 1880s and regarded it as an important avenue of self-improvement. However, after 1900 he regarded the liquor question as "the nemesis of black progress" and resolved to steer clear of moral issues that would place his political interests "in an open fight with factions of the Klan and Prohibition."[74]

Among the black intelligentsia strong lines of support for prohibition were identified only with those who took a conservative position on labor, political franchisement, and social welfare. Booker T. Washington, whose accommodationist social policies made him a favorite of southern "liberal" elites, urged acceptance of a subordinate political position for blacks and advocated education for the practical end of gaining a livelihood.[75] Echoing other southern elites, he welcomed prohibition "as a blessing to the Negro race" that would reduce crime and degradation among blacks and lower-class whites.

Probably the most profound changes in blacks' views of moral reform occurred at the popular level. The highly politicized, mass moral reform and temperance movement of the early nineteenth century was replaced by a new cultural image of liquor, one that was sensual and titillating, complete with a folklore of heavy drinking and pleasure seeking. Cabarets and nightclubs rose to preeminence as havens of excitement and exotic pleasure. Within these nightspots liquor flowed freely as an elixir of gaiety and sensuality.[76] Langston Hughes's portrait of a northern city "Juice Joint" as a "gin mill on the avenue" with "singing black boys" and "gay dancing feet" is part of a larger genre of romantic portrayals of black nightlife in this era.[77]

The new cultural fascination with drinking was in part a reflection of actual demographic and socioeconomic changes in the black population. Beginning around 1900, thousands of blacks began to leave the South in the great migration to northern cities. As blacks moved from rural "dry" areas to the urban scene, they became a focus of the nightlife culture and the illegal liquor trade that flourished in those areas. They also became a target of economic exploitation in the market for illegal alcohol, which was run mostly by white ethnics.[78] In addition, blacks themselves turned to bootlegging and rumrunning because it was much more profitable than farming and unskilled labor.[79]

By the early decades of the twentieth century liquor reform had vanished as a meaningful political issue in the black population. Although there was, and still is, a large reservoir of abstinence sentiment among blacks, it was expressed at the informal and private social level. Publicly, abstinence sentiment was overshadowed by a social mythology wherein liquor was a necessary lubricant for an expressive, sensual life-style. The black masses had become depoliticized directly through disfranchisement and indirectly through a new cultural ideology of pleasure seeking. However, the new idealization of drinking may have in fact served as an "expressive" protest against the social domination associated with the prohibition movement.[80] In other words, drinking had become a way to show defiance against an oppressive legal system, much as abstinence had a hundred years earlier. It had now acquired the connotation of personal liberty that could not be achieved through the political process.

CONCLUSION

Within a hundred years the dominant images associated with the alcohol question and with blacks changed from one emphasizing alcohol as enslaver to one emphasizing alcohol as disinhibitor. Although both images were rooted in nineteenth-century ideas about the perfectability of human society, they were associated with divergent instrumental functions and different ideological approaches to the problem of social order. The image of alcohol as enslaver was a self-designated symbol adopted by the middle classes struggling for social mobility and humanistic social changes. This image left intact the Enlightenment ideal that man was inherently virtuous and capable of ultimate freedom—self-mastery—while damning alcohol as the culprit that overpowered and reduced the drinker to wretchedness. Abstinence provided men and women with the ultimate power of control. By saying no, they could overpower a virtually uncontrollable substance.

The program of social reform and self-help associated with this phase of the temperance movement apparently had great appeal for blacks, who regarded the close association of the movement with abolition and its ethic of human perfectability as an avenue of social transformation. Bourgeois values had revolutionary implications for blacks, who saw in them a means of achieving emancipation and gaining political and economic parity in the society. The image of alcohol the enslaver thus was eagerly adopted and literally transposed to symbolize all the barbaric and oppressive forces that kept blacks in bondage. The pledge of abstinence in its positive sense affirmed the overwhelming sentiment among blacks that they were capable of self-government and therefore of freedom.

In contrast to the ethic of self-determination and inner reform suggested by the image of alcohol as enslaver, images of alcohol and disinhibition were closely associated with the efforts of one class to dominate and control another class. The images of disinhibition appearing in the nineteenth century were not self-designated; rather, they were applied to groups different from, and less powerful than, those in the dominant class. Theories of disinhibition emphasized the cultural and biological inferiority—the "savage potential"— of lower-class groups. The idea drew on the scientific dogma of social Darwinism and evolutionary theory. It was fundamentally tied to a fixed, hierarchical vision of society, one with a small governing elite and a large, docile underclass.

The conservative, repressive bias reflected in this period of alcohol reform caused a fundamental cleavage in the politics of morality from those of liberal social change. Among blacks the movement vanished as a public symbol and remained influential only in religious values. In the broader social domain it was replaced by a diffuse and fragmented political consciousness, overshadowed by a more powerful cultural image associating alcohol with personal pleasure and individual freedom.

NOTES

1. Harry G. Levine, "The Discovery of Addiction," *Journal of Studies on Alcohol* 40 (January 1978): 143–173.

2. George M. Fredrickson, *The Black Image in the White Mind* (New York: Harper and Row, 1971), 105–109, 275–282.

3. Henry S. Cooley, "A Study of Slavery in New Jersey," in *Slavery, and Constitutional History,* Johns Hopkins University Studies in Historical and Political Science, vol. 14, ed. Herbert B. Adams (Baltimore, Johns Hopkins University Press, 1896), 36–37.

4. John R. Larkins, *Alcohol and the Negro: Explosive Issues* (Zebulon, N.C.: Record Publishing, 1965), 6–11.

5. Eugene D. Genovese, *Roll, Jordan, Roll: The World the Slaves Made* (New York: Vintage Books, 1976), 642.

6. William W. Freehling, *Prelude to Civil War* (New York: Harper and Row, 1965), 334.

7. Richard C. Wade, *Slavery in the Cities: The South, 1820–1860* (London: Oxford University Press, 1964), 158.

8. Daniel R. Hundley, *Social Relations in Our Southern States,* ed. by William J. Cooper, (1860; rpt. Baton Rouge: Louisiana State University Press, 1979), 231.

9. Frederick Douglass, *My Bondage and My Freedom* (New York: Miller, Orton and Mulligan, 1855), 253, 256.

10. Benjamin Quarles, *Black Abolitionists* (New York: Oxford University Press, 1969), 93.

11. Henry F. May, *The Enlightenment in America* (New York: Oxford University Press, 1976).

12. Levine, "Discovery of Addiction," 164–165.

13. William J. Rorabaugh, *The Alcoholic Republic* (New York: Oxford University Press, 1979), 32–35.

14. Ann Pinson, "The New England Rum Era: Drinking Styles and Social Change in Newport, R.I., 1720–1770," Working Papers on Alcohol and Human Behavior, no. 8 (Brown University, 1980), 24–28.

15. Harry G. Levine, "Demon of the Middle Class: Self-Control, Liquor and the Ideology of Temperance in Nineteenth-Century America" (Ph.D. diss., University of California, Berkeley, 1978), 87–96.

16. Levine, "Demon of the Middle Class," 31–35.

17. David Brion Davis, *The Problem of Slavery in Western Culture* (New York: Cornell University Press, 1966), 407.

18. Rorabaugh, *Alcoholic Republic,* 200.

19. Heman Humphrey, *Parallel between Intemperance and the Slave Trade* (Amherst, Mass.: J. S. and C. Adams, 1828), 4–5.

20. John L. Thomas, "Romantic Reform in America, 1815–1865," *American Quarterly* 17 (Winter 1965): 656–681; Bernard A. Weisberger, *They Gathered at the River* (Boston: Little, Brown, 1958); Clifford S. Griffin, *The Ferment of Reform: 1830–1860* (New York: Crowell Press, 1967); Clifford S. Griffin, *Their Brothers' Keepers: Moral Stewardship in the United States, 1800 to 1865* (1960; rpt. Westport, Conn.: Greenwood Press, 1983).

21. Ian R. Tyrrell, *Sobering Up: From Temperance to Prohibition in Antebellum*

America, 1800–1860, Contributions in American History, no. 82 (Westport, Conn.: Greenwood Press, 1979), 67.

22. Thomas, "Romantic Reform," 657–659, 665–666.

23. Stanley M. Elkins, *Slavery: A Problem in American Institutional and Intellectual Life* (1959; rpt. Chicago: University of Chicago Press, 1968), 167–170.

24. Tyrrell, *Sobering Up,* 96–98, 107–108, 127–128.

25. *African Repository* 6 (March 1830): 12.

26. Lydia Maria Child, *An Appeal in Favor of That Class of Americans Called Africans* (New York, 1836), 16.

27. Fredrickson, *Black Image,* 35.

28. Carol V. R. George, *Segregated Sabbaths: Richard Allen and the Emergence of Independent Black Churches, 1760–1840* (New York: Oxford University Press, 1973), 60–61.

29. See Denise A. Herd, "We Cannot Stagger to Freedom: A History of Blacks and Alcohol in American Politics," in *Yearbook of Substance Use and Abuse,* ed. L. Brill and C. Winick (New York: Human Sciences Press, 1985), 3:141–186, for a more detailed analysis of the development of the black temperance movement from the early nineteenth century to the turn of the twentieth century. Herd's essay and the following account draw heavily from, and take a similar perspective as, Quarles, *Black Abolitionists,* 93–101, which argues that the temperance movement among antebellum blacks was primarily an outgrowth of, and complement to, the black abolitionist movement.

30. Quarles, *Black Abolitionists,* 93–100; Roslyn U. Cheagle, "The Colored Temperance Movement," Master's thesis, Howard University, 1969).

31. Quarles, *Black Abolitionists,* 94.

32. Quarles, *Black Abolitionists,* 96..

33. "Colored Temperance Convention," *The Liberator* 6 (July 30, 1836): 122.

34. Genovese, *Roll, Jordan, Roll,* 643–644.

35. Wade, *Slavery in the Cities,* 156.

36. Health statistics from the period supported these observations. The 1850 census reported that blacks died of intemperance at the rate of 1.75 per 100,000 persons, whereas deaths from alcoholism among whites was 2.52 per 100,000 persons. The mortality of blacks due to liver disease was about half that of whites, 4.47 per 100,000 as compared to 8.63 per 100,000. See U.S. Census Office, *Seventh Census (1850) Mortality Statistics* (Washington, D.C.: Nicholson, 1855), 27–28, 35.

37. "An Address Delivered by Thomas Cole, of Boston, before the N. England Colored Temperance Convention Held in Boston, Sept. 1837," *The Liberator* 7 (October 13, 1837), 166.

38. *Minutes of a Convention of Color for the Promotion of Temperance in New England* (Providence, R.I., Brown, 1836), 12.

39. John A. Krout, *The Origins of Prohibition* (New York: Knopf, 1925), 289.

40. Quarles, *Black Abolitionists,* 93.

41. *Minutes of a Convention of Color for the Promotion of Temperance in New England,* 9.

42. "Temperance Convention," *The Liberator* 7 (September 29, 1837), 159.

43. *Minutes of a Convention of Color for the Promotion of Temperance in New England,* 15.

44. American Temperance Union, *Temperance Tract for the Freedmen* (New York: American Temperance Union, n.d.), 4.

45. *Northern Star and Freeman's Advocate* 1 (February 17, 1842), 17. For another example, see "The Delevan Temperance Union," *North Star* 1 (July 28, 1848), 2.

46. Genovese, *Roll, Jordan, Roll,* 645–646; Douglass, *My Bondage and My Freedom,* 255–256.

47. Douglass, *My Bondage and My Freedom,* 252–254.

48. Wade, *Slavery in the Cities,* 90–91.

49. Robert A. Warner, "Amos Gerry Beman, 1812–1874: A Memoir on a Forgotten Leader," *Journal of Negro History* 22 (April 1937): 200–221.

50. "Temperance Meeting," *The Liberator* 6 (December 5, 1836), 195.

51. "Goshen Butter," *Rights of All* 1 (October 9, 1829), 43.

52. "Temperance Convention," *The Liberator* 7 (September 29, 1837), 159.

53. Mark H. Haller, *Eugenics: Hereditarian Attitudes in American Thought* (New Brunswick, N.J.: Rutgers University Press, 1963), 50–52.

54. Winthrop Jordan, *White over Black,* (1968; rpt. Baltimore: Penguin Books, 1969), 305–308.

55. Fredrickson, *Black Image,* 53–54.

56. Levine, "Demon of the Middle Class," 104–105.

57. Jordan, *White over Black,* 40–42.

58. George Winston, "The Relations of the Whites to the Negroes," *Annals of the American Academy of Political and Social Science* 17 (July 1901): 108–109.

59. Richard Hofstadter, *Social Darwinism in American Thought,* rev. ed. (Boston: Beacon Press, 1955), 6–7, 41, 61.

60. Harry G. Levine, "Presenter's Comments," in *Alcohol and Disinhibition: Nature and Meaning of the Link,* ed. R. Room and Gary Collins, Research Monograph no. 12 (Rockville, Md.: U.S. Department of Health and Human Services, NIAAA, 1983), 162–171.

61. "The Tennessean, 1908," quoted in P. E. Isaac, *Prohibition and Politics in Tennessee 1885–1920* (Knoxville, Tenn.: University of Tennessee Press), 48.

62. Will Irwin, "Who Killed Margaret Lear?" *Collier's Weekly* 41 (May 16, 1908), 10; Will Irwin, "More about Nigger Gin," *Collier's Weekly* 41 (August 15, 1908), 28, 30. See also Isaac, *Prohibition and Politics,* 147.

63. Charles Crowe, "Racial Violence and Social Reform: Origins of the Atlanta Riot of 1906," *Journal of Negro History* 53 (July 1968): 234–256.

64. Dr. and Mrs. Wilbur F. Crafts, *World Book of Temperance,* 3d ed. (Washington, D.C.: International Reform Bureau, 1911), 58.

65. Crowe, "Racial Violence and Social Reform," 237.

66. See Denise Herd, "Prohibition, Racism and Class Politics in the Post-Reconstruction South," *Journal of Drug Issues* 13 (1983): 77–94, for a complete discussion of the political context of blacks and prohibition in the post-Reconstruction south.

67. John Koren, *Economic Aspects of the Liquor Problem* (Boston: Houghton Mifflin, 1899), 163, 176–177.

68. U.S. Census Office, *Tenth Census (1880),* vol. 12, *Report on the Mortality and Vital Statistics of the United States* (Washington, D.C.: Government Printing Office, 1886), lxvii.

69. *A Documentary History of the Negro People in the United States,* ed. Herbert Aptheker (1951; rpt. New York: Citadel Press, 1968), 2:685.

70. James Benson Sellers, *The Prohibition Movement in Alabama,* The James Sprunt Studies in History and Political Science, vol. 26, no. I (Chapel Hill, N.C.: University of North Carolina Press, 1943), 75.

71. Sellers, *Prohibition Movement in Alabama,* 44–45; Daniel J. Whitener, *Prohibition in North Carolina, 1715–1945* (Chapel Hill, N.C.: University of North Carolina Press, 1946), 56.

72. W. E. B. DuBois, "Drunkenness," *The Crisis* 35 (October 1928): 348.

73. This transition is aptly illustrated by a "temperance" speech written by Douglass, probably during the 1880s:

> Three very grave obstacles in the way of temperance reform and of a general social improvement among the ignorant blacks of the South confront us, and until these evils are to a considerable degree eliminated, we cannot hope for great success—[the] liquor license of the road corners grocery—an illiterate and immoral ministry—and that device of Satan for the grinding down of the poor. The other system, a system so degrading to the victim that it is forbidden by law in monarchial England, but practiced unblushingly in Republican America—a system by which the laborer is paid in orders upon a certain share...[by] his employer, and in goods of any quality or price the share keeper may choose or impose—thus keeping the laborer always in debt and binding him to a...serfdom from which there is no release.
>
> What work is first to be done in such a case? It is to change the conditions. If we find a man pinned to the ground under the teeth of a harrow, [do] we first present him with a temperance pledge to sign, or argue with him upon the benefits of prohibition? No, first lift off the harrow. The harrow must be lifted from our black fellow citizens. The first requirement is that [he] be treated justly. Just so far as we fail to deal justly—just so far we shall fail to deal righteously—and just so far will our efforts in temperance or any other reform, fail of fruition. (Unpublished speech, microfilm, The Frederick Douglass Papers, University of California, Berkeley)

74. *The Correspondence of W. E. B. DuBois* ed. Herbert Aptheker (Amherst, Mass.: University of Massachusetts Press, 1973), 1:293.

75. *The Booker T. Washington Papers,* ed. Louis R. Harlan (Urbana, Ill.: University of Illinois, 1974), 3:86.

76. Jervis Anderson, *This Was Harlem, 1900–1950* (New York: Farrar Straus Giroux, 1981), 168–178.

77. Langston Hughes, *One-Way Ticket* (1936; rpt. New York: Knopf, 1949), 67.

78. Claude McKay, *Harlem: Negro Metropolis* (New York: Harcourt Brace Jovanovich, 1968), 117–118; St. Clair Drake and Horace Cayton, *Black Metropolis: A Study of Negro Life in a Northern City* (New York: Harcourt, Brace, 1945), 485.

79. S. Winston and M. Butler, "Negro Bootleggers in Eastern North Carolina," *American Sociological Review* 8 (1943): 692–697.

80. Nancy O. Lurie, "The World's Oldest On-Going Protest Demonstration: North American Indian Drinking Patterns," *Pacific Historical Review* 40 (1971): 311–332.

SEVENTEEN

From Symbolic Exchange
to Commodity Consumption:
Anthropological Notes on Drinking as
a Symbolic Practice

Marianna Adler

This essay draws on historical accounts of drinking in British society in an effort to shed light on the symbolic nature of drinking in modern Western societies. My approach reflects a growing anthropological interest in the cultural interpretation of historical data.[1] In keeping with a Marxist approach to the analysis of culture, I assume that an examination of drinking as symbolic practice requires such a historical approach for the critical illumination of our ethnographic present. To this end I will begin here with reflections on a contemporary advertisement for tequila, proposing an interpretation that reads this ad as myth. Then I will argue that the social production of this myth can be traced through the ideological processes that transformed the symbolic terrain of drinking in nineteenth- and twentieth-century England.

The ad of which I speak (and it comes in several versions) is for Cuervo Premium Tequila. The setting changes. Sometimes it is a vast expanse of sandy desert, sometimes a patio high on a hill looking out over the glittering night lights of a city far below, sometimes the white sands of a beach at sunset. Whatever the setting, the evocation is of a dream. The colors are flushed and sensual; time appears suspended. In one version a bottle of tequila, swollen to a size that can only evoke mythic presence and glowing with an interior light, hovers above the heads of the small group of young men and women intensely absorbed in the collective effervescence of each other's company. At their feet is a life-sized "real" version of the tequila bottle, hazy and indistinct compared to its illuminated mythic counterpart. Similarly, the people, holding glasses of tequila, are depicted without much distinction or graphic detail. By contrast, a gold and shimmering glass of tequila on ice rises against the pink and blue sky above the ocean at the horizon. Overhead a green lime hangs suspended; a saltshaker with a phallic silver head angles suggestively inward. A brilliant red parrot, florid and primitive, takes flight across the sky. Parrot, glass, saltshaker, and lime share the same mythic proportions, dwarfing the small group of revelers. In fact, the human party going on is so insignificant that in one version of the ad it is completely absent and only the objects themselves remain, lifelike, powerful, and dominating against an empty, surreal landscape. In contrast to the richly elaborated imagery, the words of the ad are minimal. The most telling version of this ad-myth simply reads "It's all true."

What's all true? And what is the source of the disturbing, yet compelling, imagery of this text? Let me suggest that this mythic text is a symbolic representation of the cosmology of capitalist society, the representation of itself to itself, which reveals (more than it knows) the truth of its own internal logic of production. The objects of the picture —the bottle of tequila, the lime, the saltshaker, and the glass—exude an animate, spiritual force; they are in fact the source of the life force that animates the small party of drinkers. What we are given is the mythic expression of commodity fetishism, which in the processes of everyday life informs the symbolic terrain of the lived experience of capitalist relations of production and consumption. Fetishization connotes the attribution of life and power to inanimate objects. Commodity fetishism, as a specific form of fetishization, presupposes the draining of these qualities from the human actors who bestow such attributions. Social relationships are emptied of significance and reconstituted only as secondary attributes of the relations maintained between things, that is, the products of labor exchanged and consumed. In the case of the tequila liquor ad the social quality of collective effervescence is attributed to the commodity Cuervo Premium Tequila, which is then consumed in its miniaturized iconic form by the group to attain its effect. "It's all true" is the mythical affirmation of the everyday experience of commodities as having value and lifelike qualities with the power to dominate and transform human existence. The acceptance of this experience as the "real" or "true" perception of the phenomenal world is, moreover, the necessary psychic component for the continued hegemony of capitalist relations.

Fetishization as such is not confined to capitalist society. Marcel Mauss explored the fetishized nature of the gift that binds men in relations of symbolic exchange in primitive and archaic societies.[2] The belief that an article exchanged contains the life force of the person who first created it and subsequently gave it away forms the basis of the symbolic power of the gift to bind people into relations of continued reciprocity, the foundation of society itself. But as Michael Taussig explains, commodity fetishism is a function of the initial alienation of the person from the object of his creation in keeping with the bourgeois norms of private property:

> In the capitalist lexicon to buy or sell means to claim or lose all attachment to the article that is transferred. The relations of product to producer and the productive social milieu, as well as to nature, are forever sundered. The commodity assumes an autonomy apart from human social activities, and in transcending that activity the relations between commodities subjugate persons, who become dominated by a world of things—things that they themselves created.[3]

Taussig argues that the fetishization of the commodity corresponds to a general principle underlying capitalist culture and serving as the basis of awareness within that culture. According to this principle, "the social relation is consummated in the relationship of a thing to itself and...ontology lies not in a relational gestalt but squarely within the thing itself." The consequence is that parts of a living system are "thingified" and appear independent of the context of which they are a part. Things indeed appear as though they were animate, and the logical and perceptual basis is established for fetishization.[4] The result of this cultural construction is the projection of an atomized, self-encapsulated world of things whose meanings and properties appear to be self-contained. This construction, however, is necessarily a deception inasmuch as what appear as self-bounded things are merely the embodiment and concretization of social relationships that bind them to a larger whole.

As originally analyzed by Marx, commodity fetishism is rooted in the alienation of the laborer from his labor and from the products of his labor. Baudrillard, who extends Marx's critique of the political economy of production to a critique of the political economy of consumption, further argues that the fetishization of the object under capitalism hides not only the relations of production but also the relations of symbolic exchange.[5] The latter, as exemplified by the process of primitive gift exchange, is a moral or jural transaction that initiates and sustains personalized and humanized relations among women and men and among groups. It is hidden by what appears as "rationalized" market exchange, exchange that proposes to substitute equivalents (labor for a wage) to deny the social relation initiated by the transaction. Under capitalism the gift is transposed into the commodity, a thing whose value is self-contained, that can be alienated by the simple substitution of its value equivalent, and that appears to exist independently of any human moral relation. The ideological process effected in this conversion is a transposition of the process by which social relations, and thus subjectivity itself, are produced and reproduced in society. Rather than appearing as emanating from relations among men and women, identity appears as grounded in the relationship between the individual and the objects of his or her consumption. This transposition of meaning accomplishes the conversion of symbolic exchange into the political economy of consumption. The latter is nothing less than the cultural production of the atomized individual, the consumer with needs to be satisfied. It is at the same time the production of the individual laborer with labor power to be sold on the market and expended on the production of an object that as self-contained value, can enter into the market circulation of commodities. The political economy of consumption is thus the ideological basis of an entire social formation grounded in the construction of a particular pattern of subjectivity.

My argument is that an initial examination of the symbolic history of alcohol and drinking in the period covering the emergence and consolidation of capitalist culture will at least partially reveal this same ideological process. As I shall suggest, under precapitalist social relations in England drinking was defined by relations of symbolic exchange analogous to gift exchange. As both symptom and agency of the emergence of industrial capitalism in the nineteenth and twentieth centuries, drinking was symbolically redefined, first as moral deviance and later as legitimate consumption circumscribed within the emergent leisure domain. However, I would propose that drinking in our culture still has the ability to recall, and at times even reproduce momentarily, the relations of symbolic exchange that informed its preindustrial history. The commodification of drinking, its conversion to the activity of consumption that we witness in the tequila ad, operates by recalling relations of symbolic exchange only to fetishize them within the mythic discourse of capitalist social relations. This process of fetishization is the basis of the symbolic power of the ad, a power that harnesses the primary truth of the gift to the reproduction of a specific political economy.

DRINKING, SYMBOLIC EXCHANGE, AND THE MORAL ECONOMY OF PREINDUSTRIAL SOCIETY

The defining characteristics of modern industrial society as it emerged in the nineteenth century was its cultural and social organization according to the principles of a market economy. This "fact" of nineteenth-century society concealed not only a social history but also an

ideological history in which the very category of economy as a self-de-
fining whole apart from other socially constituted domains emerged as
a phenomenon of consciousness and experience. Louis Dumont has
traced this slow recognition and subsequent disembedding and recon-
stituting of the raw phenomena of economic perception.[6] He equates
this process with the transition from traditional society, ordered according to holistic principles, to modern society, whose fundamental
unit for organization is the individual. In the first case the stress is on
the relations between men and women ordered according to principles
of hierarchy and subordination within a social whole; in the second
case the stress is on the relation between people and things or property.
The effect of this shift transforms not only the principles for the
organization of human society but also human nature, on which those
principles must operate. In this historical process the traditional
meanings attached to drink as a symbolic medium for the social relations among men and women were displaced.

The market economy that emerged in England in its mature form
only after 1830 took as its normative model the self-regulating market,
wherein nothing but market prices were to be allowed to regulate the
economic life of the nation. Under such a system economic relations
became the norm and the measure of all other forms of social relationships. Although, as Dumont has shown, the ideological precedent for
market hegemony was unsystematically present in the work of such
seventeenth- and eighteenth-century philosophers as Locke and Mandeville, it was not until the nineteenth century that economic principles, disengaged from both religious and political forms, gained
their ascendancy.[7] In this sense nineteenth-century capitalist society
differed from any society that had ever before existed in the history of
mankind. In all previous forms of society, and in those few societies
that even today remain marginal to the world market, economy has
been subsumed in social relationships. In consequence the motivations
that govern human activity have differed fundamentally from those
characteristic of a market economy. As Karl Polanyi argues, in precapitalist society men and women do not act to safeguard personal interests
in the accumulation of material goods but rather act to secure their
social interests:

> He acts so as to safeguard his social standing, his social claims, his social
> assets. He values material goods only in so far as they serve this end.
> Neither the process of production nor that of distribution is linked to
> specific economic interests attached to the possession of goods; but
> every single step in that process is geared to a number of social interests
> which eventually ensure that the required steps be taken.[8]

The point is not that individual acts of barter do not exist in such societies but rather that such acts are deeply embedded in social and symbolic transactions. As such, the act of barter is subordinated to custom and law, religion and magic. The economic transaction is kept secondary to the social relation, whose vitality depends on trust and confidence organized according to principles of reciprocity, autarchy, and redistribution. Only by devoting primary attention to the maintenance of social ties can the necessary exchange and transactions involving material goods be assured. Even under mercantilism in England the state acted to regulate the growing national market so as to assure the continued primacy of social relations organized according to principles other than those of the market. Phenomena that today are separated out as economic on the one hand or as political on the other remained intermingled. Economic phenomena were still considered to be means to what were recognized as fundamentally political ends: "Wealth remained on the whole subordinated to or encompassed in power."[9]

Not until 1830 was the transition to the free market economy completed in England, the critical stage being reached when the Poor Laws were reformed so as to allow the unrestricted commodification of free labor, whose price was to be completely determined by the action of the unrestricted market. Older principles that had previously organized the rights and obligations of a reciprocally constituted social hierarchy were dissolved. E.P. Thompson, who has called this premarket society a moral economy,[10] has argued that the widespread resistance to the emergence of the early capitalist economy was inspired by the sense of the violation of the principles of this older moral order. What I wish to focus on is the symbolic significance of drink in the moral economy of precapitalist society so that we may understand the increasing marginalization and repudiation of older drinking practices as a function of the transformation to capitalist economy and culture.

"WITH BEER ONE THANKS, BUT WITH MONEY ONE PAYS"

Before the 1830s, the shared practice of daily drinking was a primary symbolic vehicle for the generation and affirmation of the social relations of community that formed the basis of English preindustrial society. *Not* to drink was tantamount to a complete withdrawal from socially meaningful existence as it was then defined. John Dunlop, a temperance advocate and chronicler of the drinking customs of the British Isles, repeatedly recorded instances of laboring men and women being ostracized and denied assistance in their work for refusing to participate in reciprocal drinking rituals. In one case a man's shoes were nailed to the floor; in another a man's tools were stolen. A woman in domestic service was made so miserable by her working companions that she finally quit. In at least one instance the offense was considered so serious that a man received a beating for antisocial behavior. Dunlop observed that such drink customs operated like a tax, and in many cases men and women longed to be freed from the obligation but were unable to resist the social demands for conformity. The compulsory quality of these drink rituals make it abundantly clear that their observance was motivated by far more than simply a national proclivity for the taste of alcohol. Dunlop himself observed that these rituals were in essence a "metaphysical agency" for the observance of manners of social etiquette and courtesy. But in fact such drink rituals were more than the medium for the exchange of social niceties. They occupied a significant symbolic place in the affirmation and reproduction of the social relations that formed the basis of preindustrial English society. The ritual occasions for drinking served to reaffirm principles for the organization of social relations of exchange in a precapitalist economy.[11] With the transformation to full-scale industrial capitalism these principles would necessarily be superseded or at best remain marginalized, counterhegemonic themes in a society whose organization was overwhelmingly governed by a different order.

Unlike the rationalized workplace of industrial society, whose primary function is to maximize production, the workplace of the artisan group was first and foremost a social community. The symbolic acts that created and reaffirmed social ties took precedence over the productive activity that was dependent on them. It was through drink rituals that the social world of the artisan work group was reproduced. Through the giving and exchange of drinks social ties of obligation and reciprocity were established. Such was the meaning of the elaborate drink practices surrounding the integration of the new apprentice into the work group. In almost all trades apprentices were expected to pay a drink fine commencing their service in a shop. Other drink fines in the trades were occasioned by "loosening", or the completion of apprenticeship. Drink fines were also due on completion of various stages in the work process. Among calico printers, when a man changed from one department to another, he was assessed a drink fine. Aside from assuring the internal solidarity of the work group, the practice of drink fines, especially those due on the initiation of a new apprentice, served to restrict entry into trade guilds and thus strengthened guild monopoly.[12] Only those who could afford to pay the fine could enter on an apprenticeship, and for a poor family, the cost could be prohibitive.

Some sense of the internal cohesion and strength of the work group can be had by examining other circumstances for levying drink fines.

Not only did the fine establish the structure of loyalties, but the very ability to exact the payment was indicative of the moral hegemony of the group. As reported by Dunlop,

> if any man inform on another to the master (called "sucking" the master), the case is brought before the trade club, and decided; if any penalty ensue, it is generally a drink fine. If an apprentice neglects to watch the fire properly, he incurs a drink fine. When a man is made foreman he must pay 5s. for a drink....If fines and footings are not paid, tools are bid; particularly the special tools required at the time. This is called "making an old woman on one." If the recusant acquaints the master, the fine is just doubled....The same informant mentions, that if fines and footings were not paid, after all other schemes fail, a strike would ensue, and the employer be forced to dismiss the operative. As we before had occasion to state, with regard to the regulations of various trades in Ireland and Scotland, there is here a tribunal for the purpose of trying all questions which infer drink fines. A man is said, under these circumstances, to be tried under the Strong Beer Act. Sometimes, the court is formed of men in the same workshop, at other times, of persons selected from various shops. One informant has seen a man fined in four gallons of ale; and a foreman in eight gallons, on such an occasion.[13]

On all these occasions the fine was owed to the group as a whole and was consumed collectively, generally at the local tavern.

Communal drinking also functioned to organize ceremonies of redistribution that simultaneously affirmed principles of reciprocity and communality. According to Harrison, in times of economic hardship, when one member of the community was particularly hard hit, organized drinking, or "whip-rounds", were held in the local tavern to raise funds for the impoverished member.[14] Thus, as opposed to an individualistic principle of accumulation, drinking served the principle of redistribution, sustaining and reaffirming the hegemony of the group. The symbolic affirmation of redistribution as opposed to accumulation can be observed in other drink fines imposed by the work group. For example, in many trades any purchase of new clothes by an individual required that they be "wetted," that is to say, a drink fine was owed on their account. Among platers the purchase of a pig cost a man 1s. in drink fine; a cow, 2s. 6d. If he bought a pair of top boots he had to pay 6d. for drink. Similarly, any time a man made a good bargain in the process of buying or selling he had to pay from 6d. to 1s. in drink fine.[15] In all these cases it appears that any hint that a man might be advancing his own interests at the expense of group identification met with at least the symbolic requirement that parity be restored.[16]

The mutual obligation to treat at drinking extended beyond the community of status equals. Employers were also expected at ritually defined times to supply drink to their employees. Unlike the wage, which buys labor at its market value unencumbered by the obligation of custom, the drink payment retained elements of the older paternalistic bond that linked men of unequal status in relations of exchange. A successful transaction between bargainers was also accompanied by a drink exchange, the latter standing as symbolic pledge that the commercial transaction was protected by the primary obligation of the social bond. As Harrison has noted, "Cold cash payments without drink exchange, signified either the presence of an outsider, or desire to conclude the relationship." Paying in cash for personal favors such as help in plowing "would have been a gross insult" because "with beer one thanks, but with money one pays." Transactions were "only part of a sequence of mutual favors" and were "still not exclusively a search for better goods at lower prices: it was first of all a technique in social relations."[17]

In a society where the fabric of social relations rested on claims to rights and obligations legitimated in appeals to religious and traditional forms of authority, seasonal festivities, in which alcohol played a prominent part, served to regenerate ritually the politically constituted social order. Bacchanalian festivals were the scenes of orgiastic inversions that temporarily inverted the social hierarchy to reestablish its legitimacy once again as the "natural" manifestation of the order that would follow on the heels of ritual chaos. Peter Bailey, writing of such preindustrial festivities, describes them as an instance of that "ancient license of carnival when all social restraints on the human appetite were lifted and eating, drinking, fighting, and lovemaking were celebrated in orgiastic fashion." On such occasions, he continues,

> the authority structure of village society could be temporarily inverted in the time-honored ceremonies of Saturnalia—the common man was king for the day and the world was turned upside down, as villagers thumbed their noses (and worse) at their betters. Far from taking offense, the governing classes tolerated and often patronized these and other popular festivities; their goodwill was in part a reflection of their own membership in the village community, in part a recognition of the utility of such rites in dissipating popular frustration and thus reinforcing the authority of the rural oligarchy.[18]

Despite the role that such festivals played in the maintenance of the dominant hierarchy, they were not always able to contain expressions of protest within ritualized forms. Referring to popular festivals in Europe, Peter Burke emphasizes the manner in which the popular classes took advantage of festivals to express their hostility to the person or acts of those in power:

Festival meant that peasants came to town and that everyone took to the streets. Many people were masked, some were armed. The excitement of the occasion and the heavy consumption of alcohol meant that inhibitions against expressing hostility to the authorities or private individuals would be at their weakest. Add to this a bad harvest, an increase in taxes, an attempt to introduce, or to forbid, the Reformation; the resulting mixture could be explosive. There might be a "switching" of codes, from the language of ritual to the language of rebellion. To move from the point of view of the authorities to that, more elusive, of ordinary people, it may well have been that some of those excluded from power saw Carnival as an opportunity to make their views known and so to bring about change.[19]

Whatever the precarious mix of rebellion and ritual in early modern Europe, by the middle of the eighteenth century in England the social changes resulting from the cumulative effects of enclosures, urbanization, and changing economic relations had begun to undermine the material and ideological basis that had sustained the paternalistic tolerance of the older ruling order. By the early nineteenth century the bourgeoisie, whose ruling hegemony was not yet tightly secured, found the license and disorder of festival behavior fearfully close to class rebellion, although there were already such anticipations in the 1700s. Increasingly the moralists attacked the popular recreation styles of the lower orders. By the 1850s reformers were making concerted attempts to reconstruct popular recreational patterns. These efforts in turn were part of a still wider campaign among bourgeois reformers to encourage the acceptance and imitation of bourgeois values among the growing ranks of the proletariat. During the 1830s working people were subject to increasing pressure to regulate their sexual life in accordance with middle-class morals and to conform to a middle-class model of a postponed and provident marriage. The Lord's Day Observance Society, the Society for the Prevention of Cruelty to Animals, and the Anti-Spirits Movement were all founded within a six-year period.

However, in judging the motivation of middle-class reformers, one should also acknowledge that their reform efforts were to some degree a response to a perception of appalling conditions of health and welfare among the popular classes. To the extent that the transformations and dislocations of early industrialization had destroyed the communal context for drinking, and to the extent that distilled beverages (in particular gin) were the drink of large sections of the urban poor, there were problems of health, squalor, and violence associated with (but not necessarily caused by) alcoholic consumption. Insofar as this was true, middle-class reform efforts found a sympathetic response among the industrial poor and working classes, especially among women, who frequently suffered the consequences of men's drinking. Antidrinking sentiment among women was in part a function of the changing nature of domestic relations in the transition to industrial society. Often, within both the domestic and the public spheres, preindustrial cultural patterns persisted into the nineteenth century alongside new, emergent cultural patterns. However, the changed context within which the older drinking patterns persisted altered their effects and raised new or latent contradictions. Even while recognizing the conditions to which middle-class reformers responded and the sympathetic response that such efforts may have garnered among the working classes, we note that this concern and response was itself a sign of the emergence of a society where increasingly the moral unit was the individual rather than the group.

TEMPERANCE AND INDUSTRIALIZATION: FROM MORAL ECONOMY TO POLITICAL ECONOMY

The temperance movement that arose in England and America in the first half of the nineteenth century was closely linked to the needs of an emergent industrial economy. In England the movement was allied particularly with the development of the textile manufacturing industry. It was in the textile manufacturing centers of Ulster and Glasgow that the earliest teetotal societies appeared. From the textile centers of Preston, Bradford, and Leeds the movement spread through England. It flourished especially among the nonconformist trading and manufacturing classes. As Brian Harrison notes, these classes stood directly to gain from temperance propaganda in that the movement offered a moral platform legitimating the demand for security of property, a disciplined labor force, and an expanded home market:

> Every citizen with property gained from a movement which helped to maintain law and order. "Are you a CAPITALIST?" asked Joseph Livesey in his "Malt Lecture," the manifesto of teetotalism: "What a comfort to live in the midst of a sober population. The Temperance Society is an insurance for the safety of every man's property. Drunkenness and disorder are sure to drive capital away. . . ." The movement sought to base public order on individual self-discipline: for Thomas Spencer, every teetotaler "was a policeman engaged in repressing crime, and preserving the peace." To all rate-payers, the temperance movement offered a solution to the problem of pauperism.[20]

It was in the textile industry that large-scale factory organization first developed, and nowhere, as A. Ure commented in 1835, was the gospel truth "Godliness is great gain" more appropriate than in the administration of a large factory.[21] In 1829, the year that the temperance movement was launched in the industrial north, depressed conditions in the textile industry made acute the need for a disciplined labor force.[22] By preaching discipline, sobriety, and self-control, the temperance movement protected capitalist investment. Furthermore, by urging thrift and the imitation of a middle-class home life, it helped establish a home market for consumer goods. Rather than spending their wages at the local tavern, the workers were urged to save toward the elaboration and decoration of the home. Thus, the temperance movement in England served as a significant institutional vehicle for the production of the new man: a man with labor power to sell and expend efficiently and a consumer with "needs."

However, the antispirits movement in England arose at a time when drunkenness was becoming increasingly unfashionable and appeared to be decreasing among the working classes. Frances Place, himself born of the working class and a chronicler of its early history, estimated that between 1800 and 1830 a sober and self-improving aristocracy of labor had emerged from the generalized culture of artisans and working men. Thus, it appears that the temperance movement was but one symptom of a much larger transformation whose sources lay in various historical trends converging within the emergent capitalist political economy. Moreover, secularization and individuation repeatedly emerged as the dominant themes, whether articulated through reform movements such as temperance or through radical working-class politics of the period. Similarly, utilitarianism, and thus the cardinal principle of use value, increasingly held hegemonic sway. The important point to be noted here is that the principles of thrift, sobriety, and self-control, which were aimed at the reform of drinking practices, were not simply an ideological tool by which the capitalist class controlled the proletariat but were fundamentally an instance of a much larger historical transformation involving a changed conception of man's relationship to the natural world (the process of secularization) and the social world (the process of individuation). They are analogous processes, expressing the same movement on different analytical levels. Both are aspects of what Louis Dumont has identified as the ideological transformation from a society whose organizational principles are based on relations between men to one based on relations between men and things.[23] In this process man's own conception of his self was taking on increasingly thinglike qualities. From being the hallowed vessel of God, the body was becoming a machine whose integrity was defined by the smooth functioning of its parts rather than by the moral or jural bond linking self to other. "If inanimate machines worked so well with constant attention," asked Robert Owen, "what may not be expected if you devote equal attention to your vital machines, which are far more wonderfully constructed?"[24]

As the nineteenth century advanced, the ascendant capitalist order gradually secured its dominance. The older social forms that had organized and sustained social life either disappeared or remained on as marginal "folk" practices. In other cases they persisted, though in new modes, as elements of working-class culture, a culture that, to use Antonio Gramsci's terms, retained at least for a time a corporate identity in the face of bourgeois hegemony.[25] Drinking practices, which had figured centrally in the symbolic exchanges of a precapitalist economy embedded in the social relations that bound men into relations of exchange and production, were delegitimated by the ascendant rationalist utilitarian order. The wage relation, rather than the political relation, now defined the mode of exchange between men. "With beer one thanks, but with money one pays"—and the point was now to pay. Measured time, the machine, and the self were not only the organizing social units but also the symbolically productive metaphors of the nineteenth century capitalist society. Drink and inebriety blurred time and made a mockery of its efficient "use"; it threatened the repression of affect by which the self of the bourgeois world was made self-evident; and it subverted the rationalistic order of the age of the machine by evoking older memories of relations among men and women under a different moral order.

FROM RITUALS OF COMMUNALISM TO LEISURE STYLES: WORKING-CLASS MALE CULTURE

I have argued that the temperance movement in the nineteenth century represented part of the overall processes of secularization and individuation. By then these processes were clearly operating as ideological accompaniments to the rise of industrial capitalism. A central tenet of this changed conception of the world was the transference of thinglike qualities to the individual's conception of himself or herself and his or her relation to the world. At the same time men's and women's own objective creations took on increasingly animistic qualities: capital grew and multiplied, markets were conceived of as self-regulating natural systems, and commodities promised magical transformations. However, in spite of the hegemonic dominance of such metamorphic constructions (and the fact that they are metaphors does not alter their very real *material* effect in the production and reproduction of the capitalist social formation), their displacement of older principles for governing social relations proceeded at different rates and to different degrees throughout society. Like pieces in a kaleidoscopic pattern, elements in the evolution of a new cultural personality had no necessary order of emergence. Traditional modes and mentalities persisted among English workers even as newer forms were coming into being. In this section I wish to explore the way in which the pub, as it historically evolved as a nineteenth-century male working-class institution, preserved, albeit in changing modalities, the affirmation of communal values grounded in the processes of symbolic exchange that had nurtured early English peasant and artisan culture. The further decline of the pub in the twentieth century and its replacement by such institutions as the cinema, dance hall, and television signaled the collapse of the cultural institutions that had sustained a particular historically developed form of working-class life. The effect was to weaken those counterhegemonic forms of symbolic practice that had sustained, in the face of the political economy of consumption, alternative meanings and identities.

The French anthropologist Maurice Godelier has suggested that the power of domination consists of two equally necessary relations: violence and consent.[26] Although ultimately always backed by the threat of violence, consent is the more binding of the two. I would suggest that under relations of capitalist domination it is within the realm of consumption that consent is secured. Raymond Williams has written that true hegemony consists of "effective self-identification with the hegemonic forms: a specific and internalized 'socialization,' which is expected to be positive but which if that is not possible, will rest on a (resigned) recognition of the inevitable and the necessary."[27] I contend that private life, and more specifically leisure consumption as constituted under the regime of capitalist hegemony, was one of the major domains within which positive identification was achieved. This is another way of saying what Jean Baudrillard has argued, namely, that the political economy of consumption entails the creation of specific subjects with needs appropriate for the reproduction of the generalized form of capitalist political economy. By examining the English pub as a cultural institution, we may observe this process as it has transformed the symbolic terrain of drinking practices.

If the temperance movement reflected the values of the bourgeoisie and often the aristocracy of labor as well, the pub, with its synthesis of both older traditional forms and newer working-class patterns, stood in similar symbolic relation to the evolving working-class culture of the nineteenth and early twentieth centuries. By the first quarter of the nineteenth century the cumulative effects of the breakup of older stable communities, the inroads of Methodism, the success of reforms aimed at the elimination of older festive styles, and the enclosures of the common lands had gone far toward constricting the older patterns of popular play. At the same time the demands of mechanized factory production and the accelerated pace of urbanization contributed to the radical restructuring of social patterns of work and leisure. The result was that the pub, as a center of working-class social life in the nineteenth century, both sheltered what was left of the older patterns of play and festival behavior and assured a kind of free space where working-class popular culture could define itself in an environment at least somewhat buffered from the insistent hegemony of bourgeois culture. For if the rise of industrial society entailed on the one hand an attempt by the bourgeoisie to impose its own moral standards on the working class through both legislative and moral reforms, it also entailed an increasing cultural and spatial segregation of the classes, permitting working-class culture to develop a restricted self-identity.

English radicals of the 1820s asserted that the enclosures had forced working people into the drinking places for recreation. The few public parks that did exist were often closed to working people, whose homes were generally cramped, cold, and uncomfortable. Where else was the workingman to go to find such necessities as light, heat, lavatories, newspapers, cooking facilities, sociability, and the communal festivities that relieved the harshness of early industrial life? As an old working-man, remembering conditions in industrial Yorkshire in the 1830s, recalled, "There were only two places to go in spending spare time away from one's house—church, chapel, or alehouse; the former were seldom open, while the latter were seldom closed. The first was not attractive, the second was made attractive."[28] Among those aspects that made the tavern attractive for the workingman was the wide variety of sports and entertainment that could be found in local taverns. Older popular sports involving gambling and cruelty to animals persisted in the taverns of the early nineteenth century despite the growing agitation of moral reformers. In addition, tavernkeepers would sponsor such recreational activities as bowling, quoits, glee clubs, free and easies, amateur and professional dramatics, fruit and vegetable shows, and sweepstakes clubs. By 1851 a survey of adult education in Nottingham reported the presence of workingmen's libraries in public houses. Local drinking places in many cases were the centers of intellectual life among workingmen. Political discussions held at public houses continued the traditions of radical artisans. A churchman in Bolton reported that two workingmen had explained their absence from Sunday chapel by saying that they had been attending a discussion at their local pub concerning the existence of God.

On into the nineteenth century the tavern continued to serve as a labor exchange, a pay station, and a stopping place for tramping artisans. Furthermore, as the social dislocations of the industrial revolution proceeded, the community of the tavern offered to the urban migrant a haven in an otherwise anonymous urban environment.

Throughout the first half of the century the tavern remained closely integrated with the social life of working-class culture, in part through the continuing close association between pub and work group. The many drinking rituals of the workplace that involved treating one's workmates to drinks further tied men to the credit of the pub. But perhaps more important, the pub was the place where workingmen's savings and burial clubs met, where Friendly Societies, Hampden Clubs, and the trade unions held their meetings. Workingmen generally lived close by their place of work, so that the community served by the local pub was one in which overlapping ties articulated through shared work and residential propinquity bound men to one another in rich layers of relationship. The pub, as a central node in this community of men, served as the center for conviviality, political discussion, and the rituals of drinking through which men affirmed in shared communion a collective identity.

The years 1820 to 1870 witnessed an increasing specialization and differentiation of economic and social functions throughout English society. One of the effects of the trend was to diminish substantially the role of the drinking place as a central public institution, leaving it to function primarily as a recreation center. The role of the tavern as news center, public meeting house, and center for economic transactions declined as alternative social institutions came into being. Also by 1870 popular beliefs in the restorative functions of alcohol had weakened as new attitudes toward health and the body disseminated through popular culture in the wake of scientific medical advances. An improvement in working conditions also lessened the need for the narcotic and anesthetic effects of alcohol. The availability of safe and nonintoxicating beverages, a large per capita increase in tea consumption after 1840, and the establishment of eating and drinking places besides the public house all contributed to reducing the significance of alcohol as beverage and nutrient.[29] The standardization of holidays and the shortened working day contributed to regularizing the habits of the working class. Although as late as 1912 "Saint Monday" was still being observed in places, workers were coming to accept the substitution of the Saturday half-holiday. Both temperance reformers and educated workingmen had been active in the factory reform movements that had pushed for a limit to the working day. The Ten Hours Bill, which had been seen by many as a temperance measure in that it ameliorated the social miseries believed to drive men to drink, was also a tacit acceptance by much of the working class of new industrial definitions of the appropriate separation of work and leisure. According to Bailey, the struggle of northern textile workers for the Ten Hours Bill, passed into law in 1847, "implicitly acknowledged the separation of work and leisure into exclusive domains while trying to negotiate a more humane balance between the two"; workers were "now prepared to accept the austere regimen of factory production in return for the simultaneous demand for a Saturday half-holiday." Bailey concludes that such workers came to tacit agreement with a "substantial minority of employers" who saw that in making such a concession, they "might not only win better attendance and punctuality in working hours, but might also effectively stabilize the worker's leisure within the fixed limits of a mutually defined weekend."[30]

The decline of skilled trades under the pressures of advancing industrialization had progressively undermined the artisan culture of the early part of the century, which had found its strength in the political and social solidarity of the work group. The shortening of the working week and a rise in real wages had contributed not only to an emphasis on recreation but also to the increasing significance of home and family life. As workers lost control over their labor, middle-class values of autonomy in the private sphere of the home took on a compensatory meaning. With the opportunity for improved housing, working people had begun to move to the suburbs, imposing a geographical separation between home and work that was mirrored in the association of leisure activities with the embellishment of home life rather than as the extension of the social relations of the workplace. According to Stedman Jones,[31] this social and geographical shift was evident in the changing place of the pub and pub culture in the workingman's life. Whereas previously the close geographical association of pub and workplace had reinforced the social and political bonds between the community of pubgoers and the community of workmates, now, with the geographical separation of home and work reproducing the growing ideological significance of family life, the pub to which men repaired after the evening meal was no longer the trade pub near work but the "local." Here a man would pass the evening with fellow workingmen of different trades and occupations. Occasionally wives would accompany their husbands to the local, although the sexes kept to different rooms.[32] The topics of conversation within the pub also shifted in response to the changed social conditions. Now the talk was less likely to reflect shared concerns of trade matters and more likely to draw on generalized interests of sports, entertainment, and politics, although the last to a lesser extent.[33]

Both Gareth Stedman Jones and Brian Harrison comment on the conservative implications of the privatizing trend in working-class life that increasingly linked leisure and recreation to the depoliticized private sphere of family life. For Stedman Jones, the change signaled the decline of the artisan work group whose culture had sustained the older radical traditions. For Harrison, identification with the domestic sphere discouraged the articulation of grievances against social conditions. To the extent that the temperance reformers succeeded in drawing workingmen away from the public house, they succeeded in removing them from the very community that sustained the forms and rituals of public life.

Although the public life of the pub had by 1870 been transformed, it continued to be a central institution in working-class life into the first quarter of the twentieth century. But the rise of the new housing estates beginning after World War I undermined the social relations of kin and neighbor. It was these relations that had formed the basis of the pub drinking group, replacing the older community of workmates. Moreover, the number of pubs fell off dramatically, as they were not being built on the new housing estates. So far as the pub community was able to sustain itself around its now-limited definition as a recreational center, it did so in competition with new forms of mass entertainment based on new principles for the management of identity and social life.

Studies of English working-class culture in the twentieth century have noted the decline of the pub and the chapel relative to the growth of cinema, dance hall, and television as central institutions in working-class life. A pre–World War Two study of a working-class community, *Worktown*, noted that the shift in institutional forms within which leisure time was structured fundamentally altered the relationship between the social community and its cultural expressions. In the case of the pub the internal character and dynamics were shaped by the community of patrons; but cinema, dance hall, television, and other modern forms of "spending" leisure time were institutions whose character was shaped by a commercial logic, a concern for sales success. According to this study, whereas older institutions such as the pub "by a long process of adjustment and attrition [had] developed defined functions which include always cooperation for common ends of social groups," newer institutions were quite different. They were willing, and often able, to put out any social doctrine or have any sort of effect, irrespective of obligation to society and often unaware of that effect. Even the pub became a site for conflict between brewers, who thought of it as a "place of profits," and landlords, who saw it as a "place of friends."[34] The pubs, the authors note, were succumbing to the pressures of centralization and economic competition. The old sort of landlord was gradually being squeezed out as competition between pubs and the alternatives—pool halls, cinema, dance halls—became fiercer. In the process the values of community and continuity were being sacrificed to the values of efficiency. In the same way that the old mills and the mill-home-district relationship gave way to the new cotton combines "in the interests of new industry," the brewers were forced to "eradicate the small and perhaps inefficient old-style" pub and develop a mass-efficiency mode of distribution and sales that effectively destroyed the social character of the pub,[35] indeed making its full name, *public house,* an ironical utterance.

Unlike the older institutions of the culture, the authors argue, the newer institutional forms were in no way concerned with the making of a social group except insofar as it was necessary to make patrons believe that they were in step with fashion or with their peers. The new consumers need not have any ongoing verbal or physical relationship with each other; the activities neither depended on, nor served to reproduce, primary group relations. By contrast, the pub, the church, politics, sports, and clubs depended fundamentally on the participation of people in active groups whose whole basis for relationship consisted in the sharing of similar interests and experiences. The effect of participation was thus to bind the men and women more firmly to the social community from which flowed the shared meanings that gave form to experience.

Considering the association previously noted between temperance sentiment and secularization, it is interesting that among Worktowners there existed a folk belief that symbolically linked the pub with the parish church. According to this belief, there was a secret passageway that ran from under the vault of the Man and the Scythe, the oldest pub in the town, to the parish church two hundred yards away. The passage, as the authors of the study observe, symbolized the cord linking the two spatial representations of community; the pub thereby acquired the religious associations of the still-older symbol of the communal presence. The symbolic association was carried yet further in the architectural mimicking of pub and church:

> The whole set-up of the vault, the bar severing the landlord from the ordinary folk, the arrangements of the bottles on the shelves, the often ornate windows, the beer-engine handles (generally three or four) sticking up like tapered candles, the rituals of toasting, rounds, glass-swigging—have much in common with forms of religious rite and invocation. The intricate build-up of pub rooms around the exclusive landlord sections is faintly reminiscent of the Catholic church. And in each you come to the dividing-line between minister and ministered to for alcoholic liquor.[36]

For men whose lives were regulated by the demands of factory labor, the pub with its rituals of communal affirmation offered an alternative vision to that of the incessant round of weekly labor. In the communal drinking that peaked at week's end, the laborer obliterated the careful, measured rhythm of factory time; but the context still evoked the collective and communal rather than the private and individualistic:

> The pub stresses the fact that you are living among your fellow men, that the issues of life, whether faced or escaped, are not solitary but communal. The church and the political party say the same thing, in a different way. The films and pool do not. They emphasize the separateness of the individual, and they do not ask him to know anyone. They do not suggest that he has any duty to help anyone but himself, and maybe his wife and kids and old sick mother.[37]

Following World War II the transformation of the institutions of working-class culture proceeded at an even greater pace. John Clarke, commenting on these changes, argues that their full effect was to transform the drinker from member to consumer.[38] Citing the rise of the oligopolistic brewing industry after the war, Clarke notes the same erosion of local control and the decreasing ability of patrons to shape the internal dynamics of the pub environment. Owners or tenants were replaced by brewery-controlled managers. Relations of patronage between clientele and publican were interrupted, with the result that industrial concerns increasingly determined the internal dynamics and patterns of the pub. The tendency of brewers to rationalize the industry, that is, to close or "improve" the pub, led to a series of design changes, such as the substitution of large lounges for a series of snugs, public bars, and taprooms. These changes had important consequences for the patterns and experience of drinking. As Clarke observes:

> Much of this [design change] has been done in accordance with an image of a changing clientele identified by the breweries. The new consumer differs from the old in terms of age (s/he is young), class (s/he is classless) and taste (campari not beer). The effect of this attempt to address the new consumer is to fundamentally change the social and economic conditions under which drinking takes place, that is, to change the determinants of a particular historically developed form of reproduction. We may borrow from Althusser to suggest that these changes in material conditions and signifying practices (and the commercial ideologies which guide them) function to interpellate a new identity for the drinker —that of the "consumer" rather than the "member." This newly forged interpretation dissolves previous patterns and habits of "how to drink" and substitutes for them new "preferred styles of drinking."[39]

As has been my argument throughout this paper, the assumption of the positive identity of consumer represents within the domain of

drinking practices the extension of the hegemonic logic of the capitalist political economy. Furthermore, it represents the extension of this
logic to the domains of leisure and recreation, domains I have suggested that are critical for producing popular consent, the necessary
condition for the nonviolent reproduction of political relations of
domination. I do not mean to suggest that drinking practices, as they
existed before capitalist political economy, were independent of the
reproduction of relations of domination and subordination. In fact, I
hope to have demonstrated that such practices were central to the
symbolic affirmation of political relations among men and women,
relations that were hierarchical as well as egalitarian. It was perhaps
only with the marginalization of such practices within the working-
class culture of industrial capitalism that they functioned to affirm
egalitarian communal relations of shared membership *within* a community whose identity presumed its subordination to middle- and
upper-class culture. But if drinking practices have functioned to produce consent within the politically subordinated classes in both precapitalist and capitalist society, I have tried to suggest that the consent
extracted was based on fundamentally different principles for the
management of identity and social intercourse. In the first case identity was symbolically constructed on the basis of relations among men
and women. In this context drink was the symbolic medium by which
men and women were joined in relations of exchange that served as the
formal grid for articulating principles of membership, difference, and
identity. Under capitalism, I have argued, the locus of identity is
shifted from the *relations* that the object of exchange serves to articulate, to the *object itself*. "I have, therefore I am" and "You are what you
eat (and drink)" are appropriate mottoes for the modern subject of
political economy. However, lest we fall into totalistic theories of power
and domination, we must remember that hegemony, even in its most
effective form as internalized will or consent, must continually be
renewed, defended, and modified. A lived hegemony, as Williams has
told us, is neither uniform nor static but is always a process.[40] It does
not simply exist as a structure of domination but must constantly be
reestablished in the face of alternative and counter processes that
resist, limit, and alter it. Such counter pressures are indications of
what the hegemonic process must constantly work to control and contain. In a society that defines itself primarily by relations between
persons and things, relations of symbolic exchange challenge the dominant logic. At the same time, however, the power of this dominant
logic consists in its continued ability to play on the symbols of symbolic
exchange in the interests of its own continued domination. Returning
to the tequila ad, we can understand it more fully now as a myth, a

myth that sustains (by affirming as truth) a particular form of political economy. But it does so by harnessing those counter hegemonic moments to the symbolic logic of its own continued reproductions.

NOTES

1. For example, see Richard N. Adams, *Paradoxical Harvest: Energy and Explanation in British History* (New York: Cambridge University Press, 1982); Richard Bauman, *For the Reputation of Truth: Politics, Religion, and Conflict among the Pennsylvania Quakers, 1750–1800* (Baltimore: Johns Hopkins University Press, 1971); Eric Wolf, *Europe and the People without History* (Berkeley and Los Angeles: University of California Press, 1982).

2. Marcel Mauss, *The Gift* (New York: Norton, 1967).

3. Michael Taussig, *The Devil and the Commodity Fetishism* (Chapel Hill: University of North Carolina Press, 1980), 26.

4. Taussig, *Devil and the Commodity Fetishism*, 36.

5. Jean Baudrillard, *For a Critique of the Political Economy of the Sign* (Saint Louis: Telos Press, 1981).

6. Louis Dumont, *From Mandeville to Marx* (Chicago: University of Chicago Press, 1977), 34.

7. Dumont, *From Mandeville to Marx*.

8. Karl Polanyi, *The Great Transformation* (New York: Farrar and Rinehart, 1944), 46.

9. Dumont, *From Mandeville to Marx*, 34.

10. E. P. Thompson, "The Moral Economy of the English Crowd in the Eighteenth Century," *Past and Present* 50 (1971): 76–136.

11. Alcohol served many other functions as well. It was taken as both thirst quencher and nutrient. It was valued for its medicinal qualities as well as for its ability to impart strength. Its consumption was also seen as a marker of virility. For a fuller discussion of the usages of alcohol, see Brian Harrison, *Drink and the Victorians* (Pittsburgh: University of Pittsburgh Press, 1971).

12. John Dunlop, *The Philosophy of Artificial and Compulsory Drinking Usages in Great Britain* (London: Houlston and Stoneman, 1839).

13. Dunlop, *Drinking Usages*, 186–187.

14. Harrison, *Drink and the Victorians*.

15. Dunlop, *Drinking Usages*, 187.

16. A principle of ritual balancing appears to be operating in other drink fines as well. For example, it was common practice within work groups to impose a fine to mark a man's marriage, the birth of a child, and the occasion of a youth past sixteen years of age seen walking with a woman. Any of these events might disturb the preestablished pattern of alliances and social relationships. I hesitate to push this point too far, however, as there were other events occasioning a fine that conform to this principle only if one stretches its meaning past the point of any explanatory value. For example, in the plainting trade a man was fined if he reached age twenty-four without being married, as well as being fined when he did get married. A drink fine was also imposed if anyone traveled out into the countryside more than twenty-four miles on a visit.

17. Harrison, *Drink and the Victorians,* 55.

18. Peter Bailey, *Leisure and Class in Victorian England: Rational Recreation and the Contest for Control, 1830–1885* (Toronto: University of Toronto Press, 1978), 3.

19. Peter Burke, *Popular Culture in Early Modern Europe* (New York: Harper and Row, 1978), 203.

20. Harrison, *Drink and the Victorians,* 95.

21. Quoted in Harrison, *Drink and the Victorians,* 96.

22. "In the difficult years 1827–32, the demand for cotton goods was rising more slowly than production. Cotton mill owners were experiencing rising outputs but falling profits—a falling return on fixed capital; yet however low the ceiling price obtainable, high overheads demanded full-capacity output. The only possible remedies were further mechanization, reduced wages, improved manufacturing efficiency or enlarged consumer demand. In the woollen industry too, falling prices accompanied increasing output at this time, and both the woollen and cotton industries were depressed during 1829, the year of the Anti-Spirits movement's successful launching in the textile districts of Northern Ireland and the Scottish Lowlands" (Harrison, *Drink and the Victorians,* 96).

23. Dumont, *From Mandeville to Marx.*

24. Harrison, *Drink and the Victorians,* 185.

25. Gramsci's concept of a corporate class is best understood in relation to his concept of a hegemonic class. A hegemonic class imposes its own vision of things and its own ends on the society as a whole. A corporate class, by contrast, pursues a defensive, yet active, course within the social totality, the determinations of which lie outside its control. A corporate class defines and pursues its own ends within the limits of the social order as hegemonically defined. Within those limits it seeks to define and improve its own condition.

26. Maurice Godolier, "Infrastructures, Societies, and History" *Current Anthropology* 19 (1978): 763–771.

27. Raymond Williams, *Marxism and Literature* (Oxford: Oxford University Press, 1977).

28. Bailey, *Leisure and Class.*

29. Harrison, *Drink and the Victorians.*

30. Bailey, *Leisure and Class,* 14.

31. Gareth Stedman Jones, "Working Class Culture and Working Class Politics in London, 1870–1900," *Journal of Social History* 7, no.4 (Summer 1974).

32. Mass-Observation, *The Pub and the People: A Worktown Study* (1943; rpt. Seven Dials Press, 1970).

33. Stedman Jones, "Working Class Culture."

34. Mass-Observation, *Pub and the People,* 76–77.

35. *Pub and the People,* 77.

36. *Pub and the People,* 93.

37. *Pub and the People,* 218.

38. John Clarke, "Capital and Culture: The Post-War Working Class Revisited," in *Working Class Culture: Studies in History and Theory,* ed. John Clarke, Chas Critcher, and Richard Johnson (London: Hutchinson, 1979).

39. Clarke, "Capital and Culture," 245.

40. Williams, *Marxism and Literature.*

EIGHTEEN

Benevolent Repression:
Popular Culture, Social Structure,
and the Control of Drinking

Joseph Gusfield

In the sequence of festivities in many European countries, Carnival, with its licensed release from many prohibitions on eating, sexuality, aggression, and social hierarchy, occurs before and contrasts with the ascetic period of Lent. The two holidays also appear as metaphors and figures for alternating and opposed attitudes toward life. In his detailed study of popular culture in early modern Europe Peter Burke points to a Brueghel painting in which a fat man sitting on a barrel combats a thin old woman on a chair. The historian remarks that it is a literal enactment of a common battle in Shrovetide rituals. He interprets Carnival, "who belongs to the tavern side of the picture," as symbolic of the traditional popular culture; Lent, however, he associates with the "high culture" of the church clergy, who were then (1559) attempting to reform, if not suppress, many popular festivities.[1]

This association between modes of drinking and modes of sobriety, on the one hand, and divisions in the social structure, on the other, is both the inciting point as well as the subject matter of this chapter. Attempts by officials and established institutions to limit, control, and repress drinking and drinking patterns run through the history of many countries like rivers winding through the landscape, now swollen by spring rains, now dried and thin by the heat of summer. Social scientists are interested in explaining and understanding the flow of drinking controls. They find themselves equipped with a set of conflicting and contrasting perspectives with which to study social hydrodynamics. This paper is about structural explanations and opposing frameworks for understanding alcohol controls.

SOCIAL CONTROL AND MORAL REFORM

On my study wall there is a framed slogan, "Work is the curse of the drinking classes." It is an appropriate text with which to begin. Within those few words are several ways in which issues of regulating drinking are frequently treated. First, there is the importance of social structure. Descriptions of drinking involve classes in conflict rather than a societal consensus that is shared throughout society and from which a special category of persons deviates. Second, in transmuting and transvaluing the parent phrase, "Drink is the curse of the working classes," it reverses the usual view of the problem of alcohol use by locating it among the sober and the orderly. It is the view of those inside the drinking culture, not outside of it. Third, the slogan asserts an opposition between work and drink, an irreconcilability often fundamental to Temperance adherents. What makes it funny is its agreement with the parent phrase in viewing drinking problems as differentiated by class and its reversal of values. It is the view of Carnival, not of Lent.

Implicitly the two slogans are not mirror images. The more conventional view is that of the altruist for whom the regulation and control of drinking is a matter of helping sufferers, people in trouble. For the humorous sloganeer, the control of drinking is something other people impose on him; the alcohol abuse is something that affects the controllers, not the controlled. The crux of the problem, both as a matter of policy and as an analytical issue, is evidenced in the attempted regulation of dance hall and liquor sale hours in Milwaukee in 1912.[2] Frequently the dance halls were part of, or next to, saloon premises. Opponents of restrictive local ordinances, especially the unions, charged that they constituted class legislation since the dance halls were a major form of recreation for working-class youth. A social worker declared: "This is not a fight against the Germans or the Poles. It is not a fight against the pleasures of the working class. All we want to do is lift the moral standards of the city. Give our working girls the liberty of a pure city, pure enjoyment, rather than this personal liberty the opposition speaks of."[3]

Analyses by historians and sociologists of what is called moral reform, or sometimes humanitarian reform, often demonstrate one or the other of these polar perspectives. One school, perhaps most frequent among historians, views reforms as actions in which the reformers are inspired by visions of a new and better world for those to be reformed. The relevant questions concern ideas of reformers about what it is that makes some people suffer and what can be done about their suffering. In the opposite perspective attempts to reform others, including drinkers, are inspired by the trouble that they (those being reformed) create for the controllers. These are to be seen as efforts at social control of troublesome behavior. As William Muraskin has put it in characterizing the social control approach, "the first question to ask is: 'Who are the reformers and of what are they specifically afraid.' "[4]

Such considerations raise the question, For whom is alcohol a source of trouble? In this chapter I examine a group of materials, largely by historians, bearing on the ways, times, and places in which drinking has been troubling. I hope to shed some light on the structural contexts in which policies of alcohol control emerge. This chapter calls attention to the settings in which drinking occurs. The act of drinking, and even drunkenness, has not been the major target of efforts to control alcohol. Such efforts are fruitfully seen as directed against particular forms of usage embodied in particular times and places and involving particular groups. This paper focuses on the context of drinking as part of popular culture, as distinguished from "official" and "high" culture, and its relation to divisions within the social structure.

My attention is drawn to discussions among sociologists and social historians working in other, though allied, fields—the history of crime, deviance, law enforcement, urbanization, popular culture, and what is now termed social control. Those discussions are fertile sources for alcohol studies, both in the theoretical questions they raise and in the sometimes explicit, often implicit material bearing on the social history of drinking.

SOCIAL STRUCTURE AND SOCIAL CONTROL

Like most concepts, social control is one with a long history, though its users often have a short memory. Early sociologists used it as a contrast to governmental, legal, and coercive controls. They emphasized the normative and interactive sources of human coordination as opposed to legal and institutional sources of compliance.[5] In recent years the term appears in two different forms, each a sharp contrast with its earlier uses.[6]

Social control has become a buzzword of the alcohol field. Several major reports have stressed the reconsideration of controls as the outstanding development of the 1980s in Europe and America.[7] Here the reference is to the use of law and institutional regulations in establishing a continuing framework for the availability and use of alcohol. In another arena, among sociologists and social historians, the term has come to mean almost the equivalent of suppression or repression. To show social control is to diminish its claim to do something else—to reform or to help, for example.

Such meanings are observable in the recent stream of sociological materials about health and medicalization. The message has been clear: aspects of medicine such as treatment of mental illness, alcoholism, homosexuality, and drug addiction are construable as means of controlling behavior rather than curing illness.[8] The matter is summed up in a now-classic essay by Irving Zola, "Medicine as an Institution of Social Control."[9] The imputation that a particular professional practice is a means of social control serves to impeach its claim to social neutrality. What professes to be a way of helping sick people is then interpreted as a way in which one part of society is trying to enforce its interests, its standards, and its values over the opposite values, standards, or interests of another. What is presented from a posture of benevolent consensus between doctor and patient, reformer and reformed, is unmasked (demystified) as conflict repressed.

My preference for the term *public controls* to refer to this newer usage and *communal controls* to describe the older form is more than a compulsion for clarity and neatness. It calls attention to a feature of human social life that I will explore later, perhaps ad nauseam. Here it is used to distinguish the official, deliberate acts of institutional policy from the normative and structured patterns of social interaction that constitute facets of situated, particular action. The latter—the social controls of specific settings, of popular and often unofficial culture—must be contrasted with the official, public controls of governments and laws as well as church officials and others in public positions. At least since Sumner's *Folkways* the relation between these two levels of collective life has been a major problem of modern sociology.

I have been recounting a typical intellectual history. Concepts and counterconcepts go together like husband and wife, locked in loving conflict. In the narrow field of alcohol studies today we use controls to contrast preventive measures with treatment approaches. What then is their usage among the social historians and sociologists in allied domains?

Consider the study of mental illness/madness/insanity (the choice of descriptive term is significant, of course). David Rothman's research into the development of asylums in the United States is a study of reformers in the first half of the nineteenth century and why they believed as they did in the then-new idea of asylum: "The asylum was to fulfill a dual purpose for its innovators. It would rehabilitate inmates and then, by virtue of its success, set an example of right action for the larger society."[10] Even though he casts much doubt on its progressive character, Rothman's view of his subject matter is nonetheless that of his subjects; his is a study of reform, of aid to people with troubles. Andrew Scull, in his analysis of the treatment of insanity in nineteenth-century England, shares common ground with Rothman but approaches the subject matter from another perspective. He draws attention to the differentiation that occurred between being employed or unemployable, especially in respect to the indigent poor and the insane. He sees the problem posed by the conditions of economic life: "The establishment of a market economy and, more particularly the emergence of a market in labor, provided the initial incentive to distinguish far more carefully than hitherto between different categories of deviance.... [To distinguish] the able-bodied from the non-able-bodied poor,...to provide aid to the able-bodied poor threatened to undermine...the whole notion of a labor market."[11]

These diverse formulations supply differing perspectives and raise different kinds of questions. What one sees as asylum another sees as incarceration. Rothman's subjects see the deviant as a troubled person; Scull sees persons whose existence creates trouble for others. Rothman's emphasis is on cultural meaning, on how mental illness was defined and understood. Scull's is on structure, on the problem posed for others by the ways in which mental illness and poverty were handled in England.

Thus, recent public control perspectives redefine the reform of deviance. Where the rhetoric of reform talks of helping others, the redefinition raises doubts and queries, finding interests and functions at work that contrast with the consensus that the concept of deviance itself implies. As the material on medicalization indicates, the control perspective uncovers social conflicts where consensus was thought to lie.

How, then, shall we go about studying drinking from these different perspectives? In much of the remainder of this essay I will examine some of the efforts to study drinking in the context of how it creates troubles for other people and of how sociologists and social historians have been utilizing ideas of social conflict in the analysis of drinking and deviance. Implicit, and sometimes explicit, in this analysis is a perspective that asserts that the problems of public control of alcohol are seldom those of drinking per se but rather of the contexts and groups within which drinking and drinking behavior occur. It is these contexts that give meanings to, and create troubles for, specific parts of social structures within particular historical circumstances.

THE RATIONALIZATION OF LEISURE

Deep in the conscious experience of modern people is the division of time into distinct periods—minutes, hours and days. Equally as significant is the overarching difference between times of work and times of play—day and night, week and weekend. As Lewis Mumford and, later,

David Landes have pointed out, the clock and the watch are the symbols of modern, organized, systematized life.[12] The contrast between Carnival and Lent has its analogue in the separation of daily work from daily leisure.[13]

Leisure is more than play. It is a discrete period set aside for play, a systematized way in which time is divided. It is the counterpart to work. As such, it emerges into the consciousness and daily routine as a consequence of the transition from the home-centered workplace to the workplace—the factory, the office—outside the family and the household.[14] It represents a paradox of mere existence—routinization of the time for play. It is here that the major issues of popular culture and drinking are found.

This is not to say that drinking and drunkenness have been issues only in industrialized, modern societies. The attempts to limit the "excesses" of festival and carnival behavior beginning in the sixteenth century in Europe are instructive in two respects. First, they demonstrate a perceived sacrilegious and immoral behavior. A focus on drinking as the source of the gluttony, lechery, and violence of Carnival is part of the efforts of the Protestant and Counter-Reformation Catholic churches to limit the occurrence and activities of Carnival. The ethics and religious sensibilities of the reformers were in conflict with the ethics and sensibilities of popular tradition, "which involved more stress on the values of generosity and spontaneity and a greater tolerance of disorder."[15] The persistence of this competition for the control of popular recreation is a major theme of this essay.[16]

The second lesson in the early attempts to control drinking and drunkenness is the division between popular culture and high culture. The rowdiness with which Carnival is associated had become less and less a shared sacred quality of holidays, festivals, and holy days. Sobriety had been more successful at the higher levels of society.[17] It gave to drunkenness and festival behavior an added feature of social protest that made the emergence of rowdy behavior even more fearful to those who sought to control it. The content of holiday parades, rituals, and other behavior expressed itself in symbolized protests and sometimes in crowd violence. A similar point about the symbolic content of peasant culture has been made by E. P. Thompson in his distinction between polite culture and plebeian culture.[18]

To what extent are the troubles created by drinking related to its context, to the settings in which drunkenness occurs? For whom are drunken acts troubles? Are they understandable as encounters between cultures—between classes, ethnic groups, and religions—in which what is presented as reform, as aid to troubled persons, can be interpreted as troublesome to controllers?

The conditions of agrarian life and the diffuse character of peasant-patrician relations nevertheless made for a social framework that operated to contain and limit the collision between the forces of Carnival and Lent. One form of the argument about drinking and public controls has been that the rise of industrial work led employers to change the traditional acceptance of alcohol as a feature of the workplace. The resistance of the preindustrial community to the rational conduct of life in an industrial society has often been epitomized in the Saint Monday phenomenon, absenteeism or drunkenness of workers after the weekend. Unaccustomed to a time sequencing that required planning and pacing of the total daily agenda, workers continued to declare holidays and sought to work when they saw fit rather than follow the systematic organization of daily and weekly time that the industrial process made dominant.[19]

Another way of seeing these processes is to recognize that what was threatening to the development of industrial production was the timing and location of drinking. The new industrial work force had to learn the disciplines of routine, punctuality, and perseverance while overcoming the traditional habits of spontaneity, indefiniteness, and the mix of work and play.[20] Drinking at work became anathema not because it had increased in frequency but because it conflicted with the demands of new forms of coordinating labor into a more routinized life.[21] What had to be learned was a new industrial morality that prescribed a more routinized and disciplined use of time.[22] As Harrison remarks, the nineteenth-century Temperance debate in England was really an argument about how leisure was to be spent. My previous study of the American case is very similar.[23]

These perspectives toward emergent controls over alcohol use are two somewhat different forms of class interest theory. The first finds impediments to good workers largely in the physiological effects of alcohol on work. It is the employer who finds in control of drinking means for improving the productivity of an industrial labor force. His conflict is epitomized in the move to end both drinking on the job and payment of wages in whiskey.[24] In the United States this exclusion of drinking from the workplace, so contrary to earlier practice, was well under way by the 1830s and had become an accomplished fact of American life by the late nineteenth century.[25]

A second form of the theory of class interest in the rationalization of leisure focuses attention on the culture of the working classes as it exists in congruence or in conflict with the demands of organized productivity under an industrial capitalism. Here rationalized industry and agriculture are predicated on the existence of a particular kind of person as worker and as citizen—one whose values and habits form the self-discipline, ambition, individualism, and ethical probity that ensure both loyal and competent laborers and neighbors. The interest of the industrial and employing class is in the total way of life of employees, in ensuring that the culture of the working class is consistent with the need of employers for a consistent and productive work force.[26] The control of drinking is one means for inculcating a new culture in the working class, a means that benefits the employers by providing the recreation that ensures a more stable and self-motivated work force.

A crude form of this class struggle analysis is found in Sydney Harring's historical study of police in several American cities in the nineteenth century. Harring describes police as primarily engaged in an effort to control working-class life and leisure for the benefit of employers and elites: "Increasing the degree of exploitation of labor means that the police institution provides a measure of discipline and control over the working class that permits a wider measure of exploitation through the labor process—that is, more work with less resistance."[27] From this standpoint the functions of "the suppression of working class recreational activity" can be seen, in part, as making the total society more rational with respect to the interests of employers or, as some might interpret it, with respect to the productivity of the total economy.[28] Others have presented a more sophisticated form of the argument in relation to crime control in general. Surveying the development of a professional, bureaucratized, and public police force, they have concluded that the move to an efficient and organized police was motivated by a demand for both a more orderly form of protection and a more recurrent and predictable social order, one that was not vulnerable to unpredictable work stoppages and political demonstrations.[29]

This account of the rationalization process extended to alcohol use assesses social controls as aspects of a wider domination of elites. It defines the troublesome character of alcohol as the troubles that one class creates for another. Elites institute drinking controls that benefit themselves and do so in the name of helping others. From another standpoint leisure is itself affected by the same rationalistic impulses that characterize capitalism and Western culture. Here the attempt to curtail drinking and drunkenness in its leisure-time uses is part of the moral demands of a civilization that prizes self-control and organization. Harry Levine's analysis of the pre–Civil War temperance movement is based on a description of the efforts of middle-class people to instill a new psychology of self-control in the middle class, to place the burden of social controls on the individualistic self rather than on the domination of external authority.[30] From a similar viewpoint Paul Boyer suggests that participation in, and support of, moral-reform societies was also "less the wish to control others than an impulse toward self-definition, a need to avow publicly one's own class aspirations."[31]

There are many difficulties with explaining drinking controls as serving the interests of employers in employee productivity. For one thing, preindustrial groups do not necessarily resist industrial work. Studies of contemporary industrializing societies do not find the same problems reported for England and the United States. India, for example, appears to experience little intractability in industrial labor.[32] The capacities of people to seal off new from old habits is greatly underestimated.[33]

What alternatives are available and how effective are they for solving problems or troubles posed by drinking? Samuel Cohn's study of British railway workers, for example, shows that employers made small use of "cultural monitors" (clergymen) to discipline worker drunkenness, although it was an element in the labor problems they encountered. They did, however, utilize the existence of competition from Irish migrant labor to establish systems of wage payment that made the worker avoid absenteeism.[34] In other cases, as in Pullman, Illinois, in the late nineteenth century, the attempt to create a moral atmosphere in the worker community, for whatever motives, led to a fringe suburb of evangelical churches, whorehouses, saloons, and union halls, all outlawed or discouraged in the clean air of the pure residential and paternalistic factory town.[35]

More significant are Alan Dawley and Paul Faler's studies of working-class culture and labor protest in Lynn, Massachusetts, in the nineteenth century. Similar to Gutman's study of work habits, their work distinguishes between a preindustrial morality associated with traditional culture and an industrial morality associated with modernity and industrial life.[36] The traditional preindustrial work ethic in America welcomed spontaneity and a life-style in which drinking played an important part. The Temperance movement found strong support among modern workers imbued with an industrial morality they shared with their industrial employers. However, although they shared that morality, it was neither a matter of employer dominance nor support for employer interests.

Paradoxically, the new industrial morality emerged as much from the rural, property-oriented segment of the population as from the working classes. It developed independently of employers. Daniel Rodgers, in his history of the work ethic in America, argues that the ethic of work arose in the agricultural communities of America before industrialization.[37] Moreover, the same qualities that characterized good factory workers also characterized workers who were less obedient and possessed other qualities that made it easier for them to organize. It was among the group most receptive to temperance habits that Dawley and Faler found sources of labor unrest. The more traditional workers were more ready to take orders and more subservient to paternal patterns of labor relations.

There is a vagueness to general concepts like class, capitalism, or industrialism that bedevils much of sociological history in alcohol studies. We need a microhistorical approach that specifies time, place, and group. In the same period that employers of factory labor might be seen as having had an interest in minimizing drinking among workers, commercial farmers had an interest in transporting grain in the form of alcohol.[38] The interests of the liquor industry, the glass-blowers union, and the steel manufacturers are by no means either all alike or necessarily in conflict. To assume a homogeneity of diverse or similar interests on alcohol questions because of position in the social relations of production is an illusion.

THE PROBLEM OF PUBLIC ORDER

In 1826 the Federalist preacher Lyman Beecher voiced his fears of the new electorate: "The laws are now beginning to operate extensively upon necks unaccustomed to their yoke....Drunkards reel through the streets day after day...with entire impunity. Profane swearing is heard."[39] In this sermon, one of his famous "Six Sermons on Intemperance," Beecher saw drunkenness as a political problem, a symbol of the power of a voting public that rejected the authority of the church and the cultural elite. Yet his fears of the "lower orders" are strikingly contemporary. For much of the nineteenth and twentieth centuries writers, political officials, and public figures found the sources of crime and public disorder among the lower social levels. The poor, the immigrant, and the outcast race or religion have appeared to those in higher positions as threats to personal safety, public order, and established government. In 1872 Charles Loring Brace wrote a widely read book called "The Dangerous Classes of New York City," borrowing a term long in use in England as well.[40] The term not only has a tone of class antipathy but also conveys a sense of societal crisis. As Alan Silver remarks, "It was much more than a question of annoyance, indignation or personal insecurity. The social order itself was threatened."[41] The theme persisted throughout the nineteenth century as cities grew in number and size.[42]

In most of the accounts of the "dangerous classes," "the lower orders," or, in contemporary language, "the underclass," drunkenness appears as a necessary, if insufficient, part of the descriptions. How to contain the threat of riot, crime, or just rowdiness is a major problem in the growth of American cities.[43] Both as cause and as content, alcohol and drunkenness are associated aspects of the problem of public order. Some have even related the emergence of a crime problem in European cities to the distillation of gin, its lowered price, and the increased use of liquor among the lower classes.[44]

Although drinking is always a matter of concern, it is seldom treated in isolation from other acts with which it is associated as cause or catalyst. Concern with drinking is entangled with concern for the moral and, as we shall see, the political character of drunken action. A line of continuity runs across centuries and an ocean to the British Act of 1606 controlling the operation of alehouses. It described drunkenness as the cause of "Bloodshed, Stabbings, Murder, Swearing, Fornication, Adultery and such like."[45]

The image of drunkenness as an adjunct to crime and urban disorder is deeply embedded in the repertoire of middle-class and upper-class perceptions of the social structure, augmented by the growing gap in drinking habits between the classes during the nineteenth century.[46] Susanna Barrows has shown how the French crowd and the mob were perceived in the last half of the nineteenth century as irrational and violent and explained as a consequence of male drunkenness, alcoholism, and the irrational character of women. She quotes the historian Maxime du Camp as describing the Communards as "chevaliers of debauchery; apostles of absinthe."[47] The poor and the outcast were the drunken enemies of public order.

Public order is, however, a term that means and has meant different things to different people at different times. How much orderliness is demanded, and by whom? The central work of George Rudé and Eric Hobsbawm on preindustrial crowds has made the important point that the rioting and violence of such crowds was often acceptable and expected. It was neither viewed as a threat to the social order nor as abnormal.[48] Rudé has also revised the image of the mob as undifferentiated riffraff.[49] In neither England nor France of the seventeenth and eighteenth centuries were crowds irrational, unstable, or drunken. As long as they were not seen as a threat to existing institutions, they could be accepted and rioting seen as a cry of protest falling on often-sympathetic ears. Rudé suggests that the frequent bread riots of eighteenth-century France were a form of price maintenance.[50] The control of public crime and disorder was often singularly lax by current American standards. Colonial America accepted a much higher level of disorder, including public drunkenness, than did the nineteenth-century United States.[51]

According to Silver, it was the emergence of a professional and municipal police force that raised the standards of public order.[52] As regular contact between public authority and the citizenry began to occur, the demands for greater safety, legality, and stability increased. Since the development of regularized police forces the standards of public sobriety appear to have made public drunkenness the major nontraffic violation of law in many Western societies.[53]

Yet a common standard of public order is by no means the case. Public drunkenness, for example, is not accorded the same degree of antipathy everywhere as it has been accorded in the United States. David Bayley's comparison of Japanese and American police reveals a greater acceptance of drunkenness in public areas in Japan than in America. The Japanese take a protective attitude toward fellow citizens drunk in public.[54] The sight of drunken men does not create fear in the general public in Japan as it often does in the United States.[55]

POLICE AND PUBLIC ORDER: ROWDINESS AND DISSIDENCE

Until recent decades policing has chiefly involved control of lower-class citizens. However, a close analysis of police and the maintenance of public order indicates that the problem of order and the role of alcohol in it is more complex than generalities of class and class struggle indicate. I find it useful to approach this study with some analysis of both sides of the social equation—the institution of policing and the class and ethnic character of leisure.

Studies of police and policing in the United States have been consistent in pointing out two features of law enforcement. First, policing is largely a reactive, rather than a proactive, procedure. The limitations on entry into what is defined as private spaces prevent police from responding to potential or actual crime unless it is reported or observed.[56] The second feature follows from the first and is a key element in understanding the problem of public order and alcohol. Police can best control and supervise events they can observe and to which they can react. The area in question, then, is largely public and observable territory. Streets, sidewalks, parks, alleys, and public plazas are the venue of police.[57] In the daily activities of police, public order is a matter of keeping the streets and sidewalks safe from crime and minimizing the public's fear of crime or danger.

Where, then, are points of contact between police and citizenry? An understanding of the relation of alcohol to public order would require knowledge about the life-styles of different groups in specific historical periods. Where do patterns of leisure bring people into public arenas? Are these patterns unique to particular classes or other social groups? Are they socially structured? Much of the work on nineteenth-century policing and regulation of leisure has stressed the role of public

drunkenness as a major source of arrests and the regulation of drinking areas—pool halls, dance halls, bars, streets—as a major preoccupation of police and a source of pressure on them.[58]

Are the sites of leisure class-patterned? In earlier periods there was
apparently more interclass drinking than there is today.[59] If so, are
alcohol controls only artifacts of class styles of leisure or do they
maintain the interests of one class against another? The leisure-time
pursuits of Americans bear some relationship both to cultural aspects
of immigrant and native populations and to the uses of public areas
and public places. Although the latter relate to cultures, they are also
consequences of income. That most of the arrests for public drunkenness in Milwaukee and Chicago in the late nineteenth century should
have been among the working classes is not surprising.[60] The amalgam
of class and ethnic imageries and the problems posed for police by
concerns for public order provided a situation in which drinking became a point of tension between police and the working class. It should
be pointed out, however, that such regulation was usually itself limited
both by working-class resistance and by police indifference to laws with
which they had little sympathy, being of the working class themselves.
Here the difference between highly professionalized police forces and
those with limited training and professional self-conceptions may be
considerable.

The rise of professionalized police forces is by no means adequate to
describe or explain the attempts to control, regulate, and limit drinking in such periods as the late nineteenth and early twentieth centuries
in the United States. I have elsewhere analyzed the American Temperance movement,[61] but here I want to view the public controls from a
slightly different perspective—as aspects of urban history and the control of popular culture closely related to the form in which drinking
occurs.

The theory of police control of alcohol as class struggle has another,
and perhaps more crucial, dimension. The issue here is less that of
public order in the daily sense than in the political sense. Interest in
order too has two dimensions or levels. One is the concern for the
prevention of riots, demonstrations, and dissidence. American life, as
we have come to be aware, has experienced a multitude of violent
crowd events.[62] These have lacked the acceptance of lower-class rioting
by elites that existed in Europe and England.[63]

The disposition of authorities and established groups to see political
dissent as irrational, insane actions of impulsive or drunken mobs is
one way of avoiding a confrontation with the issues and conflicts posed
by dissidence.[64] As Ted Gurr has put it, "One group's 'political violence' is another group's 'legitimate protest.' "[65] Here too there is great

need for careful examination of the role of alcohol in acts of collective behavior and the ways in which the events are interpreted by different observers. What constitutes political disorder and what constitutes crime is also at issue. Is Pearson correct in maintaining that "there is...historical continuity between this [traditional] response to the 'mob' and modern accounts of hooliganism and crime as senseless?"[66] How is the description of the presence of drinking used to strengthen or weaken interpretations?

A second form of political interest, however, is given by a different concern—the political function of the drinking place. Styles of leisure among classes or other politically significant groups are often seen as important to the power aspirations of elites. Here Gareth Stedman Jones seems mistaken when he writes, "Struggles over leisure time do not have...inherent antagonism built into them."[67] Any point of gathering that is exclusive or mostly so for a specific group becomes a potential and actual source of political mobilization for a class, an ethnic group, or an aggregate. Susanna Barrows, for France, and Patricia Morgan, for Italy, have shown how government opposition to the French working-class cabaret and the Italian laborer's *bettoja* were motivated by the fears of working-class political dissidence.[68] The drinking place may not be the workingman's club, but it has been a location particularly open to political development. In the attack on the saloon the Progressive movement found a way to challenge the supremacy of the urban political machines. By no means, however, do these considerations explain the prohibition movement and its multiple rural and urban supports. Neither do they, without much more study, explain police attention and inattention to drinking and drinking places.

In this discussion of the problem of public order and drinking I have been stressing the complexity of the act of drinking in relation to social institutions and social structure. Class, as a descriptive term, is itself often too broad for practicable analysis. The distinction made by Britons in the eighteenth century has remained in use, although with different terms: they distinguished between the "rough" and the "respectable" poor.[69] Drinking may also be seen as troublesome to those within as well as outside the lower class.[70] Within segments of the lower classes in the nineteenth century there also existed strong normative systems that enjoined abstinence or decried frequent insobriety. The social controls supported by the middle classes, in turn, were self-oriented, expressing concern about the dangers of drunkenness for their relatives, colleagues, and friends.[71]

Since the 1960s America has witnessed the rise of a new "dangerous class" whose relation to the social structure is less determined by the division of labor than by the division of age. The invention of adolescence as a distinct social category in the twentieth century has provided a new image of the criminal class and a new source of threat and fear. Although in the nineteenth century young people were frequently seen as sources of crime and disorder, they were viewed as part of a discrete class. In the past three decades, however, youth has emerged as a distinct part of the social structure. Diversities of occupation and class are submerged in a general category of age.[72]

Crime studies highlight the role of youth and the imagery of crime, delinquency, violence, and disorder. After the repeal of Prohibition minimum-age laws were one of the few limitations on alcohol availability that were upheld.[73] The major recommendation of the 1983 Presidential Commission on Drunk Driving has been the strengthening of such laws. Youth is becoming, if not a substitute for, than at least an addition to, "the dangerous class."

The contact between youth and police is accentuated both by the use of the automobile and by the leisure patterns of youth and youth communities. Adolescents are today a major user of streets in American society and a major target of police regulation. The control of adolescent leisure has become recognized as a unique area of police activity.

PUBLICIZATION OF DRINKING:
CLASS, CULTURE, AND THE SALOON

Studies of antialcohol movements as an arena of political or community conflict have depicted the clash between "dry" and "wet" forces as an outcome of differences between diverse cultures. Various distinctions have been made: the diversity between evangelical and ecclesiastical religions;[74] between pietistic and ritualistic religious perspectives;[75] between natives and immigrants, Catholics and Protestants, and urban and rural groups;[76] and between preindustrial and industrial cultures.[77] While this emphasis on the continuity of cultural elements is not misplaced, it ignores the specific history of the time and place of conflict. Others are more perceptive in stressing the way in which the experience of both the controllers and the would-be controlled respond to new conditions and experiences in their use of alcohol.[78]

The saloon represents a significant institution in the American history of drinking as well as a lesson in how particular periods of historical existence shape the meanings of alcohol among diverse groups. The saloon (a corruption of the word *salon,* denoting an elegant room in an upper-class home or establishment for dining or for receiving guests) was an invention of the late nineteenth century in America.[79] Many conditions of urban and industrial life contributed to its rise to a place of importance in the leisure of Americans, especially the working class. Although continuity with a preindustrial life was apparent, the place and meaning of alcohol consumption was shaped by the experience of life in the cities of industrial America.[80]

The importance of the saloon both in the imagery and the focus of alcohol controls is a reflection of the public character of the popular culture implicated in those controls. The bar is a quasi-public institution, accessible to strangers and, as a business, adaptable to changes in neighborhoods. Unlike private drinking, drinking in bars is both observable and closely related to public spaces such as streets, squares, and plazas. As Duis remarks, "The disorderly activities inside spilled onto the sidewalk."[81] In the long effort of middle-class America to cope with the moral disorder it attributed to urban growth, the saloon was imagined as the home of the dangerous classes and the vivid symbol of a popular culture that spawned immorality.

For the poor and the immigrant, the narrowed confines of housing, a need for social services, and even a concern for the purity of water and milk prevented him from privatizing his life in the same fashion as the native, middle-class American. "English-speaking or native-born predominated at the coffeehouse," reports Duis, "while the immigrants went to their respective saloons."[82] Within the saloon the worker could also find a multiplicity of functions often not available elsewhere. They ranged from advice on adapting to the city, check cashing, union meetinghalls, and information networks to free lunches, a telephone, conviviality, and more pleasing furnishings than the home could supply. Overall the saloonkeeper, often romanticized by journalists, played an important role in the processes by which what Duis calls a stubborn parochialism supported the autonomy of the ethnic culture and community, apart from the wider metropolitan concerns of the native American middle class.[83]

Drinking was not limited to the poor and the working class, but saloon patronage largely was. Law and public policy played a role in the development of the saloon as a commercial enterprise. In Worcester, for example, the high cost of licenses effectively spelled the death of the *shebeen*, the Irish institution of selling liquor and drinking in homes, usually a monopoly of widows. Whereas at other levels of urban communities Americans were moving in the direction of family life focused on the nuclear unit with a narrowing of the gender gap, the saloon fostered an isolated male recreational group.[84] It came to be a space and a time apart both from job and home as well as a refuge from both: "Men left the home as much in search of a place to drink as of something to drink."[85]

As Rosenzweig suggests, the saloon can be seen as an embodiment of what Raymond Williams, following Gramsci, calls an alternative culture.[86] With the increase in discretionary income accompanying the industrial organization of the late nineteenth century, the worker was able to support a social milieu that provided a sharp contrast to the discipline, individualism, and hierarchy represented by the factory model of the rational, market-oriented society. The communal values represented in "treating" were an opposite of the savings ethic that was so much the standard of middle-class advice on achieving mobility.[87] The values of mutual support, equality, and group solidarity were clearly polar to the individualistic refrain of a market-centered American morality of personal achievement.

One should recognize that what is construed as "public area" is itself not clearly given. For most of their history, colleges in the United States have been places of disorderly conduct and rioting, and college authorities have been ineffective in regulating drinking.[88] For many reasons, including their origins outside the political structure of municipalities, colleges have had an enclave status; they have been permitted to control their own affairs. With campus officials acting in place of parents, police have refrained from entering college campuses and have frequently left disciplinary problems, including drunkenness, to college authorities. The military have similarly occupied a less public position than most of the citizenry.

Such enclaving was less possible in the density and public-transportation patterns of American cities in the 1880s and 1890s. The saloon itself was an institution that always threatened to move into middle-class neighborhoods. It did find a congenial location on major thoroughfares joining urban sections to one another.[89] It is not that there was necessarily more or less drinking associated with urbanization but that the character of public drinking made the issues of popular culture and group divisions a center of heightened concern for the preservation of moral standards. The effort to control drinking was isolated neither from the general Progressive movement against political corruption nor from the movements to preserve moral purity, which was felt to be waning among the middle classes. The sense of a traditional moral order under siege pervaded the urban middle classes of the late nineteenth and early twentieth centuries in the United States.[90] It is consistent with this view of the context of drinking that the major arm of the Prohibition movement was called the Anti-Saloon League.

PRIVATIZATION OF DRINKING AND THE INDIVIDUALIZING OF LEISURE

Prohibition may have sounded the demise of the saloon, but it was well on its way out as a central institution of working-class life even before the 1920s. American leisure was undergoing profound changes as new technologies, urban communities, and rising discretionary incomes made new forms of recreation more attractive. A growing egalitarianism between husband and wife added to the emergence of other forms of public leisure, of which the movies were the most striking.[91] The development of such urban institutions as amusement parks and spectator sports added to the new commercial leisure that attracted both middle and working classes.[92] The saloon was not as vital to a working class now more accustomed to city life and new consumption patterns. The outlines of contemporary American society and culture were discernible even as the Eighteenth Amendment was passed.

The America of the past fifty years is sharply at variance with the society of the pre-Prohibition eras. A middle class of small-business and free-lance professionals has been replaced by one dependent on jobs in organizational workplaces. The dominance of agricultural ideals has given way to rhythms of life in which consumption is as much a delineator of identity as production. A rise in the general standard of living and a decline in hours of work have meant a standardization of leisure that diminishes the gap between classes in American life.

Such profound changes have sharpened the boundaries between work and leisure in their role both as symbols of character and as times of the day and the week. A description like the following would hardly be expected to gain general assent today as it did in nineteenth-century America: "The responsible young man was the one who knew that his obligations to his employer extended through his off-duty hours as well as through his working-day."[93] It is not that the ethic of work has disappeared in America, but belief in the moral significance of continuity between spheres of life, of being a person whose work and play are consistent, has become less dominant.

The very notion of rationalizing leisure contains an instructive ambiguity. With the successful eradication of drinking from the workplace the conflicts over the use of alcohol in American life have been about leisure and how it should be used. For some, the world is rationalized by being the arena of a consistent character. Sobriety is enjoined as a sign of the self, of a consistent and continuing person. To rationalize leisure is to make it the locus of the same kind of person, subject to the same set of values and judged by the same criteria. For others, work and play are two different and even contrasting spheres of life. The rational being keeps them separate. Studies of bar behavior and drinking-driving by myself and associates suggest that many drinkers utilize a typology of competence and incompetence in perceiving themselves and other drinkers.[94] Competent drinkers recognize and respect the division between the two worlds and act in accordance with a different normative system in each. Work is work and leisure is leisure, and the twain need never meet.

It may be profitable to speculate on the shift in presentation of moral character implied by these polarities. The relationship between economic activity and moral character was perhaps far more strident in America before the 1930s than it has become today. Daniel Rodgers observes that "to doubt the moral preeminence of work was the act of a conscious heretic."[95] The assumption that a consistent self is essential to either job success or the work life as indicative of other areas of life is by no means routine today.

CULTURAL HEGEMONY: CARNIVAL AND LENT REVISITED

The description of diverse meanings of leisure and play in American life suggests still another way of studying social control, by focusing on the cultural categories and meanings that constitute the tacit sources of aspiration and evaluation. Viewed from the systemic perspectives of Parsonian sociology, these sources point to the elements of a common culture. Viewed from the standpoint of social structure, especially in Marxian orientations, norms of drinking and drunkenness can be seen as ways of achieving, through culture, a social control without force and without the appellation of repression at all. The terms used here have been *dominant ideology, cultural hegemony,* or *legitimization.*[96] Has some group or class—religious, ethnic, or other—achieved control by having others embrace its beliefs, values, and categories to such an extent that control through repressive means has not been necessary?

Has there been, and is there now, a common set of beliefs and values about beverage alcohol that cuts across major diversities in American life? Do such similarities, if they exist, serve the interests of some groups and work to the disadvantage of others? Elsewhere I have discussed this issue in particular in regard to law as symbolic and to the impact of Temperance ideas on the middle classes themselves.[97] Here I will examine temperance ideas and beliefs with reference to the theme of leisure-time uses, especially in relation to the contemporary New Temperance movement.

The focus of this essay has been on drinking as part of a total context in the emergence of leisure and its uses. By the mid-nineteenth century three aspects of drinking and social control were dominant in American life in the sense that they were shared by most groups, whatever their support of, or hostility toward, the public controls represented by Temperance and Prohibitionist policies. One, as Levine has pointed out, was the belief in the disinhibiting effects of alcohol as the cause of drunkenness, accidents, and immorality.[98] Second was adherence to norms that enjoined the mix of working and drinking. Even among the nonabstinent, drinking had become defined as an after-hours matter. The third aspect was a general attitude of rejection of, disappointment in, and concern for the "habitual drunkard," or, in mid-twentieth-century terms, the "alcoholic." Despite qualifications and marginal groups, these areas of agreement have set outer limits to the conflicts over drinking and public controls in the United States for the past hundred years.

Within these limits, however, there has been active conflict over the systems of public controls. As I have maintained in this essay, such controls have found their battlefield in the efforts to control and constrain playtime. If alcohol is seen as disinhibiting, that fact has caused it to be embraced by some and repulsed by others. It is in the meanings of leisure that struggles over the uses of alcohol have been most productive of political conflict.

In the symbolism with which American culture has invested the use of alcohol, drinking and abstinence have come to be definers of moral character.[99] The respectable leisure habits of some are the disrespectable habits of others. The abstinence and inhibition that mark the Temperance ethic is decried as blue-nose intolerance, whereas boisterousness and uninhibited camaraderie are seen by others as irresponsibility and an invitation to the immoral.

The Weberian *geist* of bureaucratization and utilitarian rationality assumes much more system and unity than societies or cultures demonstrate. Whether as a dialectical response to capitalist culture and industrial organization or as historical continuity, the romantic resistance to rationalization has been a recurrent theme of modern thought.[100] Drinking has become, especially in the United States, a symbol of the irrational, the impulsive, the "free" side of life. Its association with the uncontrolled and irresponsible, with the unpredictable appearance of trouble, is part of its appeal and danger. There is a constant theme in modern literature that identifies the romantic opposition to a world of calculation, responsibility, and cooperation with the underclass, with youth, and with the dangerous classes. Efforts to rationalize leisure by responsible drinking, for example, are often chasing a contradiction in terms.

The nineteenth-century battlefields have given way to different arenas of contention. Although clear pockets of division still exist (Protestant fundamentalism, for example), the distinctions of American society along cultural lines are no longer as clearly matters of religion, class, region, or even ethnicity as they were in the nineteenth century.[101] The greater standardization of American life has meant that whatever the divisions over alcohol use, they no longer clearly follow nineteenth-century boundaries.

As I argued a number of years ago, the effort to freeze American drinking through the Eighteenth Amendment was an admission of the failure of the Temperance ethic to achieve the status of dominance through American society.[102] Neither Prohibition nor its repeal appears to have changed the conflictual status of alcohol in American life. What has changed is the structure of public controls. From 1933 until the late 1970s the repressive character of public controls toward drinking was minimized, although the United States, as compared to other capitalistic and industrialized societies (excepting the Scandinavian) retained a public definition of alcohol as a dangerous commodity. A more permissive and tolerant orientation toward leisure replaced the constraints of the Prohibition era. The "alcohol problem" became the problem of the alcoholic and was thereby sealed off from the playtime activities of most Americans and defined as a medical rather than a political issue.

The recent renaissance of prevention policies means also the return of drinking as a political issue. Measures to restrict the availability or sale of alcohol to the general public or to special groups, such as young adults, restore the effort to define leisure-time drinking and its locations as less than respectable. Yet at no time can we find a dominant or culturally hegemonic ethic. If the achievement ethic or individualism can be construed as dominant in American life, its relation to drinking is by no means clear. As an issue it remains a matter of conflict and opposition.

NOTES

1. Peter Burke, *Popular Culture in Early Modern Europe* (New York: Harper Torchbooks, 1978), 207.

2. Sidney Harring, *Policing a Class Society: The Experience of American Cities, 1865–1915* (New Brunswick, N.J.: Rutgers University Press, 1983), chap. 8.

3. Harring, *Policing a Class Society,* 185.

4. William Muraskin, "The Social Control Theory in American History: A Critique," *Journal of Social History* 2 (1976): 559–568.

5. Morris Janowitz, *The Last Half-Century: Societal Change and Politics in America* (Chicago: University of Chicago Press, 1978), chap. 2.

6. *Social Control and the State,* ed. Stanley Cohen and Andrew Scull (Oxford: Martin Robertson, 1983), esp. David Rothman, "Social Control: The Uses and Abuses of the Concept in the History of Incarceration."

7. Kettil Bruun, Griffith Edwards, Martti Lumrio, Klaus Mäkelä, Lynn Pan, et al., *Alcohol Control Policies in Public Health Perspective* (New Brunswick,

N.J.: Rutgers University Center for Alcohol Studies, 1975); Klaus Mäkelä, Robin Room, Eric Single, Pekka Sulkunin, Brendan Walsh, et al., *Alcohol, Society and the State*, vol. 1 (Toronto: Addiction Research Foundation, 1981); Mark Moore and Dean Gerstein, *Beyond the Shadow of Prohibition* (Washington, D.C.: National Academy Press, 1981).

8. Thomas Szasz, *Ideology and Insanity* (Garden City, N.Y.: Doubleday, 1970); Peter Conrad and Joseph Schneider, *Deviance and Medicalization: From Badness to Sickness* (Saint Louis: Mosby, 1980).

9. Irving K. Zola, "Medicine as an Institution of Social Control" *Sociological Review* 20 (1972): 487–504.

10. David Rothman, *The Discovery of the Asylum: Social Order and Disorder in the New Republic* (New York: Little, Brown, 1970), xix.

11. Andrew Scull, *Museums of Madness: The Social Organization of Insanity in Nineteenth Century England* (London: Allen Lane, St. Martin's Press, 1979), 37.

12. Lewis Mumford, *The Culture of Cities* (New York: Harcourt, Brace, 1938); David Landes, *Revolution in Time: Clocks and the Making of the Modern World* (Cambridge, Mass.: Harvard University Press, 1983).

13. Murray Melbin, "Night as Frontier," *American Sociological Review* 43 (February 1978): 3–22; Daniel Rodgers, *The Work Ethic in Industrial America, 1850–1920* (Chicago: University of Chicago Press, 1978), 18–19: Eviatar Zerubavel, *Hidden Rhythms* (Chicago: University of Chicago Press, 1981); idem, *The Seven Day Circle: The History and Meaning of the Week* (New York: The Free Press, 1985).

14. Michael Marrus, *The Emergence of Leisure* (New York: Harper and Row, 1974).

15. Burke, *Popular Culture in Early Modern Europe*, 213.

16. Brian Harrison, "Religion and Recreation in Nineteenth Century England," chap. 3 of *Peaceable Kingdom: Stability and Change in Modern Britain* (Oxford: Clarendon Press, 1982).

17. Burke, *Popular Culture in Early Modern Europe*, chaps. 8 and 9.

18. E. P. Thompson, "Eighteenth Century English Society: Class Struggle without Class?" *Social History* 3 (1978): 133–165.

19. Herbert Gutman, *Work, Culture and Society in Industrializing America* (New York: Vintage Books, 1977), 68–74; Brian Harrison, *Drink and the Victorians: The Temperance Question in England, 1815–1872* (Pittsburgh: University of Pittsburgh Press), 1971, 40; E. P. Thompson, "Time, Work-Discipline and Industrial Capitalism," *Past and Present* 38 (1967): 56–97; Jeffrey Kaplow, "Saint Monday and the Artisanal Tradition in Nineteenth Century France," unpublished paper presented to the Department of History, University of California, San Diego, 1980; James Roberts, "Drink and Industrial Work Discipline in Nineteenth Century Germany," *Journal of Social History* 15 (1982): 25–38.

20. Reinhard Bendix, *Work and Authority in Industry* (New York: Wiley, 1954), chap. 2; Paul Boyer, *Urban Masses and Moral Order in America, 1820–1920* (Cambridge, Mass.: Harvard University Press, 1978), chap. 3; Gutman, *Work, Culture and Society;* Alan Dawley and Paul Faler, "Working Class Culture and Politics in the Industrial Revolution: Sources of Loyalism and Rebellion" *Journal of Social History* 9 (Summer 1976).

21. Edwin Lemert, "Drinking in Hawaiian Plantation Society," chap. 2 of *Human Deviance, Social Problems and Social Control* (Englewood Cliffs, N.J.: Prentice-Hall, 1967).

22. Dawley and Faler, "Working Class Culture and Politics"; Thompson, "Time Work-Discipline and Industrial Capitalism," 56–97.

23. Brian Harrison, *Drink and the Victorians,* chap. 1; Joseph Gusfield, *Symbolic Crusade: Status Politics and the American Temperance Movement* (Urbana: University of Illinois Press, 1963), chap. 7.

24. Ian Tyrrell, "Temperance and Economic Change in the Ante-Bellum North," in *Alcohol, Reform and Society,* ed. Jack Blocker, Jr. (Westport, Conn.: Greenwood Press, 1979); William Rorabaugh, *The Alcoholic Republic: An American Tradition* (New York: Oxford University Press, 1979); Mark Lender and James Martin, *Drinking in America* (New York: The Free Press, 1982).

25. Roy Rosenzweig, *Eight Hours for What We Will: Workers and Leisure in an Industrial City, 1870–1920* (New York: Oxford University Press, 1983), chap. 2.

26. Gutman, *Work, Culture and Society;* Dawley and Faler, "Working Class Culture and Politics."

27. Harring, *Policing a Class Society,* 13.

28. Harring, *Policing a Class Society,* 151.

29. Steven Spitzer and Andrew Scull, "Social Control in Historical Perspective: From Private to Public Responses to Crime," in *Corrections and Punishment,* ed. David Greenberg (Beverly Hills, Calif.: Sage Publications, 1977); Steven Spitzer, "The Rationalization of Crime Control in Capitalist Society," in *Social Control and the State,* ed. Stanley Cohen and Andrew Scull (Oxford: Martin Robertson, 1983).

30. Harry G. Levine, "Demon of the Middle Class: Self-Control, Liquor and the Ideology of Temperance in Nineteenth Century America" (Ph.D. diss., University of California, Berkeley), 1979.

31. Boyer, *Urban Masses and Moral Order,* 161.

32. Richard Lambert, *Workers, Factories and Social Change in India* (Princeton, N.J.: Princeton University Press, 1963); Morris D. Morris, "The Recruitment of an Industrial Labor Force in India with British and American Comparisons," *Comparative Studies in Society and History* 2 (1960): 305–328.

33. Joseph Gusfield, "Tradition and Modernity: Misplaced Polarities in the Study of Social Change," *American Journal of Sociology* 72 (1967): 351–362.

34. Samuel Cohn, "Keeping the Navies in Line," in *Class Conflict and Collective Action,* ed. Charles Tilly and Louise Tilly (Beverly Hills, Calif.: Sage Publications, 1981).

35. Everett Hughes, "Pullman, Illinois" (unpublished manuscript); Ray Hutchison, chapter 9 in this volume.

36. Dawley and Faler, "Working Class Culture and Politics"; Paul E. Johnson, *A Shopkeeper's Millennium* (New York: Hill and Wang, 1978), chaps. 1, 2.

37. Daniel Rodgers, *The Work Ethic in Industrial America, 1850–1920* (Chicago: University of Chicago Press, 1978).

38. Rorabaugh, *Alcoholic Republic,* chap. 3.

39. Lyman Beecher (1864), quoted in Gusfield, *Symbolic Crusade,* 42.

40. Eric Monkkonen, *The Dangerous Class* (Cambridge, Mass.: Harvard University Press, 1975), chap. 2.

41. Alan Silver, "The Demand for Order in Civil Society," in David Bordua, ed. *The Police* (New York: Wiley, 1967), 3.

42. Paul Boyer, *Urban Masses and Moral Order*, 161.

43. Gutman, *Work, Culture and Society*; Charles Tilly, "The Web of Contention in Eighteenth Century Cities," in *Class Conflict and Collective Action*, ed. Charles Tilly and Louise Tilly (Beverly Hills, Calif.: Sage Publications, 1981); Richard Wade, "Violence in Cities," in *Riot, Rout and Tumult*, ed. Roger Lane and John J. Turner (Westport, Conn.: Greenwood Press, 1978); Richard Brown, *Strain of Violence: Historical Studies of American Violence and Vigilantism* (New York: Oxford University Press, 1970).

44. Jonathan Rubinstein, *City Police* (New York: Ballantine Books, 1973), chap. 1; Ferdinand Braudel, *Capitalism and Material Life, c. 400–1800* (New York: Harper Torchbooks, 1973), 158.

45. Keith Wrightson, "Alehouses, Order and Reformation in Rural England, 1590–1660," in E. and S. Yeo, ed. *Popular Culture and Class Conflict, 1590–1914*, ed. Eileen Yeo and Stephen Yeo (Sussex: Harvester Press, 1981), 12.

46. Joseph Kett, *Rites of Passage: Adolescence in America* (New York: Basic Books, 1977), part 2. Brian Harrison, *Drink and the Victorians*, chap. 2.

47. Susanna Barrows, "The Uncharted Revolution: Drink and Café Life in Nineteenth Century France" (Paper presented at the annual meeting of the Alcohol Epidemiology Section, International Council on Alcohol and Addictions, June 22–July 2, 1983), 45.

48. George Rudé, *The Crowd in History* (Oxford: Clarendon Press, 1964); Eric Hobsbawm, *Primitive Rebels* (New York: Praeger, 1963).

49. George Rudé, *The Crowd in the French Revolution* (Oxford: Clarendon Press, 1959); Rudé, *Crowd in History*.

50. Rudé, *Crowd in the French Revolution*, 200–209.

51. Pauline Maier, "Popular Uprisings and Civil Authority in Eighteenth Century America," in *Riot, Rout and Tumult*, ed. Roger Lane and John J. Turner (Westport, Conn.: Greenwood Press, 1978).

52. Silver, "Demand for Order."

53. Ted Gurr, *Rogues, Rebels and Reformers* (Beverly Hills, Calif.: Sage Publications, 1976), 56; Harring, *Policing a Class Society*, chap. 7.

54. David Bayley, *Forces of Order: Police Behavior in Japan and the United States* (Berkeley and Los Angeles: University of California Press, 1976), chap. 3.

55. David Plath, *The After Hours: Modern Japan and the Search for Enjoyment* (Berkeley and Los Angeles: University of California Press, 1964).

56. Donald Black, *The Manners and Customs of the Police* (New York: Academic Press, 1980); Rubinstein, *City Police*; Richard Lundman, "Police Patrol Work: A Comparative Perspective," in *Police Behavior*, ed. Richard Lundman (New York: Oxford University Press, 1980); Peter Manning, *Police Work* (Cambridge, Mass.: MIT Press, 1977); Arthur Stinchcombe, "Institutions of Privacy in the Determination of Police Administrative Practices," *American Journal of Sociology* 69 (1963): 150–160.

57. Rubinstein, *City Police,* chap. 4.

58. Harring, *Policing a Class Society.*

59. Harrison, "Religion and Recreation," chap. 2; Sherri Cavan, *Liquor License* (Chicago: Aldine, 1966).

60. Harring, *Policing a Class Society.*

61. Gusfield, *Symbolic Crusade.*.

62. Kett, *Rites of Passage,* chap. 4; Brown, *Strain of Violence.*.

63. Silver, "Demand for Order"; Gurr, *Rogues, Rebels and Reformers,* 96.

64. Patricia Morgan, "Industrialization, Urbanization and the Attack on the Italian Drinking Culture," *Contemporary Drug Problems* 15 (1988): 607–626.

65. Gurr, *Rogues, Rebels and Reformers,* 15.

66. Geoffrey Pearson, "Goths and Vandals: Crime in History," in *Hooligan: A History of Respectable Fears,* ed. Geoffrey Pearson (London: Macmillan, 1983), 100.

67. Gareth Stedman Jones, "Class Expression versus Social Control: A Critique of Recent Trends in the Social History of 'Leisure,' " in *Social Control and the State,* ed. Samuel Cohen and Andrew Scull (Oxford: Martin Robertson, 1983), 49.

68. Susanna Barrows, *Distorting Mirrors* (New Haven, Conn.: Yale University Press, 1979); Morgan, "Attack on the Italian Drinking Culture."

69. Harrison, *Drink and the Victorians,* chap. 1.

70. Michael Ignatieff, "State, Civil Society and Total Institutions: A Critique of Recent Social Histories of Punishment," in *Social Control and the State,* ed. Samuel Cohen and Andrew Scull (Oxford: Martin Robertson, 1983).

71. Joseph Gusfield, Epilogue to *Symbolic Crusade,* 2d ed. (Urbana: University of Illinois Press, 1986); Levine, "Demon of the Middle Class."

72. Kett, *Rites of Passage,* chap. 4; John F. Gillis, *Youth and History* (New York: Oxford University Press, 1981).

73. James Mosher, "Youthful Drinking Laws", in *Minimum Drinking Age Laws,* ed. Henry Wechsler (Lexington, Mass.: Heath, 1980).

74. Richard Jensen, *The Winning of the Midwest* (Chicago: University of Chicago Press, 1971).

75. Paul Kleppner, *The Cross of Culture: A Social Analysis of Midwestern Politics* (New York: The Free Press, 1970).

76. Gusfield, *Symbolic Crusade.*

77. Gutman, *Work, Culture and Society.*.

78. Richard Stivers, *The Hair of the Dog: Irish Drinking and American Stereotype* (Pennsylvania State University Press, 1976); Perry Duis, *The Saloon: Public Drinking in Chicago and Boston, 1880–1920* (Urbana: University of Illinois Press, 1983); Rosenzweig, *Eight Hours for What We Will.*

79. Rosenzweig, *Eight Hours for What We Will,* chap. 2.

80. Boyer, *Urban Masses and Moral Order;* Rosenzweig, *Eight Hours for What We Will,* chaps. 2, 4.

81. Duis, *The Saloon,* 202.

82. Duis, *The Saloon,* 202.

83. Duis, *The Saloon,* 142.

84. Rosenzweig, *Eight Hours for What We Will*, chap. 2; Richard Sennett, *Families against the City* (New York: Vintage Books, 1974).

85. Duis, *The Saloon*, 106.

86. Raymond Williams, *Marxism and Literature* (Oxford: Oxford University Press, 1977).

87. Rosenzweig, *Eight Hours for What We Will*, 58–59.

88. Kett, *Rites of Passage*; Frederick Rudolph, *The American College and University: A History* (New York: Knopf, 1962).

89. Duis, *The Saloon*, chap. 7.

90. Boyer, *Urban Masses and Moral Order*, chaps. 13, 14.

91. Rosenzweig, *Eight Hours for What We Will*, chap. 8.

92. Gunther Barth, *City People: The Rise of Modern City Culture in Nineteenth Century America* (New York: Oxford University Press, 1980).

93. Irvin Wyllie, *The Self-Made Man in America* (New Brunswick, N.J.: Rutgers University Press, 1954), 49.

94. Joseph Gusfield, Joseph Kotarba, and Paul Rasmussen, *The World of the Drinking Driver: An Ethnographic Study*, report to the National Science Foundation, May 1979; Joseph Gusfield "Managing Competence: An Ethnographic Study of Drinking-Driving and Barroom Behavior," in Thomas Harford, ed., *Social Drinking Contexts* (Washington, D.C.: Department of Health and Human Services, 1981).

95. Rodgers, *Work Ethic*.

96. Nicholas Abercrombie, Stephen Hill, and Bryan S. Turner, *The Dominant Ideology Thesis* (London: Allen and Unwin, 1980); Williams, *Marxism and Literature*.

97. Gusfield, Epilogue to *Symbolic Crusade*, 2d ed.

98. Levine, "Demon of the Middle Class."

99. Gusfield, *Symbolic Crusade*.

100. Spitzer, "The Rationalization of Crime Control"; T. J. Jackson Lears, *No Place of Grace: Antimodernism and the Transformation of American Culture, 1880–1920* (New York: Pantheon Books, 1981); Daniel Bell, *The Cultural Contradictions of Capitalism* (New York: Basic Books, 1976); Alvin Gouldner, *The Two Marxisms* (New York: Oxford University Press, 1980).

101. Gusfield, *Symbolic Crusade*, chap. 6.

102. Gusfield, *Symbolic Crusade*, chap. 6.

Sources for the
Social History of Alcohol

Jeffrey Verhey

A. GENERAL REFERENCES AND BIBLIOGRAPHIES

The best bibliographical source is the *Social History of Alcohol Review,* a newsletter published by the Alcohol and Temperance History Group and edited by Geoffrey J. Giles (available from David Gutzke, Department of History, Southwest Missouri State University, 901 South National Avenue, Springfield, Mo., 65804-0089). Each newsletter contains a useful ongoing bibliography of all recent work pertaining to the social history of alcohol. The newsletter also publishes comprehensive bibliographies on special topics, such as a bibliography of the social history of alcohol in France by Thomas Brennan (no. 3, Spring 1981), a bibliography on Australia and New Zealand by David M. Fahey (no. 11, Spring 1985), "Drink and Temperance in the United Kingdom: Works Appearing in 1940–1980," also by David M. Fahey (no. 3, Spring 1981), and "Social History of Alcohol and German Social Historiography—A Bibliographical Report on German Alcohol History Research," by Alfred Heggen (no. 10, Autumn 1984). See also Brian Harrison, "Drink and Sobriety in England, 1815–1872: A Critical Bibliography," *International Review of Social History* 12 (1967): 207–210; E. J. Higgs, "Research into the History of Alcohol Use and Control in England and Wales: The Available Sources in the Public Record Office," *British Journal of Addiction* 79 (1984): 41–47; and Jacquie Jessup, "The Liquor Issue in American History: A Bibliography," in *Alcohol, Reform and Society,* ed. Jack S. Blocker (Westport, Conn.: Greenwood Press, 1979), 259–279. Dwight A. Heath and D. M. Cooper have compiled an exhaustive bibliography of the anthropological literature in *Alcohol Use and World Cultures: A Comprehensive Bibliography of Anthropological Sources* (Toronto: Addiction Research Foundation, 1981; now being updated).

Other useful reference works include Mark Edward Lender, *Dictionary of American Temperance Biography: From Temperance Reform to Alcohol Research, the 1660s to the 1980s* (Westport, Conn.: Greenwood Press, 1984), and an older work, with Edward Hurst Cherrington as the editor in chief, *Standard Encyclopedia of the Alcohol Problem*, 6 vols. (Westerville, Ohio: American Issue Publishing, 1925–1930). Cherrington's work contains many useful short chapters on different groups, temperance leaders, and the liquor problem in different states (especially useful for the United States, Canada, Australia, New Zealand, and the United Kingdom). Gregory A. Austin and the staff of the Southern California Research Institute have written a wonderful short encyclopedic history, which also has an excellent bibliography, *Alcohol in Western Society from Antiquity to 1800: A Chronological History* (Santa Barbara, Calif.: ABC-Clio Information Services, 1985). Also useful for historians is *Guide to the Microfilm Edition of Temperance and Prohibition Papers,* ed. Randall C. Jimerson, Francis X. Blouin, and Charles A. Isetts (Ann Arbor: University of Michigan Press, 1977).

B. APPROACHES TO A SOCIAL HISTORY OF ALCOHOL

Jed Dannenbaum has written an interesting quantitative analysis of the recent historiography, "The Social History of Alcohol," *Drinking and Drug Practices Surveyor* 19 (April 1984): 7–11.

Marxism

The Marxist position is stated first and most cogently in Friedrich Engels, *The Condition of the Working Class in England* (Stanford, Calif.: Stanford University Press, 1968). See also the important article by Karl Kautsky, "Der Alkoholismus und seine Bekämpfung" *Die Neue Zeit* 9, pt. 2, nos. 27–30 (1890–1891). For a history of the socialist position, see James S. Roberts, "Alcohol, Public Policy and the Left: The Socialist Debate in Early Twentieth-Century Europe," *Contemporary Drug Problems* 12 (1985): 309–330.

Industrial Discipline

Much profitable work has been done on the history of the alcohol problem by studying it as part of the general problematic of industrialization and, especially, industrial discipline. For one of the first works in this field, see Sidney Pollard, "Factory Discipline in the Industrial Revolution," *Economic History Review*, 2d ser. 16 (1963): 254–271, as well as his *Genesis of Modern Management: A Study of the Industrial Revolution in*

Great Britain (Cambridge, Mass.: Harvard University Press, 1965). Some of the most important work in this area has centered around the Blue Monday phenomenon—see, for example, E. P. Thompson. "Time, Work-Discipline, and Industrial Capitalism," *Past and Present* 38 (1967): 59–97, and Douglas A. Reids, "The Decline of Saint Monday: 1776–1876," *Past and Present* 71 (1976): 76–101. (See also work cited below under the individual countries.)

Culture

On a more general level historians have used alcohol to study "culture"—a term that itself needs some definition. E. P. Thompson has done some important work in this direction. See especially his "Patrician Society, Plebeian Culture," *Journal of Social History* 7 (1973–1974): 382–405, and its companion piece, "Eighteenth Century English Society: Class Struggle without Class?" *Social History* 3 (1978): 133–165. But see also the somewhat different ideas of Gareth Stedman Jones, "Working-Class Culture and Working-Class Politics in London, 1870–1900: Notes on the Remaking of a Working Class," *Journal of Social History* 7 (1974): 460–508, and his "Class Expression versus Social Control: A Critique of Recent Trends in the Social History of 'Leisure,' " in *Social Control and the State*, ed. Samuel Cohen and Andrew Scull (Oxford: Oxford University Press, 1983), 39–49. See also Herbert Gutman, *Work, Culture and Society in Industrializing America* (New York: Vintage Books, 1977), and Hans Medick, "Plebeian Culture in the Transition to Capitalism," in *Culture, Ideology and Politics*, ed. Ralph Samuel and Gareth Stedman Jones (Boston: Routledge and Kegan Paul, 1982), 84–112. Anthropologists, too, have turned their attention to the history of alcohol use, and the results are very interesting indeed. See *Constructive Drinking: Perspectives on Drink from Anthropology*, ed. Mary Douglas (New York: Cambridge University Press, 1987), and Thomas W. Hill, "Ethnohistory and Alcohol Studies," in *Recent Developments in Alcoholism*, ed. Marc Galanter (New York: Plenum, 1984), 2:313–337.

Discourse

Especially since the 1970s historians have emphasized the significance of the conceptualization of the alcohol problem in any discussion of the problem itself. The work of Michel Foucault has been especially important here. Almost all of his work is interesting and relevant, but the book that most directly addresses medical issues is *The Birth of the Clinic* (New York: Pantheon Books, 1973). For the United States, see Harry Levine, "The Discovery of Addiction: Changing Conceptions of Habitual Drunkenness in America," *Journal of Studies on Alcohol* 39 (1978): 143–174, along with A. Jaffe, "Reform in American Medical

Science: The Inebriety Movement and the Origins of the Psychological Theory of Addiction, 1870–1920," *British Journal of Addiction* 73 (1978): 139–147. For a comparative discussion of the history of alcohol inebriate homes, see Jim Baumohl and Robin Room, "Inebriety, Doctors and the State: Alcoholism Treatment Institutions before 1940," in *Recent Developments in Alcoholism,* ed. Marc Galanter (New York: Plenum, 1987), 5:135–174.

C. THE SOCIAL HISTORY OF
INDIVIDUAL COUNTRIES AND REGIONS

United States

Harry Levine, "The Alcohol Problem in America: From Temperance to Alcoholism," *British Journal of Addiction* 79 (1984): 109–119, offers a good general historical overview. The collection *Alcohol, Reform and Society,* ed. Jack S. Blocker (Westport, Conn.: Greenwood Press, 1979) includes a number of essays treating different aspects of the liquor problem in American history. Other good, broad accounts include W. J. Rorabaugh, *The Alcoholic Republic: An American Tradition* (New York: Oxford University Press, 1979); Hermann Fahrenkrug, *Alkohol, Individuum und Gesellschaft—Zur Sozialgeschichte des Alkoholismus in der USA* (Frankfurt: Campus Verlag, 1984); Jack S. Blocker, Jr., *American Temperance Movements: Cycles of Reform* (Boston: Twayne Publishers, 1989); and Mark Lender and James Kirby Houston, *Drinking in America: A History* (New York: Free Press, 1982).

Prohibition has naturally attracted the most attention of all alcohol problems in the United States. Jack Krout, *The Origins of Prohibition* (New York: Knopf, 1925) remains a fine account. Other standard narrative accounts include Andrew Sinclair, *Era of Excess: A Social History of the Prohibition Movement* (New York: Harper and Row, 1962); Sean Cashman, *Prohibition: The Lie of the Land* (New York: Free Press, 1981); and Thomas Coffey, *The Long Thirst: Prohibition in America, 1920–1933* (New York: Norton, 1975). The study of prohibition has profited from many local histories. For a study of prohibition in Michigan, see Larry Engelmann, *Intemperance: The Lost War against Liquor* (New York: Free Press, 1979); for Washington, see Norman Clark's seminal work *The Dry Years: Prohibition and Social Change in Washington,* 2d ed. (Seattle: University of Washington Press, 1988); for Kansas, see Robert Smith Bader, *Prohibition in Kansas: A History* (Lawrence, Kans.: University Press of Kansas, 1986). For the history of the end of prohibition, see David E. Kyvig, *Repealing National Prohibition* (Chicago: University of Chicago Press, 1979).

Richard Hofstadter, *The Age of Reform* (New York: Vintage Books,

1955), established the standard interpretative framework for subsequent investigation of the temperance movement in the United States. Joseph Gusfield developed many of these ideas further in his rich *Symbolic Crusade: Status Politics and the American Temperance Movement*, 2d ed. (Urbana: University of Illinois Press, 1988), as did James Timberlake in his *Prohibition and the Progressive Movement, 1900–1920* (Cambridge, Mass.: Harvard University Press, 1963).

Subsequent work, however, has retreated from Hofstadter's characterization of the temperance movement as "the rural-evangelical virus" that "the country Protestant frequently brought with him to the city" (290) by examining in greater detail exactly who were the members of the early temperance organizations. Important here are K. Austin Kerr's discussion of the social backgrounds of the members of the Anti-Saloon League, *Organized for Prohibition: A New History of the Anti-Saloon League* (New Haven, Conn.: Yale University Press, 1985); Jack S. Blocker, Jr., *Retreat from Reform: The Prohibition Movement in the United States, 1890–1913* (Westport, Conn.: Greenwood Press, 1976); and Norman Clark, *Deliver Us from Evil: An Interpretation of American Prohibition* (New York: Norton, 1976). Jed Dannenbaum, *Drink and Disorder: Temperance Reform in Cincinnati from the Washingtonians to the WCTU* (Urbana: University of Illinois Press, 1984) examines temperance reform in Cincinnati. See also the collection of essays in *Law, Order, and Alcohol*, ed. David E. Kyvig (Westport, Conn.: Greenwood Press, 1985).

In continuing the trend toward investigating the social history of alcohol in the eighteenth and nineteenth centuries, historians are beginning to pay more attention to early temperance movements, especially to their social makeup and their social significance. The most important work here is Ian Tyrrell, *Sobering Up: From Temperance to Prohibition in Antebellum America, 1800–1860* (Westport, Conn.: Greenwood Press, 1979). See also Jill Siegel Dodd, "The Working Classes and the Temperance Movement in Ante-Bellum Boston," *Labor History* 19 (1978): 510–531, and Robert Hampel, *Temperance and Prohibition in Massachusetts, 1813–1852* (Ann Arbor: UMI Research Press, 1982).

Some of the most interesting work on the history of alcohol uses the liquor question as an entry into a broader set of problems. Richard Stivers, a sociologist, uses drinking to examine the creation of a stereotype in *A Hair of the Dog: Irish Drinking and American Stereotype* (University Park: Pennsylvania State University Press, 1976). Ruth Bordin examines the role of women in the temperance movement in *Women and Temperance: The Quest for Power and Liberty, 1873–1900* (Philadelphia: Temple University Press, 1981). Other works employing alcohol as a window to issues of gender include Barbara Epstein, *The Politics of*

Domesticity: Women, Evangelism and Temperance in Nineteenth-Century America (Middletown, Conn.: Wesleyan University Press, 1981); Jack S. Blocker, Jr., *"Give to the Winds Thy Fears:" The Women's Temperance Crusade, 1873–1874* (Westport, Conn.: Greenwood Press, 1985); Jack S. Blocker Jr., "Separate Paths: Suffragists and the Women's Temperance Crusade," *Signs: Journal of Women in Culture and Society* 10 (1985): 460–476; Ruth M. Alexander, "'We Are Engaged as a Band of Sisters.' Class and Domesticity in the Washingtonian Temperance Movement, 1840–1850," in *Journal of American History* 75, no. 3 (1988): 763–786; and Lori C. Ginzberg, "'Moral Suasion is Moral Balderdash': Women, Politics and Social Activism in the 1850s," in *Journal of American History* 73, no. 3 (1986): 601–622.

Paul Boyer uses the discourse on the liquor problem in his fascinating study of urban problems, *Urban Masses and Moral Order in America, 1820–1920* (Cambridge, Mass.: Harvard University Press, 1978). Roy Rosenzweig discusses alcohol as an aspect of the culture of workers' leisure in his masterly *Eight Hours for What We Will: Work and Leisure in an Industrial City, 1870–1920* (Cambridge, Mass.: Harvard University Press, 1983). Paul Faler addresses many of the same sort of issues for an earlier period in his "Cultural Aspects of the Industrial Revolution: Lynn, Massachusetts, Shoemakers and Industrial Morality, 1826–1860," *Labor History* 15 (1974): 367–394, as does Paul E. Johnson for an earlier period still in "The Modernization of Mayo Greenleaf Patch: Land, Family, and Marginality in New England, 1776–1818," *New England Quarterly* 55 (1982): 488–516.

No discussion of the historiography of the liquor question would be complete without including work on the American saloon, especially Perry Duis, *The Saloon: Public Drinking in Chicago and Boston, 1880–1920* (Urbana: University of Illinois Press, 1983), as well as Elliot West, *The Saloon on the Rocky Mountain Mining Frontier* (Lincoln, Neb.: University of Nebraska Press, 1979); Thomas J. Noel, *The City and the Saloon: Denver, 1858–1916* (Lincoln, Nebr.: University of Nebraska Press, 1982); and David Brundage, "The Producing Classes and the Saloon: Denver in the 1880s," in *Labor History* 26, no. 1 (1985): 29–52. Ernest Kurtz, *A.A.: The Story* (San Francisco: Harper & Row, 1988), considers both the history and the worldview of the dominant social movement in the alcohol field in recent decades.

United Kingdom

Brian Harrison, *Drink and the Victorians* (Pittsburgh: University of Pittsburgh Press, 1971), is one of the seminal works in the social history of alcohol and has inspired much interest in the problem. Lilian L. Shiman, in her *Crusade against Drink in Victorian England* (New York: St.

Martin's Press, 1986), examines the efforts to control such drinking. A. E. Dingle examines one aspect of Harrison's study in far greater detail in his *Campaign for Prohibition in Victorian England: The United Kingdom Alliance 1872–1875* (New Brunswick, N.J.: Rutgers University Press, 1980). Peter Clark looks at an earlier discussion on alcohol in his "The 'Mother Gin' Controversy in Early Eighteenth-Century England," *Transactions of the Royal Historical Society*, 5th ser., 38 (1988): 63–84. Stephen Jones considers the response of a working-class party to the drinking habits of its members in "Labor, Society and the Drink Question in Britain, 1918–1939," *Historical Journal* 30, no. 1 (1987): 105–122. Peter Matthias's *The Brewing Industry in England, 1700–1830* (Cambridge: Cambridge University Press, 1959) remains the standard work by a famous economic historian on the development of the brewing industry. See also his "Brewing Industry, Temperance, and Politics," *Historical Journal* 1 (1958): 97–114. The eminent labor historian Asa Briggs has taken a look at a different industry in his *Wine for Sale: Victoria Wine and the Liquor Trade, 1860–1984* (Chicago: University of Chicago Press, 1985). Peter Clark has written the history of the institution of the alehouse in England in his *English Alehouse: A Social History, 1200–1830* (London: Longman, 1983) as well as in "The Alehouse and Alternate Society," in *Puritans and Revolutionaries: Essays Presented to Christopher Hill*, ed. Donald Pennington and Keith Thomas (Oxford: Oxford University Press, 1978), 41–72. Marc Girouard has described the style and architecture of the pubs, providing many interesting photographs, in his *Victorian Pubs* (London: Studio Vista, 1975). For a useful sourcebook, heavy in statistical tables, concerning the twentieth-century history of drinking in Great Britain, see Gwylmor P. Williams and George T. Brake, *Drink in Great Britain, 1900–1979* (London: Edsall, 1980).

Older works from which one can still profit include A. Shadwell, *Drink in 1914–1918—A Lesson in Control* (London: Longmans, Green, 1923); G. B. Wilson, *Alcohol and the Nation: A Contribution to the Study of the Liquor Problem in Great Britain from 1800 to 1935* (London: Nicholson and Watson, 1940); and the famous Mass Observation Study, *The Pub and the People* (London: Boyers, 1943; rpt. London: Hutchinson, 1987).

For Wales, see William R. Lambert, *Drink and Sobriety in Victorian Wales circa 1820–circa 1895* (Cardiff: University of Wales Press, 1983). For Scotland, see S. Mechie, *The Church and Scottish Social Development, 1780–1880* (Oxford: Oxford University Press, 1960) and I. Donnachie, "Drink and Society, 1750–1850: Some Aspects of the Scottish Experience," *Scottish Labour History Society Journal* 13 (1979): 5–22.

Much of the work on the liquor problem in England has treated it as an aspect of the history of industrialization. In addition to the works of

Pollard, Thompson, and Reid cited above, see William R. Lambert, "Drink and Work-Discipline in Industrial South Wales, circa 1800–1870," in *Welsh History Review* 6 (1972): 289–306. A. E. Dingle gives useful statistics on the portion of income that the workers spent on alcohol in "Drink and Working-Class Standards in Britain, 1870–1914," *Economic History Review*, 2d ser., 25 (1972): 289–306.

Ireland

For works treating Ireland, see K. H. Connell's excellent articles "Ether-Drinking in Ulster" and "Illicit Distillation," both in his collection of essays *Irish Peasant Society* (Oxford: Oxford University Press, 1968), as well as Elizabeth Malcolm, *Ireland Sober, Ireland Free: Drink and Temperance in Nineteenth-Century Ireland* (Syracuse, N.Y.: Syracuse University Press, 1986), and her article "The Catholic Church and the Irish Temperance Movement, 1838–1901," *Irish Historical Studies* 89 (1982): 11–19. E. B. McGuire has written a fine history of distilling in Ireland, *Irish Whiskey* (New York: Barnes & Noble Books, 1973). See also Patrick Lynch and John Vaizey, *Guinness's Brewery in the Irish Economy, 1759–1876* (Cambridge: Cambridge University Press, 1960).

Australia and New Zealand

A good introduction to the history of alcohol issues in Australia is provided by three articles in the bicentennial issue of the *Australian Drug and Alcohol Review* (7, no. 4 [1988]): Milton Lewis, "Alcoholism in Australia, the 1880s to the 1980s: From Medical Science to Political Science" (391–401); Keith Powell, "Alcohol and the Eastern Colonies, 1788–1901" (403–411); and Robin Room, "The Dialectic of Drinking in Australian Life: From the Rum Corps to the Wine Column" (413–437). Gar Dillon has written, from a temperance perspective, a detailed history of "the clash with alcohol in New South Wales" from 1788 to 1983 in *A Delusion of the Australian Culture* (Sydney: Star Printery, 1985). For a more judicious account, see David Bollen, *Protestantism and Social Reform in New South Wales, 1890–1910* (Clayton, Vic.: Melbourne University Press, 1972). Diametrically opposed to Dillon is Keith Dunstan's lighthearted account of "the prudery exhibited by certain outstanding men and women in such matters as drinking, smoking, prostitution, censorship, and gambling" in *Wowsers* (Sydney: Angus & Robertson, 1974). See also A. E. Dingle, " 'The Truly Magnificent Thirst': An Historical Study of Australian Drinking Habits," *Historical Studies* 19 (1980): 227–249, and Anthea Hyslop, "Temperance, Christianity, and Feminism: The Women's Christian Temperance Union of Victoria," *Historical Studies* 17 (1976): 27–49.

On New Zealand, for a study of the history of liquor licensing, see

Conrad Bollinger, *Grog's Own Country* (Wellington: Price Milburn, 1959). A. R. Grigg has written two interesting articles on aspects of the history of temperance, "Prohibition, the Church and Labour: A Programme for Social Reform, 1890–1914," *New Zealand Journal of History* 17 (1981): 135–154, and "Prohibition and Women: The Preservation of a Myth," *New Zealand Journal of History* 17 (1983): 144–165. See also Phillida Bunkle, "The Origins of the Women's Movement in New Zealand: The Women's Christian Temperance Union, 1885–1895," in *Women in New Zealand Society*, ed. Phillida Bunkle and Beryl Hughes (Auckland: Allen & Unwin, 1980).

Canada

James Gray, a former newspaperman, has written two enjoyable and popular works: *Booze: The Impact of Whisky on the Prairie West* (Toronto: Macmillan, 1972), a work devoted mostly to prohibition, its effect, and its popularity; and *Bacchanalia Revisited: Western Canada's Boozy Skid to Social Disaster* (Saskatoon: Western Producer Prairie Books, 1982). See also F. L. Barron, "The American Origins of the Temperance Movement in Ontario, 1828–1850," *Canadian Review of American Studies* 11 (1980): 131–150, and Wendy Mitchinson, "The WCTU: 'For God, Home and Native Land': A Study in Nineteenth-Century Feminism," in *A Not Unreasonable Claim: Women and Reform in Canada, 1880–1920*, ed. Linda Kealey (Toronto: Women's Press, 1979). Some older works include Reginald E. Hose, *Prohibition or Control? Canada's Experience with the Liquor Problem 1921–1927* (New York: Longmans, Green, 1928), and J. K. Chapman, "The Mid-Nineteenth-Century Temperance Movement in New Brunswick and Maine," *Canadian Historical Review* 35 (1954): 43–60.

France

Naturally, there are some excellent books on the history of wine and vineyards in France. See Roger Dion, *Histoire de la vigne et du vin en France* (Paris: Flammarion, 1977); Georges Durand, *Vin, vigne, et vignerons en Lyonnais et Beaujolais* (Hawthorne, N.Y.: Mouton, 1979); and Marcel Lachiver, *Vin, vigne et vignerons dans la région parisienne du XVIIe au XIXe siècles* (Pontoise, 1982). For a good work in English, consult L. Loubere, *The Red and the White: A History of Wine in France and Italy in the Nineteenth Century* (Albany, N.Y.: State University of New York Press, 1978). Marie Claude Delahaye has written an interesting social history of the rise and fall of absinthe in *L'absinthe: Histoire de la fée verte* (Paris: Berger-Levrault, 1983). See also Barnaby Conrad III, *Absinthe: History in a Bottle* (San Francisco: Chronicle Books, 1988).

One of the first to treat the social history of alcohol in France was

Michael Marrus, "Social Drinking in the Belle Epoque," *Journal of Social History* 7 (1974): 115–141. See also Thomas Brennan, "Beyond the Barriers: Popular Culture and Parisian Guinguettes," *Eighteenth-Century Studies* 18 (1984–1985): 153–169; Patricia E. Prestwich, "French Workers and the Temperance Movement," *International Review of Social History* 28 (1980): 36–52; Patricia E. Prestwich, *Drink and the Politics of Social Reform: Antialcoholism in France since 1870* (Palo Alto, Calif.: Society for the Promotion of Science and Scholarship, 1988); and Susanna Barrows, "After the Commune: Alcoholism, Temperance, and Literature in the Early Third Republic," *Consciousness and Class Experience in Nineteenth-Century Europe*, ed. John Merriman (New York: Holmes and Meier, 1979), 205–218.

Germany

The recent interest in the history of alcohol in Germany began with the work of James Roberts. See especially his *Drink, Temperance, and the Working Class in Nineteenth-Century Germany* (Boston: George Irwin, 1984). See also his articles "Drink and Working-Class Living Standards in Late Nineteenth-Century Germany," in *Arbeiterexistenz im 19. Jahrhundert,* ed. Werner Conze and Ulrich Engelhardt (Stuttgart: Klett-Cotta, 1981), 74–91; "Drink and Industrial Work Discipline in Nineteenth-Century Germany," *Journal of Social History* 15 (1981): 25–38; "Wirtshaus und Politik in der deutschen Arbeiterbewegung," in *Sozialgeschichte der Freizeit,* ed. Gerhard Huck (Wuppertal: Peter Hammar Verlag, 1980): 123–140; and "Drink and the Labour Movement: The Schnaps Boycott of 1909," in *The German Working-Class, 1888–1933,* ed. Richard J. Evans (London: Croom Helm, 1982), 80–107. Roberts's "Der Alkoholkonsum deutscher Arbeiter im 19. Jahrhundert," *Geschichte und Gesellschaft* 6 (1980): 220–242, claims that the drinking habits of workers differed from those of the rest of society, and it provoked a reply from Irmgard Vogt, "Einige Fragen zum Alkoholkonsum der Arbeiter: Kommentar zu J. S. Roberts Alkoholkonsum der Arbeiter im 19. Jahrhundert," *Geschichte und Gesellschaft* 8 (1982): 134–140, and from Hermann Wunderer, "Alkohol und Arbeiterschaft im 19. Jahrhundert: Kritische Anmerkungen zu James S. Roberts" *Geschichte und Gesellschaft* 8 (1982): 141–144. Roberts defended his position in "Alkohol und Arbeiterschaft: Eine Erwiderung," *Geschichte und Gesellschaft* 8 (1982): 427–433.

For a good general study of the role of alcohol in the lives of Hamburg workers during industrialization, see Alfred Heggen, "Alkohol," in *Industriekultur in Hamburg,* ed. Volker Plagemann (Munich: C. H. Beck, 1984). For a discussion of the role of alcohol control in industrial discipline, see Jutz Jeggie, "Alkohol und Industrialisierung," in *Rausch-Ekstase-Mystik: Grenzformen religiöser Erfahrung*, ed. Herbert Cancik (Düsseldorf: Patmos, 1978), 78–94. Eleanor L. Turk discusses the German Socialist party position on the liquor question in the Wilhelmine empire in "The Great Berlin Boycott of 1894," *Central European History* 15 (1982): 377–397. See also Irmgard Vogt, "Defining Alcohol Problems as a Repressive Mechanism: Its Formative Phase in Imperial Germany and Its Strength Today," *International Journal of the Addictions* 19 (1984): 551–569.

Fascinating descriptions of early modern German drinking are interspersed in Martin Luther's works. See especially his "Sermon on Soberness and Moderation," in *Luther's Works, vol. 51, Sermons* (Philadelphia: Muhlenberg Press, 1959), 291–299; "Drunkenness a Common Vice of Germans," in vol. 54, *Table Talk* (no. 4917, May 16, 1540), 205–206; and "Drunkenness at the Saxon Court and Elsewhere," in vol. 54, *Table Talk* (no. 3468, October 27, 1536), 371–372.

Sweden, Norway, Finland, and Iceland

There is of course a substantial literature on Scandinavia in the native languages. Below only a few of the most important works are cited.

Sweden was one of the first countries to experiment with alcohol control. For an older but still useful discussion, see Walter Thompson, *The Control of Liquor in Sweden* (New York: Columbia University Press, 1935). For a more recent discussion, see Ilpo Koskikallio, "The Social History of Restaurants in Sweden and Finland—A Comparative Study," in *Contemporary Drug Problems* 12 (1985): 11–30, and, in the same issue, Per Frånberg, "The Social and Political Significance of Two Swedish Restrictive Systems," 53–62. For those who read Swedish, see especially the excellent book edited by Kettil Bruun and Per Frånberg, *Den Svenska Supen: En Historia om Brannvin, Bratt och Byrakrati* [Swedish shots: a history of liquor, Bratt, and bureaucracy] (Stockholm: Bokforlaget Prisma, 1985). The book is summarized in English by Per Frånberg, "The Swedish Snaps: A History of Booze, Bratt, and Bureaucracy," *Contemporary Drug Problems* 14 (1987): 557–612.

Ragner Hauge discusses a part of the Norwegian history of alcohol control in his *Alcohol Research in Norway* (Oslo: National Institute for Alcohol Research, 1978). See also his short pamphlet *Alcohol Policy in Norway: A Historical Outline* (Oslo: National Institute for Alcohol Research, 1978). Those who read Norwegian should consult Per Fuglum, *Kampen om alkoholen: Norge 1816–1904* [The conflict over alcohol in Norway, 1816–1904] (Oslo: Universitetsforlaget, 1972).

For an older general overview of early Finnish attempts to address the liquor problem, see John Wuorinen, *The Prohibition Experiment in*

Finland (New York: Columbia University Press, 1931). Esa Österberg has argued that the features of the modern state monopoly reflect previous Finnish traditions in "From Home Distillation to the State Alcohol Monopoly," *Contemporary Drug Problems* 12 (1985): 31–52. See also, in the next issue of the same journal, Irma Sulkunen, "Temperance as a Civic Religion: The Cultural Foundation of the Finnish Working-Class Temperance Ideology," *Contemporary Drug Problems* 12 (1985): 267–287.

For Iceland, Ann Pinson provides a good summary of the issues in "Temperance, Prohibition, and Politics in Nineteenth-Century Iceland," *Contemporary Drug Problems* 12 (1985): 249–266.

Eastern Europe

Rather little research has been published in English on the history of alcohol problems in Eastern Europe. See, however, R. E. F. Smith, "Drink in Old Russia," in *Peasants in History: Essays in Honour of David Thorner,* ed. E. J. Hobsbawm, Witold Kule, Ashok Mitra, K. N. Raj, and Ignacy Sachs (Calcutta: Oxford University Press, 1980), 42–54; R. E. F. Smith and David Christian, *Bread and Salt: A Social and Economic History of Food and Drink in Russia* (Cambridge: Cambridge University Press, 1984); George E. Snow, "The Temperance Movement in Russia," *Modern Encyclopedia of Russian and Soviet History,* 38:226–233; Neil Weissman, "Prohibition and Alcohol Control in the USSR: The 1920s Campaign against Illegal Spirits," *Soviet Studies* 38, no. 3 (July 1986): 349–368; David Christian, "Vodka and Corruption in Russia on the Eve of Emancipation," *Slavic Review* 46 (1987): 471–488; and J. F. Hutchinson, "Science, Politics and the Alcohol Problem in Post-1905 Russia," *Slavonic and East European Review* 58 (1980): 232–254. A useful discussion of the recent literature is George E. Snow's "Change and Continuity: Alcohol and Alcoholism in Russia and the Soviet Union," *The Social History of Alcohol Review* 17 (1988): 7–15. For two older but still interesting works, see William E. Johnson, *The Liquor Problem in Russia* (Westerville, Ohio: American Issue Publishing, 1913), and Louis P. Skarzhinskii, *L'alcool et son histoire en Russie: étude économique et sociale* (Paris: A. Rousseau, 1902).

For works in Russian, see Nikolai I. Grigor'ev, *Russkiia obshchestva trezvosti: ikh organizatsiia i deiatel'nosti v 1892–1893.* [Russian temperance societies: their organization and activity, 1892–1893] (Saint Petersburg, 1894); I. G. Pryzhov, *Istoriia kabakov v Rossii* [A history of taverns in Russia], 2d ed. (Kazan, 1914); I.G. Pryzhov, "Korchma: istoricheskii ocherk" [The illegal sale of drink: a historical sketch], *Ruskii Arkhiv* 7 (1966): 1053–1064; and I. G. Pryzhov, "Ocherki po istorii kabachestva" [Sketches on the history of tavernkeeping], in his *Ocherki, stat'i, pis'ma* [Sketches, articles, letters] (Moscow and Leningrad, 1934).

For Poland, see Jacek Moskalewicz, "The Monopolization of the Alcohol Arena by the State," *Contemporary Drug Problems* 12 (1985): 117–128; and Antoni Bielewicz, "Mässigkeitsarbeit der katholischen Kirche und nationale politische Identität in Polen zu Beginn des 19. Jahrhunderts," *Drogalkohol*, 1986, no. 3: 237–247.

Third World

Historians are beginning to pay more attention to the role of alcohol in the development of European imperialism. For Africa, see Lynn Pan, *Alcohol in Colonial Africa*, Finnish Foundation for Alcohol Studies, vol. 22 (Helsinki, 1975); Michael Schatzberg, *Politics and Class in Zaire: Business, Bureaucracy, and Beer in Lisala* (New York: Africana, 1980); Thomas J. Herleny, "Ties that Bind: Palm Wine Blood Brotherhood on the Kenyan Coast during the Nineteenth Century," *International Journal of African Historical Studies* 17 (1984): 285–308; David Parkin, *Palms, Wine and Witnesses* (San Francisco: Chandler, 1972); Raymond E. Dummett, "The Social Impact of the European Liquor Trade on the Akan of Ghana (Gold Coast and Asante), 1875–1910," *Journal of Interdisciplinary History* 5 (1974): 69–101; and A. Olorunfemi, "The Liquor Traffic Dilemma in British West Africa: The South Nigerian Example, 1895–1918," *International Journal of African Historical Studies* 17 (1984): 229–241. Henry F. Wollcott provides an interesting study of race relations in Rhodesia (now Zimbabwe) in *The African Beer Gardens of Bulwayo: Integrated Drinking in a Segregated Society* (New Brunswick, N.J.: Rutgers Center of Alcohol Studies, 1974). For South Africa, see Charles van Onselen, "The Randlord and Rotgut, 1886–1903: An Essay on the Role of Alcohol in the Development of European Imperialism and South African Capitalism, with Special Reference to Black Mineworkers in the Transvaal Republic," *History Workshop Journal* 2 (1976): 33–89; Paul La Hausse, *Beerhalls and Boycotts: A History of Liquor in South Africa* (Johannesburg: Raven Press, 1988); and Wallace Mills, "The Roots of African Nationalism in the Cape Colony: Temperance, 1866–1898," *International Journal of African Historical Studies* 13 (1980): 229–241.

For anthropological points of view, see Elizabeth Colson and Thayer Scudder, *For Prayer and Profit: The Ritual, Economic and Social Importance of Beer in Gwembe District, Zambia, 1950–1982* (Stanford, Calif.: Stanford University Press, 1988); Ivan Karp, "Beer Drinking and Social Experience in an African Society," in *Explorations in African Systems of Thought*, ed. Ivan Karp and Charles S. Beard (Bloomington, Ind.: University of

Indiana Press, 1980), 83–119; Robert Netting, "Beer as a Locus of
Value among the West African Kofyar," *American Anthropologist* 66
(1964): 375–384; and Walter Sangree, "The Social Function of Beer
Drinking in Bantu Tiriki," in *Society, Culture, and Drinking Patterns,* ed.
David J. Pittman and Charles S. Snyder (New York: Wiley, 1962), 6–21.

Scholars other than anthropologists ignore drinking in Latin America. William B. Taylor's excellent study is the exception: *Drinking,
Homicide and Rebellion in Colonial Mexican Villages* (Stanford, Calif.: Stanford University Press, 1979). See also M. C. Scardaville, "Alcohol Abuse
and Tavern Reform in Late Colonial Mexico City," *Hispanic American
Historical Review* 60 (1980): 643–671.

For Oceania, see several publications by Mac and Leslie Marshall:
"Opening Pandora's Bottle: Reconstructing Micronesians' Early Contacts with Alcoholic Beverages," *The Journal of the Polynesian Society* 84
(1975): 441-465; "Holy and Unholy Spirits: The Effects of Missionization on Alcohol Use in Eastern Micronesia," *Journal of Pacific History* 11
(1976): 135–166; and *Silent Voices Speak: Women and Prohibition in Truk*
(Belmont, Calif.: Wadsworth, 1990).

D. COMPARATIVE HISTORY

Much work remains to be done in the comparative social history of
alcohol. A good place to begin is still E. M. Jellinek's "Cultural Patterns
in the Meaning of Alcoholism," in *Society, Culture and Drinking Patterns,*
ed. David J. Pittman and Charles R. Snyder (New York: Wiley, 1962).
For the period after World War II, see *Alcohol, Society, and the State, vol. 1,
A Comparative Study of Alcohol Control,* by Klaus Mäkelä, Robin Room,
Eric Single, Pekka Sulkunen, and Brendan Walsh, with thirteen others
(Toronto: Addiction Research Foundation, 1981), and vol. 2, *The Social
History of Alcohol Control Experiences in Seven Countries,* ed. Eric Single,
Patricia Morgan, and Jan de Lint (Toronto: Addiction Research Foun-
dation, 1981). Much of the recent work in comparative alcohol studies
figures in works devoted to the broader problem of drug addiction,
such as, for example, W. Schivelbusch, *Das Paradies der Geschmack und die
Vernunft: Eine Geschichte der Genussmittel* (Munich: S. Hanser, 1980); the
excellent collection of essays in *Rausch und Realität: Drogen im Kultur-
vergleich,* ed. Gisela Völger (Köln: Gesellschaft für Volkerkunde, 1981);
and Brian Inglis, *The Forbidden Game: A Social History of Drugs* (New
York: Scribner, 1975).

For a study that analyzes the use of alcohol in comparing the lives of
the working class in different nations, see Peter N. Stearn, *Lives of
Labor: Work in Maturing Industrial Society* (New York: Holmes and Meier,
1975). For a comparative study on the relationship between woman

suffrage and prohibition, see Ross Evans Paulson, *Women's Suffrage and Prohibition: A Comparative Study of Equality and Social Control* (Glenview, Ill.: Scott, Foresman, 1973). For comparisons between colonial empires, see Lynn Pan, *Alcohol in Colonial Africa*, noted above, and Robin Room, "Drink, Popular Protest and Government Regulation in Colonial Empires: A Comment on Papers by Kicza, Penvenne and Ambler," *The Drinking and Drug Practices Surveyor* 23 (1990): 3–6.

Some earlier work includes Guy Hayler, *Prohibition Advance in All Worlds: A Study of the World-wide Character of the Drink Question* (London, 1913); P. T. Wineskill, *The Temperance Movement and Its Workers: A Record of Social, Moral, and Political Progress*, 4 vols. (London, 1892); and Ernest Gordon, *The Anti-Alcohol Movement in Europe* (New York: Revell, 1913).

Recent relevant cross-cultural collections of essays on alcohol history include an issue of *Drogalkohol*, 1986, no. 3:141–283, edited by Hermann Fahrenkrug and entitled "The Social History of Alcohol in Modern Europe," covering eight nations in three languages; several issues of *Contemporary Drug Problems*: "The Liquor Question and the Formation of Consciousness: Nation, Ethnicity, and Class at the Turn of the Century" (12 [1985]: 165–330); "The Formulation of State Alcohol Monopolies and Controls: Case Studies in Five Nations" (12 [1985]: 1–158); "Historical Perspectives on the Treatment Response to Alcohol Problems: Case Studies in Six Societies" (13 [1986]: 387–583); and "International Studies of the Development of Alcohol Treatment Systems" (14 [1987]: 1–123); and the proceedings of a conference, *The Social History of Alcohol: Drinking and Culture in Modern Society*, ed. Susanna Barrows, Robin Room and Jeffrey Verhey (Berkeley: Alcohol Research Group, 1987; available from Alcohol Research Group, 2000 Hearst Ave., Berkeley, Calif., 94709).

Contributors

Marianna Adler holds an M.A. in anthropology from the University of Texas, Austin, and a master's in public health from the University of California, Berkeley. She is currently contemplating a return to graduate school to study psychoanalytic theory.

Charles H. Ambler is an associate professor and chair of the Department of History at the University of Texas, El Paso. His publications include *Kenyan Communities in the Age of Imperialism* (New Haven, 1988) and several articles. He is currently coediting a volume of essays on alcohol, labor, and the state in southern African history, to be published by Ohio University Press, and is continuing research for a social history of alcohol use in nineteenth- and twentieth-century Africa.

Thomas F. Babor is a professor of psychiatry at the University of Connecticut School of Medicine. He currently serves as associate scientific director of the university's Alcohol Research Center, where his research interests include treatment evaluation as well as cultural and historical factors related to alcohol problems.

Susanna Barrows is an associate professor of history at the University of California, Berkeley. Author of *Distorting Mirrors: Visions of the Crowd in Late Nineteenth-Century France* (New Haven, 1981), she is presently working on a series of historical studies on the role of the café in nineteenth-century France.

Joel Bernard is a visiting assistant professor of history at Reed College.

He is writing a book on the origin of the American temperance movement.

Thomas Brennan is a professor of history at the U.S. Naval Academy. Author of *Public Drinking and Popular Culture in Eighteenth-Century Paris* (Princeton, 1988), he has also published several articles on the history of alcohol.

George Bretherton teaches in the Department of History at Montclair State College. In 1986 he was a postdoctoral fellow with the Alcohol Research Group in Berkeley, and during 1988–89 he was a New Jersey State College Faculty Fellow at Princeton University. He is currently completing a study of Father Mathew's temperance movement.

David W. Conroy is a member of the Alliance of Independent Scholars in Cambridge, Massachusetts. He has taught at local universities, worked as a consulting historian for the state of Connecticut, and recently finished a chapter for the forthcoming *Blackwell's Encyclopedia of the American Revolution*. Presently he is working on a book on the culture and politics of drink in colonial and Revolutionary Massachusetts and on a history of the relationship between the Mohegan Indians and the colony of Connecticut.

Hermann Fahrenkrug is a research sociologist at the Swiss Institute for the Prevention of Alcohol Problems, Lausanne. He has published a study of the history of the American alcohol problem (*Alkohol, Individuum und Gesellschaft: Zur Sozialgeschichte des Alkoholproblems in den USA* [Frankfurt, 1984]) and edited a special issue of the Swiss journal *Drogalkohol* on the history of alcohol (*Zur Sozialgeschichte des Alkohols in der Neuzeit Europas* [Lausanne, 1986]).

Geoffrey J. Giles teaches in the Department of History at the University of Florida and also edits the *Social History of Alcohol Review*. Author of *Students and National Socialism in Germany* (Princeton, 1985), he has completed research as an Alexander von Humboldt Fellow at the University of Freiburg for a book on the social history of alcohol in Germany from 1870. His next project will be a comparative and historical study of alcohol, drug, and sex education for young people.

Joseph Gusfield is a professor of sociology at the University of California, San Diego. He is the author of *Symbolic Crusade: Status Politics and the American Temperance Movement* (Urbana, Ill., 1963, 1986), *The Culture of Public Problems: Drinking-Driving and the Symbolic Order* (Chicago, 1981), and other books.

Denise Herd is an assistant professor in the School of Public Health at the University of California, Berkeley. Her research has focused on ethnicity and drinking behavior and on the cultural representation of alcohol in the United States. She has published research on the black temperance movement, contemporary black drinking patterns, and changing alcohol and health in American society.

Ray Hutchison is an associate professor of sociology in the Department of Urban and Public Affairs at the University of Wisconsin, Green Bay, and series editor of Research in Urban Sociology (JAI Press). His research has focused on race and ethnic relations and includes published work on the Hispanic population in Chicago. He is currently editing a volume of historical and contemporary research on the Mexican community in Chicago.

Patrick M. McLaughlin is a lecturer in sociology and social policy at the University of Stirling. His research interests include alcohol control policies, criminal justice, and victims of crime. He has recently published a research monograph, *Managing Drunkenness in Scotland: Criminal Justice and Social Service Responses to Alcohol Problems* (Edinburgh, 1989).

Madelon Powers is a graduate student in the Department of History at the University of California, Berkeley, and is currently completing her dissertation, "Faces along the Bar: Lore and Order in the Working-man's Saloon, 1870–1920."

James S. Roberts is an adjunct associate professor of history at Duke University, where he teaches a course on the social history of alcohol. He is the author of *Drink, Temperance, and the Working Class in Nineteenth-Century Germany* (Boston, 1984) and numerous articles on alcohol and social history.

Robin Room is scientific director of the Alcohol Research Group, Medical Research Institute of San Francisco, and an adjunct professor in the School of Public Health, University of California, Berkeley. He is coauthor of *Problem Drinking among American Men* (New Brunswick, N.J., 1974) and coeditor of *Alcohol and Disinhibition: Nature and Meaning of the Link* (Washington, D.C., 1983).

Barbara Gutmann Rosenkrantz is a professor of history of science at Harvard University. She has written on relationships between changing definitions of disease and public health practice in the nineteenth and twentieth centuries.

George E. Snow is a professor of Russian and Soviet history at Shippensburg University of Pennsylvania. He is the author of *"The Years 1881–1894 in Russia": A Memorandum Found in the Papers of N. Kh. Bunge. A Translation and Commentary* (Philadelphia, 1981), and articles on prerevolutionary Russian bureaucratic reform. He is currently writing a book on the prerevolutionary Russian temperance movement and also doing research on prerevolutionary criminal anthropology in Russia.

Ian Tyrrell teaches American history and comparative women's history and historiography at the University of New South Wales. He is the author of *Sobering Up: From Temperance to Prohibition in Antebellum America, 1800–1860* (Westport, Conn., 1979), *The Absent Marx: Class Analysis and Liberal History in Twentieth-Century America* (Westport, Conn., 1986), and other works.

Jeffrey Verhey is a graduate student in the Department of History at the University of California, Berkeley. He is completing his dissertation on the "Spirit of 1914" in Germany.

Index

Abolition, 359–360, 361–362, 364, 373n
Ackermann, Jessie, 219, 231
Adams, John, 54
Addams, Jane, 117, 213n
Adler, Marianna, 3, 9
Adolescence, 413
African Methodist Evangelical church, 198
Ainsworth, John, 169
Alcohol and Public Policy: Beyond the Shadow of Prohibition (National Academy of Sciences), 7
Alcohol control movements, and characteristic images of alcohol, 354–355, 356–359, 370–371
Alcohol controls, 405, 411, 419; in Massachusetts, 38–56, 265–284; in Nazi Germany, 315–332; state, 5
Alcohol disinhibition, 366–367, 371, 417, 418
Alcoholic as Seen in Court (Anderson), 274
Alcoholic beverage control (ABC) legislation, 265–267, 277, 282, 284
Alcoholism, 4–5, 6, 16, 17, 49, 65, 72, 83n, 180n, 243–258, 306, 338, 349, 368, 402, 409, 418; and criminality, 248; in Nazi Germany, 318–319, 321–323, 326–327
Alcoholism movement, 5, 6–7
Alcohol licensing: in Britain, 313n; in

Kenya, 178; in Massachusetts, 39–41, 45–51, 53–54, 58–59n, 277; and Massachusetts local option system, 276, 277, 279, 284; in Scotland, 307, 314n
Alcohol regulation: in Kenya, 165–178, 183n; in Massachusetts, 38–56
Alcohol, Science and Society, 6
Ale, 40, 47, 58n
Alehouse, 35–36, 40, 57n, 58n, 409
Alkohol, Volk und Staat (Bracht), 319
Althusser, Louis, 395
Ambler, Charles H., 10, 11, 14
American Statistical Association, 273
American Temperance Union, 362
American War of Independence, 355
Anderson, Victor V., 274; *The Alcoholic as Seen in Court,* 274
Andros, Edmund, 45
Anglicans, 340, 341
Anti-Cigarette League, 202
Antinomians, 37
Anti-Saloon League, 207, 415
Anti-Semitism, 243, 244
Anti-Spirits Movement, 385
Arkhiv sudebnoi meditsiny i obshchestvennoi gigieny (Archive of Forensic Medicine and Public Hygiene), 244, 245
Asylums, 17, 18
An Attempt at a Theory of Mass Alcoholism in Connection with the Theory of Demand:

Toward the Question of the Construction of a Theory of Alcoholism as a Mass Phenomenon (Pervushin), 256

Auberges, 88, 95, 97n

Austen, Jane, 10

Babor, Thomas F., 18

Bacon, Selden D., 4

Bailey, Hannah Clark, 225

Bailey, Peter, 384, 392

Balgarnie, Florence, 219, 227

Balzac, Honoré de, 87

Bands of Hope, 233

Barney, Susan, 219

Barrows, Susanna, 8, 9, 14, 409, 412

Barthes, Roland, 76

Baudrillard, Jean, 378, 389

Bayley, David, 410

Bean, Walton, 131n

Beecher, Lyman, 343–344, 408

Beer, 11, 40, 42, 47, 51, 58n, 82n, 102, 118, 119, 132, 165–171, 174, 176, 177, 257, 319, 348

Beer halls, 134

Beers, Kenneth, 202

Bekhterev, V. M., 247, 252

Belcher, Andrew, 51

Beman, Amos, 364

Berlanstein, Lenard, 2

Bernard, Joel, 13, 14

Bettoja, 412

Bianconi, Charles, 157

Bishop, J. P., 193

Bismarck, Prince Otto von, 103

Black, Peter, 287, 293, 300

Bloch, Marc, 19

Blocker, Jack S., Jr., 20

Bolsheviks, 247

Bömelburg, Theodor, 102, 103

Bordin, Ruth, 200, 221, 230, 233; *Women and Temperance*, 233

Borodin, D. N., 247, 252, 255

Boston Caucus, 54

Boyer, Paul, 406

Brace, Charles Loring, 408; "The Dangerous Classes of New York City," 408

Bracht, Werner, 319; *Alkohol, Volk und Staat*, 319

Brandy, 51

Breck, Robert, 53

Brennan, Thomas, 8, 9, 10

Bretherton, George, 9, 13, 14, 17

British Journal of Addiction, 310n

British Journal of Inebriety, 288, 310n

British Woman's Total Abstinence Union, 229

British Women's Temperance Association (BWTA), 221, 226, 227, 229, 231, 232

Bromfield, Edward, 29, 49

Brownrigg, John, 150

Brueghel, Pieter the Elder, 399

Buddhism, 338

Buder, Stanley, 211

Burke, Peter, 384, 399

Burke's Irish Peerage and Baronetage, 149

Butler, Josephine, 223

Byrne, Frank L., 225

Cabarets, 61–64, 68, 69, 71, 74, 77, 78, 80, 81n, 88, 119, 127n, 370, 412

Cafés, 68, 87–96, 97n

Cailleau, André Charles, 64

Calkins, Raymond, 114, 116, 121, 279–280, 281, 283

Camp, Maxime du, 409

Canary, 51

Carbury and Edenderry Temperance Society, 150

Carlisle, Lady Rosalind, 218, 226, 231

Carnival, 399–400, 404, 405, 417

Carswell, John, 299, 300, 306

Cartwright, Samuel, 361

Catholic Association, 157

Catholic Emancipation, 147–148, 157

Catholics, 13, 148, 153, 155, 159–162, 196, 197, 323, 339, 340, 404, 413

Catt, Carrie Chapman, 233

Caylus (Claude-Philippe de Tubières), 75; *Le Correspondant de la guinguette*, 75

Chernyshev, I., 257

Cherrington, Ernest, 217

Chicago Evangelical Society, 188, 207

Child, Lydia Maria, 359

Chirkin, V. G., 243, 255

Cider, 11, 42, 47, 49, 51, 58n

Civil War, 116, 128n, 184, 198

Clark, Peter, 36

Clarke, John, 395

Clay, Henry, 359

Cobden, Richard, 237, 349

Code de la police (Duchesne), 66, 71

Cohn, Samuel, 407

Colbert, Jean Baptiste, 66

Cole, Thomas, 361

Cole, William, 279–280

Collier's Weekly, 367
Collins, Ellen, 117
Colonialism, 9–10
Colored American, 360
Colored American Temperance society, 360
Columbian Exposition, 189, 192
Commercial and Financial Chronicle, 203
Commitment mechanisms, 208–210, 212
Committee of Fifty, 267, 272, 281
Commodity Fetishism, 377–379
Commune of Paris, 89
Communes, 208–209
Communitarianism, 186
Communitarian settlements, 208, 210
Company towns, 187, 201
Condition of the Working Class in England in 1844 (Engels), 3, 244
Congregationalists, 37, 344
Connecticut Total Abstinence Society, 360
Connelly, Mark, 224
Conroy, David W., 8, 10, 13, 14
Contagious Diseases Acts, 228
Conti-Aufruf, 330
Conway, F. L., 161
Cook, Tim, 309
Cook County Prohibition Committee, 193
Cooke, Elisha, 53–55
Cooke, Elisha, Jr., 53–54
Copp, David, 51
Cork Total Abstinence Society, 155–156
Corporate towns, 187, 205
Correspondant de la guinguette (Caylus), 75
Courtwright, David, 223; *Dark Paradise*, 223
Crafts, Wilbur Fisk, Rev., 367
Crowe, Charles, 367
Crusade against Drink in Victorian England (Shiman), 210
Cuervo Premium Tequila, 376, 377
Cunningham, Dr., 294
Cutlove, William, 49
Cyclopedia of Temperance, 225

Dahrendorf, Ralf, 315
Dalrymple, Donald, 311n
Danforth, Samuel, 44–45
"Dangerous Classes of New York City" (Brace), 408
Dark Paradise (Courtwright), 223
Dawley, Alan, 407, 408
Débits (public houses), 88, 90, 94, 95
Debs, Eugene V., 122

Decarie, Graeme, 14
Delamare, Nicolas, 83n
Dembo, G. I., 247, 250, 251, 252
Dement'ev, E. M., 247
Demorest, William Jennings, 219
Development of Capitalism in Russia (Lenin), 250
Dickens, Charles, 9, 10
Dictionnaire économique, 66
Dini ya Msambwa protest movement, 173
Dion, Roger, 65, 72
Dipsomania, 17
"Discovery of Addiction" (Levine), 5
Distilled liquors, 40, 47, 49, 51
Dobash, Russell, 295
Dodd, Jill Siegel, 9
Dogel', I. M., 247
"Dooley, Mr." (Dunne), 120
Douglass, Frederick, 356, 363, 369
Doz, Vivian, 85n
Dril', D. A., 247, 248, 249, 250, 252
Drink and the Victorians (Harrison), 9
Drink fines, 382–383, 397n
Drinking: collective, 33–34; health drinking, 34, 35, 38, 41; and problem drinkers, 282; social, 61–81; societal responses to, 12; solitary, 7; student, 132–142
Drunkenness, 180n, 281, 404–405, 406, 417, 418; and American blacks, 355–358, 360–361, 363–364, 366–367; in Britain, 287, 313n; in France, 65–77, 80–81, 81n, 83n, 84n, 85n, 89; in Germany, 136, 138; in Kenya, 169, 171–172, 180n; in Massachusetts, 273–276, 282–284; and offenders within Massachusetts penal system, 273–276; in Scotland, 287, 290, 299–300, 307–309; in U.S., 408–410, 411, 412
Dublin Evening Mail, 158
Dublin Evening Post, 161
DuBois, W. E. B., 369
Duchesne, Etienne, 66–67, 71, 83n; *Code de la police*, 66, 71
Dudley, Joseph, 53
Dudley, Paul, 49
Duis, Perry, 414
Dumont, Louis, 380, 387
Dunlop, John, 9, 290, 305, 310n, 381–382, 383
Dunne, Finley Peter, 120
Durant, Edward, 51
Durkheim, Emile, 4

Durland, Kellogg, 279–280
Duster, Troy, 1

Earhart, Mary, 221, 230
Eau-de-vie, 85n
Ebert, Friedrich, 111n
Eighteenth Amendment, 416, 419
Eliot, Charles W., 267
Eliot, T. S., 96
Ely, Richard T., 213n
Emons, Nathaniel, 51
Emmons, Nathanael, Rev., 343–344
Encyclopédie méthodique, 66–68
Engels, Friedrich, 3, 244, 249, 258; *The Condition of the Working Class in England in 1844*, 3, 244
Enlightenment, 345, 357, 358, 364
Epstein, Barbara, 230
Erisman, F. F., 245
Essay, Medical, Philosophical, and Chemical, on Drunkenness (Trotter), 288
Ether, 15
Ethnic groups: American Indian, 355; Austrians, 273; blacks, 165–178, 198, 354–371; Czechs, 197; Eastern Europeans, 197; English, 200, 283, 376–397; French, 61–81; Germans, 98–108, 119, 132–142, 196, 270, 271, 283, 315–332, 368, 400; Irish, 118, 119, 120, 147–162, 197, 200, 271, 273, 274, 283–284, 368, 369, 407; Italians, 118, 119, 120, 129n, 197, 271, 273, 283; Jews, 118, 120, 274; Mexicans, 119; Poles, 197, 273, 400; Russians, 243–258, 271, 273, 283; Scotch, 200, 287–309; Serbians, 119, 129n; Slovaks, 197; Swedish, 196
Evangelical movement, 184, 221
Evans, Richard, 232

Fahrenkrug, Hermann, 15, 17, 135
Faler, Paul, 407, 408
Fasting, 339–341, 342, 348, 350–351n
Feickert, Andreas, 136
Fetishization, 377–379
First World War. *See* World War I
Fisk, Clinton B., 186
Fitzpatrick, Andre, 163n
Flandrin, Jean Louis, 72
Flexner, Abraham, 224; *Prostitution in Europe*, 224
Folkways (Sumner), 402
Ford, James, 275, 281
Foucault, Michel, 5, 72, 289, 308

Franco-Prussian War, 89
Frankfurt School, 317
Franklin, Benjamin, 9
Frederickson, George M., 359, 365
Freedom's Journal, 360
Freehling, William W., 356
Friends of Temperance, 368
Fry, Elizabeth, 308
Fürsorgestellen (outpatient advice bureaus for alcohol problems), 18

Gamalia, N. F., 247, 254
Garner, John S., 187, 206, 209
Gaston, Lucy Page, 202, 204, 207
Gay, Peter, 10
Geertz, Clifford, 8
Genovese, Eugene D., 355, 360
George, Lloyd, 313
German Association against Alcoholism, 327
German labor movement, 98–108, 109n
German Social Democrats, 244
German Society against Alcohol Abuse, 327
German Students' Union, 136
Gertsenshtein, G. M., 250
Gestapo, 140
Giele, Janet, 230
Gilbert, Thomas, 51
Gilded Age, 201
Giles, Geoffrey J., 15
Gin, 11, 367, 385, 409
Gin Lane, 73, 84n, 85n
Glorious Revolution, 45
Godelier, Maurice, 389
Goguette, 88
Göhre, Paul, 100, 104–105
Gololobov, A. Ia., 247
Goncourt, Edmond and Jules de, 10
Good Templars, 233
Gordon, Anna, 220, 234
Gothenberg system, 226, 255, 272
Graf, O., 328–329
Gramsci, Antonio, 388, 398n, 415
Grayson, Victor, 308
Grigor'ev, N. I., 247, 248, 249, 250
Grimshaw, Patricia, 232
Grotjahn, Alfred, 256
Guardianships of Popular Sobriety, 252, 254, 255, 256
Guinguettes, 63, 70
Gurr, Ted, 411
Gusfield, Joseph R., 5, 184, 197, 212n,

230, 247; *Symbolic Crusade,* 5
Gutman, Herbert, 407
Gütt, Arthur, 322

Habermas, Jürgen, 316–317
Habitual Drunkards Act, 306, 307, 311n
Hall, David, 44
Hardy, Dennis, 186, 187
Harring, Sydney, 406
Harrison, Brian, 3, 9, 13, 154, 189, 258,
   383, 384, 386, 392–393, 405: *Drink and
   the Victorians,* 9
Harvey, Turlington, 184, 188–189, 207
Harvey Citizen, 202
Harvey Land Association, 188–194, 199,
   200, 201, 202, 203, 204–206, 209–210,
   213n
Haselmayer, Heinz, 136
Hausmann, Margaret, 285
Hautemar, Farin de, 75; *L'Impromptu des
   harangères,* 75
Hayden, Dolores, 186, 211
Haywood, William ("Big Bill"), 122
Herd, Denise, 14, 15
Hibernian Temperance Society, 147, 149
Hillsboro Women's Temperance Crusade,
   200
Himmler, Heinrich, 134, 315
Hinduism, 338
Hitler, Adolf, 134, 135, 140
Hobsbawm, Eric, 2, 409
Hochland organization, 133
Hockings, John, 155
Hoffmann, Ottilie, 231
Hofstadter, Richard, 5
Howard, John, 308
How the Other Half Lives (Riis), 117
Hudson, William, 42
Hughes, Langston, 370
Hutchinson, Elisha, 49
Hutchison, Ray, 14, 18
Hypnotism, 6

Ianzhul, I. I., 250
Impromptu des harangères (Hautemar), 75
Independent Order of Good Templars,
   368
Inebriate reformatories: in Ireland, 312n;
   in Scotland, 287–309, 310n, 311n, 312n,
   314n; in U.S. and Canada, 311n
Inebriates Acts, 287, 288, 289, 291, 298,
   300, 302, 303, 304, 305, 306, 307, 309,
   310n

Inebriety, 16
Inebriety in Boston (Parmelee), 273–274
Inns, 40
Inquiry into the Effects of Spirituous Liquors
   (Rush), 217, 345
International Congresses on Alcoholism,
   225
International Council of Women, 218
International Woman Suffrage Alliance,
   233
Irish Temperance and Literary Gazette, 149,
   150
Isetts, Charles A., 200
Islam, 338
Ivrognerie, 65–67

James I (king of England), 35
Jellinek, E. M., 6
Jones, Sam, Rev., 367
Jones, Gareth Stedman, 392–393, 412
Jordan, Winthrop, 365

Kabaks (taverns), 244, 249, 255
Käferstein, Georg, 103
Kalle, Fritz, 106
Kamp, Otto, 106
Kanatchikov, S. I., 255
Kantor, Rosabeth Moss, 208, 209
Karp, Ivan, 167
Kaspar'iants, O. A., 254–255
Kautsky, Karl, 101, 105
Keeley, L. E., 294
Kenna, Michael ("Hinky Dink"), 123, 131n
Kikuyu Central Association (KCA), 176,
   177–178
Knights of Pythias, 122, 129n
Koller, Siegfried, 331
Koren, John, 272–273, 277–278, 279,
   282, 284, 368; *A Study of the Economic
   Aspects of the Liquor Problem,* 272–273
Korovin, A. M., 247, 251, 252, 257
Kranz, Hans Werner, 331
Krout, John, 362

Labor issues, 184
Laffemas, Bernard de, 65–67
Lambert, Arsène, 90, 92
Landes, David, 404
Landis, Charles, 185
Landsdowne, Lord, 157
Lavoisier, Antoine, 63
League of Nations, 225
League of the Opponents of Alcohol, 133

Leavitt, Mary Clement, 217–218, 219, 220, 225, 228, 229, 231
Leiner, Otto von, 106
Leinster, duke of, 149
Leisure, 183n, 403–406, 410–411, 414, 416–417, 418; adolescent, 413
Lenin, V. I., 249–250; *The Development of Capitalism in Russia*, 250
Lent, 399–400, 404, 405, 417
Leopold II (king of Belgium), 231
Levine, Harry Gene, 5, 354, 357, 365, 366, 406, 417; "The Discovery of Addiction," 5
Lewis, J. W., 361
Ley, Erich, 315, 329
Ley, Robert, 142
Liberator, 361
Liberty Leagues, 131
Lindblom, Gerhard, 172
Liqueur, 85n
Liquor Problem in Its Legislative Aspects, 277
Livesey, Joseph, 386
Locke, John, 380
Loguen, Jermain, 362
Lositskii, A. E., 256, 257
Lynching, 227

MacDonald, Ramsay, 291
McGee, Christopher ("Chris"), 123
McGerr, Michael E., 126n
McLaughlin, Patrick M., 5, 16, 18
MacMahon, Maréchal, 87–88, 89, 91, 92, 94, 95, 96n
Madden, Daniel Owen, 157
Maguire, John Francis, 156, 159
Making of the English Working Class (Thompson), 2
Malcolmson, David, 151, 163n
Mandeville, Bernard, 380
Mansfield, Lord, 309
Martin, William, 155, 157
Marx, Karl, 104, 244, 378
Masons, 121–122, 129n, 130n
Mather, Cotton, 44–45, 49
Mather, Increase, 44
Mathew, Father Theobald, 19, 155–162, 164n
Mathewite movement, 159–162
Mathews, Jonathan, 202
Mauss, Marcel, 377
Maynooth Temperance Society, 149
Mears, Samuel, 51
Medick, Hans, 86n

Meggendorfer, Friedrich, 317–319
Melendy, Royal L., 113, 120
Ménétra, Jacques Louis, 74–75
Mercier, Sébastien, 62, 64
Messer, W., 331
Meyendorf, Baron A. F., 247
Michels, Robert, 105
Middle class, 199, 392, 396, 412, 417
Milhaud, Edgard, 103–104
Miliutin, V. P., 255
Minor, L. S., 247, 252, 257
Moderation Press, 133
Monck, George, 31–32, 42, 46
Montaigne, Michel de, 65–67
Montesquieu, Charles de Secondat, Baron de la Brède et de, 358
Moody, Dwight L., 188
Moore, Barrington, 316
Moore, E. C., 117
Moral societies, 344, 353n
Morgan, Patricia, 8, 412
Morley, John, 349
Mothers Against Drunk Driving, 19
Mumford, Lewis, 403
Muraskin, William, 401

Napoleon III, 88, 94
Narcomania, 17
Nash, Gary B., 31
National Educator (WCTU), 219
National Reformer, 360
National Socialist Students' Association (NSDStB), 134–135, 137, 138, 141
Nazi Germany, 15, 17, 132–142
New England Temperance Society of Colored People, 362
Nightclubs, 370
Nizhegorodtsev, M. N., 246–247, 252, 256
North American Review, 346
Northern Star and Freeman's Advocate, 363

Obozrenia Psikhiatr (Psychiatrist's Review), 246
O'Connell, Daniel, 148, 157, 159
Odd Fellows, 122, 129n
Ol'denburg, Prince Aleksandr, 246
O'Neill, Eugene, 127n
Opium, 222–223
Opportunists, 95
Origins of Prohibition (Krout), 6
Owen, Robert, 387
Owst, G. R., 338

Page, Edward, 202, 204, 207
Pan, Lynn, 10
Parmelee, M. F., 273–274; *Inebriety in Boston*, 273–274
Peabody, Francis G., 281
Pearson, Geoffrey, 412
Peasant Farming in South Russia (Postnikov), 249
Penny, Joseph, Rev., 147
Perrot, Michelle, 2
Pervushin, S. A., 256; *An Attempt at a Theory of Mass Alcoholism in Connection with the Theory of Demand*, 256
Phrenology, 337, 349
Pitson, James, 49, 51
Place, Frances, 387
Plunkitt, George Washington, 130n
Poaching, 57n
Poisons of Pleasure, 317
Polanyi, Karl, 380
Police, 409–413, 415
Police des débits de boisson, 88, 95
Pope's game, 132
Popp, Adelheid, 107
Posse, V. A., 255
Postnikov, V. I., 249; *Peasant Farming in South Russia*, 249
Powers, Madelon, 8, 9, 18
Presbyterians, 157, 344
Price, David, 85n
Progressive movement, 412, 415
Prohibition, 3, 6, 115, 123, 125, 276, 348, 413, 415, 419, 265
Prostitution, 223–224, 227–228, 238n, 300, 307
Prostitution in Europe (Flexner), 224
Protestant ethic, 363
Protestant Reformation, 310n, 385
Protestants, 13, 148, 153, 157, 160–162, 176, 191, 196, 197, 200, 339, 343, 359, 404, 413, 418
Protestant Total Abstinence Society, 161
Pryzhov, I. G., 244
Pub, 389–391, 392, 393–395
Public house, 394
Pullman, George, 189, 213n
Puritans, 29–56, 58n, 341

Quakers (Society of Friends), 155, 157, 163n
Quarterly Journal of Studies on Alcohol, 6

Rabelais, François, 72, 84n
Rahn, Carol, 201, 213n

Ramabai, Pundita, 224
Ramabai Association, 224
Ranger, Clark W., 202
Real and Imaginary Effects of Intemperance (Thomann), 267, 270
Rechabites, 233
Reconstruction, 365, 369
Reformation, 36
Reich Student Leadership, 141
Relief and Aid Society, 188
Report of the Massachusetts Bureau of Statistics of Labor, 270–272
Restrictive System in Massachusetts, 1875–1894, 276–277
Revel, F. H., 188
Riis, Jacob, 117; *How the Other Half Lives*, 117
Roberts, James S., 8, 14, 207
Rodgers, Daniel, 407, 417
Röhm, Ernst, 134
Rosen, George, 280
Rosenbach, P. Ia., 248
Rosenkrantz, Barbara G., 18, 285
Rosenzweig, Roy, 9, 14, 415
Rothman, David J., 5, 402–403
Rudé, George, 409
Rüdin, Ernst, 322, 325
Ruef, Abraham, 123, 131n
Ruggles, David, 364
Rum, 11, 47, 48, 49, 51, 55
Rush, Benjamin: *Inquiry into the Effects of Spirituous Liquors*, 217, 345
Russian Orthodox church, 248
Russian Society for the Protection of Public Health, 246
Russkii vrach' (Russian Physician), 246
Russo-Turkish War, 246
Rust, Bernhard, 140–141, 142
Rüttig, W., 330
Ryder, Emma Brainerd, 224

Saint-Germain, Jacques, 61
Saint Monday, 405
Saloon, 8, 18, 112–125, 126n, 127n, 128n, 191, 202, 203, 204, 274, 276, 279–280, 283, 366, 412, 413–416
Saltonstall, Nathaniel, 44, 46, 49
Salvation Army, 231
San Francisco Bulletin, 131n
Sargent, Ellen, 234
Sargent, J. P., 161
Sbornik sochinenii po sudebnoi meditsine, sudebnoi psikhiatrii, meditsinskoi politsii,

obshchestvennoi gigiene, epidemiologii, meditsinskoi geografii i meditsinskoi statistike (Collection of Works on Forensic Medicine, Forensic Psychiatry, Medical policy, Public Hygiene, Epidemiology, Medical Geography and Medical Statistics), 245
Schmitz, Eugene E., 123
Schnaps, 102
Schoenbaum, David, 316
Schreibenhuber, Elise, 108
Schulze, Reinhold, 136
Schüz, Alfred, 137
Scull, Andrew, 402–403
Second World War. *See* World War II
Selby, Thomas, 51
Sewall, Samuel, 29–33, 36–37, 46, 48, 49–50, 56, 56n
Shame of the Cities (Steffens), 117
Shattuck, Lemuel, 272
Shaw, Anna, Rev., 225
Shebeen, 414
Sherry, 51
Shiman, Lillian Lewis, 210; *Crusade against Drink in Victorian England,* 210
Shute, Samuel, 53, 55
Silver, Alan, 408, 409
Simon, Jules, 96n
Slack, Agnes, 229
Slavery, 354–359, 362, 363–365
Smith, Amanda, 185, 198
Smith, Thomas, 55
Snow, George E., 9, 11, 13, 14, 15
Social Darwinism, 364, 366, 368, 371
Social Democratic party (SPD), 98–99, 107, 111n
Socialism, 243–258
Society of Russian Physicians in Memory of N. I. Pirogov, 246
Somerset, Lady Isobel, 218, 221, 222, 226, 227–228, 229, 231
Sons of Temperance, 217, 233, 235n, 368
Sotsial' demokrat, 253, 256
Southern Literary Messenger, 364
Spalding, A. G., 188
Spartans, 155
Spencer, Thomas, 386
Stäbel, Oskar, 134–135
Standard Encyclopedia of the Alcohol Problem, 6
Stanford, Mrs. Leland, 186
State Temperance Society of Colored People, 360

Steffens, Lincoln, 117, 123; *Shame of the Cities,* 117
Sterilization, 321–323, 324, 325
Stevenson, Robert Louis, 365
Stewart, Jane, 219
Stolypin, P. A., 251
Study of the Economic Aspects of the Liquor Problem (Koren), 272–273
Sulkunen, Irma, 14
Summer School of Alcohol Studies (1944), 6
Sumner, William G., 402; *Folkways,* 402
Symbolic Crusade (Gusfield), 5

Tait, Irene, 301
Tammany Hall, 123
Tarnovskii, E. N., 248
Taussig, Michael, 378
Taverns, 14, 113, 126n, 355; in colonial Massachusetts, 29–56, 57n, 58n; in England, 390–391; in Germany, 98–108, 109n; John Wallis's tavern, 29, 32, 48, 50; Monck's Blue Anchor Tavern, 32; in Paris, 8, 61–64, 65, 68, 71, 77, 80, 81, 81n, 82n, 83n; Richard Hall's tavern, 54
Taylor, Christopher, 54–55
Taylor, Graham, 189
Taylor, William, 172
Teetotalers, 153–155, 158, 160, 364, 386
Temperance, 3, 13, 56, 417, 418; among American blacks, 14, 15, 354–371, 373n; temperance debate, 405; temperance fraternities, 16
Temperance Legislation League, 226
Temperance movements, 5, 6, 11, 12–15, 239n, 389; black temperance societies, 356; in Catholic countries, 13; in colonized or dependent nations, 14; in Eastern Europe, 13; in England, 13, 290, 387; in France, 8, 13; in Germany, 13, 101, 106; in Iceland, 14; in Ireland, 13, 14, 147–162; in Italy, 8, 13; in Kenya, 14; in Netherlands, 13; New Temperance Movement, 417; in Nordic countries, 13; in Ontario, 14; in Protestant countries, 13; in Russia, 9, 13, 14, 15, 261n; in Scandinavia, 13; in Scotland, 287–288, 290; in Southern Europe, 13; in Switzerland, 13; in U.S., 5, 14, 16, 19, 20, 29–56, 184–212, 233, 337–349, 407, 411
Temperance towns, 184–212
Thiers, Adolphe, 89

Thomann, Gallus, 267, 270, 281, 282; *Real and Imaginary Effects of Intemperance*, 267, 270
Thompson, E. P., 2, 4, 381, 404; *Making of the English Working Class*, 2
Tilly, Charles, 2
Times (London), 227
Tönnies, Ferdinand, 4
Trezvost' i berezhlivost' (Temperance and Thrift), 246, 247
Trotter, Thomas, 288; *Essay, Medical, Philosophical, and Chemical, on Drunkenness*, 288
Turner, John, 31–32, 42
Tyrrell, Ian R., 13, 14, 17, 200

Ulster Temperance Society, 147
Union Labor party, 130n
Unions, 122–124, 213n
Union Signal, 186, 191, 192, 193, 194, 195, 207, 218, 219, 226, 228, 229
United States Brewers' Association, 266–267, 272, 284
Universal Races Congress, 225
Ure, A., 386
Utopian community, 205
Utopian movements, 208
Utopian settlements, 204

Vadé, Jean-Joseph, 64
Van Onselen, Charles, 178
Vestnik obshchestvennoi gigieny, sudebnoi i prakticheskoi meditsiny (Herald of Public Hygiene, Forensic and Practical Medicine), 245
Vestnik sudebnoi meditsiny i obshchestvennon gigieny (Herald of Forensic Medicine and Public Hygiene), 245
Vestnik trezvosti (Temperance Herald), 246, 247
Vodka, 257
Volstead Act, 220
Voltaire, 84n
von Gruber, Max, 332
Vrachebnaia gazeta (Medical Daily), 246
Vvedenskii, N. B., 247

Wade, Richard C., 356, 364
Wadlin, Horace G., 282, 284
Wadsworth, Benjamin, 44, 49, 52
Wagner, Gerhard, 142
Walker, Francis Amassa, 267
Walley, John, 49

Wandervogel youth movement, 133
Ward, Edward, 43
Warden, G. B., 31, 54
War of 1812, 344
Washington, Booker T., 369
Weber, Max, 4, 316
Weimar Republic, 133
Wells, Ida, 227
Westphal, Otto, 137
Whipper, William, 362
Whiskey, 11, 147, 348
White, Alfred T., 117
White, Jacob C., 362
White Ribbon (Britain), 218
White Ribbon Bulletin (World's WCTU), 218, 228
Whyte, William, 41
Widmark's blood analysis test, 321
Willard, Frances, 14, 185, 204, 207, 217–218, 220–234 passim
William II (emperor of Prussia), 106
Williams, Raymond, 389, 396, 415
Wilmot, Nicholas, 42
Wine, 40, 42, 47, 51, 58n, 62–64, 77–80, 82n, 85n, 319; palm wine, 181n
Wines, Fredrick H., 279
Winston, George, 365
Winthrop, John, 43
Wittenmyer, Annie, 230
Wolfson, Amy, 285
Woman suffrage, 184, 219–220, 357, 359
Women, 14, 15, 18, 107–108, 111n, 114–115, 127n, 166, 217–235, 275, 290, 291, 292, 294, 299–302, 312n, 347, 348, 358, 385–386, 409
Women and Temperance (Bordin), 233
Women's Christian Temperance Union (WCTU), 185, 191, 200, 202, 207, 208, 211, 368; American, 217, 219, 220, 222, 223, 224, 226, 227–228, 229, 230, 232, 234; Indian, 224; *National Educator*, 219; Ontario, 221. *See also* World's WCTU
Women's Crusade, 222
Women's International League for Peace and Freedom, 234
Women's International Temperance Convention, 221
Woods, Robert A., 118
Working class, 7–8, 98, 109n; in America, 112–125, 127n, 130n, 200, 213n, 400, 411, 414; in England, 389–395; in Russia, 243–258

Worktown, 393
World Health Organization, 6
World League against Alcoholism, 217,
    233, 235n
World Prohibition Federation, 202
World's WCTU, 17, 217–235; *White Ribbon
    Bulletin*, 218, 228. *See also* Women's
    Christian Temperance Union
World War I, 17, 101, 116, 128n, 133, 165,
    169, 218, 224, 225, 257, 303, 307
World War II, 19, 395
Wormall, Sarah, 51
Wright, Carroll D., 267, 273
Wright, Gordon, 87

Yale Center of Alcohol Studies, 4

Year Book of the U. S. Brewers' Association,
    277
Youmans, Letitia, 221
Young, Arthur, 62
Young Men's Christian Association
    (YMCA), 188, 207

Zdravie (Health), 246
Zelnik, Reginald, 244
Zemskii vrach (Zemstvo Physician), 246
*Zhurnal nevropatologii i psikhiatrii imeni S.
    S. Korsakove* (Journal of Neuropathology
    and Psychiatry in Honor of S. S.
    Korsakov), 246
Zola, Emile, 9, 10, 84n
Zola, Irving K., 402